*f***P**

Down to Earth Sociology

Introductory Readings
FOURTEENTH EDITION

JAMES M. HENSLIN
Editor

FREE PRESS

New York London Toronto Sydney

FREE PRESS
A Division of Simon & Schuster, Inc.
1230 Avenue of the Americas
New York, NY 10020

First Free Press trade paperback edition 2007

FREE PRESS and colophon are trademarks
of Simon & Schuster, Inc.

For information regarding special discounts for bulk purchases,
please contact Simon & Schuster Special Sales at 1-800-456-6798
or business@simonandschuster.com

Designed by Publications Development Company

Manufactured in the United States of America

20 19 18 17 16 15 14 13 12

ISBN-13: 978-1-4165-3620-8
ISBN-10:   1-4165-3620-5

Credits and Acknowledgments

Grateful acknowledgment is made to the authors and publishers who have granted permission to reprint these selections:

ARTICLE
1   Excerpts from *Invitation to Sociology* by Peter L. Berger. Copyright © 1963 by Peter L. Berger. Reprinted by permission of Bantam Doubleday Dell Publishing Group, Inc.
2   Copyright © 2007 by James M. Henslin.
3   "The Promise," from *Sociological Imagination* by C. Wright Mills. Copyright © 1959, 2000 by Oxford University Press, Inc. Used by permission of Oxford University Press, Inc.
4   Copyright © 2007 by James M. Henslin.
5   Copyright © 1985 by The Society for the Study of Social Problems. All rights reserved. Reprinted from *Social Problems*, Vol. 32, No. 3, February 1985, pp. 251–63.
6   Reprinted by permission of Candace Clark and the University of Chicago Press, excerpts from "The Mark of a Criminal Record" in *American Journal of Sociology, 108*, 5: 937–975. Copyright © 2003 by the University of Chicago Press.
7   Reprinted by permission of Bruce Jacobs.
8   Reproduced by permission of the American Anthropological Association from *American Anthropologist*, 58:3, June 1956.
9   From *Yąnomamö*, 2nd Edition by Chagnon. Copyright © 1977. Reprinted with permission of Wadsworth, a division of Thompson Learning: www.thompsonrights.com.

27 Published by permission of Transaction Publishers, from *Society,* Vol. 9, No. 6. Copyright © 1972 by Transaction Publishers.

28 Reprinted with permission from the author and publisher from *Science,* Vol. 179 (January 19, 1973), pp. 250–58. Copyright © 1973 AAAS.

29 Reprinted by permission of Sidney Katz.

30 From *Gender and Society,* 3 (4). Copyright © 1989 by Sage Publications. Reprinted by permission of Sage Publications, Inc.

31 Reprinted by permission of Clarence Page.

32 From *Racist Mind* by Raphael S. Ezekiel. Copyright © 1995 by Raphael S. Ezekiel. Used by permission of the author and Viking Penguin, a division of Penguin Group (USA), Inc.

33 From *Social Policy,* July/August 1971, pp. 20–24. Published by Social Policy Corporation, New York, NY 10036. Copyright © 1971 by Social Policy Corporation.

34 Reprinted with the permission of the editor of *Race, Gender, and Class.* Excerpts from Vol. 4, No. 1, pp. 63–81.

35 Reprinted by permission of Rowman & Littlefield Publishers, Inc.

36 From "Nickel and Dimed: On Not Getting By in America," *Harper Magazine,* January 1999. Copyright © Barbara Ehrenrich. Reprinted by permission.

37 Reprinted by permission of the author.

38 Copyright © by Robbie E. Davis-Floyd. Reprinted with permission.

39 Reprinted by permission of Harry L. Gracey.

40 From *Human Nature Magazine* 1 (2), pp. 28, 30–36, February 1978. Copyright © by Human Nature, Inc.

41 Jennifer Hunt, *Urban Life,* Vol. 13, No. 4 (January 1985). Copyright © 1985 by Sage Publications, Inc. Reprinted by permission of Sage Publications, Inc.

42 From *War: Past, Present, and Future* by Gwynne Dyer. Copyright © 1985 by Media Resources. Used by permission of Crown Publishers, a division of Random House, Inc.

43 Excerpts reprinted by permission from pp. 44–52, 53–55, 60, 65, 72–76, 82–85 of *Fast Food, Fast Talk: Service Work and the Routinization of Everyday Life,* Robin Leidner. Copyright © 1993 The Regents of the University of California.

44 Reprinted by permission of the Lancaster Mennonite Historical Society, from *Pennsylvania Mennonite Heritage,* Vol. 13, No. 3, July 1990.

45 Reprinted by permission of the author and publisher from *Social Psychology Quarterly,* 60 (1), March 1997, excerpts from various pages. Copyright © 1997 by the American Sociological Association.

46 Reprinted by permission of the author.

For those who are studying to be sociologists—

whose unbridled curiosity will continue
to contribute to our knowledge of society

Contents

Preface to the Fourteenth Edition

Sociology has the marvelous capacity to open new windows of perception on our familiar worlds, leaving no aspect of our lives unexamined.
—Author

IT IS WITH PLEASURE that I introduce the fourteenth edition of *Down to Earth Sociology,* a pleasure akin to seeing a dear friend reach another cheerful milestone in his or her life. Adopters of earlier editions will find themselves at home in this latest edition. They will see many selections that they have used successfully in the classroom, and I trust they will welcome the newcomers.

Following the suggestions of those who have used earlier editions of *Down to Earth Sociology,* I have strived to continue to present down to earth articles in order to make the student's introduction to sociology enjoyable as well as meaningful. These selections narrate the first-hand experiences of their authors—researchers who put a human voice on sociological experiences—those who have "been there" and who, with a minimum of jargon and quantification, insightfully share their experiences with the reader.

Focusing on social interaction in everyday activities and situations, these selections not only share some of the fascination of sociology, but also they reflect both the individualistic and the structural emphases of our discipline. They make clear how social structure is not simply an abstract fact of life, but how it vitally affects our everyday lives. These selections help students become more aware of how the decisions of the rich, the powerful, and the bureaucrats provide social constraints that add to those dictated by birth (especially gender and race–ethnicity), social class, and other circumstances of our lives. They help students understand how their location in a social structure lifts or limits their vision of life, closes or opens their chances of success, and, ultimately, brings tears and laughter, hope and despair.

So much of sociology, however, goes about its business as though data were unconnected to people, as though the world consists of abstract social facts. Yet from our own experiences in social life, we know how far these

xvii

suppositions are from the truth—how divorced they are from real life. Consequently, I have sought to include authors who are able to share the realities that directly affect people's lives. As I see it, sociology is the most fascinating of the social sciences, and it is this fascination that these selections are designed to convey.

It is my hope that I have succeeded in accomplishing this goal, because sociology has the marvelous capacity to open new windows of perception on our familiar worlds, leaving no aspect of our lives unexamined. If these readings come even close to this goal, I am indebted to the many adopters of earlier editions, whose reactions and suggestions have helped shape this one. To all of you, a sincere and fond thank you.

I owe a special debt of gratitude to the instructors who shared with me their experiences with earlier editions. Their sharing proved invaluable in shaping this present version. I wish to acknowledge the help of

Richard Ambler, Southern Arkansas University
Julie E. Artis, DePaul University
Joe Bishop, Dakota State University
John Bowman, University of North Carolina at Pembroke
Tom Boyd, Berea College
Suzanne Brandon, College of St. Catherine
John C. Bridges, Immaculata College
Grace Budrys, DePaul University
Meryl Cozart, Towson University
Rolf Diamon, University of Southern Maine
Merl Dirksen, Lee University
Robert B. Enright, Jr., University of Wisconsin–Stevens Point
David C. Erickson, Northwest College
Kerry Ferris, Bradley University
Richard Gendron, Assumption College
Frank Glamser, University of Southern Mississippi
Peter R. Grahame, Mount Saint Mary's College
Susan F. Greenwood, University of Maine–Orono
Larry D. Hall, Spring Hill College
Terrell A. Hayes, Davis & Elkins College
Ines W. Jindra, Bethany Lutheran College
Cathryn Johnson, Emory University
Susan L. Johnson, Carl Sandburg College
James W. Jordan, Longwood College

Quintus Joubeve, Rutgers University
Mariame Kaba, Northeastern Illinois University
Meg Wilkes Karraker, University of St. Thomas
Margot Kempers, Fitchburg State College
Marilyn Krogh, Loyola University of Chicago
Anthony Lack, Lee College
Helene M. Lawson, University of Pittsburgh
Bill Lockhart, New Mexico State University
Jerry Lowney, Carroll College
Philip Luck, Georgia State University
Kristin Marsh, Emory University
Tina Martinez, Blue Mountain Community College
R. Robin Miller, Drury University
Sharon L. Miller, Hope College
Janine Minkler, Northern Arizona University
Elizabeth J. Mitchell, Rutgers University
Thomas S. Moore, University of Wisconsin–Milwaukee
Christopher W. Mullins, Southwestern Illinois College
Peter F. Parilla, University of St. Thomas
Kristin Park, Westminster College
Tim Pippert, Augsburg College
Paul-Jahi Price, Pasadena City College
Pam Rosenberg, Gettysburg College
Richard Rubinson, Emory University
Ross T. Runfola, Medaille College
Allen Scarboro, Augusta State University
Richard Senter, Jr., Central Michigan University
Ryan Sheppard, King's College
Rick L. Shifley, Montserrat College of Art
Thomas Soltis, Westmoreland County Community College
Marybeth C. Stalp, University of Georgia
Judith Stepan-Norris, University of California–Irvine
Jordan J. Titus, University of Alaska
Kathy Trosen, Muscatine Community College
Suzanne Tuthill, Delaware Technical and Community College
Judy C. Vaughan, Arkansas Tech University
Anita Veit, University of North Carolina
Abram Lawrence Wehmiller, Greenhill School
Clovis L. White, Oberlin College
Fred Zampa, Macon State College

One of the more interesting tasks in preparing this book is to gather information on the contributors' backgrounds. In addition to biographical data concerning their education, teaching, and publishing, this section also contains their statements telling us why they like sociology or became sociologists. You may want to assign this section with the articles to help personalize the readings and to increase the student's awareness of biographical factors that go into the choice to become a sociologist.

The selections in this edition continue to be organized to make them compatible with most introductory textbooks. Through subjects that are inherently interesting, we cover the major substantive areas of sociology. Part I, an introduction to the sociological perspective, invites students to view the world in a new way by participating in this exciting enterprise we call sociology. Part II is designed to answer the basic question of how sociologists do research. Part III examines the cultural underpinnings of social life, those taken-for-granted assumptions and contexts that provide the contours of our everyday lives. Part IV focuses on that essential component of our beings, gender and sexuality. There we look at both the process by which we assume the social identity of male or female and how those identities provide the basis for interaction among adults.

In Part V, we examine social groups and social structure, looking behind the scenes to reveal how people's assumptions, their location on social hierarchies, and the features of social settings establish both constraints and freedoms in human relationships. In Part VI, we consider the relativity of deviance and the process of becoming deviant, especially the social context that shapes deviance and conformity. We also examine features of social control, those aspects of social groups that are designed to minimize deviance. In Part VII, we focus on social stratification, beginning with the micro level of physical appearance and then looking at gender, race–ethnicity, poverty, wealth, and power as dimensions of social inequality. In Part VIII, we analyze the social institutions of economics, marriage and family, medicine, education, religion, law, and the military. We conclude the book with a look at social change, the focus of Part IX. After examining how everyday life is being rationalized in a process called McDonaldization, we look at resistance to social change—how the Amish withdraw from mainstream society and how male soldiers undermine the integration of women in the military. We then conclude the book with a look at globalization, one of the major social forces that is both driving global social change and having a profound impact on our own lives.

These selections bring the reader face-to-face with the dual emphases of contemporary sociological research: the focus on the individual's experiences and the analysis of social structure. These articles not only uncover the basic expectations that underlie routine social interaction, but also they emphasize the ways in which social institutions are interrelated. It is to their authors' credit that we lose sight of neither the people who are interacting nor the structural base that so directly influences the form and content of their interactions.

Jim Henslin
January 2007

About the Contributors

Peter L. Berger (article 1) received his Ph.D. in Sociology from the New School for Social Research. He is Professor of Sociology and Theology at Boston University, where he is also Director of the Institute for the Study of Economic Culture. He is the author of numerous books, including *The Social Construction of Reality: A Treatise in the Sociology of Knowledge* (with Thomas Luckmann), *A Far Glory: The Quest for Faith in an Age of Credulity,* and *Invitation to Sociology,* from which his selection in this book is taken.

Berger says, "I was born in Austria and came to the United States with my parents after the war [World War II]. You might say that I became a sociologist by accident. I took some courses in sociology and liked them. I have always been curious about what makes people tick, and that is what sociology is all about."

Mae A. Biggs (article 20) earned her M.A. in Sociology at Southern Illinois University, Edwardsville, and is an associate of the Masters-Johnson Institute (Biological Research Institute) in St. Louis, Missouri.

Napoleon A. Chagnon (article 9) earned his Ph.D. in Anthropology at the University of Michigan. He is Professor Emeritus of Anthropology at the University of California at Santa Barbara and the author of *Yąnomamö: The Last Days of Eden; Yąnomamö Warfare, Social Organization and Marriage Alliances;* and the book from which his selection is taken, *Yąnomamö: The Fierce People.*

William J. Chambliss (article 26) received his Ph.D. in Sociology at Indiana University and is Professor of Sociology at George Washington University. His books include *On the Take: From Petty Crooks to Presidents, Law, Order and Power,* and *Power, Politics, and Crime.* Professor Chambliss is a past President of the American Society of Criminology (1987–88) and a past President of the Society for the Study of Social Problems (1992–93).

Chambliss says, "I became a sociologist out of an interest in doing something about crime. I remained a sociologist because it became clear to me that until we have a greater understanding of the political and economic conditions that lead some societies to have excessive amounts of crime we will never be able to do anything about the problem. Sociology is a beautiful discipline that affords an opportunity to investigate just about anything connected with human behavior and still claim an identity with a discipline.

This is its strength, its promise, and why I find it thoroughly engaging, enjoyable, and fulfilling."

Candace Clark (article 11), who was Professor of Sociology at Montclair State University before she took an extended leave for disability, earned a Ph.D. in Sociomedical Sciences from Columbia University and a Ph.D. in Sociology at the University of Chicago. She is the editor of *Social Interaction: Readings in Sociology* (with Howard Robboy) and the author of *Misery and Company: Sympathy in Everyday Life*.

When I asked Clark why she became a sociologist, she said "Because sociology made more sense of social life than the taken-for-granted explanations that others around me seemed to swallow whole. I was drawn to a way of thinking that questioned the assumptions and addressed them with evidence. Being exposed to the concepts of culture and social structure (such as population pyramids and models of social class) helped me to realize that much was going on behind the scenes of the social world—and I could study it."

Stephanie Coontz (article 37) received her master's in history at the University of Washington. She is Professor of History and Family Studies at The Evergreen State College and Director of Research and Public Education at the Council on Contemporary Families. Her books include *Marriage, A History: How Love Conquered Marriage, American Families,* and *The Way We Never Were: American Families and the Nostalgia Trap*.

Coontz says that she likes sociology because "Sociology helps me understand not only how society works today but also what forces propelled us here. I am convinced that our understanding of contemporary dilemmas and choices are deeper if we know what dilemmas we faced and choices we made in the past. Although those choices often solved old problems, they created new challenges in the process. It is the same today."

Kingsley Davis (article 13) received his Ph.D. in Sociology at Harvard University. At the time of his death in 1997, he was Distinguished Professor of Sociology at the University of Southern California and Senior Research Fellow at the Hoover Institution on War, Revolution and Peace at Stanford University. His books include *Human Society, The Population of India and Pakistan,* and *Below-Replacement Fertility in Industrial Societies: Causes, Consequences, Policy*.

Davis, who often traveled to remote places on the globe, said that he liked sociology because "first, sociology deals with all aspects of society, not just economic behavior or political matters; second, in regard to social change, sociology takes a longer view than most other social science fields. I became a sociologist because I wanted to write and decided that I had better learn something to write, so I elected to learn sociology. Also, I wanted to know how the social system works. We were in the Great Depression at the time, so a social science should be able to analyze and explain that terrible catastrophe."

Robbie E. Davis-Floyd (article 38) earned her Ph.D. in Anthropology at the University of Texas. She is Senior Research Fellow in the Department of Anthropology at the University of Texas, Austin. Among her books are *Birth as an American Rite of Passage, From Doctor to Healer: The Transformative Journey* (with Gloria St. John), and (with Christina Johnson) *Mainstreaming Midwives: The Politics of Professionalization.*

Davis-Floyd says that she likes sociology and anthropology because they answer a question that bothered her. She says, "I became a social scientist because my parents, otherwise very decent human beings, were white Southern racists. During my teenage years, I became desperate to understand why such good people treated and spoke about other people of different skin tones so badly. During my first year in college, I took an anthropology course and discovered that the question, 'Why do people behave as they do?' is central to the social sciences. Not only did I get my answer to my burning personal question, but also I fell in love with this field of study that can take on any aspect of human existence or behavior and seek to make sense of it across cultures."

Gwynne Dyer (article 42) is a London-based independent journalist writing on current social issues. His articles appear in many newspapers and magazines.

Donna Eder (article 15), who earned her Ph.D. in Sociology at the University of Wisconsin, is Professor of Sociology at Indiana University. She has written *School Talk: Gender and Adolescent Culture,* the book from which her selection is taken.

When asked why she became a sociologist, Eder said, "I thought that by understanding school dynamics we could change society through improving our schools. I have since found that sociological research often focuses too much on social problems. Now I am trying to study solutions to social problems, not just the problems."

Barbara Ehrenreich (article 36) is a freelance writer and political satirist who has published widely. Her books include *Debating P.C.: The Controversy over Political Correctness on College Campuses; Fear of Falling: The Inner Life of the Middle Class,* and *Nickel and Dimed: On (Not) Getting by in America,* from which her selection in this book is taken.

Raphael Ezekiel (article 32), who received a Ph.D. in Psychology at the University of California at Berkeley, is a Research Associate at the Harvard School of Public Health. He has published *Voices from the Corner: Poverty and Racism in the Inner City, Cross-National Encounters* (with Herb Kelman), and *The Racist Mind,* the book from which his selection is taken.

When I asked Ezekiel why he likes sociology, he replied: "I am fascinated by the way life histories and broader history intersect. It's how I think about things. Doing fieldwork means that I am constantly being surprised. I run into astonishing things all the time. Reality is terribly different from our broad assumptions and from glib generalizations. Reality is fascinating to me, and relating the specific realities to the broader march of history is absorbing."

Herbert J. Gans (article 33) received his Ph.D. in City Planning and Sociology from the University of Pennsylvania. He is Robert S. Lynd Professor of Sociology at Columbia University and has written such books as *The Urban Villagers; The War against the Poor: The Underclass and Antipoverty Policy;* and *Popular Culture and High Culture: An Analysis and Evaluation of Taste.* Professor Gans is a past President of the American Sociological Association (1987–88).

Why did Gans become a sociologist? He says: "When I was in high school, I thought I would become a journalist, but then when I got to college I discovered that the articles I enjoyed writing most were sociology. From then on I was pretty sure I would become a sociologist." He adds, "The deeper reason I became a sociologist is because I am a refugee from Nazi Germany, and ever since I came to the United States as a teenager in 1940, I have been trying to understand the country which took me in." Whenever possible—and his family agrees—Gans rents an apartment for a month in a European city or medieval town and "explores it, living in it fully."

Erving Goffman (article 12) earned his Ph.D. in Sociology at the University of Chicago and at the time of his death in 1982 was Director of the Center for Urban Ethnography at the University of Pennsylvania. His many books include *Stigma: Notes on the Management of a Spoiled Identity; Behavior in Public Places: Notes on the Social Organization of Gatherings;* and the book from which his selection is taken, *The Presentation of Self in Everyday Life.*

Harry L. Gracey (article 39) received his Ph.D. in Sociology at the New School for Social Research. He is in private practice in organizational development in Cambridge, Massachusetts, and has published *Curriculum or Craftsmanship?: Elementary School Teachers in a Bureaucratic System,* and *Readings in Introductory Sociology* (with Dennis H. Wrong).

Gracey says, "What led me to study sociology was a curiosity about how things work, which in my case got focused on the world of social life, rather than on the physical or biological world. Sociology, uniquely among the social sciences, I think, 'lifts the veil of ideology' on the working of society to see what is really going on—and who is doing it and how it is being done."

Michael D. Grimes (article 34), who earned his Ph.D. at the University of Texas at Austin, is Professor of Sociology at Louisiana State University. He is the author of *Patching Up the Cracks: A Case Study in Juvenile Court Reform, Class in Twentieth Century American Sociology: An Analysis of Theories and Measurement Strategies,* and (with Joan M. Morris) *Caught-in-the-Middle: Contradictions in the Lives of Sociologists from Working-Class Backgrounds.*

Why did Grimes become a sociologist? He says, "Coming from a working-class family, I found it difficult to understand why my family and I were undervalued and treated differently by others, and why we, in turn, undervalued those who were even poorer than we were. I also grew up in a segregated society, and slowly I began to realize that blacks, like us, were somehow victims of the same system. As I grew older, the issues of class and race became almost an obsession. Sociology seemed like a place where I could both understand and, perhaps, help others understand these consequences of life in a democratic capitalist society. On the surface at least, our society stresses equality of opportunity for all, but then it 'blames the victims' for their failures. Not examined are the myriad ways in which society itself assures that the children of the rich remain so, and why the children of the poor are not likely to get as far in life."

Edward T. Hall (article 10) was awarded his Ph.D. in Anthropology at Columbia University. As Emeritus Professor of Anthropology at Northwestern University, he is enjoying retirement in Santa Fe, New Mexico. His books include *The Silent Language, The Hidden Dimension*, and *Beyond Culture*.

Mildred R. Hall (article 10) received her B.A. from Barnard College and (with Edward T. Hall) has written *The Fourth Dimension in Architecture; Hidden Differences: Doing Business with the Japenese;* and *Understanding Cultural Differences: German, French, and American*.

Marvin Harris (article 40) received his Ph.D. from Columbia University. He was Graduate Research Professor of Anthropology at the University of Florida until his death in 2001. Following his primary interest, cultural anthropology, Harris searched for the practical reasons that underlie customs that on the surface seem unreasonable or even bizarre. His books include *Cows, Pigs, Wars, and Witches: The Riddles of Culture; Cannibals and Kings: The Origins of Cultures;* and *Good to Eat: Riddles of Food and Culture*.

James M. Henslin (articles 2, 4, 14, 20, and 24) earned his Ph.D. in Sociology at Washington University in St. Louis. He is Professor Emeritus of Sociology at Southern Illinois University, Edwardsville. His books include *Social Problems; Sociology: A Down-to-Earth Approach;* and *Essentials of Sociology: A Down-to-Earth Approach*.

Henslin says, "My early childhood was marked by poverty. I was born in a rented room in a minister's parsonage. Then my parents made a leap in their economic status—we moved into our own home, a converted garage, with no running water or indoor plumbing! My parents continued their climb in status, and when I was thirteen they built one of the nicest houses in town. These experiences helped make me keenly aware of the significance of 'place' and opportunity in social life." He adds, "I like sociology because of its tremendous breadth—from social class and international stratification to the self and internal conflicts. No matter how diverse your curiosities, you can follow them and they are still part of sociology. Everything that is part of the landscape of human behavior comes under the lens of sociology."

Stephen Higley (article 35) received his Ph.D. in Geography from the University of Illinois at Urbana-Champaign. He is Associate Professor of Geography at the University of Montevallo. Higley wrote *Privilege, Power, and Place: The Geography of the American Upper Class,* the book from which his selection is taken.

As an urban social geographer, Higley's approach to geography is close to sociology. He stresses the consequences of the stratification (or geographical structure) of U.S. metropolitan areas on school systems, public amenities, social services, and even for stereotyping people from different social classes. He says, "The upper class has the means and the influence to create a distinct style of life that minimizes their contact with other social classes. One of the most important vehicles for this separation is where they live and how they control it (of course, with the help of the upper middle class)."

Robert A. Hummer (article 30), who received his Ph.D. from Florida State University, is Associate Professor in the Department of Sociology at the University of Texas, Austin. He has published (with Richard Rogers and Charles Nam) *Living and Dying in the U.S.A.: Behavioral, Health, and Social Differentials of Adult Mortality.*

Hummer says he became a sociologist because "sociology provides me a better way of understanding the complex world in which I live." He enjoys traveling with his wife and daughter, fishing, and watching the Detroit Tigers.

Jennifer Hunt (article 41) received her Ph.D. in Sociology from the City University of New York and is Professor of Sociology at Montclair State University. She has also completed certification in the clinical training program at The Psychoanalytic Institute at the New York University Medical Center.

Hunt has written *Psychoanalytic Aspects of Fieldwork.* She likes sociology because "it provides an unusual opportunity to explore other cultural worlds by doing in-depth fieldwork."

Bruce A. Jacobs (article 7), who received his Ph.D. in Sociology from the University of Southern California, is Associate Professor in Sociology at the University of Texas at Dallas. He is the author of *Robbing Drug Dealers: Violence Beyond the Law* and *Dealing Crack: The Social World of Streetcorner Selling,* the book from which his selection is taken.

Sidney Katz (article 29), who earned a Bachelor in Social Sciences from Carleton University and a Master of Social Work at the University of Toronto, is a professional writer. He has published hundreds of articles and two books and has done considerable radio and TV broadcasting. He has been a columnist, a feature writer, and an editor at the *Toronto Star* and at *Maclean's Magazine.* He says, "I have retired several times, but it hasn't stuck."

Helene M. Lawson (article 18) earned her Ph.D. in Sociology at Loyola University. She is Professor of Sociology at the University of Pittsburgh at Bradford. She has edited *The Cultural Study of Work* (with Doug Harper) and written *Ladies on the Lot: Women, Car Sales, and the Pursuit of the American Dream,* the book from which her selection is taken.

Lawson says, "I decided to become a sociologist after getting a B.A. in Elementary Education and two M.A. degrees, one in Early Childhood and one in Gerontology. I was teaching people about human behavior, but I was not content with the explanations I gained from psychology, biology, or education. Sociology gave me a broader view of social institutions and the motivations for individual behavior, and, through its encompassing view of human institutions, even a vision of progress in which I find hope." Lawson's interests are broad, and, as she says, "My writings range from stories about gender equality in blue-collar families to what it's like to work on hair, and even the interactions of conservation officers with hunted animals."

Robin Leidner (article 43), who earned her Ph.D. in Sociology at North-western University, is Associate Professor of Sociology at the University of Pennsylvania.

Leidner says, "I became a sociologist after concluding that acting was unlikely to be my life's work. I have carried my interest in acting into sociology, and I am now doing research on work, identity, and scripts in professional theater. Questions about how much acting is asked of work-ers in other jobs, and about how people reconcile who they want to be with what they have to do to make a living, are central to my sociolog-ical work."

Elliot Liebow (article 21) earned his Ph.D. in Sociology at the Catholic University of America. Until his death in 1994, he was a social anthropolo-gist with the National Institute of Mental Health. He is the author of *Tally's Corner* and *Tell Them Who I Am: The Lives of Homeless Women,* the book from which his selection is taken.

Zella Luria (article 16) received her Ph.D. in Psychology at Indiana Uni-versity and is Professor of Psychology at Tufts University. She is the author of *The Psychology of Human Sexuality* (with Mitchel D. Rose) and *Human Sexuality* (with S. Friedman and Mitchel D. Rose).

Luria says, "What I appreciate about sociology is its exquisite attention to the group context for explanations of behavior."

Joseph Marolla (article 5) earned his Ph.D. in Sociology at the University of Denver. He is Professor of Sociology at Virginia Commonwealth University. He has published articles in social psychology, criminology, sociology of education, symbolic interaction, and self-esteem.

Marolla says, "I suppose, as much as anything else, I became a sociologist because my draft lottery number was 315 in the winter of 1969—which meant that I would not be going to Vietnam. At the time, I had given very little thought to life beyond the war. Once handed the option, school seemed the reasonable thing to do since I had been doing it for a while. I was an English major, and I moved to sociology because I thought it would broaden my creative writing. . . . What I most like about sociology is that it provides a broad picture and helps us see through the facade of life as we live it. This was appealing to me, and still is. Our research on rape is an example. Psychologists are convinced that rape is due to psychological dysfunction. We have demonstrated that rape is dramatically embedded in the culture."

Patricia Yancey Martin (article 30), who received her Ph.D. from Florida State University, is Professor of Sociology at Florida State University. Her books include *Feminist Organizations: Harvest of the New Women's Movement* (with Myra M. Ferree) and *The Social Environment: Open Systems Applications* (with Gerald O'Connor).

Martin, whose favorite activity outside of teaching, gardening, and the arts, is traveling to Europe, says that she majored in English literature, but didn't like it enough to pursue it after the bachelor's degree. She thought she might be interested in sociology, and tried graduate school. "After I was in sociology a few years," she says, "I came to see the power of the sociological perspective." She adds, "I love trying to observe and explain the social world around me."

Philip Meyer (article 23) earned an M.A. in Political Science at the University of North Carolina at Chapel Hill, where he is now Knight Chair in Journalism. His books include *Precision Journalism: A Reporter's Introduction to Social Science Methods; Ethical Journalism: A Guide for Students, Practitioners, and Consumers;* and *The Vanishing Newspaper: Saving Journalism in the Information Age.*

Meyer says, "I became interested in sociology because, as a journalist, I envied its research tools. I spent a postgraduate year at Harvard learning about those tools and thinking of ways to apply them to news reporting. In the course of that work, I learned about the Milgram experiments."

Laura L. Miller (article 45), who received her Ph.D. from Northwestern University, is Assistant Professor of Sociology at Brandeis University. She has published *New Opportunities for Military Women: Effects Upon Readiness, Cohesion, and Morale* (with Margaret C. Harrell).

Miller, whose primary focus is human relations in the military, has done research on peacekeeping operations in Somalia, Macedonia, Haiti, and Bosnia. She also enjoys snowboarding, international travel, live music, and playing at the beach. She says, "In college I was interested in so many different subjects. Sociology was the answer for me, because as a sociologist I can study anything I want and never have to change jobs."

C. Wright Mills (article 3) received his Ph.D. in Sociology from the University of Wisconsin. His scathing criticisms of U.S. society in such books as *White Collar, The Causes of World War III*, as well as the book from which his article is taken, *The Sociological Imagination*, made him one of the most controversial sociologists in the United States. At the time of his death in 1962, he was Professor of Sociology at Columbia University.

Horace Miner (article 8) earned his Ph.D. in Social Anthropology at the University of Chicago. Until his death in 1993, he was Professor Emeritus of Anthropology at the University of Michigan. His books include *The Primitive City in Timbuctoo, St. Denis: A French Canadian Parish*, and *The City in Modern Africa*.

Miner said, "It was by accident that I became a sociologist. Having received my degree in social anthropology, it was easy to teach sociology when I received an offer. My courses were listed in both anthropology and sociology."

Joan M. Morris (article 34), who received her Ph.D. from Louisiana State University, is Associate Professor of Sociology at University of Central Florida. She has written (with Michael D. Grimes) *Caught in the Middle: Contradictions in the Lives of Sociologists from Working-class Backgrounds*.

When asked why she became a sociologist, Morris said: "I became a sociologist so I could teach. I hoped to share the fascination I have with social processes and the excitement I felt when I first learned the basic concepts of sociology. I wanted to help others understand social inequality and to offer an alternative view—or a fuller understanding of why there is so much inequality in American society—one that focuses so much on individualism and competition. After years in graduate school and teaching, I am still moved when I read the kind of sociology that helps us understand the world around us. I still get that 'aha' experience sometimes—and the benefit of teaching is that it now sometimes comes from my students."

Clarence Page (article 31) is the editor of *A Foot in Each World: Essays and Articles* (with Leanita McClain), and the author of *Freedom's Champion:*

Elijah Lovejoy (with Paul Simon), and *Showing My Color: Impolite Essays on Race and Identity*, the book from which his selection is taken.

Page says, "My interest in sociology dates back to my high school years. It is grounded in the same curiosity that informed my book of essays on race." He adds, "I like sociology because it tries to analyze and explain the group behaviors, attitudes, and relationships that raise the sort of questions I try to answer in my book."

Devah Pager (article 6), who earned her Ph.D. in Sociology at the University of Wisconsin-Madison, is Assistant Professor of Sociology at Princeton University. She is the author of *Marked: Race, Crime, and Finding Work in an Era of Mass Incarceration.*

Pager, who originally wanted to be a psychologist, lived in Los Angeles while she was studying for her undergraduate degree. "This," she says, "exposed me to a world of urban inequality, racial segregation, and social problems that extended far beyond the individual focus of psychology. Sociology provides the tools to understand these broader social and structural forces that create and perpetuate racial inequality."

David L. Rosenhan (article 28), who received his Ph.D. in Psychology from Columbia University, is Professor Emeritus of Psychology and Law at Stanford University. His books include *Foundations of Abnormal Psychology* (with Perry London), *Theory and Research in Abnormal Psychology,* and (with Martin Seligman and Elaine Walker) *Abnormal Psychology.*

Jerry Savells (article 44) received his Ph.D. in Sociology at Louisiana State University. He is Professor of Sociology at Wright State University. He has edited (with Larry Cross) *The Changing Family: Making Way for Tomorrow,* and *Marriage and the Family in a Changing Society.*

Savells, whose favorite activity outside of teaching and doing sociology is fishing, earned his bachelor's degree in chemistry and biology at Murray State University. He says, "After working for a few years, I found the chemistry laboratory too confining. I decided that I wanted to move into an area where I could have more impact on people, and I returned to graduate school and studied sociology. I also served as an officer in the army, where I did some teaching, and thought that I would like to teach in an academic setting. I am fascinated with human behavior, with how people get together in social groups, and I have focused on families, especially on how families respond to social change."

Diana Scully (article 5) earned her Ph.D. in Sociology at the University of Illinois. She is Professor of Sociology and Coordinator of Women's Studies at Virginia Commonwealth University. She has written *Understanding Sexual Violence: A Study of Convicted Rapists,* and *Men Who Control Women's Health: The Miseducation of Obstetrician Gynecologists.*

Scully says, "I changed my undergraduate major to sociology on the day that Martin Luther King was assassinated. I felt then and continue to believe that because of its focus on social structure sociology has a greater potential than other disciplines for understanding complex problems, such as racism and sexism, and therefore can be used as a tool for accomplishing change that is meaningful collectively and individually."

Kandi M. Stinson (article 19), who earned her Ph.D. at the University of North Carolina at Chapel Hill, is Professor of Sociology at Xavier University. She has published *Adolescents, Family, and Friends: Social Support after Parents' Divorce or Remarriage* and *Women and Dieting Culture: Inside a Commercial Weight Loss Group.*

Stinson says that English was her first major as an undergraduate, but that her introductory sociology class changed her course in life. "I soon 'converted' to sociology after reading C. Wright Mills, *The Sociological Imagination,* in an introductory course. I was struck by his thoughtful critique of American society and deep insights into the relationships between individuals and society. I was also desperately looking for a career that would somehow combine my love for people watching, my fascination with culture, especially popular culture, and my interest in and talent for writing. I found all these in sociology."

Deborah Tannen (article 17) earned a Ph.D. in English literature at the University of California at Berkeley. After teaching English at several universities in the U.S. and Greece, she joined the Linguistics Department at Georgetown University, where she is University Professor. Her books include *Talking from 9 to 5; You Just Don't Understand: Women and Men in Conversation;* and *That's Not What I Meant: How Conversational Style Makes or Breaks Relationships.*

William E. Thompson (article 22) earned his Ph.D. in Sociology at Oklahoma State University and is Professor of Sociology and Criminal Justice at Texas A&M University at Commerce. He has edited *Juvenile Delinquency: Classic and Contemporary Readings* (with Jack E. Bynum) and written *Juvenile Delinquency: A Sociological Approach* (with Jack E. Bynum), and *Society in Focus* (with Joseph V. Hickey).

Coming from a working-class background, Thompson is the first in his immediate family to graduate from high school. He says that he is attracted to sociology because "sociology makes the entire world your laboratory."

Barrie Thorne (article 16) earned her Ph.D. in Sociology at Brandeis University. She is Professor of Sociology and of Women's Studies at the University of California at Berkeley. Thorne is the author of *Gender Play: Girls and Boys in School,* and (with Barbara Laslett) the editor of *Feminist Sociology: Life Histories of a Movement,* and *Language, Gender and Society.*

When asked why she became a sociologist, Thorne said, "Existing arrangements aren't fixed; they're the result of and can be changed by human action. Sociology provides tools for digging beneath the surface of the 'given'—such as arrangements of schooling. This helps us see underlying structures of inequality, enabling us to learn more about the perspectives of groups, like women and children, who have historically been relatively invisible in knowledge. Critical sociological perspectives connect empirical inquiry with visions of justice—a useful path for both understanding and action."

William van Dusen Wishard (article 46) graduated from high school in Richmond, Virginia. After that, he traveled the world, working and living in thirty countries. The founder of World Trends Research, from which he is semi-retired, he lectures on the major cultural and technological trends reshaping the global landscape. He is the author of *A Perspective for the '90s: A World in Search of Meaning, The American Future: What Would George and Tom Do Now?*, and *Between Two Ages: The 21st Century and the Crisis of Meaning.*

When I asked van Dusen Wishard why he liked sociology, he said, "Sociology engages me because it is the only academic discipline that incorporates all areas of life into one comprehensive perspective. It helps give us a view of where humanity is in its historic trajectory, and where we might be headed."

Philip G. Zimbardo (article 27) earned his Ph.D. in Social Psychology at Yale University and is Professor of Social Psychology at Stanford University. He is a past president of the American Psychological Association (2002). His books include *Psychology and Life* (with Richard J. Gerrig), *The Shy Child: Overcoming and Preventing Shyness from Infancy to Adulthood* (with Shirley Radl), and (with Michael R. Leippe) *The Psychology of Attitude Change and Social Influence.*

Zimbardo, who has taught in Italy and enjoys collecting and studying the arts and crafts of the Native Americans of the Northwest and Southwest, says that he likes sociology because of "the scope of the significant questions it raises about human behavior."

The Sociological Perspective

Sociology is an invitation to look behind the scenes of the social world—a passport, as it were, to a different way of viewing life.

—Author

I WOULD LIKE TO BEGIN this introduction on a personal note. Since my early school days, reading has been one of my favorite pastimes. I used to read almost anything I could lay my hands on, but I was especially fascinated by books that explored people's lives—especially novels that described people's life situations, thoughts, relationships, hopes and dreams, challenges and obstacles. Without knowing it, I was gaining an appreciation for understanding the social context in which people live out their lives—for seeing how important that context is in determining what people are like.

When I went to college, I discovered that there was a name for my interests: sociology. What an exciting revelation: I had found an entire academic discipline centered on understanding the general context in which people live and analyzing how their lives are influenced by it! I could not help wanting to read sociology, to take more courses, to immerse myself in it. I was hooked—so thoroughly, in fact, that eventually I decided to become a sociologist and spend my life in this fascinating endeavor.

The intention of this book is fourfold. First, I want to share some of the excitement and fascination of sociology. Second, through these readings, I want to make more visible the context of social life that affects us all. Third, if this is successful, you will gain a better understanding not only of people in general, but of your own self as well. Finally, I hope to whet your appetite for more sociology.

As Peter Berger says in the opening selection, the discovery of sociology can change your life. It can help you to understand the social forces you confront, the forces that constrain and free you as you go about living your life.

This understanding offers a liberating potential: To gain insight into how these social forces influence your life allows you to stand somewhat apart from at least some of them and thereby to exert more creative control over your own life.

But just what is sociology? In my teaching I have found that introductory students often find this a vexing question. To provide a better grasp of what sociology is, then, in the second selection I compare sociology with the other social sciences. One of the main points of this article is that sociology casts an intellectual net that provides an unparalleled approach to understanding social life.

In the third and last article in this first part of the book, C. Wright Mills turns again to this liberating potential that sociology offers. As he points out, this capacity centers on understanding three main issues: (1) the structure of society—that is, how society's components are interrelated; (2) where one's society stands in human history and the changes that are occurring in it; and (3) what type of people prevail in one's society, how they are selected for prevalence, and what types are coming to prevail.

Thinking of life in these terms, says Mills, is a quality of mind that we should strive for. This *sociological imagination,* to use his term for the socio-logical perspective, allows us to peer beyond our immediate confines, to seek out and understand the broader social and historical forces at work in our lives. One of the rewarding consequences of this perspective, he says, is that it en-ables us to see ourselves in a different light.

It is the goal of Part I, then, to let you dip your feet in the sociological waters, to challenge you to venture into sociology, and, while venturing, to stimulate your sociological imagination.

1   Invitation to Sociology

PETER L. BERGER

Motivated by an intense desire to know what is "really happening," what goes on "behind the scenes," sociologists study almost every aspect of life in society. As Berger indicates, nothing is too sacred or too profane to be spared the sociologist's scrutiny. But when you penetrate the surface and peer behind the masks that individuals and organizations wear, you find a reality quite unlike the one that is so carefully devised and, just as carefully, put forward for public consumption.

This changed angle of vision, however, poses a danger. Once you have peered behind the scenes and viewed life in a new light, it is nearly impossible to revert to complacent assumptions. The old, familiar, and so very comfortable ways of looking at life become upset when your angle of vision changes. This potential of sociology is also part of its attraction.

THE SOCIOLOGIST (that is, the one we would really like to invite to our game) is a person intensively, endlessly, shamelessly interested in the doings of men.* His natural habitat is all the human gathering places of the world, wherever men come together. The sociologist may be interested in many other things. But his consuming interest remains in the world of men, their institutions, their history, their passions. And since he is interested in men, nothing that men do can be altogether tedious for him. He will naturally be interested in the events that engage men's ultimate beliefs, their moments of tragedy and grandeur and ecstasy. But he will also be fascinated by the commonplace, the everyday. He will know reverence, but this reverence will not prevent him from wanting to see and to understand. He may sometimes feel revulsion or contempt. But this also will not deter him from wanting to have his questions answered. The sociologist, in his quest for understanding, moves through the world of men without respect for the usual lines of demarcation. Nobility and degradation, power and obscurity, intelligence and folly—these are equally *interesting* to him, however unequal they may be in his

*Some of the classic articles in this book (selections 1, 3, 8, 9, 10, 12, and 28) were written before linguistic styles changed, when "men" was generic, referring to both men and women. So it was with "he, his, him," and so on. Although the writing style has changed, the sociological ideas have not.

personal values or tastes. Thus his questions may lead him to all possible levels of society, the best and the least known places, the most respected and the most despised. And, if he is a good sociologist, he will find himself in all these places because his own questions have so taken possession of him that he has little choice but to seek for answers.

It would be possible to say the same things in a lower key. We could say that the sociologist, but for the grace of his academic title, is the man who must listen to gossip despite himself, who is tempted to look through key-holes, to read other people's mail, to open cabinets. Before some otherwise unoccupied psychologist sets out now to construct an aptitude test for sociologists on the basis of sublimated voyeurism, let us quickly say that we are speaking merely by way of analogy. Perhaps some little boys consumed with curiosity to watch their maiden aunts in the bathroom later become inveterate sociologists. This is quite uninteresting. What interests us is the curiosity that grips any sociologist in front of a closed door behind which there are human voices. If he is a good sociologist he will want to open that door, to understand these voices. Behind each closed door he will anticipate some new facet of human life not yet perceived and understood.

The sociologist will occupy himself with matters that others regard as too sacred or as too distasteful for dispassionate investigation. He will find rewarding the company of priests or of prostitutes, depending not on his personal preferences but on the questions he happens to be asking at the moment. He will also concern himself with matters that others may find much too boring. He will be interested in the human interaction that goes with warfare or with great intellectual discoveries, but also in the relations between people employed in a restaurant or between a group of little girls playing with their dolls. His main focus of attention is not the ultimate significance of what men do, but the action in itself, as another example of the infinite richness of human conduct.

In these journeys through the world of men the sociologist will inevitably encounter other professional Peeping Toms. Sometimes these will resent his presence, feeling that he is poaching on their preserves. In some places the sociologist will meet up with the economist, in others with the political scientist, in yet others with the psychologist or the ethnologist. Yet chances are that the questions that have brought him to these places are different from the ones that propelled his fellow-trespassers. The sociologist's questions always remain essentially the same: "What are people doing with each other here?" "What are their relationships to each other?" "How are these relationships organized in institutions?" "What are the collective ideas that move men and institutions?" In trying to answer these questions in specific instances, the sociologist will, of course, have to deal with economic or political matters, but he will do so in a way rather different from that of the economist or the political scientist. The scene that he contemplates is the same human scene that these other scientists concern themselves with. But the sociologist's angle of vision is different. When this is understood, it becomes clear that it makes little sense to try to stake out a special enclave within which the sociologist will carry on business in his own right. Like Wesley the sociologist will have to confess that his parish is the world. But unlike some latter-day Wesleyans he will gladly share this parish with others. There is, however, one traveler whose path the sociologist will cross more often than anyone else's on his journeys. This is the historian. Indeed, as soon as the sociologist turns from the present to the past, his preoccupations are very hard indeed to distinguish from those of the historian. [T]he sociological journey will be much impoverished unless it is punctuated frequently by conversation with that other particular traveler.

Any intellectual activity derives excitement from the moment it becomes a trail of discovery. . . . The excitement of sociology is [not always to penetrate] worlds that had previously been quite unknown . . . for instance, the world of crime, or the world of some bizarre religious sect, or the world fashioned by the exclusive concerns of some group such as medical specialists or military leaders or advertising executives. [M]uch of the time the sociologist moves in sectors of experience that are familiar to him and to most people in his society. He investigates communities, institutions, and activities that one can read about every day in the newspapers. Yet there is another excitement of discovery beckoning in his investigations. It is not the excitement of finding the familiar but becoming transformed in it. The fascination of sociology lies in the fact that its perspective makes us see in a new light the very world in which we have lived all of our lives. This also constitutes a transformation of consciousness. Moreover, this transformation is more relevant existentially than that of many other intellectual disciplines, because it is more difficult to segregate in some special compartment of the mind. The astronomer does not live in the remote galaxies, and the nuclear physicist can, outside his laboratory, eat and laugh and marry and vote without thinking about the insides of the atom. The geologist looks at rocks only at appropriate times, and the linguist speaks English with his wife. The sociologist lives in society, on the job and off it. His own life, inevitably, is part of his subject matter. Men being what they are, sociologists too manage to segregate their professional insights from their everyday affairs. But it is a rather difficult feat to perform in good faith.

The sociologist moves in the common world of men, close to what most of them would call real. The categories he employs in his analyses are only refinements of the categories by which other men live—power, class, status, race, ethnicity. As a result, there is a deceptive simplicity and obviousness about some sociological investigations. One reads them, nods at the familiar scene, remarks that one has heard all this before and don't people have better things to do than to waste their time on truisms—until one is suddenly brought up against an insight that radically questions everything one had previously assumed about this familiar scene. This is the point at which one begins to sense the excitement of sociology.

Let us take a specific example. Imagine a sociology class in a Southern college where almost all the students are white Southerners. Imagine a lecture on the subject of the racial system of the South. The lecturer is talking here of matters that have been familiar to his students from the time of their infancy. Indeed, it may be that they are much more familiar with the minutiae of this system than he is. They are quite bored as a result. It seems to them that he is only using more pretentious words to describe what they already know. Thus he may use the term "caste," one commonly used now by American sociologists to describe the Southern racial system. But in explaining the term he shifts to traditional Hindu society, to make it clearer. He then goes on to analyze the magical beliefs inherent in caste tabus, the social dynamics of commensalism and connubium, the economic interests concealed within the system, the way in which religious beliefs relate to the tabus, the effects of the caste system upon the industrial development of the society and vice versa—all in India. But suddenly India is not very far away at all. The lecture then goes back to its Southern theme. The familiar now seems not quite so familiar any more. Questions are raised that are new, perhaps raised angrily, but raised all the same. And at least some of the students have begun to understand that there are functions involved in this business of race that they have not read about in the newspapers (at least not those in their hometowns) and that their parents have not told them—partly, at least, because neither the newspapers nor the parents knew about them.

It can be said that the first wisdom of sociology is this—things are not what they seem. This too is a deceptively simple statement. It ceases to be simple after a while. Social reality turns out to have many layers of meaning. The discovery of each new layer changes the perception of the whole.

Anthropologists use the term "culture shock" to describe the impact of a totally new culture upon a newcomer. In an extreme instance such shock will be experienced by the Western explorer who is told, halfway through dinner, that he is eating the nice old lady he had been chatting with the previous day—a shock with predictable physiological if not moral consequences. Most explorers no longer encounter cannibalism in their travels today. However, the first encounters with polygamy or with puberty rites or even with the way some nations drive their automobiles can be quite a shock to an American visitor. With the shock may go not only disapproval or disgust but a sense of excitement that things can *really* be that different from what they are at home. To some extent, at least, this is the excitement of any first travel abroad. The experience of sociological discovery could be described as "culture shock" minus geographical displacement. In other words, the sociologist travels at home—with shocking results. He is unlikely to find that he is eating a nice old lady for dinner. But the discovery, for instance, that his own church has considerable money invested in the missile industry or that a few blocks from his home there are people who engage in cultic orgies may not be drastically different in emotional impact. Yet we would not want to imply that sociological discoveries are always or even usually outrageous to moral sentiment. Not at all. What they have in common with exploration in distant lands, however, is the sudden illumination of new and unsuspected facets of human existence in society. . . .

People who like to avoid shocking discoveries, who prefer to believe that society is just what they were taught in Sunday School, who like the safety of the rules and the maxims of what Alfred Schutz has called the "world-taken-for-granted," should stay away from sociology. People who feel no temptation before closed doors, who have no curiosity about human beings, who are content to admire scenery without wondering about the people who live in those houses on the other side of that river, should probably stay away from sociology. They will find it unpleasant or, at any rate, unrewarding. People who are interested in human beings only if they can change, convert, or reform them should also be warned, for they will find sociology much less useful than they hoped. And people whose interest is mainly in their own conceptual constructions will do just as well to turn to the study of little white mice. Sociology will be satisfying, in the long run, only to those who can think of nothing more entrancing than to watch men and to understand things human.

It may now be clear that we have, albeit deliberately, understated the case in the title of this chapter. [The chapter title from which this selection is taken is "Sociology as an Individual Pastime."] To be sure, sociology is an individual pastime in the sense that it interests some men and bores others. Some like to observe human beings, others to experiment with mice. The world is big enough to hold all kinds and there is no logical priority for one interest as against another. But the word "pastime" is weak in describing what we mean. Sociology is more like a passion. The sociological perspective is more like a demon that possesses one, that drives one compellingly, again and again, to the questions that are its own. An introduction to sociology is, therefore, an invitation to a very special kind of passion.

2 What Is Sociology? Comparing Sociology and the Other Social Sciences

JAMES M. HENSLIN

Introductory students often wrestle with the question of what sociology is. If you continue your sociological studies, however, that vagueness of definition—"Sociology is the study of society" or "Sociology is the study of social groups"—that frequently so bothers introductory students will come to be appreciated as one of sociology's strengths and one of its essential attractions. That sociology encompasses almost all human behavior is, indeed, precisely the appeal that draws many to sociology.

To help make clearer at the outset what sociology is, Henslin compares and contrasts sociology with the other social sciences. After examining similarities and differences in their approaches to understanding human behavior, he looks at how social scientists from these related academic disciplines would approach the study of juvenile delinquency.

Science and the Human Desire for Explanation

HUMAN BEINGS ARE FASCINATED with the world in which they live, and they aspire to develop ways to explain their experiences. People appear to have always felt this fascination—along with the intense desire to unravel the world's mysteries—for people in ancient times also attempted to explain their worlds. Despite the severe limitations that confronted them, the ancients explored the natural or physical world, constructing explanations that satisfied them. They also developed an understanding of their social world, the world of people with all their activities and myriad ways of dealing with one another. The ancients, however, mixed magic and superstition to explain their observations.

Today, we are no less fascinated with the world within which we live out our lives. We also investigate both the mundane and the esoteric. We cast a quizzical eye at the common rocks we find embedded in the earth, as well as at some rare variety of insect found only in an almost inaccessible region of remote Tibet. We subject our contemporary world to the constant probings of the instruments and machines we have developed to extend our senses. In our attempts to decipher our observations, we no longer are satisfied with traditional explanations of origins or of relationships. No longer do we accept unquestioningly explanations that earlier generations took for granted. Making observations with the aid of our new technology—such as electronic microscopes, satellites, and the latest generation of computers and software—we derive testable conclusions concerning the nature of our world.

As the ancients could only wish to do, we have been able to expand our objective study of the world beyond the confines of this planet. In our relentless pursuit of knowledge, no longer are we limited to speculation concerning the nature of the stars and planets. In the past couple of centuries the telescope has enabled us to make detailed and repetitive observations of the planets and other heavenly bodies. From these observations, we have reached conclusions startlingly different from those that people traditionally drew concerning the relative place of the earth in our galaxy and the universe. In just the past few years, by means of space technology, we have been able to extend our senses, as it were, beyond anything we had before dreamed possible. We now are able to reach out by means of our spaceships, satellites, and space platforms to record data from other planets and—by means of computer-enhanced graphics—to gain an intrinsically detailed and changing vision of our physical world. We have also been able to dig up and return to the earth samples of soil from the surface of the moon as well as to send mechanized vehicles to Mars and probes to the radiant and magnetic belts of Jupiter, over a distance so great (or, we could say, with our technology still so limited) that they must travel eighteen months before they can send reports back to earth. Having discovered evidence of water on Mars, we have begun to dig into its surface to find out if life exists on our "sister" planet.

A generation or so ago such feats existed only in the minds of "mad" scientists, who at that time seemed irrelevant to the public but whose ideas today are producing fascinating and sometimes fearful consequences for our life on earth. Some of those scientists are drawing up plans for colonizing space, beginning with the moon, opening still another area of exciting exploration, but one whose consequences probably will be only inadequately anticipated. Others are developing weapons for real space wars, with potential outcomes so terrifying we can barely imagine them. For good and evil, science directly impinges on our contemporary life in society, leaving none of us unaffected.

The Natural and the Social Sciences

In satisfying our basic curiosities about the world, we have developed two parallel sets of sciences, each identified by its distinct subject matter. The first is called the *natural sciences,* the intellectual and academic endeavors designed to explain and predict the events in our natural environment. The natural sciences are divided into specialized fields of research and given names on the basis of their particular subject matter—such as biology, geology, chemistry, and physics. These fields of knowledge are further divided into even more highly specialized areas, each with a further narrowing of content: Biology is divided into botany and zoology, geology into mineralogy and geomorphology, chemistry into its organic and inorganic branches, and physics into biophysics and quantum mechanics. Each area of investigation examines a particular "slice" of nature.

People have not limited themselves to investigating nature. In their pursuit of a more adequate understanding of life, they have also developed fields of science that focus on the social world. The *social sciences* examine human relationships. Just as the natural sciences attempt to understand objectively the world of nature, the social sciences attempt to understand objectively the social world. Just as the world of nature contains ordered (or lawful) relationships that are not obvious but must be discovered through controlled observation, so the ordered relationships of the human or social world are not obvious, and must be revealed by means of repeated observations.

Like the natural sciences, the social sciences are divided into specialized fields based on their subject matter. These divisions are anthropology, economics, political science, psychology, and sociology, with history sometimes included on this list. To be inclusive, I shall count history as a social science.

The social sciences are divided further into specialized fields. Anthropology is divided into cultural and physical anthropology; economics has macro (large-scale) and micro (small-scale) specialties; political science has theoretical and applied branches; psychology may be clinical or experimental; history has ancient and modern specialties; and sociology has its quantitative and qualitative branches. Because our focus is sociology, let's contrast sociology with each of the other social sciences.

Sociology Contrasted with the Other Social Sciences

The distinctions between sociology and the other social sciences are not always clear. As they practice their crafts, much that social scientists do crosses conceptual lines and blurs the distinctions among the social sciences. Yet, there are basic differences.

Let's begin with *history,* the social science that focuses on past events. Historians attempt to unearth the facts that surround an event that they are trying to explain. They attempt to establish the social context of the event— the important people, ideas, social institutions, social movements, or preceding events that appear to have influenced the outcome that they want to explain. From this context, which they reconstruct from records of the past, they abstract what they consider to be the most important elements, or *variables,* that caused the event. Using these "causal" factors or variables, historians "explain" the past.

The focus of *political science* is politics or government. Political scientists study the ways that people govern themselves—their forms of government and how these forms are related to other institutions of society. Political scientists are especially interested in how people attain ruling positions, how they maintain those positions, and the consequences of their actions for those they govern. In studying a constitutional government, such as that of the United States, political scientists also analyze voting behavior.

Economics also concentrates on a single social institution. Economists study the production and distribution of the material goods and services of a society. They want to know what goods are being produced, at what rate, and at what cost, and how those goods are distributed. Economists are also interested in what determines production and consumption; for example, what motivates people to buy a certain item instead of another? Some economists, but not nearly enough in my judgment, are also interested in the consequences for human life of the facts of production and distribution of goods and services.

Anthropology is the sister discipline of sociology. The chief concern of anthropologists is to understand *culture,* a people's total way of life. Culture includes a group's (1) *artifacts,* such as its tools, art, and weapons; (2) *structure,* that is, the patterns (such as positions that require respect) that determine how its members interact with one another; (3) *ideas and values,* especially how its belief system affects people's lives; and (4) *forms of communication,* especially language. The traditional focus of anthropology has been on tribal peoples. Anthropologists who are studying for their doctorate usually live with a group. In their reports, they emphasize the group's family (kin) relationships. Because there are no "undiscovered" groups left in the world, this focus on tribal groups is giving way to the study of people who live in industrialized societies. Anthropologists who focus on contemporary societies are practically indistinguishable from sociologists, except that they place greater emphasis on artifacts, authority (hierarchy), and language, especially kinship terms.

The focus of *psychology* is processes that occur *within* the individual, inside what psychologists call the "skin-bound organism." Psychologists study mental processes (what occurs in the brain, or the mind). They examine intelligence, emotions, perception, memory, even dreams. Some study how personality is formed. Others focus on mental aberrations (psychopathology or mental illness). Many psychologists work in private practice and as counselors in school and work settings, where they give personality tests, IQ tests, and vocational aptitude tests. As therapists, psychologists focus on resolving personal problems, whether they involve the need to recover from trauma, such as abuse, or to be freed from addiction to drugs, alcohol, or gambling.

Sociology has many similarities to the other social sciences. Like history, sociologists also attempt to establish the social contexts that influence people. Sociology is also similar to political science in that sociologists, too, study how people govern one another, especially how government affects people's lives. Like economists, sociologists are also concerned with what happens to the goods and services of a society, but sociologists place their focus on the social consequences of inequality. Like anthropologists, sociologists also study culture; they, too, have an interest in group structure and belief systems, as well as in how people communicate with one another. Like psychologists, sociologists are also concerned with how people adjust to the problems and challenges that they face in life.

With these overall similarities, then, where are the differences? Unlike historians, sociologists are primarily concerned with events in the present. Unlike political scientists and economists, sociologists do not concentrate on only a single social institution. Unlike anthropologists, sociologists primarily focus on contemporary societies. And unlike psychologists, to determine what influences people, sociologists stress variables external to the individual.

The Example of Juvenile Delinquency

Because all the social sciences focus on human behavior, they differ from one another not so much in the content of what each studies but, rather, in what the social scientists look for when they conduct their studies. It is basically their approaches, their orientations, or their emphases that differentiate the social sciences. Accordingly, to make clearer the differences between them, it might be helpful to look at how different social scientists might approach the same topic. We shall use juvenile delinquency as our example.

Historians who are interested in juvenile delinquency would examine juvenile delinquency in some particular past setting, such as New York City in the 1920s or Los Angeles in the 1950s. The historian would try to interpret the delinquency by stressing the social context of the period. For example, if delinquent gangs in New York City in the 1920s were the focus, historians might emphasize the social disruption caused by World War I; the problems of unassimilated, recently arrived ethnic groups; competition and rivalry for social standing among those ethnic groups; intergenerational conflict; the national, state, and local political and economic situation; and so on. The historian might also document the number of gangs, as well as their ethnic makeup. He or she would then produce a history of juvenile delinquency in New York City in the 1920s.

Political scientists are less likely to be interested in juvenile delinquency. But if they were, they would want to know how the existence of juvenile gangs is related to politics. For example, are the children of people who have less access to political decision making more likely to join gangs? Or political scientists might study the power structure within a particular gang by identifying its leaders and followers. They might then compare one gang with another, perhaps even drawing analogies with the political structure of some legitimate group.

Economists also are not likely to study delinquent gangs or juvenile delinquency. But if they did, they, of course, would emphasize the economic aspects of delinquency. They might determine how material goods, such as stolen property, are allocated within a gang. But they would be more inclined to focus on delinquency in general, emphasizing the relationship of gangs to economic conditions in the country. Economists might wish to examine the effects of such conditions as booms and busts on the formation of gangs or on the prevalence of delinquency. They might also wish to determine the cost of juvenile delinquency to the nation in terms of property stolen and destroyed and wages paid to police and social workers.

Anthropologists are likely to be highly interested in studying juvenile delinquency and the formation of juvenile gangs. If anthropologists were to study a particular gang, they might examine the implements of delinquency, such as tools used in car theft or in burglary. They would focus on the social organization of the gang, looking at its structure of leaders and followers. They would study the belief system of the group to see how it supports the group's delinquent activities. They would also concentrate on the ways in which group members communicate with one another, especially their *argot,* or special language. Anthropologists would stress the larger cultural context in order to see what it is about a culture, such as the ways in which it marks entry into manhood, that leads to the formation of such groups. They would compare their findings with what anthropologists have discovered about delinquency in other cultures. In making such cross-cultural comparisons, they probably would note that juvenile delinquency is not a universal phenomenon but is largely a characteristic of industrialized and post-industrialized societies. They would point out that these societies require many years of formal education for their youth. This postpones the age at which young men and women are allowed to assume the role of adults, and it is during this "in-between status" that delinquency occurs. The emphasis given by anthropologists in such a study, then, would be true to their calling; that is, anthropologists would be focusing on culture.

Psychologists also have high interest in juvenile delinquency. When psychologists approach the subject, however, they tend to focus on what exists *within* the delinquent. They might test the assumption (or *hypothesis*) that, compared with their followers, gang leaders have more outgoing personality traits, or greater hostility and aggressiveness. Psychologists might also compare the personality traits of adolescent males who join gangs with boys from the same neighborhood or in the general population who do not become gang members. They might give a series of tests to determine whether gang members are more insecure, dominant, hostile, or aggressive than nonmembers.

Sociologists are also interested in most of the aspects emphasized by the other social scientists. Sociologists, however, ordinarily are not concerned with a particular gang from some past period, as historians might be, although they, too, try to identify the relevant social context. Sociologists focus on the power structure of gangs, as would political scientists, and they also are interested in certain aspects of property, as an economist might be. But sociologists would be more interested in the gang members' attitudes toward property, why delinquents feel it is legitimate to steal and vandalize, and how they divide up the property they steal.

Sociologists would also approach delinquency in a way quite similar to that of anthropologists and be interested in the same sorts of things. But sociologists would place strong emphasis on *social class* (which is based on occupation, income, and education). They would want to know if there is greater likelihood that a person will join a gang if his or her parents have little education, and how gang membership varies with income. If sociologists found that delinquency varies with education, age, sex, religion, income, or race–ethnicity, they would want to know the reasons for this. Do children of unskilled workers have a greater chance of becoming delinquent than the children of doctors and lawyers? If so, why?

The sociologists' emphases also separate them from psychologists. Sociologists are inclined to ignore personality, the primary focus of psychologists, and instead to stress the effects of social class on recruitment into delinquency. Sociologists also examine group structure and interaction. For example, both sociologists and psychologists would be interested in differences between a gang's leaders and followers. To discover these distinctions, however, sociologists are not likely to give paper-and-pencil tests. They are much more likely to observe *face-to-face interaction* among gang members (what they do in each other's presence). Sociologists would want to see if leaders and followers uphold the group's values differently; who suggests their activities; and who does what when they do them—whether the activity be simply some form of recreation or a criminal act. For example, do leaders maintain their leadership by committing more acts of daring and bravery than their followers?

Compared with other social scientists, sociologists are more likely to emphasize the routine activities of the police, the courts, and changing norms. The police approach their job with preconceived ideas about who is likely to commit crimes and who is not. Their ideas are based on what they have experienced "on the streets," as well as on stereotypes nurtured within their occupation. The police typically view some people (usually lower-class males living in some particular area of the city) to be more apt to commit crimes than males from other areas of the city, males from a higher social class, or females in general. How do the police develop their ideas? How are such stereotypes supported in their occupational subculture? What effects do stereotypes have on the behavior of the police and on those whom they encounter? In other words, sociologists are deeply interested in finding out how the police define people and how those definitions help to determine whom the police stop, interrogate, and arrest.

Sociologists are also interested in what occurs following an arrest. Prosecutors wield much discretion. For the same act they can level a variety of charges: Prosecutors can charge an individual with first degree burglary, second degree burglary, breaking and entering, or merely trespassing. Sociologists want to know how such decisions are made, as well as their effects on the lives of those who are charged with crimes. Sociologists also study what happens when an individual comes before a judge, especially the outcome of the trial by the type of offense and the sex, age, or race–ethnicity of the offender. They also focus on the effects of detention and incarceration, as well as how people adjust when they are released back into the community.

Norms, the behaviors that people expect of others, obviously change over time. What was considered proper behavior a generation ago is certainly not the same as what is considered proper today. Consequently, the law changes, and acts that are considered to be law violations at one time are not necessarily considered to be criminal at another time. Similarly, acts that are not now considered criminal may become law violations at a later date. For example, at one point in our history drinking alcohol in public at age sixteen was within the law in many communities, while today it would be an act of delinquency. In the same way, a person under sixteen who is on the streets after 10 P.M. unaccompanied by an adult is breaking the law in some communities. But if the law is changed or if the sixteen-year-old has a birthday or moves to a different community, the same act is not a violation of the law. With marijuana, the case is similar. Tens of millions of Americans break the law when they smoke grass, but for several years Alaska allowed possession of marijuana for personal use, a legal right later revoked. From time to time, other states consider such laws, which, if passed, would affect greatly the activities of the police.

Perhaps more than any of the other social scientists, sociologists maintain a crucial interest in how changing legal definitions determine what people are arrested for and what they are charged with. In effect, sociologists are interested in what juvenile delinquency is in the first place. They take the definition of delinquency not as obvious but as problematic, something to be studied in the context of lawmaking, lawbreaking, and the workaday world of the judicial system.

By means of this example of juvenile delinquency, it is easy to see that the social sciences greatly overlap one another. Sociology, however, is an *overarching* social science, because sociologists are, for the most part, interested in the same things that other social scientists are interested in. They are, however, not as limited in their scope or focus as are the others. Except for its traditional concerns with tribal societies, anthropology is similarly broad in its treatment of human behavior.

Types of Sociology: Structural and Interactional

As sociologists study human behavior, they focus on people's *patterned* relationships; that is, sociologists study the recurring aspects of human behavior. This leads them to focus on two principal aspects of life in society: (1) *group membership* (including the *institutions* of society, the customary arrangements by which humans attempt to solve their perennial problems, such as the need for social order or dealing with sickness and death) and (2) *face-to-face* interaction, that is, what people do when they are in one another's presence. These twin foci lead to two principal forms of sociology, the structural and the interactional.

In the first type of sociology, *structural,* the focus is placed on the *group.* Structural sociologists are interested in determining how membership in a group, such as a religion, influences people's behavior and attitudes, such as how they vote, or perhaps how education affects the stand they take on social issues. For example, are there voting differences among Roman Catholics, Lutherans, Jews, Baptists, and charismatics? If so, on what issues? And within the same religion, do people's voting patterns differ according to their income and education?

Also of interest to sociologists who focus on group memberships would be how people's attitudes toward social issues (or their voting) differ according to their age, sex, occupation, race–ethnicity, or even geographical residence—both by region of the country and by urban or rural setting. As you probably have gathered, the term "group" is being used in an extended sense. People do not have to belong to an actual group to be counted; sociologists simply "group" together people who have similar characteristics, such as age, height, weight, education, or, if it is thought relevant, even those who take their vacations in the winter versus those who take them during the summer. These are known as *aggregates,* people who are grouped together for the purpose of social research because of characteristics they have in common.

Note that sociologists who have this first orientation concentrate on how group memberships affect people's attitudes and behavior. Ordinarily they do not simply want to know the proportion of Roman Catholics who vote Democratic (or, in sociological jargon, "the correlation between religious-group membership and voting behavior"); they want to determine what difference being a Roman Catholic makes in people's lives, such as their dating practices, premarital sex, birth control, abortion, what they do for recreation, or how they treat their spouses and rear their children.

In the second type of sociology, the *interactional,* greater emphasis is placed on individuals. Some sociologists who have this orientation focus on what people do when they are in the presence of one another. They observe their behavior, recording the interaction by taking notes or by using tape, video, film, or digitized technology. Other sociologists tap people's attitudes and behaviors more indirectly by interviewing them. Still others examine social records—from diaries and letters to court transcripts, even memorabilia of pop culture from *Rolling Stone* to science fiction and comic books. They may systematically observe soap operas, children's cartoons, police dramas, situation comedies, or MTV. Sociologists who focus on interaction develop ways of classifying the *data*—what they have observed, read, recorded, or been told. From their observations, they draw conclusions about people's attitudes and what significantly affects their lives.

Types of Sociology: Qualitative and Quantitative

Another division among sociologists is based on the *methods* they use to study people. Some sociologists are statistically oriented; they attempt to determine *numbers* to represent people's patterns of behavior. Sociologists who have this orientation stress that proper measurement by the use of statistical techniques is necessary if we are to understand human behavior. This emphasis is known as *quantitative* sociology.

A group of sociologists who disagree strongly with this position concentrate instead on the *meaning* of people's behavior. They focus on how people construct their worlds, how they develop their ideas and attitudes, and how they communicate with one another. Sociologists who have this orientation attempt to determine how people's meanings (called symbols, mental constructs, ideas, and stereotypes) affect their ideas about the self and their relationships to one another. This emphasis is known as *qualitative* sociology.

Conclusion

From chicken to sociology, there are many ways of dividing up anything in life. Just as those who are most familiar with chicken may disagree about the proper way of cutting up a chicken, so those who are most familiar with sociology will disagree about how to slice up sociology. From my experiences, however, the divisions that I have presented here reflect accurately what is taking place in sociology today. Inevitably, however, other sociologists probably would present another way of looking at our discipline. Nonetheless, I think that you will find this presentation helpful for visualizing sociology.

It is similarly the case when it comes to evaluating the divisions within sociology. These are *not* neutral matters for sociologists. For example, almost all sociologists feel strongly about whether a qualitative or quantitative approach is the *proper* way to study human behavior.

My own biases strongly favor qualitative sociology. For me, there simply is no contest. I see qualitative sociology as more accurately reflecting people's lives, as being more closely tied into the realities that people experience—how they make sense of their worlds, how they cope with their problems, and how they try to maintain some semblance of order in their lives. Because I find this approach fascinatingly worthwhile, the qualitative approach is stressed in this book. You should note, however, that many sociologists find the quantitative approach to be the most rewarding way to study social life.

Wherever and whenever people come into one another's presence, there are potential data for the sociologist. Sunday School and the bar, the classroom and the street—even the bedroom and the bathroom—all provide material for sociologists to observe and analyze. Nothing is really taboo for sociologists; they regularly raise questions about most aspects of social life. Simply overhearing an ordinary conversation—or catching a glimpse of some unusual happening—is enough to whet the curiosity of many sociologists. In following that curiosity, they can simply continue to "overhear" conversations, but this time purposely, or they can conduct an elaborate study with a scientifically selected random sample backed by huge funding from some government or private agency. What sociologists study can be as socially significant as an urban riot or as common but personally significant as two people greeting with a handshake or parting with a kiss.

In this sense, then, the world belongs to the sociologist—for to the sociologist everything is fair game. The all-inclusiveness of sociology, indeed, is what makes sociology so intrinsically fascinating for many: Sociology offers a framework that provides a penetrating perspective on almost everything that we do in life.

Some of you who are being introduced to sociology through this essay may find the sociological approach to understanding human life rewarding enough to take other courses in sociology and, after college, to be attracted to books of sociological content. A few, perhaps, may even make sociology your life's vocation and thus embark on a lifelong journey that takes you to the far corners of human endeavor, as well as to people's more familiar pursuits. Certainly some of us, intrigued by sociology, have experienced an unfolding panorama of intellectual delight in the midst of a fascinating exploration of the social world. And, in this enticing process, we have the added pleasure of constantly discovering and rediscovering our changing selves.

3 The Promise

C. WRIGHT MILLS

The *sociological imagination* is seeing how the unique historical circumstances of a particular society affect people and, at the same time, seeing how people affect history. Every individual lives out his or her life in a particular society, with the historical circumstances of that society influencing greatly what that individual becomes. People thus shaped by their society contribute, in turn, to the formation of their society and to the course of its history.

It is this quality of mind (termed the *sociological imagination* by Mills and the *sociological perspective* by others) that is presented for exploration in the readings of this book. As this intersection of biography and history becomes more apparent to you, your own sociological imagination will grow, bringing you a deepened and broadened understanding of social life—and of your own place within it.

NOWADAYS, MEN OFTEN FEEL that their private lives are a series of traps. They sense that, within their everyday worlds, they cannot overcome their troubles, and, in this feeling, they are quite correct: What ordinary men are directly aware of and what they try to do are bounded by the private orbits in which they live; their visions and their powers are limited to the close-up scenes of job, family, neighborhood; in other milieux, they move vicariously and remain spectators. And the more aware they become, however vaguely, of ambitions and of threats that transcend their immediate locales, the more trapped they seem to feel.

Underlying this sense of being trapped are seemingly impersonal changes in the very structure of continent-wide societies. The facts of contemporary history are also facts about the success and the failure of individual men and women. When a society is industrialized, a peasant becomes a worker; a feudal lord is liquidated or becomes a businessman. When classes rise or fall, a man is employed or unemployed; when the rate of investment goes up or down, a man takes new heart or goes broke. When wars happen, an insurance salesman becomes a rocket launcher; a store clerk, a radar man; a wife lives alone; a child grows up without a father. Neither the life of an individual nor the history of a society can be understood without understanding both.

Yet, men do not usually define the troubles they endure in terms of historical change and institutional contradiction. The well-being they enjoy, they do not usually impute to the big ups and downs of the societies in which they live. Seldom aware of the intricate connection between the patterns of their own lives and the course of world history, ordinary men do not usually know what this connection means for the kinds of men they are becoming and for the kinds of history-making in which they might take part. They do not possess the quality of mind essential to grasp the interplay of man and society, of biography and history, of self and world. They cannot cope with their personal troubles in such ways as to control the structural transformations that usually lie behind them.

Surely, it is no wonder. In what period have so many men been so totally exposed at so fast a pace to such earthquakes of change? That Americans have not known such catastrophic changes as have the men and women of other societies is due to historical facts that are now quickly becoming "merely history." The history that now affects every man is world history. Within this scene and this period, in the course of a single generation, one-sixth of mankind is transformed from all that is feudal and backward into all that is modern, advanced, and fearful. Political colonies are freed; new and less visible forms of imperialism, installed. Revolutions occur; men feel the intimate grip of new kinds of authority. Totalitarian societies rise, and are smashed to bits—or succeed fabulously. . . . After two centuries of hope, even formal democracy is restricted to a quite small portion of mankind. Everywhere in the underdeveloped world, ancient ways of life are broken up and vague expectations become urgent demands. Everywhere in the overdeveloped world, the means of authority and of violence become total in scope and bureaucratic in form. . . .

The very shaping of history now outpaces the ability of men to orient themselves in accordance with cherished values. And which values? Even when they do not panic, men often sense that older ways of feeling and thinking have collapsed, and that newer beginnings are ambiguous to the point of moral stasis. Is it any wonder that ordinary men feel they cannot cope with the larger worlds with which they are so suddenly confronted? That they cannot understand the meaning of their epoch for their own lives? That—in defense of selfhood—they become morally insensible, trying to remain altogether private men? Is it any wonder that they come to be possessed by a sense of the trap?

It is not only information that they need—in this Age of Fact, information often dominates their attention and overwhelms their capacities to assimilate it. It is not only the skills of reason that they need—although their struggles to acquire these often exhaust their limited moral energy.

What they need, and what they feel they need, is a quality of mind that will help them to use information and to develop reason in order to achieve lucid summations of what is going on in the world and of what may be happening within themselves. It is this quality, I am going to contend, that journalists and scholars, artists and publics, scientists and editors are coming to expect of what may be called the sociological imagination.

The sociological imagination enables its possessor to understand the larger historical scene in terms of its meaning for the inner life and the external career of a variety of individuals. It enables him to take into account how individuals, in the welter of their daily experience, often become falsely conscious of their social positions. Within that welter, the framework of modern society is sought, and within that framework the psychologies of a variety of men and women are formulated. By such means, the personal uneasiness of individuals is focused upon explicit troubles, and the indifference of publics is transformed into involvement with public issues.

The first fruit of this imagination—and the first lesson of the social science that embodies it—is the idea that the individual can understand his own experience and gauge his own fate only by locating himself within his period, that he can know his own chances in life only by becoming aware of those of all individuals in his circumstances. In many ways, it is a terrible lesson; in many ways, a magnificent one. We do not know the limits of man's capacities for supreme effort or willing degradation, for agony or glee, for pleasurable brutality or the sweetness of reason. But in our time we have come to know that the limits of "human nature" are frighteningly broad. We have come to know that every individual lives, from one generation to the next, in some society; that he lives out a biography, and that he lives it out within some historical sequence. By the fact of his living he contributes, however minutely, to the shaping of this society and to the course of its history, even as he is made by society and by its historical push and shove.

The sociological imagination enables us to grasp history and biography and the relations between the two within society. That is its task and its promise. To recognize this task and this promise is the mark of the classic social analyst. It is characteristic of Herbert Spencer—turgid, polysyllabic, comprehensive; of E. A. Ross—graceful, muckraking, upright; of Auguste Comte and Emile Durkheim; of the intricate and subtle Karl Mannheim. It is the quality of all that is intellectually excellent in Karl Marx; it is the clue to Thorstein Veblen's brilliant and ironic insight, to Joseph Schumpeter's many-sided constructions of reality; it is the basis of the psychological sweep of W. E. H. Lecky no less than of the profundity and clarity of Max Weber. And it is the signal of what is best in contemporary studies of man and society.

No social study that does not come back to the problems of biography, of history, and of their intersections within a society has completed its intellectual journey. Whatever the specific problems of the classic social analysts, however limited or however broad the features of social reality they have examined, those who have been imaginatively aware of the promise of their work have consistently asked three sorts of questions:

1. What is the structure of this particular society as a whole? What are its essential components, and how are they related to one another? How does it differ from other varieties of social order? Within it, what is the meaning of any particular feature for its continuance and for its change?

2. Where does this society stand in human history? What are the mechanics by which it is changing? What is its place within, and its meaning for, the development of humanity as a whole? How does any particular feature we are examining affect, and how is it affected by, the historical period in which it moves? And this period—what are its essential features? How does it differ from other periods? What are its characteristic ways of history-making?

3. What varieties of men and women now prevail in this society and in this period? And what varieties are coming to prevail? In what ways are they selected and formed, liberated and repressed, made sensitive and blunted? What kinds of "human nature" are revealed in the conduct and character we observe in this society in this period? And what is the meaning for "human nature" of each and every feature of the society we are examining?

Whether the point of interest is a great power state or a minor literary mood, a family, a prison, a creed—these are the kinds of questions the best social analysts have asked. They are the intellectual pivots of classic studies of man in society—and they are the questions inevitably raised by any mind possessing the sociological imagination. For that imagination is the capacity to shift from one perspective to another—from the political to the psychological; from examination of a single family to comparative assessment of the national budgets of the world; from the theological school to the military establishment; from considerations of an oil industry to studies of contemporary poetry. It is the capacity to range from the most impersonal and remote transformations to the most intimate features of the human self—and to see the relations between the two. Back of its use, there is always the urge to know the social and historical meaning of the individual in the society and in the period in which he has his quality and his being.

> I have never felt that much anger before. If she had resisted, I would have killed her. . . . The rape was for revenge. I didn't have an orgasm. She was there to get my hostile feelings off on.

That, in brief, is why it is by means of the sociological imagination that men now hope to grasp what is going on in the world, and to understand what is happening in themselves as minute points of the intersections of biography and history within society. In large part, contemporary man's self-conscious view of himself as at least an outsider, if not a permanent stranger, rests upon an absorbed realization of social relativity and of the transformative power of history. The sociological imagination is the most fruitful form of this self-consciousness. By its use, men whose mentalities have swept only a series of limited orbits often come to feel as if suddenly awakened in a house with which they had only supposed themselves to be familiar. Correctly or incorrectly, they often come to feel that they can now provide themselves with adequate summations, cohesive assessments, comprehensive orientations. Older decisions that once appeared sound now seem to them products of a mind unaccountably dense. Their capacity for astonishment is made lively again. They acquire a new way of thinking; they experience a transvaluation of values. In a word, by their reflection and by their sensibility, they realize the cultural meaning of the social sciences.

Perhaps the most fruitful distinction with which the sociological imagination works is between the "personal troubles of milieu" and the "public issues of social structure." This distinction is an essential tool of the sociological imagination and a feature of all classic work in social science.

Troubles occur within the character of the individual and within the range of his immediate relations with others; they have to do with his self and with those limited areas of social life of which he is directly and personally aware. Accordingly, the statement and the resolution of troubles properly lie within the individual as a biographical entity and within the scope of his immediate milieu—the social setting that is directly open to his personal experience and, to some extent, his willful activity. A trouble is a private matter: Values cherished by an individual are felt by him to be threatened.

Issues have to do with matters that transcend these local environments of the individual and the range of his inner life. They have to do with the organization of many such milieu into the institutions of a historical society as a whole, with the ways in which various milieu overlap and interpenetrate to form the larger structure of social and historical life. An issue is a public matter: Some value cherished by publics is felt to be threatened. Often, there is a debate about what that value really is and about what it is that really threatens it. This debate is often without focus, if only because it is the very nature of an issue, unlike even widespread trouble, that it cannot very well be defined in terms of the immediate and everyday environments of ordinary men. An issue, in fact, often involves a crisis in institutional arrangements, and often, too, it involves what Marxists call "contradictions" or "antagonisms."

In these terms, consider unemployment. When, in a city of 100,000, only one man is unemployed, that is his personal trouble, and for its relief we properly look to the character of the man, his skills, and his immediate opportunities. But when, in a nation of 50 million employees, 15 million men are unemployed, that is an issue, and we may not hope to find its solution within the range of opportunities open to any one individual. The very structure of opportunities has collapsed. Both the correct statement of the problem and range of possible solutions require us to consider the economic and political institutions of the society, and not merely the personal situation and character of a scatter of individuals.

Consider war. The personal problem of war, when it occurs, may be how to survive it or how to die in it with honor; how to make money out of it; how to climb into the higher safety of the military apparatus; or how to contribute to the war's termination. In short, according to one's values, to find a set of milieux and within it to survive the war or make one's death in it meaningful. But the structural issues of war have to do with its causes; with what types of men its throws up into command; with its effects upon economic and political, family and religious institutions; with the unorganized irresponsibility of a world of nation-states.

Consider marriage. Inside a marriage, a man and a woman may experience personal troubles; but, when the divorce rate during the first four years of marriage is 250 out of every 1,000 attempts, this is an indication of a structural issue having to do with the institutions of marriage and the family and other institutions that bear upon them.

Or consider the metropolis—the horrible, beautiful, ugly, magnificent sprawl of the great city. For many upper-class people, the personal solution to the problem of the city is to have an apartment with private garage under it in the heart of the city, and forty miles out, a house by Henry Hill, garden by Garrett Eckbo, on a hundred acres of private land. In these two controlled environments—with a small staff at each end and a private helicopter connection—most people could solve many of the problems of personal milieux caused by the facts of the city. But all this, however splendid, does not solve the public issues that the structural fact of the city poses. What should be done with this wonderful monstrosity? Break it all up into scattered units, combining residence and work? Refurbish it as it stands? Or, after evacuation, dynamite it and build new cities according to new plans in new places? What should those plans be? And who is to decide and to accomplish whatever choice is made? These are structural issues; to confront them and to solve them requires us to consider political and economic issues that affect innumerable milieux.

Insofar as an economy is so arranged that slumps occur, the problem of unemployment becomes incapable of personal solution. Insofar as war is inherent in the nation-state system and in the uneven industrialization of the world, the ordinary individual in his restricted milieu will be powerless—with or without psychiatric aid—to solve the troubles this system or lack of system imposes upon him. Insofar as the family as an institution turns women into darling little slaves and men into their chief providers and unweaned dependents, the problem of a satisfactory marriage remains incapable of purely private solution. Insofar as the overdeveloped megalopolis and the overdeveloped automobile are built-in features of the overdeveloped society, the issues of urban living will not be solved by personal ingenuity and private wealth.

What we experience in various and specific milieu, I have noted, is often caused by structural changes. Accordingly, to understand the changes of many personal milieu, we are required to look beyond them. And the number and variety of such structural changes increase as the institutions within which we live become more embracing and more intricately connected with one another. To be aware of the idea of social structure and to use it with sensibility is to be capable of tracing such linkages among a great variety of milieu. To be able to do that is to possess the sociological imagination.

What are the major issues for publics and the key troubles of private individuals in our time? To formulate issues and troubles, we must ask what values are cherished yet threatened, and what values are cherished and supported, by the characterizing trends of our period. In the case both of threat and of support, we must ask what salient contradictions of structure may be involved.

When people cherish some set of values and do not feel any threat to them, they experience *well-being.* When they cherish values but *do* feel them to be threatened, they experience a *crisis*—either as a personal trouble or as a public issue. And, if all their values seem involved, they feel the total threat of panic.

But suppose people are neither aware of any cherished values nor experience any threat? That is the experience of *indifference,* which, if it seems to involve all their values, becomes apathy. Suppose, finally, they are unaware of any cherished values, but still are very much aware of a threat? That is the experience of *uneasiness,* of anxiety, which, if it is total enough, becomes a deadly, unspecified malaise.

Ours is a time of uneasiness and indifference—not yet formulated in such ways as to permit the work of reason and the play of sensibility. Instead of troubles—defined in terms of values and threats—there is often the misery of vague uneasiness; instead of explicit issues, there is often merely the beat feeling that all is somehow not right. Neither the values threatened nor whatever threatens them has been stated; in short, they have not been carried to the point of decision. Much less have they been formulated as problems of social science. . . .

We are frequently told that the problems of our decade, or even the crises of our period, have shifted from the external realm of economics and now have to do with the quality of individual life—in fact, with the question of whether there is soon going to be anything that can properly be called individual life. Not child labor but comic books, not poverty but mass leisure, are at the center of concern. Many great public issues as well as many private troubles are described in terms of "psychiatric"—often, it seems in a pathetic attempt to avoid the large issues and problems of modern society. Often, this statement seems to rest upon a provincial narrowing of interest to the Western societies, or even to the United States—thus ignoring two-thirds of mankind; often, too, it arbitrarily divorces the individual life from the larger institutions within which that life is enacted, and which on occasion bear upon it more grievously than do the intimate environments of childhood.

Problems of leisure, for example, cannot even be stated without considering problems of work. Family troubles over comic books cannot be formulated as problems without considering the plight of the contemporary family in its new relations with the newer institutions of the social structure. Neither leisure nor its debilitating uses can be understood as problems without recognition of the extent to which malaise and indifference now form the social and personal climate of contemporary American society. In this climate, no problems of the "private life" can be stated and solved without recognition of the crisis of ambition that is part of the very career of men at work in the incorporated economy.

It is true, as psychoanalysts continually point out, that people do often have the "increasing sense of being moved by obscure forces within themselves that they are unable to define." But it is *not* true, as Ernest Jones asserted, that "man's chief enemy and danger is his own unruly nature and the dark forces pent up within him." On the contrary: "Man's chief danger" today lies in the unruly forces of contemporary society itself, with its alienating methods of production, its enveloping techniques of political domination, its international anarchy—in a word, its pervasive transformations of the very "nature" of man and the conditions and aims of his life.

It is now the social scientist's foremost political and intellectual task— for here the two coincide—to make clear the elements of contemporary uneasiness and indifference. It is the central demand made upon him by other cultural workmen—by physical scientists and artists, by the intellectual community in general. It is because of this task and these demands, I believe, that the social sciences are becoming the common denominator of our cultural period, and the sociological imagination, our most needed quality of mind.

PART II Doing Sociological Research

I N PART I, YOU LEARNED that sociologists are fascinated with the unknown—how we constantly want to peer behind locked doors to better understand social life. Part II will show you how sociologists open those doors. I wrote the first selection in this part to give you an overview of the research methods that sociologists use. Diana Scully and Joseph Marolla then follow with an article based on interviewing in a difficult situation. Devah Pager then reports on a field experiment she used to determine if a criminal record for drug dealing has different effects on the chances of blacks and whites being given the opportunity to work. Bruce Jacobs closes Part II with a review of his first attempts at field work. This last article gives you a glimpse of the intriguing—and sometimes dangerous—worlds that sociologists explore.

As we begin to pry open some of the doors that people so carefully lock, you will be able to catch a glimpse of what goes on behind them. For example, from Scully and Marolla's research, you will better understand why men rape, and, from Jacobs' article, why people sell illegal drugs. In and of itself, such an understanding is valuable, but the selections in this Part have an additional purpose—to introduce you to the two major activities of sociologists: (1) conducting empirical research and (2) constructing a theoretical base. Let's look at each of these activities.

When sociologists do their craft, these twin tasks merge. They are so joined to one another that neither is more important than the other—nor does one necessarily come before the other. For the sake of presentation, however, let's say that the *first* task of sociology is to conduct empirical research. *Empirical* means "based on objective observations." Sociologists cannot draw conclusions that are based on guesswork, hunches, custom, superstition, common sense, or how they would like the world to be. Sociologists must gather information that represents people's attitudes and behaviors accurately. Then they must report their observations openly, spelling out in detail how they conducted their studies so that others can test their conclusions.

Sociologists use a variety of methods to do their research, several of which are represented by articles in this book. To mention a few: an experiment (article 23, on compliance to authority), interviewing (article 45, on women in the military), and documents or secondary sources (article 13, the classic report on abused children, Anna and Isabelle). Article 14, on childhood, is even based on a method for which we have no standard name. We could make up a fancy term such as *post-event reflexivity,* or we could simply refer to it as recall and analysis.

As sociologists do their research, they often find that using just one method is not enough to accomplish their goals, and they combine methods. The studies of the American way of giving birth (article 38) and how rookie cops learn from seasoned officers *their* distinctions between brutality and justifiable force (article 41), for example, are based on interviewing combined with participant observation. Most of the articles in this book are based on participant observation, which you will read about in the selection that opens this Part (as well as a more detailed analysis in the opening to Part V).

Because no specific reading summarizes the *second* task of sociology, constructing a theoretical base, I shall provide an overview at this point.

The word *theory* sometimes scares students. It shouldn't, for *all of us are theorists.* To see what I mean by this, let's start with a basic point—how we make sense out of life. All of us want to know the meaning of the things that happen to us, but facts never interpret themselves. To find this meaning, we place our experiences (our "facts") into a conceptual framework. That is, we take a "fact" (which can be someone's behavior, something we see on television—anything that happened to us) and compare it with what we know about "that kind of thing." We then use "what we know" to interpret that "fact."

Doing this gives us an understanding of what that event or "fact" of life means. Whether our understanding is right or wrong is not the point. The point is that we all do this as a regular part of our everyday lives. We feel a need to know how "events" are related to one another. By placing them into "frameworks" that we carry around in our heads, we arrive at that meaning. This process can be called "everyday theorizing." In essence, then, all of us are theorists all the time.

So why be scared of theory? We all know how to "do" theory. Now let's consider how sociologists "do" theory.

Like the events of everyday life, sociological "facts" (the observations, measurements, or research results of sociologists) do not come with built-in meanings. They, too, must be interpreted. To make sense of them, sociologists place their findings into conceptual frameworks that they have developed. These frameworks provide explanations of how "facts" are related to one another. The basic difference between sociological theory and everyday-life theory is that sociological theory is more rigorous. Sociologists check constantly to see how the "empirical" (the things observed) match a theory—and then refine the theory to match the real world.

A *theory,* then, is a conceptual framework that interprets "facts"; it shows how "facts" (measurements, observations, or research results) are related to one another. Because each theory provides a framework that interprets sociological observations, it offers a unique explanation of reality. This will become clearer as we examine the three dominant theories of sociology. You will see how each theory reveals a contrasting picture of social life.

The *first* theory is called *symbolic interactionism* (or *symbolic interaction*). It stresses what you already know quite well—that you live in a world filled with meaning. You are surrounded by *people* who mean something to you (from your parents to your friends), by *objects* that represent something special (your clothing, your pet, your car, your room), and by *events* that are filled with meaning (first kiss, first date, first job, birthdays, holidays, anniversaries). The term *symbol* refers to the meanings that such things have for us. And symbols are what *symbolic* interactionists focus on—how we construct meanings, how we use symbols to communicate with one another, and how symbols are the foundation of our social world.

Symbolic interactionism has three major themes: (1) human beings have a self; (2) people construct meanings, and act on the basis of those meanings; and (3) people take into account the possible reactions of others. Let's look at each of these points.

1. *Human beings have a self.* This means that we have the capacity to think, to talk about, and to reflect on our own actions (what we have done), future actions (what we plan to do), even our thoughts and feelings about our actions (such as what we regret or are pleased at having done). We are even able to tell others what was going on in our mind when we did something. That is, just as we can reflect on the actions and motives of others, so we can reflect on our own actions, analyze our own motives, and evaluate how we feel about what we did or what happened to us. This is called "making the self an object."

2. *People construct meanings and act on the basis of those meanings.* As we reflect on our experiences, we interpret (or give meaning to) what happens to us. As we evaluate events and how others react to us, we further refine those meanings. The significance of this human trait is that the

meanings we give to our experiences (the objects, the important events—the "facts" of our life) become the basis for how we act.

This sounds abstract and vague, but let's consider how all of us do this all the time. For example, if someone makes physical contact with us, we want to know what it means. If we interpret the contact as an "accidental bump," it requires nothing but a mumbled apology. If we interpret the contact as a "push" or a "stomp," however, our reactions are quite different. The actual act is the same in either case, but our *interpretation* determines what that act means for us. In doing this, it also indicates what our "appropriate" reaction should be. Note that the basis for our "appropriate" reaction does not depend on the act, but on the symbols we apply—that is, how we interpret (or define) the act.

How we interpret (or "symbolize") life's events is actually a good deal more complicated than I have just sketched. While we all place our experiences into categories, the categories that we use differ from individual to individual. Even an accidental bump, for example, has different meanings to people of different backgrounds. I am reminded of this by Kody Scott's fascinating book, *Monster,* in which, among gang members, an accidental bump can be an invitation to death.

3. *People take into account the possible reactions of others.* We are aware of how others might react to something that we are thinking about doing, and we take those anticipated reactions into account as we make decisions about what to do. This is called *taking the role of others,* which simply means that we adjust our behavior according to how we think people might react.

As is apparent, taking the role of others is a regular part of everyday life. We take the role of individuals ("specific others") and of groups of people ("the generalized other"). For example, if a Chicago Bulls player were tempted to accept a bribe, he might think, "What would my coach or mom [a specific other] think if I took this?" He probably would also think, "What would my team and the American public [a generalized other] think of me if they found out?"

In sum: Central to symbolic interactionism is the principle that to understand people's behavior we must understand their symbolic worlds. That is, we must understand how people think about life, how they mentally construct their worlds. Accordingly, sociologists study the meanings that people give to things, to events, and to other people, for symbols hold the key to understanding both our attitudes and our behavior.

The *second* theory is called *functionalism.* Functionalists stress that society is an integrated system made up of many parts. When working properly, each part contributes to the stability of society: that is, each part fulfills a function that helps keep society going. Sometimes, however, a part fails to work correctly; that is, it becomes *dysfunctional*. This creates problems for other parts of the system, for they were depending on it. In short, functionalists stress how the parts of society are interrelated, and how a change in one part of society affects its other parts.

To illustrate functionalism, let's consider why divorce is so prevalent in U.S. society. Functionalists first point out that the family performs functions for the entire society. Over the millennia, the family's traditional functions have been economic production, the distribution of property, the socialization of children, reproduction, recreation, sexual control of its members, and taking care of its sick, injured, and aged. During the past couple of hundred years (especially the last hundred), as society industrialized profound changes occurred that have left no aspect of social life untouched.

The consequences for family life have been especially remarkable. Consider how industrialization has eroded the family's traditional functions. For example, medical personnel now take care of the family's sick and injured, often the family's elderly are placed in homes for the aged, and almost all economic production has moved from family to factories. As its basic functions have been taken over at least partially by other units of society, the family has been weakened. Simply put, as the "ties that bind" became fewer, that is, as traditional functions of the family were taken over by other social groups—husbands and wives had fewer functions to hold them together, and they became more prone to break up.

The *third* dominant theory in sociology is *conflict theory*. From this perspective, society is viewed as a system in which its many parts (groups) are in competition and conflict. For their survival and to improve their relative position in society, each group competes for resources. There are not enough resources to satisfy each group, however, as each group tends to want more power, more wealth, more prestige, and so on. Consequently, groups compete with one another for a larger share of these limited resources. Those groups that already have more than their share are not about to redistribute what they have willingly. Instead, they hold on to it for dear life, while trying to enlarge what they already have. Conflict is the inevitable result.

As a consequence, say conflict theorists, society is not like a smoothly running machine, as the functionalists picture it, with each part contributing to the well-being of the other parts. Rather, society is more like an imbalanced machine running wildly out of kilter and ready to break apart. The results of this inherent conflict show up as racism, with one racial–ethnic group pitted against another; sexism, with men and women squared off in the struggle for dominance; social class conflict, with the exploitation of the powerless by a ruling elite; ageism, with a struggle for finances (Social Security) and health care (Medicare) dividing the generations of workers; and so on.

Due to space limitations, I can provide only this brief sketch of these three theories that dominate sociology today. Among the many examples of *symbolic interactionism* in this book, you might look at selections by Clark (11), Goffman (12), Lawson (18), and Henslin and Biggs (20). The readings by Gans (33) and Harris (40) provide examples of *functionalism*, while the one by Gracey (39) is an example of *conflict theory*. The dominant orientation of this book is symbolic interactionism.

Part II of the book, then, builds upon Part I. I hope that it will help you to better appreciate how sociologists do their research and how they interpret what they find.

4 How Sociologists Do Research

JAMES M. HENSLIN

Guesswork does not go very far in helping us to understand our social world. Some of our guesses, hunches, and ideas that pass for common sense are correct. Others are not. And we seldom know which is which.

Sociologists must gather data in such a way that what they report is objective—presenting information that represents what is really "out there." To do so, they must use methods that other researchers can repeat (*replicate*) to check their findings. They also must tie their findings into what other researchers have already reported and into sociological theory. In this overview of *research methods*, Henslin outlines the procedures that sociologists use to gather data.

Renée had never felt fear before—at least not like this. It had begun as a vague feeling that something was out of place. Then she felt it creep up her spine, slowly tightening as it clawed its way upward. Now it was like a fist pounding inside her skull.

Renée never went anywhere with strangers. Hadn't her parents hammered that into her head since she was a child? And now, at 19, she wasn't about to start breaking *that* rule.

And yet here she was, in a car with a stranger. He seemed nice enough. And it wasn't as though he were some strange guy on the side of the road or anything. She had met George at Patricia's party, and everyone seemed to know him.

Renée had first been attracted by his dark eyes. They seemed to light up his entire face when he smiled. And when he asked her to dance, Renée felt flattered. He was a little older, a little more sure of himself than most of the guys she knew. Renée liked that: It was a sign of maturity.

As the evening wore on and he continued to be attentive to her, it seemed natural to accept his offer to take her home.

But then they passed the turn to her dorm. She didn't understand his mumbled reply about "getting something." And as he turned off on the country road, that clawing at the back of her neck had begun.

As he looked at her, his eyes almost pierced the darkness. "It's time to pay, Babe," he said, as he clawed at her blouse.

Renée won't talk about that night. She doesn't want to recall anything that happened then.

IN THIS PAPER we examine how sociologists do research. To better understand how they gather data, it is useful to focus on a single topic. Let's try to answer this question: How can we gather reliable information on rape—which is to say on both rapists *and* their victims?

Sociology and Common Sense

Common sense will give us some information. From common sense (a kind of knowledge not based on formal investigation, but on ideas that we pick up from our groups, mixed with abstractions from our own experiences), we know that Renée's rape was a significant event in her life. And from common sense we know that rape has ongoing effects, that it can trigger fears and anxieties, and that it can make women distrust men.

It so happens that these ideas are true. But many other commonsense ideas, even though glaringly obvious to us, are *not* true, and so we need research to test the validity and accuracy of our ideas. For example, common sense also tells us that one reason men rape is the revealing clothing that some women wear. And common sense may tell us that men who rape are sexually deprived. These commonsense ideas, however, are not on target. Researchers have found that men who rape don't care what a woman is wearing. Most don't even care who the woman is. She is simply an object for their lust, drives for power and exploitation, and, sometimes, frustration and anger. Researchers have also found that rapists may or may not be sexually deprived—the same as with men who do not rape. For example, many rapists have wives or girlfriends with whom they have an ongoing sexual relationship.

If it is neither provocative clothing nor sexual deprivation, then, what *does* cause rape? And what effects does rape have on victims? Phrasing the matter this way—instead of assuming that we know the answers—not only opens up our minds but also underscores the pressing need for sociological research. We need to search for empirical findings that will take us completely out of the realm of guesswork and well beyond common sense.

Let's see how sociologists do their research. We shall look first at a research model, and then at the research methods used in sociology.

A Research Model

As shown in Figure 4.1, eight basic steps are involved in social research. As you look at each of these steps, be aware that this is an ideal model. In some research these steps are collapsed, in others their order may be rearranged, while in still others one or more steps may be omitted.

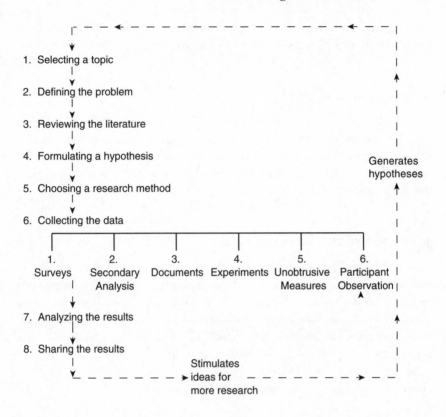

Figure 4.1 The Research Model (*Modification of Fig. 2.2 in Schaefer and Lamm 1998.*)

1. SELECTING A TOPIC

The first step is to select a topic. What is it that you want to know more about? Many sociologists simply follow their curiosity, their drive to know. They become interested in a particular topic, and they pursue it. Sometimes sociologists choose a topic simply because funds are available. At other times, some social problem, such as rape, has become a pressing issue and the sociologist wants to gather data that will help people better understand—and perhaps help solve it. Let's use rape as our example.

2. DEFINING THE PROBLEM

The second step is to define the problem, to determine what you want to learn about the topic. To develop a researchable question, you need to focus on a specific area or problem. For example, you may want to determine the education and work experiences of rapists, or the average age of their victims.

3. REVIEWING THE LITERATURE

The third step is to review the literature to see what has been published on the topic. Nobody wants to rediscover the wheel. If the question has already been answered, you want to know that. In addition, a review of what has been written on the topic can stir your ideas, help sharpen your questions, and help you accomplish the next step.

4. FORMULATING A HYPOTHESIS

The fourth step is to formulate a *hypothesis*, a statement of what you expect to find based on a theory. A hypothesis predicts a relationship between or among *variables* (factors thought to be significant). For example, the statement "Men who are more socially isolated are more likely to rape than are men who are more socially integrated" is a hypothesis. Hypotheses (the plural) need *operational definitions*—that is, precise ways to measure their concepts. In this example, you would need operational definitions for three concepts: social integration, social isolation, and rape.

5. CHOOSING A RESEARCH METHOD

The ways by which sociologists collect data are called *research methods* (also known as *research designs*). To answer the questions you have formulated, you will need to select one of these methods. I will explain what they are after we complete this review of the research model.

6. COLLECTING THE DATA

After you have selected a research method, then you gather your data. You have to take care to ensure that your data are both valid and reliable. *Validity* means the extent to which the operational definitions measure what you intend to measure. In other words, do your definitions or measures of social isolation and integration *really* measure these concepts and not something else?

The concept of rape is not as simple to define (or operationalize) as it may seem. For example, there are various degrees of sexual assault. Look at Table 4.1, which depicts a variety of forced sexual activities. Deciding which of these constitute rape for the purposes of your research project is

**TABLE 4.1 Date Rape and Other Unwanted Sexual Activities
Experienced by College Undergraduates**

UNWANTED SEXUAL ACTIVITY	WOMEN WHO REPORTED THIS HAD HAPPENED TO THEM (%)	MEN WHO REPORTED THEY HAD DONE THIS (%)
He kissed without tongue contact	3.7	2.2
He kissed with tongue contact	12.3	0.7
He touched/kissed her breasts through her clothes	24.7	7.3
He touched/kissed her breasts under her clothes	22.6	13.1
He touched her genitals through her clothes	28.8	15.3
He touched her genitals under her clothes	28.4	13.9
He performed oral sex on her	9.9	8.8
He forced her to touch his genitals through his clothes	2.9	0.7
He forced her to touch his genitals under his clothes	5.8	2.2
He forced her to perform oral sex on him	2.5	4.4
He forced her to have sexual intercourse	20.6	15.3

These are the results of a survey of 380 women and 368 men enrolled in introductory psychology courses at Texas A&M University. Percentages add up to more than 100 because often more than one unwanted sexual activity occurred on the same date.
Source: Based on Muehlenhard and Linton 1987:190.

an example of the difficulties of developing operational definitions. Certainly not all of these acts are rape—and, therefore, not all of those who did them are rapists.

Reliability means that if other researchers use your operational definitions, their findings will be consistent with yours. Inadequate operational definitions will prevent reliability. For example, if other researchers want to replicate (repeat) your study but your measure of rape is inadequate, they will exclude acts that you included, and include acts that you excluded. In that case, how can you compare the results?

7. ANALYZING THE RESULTS

After you gather the data, it is time to analyze them. Sociologists have specific techniques for doing this, each of which requires special training. They range from statistical tests (of which there are many, each with its own rules for application) to *content analysis* (examining the content of something in order to identify its themes—in this case perhaps magazine articles and television reports about rape, or even diaries kept by women who have been raped or the recounts of rapes in novels). If a hypothesis has been part of the research (and not all social research has hypotheses), it is during this step that it is tested.

8.   SHARING THE RESULTS

Now it is time to wrap up the research. In this step, you write a report to share your findings with the scientific community. You relate your findings to the literature, to show how they are connected to what has previously been discovered. You explain your research procedures so others can evaluate them. This also guides researchers who may want to *replicate* your research—that is, repeat the study to test its findings. In this way science slowly builds, adding finding to finding.

Now let's look in greater detail at the fifth step to examine the research methods that sociologists use.

Six Research Methods

Sociologists use six *research methods* (also called research designs). These *procedures for gathering data* are surveys, secondary analysis, documents, experiments, unobtrusive measures, and participant observation.

SURVEYS

Let's suppose that you want to know how many women are raped each year. The *survey*—having people answer a series of questions—would be an appropriate method to use.

Before using this method, however, you have to decide whom you will survey. What is your *population;* that is, what is the target group that you want to learn about? Is it all females in the world? Only U.S. or Canadian females? The females in a particular state, county, or city? Only females above a certain age? Or only women on your college campus?

Let's suppose that your research interest is modest—that you want only to know the extent of rape on your campus. Ideally, you would survey all women students. But let's also suppose that your college enrollment is large, making this impractical. To get the answer, then, you must select a smaller group, a *sample* of individuals, from whom you can generalize to the entire campus. How you choose your sample is crucial, for it will affect the results of your study. For example, you will get different results if you survey only freshmen or seniors—or only women taking introductory sociology or advanced physics classes.

What kind of sample will allow you to *generalize* to the entire campus? The best is a *random sample.* This does *not* mean that you stand on some campus corner and ask questions of any woman who happens to walk by. *In a random sample, everyone in your population (the target group) has the same chance of being included in the study.* In this case, since the population is all women taking classes at your college, all such women must have the same chance of being included in your research—whether they are freshmen, sophomores, juniors, seniors, or graduate students. It also means that such factors (*variables*) as a woman's choice of major, her grade point average, or whether she is a day or evening student cannot affect her chances of being a part of your sample.

How can you obtain a random sample? First, you need a list of all the women who are enrolled in your college. Then you assign a number to each name on the list. You then use random numbers to determine which particular women will become part of the sample. (Random numbers are available on tables in statistics books, or they can be generated by a computer.)

Because a random sample represents your study's population (in this case women students enrolled at your college), you can generalize your findings to all the women students on your campus, even if they were not part of your sample. This means, for example, that if 5 percent of the women in your sample have been raped, then about 5 percent of the women on campus have been raped. There is always some variation. It could be 4 percent or 6 percent, for example.

In some surveys, *questionnaires,* a list of questions, are mailed to people. Although such *self-administered questionnaires* allow a large number of people to be sampled at a lower cost, control is lost. For example, under what conditions did people (*respondents*) fill them out? Who might have influenced their answers?

Other surveys use *interviews:* Respondents are asked questions directly. This is usually done on a face-to-face basis, although some interviews are conducted over the telephone. The advantage of this type of survey is that the researchers bring control to the situation. They know the conditions under which the interviews took place and that each question was asked in the same way. Its disadvantages include not only the more limited number of questionnaires that can be completed, and the increased cost, but also *interviewer bias,* the effects that interviewers can have on respondents that lead to biased answers. For example, although respondents may be willing to write an anonymous answer, they may not want to express their opinions to another person directly. Some respondents even try to make their answers match what they think the interviewer wants to hear.

Sociologists sometimes use *closed-ended questions,* called *structured interviews.* Each question is followed by a list of possible answers. The advantages are that these are faster to administer, and make it easier for the answers to be *coded* (categorized) so they can be fed into a computer for analysis. If you use closed-ended questions, you will have to be careful to make sure that they represent people's opinions. For example, if you were to ask, "What do you think should be done to rapists?" and the only choices you provide are to castrate or kill them, you would not be taking accurate measurements of people's opinions. Similarly, if you begin a question with, "Don't you agree that" ("rapists should be locked up for life"—or whatever you want to add), you would tilt the results toward agreement with a particular position.

Questions, then, must be worded carefully so they do not slant answers—because biased findings are worthless. It takes a great deal of training to construct questions that are free of bias, and sociologists are extremely critical of both how questions are worded and how they are administered (given).

To better tap the depth and diversity of people's experiences and attitudes, you may chose to use *open-ended questions,* called *unstructured interviews,* that allow people to answer in their own words. The primary advantage of this type of interview is that it allows people to express their full range of opinions. The major disadvantage is that it is difficult to compare people's answers. For example, how would you compare these answers to the question "What do you think causes rape?"

"They haven't been raised right."
"I think they must have had problems with their mother."
"We ought to kill every one!"
"They're all sick."
"I don't want to talk about it."

The research topic we are considering also brings up another significant item. Let's suppose that you want to interview rape victims. Would they really give honest answers? Will a woman even admit to a stranger that she has been raped, much less talk about it? Wouldn't all your efforts be futile?

If you were to simply walk up to a stranger on the street and ask if she had ever been raped, you can guess the results—and they certainly would give little basis for placing confidence in your findings. Researchers must establish *rapport* (pronounced ruh–pour), a feeling of trust, with their respondents. When it comes to sensitive topics, areas about which people may feel embarrassment, shame, hostility, or other deep emotions, rapport is all the more important.

Once rapport is gained (often through building trust by explaining the significance of the research, assuring anonymity, and asking nonsensitive questions first), victims usually will talk about rape. For example, each year researchers conduct a national crime survey in which they interview a random sample of 100,000 Americans. They find that most rape victims will talk about their experiences. These national crime surveys show that rape is *three* times higher than the official statistics, and that most rape is committed by someone the victim knows (*Statistical Abstract of the United States* 2006: page 192).

SECONDARY ANALYSIS

In *secondary analysis,* a second research method, researchers analyze data already collected by others. For example, if you were to examine the basic data gathered by the interviewers who did the national crime survey just mentioned, you would be doing secondary analysis.

Ordinarily, researchers prefer to gather their own data, but lack of resources, especially money, may make this impossible. In addition, data already gathered may contain a wealth of information not pertinent to the goals of the original researchers. It simply lies there, waiting to be analyzed.

While this approach can solve problems of access, it also poses its own problems. Since you didn't do the research, how can you be sure that the data were gathered systematically and recorded accurately, and that biases were avoided? Knowing this may not be an easy task, especially if the original data were gathered by a team of researchers, not all of whom were equally qualified.

DOCUMENTS

The use of *documents,* written sources, is a third research method employed by sociologists. To investigate social life, sociologists examine such diverse sources as books, newspapers, diaries, bank records, police reports, immigration files, and records kept by schools, hospitals, and other organizations. Although they are not commonly called documents, also included here are movies, television programs, videotapes, computer disks, CDs, DVDs, and other digitized records.

To apply this method to the study of rape, you might examine police reports. They may reveal what proportion of all arrests are for rape; how many of the men arrested go to trial; what proportion is convicted, put on probation, sent to prison; and so forth. If these are your questions, police statistics could be valuable.

But for other questions, police records would be useless. For example, if you want to know about the adjustment of rape victims, such records would tell you nothing. Other documents, however, may lend themselves to this question. If your campus has a rape crisis center, for example, it might have records that would provide key information. Or you may obtain diaries kept by victims, and search them for clues to their reactions—especially how their orientations change over time. If you couldn't find such diaries, you might contact a sample of rape victims and ask them to keep diaries. Locating that sample is extremely difficult—but, again, the rape crisis center could be the key. Their personnel might ask victims to keep the diaries. (To my knowledge, however, no sociologist has yet studied rape in this way.)

I am writing, of course, about an ideal case, as though the rape crisis center is opening its arms to you. In actual fact it may not cooperate at all, refusing to ask victims to keep diaries and not even letting you near their records. Access, then, is another problem researchers constantly face. Simply put, you can't study something unless you can gain access to it.

EXPERIMENTS

A fourth research method is the *experiment*. This is the classic method of the natural sciences. Sociologists seldom use it, however, because they are more likely to be interested in broad features of society and social behavior, or in studying a social group in a natural setting, neither of which lends itself to an experiment.

The basic purpose of an experiment is to identify cause-and-effect relationships—to find out what causes what. Ordinarily, experiments are used to test a hypothesis. Experiments involve *independent variables* (those factors that cause a change in something) and *dependent variables* (those factors that are changed). Before the experiment, you must measure the dependent variable. Then, after introducing the independent variable, you again measure the dependent variable in order to see what change has occurred.

Let's assume, for example, that you want to test the hypothesis that pornography creates attitudes that favor rape. The independent variable would be pornography, the dependent variable attitudes toward rape. You can measure a group of men's attitudes toward rape and then use random numbers to divide the men into two subgroups. To one group, the *experimental group*, you introduce the independent variable (such as violent pornographic videos). The other group, the *control group*, is not exposed to the independent variable (that is, they are not shown these videos). You then measure the dependent variable in both groups. Changes in the dependent variable (in this case attitudes toward rape) are due to what only the experimental group received, the independent variable (in this case, the pornography).

Because there is always some chance that unknown third variables have not been distributed evenly among the groups, you would need to retest your results by repeating the experiment with other groups of men.

UNOBTRUSIVE MEASURES

The fifth research method is *unobtrusive measures:* observing people's behavior when they do not know they are being studied. For example, social researchers have studied the level of whiskey consumption in a "dry" town by counting empty bottles in trash cans; the degree of fear induced by ghost stories by measuring the shrinking diameter of a circle of seated children; and the popularity of exhibits at Chicago's Museum of Science and Industry by the wear upon tiles in front of the various displays (Webb et al. 1966; Lee 2000). Researchers have also gone high tech in their unobtrusive measures (Hays 2004). To trace customers' paths through stores, they have attached infrared surveillance devices to shopping carts. Retailers use these findings to place higher profit items in more strategic locations (McCarthy 1993). Casinos use chips that transmit radio signals, allowing casino operators to know exactly how much their high rollers are betting at every hand of poker or blackjack (Sanders, 2005).

Unobtrusive measures could also be used to study rape. For example, you could observe rapists in prison when they do not know they are being watched. You might arrange for the leader of a therapy group for rapists to be called out of the room. During his absence, you could use a one-way mirror to observe the men's interactions, and video cameras to preserve what they say and do. You might even have a stooge bring up a certain topic. Such an approach would probably tell you more about the men's real attitudes than most other techniques.

Professional ethics, however, probably would disallow such a study. And I know of no research that has applied this method to the study of rape.

PARTICIPANT OBSERVATION (FIELD WORK)

Let's turn to my favorite method, one that involves the researcher in the most direct way. In *participant observation* (or field work) the researcher *participates* in a research setting while *observing* what is happening in that setting.

How is it possible to study rape by participant observation? It would seem that this method would not apply. If one considers being present during rape, it certainly does not. But there are many other questions about rape that can be answered by participant observation, answers that cannot be gained as adequately by any other method.

Let's suppose that your interest is the adjustment of rape victims. You would like to learn how the rape has affected their behavior and their orientations to life. For example, how has their victimization affected their hopes and goals, their dating patterns, their ideas about men and intimacy? Participant observation can provide detailed answers to such questions.

Let's go back to your campus again. Assume that your campus has a rape crisis intervention center. This setting lends itself to participant observation, for here you can observe rape victims from the time they first report the attack to their later participation in individual and group counseling. With good rapport, you can even spend time with victims outside this setting, observing how it affects other aspects of their lives.

Participant observation has the added benefit of allowing you to study whatever happens to occur while you are in the setting. In this instance, you would also be able to study the operation of the rape crisis center. As you observe counselors at work, you could also analyze their statements and study *their* attitudes and behaviors.

As you may have noticed, in participant observation the personal characteristics of the researcher are important. Could a man, for example, conduct such research? Technically, the answer is yes. Properly introduced and with the right attitudes, men could do this research. But granted the topic, and especially the emotional states of females who have been brutally victimized by males, it may be more appropriate for women sociologists to conduct this research. Their chances of success are likely to be higher.

In conducting research, then, sociologists must be aware of such variables as the sex, age, race–ethnicity, personality, and even height and weight of the researcher (Henslin 1990). While important in all research methods (for example, in surveys men who are being interviewed may be more talkative to young, shapely women than to unkempt men with bad breath), these variables are especially important in participant observation.

Participant observers face a problem with generalizability. Although they look for principles of human behavior, it is difficult to know the extent to which their findings apply beyond the setting in which they occur. Consequently, most participant observation is exploratory in nature: The findings document in detail what people in a particular setting are experiencing and how they are reacting to those experiences, suggesting that other people who face similar situations will react in similar ways.

I find participant observation the most exciting of the methods. It is the type of sociology that I like to do and the type I like to read about. From these studies, I gain a depth of understanding of settings that I want to know more about but for whatever reason am not able to study, and in some cases am not even able to enter. If I were a woman, for example, I might have volunteered for work in my campus's rape crisis center—a technique often used by sociologists to solve the problem of access.

Conclusion: A Note on Choosing Research Methods

As you have seen, a crucial factor in choosing a research method is the questions you want to answer. Each method lends itself much better to answering particular interests or questions than do other methods. You also have seen that access to subjects is crucial in deciding which research method to use. Two other factors are also significant in this choice: the resources available to the researcher, and the researcher's background or training. For example, a researcher who prefers to conduct a survey may find that finances will not permit it, and instead turn to the study of documents. The researcher's background is similarly significant in making a choice. Researchers who have been trained in *quantitative research methods* (an emphasis on measurement, numbers, statistics) are more likely to use surveys, while researchers who have been trained in *qualitative research methods* (an emphasis on observing and interpreting what people do and say) lean toward participant observation. The particular training that sociologists receive in graduate school, which sometimes depends on capricious events, orients them toward certain research methods. They feel comfortable with those, and tend to continue to use them throughout their careers.

5 · "Riding the Bull at Gilley's": Convicted Rapists Describe the Rewards of Rape

DIANA SCULLY
JOSEPH MAROLLA

As we saw in the previous reading, sociologists can choose from a variety of research methods. Rape was used as the example to illustrate the ways in which sociologists collect data. In this selection, you can see how two sociologists used the research method known as unstructured interviewing to gather data on rape. What prompted their research was a question that many people wonder about: "Just why do men rape?"

Scully and Marolla interviewed a sample of men who had been sent to prison for rape. In what was a difficult interviewing situation, they established enough *rapport* that the men felt free to talk about their motives. From this selection, you should gain an understanding of the reasons why men commit this violent act. To determine how widespread (representative) these motives are, we need more studies, preferably with both convicted and unconvicted rapists. Perhaps you, now a student reading this book, will become a sociologist who will build on this study.

OVER THE PAST SEVERAL DECADES, rape has become a "medicalized" social problem. That is to say, the theories used to explain rape are predicated on psychopathological models. They have been generated from clinical experiences with small samples of rapists, often the therapists' own clients. Although these psychiatric explanations are most appropriately applied to the atypical rapist, they have been generalized to all men who rape and have come to inform the public's view on the topic.

Two assumptions are at the core of the psychopathological model: that rape is the result of idiosyncratic mental disease and that it often includes an uncontrollable sexual impulse (Scully and Marolla, 1985). For example, the presumption of psychopathology is evident in the often cited work of Nicholas Groth (1979). While Groth emphasizes the nonsexual nature of rape (power, anger, sadism), he also concludes, "Rape is always a symptom of some psychological dysfunction, either temporary and transient or chronic and repetitive" (Groth, 1979:5). Thus, in the psychopathological view, rapists lack the ability to control their behavior; they are "sick" individuals from the "lunatic fringe" of society.

In contradiction to this model, empirical research has repeatedly failed to find a consistent pattern of personality type or character disorder that reliably discriminates rapists from other groups of men (Fisher and Rivlin, 1971; Hammer and Jacks, 1955; Rada, 1978). Indeed, other research has found that fewer than 5 percent of men were psychotic when they raped (Abel et al., 1980).

Evidence indicates that rape is not a behavior confined to a few "sick" men, but many men have the attitudes and beliefs necessary to commit a sexually aggressive act. In research conducted at a midwestern university, Koss and her coworkers reported that 85 percent of men defined as highly sexually aggressive had victimized women with whom they were romantically involved (Koss and Leonard, 1984). A survey quoted in *The Chronicle of Higher Education* estimates that more than 20 percent of college women are the victims of rape and attempted rape (Meyer, 1984). These findings mirror research published several decades earlier which also concluded that sexual aggression was commonplace in dating relationships (Kanin, 1957, 1965, 1967, 1969; Kirkpatrick and Kanin, 1957). In their study of 53 college males, Malamuth, Haber, and Feshback (1980) found that 51 percent indicated a likelihood that they, themselves, would rape if assured of not being punished.

In addition, the frequency of rape in the United States makes it unlikely that responsibility rests solely with a small lunatic fringe of psychopathic men. Johnson (1980), calculating the lifetime risk of rape to girls and women aged twelve and over, makes a similar observation. Using Law Enforcement Assistance Association and Bureau of Census Crime Victimization Studies, he calculated that, excluding sexual abuse in marriage and assuming equal risk to all women, 20 to 30 percent of girls now 12 years old will suffer a violent sexual attack during the remainder of their lives. Interestingly, the lack of empirical support for the psychopathological model has not resulted in the de-medicalization of rape, nor does it appear to have diminished the belief that rapists are "sick" aberrations in their own culture. This is significant because of the implications and consequences of the model.

A central assumption in the psychopathological model is that male sexual aggression is unusual or strange. This assumption removes rape from the realm of the everyday or "normal" world and places it in the category of "special" or "sick" behavior. As a consequence, men who rape are cast in the role of outsider and a connection with normative male behavior is avoided. Since, in this view, the source of the behavior is thought to be within the psychology of the individual, attention is diverted away from culture or social structure as contributing factors. Thus, the psychopathological model ignores evidence which links sexual aggression to environmental variables and which suggests that rape, like all behavior, is learned.

Cultural Factors in Rape

Culture is a factor in rape, but the precise nature of the relationship between culture and sexual violence remains a topic of discussion. Ethnographic data from pre-industrial societies show the existence of rape-free cultures (Broude and Green, 1976; Sanday, 1979), although explanations for the phenomenon differ. Sanday (1979) relates sexual violence to contempt for female qualities and suggests that rape is part of a culture of violence and an expression of male dominance. In contrast, Blumberg (1979) argues that in pre-industrial societies women are more likely to lack important life options and to be physically and politically oppressed where they lack economic power relative to men. That is, in pre-industrial societies relative economic power enables women to win some immunity from men's use of force against them.

Among modern societies, the frequency of rape varies dramatically, and the United States is among the most rape-prone of all. In 1980, for example, the rate of reported rape and attempted rape for the United States was eighteen times higher than the corresponding rate for England and Wales (West, 1983). Spurred by the Women's Movement, feminists have generated an impressive body of theory regarding the cultural etiology of rape in the United States. Representative of the feminist view, Griffin (1971) called rape "The All American Crime."

The feminist perspective views rape as an act of violence and social control which functions to "keep women in their place" (Brownmiller, 1975; Kasinsky, 1975; Russell, 1975). Feminists see rape as an extension of normative male behavior, the result of conformity or overconformity to the values and prerogatives which define the traditional male sex role. That is, traditional socialization encourages males to associate power, dominance, strength, virility, and superiority with masculinity, and submissiveness, passivity, weakness, and inferiority with femininity. Furthermore, males are taught to have expectations about their level of sexual needs and expectations for corresponding female accessibility which function to justify forcing sexual access. The justification for forced sexual access is buttressed by legal, social, and religious definitions of women as male property and sex as an exchange of goods (Bart, 1979). Socialization prepares women to be "legitimate" victims and men to be potential offenders (Weis and Borges, 1973). Herman (1984) concludes that the United States is a rape culture because both genders are socialized to regard male aggression as a natural and normal part of sexual intercourse.

Feminists view pornography as an important element in a larger system of sexual violence; they see pornography as an expression of a rape-prone culture where women are seen as objects available for use by men (Morgan, 1980; Wheeler, 1985). Based on his content analysis of 428 "adults only" books, Smith (1976) makes a similar observation. He notes that, not only is rape presented as part of normal male/female sexual relations, but the woman, despite her terror, is always depicted as sexually aroused to the point of cooperation. In the end, she is ashamed but physically gratified. The message—women desire and enjoy rape—has more potential for damage than the image of the violence *per se.*

The fusion of these themes—sex as an impersonal act, the victim's uncontrollable orgasm, and the violent infliction of pain—is commonplace in the actual accounts of rapists. Scully and Marolla (1984) demonstrated that many convicted rapists denied their crime and attempted to justify their rapes by arguing that their victim enjoyed herself despite the use of a weapon and the infliction of serious injuries, or even death. In fact, many argued, they had been instrumental in making *her* fantasy come true.

The images projected in pornography contribute to a vocabulary of motive which trivializes and neutralizes rape and which might lessen the internal controls that otherwise would prevent sexually aggressive behavior. Men who rape use this culturally acquired vocabulary to justify their sexual violence.

Another consequence of the application of psychopathology to rape is that it leads one to view sexual violence as a special type of crime in which the motivations are subconscious and uncontrollable rather than overt and deliberate as with other criminal behavior. Black (1983) offers an approach to the analysis of criminal and/or violent behavior which, when applied to rape, avoids this bias. Black suggests that it is theoretically useful to ignore that crime is criminal in order to discover what such behavior has in common with other kinds of conduct. From his perspective, much of the crime in modern societies, as in pre-industrial societies, can be interpreted as a form of "self help" in which the actor is expressing a grievance through aggression and violence. From the actor's perspective, the victim is deviant and his own behavior is a form of social control in which the objective may be conflict management, punishment, or revenge. For example, in societies where women are considered the property of men, rape is sometimes used as a means of avenging the victim's husband or father (Black, 1983). In some cultures rape is used as a form of punishment. Such was the tradition among the puritanical, patriarchal Cheyenne, where men were valued for their ability as warriors. It was Cheyenne custom that a wife suspected of being unfaithful could be "put on the prairie" by her husband. Military confreres then were invited to "feast" on the prairie (Hoebel, 1954; Llewellyn and Hoebel, 1941). The ensuing mass rape was a husband's method of punishing his wife.

Black's (1983) approach is helpful in understanding rape because it forces one to examine the goals that some men have learned to achieve through sexually violent means. Thus, one approach to understanding why some men rape is to shift attention from individual psychopathology to the important question of what rapists gain from sexual aggression and violence in a culture seemingly prone to rape. In this paper, we address this question using data from interviews conducted with 114 convicted, incarcerated rapists.

Methods

SAMPLE

During 1980 and 1981 we interviewed 114 convicted rapists. All of the men had been convicted of the rape or attempted rape of an adult woman and subsequently incarcerated in a Virginia prison. Men convicted of other types of sexual offense were omitted from the sample.

In addition to their convictions for rape, 39 percent of the men also had convictions for burglary or robbery, 29 percent for abduction, 25 percent for sodomy, 11 percent for first or second degree murder, and 12 percent had been convicted of more than one rape. The majority of the men had previous criminal histories, but only 23 percent had a record of past sex offenses and only 26 percent had a history of emotional problems. Their sentences for rape and accompanying crimes ranged from ten years to seven life sentences plus 380 years for one man. Twenty-two percent of the rapists were serving at least one life sentence. Forty-six percent of the rapists were white, 54 percent black. In age, they ranged from 18 to 60 years, but the majority were between 18 and 35 years. Based on a statistical profile of felons in all Virginia prisons prepared by the Virginia Department of Corrections, it appears that this sample of rapists was disproportionately white and, at the time of the research, somewhat better educated and younger than the average inmate.

All participants in this research were volunteers. In constructing the sample, age, education, race, severity of current offense, and past criminal record were balanced within the limitations imposed by the characteristics of the volunteer pool. Obviously the sample was not random and thus may not be typical of all rapists, imprisoned or otherwise.

How Offenders View the Rewards of Rape

REVENGE AND PUNISHMENT

As noted earlier, Black's (1983) perspective suggests that a rapist might see his act as a legitimized form of revenge or punishment. Additionally, he asserts that the idea of "collective liability" accounts for much seemingly random violence. "Collective liability" suggests that all people in a particular category are held accountable for the conduct of each of their counterparts. Thus, the victim of a violent act may merely represent the category of individual being punished.

These factors—revenge, punishment, and the collective liability of women—can be used to explain a number of rapes in our research. Several cases will illustrate ways in which these factors combined in various types of rape. Revenge-rapes were among the most brutal and often included beatings, serious injuries, and even murder.

Typically, revenge-rapes included the element of collective liability. That is, from the rapist's perspective, the victim was a substitute for the woman on whom he wanted revenge. As explained elsewhere (Scully and Marolla, 1984), an upsetting event, involving a woman, preceded a significant number of rapes. When they raped, these men were angry because of a perceived indiscretion, typically related to a rigid, moralistic standard of sexual conduct, which they required from "their woman" but, in most cases, did not abide by themselves. Over and over these rapists talked about using rape "to get even" with their wives or some other significant woman. Typical is a young man who, prior to the rape, had a violent argument with his wife over what eventually proved to be her misdiagnosed case of venereal disease. She assumed the disease had been contracted through him, an accusation that infuriated him. After fighting with his wife, he explained that he drove around "thinking about hurting someone." He encountered his victim, a stranger, on the road where her car had broken down. It appears she accepted his offered ride because her car was out of commission. When she realized that rape was pending, she called him "a son of a bitch," and attempted to resist. He reported flying into a rage and beating her, and he confided,

I have never felt that much anger before. If she had resisted, I would have killed her. . . . . The rape was for revenge. I didn't have an orgasm. She was there to get my hostile feelings off on.

Although not the most common form of revenge-rape, sexual assault continues to be used in retaliation against the victim's male partner. In one such case, the offender, angry because the victim's husband owed him money, went to the victim's home to collect. He confided, "I was going to get it one way or another." Finding the victim alone, he explained, they started to argue about the money and,

I grabbed her and started beating the hell out of her. Then I committed the act. I knew what I was doing. I was mad. I could have stopped, but I didn't. I did it to get even with her and her husband.

Griffin (1971) points out that when women are viewed as commodities, "In raping another man's woman, a man may aggrandize his own manhood and concurrently reduce that of the other man" (p. 33).

Revenge-rapes often contained an element of punishment. In some cases, while the victim was not the initial object of the revenge, the intent was to punish her because of something that transpired after the decision to rape had been made or during the course of the rape itself. This was the case with a young man whose wife had recently left him. Although they were in the process of reconciliation, he remained angry and upset over the separation. The night of the rape, he met the victim and her friend in a bar where he had gone to watch a fight on TV. The two women apparently accepted a ride from him, but after taking her friend home, he drove the victim to his apartment. At his apartment, he found a note from his wife indicating she had stopped by to watch the fight with him. This increased his anger because he preferred his wife's company. Inside his apartment, the victim allegedly remarked that she was sexually interested in his dog, which, he reported, put him in a rage. In the ensuing attack, he raped and pistol-whipped the victim. Then he forced a vacuum cleaner hose, switched on suction, into her vagina and bit her breast, severing the nipple. He stated:

I hated at the time, but I don't know if it was her (the victim). (Who could it have been?) My wife? Even though we were getting back together. I still didn't trust her.

During his interview, it became clear that this offender, like many of the men, believed men have the right to discipline and punish women. In fact, he argued that most of the men he knew would also have beaten the victim because "that kind of thing (referring to the dog) is not acceptable among my friends."

Finally, in some rapes, both revenge and punishment were directed at victims because they represented women whom these offenders perceived as collectively responsible and liable for their problems. Rape was used "to put women in their place" and as a method of proving their "manhood" by displaying dominance over a female. For example, one multiple rapist believed his actions were related to the feeling that women thought they were better than he was.

> Rape was a feeling of total dominance. Before the rapes, I would always get a feeling of power and anger. I would degrade women so I could feel there was a person of less worth than me.

Another, especially brutal, case involved a young man from an upper middle class background, who spilled out his story in a seven-hour interview conducted in his solitary confinement cell. He described himself as tremendously angry, at the time, with his girlfriend, who he believed was involved with him in a "storybook romance," and from whom he expected complete fidelity. When she went away to college and became involved with another man, his revenge lasted eighteen months and involved the rape and murder of five women, all strangers who lived in his community. Explaining his rape-murders, he stated:

> I wanted to take my anger and frustration out on a stranger, to be in control, to do what I wanted to do. I wanted to use and abuse someone as I felt used and abused. I was killing my girl friend. During the rapes and murders, I would think about my girl friend. I hated the victims because they probably messed men over. I hated women because they were deceitful and I was getting revenge for what happened to me.

AN ADDED BONUS

Burglary and robbery commonly accompany rape. Among our sample, 39 percent of the rapists had also been convicted of one or the other of these crimes committed in connection with rape. In some cases, the original intent was rape, and robbery was an afterthought. However, a number of men indicated that the reverse was true in their situation. That is, the decision to rape was made subsequent to their original intent, which was burglary or robbery.

This was the case with a young offender who stated that he originally intended only to rob the store in which the victim happened to be working. He explained that when he found the victim alone,

I decided to rape her to prove I had guts. She was just there. It could have been anybody.

Similarly, another offender indicated that he initially broke into his victim's home to burglarize it. When he discovered the victim asleep, he decided to seize the opportunity "to satisfy an urge to go to bed with a white woman, to see if it was different." Indeed a number of men indicated that the decision to rape had been made after they realized they were in control of the situation. This was also true of an unemployed offender who confided that his practice was to steal whenever he needed money. On the day of the rape, he drove to a local supermarket and paced the parking lot, "staking out the situation." His pregnant victim was the first person to come along alone and "she was an easy target." Threatening her with a knife, he reported the victim as saying she would do anything if he didn't harm her. At that point, he decided to force her to drive to a deserted area, where he raped her. He explained:

I wasn't thinking about sex. But when she said she would do anything not to get hurt, probably because she was pregnant, I thought, "why not?"

The attitude of these men toward rape was similar to their attitude toward burglary and robbery. Quite simply, if the situation is right, "why not?" From the perspective of these rapists, rape was just another part of the crime—an added bonus.

SEXUAL ACCESS

In an effort to change public attitudes that are damaging to the victims of rape and to reform laws seemingly premised on the assumption that women both ask for and enjoy rape, many writers emphasize the violent and aggressive character of rape. Often such arguments appear to discount the part that sex plays in the crime. The data clearly indicate that from the rapists' point of view, rape is in part sexually motivated. Indeed, it is the sexual aspect of rape that distinguishes it from other forms of assault.

Rape as a means of sexual access also shows the deliberate nature of this crime. When a woman is unwilling or seems unavailable for sex, the rapist can seize what isn't volunteered. In discussing his decision to rape, one man made this clear.

. . . a real fox, beautiful shape. She was a beautiful woman and I wanted to see what she had.

The attitude that sex is a male entitlement suggests that when a woman says "no," rape is a suitable method of conquering the "offending" object. If, for example, a woman is picked up at a party or in a bar or while hitchhiking (behavior which a number of the rapists saw as a signal of sexual availability), and the woman later resists sexual advances, rape is presumed to be justified. The same justification operates in what is popularly called "date rape." The belief that sex was their just compensation compelled a number of rapists to insist they had not raped. Such was the case of an offender who raped and seriously beat his victim when, on their second date, she refused his sexual advances.

> I think I was really pissed off at her because it didn't go as planned. I could have been with someone else. She led me on but wouldn't deliver. . . . I have a male ego that must be fed.

The purpose of such rapes was conquest, to seize what was not offered.

Despite the cultural belief that young women are the most sexually desirable, several rapes involved the deliberate choice of a victim relatively older than the assailant. Since the rapists were themselves rather young (26 to 30 years of age on the average), they were expressing a preference for sexually experienced, rather than elderly, women. Men who chose victims older than themselves often said they did so because they believed that sexually experienced women were more desirable partners. They raped because they also believed that these women would not be sexually attracted to them.

Finally, sexual access emerged as a factor in the accounts of black men who consciously chose to rape white women. The majority of rapes in the United States are intraracial. However, for the past 20 years, according to national data based on reported rapes as well as victimization studies, which include unreported rapes, the rate of black on white (B/W) rape has significantly exceeded the rate of white on black (W/B) rape (La Free, 1982). Indeed, we may be experiencing a historical anomaly, since, as Brownmiller (1975) has documented, white men have freely raped women of color in the past. The current structure of interracial rape, however, reflects contemporary racism and race relations in several ways.

First, the status of black women in the United States today is relatively lower than the status of white women. Further, prejudice, segregation, and other factors continue to militate against interracial coupling. Thus, the desire for sexual access to higher status, unavailable women, an important function in B/W rape, does not motivate white men to rape black women. Equally important, demographic and geographic barriers interact to lower the incidence of W/B rape. Segregation as well as the poverty expected in black neighborhoods undoubtedly discourages many whites from choosing such areas as a target for housebreaking or robbery. Thus, the number of rapes that would occur in conjunction with these crimes is reduced.

Reflecting in part the standards of sexual desirability set by the dominant white society, a number of black rapists indicated they had been curious about white women. Blocked by racial barriers from legitimate sexual relations with white women, they raped to gain access to them. They described raping white women as "the ultimate experience" and "high status among my friends. It gave me a feeling of status, power, macho." For another man, raping a white woman had a special appeal because it violated a "known taboo," making it more dangerous, and thus more exciting to him, than raping a black woman.

IMPERSONAL SEX AND POWER

The idea that rape is an impersonal rather than an intimate or mutual experience appealed to a number of rapists, some of whom suggested it was their preferred form of sex. The fact that rape allowed them to control rather than care encouraged some to act on this preference. For example, one man explained,

> Rape gave me the power to do what I wanted to do without feeling I had to please a partner or respond to a partner. I felt in control, dominant. Rape was the ability to have sex without caring about the woman's response. I was totally dominant.

Another rapist commented:

> Seeing them laying there helpless gave me the confidence that I could do it. . . . With rape, I felt totally in charge. I'm bashful, timid. When a woman wanted to give in normal sex, I was intimidated. In the rapes, I was totally in command, she totally submissive.

During his interview, another rapist confided that he had been fantasizing about rape for several weeks before committing his offense. His belief was that it would be "an exciting experience—a new high." Most appealing to him was the idea that he could make his victim "do it all for him" and that he would be in control. He fantasized that she "would submit totally and that I could have anything I wanted." Eventually, he decided to act because his older brother told him, "forced sex is great, I wouldn't get caught and, besides, women love it." Though now he admits to his crime, he continues to believe his victim "enjoyed it." Perhaps we should note here that the appeal of impersonal sex is not limited to convicted rapists. The amount of male sexual activity that occurs in homosexual meeting places as well as the widespread use of prostitutes suggests that avoidance of intimacy appeals to a large segment of the male population. Through rape men can experience power and avoid the emotions related to intimacy and tenderness. Further, the popularity of violent pornography suggests that a wide variety of men in this culture have learned to be aroused by sex fused with violence (Smith, 1976). Consistent with this observation, experimental research conducted by Malamuth et al. (1980) demonstrates that men are aroused by images that depict women as orgasmic under conditions of violence and pain. They found that, for female students, arousal was high when the victim experienced an orgasm and *no* pain, whereas male students were highly aroused when the victim experienced an orgasm *and* pain. On the basis of their results, Malamuth et al. suggest that forcing a woman to climax despite her pain and abhorrence of the assailant makes the rapist feel powerful; he has gained control over the only source of power historically associated with women, their bodies. In the final analysis, dominance was the objective of most rapists.

RECREATION AND ADVENTURE

Among gang rapists, most of whom were in their late teens or early twenties when convicted, rape represented recreation and adventure, another form of delinquent activity. Part of rape's appeal was the sense of male camaraderie engendered by participating collectively in a dangerous activity. To prove one's self capable of "performing" under these circumstances was a substantial challenge and also a source of reward. One gang rapist articulated this feeling very clearly.

> We felt powerful; we were in control. I wanted sex, and there was peer pressure. She wasn't like a person, no personality, just domination on my part. Just to show I could do it—you know, macho.

Our research revealed several forms of gang rape. A common pattern was hitchhike-abduction for the purpose of having sex. Though the intent was rape, a number of men did not view it as such because they were convinced that women hitchhiked primarily to signal sexual availability and only secondarily as a form of transportation. In these cases, the unsuspecting victim was driven to a deserted area, raped, and in the majority of cases physically injured. Sometimes, the victim was not hitchhiking; she was abducted at knife or gun point from the street, usually at night. Some of these men did not view this type of attack as rape either, because they believed a woman walking alone at night to be a prostitute. In addition, they were often convinced "she enjoyed it."

"Gang date" rape was another popular variation. In this pattern, one member of the gang would make a date with the victim. Then, without her knowledge or consent, she would be driven to a predetermined location and forcibly raped by each member of the group. One young man revealed this practice was so much a part of his group's recreational routine, they had rented a house for the purpose. From his perspective, the rape was justified because "usually the girl had a bad reputation, or we knew it was what she liked."

During his interview, another offender confessed to participating in twenty or thirty such "gang date" rapes because his driver's license had been revoked, making it difficult for him to "get girls." Sixty percent of the time, he claimed, "they were girls known to do this kind of thing," but "frequently, the girls didn't want to have sex with all of us." In such cases, he said, "It might start out as rape, but, then, they (the women) would quiet down and none ever reported it to the police." He was convicted for a gang rape, which he described as "the ultimate thing I ever did," because unlike his other rapes, the victim, in this case, was a stranger whom the group abducted as she walked home from the library. He felt the group's past experience with "gang date" rape had prepared them for this crime in which the victim was blindfolded and driven to the mountains where, though it was winter, she was forced to remove her clothing. Lying on the snow, she was raped by each of the four men several times before being abandoned near a farm house. This young man continued to believe that if he had spent the night with her, rather than abandoning her, she would not have reported it to the police.

Solitary rapists also used terms like "exciting," "a challenge," "an adventure" to describe their feelings about rape. Like the gang rapists, these men found the element of danger made rape all the more exciting. Typifying this attitude was one man who described his rape as intentional. He reported:

> It was exciting to get away with it (rape), just being able to beat the system, not women. It was like doing something illegal and getting away with it.

Another rapist confided that for him "rape was just more exciting and compelling" than a normal sexual encounter because it involved forcing a stranger. A multiple rapist asserted, "It was the excitement and fear and the drama that made rape a big kick."

FEELING GOOD

When the men were asked to recall their feelings immediately following the rape, only eight percent indicated that guilt or feeling bad was part of their emotional response. The majority said they felt good, relieved, or simply nothing at all. Some indicated they had been afraid of being caught or felt sorry for themselves. Only two men out of 114 expressed any concern or feeling for the victim. Feeling good or nothing at all about raping women is not an aberration limited to men in prison. Smithyman (1978), in his study of "undetected rapists"—rapists outside of prison—found that raping women had no impact on their lives, nor did it have a negative effect on their self-image.

Significantly, a number of men volunteered the information that raping had a positive impact on their feelings. For some, the satisfaction was in revenge. For example, the man who had raped and murdered five women:

It seems like so much bitterness and tension had built up, and this released it. I felt like I had just climbed a mountain and now I could look back.

Another offender characterized rape as habit forming: "Rape is like smoking. You can't stop once you start." Finally, one man expressed the sentiments of many rapists when he stated,

After rape, I always felt like I had just conquered something, like I had just ridden the bull at Gilley's.

Conclusions

This paper has explored rape from the perspective of a group of convicted, incarcerated rapists. The purpose was to discover how these men viewed sexual violence and what they gained from their behavior.

We found that rape was frequently a means of revenge and punishment. Implicit in revenge-rapes was the notion that women were collectively liable for the rapists' problems. In some cases, victims were substitutes for significant women on whom the men desired to take revenge. In other cases, victims were thought to represent all women, and rape was used to punish, humiliate, and "put them in their place." In both cases women were seen as a class, a category, not as individuals. For some men, rape was almost an afterthought, a bonus added to burglary or robbery. Other men gained access to sexually unavailable or unwilling women through rape. For this group of men, rape was a fantasy come true, a particularly exciting form of impersonal sex which enabled them to dominate and control women, by exercising a singularly male form of power. These rapists talked of the pleasures of raping—how for them it was a challenge, an adventure, a dangerous and "ultimate" experience. Rape made them feel good and, in some cases, even elevated their self-image.

The pleasure these men derived from raping reveals the extreme to which they objectified women. Women were seen as sexual commodities to be used or conquered rather than as human beings with rights and feelings. One young man expressed the extreme of the contemptful view of women when he confided to the female researcher.

> Rape is a man's right. If a woman doesn't want to give it, the man should take it. Women have no right to say no. Women are made to have sex. It's all they are good for. Some women would rather take a beating, but they always give in; it's what they are for.

This man murdered his victim because she wouldn't "give in."

Undoubtedly, some rapes, like some of all crimes, are idiopathic [caused by a condition of unknown origin]. However, it is not necessary to resort to pathological motives to account for all rape or other acts of sexual violence. Indeed, we find that men who rape have something to teach us about the cultural roots of sexual aggression. They force us to acknowledge that rape is more than an idiosyncratic act committed by a few "sick" men. Rather, rape can be viewed as the end point in a continuum of sexually aggressive behaviors that reward men and victimize women. In the way that motives for committing any criminal act can be rationally determined, reasons for rape can also be determined. Our data demonstrate that some men rape because they have learned that in this culture, sexual violence is rewarding. Significantly, the overwhelming majority of these rapists indicated they never thought they would go to prison for what they did. Some did not fear imprisonment because they did not define their behavior as rape. Others knew that women frequently do not report rape and of those cases that are reported, conviction rates are low, and therefore they felt secure. These men perceived rape as a rewarding, low-risk act. Understanding that otherwise normal men can and do rape is critical to the development of strategies for prevention.

We are left with the fact that all men do not rape. In view of the apparent rewards and cultural supports for rape, it is important to ask why some men do not rape. Hirschi (1969) makes a similar observation about delinquency. He argues that the key question is not "Why do they do it?" but rather "Why don't we do it?" (p. 34). Likewise, we may be seeking an answer to the wrong question about sexual assault of women. Instead of asking men who rape "Why?" perhaps we should be asking men who don't "Why not?"

6 Would You Hire an Ex-Convict?

DEVAH PAGER

The question of causation is vexing, both for people in everyday life and for social scientists. How do we really know what causes something? For the most part, this question is easier to resolve in the physical sciences. Carefully measure all items in a mixture, heat the mixture to some designated temperature, and you know that the addition of heat caused the result. To be sure, you can repeat this procedure over and over.

But what is the cause of human behavior? This is infinitely more complicated and often frustrating to tease out. Consider a little game I sometimes play to amuse myself at traffic lights. In long lines at long lights, drivers sometimes edge forward, closing the gaps between their cars. As they do so, I sometimes hold back, not moving. When the space between my car and the next one ahead of me reaches a certain point, I suddenly move my car forward so it almost touches the car in front of me. I then watch in the rear-view mirror to see if the car in back of me follows. If it does, I reflect on causation. Did my increasing the space between our cars cause the driver to move his or her car forward? My musing makes me aware that I didn't cause this driver to do anything, although it appears that way. The cause is not the new distance between the cars, but something inside the driver, a choice of some sort that the driver makes. ("I can get closer to the light" or "The light's about to change and it isn't worth the effort.") My behavior, however, was both an essential condition and a stimulus for the other driver's action.

Think about this: Essential and a stimulus, but yet not the cause. It is with such questions (at times more philosophical than physical or empirical) that sociologists grapple. One way that we unravel cause and effect is through field experiments, the method used by Pager in this selection.

WHILE STRATIFICATION RESEARCHERS typically focus on schools, labor markets, and the family as primary institutions affecting inequality, a new institution has emerged as central to the sorting and stratifying of young and disadvantaged men: the criminal justice system. With over two million individuals currently incarcerated, and over half a million prisoners released each year, the large and growing numbers of men being processed through the criminal justice system raises important questions about the consequences of this massive institutional intervention.

This article focuses on the consequences of incarceration for the employment outcomes of black and white men. While previous survey research has demonstrated a strong *association* between incarceration and employment, there remains little understanding of the mechanisms by which these outcomes are produced. In the present study, I adopt an experimental audit approach to formally test the degree to which a criminal record affects subsequent employment opportunities. By using matched pairs of individuals to apply for real entry-level jobs, it becomes possible to directly measure the extent to which a criminal record—in the absence of other disqualifying characteristics—serves as a barrier to employment among equally qualified applicants. Further, by varying the race of the tester pairs, we can assess the ways in which the effects of race and criminal record interact to produce new forms of labor market inequalities.

Trends in Incarceration

Over the past three decades, the number of prison inmates in the United States has increased by more than 600%, leaving it the country with the highest incarceration rate in the world (Bureau of Justice Statistics, 2002; Barclay, Tavares, and Siddique, 2001). During this time, incarceration has changed from a punishment reserved primarily for the most heinous offenders to one extended to a much greater range of crimes and a much larger segment of the population. Recent trends in crime policy have led to the imposition of harsher sentences for a wider range of offenses, thus casting an even-widening net of penal intervention.

While the recent "tough on crime" policies may be effective in getting criminals off the streets, little provision has been made for when they get back out. Of the nearly 2 million individuals currently incarcerated, roughly 95% will be released, with more than half a million being released each year (Slevin, 2000). According to one estimate, there are currently over 12 million ex-felons in the United States, representing roughly 8% of the working-age population (Uggen, Thompson, and Manza, 2000). Of those recently released, nearly two-thirds will be charged with new crimes and over 40% will return to prison within three years (Bureau of Justice Statistics, 2000). Certainly some of these outcomes are the result of desolate opportunities or deeply ingrained dispositions, grown out of broken families, poor neighborhoods, and little social control (Sampson and Laub, 1993; Wilson, 1997). But net of these contributing factors[sic], there is evidence that experience with the criminal justice system in itself has adverse consequences for subsequent opportunities. In particular, incarceration is associated with limited future employment opportunities and earnings potential (Freeman, 1987; Western, 2002), which themselves are among the strongest predictors of recidivism (Sampson and Laub, 1993; Shover, 1996; Uggen, 2000).

The expansion of the prison population has been particularly consequential for blacks. The incarceration rate for young black men in the year 2000 was nearly 10%, compared to just over 1% for white men in the same age group (Bureau of Justice Statistics, 2001). Young black men today have a 28% likelihood of incarceration during their lifetime (Bureau of Justice Statistics, 1997), a figure that rises above 50% among young black high school dropouts (Pettit and Western, 2001). These vast numbers of inmates translate into a large and increasing population of black ex-offenders returning to communities and searching for work. The barriers these men face in reaching economic self-sufficiency are compounded by the stigma of minority status and criminal record. The consequences of such trends for widening racial disparities are potentially profound (see Freeman and Holzer, 1986; Western and Pettit, 1999).

The objective of this study is to assess whether the effect of a criminal record differs for black and white applicants. Most research investigating the differential impact of incarceration on blacks has focused on the differential *rates* of incarceration and how those rates translate into widening racial disparities. In addition to disparities in the rate of incarceration, however, it is also important to consider possible racial differences in the *effects* of incarceration. Almost none of the existing literature to date has explored this issue.

Study Design

The basic design of this study involves the use of four male auditors (also called testers), two blacks and two whites. The testers were 23-year-old college students from Milwaukee who were matched on the basis of physical appearance and general style of self-presentation. Objective characteristics that were not already identical between pairs—such as educational attainment and work experience—were made similar for the purpose of the applications. Within each team, one auditor was randomly assigned a "criminal record" for the first week; the pair then rotated which member presented himself as the ex-offender for each successive week of employment searches, such that each tester served in the criminal record condition for an equal number of cases. By varying which member of the pair presented himself as having a criminal record, unobserved differences within the pairs of applicants were effectively controlled. No significant differences were found for the outcomes of individual testers or by month of testing.

Job openings for entry-level positions (defined as jobs requiring no previous experience and no education greater than high school) were identified from the Sunday classified advertisement section of the *Milwaukee Journal Sentinel.* In addition, a supplemental sample was drawn from *Jobnet,* a state-sponsored web site for employment listings, which was developed in connection with the W-2 Welfare-to-Work initiatives.

The audit pairs were randomly assigned 15 job openings each week. The white pair and the black pair were assigned separate sets of jobs, with the same-race testers applying to the same jobs. One member of the pair applied first, with the second applying one day later (randomly varying whether the ex-offender was first or second). A total of 350 employers were audited during the course of this study: 150 by the white pair and 200 by the black pair. Additional tests were performed by the black pair because black testers received fewer callbacks on average, and there were thus fewer data points with which to draw comparisons. A larger sample size enabled me to calculate more precise estimates of the effects under investigation.

Immediately following the completion of each job application, testers filled out a six-page response form that coded relevant information from the test. Important variables included type of occupation, metropolitan status, wage, size of establishment, and race and sex of employer. Additionally, testers wrote narratives describing the overall interaction and comments made by employers (or included on applications) specifically related to race or criminal records.

Tester Profiles

In developing the tester profiles, emphasis was placed on adopting characteristics that were both numerically representative and substantively important. In the present study, the criminal record consisted of a felony drug conviction (possession with intent to distribute, cocaine) and 18 months of (served) prison time. A drug crime (as opposed to a violent or property crime) was chosen because of its prevalence, its policy salience, and its connection to racial disparities in incarceration. It is important to acknowledge that the effects reported here may differ depending on the type of offense.

The Effect of a Criminal Record for Whites

I begin with an analysis of the effect of a criminal record among whites. White noncriminals can serve as our baseline in the following comparisons, representing the presumptively nonstigmatized group relative to blacks and those with criminal records. Given that all testers presented roughly identical credentials, the differences experienced among groups of testers can be attributed fully to the effects of race or criminal status.

Figure 6.1 shows the percentage of applications submitted by white testers that elicited callbacks from employers, by criminal status. As illustrated below, there is a large and significant effect of a criminal record, with 34% of whites without criminal records receiving callbacks, relative to only 17% of whites with criminal records. A criminal record thereby reduces the likelihood of a callback by 50%.

There were some fairly obvious examples documented by testers that illustrate the strong reaction among employers to the signal of a criminal record. In one case, a white tester in the criminal record condition went to a trucking service to apply for a job as a dispatcher. The tester was given a long application, including a complex math test, which took nearly 45 minutes to

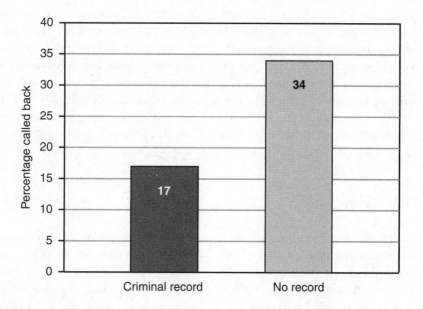

Figure 6.1   The effect of a criminal record on employment opportunities for whites.

fill out. During the course of this process, there were several details about the application and the job that needed clarification, some of which involved checking with the supervisor about how to proceed. No concerns were raised about his candidacy at this stage. When the tester turned the application in, the secretary brought it into a back office for the supervisor to look over, so that an interview could perhaps be conducted. When the secretary came back out, presumably after the supervisor had a chance to look over the application more thoroughly, he was told the position had already been filled. While, of course, isolated incidents like this are not conclusive, this was not an infrequent occurrence. Often testers reported seeing employers' levels of responsiveness change dramatically once they had glanced down at the criminal record questions.

Clearly, the results here demonstrate that criminal records close doors in employment situations. Many employers seem to use the information as a screening mechanism, without attempting to probe deeper into the possible context or complexities of the situation. As we can see here, in 50% of cases, employers were unwilling to consider equally qualified applicants on the basis of their criminal record.

Of course, this trend is not true among all employers, in all situations. There were, in fact, some employers who seemed to prefer workers who had been recently released from prison. One owner told a white tester in the criminal record condition that he "like[d] hiring people who ha[d] just come out of prison because they tend to be more motivated, and are more likely to be hard workers [not wanting to return to prison]." Another employer for a cleaning company attempted to dissuade the white noncriminal tester from applying because the job involved "a great deal of dirty work." The tester with the criminal record, on the other hand, was offered the job on the spot. A criminal record is thus not an obstacle in all cases, but on average, as we see in Figure 6.1, it reduces employment opportunities substantially.

The Effect of Race

A second major focus of this study concerns the effect of race. African-Americans continue to suffer from lower rates of employment relative to whites, but there is tremendous disagreement over the source of these disparities. The idea that race itself—apart from other correlated characteristics—continues to play a major role in shaping employment opportunities has come under question in recent years (e.g., D'Souza, 1995; Steele, 1991). The audit methodology is uniquely suited to address this question. While the present study design does not provide the kind of cross-race matched-pair tests that earlier audit studies of racial discrimination have used, the between-group comparisons (white pair vs. black pair) can nevertheless offer an unbiased estimate of the effect of race on employment opportunities.

Figure 6.2 presents the percentage of callbacks received for both categories of black testers relative to those for whites. The effect of race in these findings is strikingly large. Among blacks without criminal records, only 14% received callbacks, relative to 34% of white noncriminals. In fact, even whites with criminal records received more favorable treatment (17%) than blacks *without* criminal records (14%). The rank ordering of groups in this graph is painfully revealing of employer preferences: race continues to play a dominant role in shaping employment opportunities, equal to or greater than the impact of a criminal record.

The magnitude of the race effect found here corresponds closely to those found in previous audit studies directly measuring racial discrimination. Bendick et al. (1994), for example, found that blacks were 24 percentage points less likely to receive a job offer relative to their white counterparts, a finding very close to the 20 percentage point difference (between white and

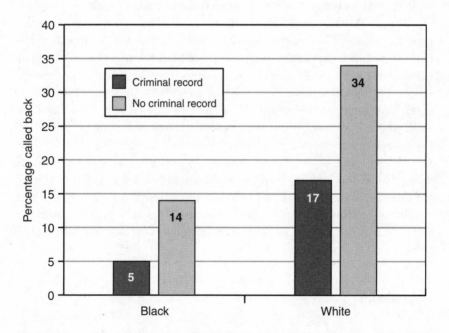

Figure 6.2 The effect of a criminal record for black and white job applicants. Dark bars represent criminal record; light bars represent no criminal record.

black nonoffenders) found here. Thus in the eight years since the last major employment audit of race was conducted, very little has changed in the reaction of employers to minority applicants. Despite the many rhetorical arguments used to suggest that direct racial discrimination is no longer a major barrier to opportunity (e.g., D'Souza, 1995; Steele, 1991), as we can see here, employers, at least in Milwaukee, continue to use race as a major factor in hiring decisions.

Racial Differences in the Effects of a Criminal Record

The final question this study sought to answer was the degree to which the effect of a criminal record differs depending on the race of the applicant. Based on the results presented in Figure 6.2, the effect of a criminal record appears more pronounced for blacks than it is for whites. While this interaction term is not statistically significant, the magnitude of the difference is nontrivial. While the ratio of callbacks for nonoffenders relative to ex-offenders for whites is 2 : 1, this same ratio for blacks is nearly 3 : 1. The effect of a criminal record is thus 40% larger for blacks than for whites.

This evidence is suggestive of the way in which associations between race and crime affect interpersonal evaluations. Employers, already reluctant to hire blacks, appear even more wary of blacks with proven criminal involvement. Despite the fact that these testers were bright articulate college students with effective styles of self-presentation, the cursory review of entry-level applicants leaves little room for these qualities to be noticed. Instead, the employment barriers of minority status and criminal record are compounded, intensifying the stigma toward this group.

The salience of employers' sensitivity toward criminal involvement among blacks was highlighted in several interactions documented by testers. On three separate occasions, for example, black testers were asked in person (before submitting their applications) whether they had a prior criminal history. None of the white testers were asked about their criminal histories up front.

Discussion

There is serious disagreement among academics, policy makers, and practitioners over the extent to which contact with the criminal justice system—in itself—leads to harmful consequences for employment. The present study takes a strong stand in this debate by offering direct evidence of the causal relationship between a criminal record and employment outcomes. While survey research has produced noisy and indirect estimates of this effect, the current research design offers a direct measure of a criminal record as a mechanism producing employment disparities. Using matched pairs and an experimentally assigned criminal record, this estimate is unaffected by the problems of selection, which plague observational data. While certainly there are additional ways in which incarceration may affect employment outcomes, this finding provides conclusive evidence that mere contact with the criminal justice system, in the absence of any transformative or selective effects, severely limits subsequent employment opportunities. And while the audit study investigates employment barriers to ex-offenders from a micro-perspective, the implications are far-reaching. The finding that ex-offenders are only one-half to one-third as likely as nonoffenders to be considered by employers suggests that a criminal record indeed presents a major barrier to employment. With over 2 million people currently behind bars and over 12 million people with prior felony convictions, the consequences for labor market inequalities are potentially profound.

Second, the persistent effect of race on employment opportunities is painfully clear in these results. Blacks are less than half as likely to receive consideration by employers, relative to their white counterparts, and black nonoffenders fall behind even whites with prior felony convictions. The powerful effects of race thus continue to direct employment decisions in ways that contribute to persisting racial inequality. In light of these findings, current public opinion seems largely misinformed. According to a recent survey of residents in Los Angeles, Boston, Detroit, and Atlanta, researchers found that just over a quarter of whites believe there to be "a lot" of discrimination against blacks, compared to nearly two-thirds of black respondents (Kluegel and Bobo, 2001). Over the past decade, affirmative action has come under attack across the country based on the argument that direct racial discrimination is no longer a major barrier to opportunity. According to this study, however, employers, at least in Milwaukee, continue to use race as a major factor in their hiring decisions. When we combine the effects of race and criminal record, the problem grows more intense. Not only are blacks much more likely to be incarcerated than whites; based on the findings presented here, they may also be more strongly affected by the impact of a criminal record. Previous estimates of the aggregate consequences of incarceration may therefore underestimate the impact on racial disparities.

Finally, in terms of policy implications, this research has troubling conclusions. In our frenzy of locking people up, our "crime control" policies may in fact exacerbate the very conditions that lead to crime in the first place. Research consistently shows that finding quality steady employment is one of the strongest predictors of desistance from crime (Sampson and Laub, 1993; Shover, 1996; Uggen, 2000). The fact that a criminal record severely limits employment opportunities—particularly among blacks—suggests that these individuals are left with few viable alternatives.

As more and more young men enter the labor force from prison, it becomes increasingly important to consider the impact of incarceration on the job prospects of those coming out. No longer a peripheral institution, the criminal justice system has become a dominant presence in the lives of young disadvantaged men, playing a key role in the sorting and stratifying of labor market opportunities. This article represents an initial attempt to specify one of the important mechanisms by which incarceration leads to poor employment outcomes. Future research is needed to expand this emphasis to other mechanisms (e.g., the transformative effects of prison on human and social capital), as well as to include other social domains affected by incarceration (e.g., housing, family formation, political participation, etc.); in this way, we can move toward a more complete understanding of the collateral consequences of incarceration for social inequality.

7 Doing Research with Streetcorner Crack Dealers

BRUCE A. JACOBS

Let's suppose that you want to study streetcorner drug dealing. How would you go about it? You could pass out questionnaires, but to whom? Considering how they might be filled out, what confidence could you have in the answers? You could interview people who have been charged with selling illegal drugs, but how would you know if they are similar to dealers who have not been arrested? If you decide to conduct a survey, whom would you survey? If you wanted to conduct an experiment, how would you do it—and how could you do it safely?

Jacobs faced this dilemma. He wanted accurate information on drug dealing, but how was he to get it? His solution was to go where the action was. He talked to dealers on the streetcorners and observed how they sold drugs. He learned about their lives and why they engage in such risky behavior. Getting dealers to open up wasn't easy, however, for this sociologist was a stranger to them—and his questions seemed too nosey. On top of this, his looks and speech marked him as someone who was not part of their world. At first, the dealers thought that he was from the police, not exactly a comfortable or safe identity in this setting. In this selection, the author focuses on how he overcame these obstacles.

Setting and Respondents

LIKE OTHER POST–WORLD WAR II rustbelt cities of its general size and type, St. Louis has suffered rapid deindustrialization, population loss, resource deprivation, and urban decay. Mobility to surrounding suburbs is high and continues unabated, taking important tax revenue and social capital with it. Since 1990, St. Louis has lost 15 percent of its population. The city's base of 341,000 makes the impact of such trends acute. St. Louis is developing a concentrated population of the truly disadvantaged—people with scarce resources and abundant social service needs that cannot be met and are getting worse. Such conditions provide an ideal context for drug use, drug selling, and other serious criminality.

Historically, St. Louis has had one of the largest illicit drug markets in the midwestern United States. In many neighborhoods, crack, heroin, marijuana, and PCP are sold openly and are available throughout the day—particularly on the troubled north side, where social disorganization and urban decay are most pronounced. St. Louis arrestees persistently have high rates of cocaine-, opiate-, and marijuana-positive urine specimens; they are among the highest of the twenty-four cities measured in the Drug Use Forecasting program. Emergency room cases involving cocaine and heroin mirror other large metropolitan areas and indicate a high degree of street drug institutionalization. Though street gangs neither control nor direct drug sales in St. Louis, the nearly 1,500 members of forty-five different gangs facilitate them by providing the microstructural networks and mass of contacts necessary for the trade to thrive.

Among the most socially distressed and impoverished areas in the St. Louis metropolitan area, the study neighborhood generally outranks other local sectors in the percentage of people living at or below poverty, proportions of citizens unemployed or on welfare, dropout rates of children of school age, drug arrests, substance abuse rates, and various indicators of poor health. The study neighborhood and contiguous blocks have all the earmarks of an "urban dead zone"—abandoned buildings, burned-out tenements, garbage-strewn vacant lots, and graffiti-splashed walls. Groups of young men collect on the street, selling crack, "insulting one another's sexual prowess, getting high, and looking for an opportunity to make some fast cash."

The study population is made up of curbside (streetcorner) distributors, consisting of persons who "routinely sell crack in the same areas, [though] each is a freelancer with his own supplier and responsible for his own profits and losses." These sellers are gang affiliated but not gang directed. This book, therefore, is not about street gang members who sell crack but about crack sellers who happen to be street gang members. Though the public widely perceives gangs to drive street drug selling, research has consistently demonstrated the rarity of such a phenomenon. Inner-city street gangs do not have exclusive control over crack distribution, and many street distributors are not gang members. Gang membership and crack selling correlate but in a facilitating way: Gangs provide the connections and criminal capital necessary to do business. Street gangs, however, are unable to develop and implement hierarchical, functionally interdependent structures that would allow a formal business of selling to happen.

As freelancers, the offenders in my sample are rarely fronted supplies (given crack to sell and allowed to pay for it later), sell for their own individual profit, and generally are in constant competition for a small number of compulsively addicted daily smokers who always try to negotiate the price down. Not infrequently, a number of sellers work the same street, corner, or vacant lot at the same time. Though not always blatant or obtrusive, transactions may easily be observed if looked for. Any organization between or among sellers tends to be crude, primitive, and fleeting. House sales are uncommon because the offenders usually lack access to private dwellings in which to do business. Their "collective orientation" as street gang members also is far too weak to support a social organization conducive to selling from private dwellings.

Entering the Setting

Studying active drug dealers is difficult and challenging precisely because their activity is criminal. Active offenders are generally "hard to locate because they find it necessary to lead clandestine lives. Once located, they are reluctant, for similar reasons, to give accurate and truthful information about themselves." By definition, criminological fieldworkers seek to explore the lives of those engaged in felonies where exposure could mean hard prison time. Outside observers represent a potential legal threat, a fact that impedes a good deal of ethnographic work. The more illegal the behavior, the more offenders have to lose if found out. Individuals may refuse to cooperate or may give less than reliable answers to protect their privacy. It is no surprise that outsiders—such as researchers—are often perceived as narcotics officers seeking to obtain damaging evidence for juridical purposes. Indeed, the most common suspicion that subjects have about fieldworkers is that they are spies of some sort.

I began frequenting a neighborhood known for open street-level crack sales. . . . For weeks, I would either walk or slowly drive through the area to try to be recognized, attempting to capitalize on what Goffman has called second seeings: "under some circumstances if he and they see each other seeing each other, they can use this fact as an excuse for an acquaintanceship greeting upon next seeing." Unfortunately, this process did not go as easily as Goffman suggests. When I drove by, crack dealers yelled "SCAT" at me, screams accentuated with derisive looks and obscene gestures. *SCAT* is an acronym for "street-corner apprehension team." This fifteen-man undercover team is charged with curbing street-level drug sales by apprehending dealers immediately after sales to one of their "buy" officers. Hiding nearby in unmarked cars, personnel swoop down on offenders in an attempt to catch them with the marked money just given to them by purchasing officers. This money has either traceable dye or serial numbers previously recorded that link dealers to undercover transactions. SCAT units were both feared and loathed, being reportedly merciless in their arrest procedures, which involved strip searches and no breaks.

A few more weeks passed and more trips, but I had yet to make any direct contact. Finally, I decided to get out of my car and approach the individuals I had seen dealing. Though this classic ethnographic technique of approaching strangers and initiating dialogue is said to be ineffective with drug dealers, I tried anyway. I told the dealers who I was and that I wished to take a few minutes out of their day to interview them about street life. Predictably they scoffed, accused me of being "the poh-lice," and instructed me to "get the hell out of here." Two days later, I tried again. I showed the dealers my university identification and told them that the interviews would be confidential and anonymous and that they would be paid for their time and effort. It was the money that was critical in generating their interest—even the modest sum that I offered. On the streets, money talks; nobody does anything for nothing.

Though I had made contact, making that contact stick proved difficult because dealers still suspected that I was tied to law enforcement in some way. Ironically, the police gave me my biggest credibility boost.

Police and Credibility

Hanging out with offenders on street corners, driving them around in my car, and visiting their homes must have been a curious sight. My appearance is somewhat like that of a college student. Shorts, t-shirts, casual boots, and baseball caps with rounded brims—"just like SCAT wear them," as one dealer put it—are my typical attire. Further, I am white, clean-cut, and affect a middle-class appearance—traits the relatively poor, African American respondents associate with the police.

To offenders who hadn't gotten to know me well or were waiting to pass judgment, I was seen as being on a deep-cover assignment designed to unearth their secrets and put them in jail. To cops on the beat, I was just another college boy driving down to crackville with a user in tow to buy for him. Such relations are commonplace in the street-level drug scene and have generalized subcultural currency: users serve as middlemen and funnel unfamiliar customers to dealers for a finder's fee, usually in drugs and without the customer's consent (for being "taxed," that is) but generally with his or her tacit permission. When cops see a nicely dressed, clean-shaven white boy, wearing a baseball cap, with a black street person in the passenger seat of a late-model car (a car with out-of-state plates, I might add), they scent that business is in the offering. . . .

My first run-in came two weeks after making initial contact with offenders. I was driving a field contact (an active crack seller) through a crack-filled neighborhood—a neighborhood that also happened to have the highest murder rate in a city with the fourth-highest murder rate in the nation. We were approaching a group of ten midteen youths and were about to stop when a St. Louis City patrol car pulled behind. Should I stop, as I planned on doing, get out, and talk with these youth (some of whom the field contact marginally knew), or would that place them in imminent danger of arrest? Or should I continue on as if nothing was really going on, even though I had been driving stop and go, under ten miles an hour, prior to and during the now slow-speed pursuit? I opted for the latter, accelerating slowly in a vain attempt to reassert a "normal appearance."

Sirens went on. I pulled over and reassured my field contact there was nothing to worry about since neither of us had contraband (I hoped). As officers approached, I thought about what to tell them. Should I say I was a university professor doing field research on crack dealers (a part I clearly didn't look), lie, or say nothing at all? "What you doin' down here?" one of the officers snapped. "Exit the vehicle, intertwine your fingers behind your heads, and kneel with your ankles crossed," he commanded. The searing June sidewalk was not conducive to clear thinking, but I rattled something off. "We used to work together at _____. I waited tables, he bussed, and we been friends since. I'm a sociology major up at _____ and he said he'd show me around the neighborhood sometime. Here I am." "Yeah right," the cop snapped again while searching for the crack he thought we already had purchased. Three other police cars arrived, as the cop baited my field contact and me as to how we really knew each other, what each other's real names were (which neither of us knew at the time), and what we were doing here. Dissatisfied with my answers, a sergeant took over, lecturing me on the evils of crack and how it would destroy a life others in this very neighborhood wished they had. I found no fault with the argument, listened attentively, and said nothing. After a final strip search in the late afternoon sun revealed nothing, they let us go, said I was lucky, and vowed to take me in if I ever showed my face again.

On a second occasion, my field contact and one of his crack-selling friends were in my car when we pulled up to a local liquor store. The two offenders became nervous on seeing two suits in a "tec" (detective) car parked at the phone booth. I told the two to wait while I went into the store. As I exited, the two men approached me and showed their badges. "What you doin' with these guys? Do you know 'em?" "Yes," I said, deciding to tell them who I *really* was and what I was doing. "Mind if we search your car?" one asked. "No problem," I replied. "Go right ahead." As one searched my car (for crack, guns, or whatever else he thought he'd find), his partner cuffed both of the offenders and ran warrants. As I soon learned, both detectives knew the two as repeat violent offenders with long rap sheets. "I respect what you're doing," the searching officer said as he finished and approached, "but you don't know who you're dealing with. These guys are no good." I told him thanks and promptly left. . . .

I did not realize it at the time, but these episodes with the police were absolutely essential to my research. Police provided the test I desperately needed to pass if my study were to be successful. The differential enforcement practices of these officers—where young minority males are singled out as the "symbolic assailants" and "suspicious characters" deserving of attention—benefited me immensely. Police detained me because I was with them. Driving alone in these same areas at the same time—though suspicious—would not likely have attracted nearly as much attention. I was "guilty by association" and "deserving" of the scrutiny young black males in many urban locales receive consistently. For my research, at least, this differential enforcement was anything but negative.

Police had treated me like just another user and did so with offenders present. This treatment provided the "actions" for me, the picture that spoke a thousand words. Offenders' accounts of my treatment spread rapidly through the grapevine, solidifying my credibility for the remainder of the project, and setting up the snowball sampling procedure I would use to recruit additional respondents.

Why police never attempted to confiscate my notes during these pullovers, I'll never know. Perhaps it was because they appeared to be indecipherable by anyone but me. Perhaps it was because they didn't reveal anything the cops did not already know or at least thought they knew. Regardless, the law is clearly against ethnographers, who can be held in contempt and sent to jail for protecting sources and withholding information. This, of course, says nothing about issues of guilty knowledge or guilty observation. Being aware of dealing operations and watching transactions take place make one an accessory to their commission, a felony whether one participates or not. Criminological fieldworkers almost inevitably will be coconspirators, no matter their motive or intent. "If one is effectively to study adult criminals in their natural settings," Polsky concludes, "he must make the moral decision that in some ways he will break the law himself."

Chain Referral and Data Collection

The first five respondents were recruited directly from the dealers I initially approached. Four of these five became contacts and provided six additional referrals. Three of these six then referred nine additional respondents. This chain referral method was carried out to secure a forty-person sample. Two contacts in particular proved critical for recruiting work. Snowball samples, after all, are only as good as the gatekeepers on the chain. These two had multiple contacts in the study neighborhood and in neighborhoods nearby with similar characteristics, forms of sales organization, and leader-customer/dealer-dealer relations. Roughly half of the forty respondents moved in different sets and lived in different parts of the city, providing the opportunity to address the problem that chain referral methods can have in creating a sample of like-minded offenders that offers limited response variance.

Contacts were given eligibility criteria before referring someone to me. Rather broad ranging and reflective of the variable and often vague nature of participation street-level crack dealing involves, these criteria called for someone who trafficked on streets and public thruways one or more days a week, who had done so for at least six months to several different customers per day (six to fifteen), and who grossed between $300 and $2,000 a month for all activity relevant to street crack sales (that is, selling crack, carrying drugs for someone, steering customers, or other assisting activities).

The first set of forty interviews focused on the social organization of street sales as it pertained to risk perception and detection avoidance. An additional fourteen interviews were structured to explore more systematically the areas that comprise the topical focus of this book—motivation, functions and roles, transactional security, and other core issues in the social organization of streetcorner crack sales. My "intensive fourteen" provided the richest source of data and primary stock of information on which the present study is based.

Ten of the fourteen were new subjects but similar to the original forty respondents on variables such as age, race, gang membership, amount of crack sold, number of hours per day and per week spent selling it, contact in which they sold it, level in the crack distribution hierarchy at which they dealt, and forms of sales activity and social organization in which they participated. I am confident that these fourteen are representative of the original sample and of similar sellers situated in other parts of the city in which streetcorner crack dealing is performed. More on the data's internal and external validity is provided below.

The intensive fourteen's self-reported estimates for the categories listed below were as follows: average gross monthly income per respondent, $1,787; average number of days per week spent selling, six; average grade completion, tenth; average age, 17.5. For the original forty, these estimated averages were as follows: gross monthly income, $2,300; days per week spent selling, 5.5; grade completion, tenth; average age, twenty. Estimations are based on respondent reports and must be interpreted with care, as independent validation of such figures is inherently difficult. All members of the intensive fourteen were African American males. All members of the original forty were African American. Thirty-four of the forty were male, and six were female.

Data were collected using an open-ended interview format guided by specific category and subject headings. This technique allows subjects a measure of latitude and flexibility in their responses. It also helps to make interviews flow much like a conversation, creating a comfort zone between researcher and respondent that facilitates collection of valid and reliable data. Most important, it permits the researcher to study crack sellers without

actually becoming one, yielding descriptive data about the dealing subculture and insights into the ways in which sellers "observe, classify, and describe their own life experiences." Interviews were not tape recorded
because respondents tended to link recording devices to undercover police.
Extensive notes were taken, and further details were filled in immediately
after interviews had finished. Interviews took place in private rooms or se-
cluded areas.

Though skeptical at first, interviewees relaxed and opened up soon after
interviews had begun. They talked with ease and comfort, apparently trusting the guarantee of anonymity and confidentiality I had given them. Offenders also seemed to enjoy speaking with someone "straight" about their
criminal experiences; it may have provided some sort of outlet for them to
share their expertise and teach me, someone supposedly "smarter" than
them (in terms of academic degrees), a thing or two about street life. Respondents also may see something in the research that benefits them or define it as an opportunity to correct faulty impressions of what it is they do.
Finally, the legitimation from my field contacts was critical; if they told others that it was "cool" to talk to me and that participants would not be
"burned" as a result, it tended to be believed.

How reliable and valid are my data? Here I was intruding into the lives
of individuals engaged in felonies for which they could receive long sentences. How could I know they were giving me the straight story? How could
it have been in their interest to provide incisive, accurate comments about
their lives when divulging such details might undermine their success as
dealers? To begin, though the inclusion criteria seem fairly straightforward,
they are inherently difficult to apply in the real world of street dealing. Some
respondents may have lied about their dealing status. Others may have failed
to meet the specified eligibility requirements: it seemed a waste, however,
to turn away potentially valuable respondents for the sake of adhering to a
somewhat arbitrary operational definition of eligibility in the first place. I
tried to compensate for possible mistakes by using unobtrusive observational
measures—a very revealing strategy. In one case, a respondent interrupted
our interview to run to a nearby restroom so that he could regurgitate two
$20 rocks he had swallowed ten minutes before in an attempt to avoid arrest.
This is one among a number of such stories. I impressed on my contacts the
importance of having referrals meet the criteria and, of course, asked
specifically targeted questions designed to screen out those who were inappropriate for the study. That I may not have been able to match every offender to the specified criteria need not be devastating. As Van Maanen
notes, imperfections are an inevitable part of fieldwork, given the complexity
of the enterprise.

Though participants in the drug market have an image of lying or evading the truth more than others (both nonoffending citizens and other offenders), there is little evidence to support this claim. Self-report data have been carefully assessed by a number of researchers, all of whom conclude that drug dealers are among the best, if not the best, source of information about the behaviors being studied. The most accurate self-report designs are those that ask questions regarding serious criminality and those that involve face-to-face data collection—my technique—rather than surveys administered impersonally. Offender reports are not always immune from "exaggerations, intentional distortions, lies, self-serving rationalizations, or drug-induced forgetfulness," but they may be less susceptible than some might think.

The fact that responses became repetitious indicated sufficient topical coverage, although such repetition could have been an artifact of the sampling design itself. Dealers may have conspired to respond only in a certain way, but their separation from each other in the interview process—both contextually and in many cases over periods of time—makes this unlikely. Reasonable effort was made to question every offender about every issue, but the nature of open-ended qualitative interviewing is such that not all topics could be anticipated and not all offenders could be asked the same questions about issues that emerged later, often serendipitously, during the research process.

The unobtrusive observation I engaged in of drug sales and interactions among dealers over the twenty-two-month research period, though unsystematic, confirmed many of the issues reported in the interviews. I have supplemented these interview and observational data with information collected during the course of several years of field research on the use, distribution, and control of street drugs—preceding and including the study period—from persons and places relevant to the present topic. Eight months of ride-alongs with officers from an elite gun and drug unit in the St. Louis City Police Department form part of this experiential reservoir. The researcher is the research instrument in qualitative research, and such experiences can be key to the form, content, and structure of the work produced.

PART III The Cultural Context of Social Life

W HAT IS CULTURE? The concept is easier to grasp by description than by definition. For example, suppose that you meet a young woman who has just arrived in the United Staters from India. That her culture is different is immediately evident. You first see it in her clothing, jewelry, makeup, and hair style. Next you hear it in her speech. Then it becomes apparent by her gestures. Later, you might hear her express unfamiliar beliefs about relationships, or voice other attitudes and opinions unlike yours. These characteristics, especially when they contrast sharply with our own, alert us to broad differences in the way that person was reared—to that person's culture.

Culture consists of *material* things, such as buildings, art, weapons, utensils, machines, clothing, makeup, and jewelry. Culture is also *nonmaterial,* consisting of the beliefs and patterns of behavior common to a group of people. Nonmaterial (or *symbolic*) culture is of primary interest to sociologists, for it provides the broad framework that people use to interpret life. Culture is the lens through which we see the world, the basis on which we construct reality and make our decisions.

Understanding how culture affects people's lives is essential to attaining a sociological imagination. But while we may become aware of culture's pervasive influence when we meet someone from a different culture, our perception of *our own* culture is quite another matter. We usually take *our* speech, *our* body language, *our* beliefs, and *our* ways of doing things for granted. We assume that these are normal or natural, and almost without exception we perform them without question. As Ralph Linton said, "The last thing a fish would ever notice would be water." So it is with us: Except for unusual circumstances, the effects of our own culture generally remain imperceptible to us.

Yet culture's significance is profound—not only for our behavior, but also for our orientations to life, and, ultimately, for our very being. It would be difficult to identify any aspect of who and what we are that is untouched by culture. We came into this life without a language, without values, with no ideas about religion, education, war, money, jobs, friendship, love, truth, honesty, honor, humor, family relationships—the stuff that life is made of. At birth, we possessed no such orientations to social life—which are so essential in determining the type of people we are. Yet now we take them for granted. This, say sociologists, is *culture within us.*

These learned and shared ways of believing and of doing things (another way to define culture) penetrate our being at an early age. They become part of our basic assumptions about what normal is. They form the screen through which we perceive and evaluate our world. Seldom do we question these assumptions, because like water for a fish, they form our framework for viewing life but remain beyond our ordinary perception.

On occasion, however, some unusual event may challenge our background assumptions. This makes our assumptions more visible to us, and, if we are fortunate, it even makes us aware of how arbitrary they are. For example, when several Americans converge at a ticket booth, they usually line up on the basis of time of arrival. The ticket seller, who shares the same culture, also assumes the normalcy of this behavior and expects to sell tickets on a "first come, first served" basis. To us, this seems the natural and right way of doing things, and we engage in this behavior routinely, and without thought.

But in northern Africa, where people's ideas of how to use space sharply contrast with ours, when several people want a ticket each pushes his or her way toward the ticket booth. With no idea similar to our "first come, first served" notion, the ticket seller first dispenses tickets to the noisiest, the pushiest, and (not incidentally) those with the longest arms.

When I traveled in northern Africa, I found this part of their culture most upsetting. It violated my basic expectations of how people *ought* to act—expectations that I did not even know I held until they were challenged so abruptly. At that point I experienced *culture shock,* the sudden inability to depend on the basic orientations to everyday life learned in childhood. That I was several inches taller than most Arabs, however, and was able to outreach almost everyone, helped me to adjust (partially) to this different way of doing things. I never did get used to the idea that pushing ahead of others was "right," though, and I always felt guilty about using the accident of my height to receive preferential treatment.

It is to sensitize us to this aspect of life in society—to how culture so fundamentally influences our lives—that the selections in this third Part are directed. Each reading introduces us to aspects of our social lives that ordinarily go unquestioned and unnoticed. Horace Miner helps make visible our basic assumptions about taking care of the body; Napoleon Chagnon exposes our taken-for-granted assumptions about sharing, making requests, and how to treat strangers and guests; Edward and Mildred Hall illustrate how culture influences our posture, gestures, eye contact, and use of space in face-to-face interaction; Candace Clark uncovers the cultural rules, many hidden beneath our consciousness, that govern our giving of sympathy; and Erving Goffman helps us to see how our nonverbal communications are intricate ways by which we attempt to manipulate people's opinions of us. These analyses of culture can serve as starting points from which we can begin to analyze other assumptions of reality that we unquestioningly hold, and thus gain a startlingly different perspective of social life—and of our own roles in it.

8   Body Ritual Among the Nacirema

HORACE MINER

As part of their culture, all peoples develop ideas about proper ways to care for their bodies. The Nacirema, however, have advanced these ideas to an extraordinary degree, and they spend a good deal of their time, energy, and income following the rituals prescribed by their culture. Taking care of the body in the manner dictated by their culture is so important to these people that even a good part of their childrearing revolves around instructing their children in how to fulfill these cultural rituals. With intense and prolonged training, accompanied by punishing children who fail to conform while shunning nonconforming adults, it is no wonder that almost all members of the Nacirema culture unquestioningly conform to their prescribed body rituals and dutifully pass them on to their own children.

A better understanding of the Nacirema culture might possibly shed some light on our own way of life.

THE ANTHROPOLOGIST HAS BECOME so familiar with the diversity of ways in which different peoples behave in similar situations that he is not apt to be surprised by even the most exotic customs. In fact, if all of the logically possible combinations of behavior have not been found somewhere in the world, he is apt to suspect that they must be present in some yet undescribed tribe. This point has, in fact, been expressed with respect to clan organization by Murdock. In this light, the magical beliefs and practices of the Nacirema present such unusual aspects that it seems desirable to describe them as an example of the extremes to which human behavior can go.

Professor Linton first brought the ritual of the Nacirema to the attention of anthropologists twenty years ago, but the culture of this people is still very poorly understood. They are a North American group living in the territory between the Canadian Cree, the Yaqui and Tarahumare of Mexico, and the Carib and Arawak of the Antilles. Little is known of their origin, although tradition states that they came from the east.

Nacirema culture is characterized by a highly developed market economy which has evolved in a rich natural habitat. While much of the people's time is devoted to economic pursuits, a large part of the fruits of these labors and a considerable portion of the day are spent in ritual activity. The focus of this activity is the human body, the appearance and health of which loom as a dominant concern in the ethos of the people. While such a concern is certainly not unusual, its ceremonial aspects and associated philosophy are unique.

The fundamental belief underlying the whole system appears to be that the human body is ugly and that its natural tendency is to debility and disease. Incarcerated in such a body, people's only hope is to avert these characteristics through the use of the powerful influences of ritual and ceremony. Every household has one or more shrines devoted to this purpose. The more powerful individuals in the society have several shrines in their houses and, in fact, the opulence of a house is often referred to in terms of the number of such ritual centers it possesses. Most houses are of wattle and daub construction, but the shrine rooms of the more wealthy are walled with stone. Poorer families imitate the rich by applying pottery plaques to their shrine walls.

While each family has at least one such shrine, the rituals associated with it are not family ceremonies but are private and secret. The rites are normally only discussed with children, and then only during the period when they are being initiated into these mysteries. I was able, however, to establish sufficient rapport with the natives to examine these shrines and to have the rituals described to me.

The focal point of the shrine is a box or chest which is built into the wall. In this chest are kept the many charms and magical potions without which no native believes he could live. These preparations are secured from a variety of specialized practitioners. The most powerful of these are the medicine men, whose assistance must be rewarded with substantial gifts. However, the medicine men do not provide the curative potions for their clients, but decide what the ingredients should be and then write them down in an ancient and secret language. This writing is understood only by the medicine men and by the herbalists who, for another gift, provide the required charm.

The charm is not disposed of after it has served its purpose, but is placed in the charm-box of the household shrine. As these magical materials are specific for certain ills, and the real or imagined maladies of the people are many, the charm-box is usually full to overflowing. The magical packets are so numerous that people forget what their purposes were and fear to use them again. While the natives are very vague on this point, we can only assume that the idea in retaining all the old magical materials is that their presence in the charm-box, before which the body rituals are conducted, will in some way protect the worshipper.

Beneath the charm-box is a small font. Each day every member of the family, in succession, enters the shrine room, bows his head before the charm-box, mingles different sorts of holy water in the font, and proceeds with a brief rite of ablution. The holy waters are secured from the Water Temple of the community, where the priests conduct elaborate ceremonies to make the liquid ritually pure.

In the hierarchy of magical practitioners, and below the medicine men in prestige, are specialists whose designation is best translated "holy-mouth-men." The Nacirema have an almost pathological horror of and fascination with the mouth, the condition of which is believed to have a supernatural influence on all social relationships. Were it not for the rituals of the mouth, they believe that their teeth would fall out, their gums bleed, their jaws shrink, their friends desert them, and their lovers reject them. They also believe that a strong relationship exists between oral and moral characteristics. For example, there is a ritual ablution of the mouth for children which is supposed to improve their moral fiber.

The daily body ritual performed by everyone includes a mouth-rite. Despite the fact that these people are so punctilious about care of the mouth, this rite involves a practice which strikes the uninitiated stranger as revolting. It was reported to me that the ritual consists of inserting a small bundle of hog hairs into the mouth, along with certain magical powders, and then moving the bundle in a highly formalized series of gestures.

In addition to the private mouth-rite, the people seek out a holy-mouth-man once or twice a year. These practitioners have an impressive set of paraphernalia, consisting of a variety of augers, awls, probes, and prods. The use of these objects in the exorcism of the evils of the mouth involves almost unbelievable ritual torture of the client. The holy-mouth-man opens the client's mouth and, using the above mentioned tools, enlarges any holes which decay may have created in the teeth. Magical materials are put into these holes. If there are no naturally occurring holes in the teeth, large sections of one or more teeth are gouged out so that the supernatural substance can be applied. In the client's view, the purpose of these ministrations is to arrest decay and draw friends. The extremely sacred and traditional character of the rite is evident in the fact that the natives return to the holy-mouth-men year after year, despite the fact that their teeth continue to decay.

It is to be hoped that, when a thorough study of the Nacirema is made, there will be careful inquiry into the personality structure of these people. One has but to watch the gleam in the eye of a holy-mouth-man, as he jabs an awl into an exposed nerve, to suspect that a certain amount of sadism is involved. If this can be established, a very interesting pattern emerges, for most of the population shows definite masochistic tendencies. It was to these that Professor Linton referred in discussing a distinctive part of the daily body ritual which is performed only by men. This part of the rite involves scraping and lacerating the surface of the face with a sharp instrument. Special women's rites are performed only four times during each lunar month, but what they lack in frequency is made up in barbarity. As part of this ceremony, women bake their heads in small ovens for about an hour. The theoretically interesting point is that what seems to be a preponderantly masochistic people have developed sadistic specialists.

The medicine men have an imposing temple, or *latipso*, in every community of any size. The more elaborate ceremonies required to treat very sick patients can only be performed at this temple. These ceremonies involve not only the thaumaturge but a permanent group of vestal maidens who move sedately about the temple chambers in distinctive costume and headdress.

The *latipso* ceremonies are so harsh that it is phenomenal that a fair proportion of the really sick natives who enter the temple ever recover. Small children whose indoctrination is still incomplete have been known to resist attempts to take them to the temple because "that is where you go to die." Despite this fact, sick adults are not only willing but eager to undergo the protracted ritual purification, if they can afford to do so. No matter how ill the supplicant or how grave the emergency, the guardians of many temples will not admit a client if he cannot give a rich gift to the custodian. Even after one has gained admission and survived the ceremonies, the guardians will not permit the neophyte to leave until he makes still another gift.

The supplicant entering the temple is first stripped of all his or her clothes. In everyday life the Nacirema avoids exposure of his body and its natural functions. Bathing and excretory acts are performed only in the secrecy of the household shrine, where they are ritualized as part of the body-rites. Psychological shock results from the fact that body secrecy is suddenly lost upon entry into the *latipso*. A man whose own wife has never seen him in an excretory act, suddenly finds himself naked and assisted by a vestal maiden while he performs his natural functions into a sacred vessel. This sort of ceremonial treatment is necessitated by the fact that the excreta are used by a diviner to ascertain the course and nature of the client's sickness. Female clients, on the other hand, find their naked bodies are subjected to the scrutiny, manipulation, and prodding of the medicine men.

Few supplicants in the temple are well enough to do anything but lie on their hard beds. The daily ceremonies, like the rites of the holy-mouth-men, involve discomfort and torture. With ritual precision, the vestals awaken their miserable charges each dawn and roll them about on their beds of pain while performing ablutions, in the formal movements of which the maidens are highly trained. At other times they insert magic wands in the supplicant's mouth or force him to eat substances which are supposed to be healing. From time to time the medicine men come to their clients and jab magically treated needles into their flesh. The fact that these temple ceremonies may not cure, and may even kill the neophyte, in no way decreases the people's faith in the medicine men.

There remains one other kind of practitioner, known as a "listener." This witchdoctor has the power to exorcise the devils that lodge in the heads of people who have been bewitched. The Nacirema believe that parents bewitch their own children. Mothers are particularly suspected of putting a curse on children while teaching them the secret body rituals. The counter-magic of the witchdoctor is unusual in its lack of ritual. The patient simply tells the "listener" all his troubles and fears, beginning with the earliest difficulties he can remember. The memory displayed by the Nacirema in these exorcism sessions is truly remarkable. It is not uncommon for the patient to bemoan the rejection he felt upon being weaned as a babe, and a few individuals even see their troubles going back to the traumatic effects of their own birth.

In conclusion, mention must be made of certain practices which have their base in native esthetics but which depend upon the pervasive aversion to the natural body and its functions. There are ritual fasts to make fat people thin and ceremonial feasts to make thin people fat. Still other rites are used to make women's breasts larger if they are small, and smaller if they are large. General dissatisfaction with breast shape is symbolized in the fact that the ideal form is virtually outside the range of human variation. A few women afflicted with almost inhuman hyper-mammary development are so idolized that they make a handsome living by simply going from village to village and permitting the natives to stare at them for a fee.

Reference has already been made to the fact that excretory functions are ritualized, routinized, and relegated to secrecy. Natural reproductive functions are similarly distorted. Intercourse is taboo as a topic and scheduled as an act. Efforts are made to avoid pregnancy by the use of magical materials or by limiting intercourse to certain phases of the moon. Conception is actually very infrequent. When pregnant, women dress so as to hide their condition. Parturition takes place in secret, without friends or relatives to assist, and the majority of women do not nurse their infants.

Our review of the ritual life of the Nacirema has certainly shown them to be a magic-ridden people. It is hard to understand how they have managed to exist so long under the burdens which they have imposed upon themselves. But even such exotic customs as these take on real meaning when they are viewed with the insight provided by Malinowski when he wrote:

> Looking from far and above, from our high places of safety in the developed civilization, it is easy to see all the crudity and irrelevance of magic. But without its power and guidance early man could not have mastered his practical difficulties as he has done, nor could man have advanced to the higher stages of civilization.

9 Doing Fieldwork Among the Yąnomamö

NAPOLEON A. CHAGNON

As stated in the second reading, the primary difference between sociology and anthropology is the choice of research setting. That is, sociologists usually study people who are members of industrialized and post-industrialized (information) societies, while anthropologists usually focus on tribal and peasant groups. The distinction does not always hold, however, because some anthropologists do research in urban settings, and occasionally a sociologist wanders into peasant society. Consequently, it makes little difference that the fieldwork reported here was done by an anthropologist, for if a sociologist had done participant observation among the Yąnomamö, he or she would have written a similar account of those experiences. (Sociologists, however, are considerably less interested in kinship and genealogy.)

Note how the culture of the Yąnomamö sets the stage for their behaviors. Although from our perspective their behaviors are strange, this is the way of life that the Yąnomamö take for granted. What they experience is as natural for them as our way of life is for us. But, as Chagnon discovered firsthand, for someone from our culture to experience Yąnomamö life is to encounter an alien world. Chagnon experienced *culture shock*—that is, the fundamentals of life that he had learned and lived with from childhood no longer applied, and he was most uncomfortable with what he confronted. How would you have felt in his place?

THE YĄNOMAMÖ INDIANS live in southern Venezuela and the adjacent portions of northern Brazil. Some 125 widely scattered villages have populations ranging from 40 to 250 inhabitants, with 75 to 80 people the most usual number. In total numbers their population probably approaches 10,000 people, but this is merely a guess. Many of the villages have not yet been contacted by outsiders, and nobody knows for sure exactly how many uncontacted villages there are, or how many people live in them. By comparison to African or Melanesian tribes, the Yąnomamö population is small. Still, they are one of the largest unacculturated tribes left in all of South America.

But they have a significance apart from tribal size and cultural purity: The Yąnomamö are still actively conducting warfare. It is in the nature of man to fight, according to one of their myths, because the blood of "Moon" spilled on this layer of the cosmos, causing men to become fierce. I describe the Yąnomamö as "the fierce people" because that is the most accurate single phrase that describes them. That is how they conceive themselves to be, and that is how they would like others to think of them.

I spent nineteen months with the Yąnomamö, during which time I acquired some proficiency in their language and, up to a point, submerged myself in their culture and way of life. The thing that impressed me most was the importance of aggression in their culture. I had the opportunity to witness a good many incidents that expressed individual vindictiveness on the one hand and collective bellicosity on the other. These ranged in seriousness from the ordinary incidents of wife beating and chest pounding to dueling and organized raiding by parties that set out with the intention of ambushing and killing men from enemy villages. One of the villages was raided approximately twenty-five times while I conducted the fieldwork, six times by the group I lived among. . . .

This is not to state that primitive man everywhere is unpleasant. By way of contrast, I have also done limited fieldwork among the Yąnomamö's northern neighbors, the Carib-speaking Makiritare Indians. This group was very pleasant and charming, all of them anxious to help me and honor bound to show any visitor the numerous courtesies of their system of etiquette. In short, they approached the image of primitive man that I had conjured up, and it was sheer pleasure to work with them. . . .

My first day in the field illustrated to me what my teachers meant when they spoke of "culture shock." I had traveled in a small, aluminum rowboat propelled by a large outboard motor for two and a half days. This took me from the Territorial capital, a small town on the Orinoco River, deep into Yąnomamö country. On the morning of the third day we reached a small mission settlement, the field "headquarters" of a group of Americans who were working in two Yąnomamö villages. The missionaries had come out of these villages to hold their annual conference on the progress of their mission work, and were conducting their meetings when I arrived. We picked up a passenger at the mission station, James P. Barker, the first non-Yąnomamö to make a sustained, permanent contact with the tribe (in 1950). He had just returned from a year's furlough in the United States, where I had earlier visited him before leaving for Venezuela. He agreed to accompany me to the village I had selected for my base of operations to introduce me to the Indians.

This village was also his own home base, but he had not been there for over a year and did not plan to join me for another three months. Mr. Barker had been living with this particular group about five years.

We arrived at the village, Bisaasi-teri, about 2:00 P.M. and docked the boat along the muddy bank at the terminus of the path used by the Indians to fetch their drinking water. It was hot and muggy, and my clothing was soaked with perspiration. It clung uncomfortably to my body, as it did thereafter for the remainder of the work. The small, biting gnats were out in astronomical numbers, for it was the beginning of the dry season. My face and hands were swollen from the venom of their numerous stings. In just a few moments I was to meet my first Yąnomamö, my first primitive man. What would it be like? I had visions of entering the village and seeing 125 social facts running about calling each other kinship terms and sharing food, each waiting and anxious to have me collect his genealogy. I would wear them out in turn. Would they like me? This was important to me; I wanted them to be so fond of me that they would adopt me into their kinship system and way of life, because I had heard that successful anthropologists always get adopted by their people. I had learned during my seven years of anthropological training at the University of Michigan that kinship was equivalent to society in primitive tribes and that it was a moral way of life, "moral" being something "good" and "desirable." I was determined to work my way into their moral system of kinship and become a member of their society.

My heart began to pound as we approached the village and heard the buzz of activity within the circular compound. Mr. Barker commented that he was anxious to see if any changes had taken place while he was away and wondered how many of them had died during his absence. I felt into my back pocket to make sure that my notebook was there and felt personally more secure when I touched it. Otherwise, I would not have known what to do with my hands.

I looked up and gasped when I saw a dozen burly, naked, filthy, hideous men staring at us down the shafts of their drawn arrows! Immense wads of green tobacco were stuck between their lower teeth and lips making them look even more hideous, and strands of dark-green slime dripped or hung from their noses. We arrived at the village while the men were blowing a hallucinogenic drug up their noses. One of the side effects of the drug is a runny nose. The mucus is always saturated with the green powder and the Indians usually let it run freely from their nostrils. My next discovery was that there were a dozen or so vicious, underfed dogs snapping at my legs, circling me as if I were going to be their next meal. I just stood there holding my notebook, helpless and pathetic. Then the stench of the decaying vegetation and filth struck me and I almost got sick. I was horrified. What sort of a welcome was this for the person who came here to live with you and learn your way of life, to become friends with you? They put their weapons down when they recognized Barker and returned to their chanting, keeping a nervous eye on the village entrances.

We had arrived just after a serious fight. Seven women had been abducted the day before by a neighboring group, and the local men and their guests had just that morning recovered five of them in a brutal club fight that nearly ended in a shooting war. The abductors, angry because they lost five of the seven captives, vowed to raid the Bisaasi-teri. When we arrived and entered the village unexpectedly, the Indians feared that we were the raiders. On several occasions during the next two hours the men in the village jumped to their feet, armed themselves, and waited nervously for the noise outside the village to be identified. My enthusiasm for collecting ethnographic curiosities diminished in proportion to the number of times such an alarm was raised. In fact, I was relieved when Mr. Barker suggested that we sleep across the river for the evening. It would be safer over there.

As we walked down the path to the boat, I pondered the wisdom of having decided to spend a year and a half with this tribe before I had even seen what they were like. I am not ashamed to admit, either, that had there been a diplomatic way out, I would have ended my fieldwork then and there. I did not look forward to the next day when I would be left alone with the Indians; I did not speak a word of their language, and they were decidedly different from what I had imagined them to be. The whole situation was depressing, and I wondered why I ever decided to switch from civil engineering to anthropology in the first place. I had not eaten all day, I was soaking wet from perspiration, the gnats were biting me, and I was covered with red pigment, the result of a dozen or so complete examinations I had been given by as many burly Indians. These examinations capped an otherwise grim day. The Indians would blow their noses into their hands, flick as much of the mucus off that would separate in a snap of the wrist, wipe the residue into their hair, and then carefully examine my face, arms, legs, hair, and the contents of my pockets. I asked Mr. Barker how to say "Your hands are dirty"; my comments were met by the Indians in the following way: They would "clean" their hands by spitting a quantity of slimy tobacco juice into them, rub them together, and then proceed with the examination.

Mr. Barker and I crossed the river and slung our hammocks. When he pulled his hammock out of a rubber bag, a heavy, disagreeable odor of mildewed cotton came with it. "Even the missionaries are filthy," I thought to myself. Within two weeks everything I owned smelled the same way, and

I lived with the odor for the remainder of the fieldwork. My own habits of personal cleanliness reached such levels that I didn't even mind being examined by the Indians, as I was not much cleaner than they were after I had adjusted to the circumstances.

So much for my discovery that primitive man is not the picture of nobility and sanitation I had conceived him to be. I soon discovered that it was an enormously time-consuming task to maintain my own body in the manner to which it had grown accustomed in the relatively antiseptic environment of the northern United States. Either I could be relatively well fed and relatively comfortable in a fresh change of clothes and do very little fieldwork, or, I could do considerably more fieldwork and be less well fed and less comfortable.

It is appalling how complicated it can be to make oatmeal in the jungle. First, I had to make two trips to the river to haul the water. Next, I had to prime my kerosene stove with alcohol and get it burning, a tricky procedure when you are trying to mix powdered milk and fill a coffee pot at the same time: the alcohol prime always burned out before I could turn the kerosene on, and I would have to start all over. Or, I would turn the kerosene on, hoping that the element was still hot enough to vaporize the fuel, and not start a small fire in my palm-thatched hut as the liquid kerosene squirted all over the table and walls and ignited. It was safer to start over with the alcohol. Then I had to boil the oatmeal and pick the bugs out of it. All my supplies, of course, were carefully stored in Indian-proof, ratproof, moisture-proof, and insect-proof containers, not one of which ever served its purpose adequately. Just taking things out of the multiplicity of containers and repacking them afterward was a minor project in itself. By the time I had hauled the water to cook with, unpacked my food, prepared the oatmeal, milk, and coffee, heated water for dishes, washed and dried the dishes, repacked the food in the containers, stored the containers in locked trunks and cleaned up my mess, the ceremony of preparing breakfast had brought me almost up to lunch time.

Eating three meals a day was out of the question. I solved the problem by eating a single meal that could be prepared in a single container, or, at most, in two containers, washed my dishes only when there were no clean ones left, using cold river water, and wore each change of clothing at least a week to cut down on my laundry problem, a courageous undertaking in the tropics. I was also less concerned about sharing my provisions with the rats, insects, Indians, and the elements, thereby eliminating the need for my complicated storage process. I was able to last most of the day on *café con leche*, heavily sugared espresso coffee diluted about five to one with hot milk. I would prepare this in the evening and store it in a thermos. Frequently, my single meal was no more complicated than a can of sardines and a package of crackers. But at least two or three times a week I would do something sophisticated, like make oatmeal or boil rice and add a can of tuna fish or tomato paste to it. I even saved time by devising a water system that obviated the trips to the river. I had a few sheets of zinc roofing brought in and made a rain-water trap. I caught the water on the zinc surface, funneled it into an empty gasoline drum, and then ran a plastic hose from the drum to my hut. When the drum was exhausted in the dry season, I hired the Indians to fill it with water from the river.

I ate much less when I traveled with the Indians to visit other villages. Most of the time my travel diet consisted of roasted or boiled green plantains that I obtained from the Indians, but I always carried a few cans of sardines with me in case I got lost or stayed away longer than I had planned. I found peanut butter and crackers a very nourishing food, and a simple one to prepare on trips. It was nutritious and portable, and only one tool was required to prepare the meal, a hunting knife that could be cleaned by wiping the blade on a leaf. More importantly, it was one of the few foods the Indians would let me eat in relative peace. It looked too much like animal feces to them to excite their appetites.

I once referred to the peanut butter as the dung of cattle. They found this quite repugnant. They did not know what "cattle" were, but were generally aware that I ate several canned products of such an animal. I perpetrated this myth, if for no other reason than to have some peace of mind while I ate. Fieldworkers develop strange defense mechanisms, and this was one of my own forms of adaptation. On another occasion I was eating a can of frankfurters and growing very weary of the demands of one of my guests for a share in my meal. When he asked me what I was eating, I replied: "Beef." He then asked, "What part of the animal are you eating?" to which I replied, "Guess!" He stopped asking for a share.

Meals were a problem in another way. Food sharing is important to the Yąnomamö in the context of displaying friendship. "I am hungry," is almost a form of greeting with them. I could not possibly have brought enough food with me to feed the entire village, yet they seemed not to understand this. All they could see was that I did not share my food with them at each and every meal. Nor could I enter into their system of reciprocities with respect to food; every time one of them gave me something "freely," he would dog me for months to pay him back, not with food, but with steel tools. Thus, if I accepted a plantain from someone in a different village while I was on a visit, he would most likely visit me in the future and demand a machete as payment for the time that he "fed" me. I usually reacted to these kinds of demands by giving a banana, the customary reciprocity in their culture—food for food—but this would be a disappointment for the individual who had visions of that single plantain growing into a machete over time.

Despite the fact that most of them knew I would not share my food with them at their request, some of them always showed up at my hut during mealtime. I gradually became accustomed to this and learned to ignore their persistent demands while I ate. Some of them would get angry because I failed to give in, but most of them accepted it as just a peculiarity of the subhuman foreigner. When I did give in, my hut quickly filled with Indians, each demanding a sample of the food that I had given one of them. If I did not give all a share, I was that much more despicable in their eyes.

A few of them went out of their way to make my meals unpleasant, to spite me for not sharing; for example, one man arrived and watched me eat a cracker with honey on it. He immediately recognized the honey, a particularly esteemed Yąnomamö food. He knew that I would not share my tiny bottle and that it would be futile to ask. Instead, he glared at me and queried icily, "Shaki![1] What kind of animal semen are you eating on that cracker?" His question had the desired effect, and my meal ended.

Finally, there was the problem of being lonely and separated from your own kind, especially your family. I tried to overcome this by seeking personal friendships among the Indians. This only complicated the matter because all my friends simply used my confidence to gain privileged access to my cache of steel tools and trade goods, and looted me. I would be bitterly disappointed that my "friend" thought no more of me than to finesse our relationship exclusively with the intention of getting at any locked up possessions, and my depression would hit new lows every time I discovered this. The loss of the possession bothered me much less than the shock that I was, as far as most of them were concerned, nothing more than a source of desirable items; no holds were barred in relieving me of these, since I was considered something subhuman, a non-Yąnomamö.

The thing that bothered me most was the incessant, passioned, and aggressive demands the Indians made. It would become so unbearable that I would have to lock myself in my mud hut every once in a while just to escape from it: Privacy is one of Western culture's greatest achievements. But I did not want privacy for its own sake; rather, I simply had to get away from the begging. Day and night for the entire time I lived with the Yąnomamö I was plagued by such demands as: "Give me a knife, I am poor!"; "If you don't take me with you on your next trip to Widokaiya-teri, I'll chop a hole in your canoe!"; "Don't point your camera at me or I'll hit you!"; "Share your food with me!"; "Take me across the river in your canoe and be quick about it!"; "Give me a cooking pot!"; "Loan me your flashlight so I can go hunting tonight!"; "Give me medicine . . . I itch all over!"; "Take us on a week-long hunting trip with your shotgun!"; and "Give me an axe, or I'll break into your hut when you are away visiting and steal one!" And so I was bombarded by such demands day after day, months on end, until I could not bear to see an Indian.

It was not as difficult to become calloused to the incessant begging as it was to ignore the sense of urgency, the impassioned tone of voice, or the intimidation and aggression with which the demands were made. It was likewise difficult to adjust to the fact that the Yąnomamö refused to accept "no" for an answer until or unless it seethed with passion and intimidation—which it did after six months. Giving in to a demand always established a new threshold; the next demand would be for a bigger item or favor, and the anger of the Indians even greater if the demand was not met. I soon learned that I had to become very much like the Yąnomamö to be able to get along with them on their terms: sly, aggressive, and intimidating.

Had I failed to adjust in this fashion I would have lost six months of supplies to them in a single day or would have spent most of my time ferrying them around in my canoe or hunting for them. As it was, I did spend a considerable amount of time doing these things and did succumb to their outrageous demands for axes and machetes, at least at first. More importantly, had I failed to demonstrate that I could not be pushed around beyond a certain point, I would have been the subject of far more ridicule, theft, and practical jokes than was the actual case. In short, I had to acquire a certain proficiency in their kind of interpersonal politics and to learn how to imply subtly that certain potentially undesirable consequences might follow if they did such and such to me. They do this to each other in order to establish precisely the point at which they cannot goad an individual any further without precipitating retaliation. As soon as I caught on to this and realized that much of their aggression was stimulated by their desire to discover my flash point, I got along much better with them and regained some lost ground. It was sort of like a political game that everyone played, but one in which each individual sooner or later had to display some sign that his bluffs and implied threats could be backed up. I suspect that the frequency of wife beating is a component of this syndrome, since men can display their ferocity and show others that they are capable of violence. Beating a wife with a club is considered to be an acceptable way of displaying ferocity and one that does not expose the male to much danger. The important thing is that the man has displayed his potential for violence and the implication is that other men better treat him with respect and caution.

After six months, the level of demand was tolerable in the village I used for my headquarters. The Indians and I adjusted to each other and knew what to expect with regard to demands on their part for goods, favors, and services. Had I confined my fieldwork to just that village alone, the field experience would have been far more enjoyable. But, as I was interested in the demographic pattern and social organization of a much larger area, I made regular trips to some dozen different villages in order to collect genealogies or to recheck those I already had. Hence, the intensity of begging and intimidation was fairly constant for the duration of the fieldwork. I had to establish my position in some sort of pecking order of ferocity at each and every village.

For the most part, my own "fierceness" took the form of shouting back at the Yąnomamö as loudly and as passionately as they shouted at me, especially at first, when I did not know much of their language. As I became more proficient in their language and learned more about their political tactics, I became more sophisticated in the art of bluffing. For example, I paid one young man a machete to cut palm trees and make boards from the wood. I used these to fashion a platform in the bottom of my dugout canoe to keep my possessions dry when I traveled by river. That afternoon I was doing informant work in the village; the long-awaited mission supply boat arrived, and most of the Indians ran out of the village to beg goods from the crew. I continued to work in the village for another hour or so and went down to the river to say "hello" to the men on the supply boat. I was angry when I discovered that the Indians had chopped up all my palm boards and used them to paddle their own canoes across the river. I knew that if I overlooked this incident I would have invited them to take even greater liberties with my goods in the future. I crossed the river, docked amidst their dugouts, and shouted for the Indians to come out and see me. A few of the culprits appeared, mischievous grins on their faces. I gave a spirited lecture about how hard I had worked to put those boards in my canoe, how I had paid a machete for the wood, and how angry I was that they destroyed my work in their haste to cross the river. I then pulled out my hunting knife and, while their grins disappeared, cut each of their canoes loose, set them into the current, and let them float away. I left without further ado and without looking back.

They managed to borrow another canoe and, after some effort, recovered their dugouts. The headman of the village later told me with an approving chuckle that I had done the correct thing. Everyone in the village, except, of course, the culprits, supported and defended my action. This raised my status.

Whenever I took such action and defended my rights, I got along much better with the Yąnomamö. A good deal of their behavior toward me was directed with the forethought of establishing the point at which I would react defensively. Many of them later reminisced about the early days of my work when I was "timid" and a little afraid of them, and they could bully me into giving goods away.

Theft was the most persistent situation that required me to take some sort of defensive action. I simply could not keep everything I owned locked in trunks, and the Indians came into my hut and left at will. I developed a very effective means for recovering almost all the stolen items. I would simply ask a child who took the item and then take that person's hammock when he was not around, giving a spirited lecture to the others as I marched away in a faked rage with the thief's hammock. Nobody ever attempted to stop me from doing this, and almost all of them told me that my technique for recovering my possessions was admirable. By nightfall the thief would either appear with the stolen object or send it along with someone else to make an exchange. The others would heckle him for getting caught and being forced to return the item.

With respect to collecting the data I sought, there was a very frustrating problem. Primitive social organization is kinship organization, and to understand the Yąnomamö way of life I had to collect extensive genealogies. I could not have deliberately picked a more difficult group to work with in this regard: They have very stringent name taboos. They attempt to name people in such a way that when the person dies and they can no longer use his name, the loss of the word in the language is not inconvenient. Hence, they name people for specific and minute parts of things, such as "toenail of some rodent," thereby being able to retain the words "toenail" and "(specific) rodent," but not being able to refer directly to the toenail of that rodent. The taboo is maintained even for the living: One mark of prestige is the courtesy others show you by not using your name. The sanctions behind the taboo seem to be an unusual combination of fear and respect.

I tried to use kinship terms to collect genealogies at first, but the kinship terms were so ambiguous that I ultimately had to resort to names. They were quick to grasp that I was bound to learn everybody's name and reacted, without my knowing it, by inventing false names for everybody in the village. After having spent several months collecting names and learning them, this came as a disappointment to me: I could not cross-check the genealogies with other informants from distant villages.

They enjoyed watching me learn these names. I assumed, wrongly, that I would get the truth to each question and that I would get the best information by working in public. This set the stage for converting a serious project into a farce. Each informant tried to outdo his peers by inventing a name even more ridiculous than what I had been given earlier, or by asserting that the individual about whom I inquired was married to his mother or daughter, and the like. I would have the informant whisper the name of the individual in my ear, noting that he was the father of such and such a child. Everybody would then insist that I repeat the name aloud, roaring in hysterics as I clumsily pronounced the name. I assumed that the laughter was in response to the violation of the name taboo or to my pronunciation. This was a reasonable interpretation, since the individual whose name I said aloud invariably became angry. After I learned what some of the names meant, I began to understand what the laughter was all about. A few of the more colorful examples are: "hairy vagina," "long penis," "feces of the harpy eagle," and "dirty rectum." No wonder the victims were angry.

I was forced to do my genealogy work in private because of the horseplay and nonsense. Once I did so, my informants began to agree with each other and I managed to learn a few new names, real names. I could then test any new informant by collecting a genealogy from him that I knew to be accurate. I was able to weed out the more mischievous informants this way. Little by little I extended the genealogies and learned the real names. Still, I was unable to get the names of the dead and extend the genealogies back in time, and even my best informants continued to deceive me about their own close relatives. Most of them gave me the name of a living man as the father of some individual in order to avoid mentioning that the actual father was dead.

The quality of a genealogy depends in part on the number of generations it embraces, and the name taboo prevented me from getting any substantial information about deceased ancestors. Without this information, I could not detect marriage patterns through time. I had to rely on older informants for this information, but these were the most reluctant of all. As I became more proficient in the language and more skilled at detecting lies, my informants became better at lying. One of them in particular was so cunning and persuasive that I was shocked to discover that he had been inventing his information. He specialized in making a ceremony out of telling me false names. He would look around to make sure nobody was listening outside my hut, enjoin me to never mention the name again, act very nervous and spooky, and then grab me by the head to whisper the name very softly into my ear. I was always elated after an informant session with him, because I had several generations of dead ancestors for the living people. The others refused to give me this information. To show my gratitude, I paid him quadruple the rate I had given the others. When word got around that I had increased the pay, volunteers began pouring in to give me genealogies.

I discovered that the old man was lying quite by accident. A club fight broke out in the village one day, the result of a dispute over the possession of a woman. She had been promised to Rerebawa, a particularly aggressive young man who had married into the village. Rerebawa had already been given her older sister and was enraged when the younger girl began having an affair with another man in the village, making no attempt to conceal it from him. He challenged the young man to a club fight, but was so abusive in his challenge that the opponent's father took offense and entered the village circle with his son, wielding a long club. Rerebawa swaggered out to the duel and hurled insults at both of them, trying to goad them into striking him on the head with their clubs. This would have given him the opportunity to strike them on the head. His opponents refused to hit him, and the fight ended. Rerebawa had won a moral victory because his opponents were afraid to hit him. Thereafter, he swaggered around and insulted the two men behind their backs. He was genuinely angry with them, to the point of calling the older man by the name of his dead father. I quickly seized on this as an opportunity to collect an accurate genealogy and pumped him about his adversary's ancestors. Rerebawa had been particularly nasty to me up to this point, but we became staunch allies: We were both outsiders in the local village. I then asked about other dead ancestors and got immediate replies. He was angry with the whole group and not afraid to tell me the names of the dead. When I compared his version of the genealogies to that of the old man, it was obvious that one of them was lying. I challenged his information, and he explained that everybody knew that the old man was deceiving me and bragging about it in the village. The names the old man had given me were the dead ancestors of the members of a village so far away that he thought I would never have occasion to inquire about them. As it turned out, Rerebawa knew most of the people in that village and recognized the names.

I then went over the complete genealogical records with Rerebawa, genealogies I had presumed to be in final form. I had to revise them all because of the numerous lies and falsifications they contained. Thus, after five months of almost constant work on the genealogies of just one group, I had to begin almost from scratch!

Discouraging as it was to start over, it was still the first real turning point in my fieldwork. Thereafter, I began taking advantage of local arguments and animosities in selecting my informants, and used more extensively individuals who had married into the group. I began traveling to other villages to check the genealogies, picking villages that were on strained terms with the people about whom I wanted information. I would then return to my base camp and check with local informants the accuracy of the new information. If the informants became angry when I mentioned the new names I acquired from the unfriendly group, I was almost certain that the information was accurate. For this kind of checking I had to use informants whose genealogies I knew rather well: They had to be distantly enough related to the dead person that they would not go into a rage when I mentioned the name, but not so remotely related that they would be uncertain of the accuracy of the information. Thus, I had to make a list of names that I dared not use in the presence of each and every informant. Despite the precautions, I occasionally hit a name that put the informant into a rage, such as that of a dead brother or sister that other informants had not reported. This always terminated the day's work with that informant, for he would be too touchy to continue any further, and I would be reluctant to take a chance on accidentally discovering another dead kinsman so soon after the first.

These were always unpleasant experiences, and occasionally dangerous ones, depending on the temperament of the informant. On one occasion I was planning to visit a village that had been raided about a week earlier. A woman whose name I had on my list had been killed by the raiders. I planned to check each individual on the list one by one to estimate ages, and I wanted to remove her name so that I would not say it aloud in the village. I knew that I would be in considerable difficulty if I said this name aloud so soon after her death. I called on my original informant and asked him to tell me the name of the woman who had been killed. He refused, explaining that she was a close relative of his. I then asked him if he would become angry if I read off all the names on the list. This way he did not have to say her name and could merely nod when I mentioned the right one. He was a fairly good friend of mine, and I thought I could predict his reaction. He assured me that this would be a good way of doing it. We were alone in my hut so that nobody could overhear us. I read the names softly, continuing to the next when he gave a negative reply. When I finally spoke the name of the dead woman he flew out of his chair, raised his arm to strike me, and shouted: "You son-of-a-bitch![2] If you ever say that name again, I'll kill you!" He was shaking with rage, but left my hut quietly. I shudder to think what might have happened if I had said the name unknowingly in the woman's village. I had other, similar experiences in different villages, but luckily the dead person had been dead for some time and was not closely related to the individual into whose ear I whispered the name. I was merely cautioned to desist from saying any more names, lest I get people angry with me.

I had been working on the genealogies for nearly a year when another individual came to my aid. It was Kaobawa, the headman of Upper Bisaasi-teri, the group in which I spent most of my time. He visited me one day after the others had left the hut and volunteered to help me on the genealogies. He was poor, he explained, and needed a machete. He would work only on the condition that I did not ask him about his own parents and other very close kinsmen who were dead. He also added that he would not lie to me as the others had done in the past. This was perhaps the most important single event in my fieldwork, for out of this meeting evolved a very warm friendship and a very profitable informant-fieldworker relationship.

Kaobawa's familiarity with his group's history and his candidness were remarkable. His knowledge of details was almost encyclopedic. More than that, he was enthusiastic and encouraged me to learn details that I might otherwise have ignored. If there were things he did not know intimately, he would advise me to wait until he could check things out with someone in the village. This he would do clandestinely, giving me a report the next day. As I was constrained by my part of the bargain to avoid discussing his close dead kinsmen, I had to rely on Rerebawa for this information. I got Rerebawa's genealogy from Kaobawa.

Once again I went over the genealogies with Kaobawa to recheck them, a considerable task by this time: they included about two thousand names, representing several generations of individuals from four different villages. Rerebawa's information was very accurate, and Kaobawa's contribution enabled me to trace the genealogies further back in time. Thus, after nearly a year of constant work on genealogies, Yąnomamö demography and social organization began to fall into a pattern. Only then could I see how kin groups formed and exchanged women with each other over time, and only then did the fissioning of larger villages into smaller ones show a distinct pattern. At this point I was able to begin formulating more intelligent questions because there was now some sort of pattern to work with. Without the help of Rerebawa and Kaobawa, I could not have made very much sense of the plethora of details I had collected from dozens of other informants.

Kaobawa is about 40 years old. I say "about" because the Yąnomamö numeration system has only three numbers: one, two, and more-than-two. He is the headman of Upper Bisaasi-teri. He has had five or six wives so far and temporary affairs with as many more women, one of which resulted in a child. At the present time he has just two wives, Bahimi and Koamashima. He has had a daughter and a son by Bahimi, his eldest and favorite wife. Koamashima, about 20 years old, recently had her first child, a boy. Kaobawa may give Koamashima to his youngest brother. Even now the brother shares in her sexual services. Kaobawa recently gave his third wife to another of his brothers because she was beshi: "horny." In fact, this girl had been married to two other men, both of whom discarded her because of her infidelity. Kaobawa had one daughter by her; she is being raised by his brother.

Kaobawa's eldest wife, Bahimi, is about thirty-five years old. She is his first cross-cousin. Bahimi was pregnant when I began my fieldwork, but she killed the new baby, a boy, at birth, explaining tearfully that it would have competed with Ariwari, her nursing son, for milk. Rather than expose Ariwari to the dangers and uncertainty of an early weaning, she killed the new child instead. By Yąnomamö standards, she and Kaobawa have a very tranquil household. He only beats her once in a while, and never very hard. She never has affairs with other men.

Kaobawa is quiet, intense, wise, and unobtrusive. He leads more by example than by threats and coercion. He can afford to be this way as he established his reputation for being fierce long ago, and other men respect him. He also has five mature brothers who support him, and he has given a number of his sisters to other men in the village, thereby putting them under some obligation to him. In short, his "natural" following (kinsmen) is large, and he does not have to constantly display his ferocity. People already respect him and take his suggestions seriously.

Rerebawa is much younger, only about twenty-two years old. He has just one wife by whom he has had three children. He is from Karohi-teri, one of the villages to which Kaobawa's is allied. Rerebawa left his village to seek a wife in Kaobawa's group because there were no eligible women there for him to marry.

Rerebawa is perhaps more typical than Kaobawa in the sense that he is concerned about his reputation for ferocity and goes out of his way to act tough. He is, however, much braver than the other men his age and backs up his threats with action. Moreover, he is concerned about politics and knows the details of intervillage relationships over a large area. In this respect he shows all the attributes of a headman, although he is still too young and has too many competent older brothers in his own village to expect to move easily into the position of leadership there.

He does not intend to stay in Kaobawa's group and has not made a garden. He feels that he has adequately discharged his obligations to his wife's parents by providing them with fresh game for three years. They should let him take the wife and return to his own village with her, but they refuse and try to entice him to remain permanently in Bisaasi-teri to provide them with game when they are old. They have even promised to give him their second daughter if he will stay permanently.

Although he has displayed his ferocity in many ways, one incident in particular shows what his character is like. Before he left his own village to seek a wife, he had an affair with the wife of an older brother. When he was discovered, his brother attacked him with a club. Rerebawa was infuriated so he grabbed an axe and drove his brother out of the village after soundly beating him with the flat of the blade. The brother was so afraid that he did not return to the village for several days. I recently visited his village with him. He made a point to introduce me to this brother. Rerebawa dragged him out of his hammock by the arm and told me, "This is the brother whose wife I had an affair with," a deadly insult. His brother did nothing and slunk back into his hammock, shamed, but relieved to have Rerebawa release the vise-grip on his arm.

Despite the fact that he admires Kaobawa, he has a low opinion of the others in Bisaasi-teri. He admitted confidentially that he thought Bisaasi-teri was an abominable group: "This is a terrible neighborhood! All the young men are lazy and cowards and everybody is committing incest! I'll be glad to get back home." He also admired Kaobawa's brother, the headman of Monou-teri. This man was killed by raiders while I was doing my fieldwork. Rerebawa was disgusted that the others did not chase the raiders when they discovered the shooting: "He was the only fierce one in the whole group; he was my close friend. The cowardly Monou-teri hid like women in the jungle and didn't even chase the raiders!"

Even though Rerebawa is fierce and capable of being quite nasty, he has a good side as well. He has a very biting sense of humor and can entertain the group for hours on end with jokes and witty comments. And, he is one of few Yąnomamö that I feel I can trust. When I returned to Bisaasi-teri after having been away for a year, Rerebawa was in his own village visiting his kinsmen. Word reached him that I had returned, and he immediately came to see me. He greeted me with an immense bear hug and exclaimed, "Shaki! Why did you stay away so long? Did you know that my will was so cold while you were gone that at times I could not eat for want of seeing you?" I had to admit that I missed him, too.

Of all the Yąnomamö I know, he is the most genuine and the most devoted to his culture's ways and values. I admire him for that, although I can't say that I subscribe to or endorse these same values. By contrast, Kaobawa is older and wiser. He sees his own culture in a different light and criticizes aspects of it he does not like. While many of his peers accept some of the superstitions and explanatory myths as truth and as the way things ought to be, Kaobawa questions them and privately pokes fun at some of them. Probably, more of the Yąnomamö are like Rerebawa, or at least try to be.

Notes

1. "Shaki," or, rather, "Shakiwa," is the name they gave me because they could not pronounce "Chagnon." They like to name people for some distinctive feature

when possible. *Shaki* is the name of a species of noisome bees; they accumulate in large numbers around ripening bananas and make pests of themselves by eating into the fruit, showering the people below with the debris. They probably adopted this name for me because I was also a nuisance, continuously prying into their business, taking pictures of them, and, in general, being where they did not want me.

2. This is the closest English translation of his actual statement, the literal translation of which would be nonsensical in our language.

10 The Sounds of Silence

EDWARD T. HALL
MILDRED R. HALL

When we refer to communication, we generally think about words. People who are talking, however, use much more than words to communicate with one another. *How* they say things is just as important—sometimes more so—than *what* they say. Their inflections, tones, pauses, cadence, and volume also convey meanings. If people are speaking face-to-face, their gestures, expressions, and use of space also contain significant messages.

Nonverbal communication is especially significant in conveying feelings and attitudes. Through ways so subtle that they lie beyond even our own perception—and ways so obvious that no one can miss the message—we communicate feelings of comfort and discomfort, trust and distrust, pleasure or tension, suspicions, uncertainties, desires, and a host of other feelings and concerns.

Yet we seldom think about our nonverbal communications. Our body language, for example, usually seems to be "just doing what is natural." Researchers, however, have found little that is "natural" about body language. Like our speech, our body language and other forms of nonverbal communication are learned. Thus, the specific ways by which people communicate these messages vary from one group to another, as the Halls make evident in this selection.

BOB LEAVES HIS APARTMENT at 8:15 A.M. and stops at the corner drugstore for breakfast. Before he can speak, the counterman says, "The usual?" Bob nods yes. While he savors his Danish, a fat man pushes onto the adjoining stool and overflows into his space. Bob scowls, and the man pulls himself in as much as he can. Bob has sent two messages without speaking a syllable.

Henry has an appointment to meet Arthur at 11:00 A.M.; he arrives at 11:30. Their conversation is friendly, but Arthur retains a lingering hostility. Henry has unconsciously communicated that he doesn't think the appointment is very important or that Arthur is a person who needs to be treated with respect.

George is talking to Charley's wife at a party. Their conversation is entirely trivial, yet Charley glares at them suspiciously. Their physical proximity and the movements of their eyes reveal that they are powerfully attracted to each other.

José Ybarra and Sir Edmund Jones are at the same party, and it is important for them to establish a cordial relationship for business reasons. Each is trying to be warm and friendly, yet they will part with mutual distrust, and their business transaction will probably fall through. José, in Latin fashion, moves closer and closer to Sir Edmund as they speak, and this movement is being miscommunicated as pushiness to Sir Edmund, who keeps backing away from this intimacy, which in turn is being miscommunicated to José as coldness. The silent languages of Latin and English cultures are more difficult to learn than their spoken languages.

In each of these cases, we see the subtle power of nonverbal communication. The only language used throughout most of the history of humanity (in evolutionary terms, vocal communication is relatively recent), it is the first form of communication you learn. You use this preverbal language, consciously and unconsciously, every day to tell other people how you feel about yourself and them. This language includes your posture, gestures, facial expressions, costume, the way you walk, even your treatment of time and space and material things. All people communicate on several different levels at the same time but are usually aware of only the verbal dialogue and don't realize that they respond to nonverbal messages. But when a person says one thing and really believes something else, the discrepancy between the two can usually be sensed. Nonverbal communication systems are much less subject to the conscious deception that often occurs in verbal systems. When we find ourselves thinking, "I don't know what it is about him, but he doesn't seem sincere," it's usually this lack of congruity between a person's words and his behavior that makes us anxious and uncomfortable.

Few of us realize how much we all depend on body movement in our conversation or are aware of the hidden rules that govern listening behavior. But we know instantly whether or not the person we're talking to is "tuned in," and we're very sensitive to any breach in listening etiquette. In white middle-class American culture, when someone wants to show he is listening to someone else, he looks either at the other person's face or, specifically, at his eyes, shifting his gaze from one eye to the other.

If you observe a person conversing, you'll notice that he indicates he's listening by nodding his head. He also makes little "Hmm" noises. If he agrees with what's being said, he may give a vigorous nod. To show pleasure or affirmation, he smiles; if he has some reservations, he looks skeptical by raising an eyebrow or pulling down the corners of his mouth. If a participant wants to terminate the conversation, he may start shifting his body position, stretching his legs, crossing or uncrossing them, bobbing his foot, or diverting his gaze from the speaker. The more he fidgets, the more the speaker becomes aware that he has lost his audience. As a last measure, the listener may look at his watch to indicate the imminent end of the conversation.

Talking and listening are so intricately intertwined that a person cannot do one without the other. Even when one is alone and talking to oneself, there is part of the brain that speaks while another part listens. In all conversations, the listener is positively or negatively reinforcing the speaker all the time. He may even guide the conversation without knowing it, by laughing or frowning or dismissing the argument with a wave of his hand.

The language of the eyes—another age-old way of exchanging feelings—is both subtle and complex. Not only do men and women use their eyes differently, but there are class, generational, regional, ethnic, and national cultural differences. Americans often complain about the way foreigners stare at people or hold a glance too long. Most Americans look away from someone who is using his eyes in an unfamiliar way because it makes them self-conscious. If a man looks at another man's wife in a certain way, he's asking for trouble, as indicated earlier. But he might not be ill-mannered or seeking to challenge the husband. He might be a European in this country who hasn't learned our visual mores. Many American women visiting France or Italy are acutely embarrassed because, for the first time in their lives, men really look at them—their eyes, hair, nose, lips, breasts, hips, legs, thighs, knees, ankles, feet, clothes, hairdo, even their walk. These same women, once they have become used to being looked at, often return to the United States and are overcome with the feeling that "No one ever really looks at me anymore."

Analyzing the mass of data on the eyes, it is possible to sort out at least three ways in which the eyes are used to communicate: dominance vs. submission, involvement vs. detachment, and positive vs. negative attitude. In addition, there are three levels of consciousness and control, which can be categorized as follows: (1) conscious use of the eyes to communicate, such as the flirting blink and the intimate nosewrinkling squint; (2) the very extensive category of unconscious but learned behavior governing where the eyes are directed and when (this unwritten set of rules dictates how and under what circumstances the sexes, as well as people of all status categories, look at each other); and (3) the response of the eye itself, which is completely outside both awareness and control—changes in the cast (sparkle) of the eye and the pupillary reflex.

The eye is unlike any other organ of the body, for it is an extension of the brain. The unconscious pupillary reflex and the cast of the eye have been known by people of Middle Eastern origin for years—although most are unaware of their knowledge. Depending on the context, Arabs and others look directly at the eyes or deeply into the eyes of their interlocutor. We became aware of this in the Middle East several years ago while looking at jewelry. The merchant suddenly started to push a particular bracelet at a customer and said, "You buy this one." What interested us was that the bracelet was not the one that had been consciously selected by the purchaser. But the merchant, watching the pupils of the eyes, knew what the purchaser really wanted to buy. Whether he specifically knew how he knew is debatable.

A psychologist at the University of Chicago, Eckhard Hess, was the first to conduct systematic studies of the pupillary reflex. His wife remarked one evening, while watching him reading in bed, that he must be very interested in the text because his pupils were dilated. Following up on this, Hess slipped some pictures of nudes into a stack of photographs that he gave to his male assistant. Not looking at the photographs but watching his assistant's pupils, Hess was able to tell precisely when the assistant came to the nudes. In further experiments, Hess retouched the eyes in a photograph of a woman. In one print, he made the pupils small, in another, large; nothing else was changed. Subjects who were given the photographs found the woman with the dilated pupils much more attractive. Any man who has had the experience of seeing a woman look at him as her pupils widen with reflex speed knows that she's flashing him a message.

The eye-sparkle phenomenon frequently turns up in our interviews of couples in love. It's apparently one of the first reliable clues in the other person that love is genuine. To date, there is no scientific data to explain eye sparkle; no investigation of the pupil, the cornea, or even the white sclera of the eye shows how the sparkle originates. Yet we all know it when we see it.

One common situation for most people involves the use of the eyes in the street and in public. Although eye behavior follows a definite set of rules, the rules vary according to the place, the needs and feelings of the people, and their ethnic background. For urban whites, once they're within definite recognition distance (sixteen to thirty-two feet for people with average eyesight), there is mutual avoidance of eye contact—unless they want something specific: a pickup, a handout, or information of some kind. In the West and in small towns generally, however, people are much more likely to look and greet one another, even if they're strangers.

It's permissible to look at people if they're beyond recognition distance, but once inside this sacred zone, you can only steal a glance at strangers. You must greet friends, however; to fail to do so is insulting. Yet, to stare too fixedly even at them is considered rude and hostile. Of course, all of these rules are variable.

A great many blacks, for example, greet each other in public even if they don't know each other. To blacks, most eye behavior of whites has the effect of giving the impression that they aren't there, but this is due to white avoidance of eye contact with anyone in the street.

Another very basic difference between people of different ethnic backgrounds is their sense of territoriality and how they handle space. This is the silent communication, or miscommunication, that caused friction between Mr. Ybarra and Sir Edmund Jones in our earlier example. We know from the research that everyone has around himself an invisible bubble of space that contracts and expands depending on several factors: his emotional state, the activity he's performing at the time, and his cultural background. This bubble is a kind of mobile territory that he will defend against intrusion. If he is accustomed to close personal distance between himself and others, his bubble will be smaller than that of someone who's accustomed to greater personal distance. People of northern European heritage—English, Scandinavian, Swiss, and German—tend to avoid contact. Those whose heritage is Italian, French, Spanish, Russian, Latin American, or Middle Eastern like close personal contact.

People are very sensitive to any intrusion into their spatial bubble. If someone stands too close to you, your first instinct is to back up. If that's not possible, you lean away and pull yourself in, tensing your muscles. If the intruder doesn't respond to these body signals, you may then try to protect yourself, using a briefcase, umbrella, or raincoat. Women—especially when traveling alone—often plant their pocketbooks in such a way that no one can get very close to them. As a last resort, you may move to another spot and position yourself behind a desk or a chair that provides screening. Everyone tries to adjust the space around himself in a way that's comfortable for him; most often, he does this unconsciously.

Emotions also have a direct effect on the size of a person's territory. When you're angry or under stress, your bubble expands and you require more space. New York psychiatrist Augustus Kinzel found a difference in what he calls body-buffer zones between violent and nonviolent prison inmates. Dr. Kinzel conducted experiments in which each prisoner was placed in the center of a small room, and then Dr. Kinzel slowly walked toward him. Nonviolent prisoners allowed him to come quite close, while prisoners with a history of violent behavior couldn't tolerate his proximity and reacted with some vehemence.

Apparently, people under stress experience other people as looming larger and closer than they actually are. Studies of schizophrenic patients have indicated that they sometimes have a distorted perception of space, and several psychiatrists have reported patients who experience their body boundaries as filling up an entire room. For these patients, anyone who comes into the room is actually inside their body, and such an intrusion may trigger a violent outburst.

Unfortunately, there is little detailed information about normal people who live in highly congested urban areas. We do know, of course, that the noise, pollution, dirt, crowding, and confusion of our cities induce feelings of stress in most of us, and stress leads to a need for greater space. The man who's packed into a subway, jostled in the street, crowded into an elevator, and forced to work all day in a bull pen or in a small office without auditory or visual privacy is going to be very stressed at the end of his day. He needs places that provide relief from constant overstimulation of his nervous system. Stress from overcrowding is cumulative, and people can tolerate more crowding early in the day than later; note the increased bad temper during the evening rush hour as compared with the morning melee. Certainly one factor in people's desire to commute by car is the need for privacy and relief from crowding (except, often, from other cars); it may be the only time of the day when nobody can intrude.

In crowded public places, we tense our muscles and hold ourselves stiff, and thereby communicate to others our desire not to intrude on their space and, above all, not to touch them. We also avoid eye contact, and the total effect is that of someone who has "tuned out." Walking along the street, our bubble expands slightly as we move in a stream of strangers, taking care not to bump into them. In the office, at meetings, in restaurants, our bubble keeps changing as it adjusts to the activity at hand.

Most white middle-class Americans use four main distances in their business and social relations: intimate, personal, social, and public. Each of these distances has a near and a far phase and is accompanied by changes in the volume of the voice. Intimate distance varies from direct physical contact with another person to a distance of six to eighteen inches and is used for our most private activities—caressing another person or making love. At this distance, you are overwhelmed by sensory inputs from the skin, the fragrance of perfume, even the sound of breathing—all of which literally envelop you. Even at the far phase, you're still within easy touching distance. In general, the use of intimate distance in public between adults is frowned on. It's also much too close for strangers, except under conditions of extreme crowding.

In the second zone—personal distance—the close phase is one and a half to two and a half feet: it's at this distance that wives usually stand from their husbands in public. If another woman moves into this zone, the wife will most likely be disturbed. The far phase—two and a half to four feet—is the distance used to "keep someone at arm's length" and is the most common spacing used by people in conversation.

The third zone—social distance—is employed during business transactions or exchanges with a clerk or repairman. People who work together tend to use close social distance—four to seven feet. This is also the distance for conversation at social gatherings. To stand at this distance from someone who is seated has a dominating effect (e.g., teacher to pupil, boss to secretary). The far phase of the third zone—seven to twelve feet—is where people stand when someone says, "Stand back so I can look at you." This distance lends a formal tone to business or social discourse. In an executive office, the desk serves to keep people at this distance.

The fourth zone—public distance—is used by teachers in classrooms or speakers at public gatherings. At its farthest phase—twenty-five feet and beyond—it is used for important public figures. Violations of this distance can lead to serious complications. During his 1970 U.S. visit, the president of France, Georges Pompidou, was harassed by pickets in Chicago, who were permitted to get within touching distance. Since pickets in France are kept behind barricades a block or more away, the president was outraged by this insult to his person, and President Nixon was obliged to communicate his concern as well as offer his personal apologies.

It is interesting to note how American pitchmen and panhandlers exploit the unwritten, unspoken conventions of eye and distance. Both take advantage of the fact that once explicit eye contact is established, it is rude to look away, because to do so means to brusquely dismiss the other person and his needs. Once having caught the eye of his mark, the panhandler then locks on, not letting go until he moves through the public zone, the social zone, the personal zone and, finally, into the intimate sphere, where people are most vulnerable.

Touch also is an important part of the constant stream of communication that takes place between people. A light touch, a firm touch, a blow, a caress are all communications. In an effort to break down barriers among people, there's been a recent upsurge in group-encounter activities, in which strangers are encouraged to touch one another. In special situations such as these, the rules for not touching are broken with group approval, and people gradually lose some of their inhibitions.

Although most people don't realize it, space is perceived and distances are set not by vision alone but with all the senses. Auditory space is perceived with the ears, thermal space with the skin, kinesthetic space with muscles of the body, and olfactory space with the nose. And, once again, it's one's culture that determines how his senses are programmed—which sensory information ranks highest and lowest. The important thing to remember is that culture is very persistent. In this country, we've noted the existence of culture patterns that determine distance between people in the third and fourth generations of some families, despite their prolonged contact with people of very different cultural heritages.

Whenever there is great cultural distance between two people, there are bound to be problems arising from differences in behavior and expectations. An example is the American couple who consulted a psychiatrist about their marital problems. The husband was from New England and had been brought up by reserved parents who taught him to control his emotions and to respect the need for privacy. His wife was from an Italian family and had been brought up in close contact with all the members of her large family, who were extremely warm, volatile, and demonstrative.

When the husband came home after a hard day at the office, dragging his feet and longing for peace and quiet, his wife would rush to him and smother him. Clasping his hands, rubbing his brow, crooning over his weary head, she never left him alone. But when the wife was upset or anxious about her day, the husband's response was to withdraw completely and leave her alone. No comforting, no affectionate embrace, no attention—just solitude. The woman became convinced her husband didn't love her, and in desperation she consulted a psychiatrist. Their problem wasn't basically psychological but cultural.

Why has man developed all these different ways of communicating messages without words? One reason is that people don't like to spell out certain kinds of messages. We prefer to find other ways of showing our feelings. This is especially true in relationships as sensitive as courtship. Men don't like to be rejected, and most women don't want to turn a man down bluntly. Instead, we work out subtle ways of encouraging or discouraging each other that save face and avoid confrontations.

How a person handles space in dating others is an obvious and very sensitive indicator of how he or she feels about the other person. On a first date, if a woman sits or stands so close to a man that he is acutely conscious of her physical presence—inside the intimate-distance zone—the man usually construes it to mean that she is encouraging him. However, before the man starts moving in on the woman, he should be sure what message she's really sending; otherwise, he risks bruising his ego. What is close to someone of northern European background may be neutral or distant to someone of Italian heritage. Also, women sometimes use space as a way of misleading a man, and there are few things that put men off more than women who communicate contradictory messages, such as women who cuddle up and then act insulted when a man takes the next step.

How does a woman communicate interest in a man? In addition to such familiar gambits as smiling at him, she may glance shyly at him, blush, and then look away. Or she may give him a real come-on look and move in very close when he approaches. She may touch his arm and ask for a light. As she leans forward to light her cigarette, she may brush him lightly, enveloping him in her perfume. She'll probably continue to smile at him, and she may use what ethologists call preening gestures—touching the back of her hair, thrusting her breasts forward, tilting her hips at she stands, or crossing her legs if she's seated, perhaps even exposing one thigh or putting a hand on her thigh and stroking it. She may also stroke her wrists as she converses or show the palm of her hand as a way of gaining his attention. Her skin may be unusually flushed or quite pale, her eyes brighter, the pupils larger.

If a man sees a woman whom he wants to attract, he tries to present himself by his posture and stance as someone who is self-assured. He moves briskly and confidently. When he catches the eye of the woman, he may hold her glance a little longer than normal. If he gets an encouraging smile, he'll move in close and engage her in small talk. As they converse, his glance shifts over her face and body. He too, may make preening gestures—straightening his tie, smoothing his hair, or shooting his cuffs.

How do people learn body language? The same way they learn spoken language—by observing and imitating people around them as they're growing up. Little girls imitate their mothers or an older female. Little boys imitate their fathers or a respected uncle or a character on television. In this way, they learn the gender signals appropriate for their sex. Regional, class, and ethnic patterns of body behavior are also learned in childhood and persist throughout life. . . .

Nonverbal communications signal to members of your own group what kind of person you are, how you feel about others, how you'll fit into and work in a group, whether you're assured or anxious, the degree to which you feel comfortable with the standards of your own culture, as well as deeply significant feelings about the self, including the state of your own psyche. For most of us, it's difficult to accept the reality of another's behavioral system. And, of course, none of us will ever become fully knowledgeable of the importance of every nonverbal signal. But as long as each of us realizes the power of these signals, the society's diversity can be a source of great strength rather than a further—and subtly powerful—source of division.

11 Sympathy in Everyday Life

CANDACE CLARK

To learn a culture is to learn a set of background expectations for living, and by now you have a good idea of how pervasive culture is. From the attitudes we have toward our own bodies (selections 8 and 19) to our propensity toward and expectations of violence and gender (selection 9) and the personal bubbles that we carry around with us in our everyday lives (selection 10)—all these, as you have seen in preceding selections, are rooted in culture. The guidelines, rules, and expectations that become a part of us as we learn a culture are so thorough that they cover our interactions with others in almost every situation. They even include our emotions or feelings, both what we should feel under varying circumstances and how we should express those feelings.

Sympathy, as Clark analyzes in this selection, is not simply a natural outpouring from within, but is a reflection of the culture we learn. Although we seldom recognize it, we live within an elaborate system of rules regarding feeling and expressing sympathy. As you read this article, consider these questions: When *should* you feel sympathy about someone's plight? How *should* you show your feelings? When do you have a right to *not* feel or express sympathy toward another person who is experiencing problems? Do you *owe* people sympathy? If so, how does the sympathy that you owe depend on someone's relationship to you? How much right do people have to claim your sympathy? What boundaries ordinarily limit people from claiming more sympathy than they have a right to?

SYMPATHY, FEELING SORRY FOR or with another person . . . is basic to human society. . . . In the course of everyday encounters, people enter and enact the reciprocal roles-within-roles of sympathy donor and recipient, "sympathizer" and "sympathizee." In my research, I explore the roles of sympathizer and sympathizee in the United States today. . . .

I gathered data eclectically. . . . First, I sought expressions of sympathy in greeting cards, newspaper and television reports, advice columns, etiquette books, song lyrics, and literature. . . . A second source of data is the ethnographic materials produced by generations of sociologists studying victims, the downtrodden, the bereaved, the sick, and other underdogs and potential sympathizees. . . . I also involved myself as a participant observer (sometimes more as participant, others more as observer) of sympathy interactions in natural settings (e.g., hospitals, funeral homes, offices, etc.) over a period of two years. . . . A fourth source of data is a survey of northern New Jersey residents (hereafter designated "respondents"). Student interviewers presented vignettes depicting three plights to a cross section of adult nonstudents. The 877 respondents were predominantly Catholics, ranged in age from 18 to 77, and came mostly from the working and middle classes. In one of the vignettes, a hurricane has damaged a family's house; in another, a woman is brutally beaten by a man she "met in passing in a bar"; in the third, a young couple's marriage is jeopardized by one spouse's problems with alcohol. Respondents were asked to read one of these vignettes, to indicate the degree of sympathy they felt for the character(s) (from "extremely sorry" to "somewhat sorry" to "not sorry at all"), and to describe what aspects of the story had affected their responses. . . . Finally, four trained male and female interviewers and I conducted intensive interviews with 12 men and 13 women (hereafter termed "interviewees") between the ages of 25 and 80 living in New Jersey. . . . The interview schedule asked people to describe specific cases in which they had given, not given, received, rejected, expected, feigned, and "worked on" (Hochschild, 1983, pp. 35–55) sympathy. . . .

Sympathy Flow

A set of loose, unwritten rules—an "emotional economy" (Collins, 1981)—governs how feelings flow. I am using the term socioemotional economy to mean a system, produced and reproduced by interacting group members, for regulating emotional resources in a community. It promotes group survival just as a money-based, goods-and-services economy does.

The people I observed, interviewed, and read about followed a sympathy economy based on two principles. Sympathizers should adhere to the tenet of the strong supporting the "deserving" weak. Recipients should reciprocate.

Sympathizers are expected to display sympathy, not indiscriminately, but in a manner appropriate to the person and to the plight. In what may be a split second, a potential sympathizer considers the other's plight, the other's complicity in the plight, and one's own situation relative to the other's. The outcome may or may not be sympathy.

One of the first principles for sympathizers is to determine whether the other person's plight is included in the *grounds* that the society considers sympathy worthy. My data show that in our culture these grounds include loss of a loved one, illness, divorce, loss of one's job, crime victimization, car trouble, and even noisy neighbors or fatigue. . . . Grounds, of course, change over time and vary [from group to group].

My evidence also indicates that sympathizers are influenced by people's social statuses. Children, for instance, often elicit more sympathy than adults with the same problems, and perhaps the middle class elicit more than either the wealthy or the destitute. More sympathy and aid go to the disaster victims in friendly nations such as Mexico and Colombia than to those in disliked nations. Further, statuses and plights can interact to produce very specific sympathy norms. For my interviewees, women with car trouble warrant more sympathy than men because of men's presumably superior mechanical skills. Widowers with small children often rate more sympathy than widows with children because of women's presumably greater talents in child care.

The giving of sympathy, in addition to being subject to a battery of norms, also has unique meanings for the donor. Giving sympathy sends a dual message: it is a sign of caring or connectedness, and of the superiority or moral worth of the donor. . . .

As it flows from donor to recipient, sympathy leaves invisible but important ties and debts marking its path. Receiving sympathy can both benefit and obligate the recipient. It benefits, because normal role obligations and standards are relaxed. In addition, the acceptance, caring, and validation, demonstrated by others are rewarding. Beneficial consequences include the tangible as well as the psychological. Receiving sympathy can make the difference between getting fired and not getting fired, between going to prison and going free. . . .

Receiving sympathy obligates, because accepting the role of sympathizee requires one to reciprocate for the gifts of sympathy and acceptance (Simmel, 1971, pp. 150–178). . . . A variety of emotional commodities, such as gratitude, deference, and future sympathy, serve as returns on the original gift.

Many other social variables—such as how intimate a relationship is and how power is configured—affect complex processes of giving and taking sympathy. Space does not permit analysis of them all. The variable to which I turn now is the sympathy margin, or account, set up by the donor for the recipient. Sympathy flow in the socioemotional economy works via sympathy margins. . . .

Sympathy Margin

In life, as in the literature that socializes us, to receive sympathy one must be a "sympathetic character." But what constitutes a sympathetic character? Part of the answer has to do with one's social statuses, and my data suggest that another part is related to relationships built up over time and involving considerable reciprocity. Jacqueline Wiseman (1979), in her analysis of the plight of skid row men and of the agents of social control who deal with them, points to a concept that helps us understand how sympathy and compassion come about. That concept is "social margin," that is, ". . . the amount of leeway a given individual has in making errors on the job, buying on credit, or stepping on the toes of significant others without suffering such serious penalties as being fired, denied credit, or losing friends and family. . . . A person with margin can get help" (1979, p. 223). Wiseman claims that respectability, especially in work and family careers, must be maintained to acquire margin (Wiseman, 1979, p. 224).

Wiseman's insights have general utility in explaining interaction in the socioemotional economy of everyday life. One's moral worth and network ties affect how many emotional commodities, including "units" of sympathy and compassion, can be claimed from others and that others feel they owe. Social margin thus includes sympathy margin. Margin (social and otherwise) must be *ascribed by others*. Since we all interact with a variety of others, we may speak of people as having many margins of variable widths—one with each specific other in one's network.

In keeping with Wiseman's terminology, I have drawn a banking analogy with sympathy flow. Each group member has, I maintain, what amounts to an "account" of "sympathy credits" . . . held for him or her by each other group member. A certain number of sympathy credits are automatically on deposit in each of the sympathy accounts of the ordinary group members, available for cashing in when they are needed. They are a right of group membership.

The right to sentiment.—Simply put, group members are expected to feel some sympathy toward each other. How much sympathy (how many credits) each member can claim from each other member varies, but there is some minimum, albeit an unspecifiable and unquantifiable one. In general, people involved in "close" or "deep" relationships have an obligation to create wider sympathy margins for each other than do acquaintances or secondary group members. . . . More sympathy is due per occasion, more *genuine* sympathy is due, and it is due in a wider range of circumstances. We may, for example, feel sympathy for strangers or even enemies in what are considered disastrous or freak circumstances (being pushed under a subway car or being

122 / *Candace Clark*

subjected to an earthquake or a terrorist attack), yet our friends and loved ones can call out, and count on, our sympathies for their minor problems as well as for their disasters. Also, credit is more freely given to an intimate than to an acquaintance, even before accounts have been settled.

The right to empathy.—Furthermore, there is an obligation to be empathic and to search for evidence that group members, especially intimates, have problems that merit sympathy. . . . When Goffman (1983, p. 13) discusses the role of "knowership," he recognizes this point, noting that in close relationships one is supposed to keep the friend's biography in mind, ask questions about how issues in that person's life have been resolved, refer to his or her past illnesses, and the like. Focusing conversation on each other's biographies enhances communication and empathy between "knowers."

The right to display.—Abundant evidence also exists to show that group members are obligated to display sympathy appropriate to the person and the plight. Sometimes words of sympathy are expected, sometimes nonverbal messages and kid glove treatment. Some problems call for "off-the-rack" sentiments available in greeting cards.

Sudnow's (1967) study of hospital staff provides examples of the display norms expected of those dealing face to face with bereaved family members. Physicians giving "bad news" to relatives "cannot, like the telegram deliverer, merely present the news and leave the scene, but must evidence some degree of general concern and responsibility" (p. 129). The relative has the right to cry, moan, scream out, in other words, "to suspend his concern for normally enforceable requirements of . . . composure" (p. 136) on hearing of the death. He or she also has the right to indicate when interaction may proceed after the period of "carrying on" (p. 142). The staff member has the obligation to defer to the other, to present himself or herself solemnly, with appropriate tone of voice, facial expression, and the like.

Among my own interviewees, a 40-year-old professional woman, in reporting her reaction to a friend's illness, said: "I can remember saying to myself, 'Now, this is a shock, and you haven't taken it in yet, but you'd better look serious.'" Another woman, a 36-year-old waitress and college student, in noting violations of display norms, said: "My children were shocked to see [distant relatives] laughing and drinking at *their grandma's* funeral. In fact, so was I!" Interestingly enough, when my interviewees merely began to think, in the interview situation, about their reactions to others' plights, they frequently adopted the facial expressions, postures, and tones of voice appropriate to sympathy display—erasing smiles, knitting eyebrows, sitting up straighter, and speaking in "concerned" tones.

A given sympathy account or margin held by a specific other does not always remain constant. It is continually negotiated and may be increased, decreased, replenished, or used up entirely. Beyond the number of sympathy credits automatically "on account" in one's margins, a group member can earn credits, for example, by investing sympathy, help, and concern in others. The nature of the relationship between the two parties may also change as the sympathy margins of one or both change. Investing in another usually implies (whether as a consequence or a cause) a greater degree of intimacy between the parties.

Sympathy credits can also be cashed in. Claiming or accepting sympathy reduces one's margins, and one should draw against accounts that are solvent. The sick person who does not try to get well, like the skid row man who does not try to reform, may soon find his or her sympathy accounts depleted or even withdrawn (Parsons, 1951; Wiseman, 1979, p. 223). The number of sympathy credits is limited.

Of course, it is possible to overdraw one's accounts with some people in one's network but not with others. One might, for instance, try to claim equal amounts of sympathy from an acquaintance and from an intimate and find that the former claim is not honored while the latter is. Further, a given sympathy account sometimes depends on the total amount of sympathy a person is receiving. Thus, as several interviewees stated, co-workers may believe that married people will get sympathy from their spouses and, consequently, offer little themselves. My observations show that the members of a network often know each other and discuss among themselves how much sympathy a given member has claimed and how much others have given. The accounts held by some of these people are small because they believe that others are offering "enough." Accounts were drained completely in several cases involving prolonged periods of unemployment, divorce, extended illness, series of mishaps, and claims felt to be exaggerated. The potential sympathizee had to find new networks of significant others—open new accounts—when sympathy was still desired.

To be ascribed sympathy margin by others, one must have dealt properly with sympathy in the past. That is, sympathy margins are affected by one's sympathy biography—previous adherence to the protocols or etiquette for owing, giving, claiming, and accepting sympathy per se. I will now present the rules of sympathy etiquette that my research has uncovered.

Sympathy Etiquette

RULE 1: DO NOT MAKE FALSE CLAIMS TO SYMPATHY

The foremost rule of sympathy etiquette is not to falsely manipulate others' sympathy by pretending to need it, by exaggerating claims, or by courting disaster with the intent of calling out emotions in others. In short, one should not claim another's sympathy needlessly.

Aesop provides an interesting illustrative case, the familiar tale of the boy who cried wolf. The boy's first cries were heeded, but in each case no concrete evidence of the wolf's visit could be found. He was given some margin by others, but eventually his sympathy accounts disappeared. When the wolf actually threatened, the boy was judged to be lying and undeserving of sympathy.

A person who engages in any of the above practices, and who is caught out, erodes bases for trust. All of his or her claims may be called into question. Sympathy accounts may be closed. Others will find themselves not making efforts to empathize, not feeling sympathy sentiments, and/or not feeling obligations to display sympathy in otherwise sympathy-worthy situations. A young working-class man explained his reactions to a co-worker's claims: "I can't take the time to sort out which things she claims are real. Now everything she says is suspect to me."

My interviewees were, on the whole, quite concerned about violations of this rule. They reported feeling "taken advantage of," "betrayed," and "conned" when other people played on their sympathies for their own gain. A psychologist in her 50s said of her sister:

> Amy's a disaster area! But . . . she makes her own problems. She calls collect from Hawaii to tell me that her husband is selling the house out from under them. She wants me to say, "Poor Amy!" I have to say to her, "He can't do that unless you sign the papers too." But she won't think or do anything for herself. . . . She makes things bad for herself to get sympathy. . . . I used to feel sorry for her, but now I try to avoid her.

Another interviewee, a 37-year-old real estate agent, spoke heatedly of a man who had got his friend's parents to feel sorry for him because his wife divorced him. The friend's parents were quite sympathetic. They rented him a house cheaply and then sold it to him for half the market value. The interviewee complained: "He just used the [former landlords], and I could never help him out again knowing what he's like."

What is at issue here is a breach of public trust, a loss of faith that others will play by the rules. Despite the fact that we know to expect cynical and manipulative performances in everyday encounters, it comes as a shock when our expectations are realized and cannot be overlooked or explained away—when the fictions that make interaction easier are shattered. The tags "untrustworthy" and "con artist" are affixed to those who mishandle others' emotions as well as to those who abuse their money or property. One with such a reputation will have little sympathy margin.

RULE 2: DO NOT CLAIM TOO MUCH SYMPATHY

Even when legitimate grounds exist, do not claim "too much" sympathy "too often" or for "too long." That is, one should not overdraw one's sympathy accounts. The person who does so risks receiving sympathy displays with less sentiment than would be forthcoming otherwise, displays without sentiment, or worse, no displays at all.

Although the point of Aesop's story was that pretense to sympathy are interpersonally dangerous, I contend that even if there had actually been an unlimited number of wolves, the boy could not have hoped to receive unlimited sympathy. In our terminology here, the boy had cashed in his sympathy credits. After his first few claims were honored, he had already received his sympathy allotment and depleted his sympathy accounts.

There are a variety of ways to ask for too much sympathy. First, one can ask too much for a particular problem. One's own plight may seem dire, but others may have perceived it as low in sympathy-worthiness. For example:

> Every time I see her, I think, "Here we go again!" She's like a broken record. "Sam did this to me; Sam didn't do that for me." I'm sorry, but a lot of us have been through divorces and survived. She's gone completely overboard. [Field notes, teacher in his 30s]

And:

> She looks like she's about 30. I mean, what does she want? Why should I feel sorry for her just because she's having her fortieth birthday? [Field notes, 45-year-old woman]

Second, one can ask for too much for a particular other's present situation. People who have their own problems are, to some extent, exempt from the obligation to feel or display sympathy to others—especially to others in less serious plights. These comments of a survey respondent, a Hispanic custodian in her 50s, show that she applied this "rule for breaking rules" to herself: "Why should I feel sorry for those people in that story [about hurricane damage]? I've got no job, and my husband died."

Third, in specific encounters and relationships, claims to sympathy may be considered excessive, as panhandlers regularly discover. Fourth, one can ask for too much sympathy for a particular setting. For instance, a claim that would be honored at lunch may not be honored in the office. Finally, sympathy may be claimed over too long a period of time—a point that merits further comment.

The estimated duration of a problem is related to the size of one's sympathy accounts in a curvilinear fashion. Problems of either very short or very long duration will engender less, or less consistent, sympathy than intermediate-range problems. Problems that are over quickly, such as a painful medical test lasting only a few moments, elicit minimal sympathy because these situations are not "worth" much. Long-term problems, while they may be worth more sympathy, may call for greater emotional expenditures than others can or will put forth. For instance, those who grieve too long or who cannot recover from a divorce or disaster in a timely fashion may find their margins diminished. Chronic illness—arthritis, for example—may thus be awarded less sympathy than an intermediate-range, acute illness, such as pneumonia. . . .

Regardless of one's misfortune, then, claiming and accepting sympathy can seriously diminish others' capacity to sympathize. George Eliot speaks of physical limits on how much sympathy can be felt or displayed:

> If we had a keen vision and feeling for all ordinary human life, it would be like hearing the grass grow and the squirrel's heart beat, and we should die of that roar which lies on the other side in silence. [(1872) 1981, p. 191]

Wiseman concurs:

> Charity and compassion are not available in unlimited supply, the Bible notwithstanding. Like so many other strong emotions, compassion cannot be called forth on every possible occasion without exhausting the giver. [1979, p. 242]

Sympathy recipients are expected to be sensitive to the sacrifices of sympathizers. If they are not, they may diminish others' willingness to sympathize. For both physical and cultural reasons, then, there appears to be a maximum amount of sympathy that an individual may claim from a specific other in a given period.

Those I observed and interviewed recognized these limits on others' sympathy. Several noted that, if they had recently received sympathy, help, time off from work, and the like, they were reluctant even to mention new problems that cropped up soon after. As one man, a carpenter in his 50s, put it,

> That month when I had three deaths in the family and my car broke down and my mother-in-law needed constant care and the kids were sick, well, it was too unbelievable. I was embarrassed to even tell people what was happening. I didn't bring up all the details.

An interviewee in her 30s, who had experienced surgery, a death in the family, and job problems, stated,

I had to deal with it jokingly. I'd list all the terrible things and laugh. There were just too many things all at once.

She takes care to protect her significant others, thereby protecting her sympathy margins as well.

The other side of this sympathy rule is that, if one does not claim very much sympathy or help very often, one may be, in commonsense terms, "due for" it. Note the case of Mr. F, cited by Locker (1981). He is a stoic who has very rarely claimed sympathy and attention for illness and who is thought by his wife to deserve some:

> . . . . he had very bad flu, it's the first time he's been ill since we've been married, and I couldn't get the doctor to come and see him. OK, so everybody has flu, but he had a high temperature. . . . I felt that if Dr. M. [their former physician] and his old receptionist had been there . . . they would have thought: Mr. F never ever comes near us, he must really not be well, or even if he's not . . . we owe him a visit. [p. 108]

Many of us, like Mr. F, may store up sympathy credits by being competent, functioning group members. (That we can go too far with this practice is the subject of rule 3 below.)

Corollary 2a: Do not accept sympathy too readily.—In addition to not needing too much sympathy, one should not appear to want it too much. One should not expect, take for granted, or demand sympathy but, rather, underplay problems and count blessings.

Giving expressions of strength, independence, and bravery helps one avoid being perceived as self-pitying or as enjoying others' displays of sympathy. The oft-repeated question, "How are you bearing up?" implies that one should be trying to bear up. The appropriate response is, "I'm okay," or "Pretty well." One's tone of voice, energy level, and other nonverbal cues may indicate otherwise. . . . But verbal expressions of bravery are expected. One interviewee pointed out that she often catalogs her misfortunes and problems for others but expressly declines sympathy:

> I guess I'm conveying that I could ask for their sympathy, but I'm not. I'm being brave. (youth typist)

Underplaying problems is quite common, as Sudnow also found in his (1967) research on dying and the bereaved. "Persons are engaged, so it seems, in the continual de-emphasis of their feelings of loss, out of respect for the difficulties of interaction facing those less intimately involved in the death than themselves" (p. 140). For instance, sympathy phone calls which

Sudnow managed to overhear included remarks initiated by the bereaved about the concerns of the sympathizer: "How are your children these days?" (p. 137). Underplaying represents, first, significant emotion work undertaken to align feelings with the norms of various interactional settings and, second, a meaningful gesture to the nonbereaved.

On those occasions when people do not "keep a stiff upper lip," sympathy is, in effect, claimed. And, of course, claims diminish margins. An interviewee, a medical researcher in his 40s, reacted to a sympathy-demanding co-worker as follows: "I always tell people to watch out for Josh. He can be quite a leech if you let him. His problems are endless. You just have to keep your distance." The "greedy" sympathizee is shunned.

The victim of circumstances is also commonly expected to focus on other good luck or blessings that are thought to compensate for the present bad luck. Hurricane victims, interviewed by network newscasters in the fall of 1984, lived up to this expectation. Indeed, none whose interviews were aired failed to strike a positive note. For example: "It could have been worse" (middle-aged woman). "At least we're still alive" (middle-aged man). "We'll just start rebuilding and try to forget all this" (elderly man).

My survey respondents reacting to the vignette about the hurricane victims echoed this theme: "I feel sorry, but at least they've got each other and no one was killed" (housewife in her 50s). "Sometimes a disaster like this draws people together. They're fortunate because they'll probably be closer now" (young secretary).

One typical get well card from Hallmark makes the count-your-blessings norm explicit. It attempts to convince the "unlucky" sufferer that he or she is really "lucky."

CHEER UP!
Things could be worse!
Suppose you had a SNEEZING FIT
Or you maybe had the GOUT,
Suppose your ARCHES all FELL IN
Or all your HAIR FELL OUT—

. . .

You're really lucky when you think
Of what it MIGHT HAVE BEEN—
But just the same, here's hoping
You will SOON BE WELL AGAIN!

Other cards, presumably for a male audience, exhort the hospitalized person to pay attention to the nurses rather than to the pain and danger.

To summarize this corollary, one who eagerly and openly accepts sympathy is an embarrassment because she or he is not meeting the role obligations of the sympathizee. Each of us has a right to some sympathy, but interactional strategies that explicitly call for these rights to be honored will diminish sympathy margins rapidly. The resulting sentiment is usually less sincere, and display, if there is any, may be empty.

RULE 3: CLAIM SOME SYMPATHY

Prescriptions of bravery notwithstanding, to keep sympathy margins viable one should claim and accept some sympathy from others when circumstances are appropriate. This sympathy rule is perhaps less obvious than the others. Taken together with rule 2, it suggests that there is some optimal amount of sympathy to claim. The self-reliant—who remain independent, pay cash, and do not develop credit ratings by borrowing and repaying—may not have sympathy accounts in times of need. Paradoxically, those who have histories of never crying wolf may find no one heeding their legitimate cries. This rule is most clearly applicable in relationships involving intimates or equals, but it operates to some extent for nonintimates, subordinates, and superiors as well.

Just as the act of claiming sympathy has a variety of meanings, so, too, does not claiming or accepting sympathy. In general, one who never claims or accepts sympathy from another over a period of time in a stable relationship may simply come to be defined as an inactive member of the interaction network. (This definition results especially, but not only, when one gives little sympathy to others as well.) Nonaccepters are of the group but not in it. When roles have solidified and become habitual, an out-of-character claim for sympathy may not "compute."

As my interviewees indicated, a number of signals may be sent if one does not, from time to time, claim and accept some sympathy. One may appear too lofty or too self-possessed. In the former case, one is unworthy of sympathy; in the latter, not in need. Or, like a rate-buster's, one's fortune is too good or the ability to cope too expert compared with that of the average person. The following case shows that highly competent people who rarely claim sympathy can easily find themselves defined as not needing sympathy, as not having the problems, worries, or stage fright common among the less able:

> I was so surprised—shocked—at the reaction of my colleagues last week. I had to give a big presentation that lasted two days. I've done shorter ones before, but this was frightening. I found myself getting nervous and tried to talk to my

friends about it. They just said, "Oh, you'll do okay. You always do." Not an ounce of sympathy! And these were "near" friends, too, not just people I know.

Although this young editor gives sympathy to others, she rarely finds the need to claim it. The event she describes led her to recognize that she had no sympathy accounts with her co-workers. She reported that she intends to change their perceptions of her by letting them know more about her insecurities—that is, by claiming some sympathy.

My interviewees also attributed such meanings to not accepting sympathy as the unwillingness to incur obligations, the unwillingness to allow others to discharge obligations, and the unwillingness to admit others into backstage regions where problems and vulnerabilities are apparent. Finally, nonclaimers may give the impression that they feel too "lowly" to expect others' attention and sympathy.

Rule 3 shows that, as a particular sympathy exchange unfolds, group boundaries are created. Insiders and outsiders, intimates and nonintimates are defined. At the same time, group structure—the system of power and status relationship—is affected.

To begin with, A's claim and B's subsequent gift of sympathy create (1) a bond of "knowership" (Goffman, 1983, p. 13) or intimacy between them and (2) trust on the part of the sympathizee. Further, the direction of the exchange crystallizes the statuses and roles of those in the relationship along a *superordinate-subordinate* dimension. Mutual exchanges of sympathy commonly symbolize equality, whereas one-way gifts of sympathy usually signify inequality.

If one gives and receives sympathy, one is a friend, intimate, or peer. Former acquaintances who have not been particularly close may find their relationship taking on a more intimate cast, once sympathy has been exchanged.

On the other hand, the person who gives without claiming or accepting sympathy in return does not allow recipients a chance to discharge their obligations. Rather than enhancing equality, these situations engender the "parent-child" relationship between donor and recipient that Mead (1962, p. 367) saw as the essential form of sympathy. And the "parent" may be rightly or wrongly perceived as not requiring or needing sympathy for himself or herself. Furthermore, the state of owing engendered in the "child" (recipient) may be so uncomfortable as to cause resentment against the donor, providing justification for not returning sympathy or actually interfering with feeling it.

To recap, there appears to be an optimal amount of sympathy to claim and/or receive (depending on the relative power and authority of the actor and the desired closeness of the relationship), if one wants to keep accounts open. Claiming too little, as well as claiming too much, may diminish margins.

RULE 4: RECIPROCATE TO OTHERS FOR THE GIFT OF SYMPATHY

A final rule for maintaining an adequate supply of sympathy credits is that one must reciprocate. Depending in part on one's position vis-à-vis the donor, one may be expected to repay the gift of sympathy with gratitude, deference, and esteem, or to pay back sympathy. Whether conscious of the fact or not, people usually expect returns when they give sympathy. . . .

As Levi-Strauss (1969, p. 54) points out, returns for social "gifts" do not have to accrue to the original donor to be considered valuable. Returns to family members, friends, and even to charities or the community at large may serve to erase obligations. For instance, if A receives sympathy from B, A can discharge the debt by showing gratitude to B's spouse or by giving sympathy to B's children should they experience problems. But a recipient who never makes a good-faith effort to show appreciation to the group may come to be ignored.

The minimal and most immediate type of return expected for sympathy is gratitude. Paying gratitude for sympathy signifies that one is in, and acknowledges being in, a position of need. She or he is "one-down" or "one-less up." First, the recipient is in trouble, ailing, or otherwise not able to function in usual social roles, or the sympathy would not be needed. Second, he or she has "burdened" the sympathizer because of these difficulties. Third, the recipient knows that the sympathizer well could have "believed in a just world" and offered blame rather than sympathy. To refuse to pay gratitude can imply, then, a refusal to recognize the state of need, a refusal to accept the sympathy and well-wishes of other group members, or an expectation that sympathy is a right involving no obligations. Any of these signals can create a gap between the sympathizee and the sympathetic other, who may feel (to use my interviewees' words) "used," "taken for granted," or "unappreciated." On the other hand, showing gratitude, even minimally with a nod or a look, can serve to cement ties. In the Outer Hebrides of Scotland and some rural communities in the United States, a gratitude column in which recipients of sympathy visits and flowers publicly give acknowledgments and thanks is a regular feature of weekly newspapers. Some potential sympathizees—students, skid row residents, low-income crime victims—may even be required to display gratitude before they receive sympathy (see Wiseman, 1979, p. 243).

The type of gratitude expected in return for sympathy varies with the relative social standings of donor and recipient. Those whom I observed and interviewed rarely mentioned receiving sympathy from a subordinate but noted receiving it from "personages." They remembered and remarked on baskets of fruit sent by company presidents at times of bereavement and cards sent to former pet owners by veterinarians (even though such cards were routinely signed and mailed by secretaries). Gifts of sympathy given by superiors (especially when the superior is frugal with such gifts) are imbued with greater value than the same gift from an equal or an inferior. For this reason . . . the returns appropriate for a gift from a superior differ from the returns appropriate for peers. What is owed a superior is gratitude cum deference. Deference is a weightier and dearer commodity than gratitude. Deferential behavior implies that one is inferior to the recipient in a fundamental and perhaps permanent way, grateful for the valuable gift from the superior, and unable to repay the debt with an equally valuable gift. A lack of deference and gratitude is often seen as arrogance, and arrogance can diminish sympathy margin. . . .

Sympathizees must not only show gratitude and deference, they must show them even when the sympathy displays they have received are crude, inept, hurtful, or unwanted. Sudnow's research on bereavement suggests that "offers of sympathy must be accepted without invitation" (1967, p. 156). In some of his cases, an open door policy existed that allowed anyone to enter the house of the bereaved to offer sympathy, whether it was timely or not. Moreover, the awkwardness often felt by sympathizers may result in bungled communications, empty phrases ("I just don't know what to say"), jocular attempts to cheer up the victim that actually induce tears of horror, and the like. Another common mode of sympathizing is the recitation of the sympathizer's own problems ("I know just how you feel, because the same thing has happened to me and I . . ."). This sort of communication is intended, one may assume, to refocus the sympathizee's attention and to indicate that one is not alone in misfortune. (A sympathy recipient may feel compelled to listen to or even to elicit such remarks, thereby switching roles with the sympathizer.) The sympathizee must put up with all of the above types of communications, because the mere fact of expressing some sympathy is thought to indicate that the sympathizer means well.

Beyond gratitude, another important type of return is sympathy itself. Paying back past awards replenishes sympathy credits, a fact that I infer from contrary evidence:

He's having a hard time, but I'm keeping my distance. . . . I gave him a lot of sympathy . . . but he didn't even notice when I needed it. [25-year-old man, teacher]

I was by her side at her mother's funeral. Where was she when my brothers died? I don't count her as part of the family any more. [Retired secretary, age 70]

Although these people feel that their past investments entitle them to sympathy, there is no FDIC to guarantee emotional returns. The people who failed to repay debts when an occasion arose risked and got closed accounts.

Rules for repaying sympathy with sympathy, like those for paying gratitude, are contingent on power relations. For example, repaying a superior with sympathy (an equal return) may be considered an insult; gratitude is often preferred. The peer or intimate is more likely to receive sympathy for sympathy.

In general, then, sympathizers expect recognition of their gifts of sympathy, and sympathizees acknowledge the fact that they incur debts when they accept such gifts. The rules do not specify commensurate returns in every case, because it is hard to measure how much has been received (and is therefore owed) and because people may want to maintain rather than erode power differences. On the whole, though, most people do not receive much more sympathy than they repay with their gratitude or their own sympathy. Margins not replenished soon become overdrawn. . . .

Conclusions

I have argued that sympathy sentiment and display flow unevenly among group members. People who have acceptable sympathy biographies are ascribed margin by others—they have a right to sympathy in appropriate circumstances. Having an acceptable sympathy biography means following rules of etiquette: not making fraudulent claims, not claiming too much too readily, claiming some sympathy, and reciprocating for sympathy gifts. A flawed sympathy biography leads to closed accounts, except when rules of niceness or goodness, perhaps combined with duty, motivate people to keep margins open.

Because of an awareness of sympathy rules, some people may, consciously or unconsciously, give sympathy to manipulate others into positions of closeness or positions of owing. Indebtedness affects power and status relationships. The debt may not be one that the debtor freely contracts; it can be imposed by the sympathizer. Furthermore, giving sympathy may belittle the recipient because it points up problems and insufficiencies. The following case explicitly illustrates the conscious manipulation of sympathy by a worker to belittle a boss:

I remember that I once used sympathy on purpose to try to knock someone down a peg. I had a boss who was always doing and saying things to put me down in a semi-nice way. . . . I got tired of it, so I turned it around on him. I was in his office, and I said, "Oh, Mr. Wall, look at all those reports you have to get done. I feel so sorry for you. I wouldn't want your job for the world." He changed colors, and I could see he was mad. He just said, "Oh, I can get this done in a snap. Nothing to it!" and edged me out the door. Normally he would have chatted a while. So I really got in a good zinger. [Middle-aged professional woman]

Not claiming or accepting sympathy may similarly play a part in power relationships. Refusing to accept sympathy though engaging in one-way sympathy displays can reduce the other's social power and raise or reinforce one's own. In some cases, giving sympathy without receiving it in return becomes "a part of the job" if one is a supervisor, parent, or teacher. A young college professor, normally sympathetic toward students in her course on death and dying, illustrated this link between power and sympathy when a student offered to give her sympathy.

He wanted me to start telling him all my problems. I thought to myself, "I don't want to get any closer to you. I don't want to tell you any more about myself. And what makes you think *you* can help me?" . . . I knew what I was doing: trying to preserve my position as professor. [Field notes]

Accepting the student's sympathy would have altered the relationship irrevocably, making it closer and jeopardizing her superior standing. Thus, she refused the offered sympathy. The student quickly left, apparently embarrassed by his misstep. The sympathy margin he tried to open for the professor had been purposely rejected.

Finally, people can even pay gratitude in return for sympathy to enhance their prestige in cases where public displays of thanks link the sympathizee with powerful or prestigious others. Gratitude column contributors, for example, show the community that they are worthy of worthy people's sympathy. The ads often thank "friends" anonymously but name superordinate sympathizers.

12 The Presentation of Self in Everyday Life

ERVING GOFFMAN

All the world's a stage
And all the men and women merely players.
They have their exits and their entrances;
And one man in his time plays many parts. . . .
William Shakespeare
As You Like It, Act 2, Scene 7

This quotation from Shakespeare could well serve as the keynote for the following selection. Taking Shakespeare's statement seriously, Goffman presents a dramaturgical model of human life and uses it as the conceptual framework for understanding life-in-society. In this view, people in everyday life are actors on stage, the audience consists of those who observe what others are doing, the parts are the roles that people play (whether work, familial, friendship roles, or whatever), the dialogue consists of ritualized conversational exchanges ("Hi. How ya doin'?"; "How's it goin'?"; "Slip me five"; the hellos, the goodbyes, and the in-betweens), while the costuming consists of whatever clothing happens to be in style.

Goffman's insightful analysis provides a framework from which we can gain a remarkably different perspective of what we do in life—at home, at school, with friends, while on a date, or while shopping. When you probe the depths of this analysis, however, you may find this approach to understanding human behavior disturbing. For example, if we are all actors playing roles on the stage of life, where is the "real me"? Is all of life merely a "put-on," play acting, a masquerade of some sort? Does this framework for understanding human interaction constitute an essentially cynical and manipulative approach to life, a sort of everyday Machiavellianism?

WHEN AN INDIVIDUAL ENTERS the presence of others, they commonly seek to acquire information about him or to bring into play information about him already possessed. They will be interested in his general socio-economic status, his conception of self, his attitude toward them, his competence, his trustworthiness, etc. Although some of this information seems to be sought almost as an end in itself, there are usually quite practical reasons for acquiring it. Information about the individual helps to define the situation, enabling others to know in advance what he will expect of them and what they may expect of him. Informed in these ways, the others will know how best to act in order to call forth a desired response from him.

For those present, many sources of information become accessible and many carriers (or "sign-vehicles") become available for conveying this information. If unacquainted with the individual, observers can glean clues from his conduct and appearance which allow them to apply their previous experience with individuals roughly similar to the one before them or, more important, to apply untested stereotypes to him. They can also assume from past experience that only individuals of a particular kind are likely to be found in a given social setting. They can rely on what the individual says about himself or on documentary evidence he provides as to who and what he is. If they know, or know of, the individual by virtue of experience prior to the interaction, they can rely on assumptions as to the persistence and generality of psychological traits as a means of predicting his present and future behavior.

However, during the period in which the individual is in the immediate presence of the others, few events may occur which directly provide the others with the conclusive information they will need if they are to direct wisely their own activity. Many crucial facts lie beyond the time and place of interaction or lie concealed within it. For example, the "true" or "real" attitudes, beliefs, and emotions of the individual can be ascertained only indirectly, through his avowals or through what appears to be involuntary expressive behavior. Similarly, if the individual offers the others a product or service, they will often find that during the interaction there will be no time and place immediately available for eating the pudding that the proof can be found in. They will be forced to accept some events as conventional or natural signs of something not directly available to the senses. In Ichheiser's terms,[1] the individual will have to act so that he intentionally or unintentionally *expresses* himself, and the others will in turn have to be *impressed* in some way by him.

The expressiveness of the individual (and therefore his capacity to give impressions) appears to involve two radically different kinds of sign activity: the expression that he *gives,* and the expression that he *gives off.* The first involves verbal symbols or their substitutes which he uses admittedly and solely to convey the information that he and the others are known to attach to these symbols. This is communication in the traditional and narrow sense. The second involves a wide range of action that others can treat as symptomatic of the actor, the expectation being that the action was performed for reasons other than the information conveyed in this way. As we shall have to see, this distinction has only an initial validity. The individual does of course intentionally convey misinformation by means of both of these types of communication, the first involving deceit, the second feigning.

Taking communication in both its narrow and broad sense, one finds that when the individual is in the immediate presence of others, his activity will have a promissory character. The others are likely to find that they must accept the individual on faith, offering him a just return while he is present before them in exchange for something whose true value will not be established until after he has left their presence. (Of course, the others also live by inference in their dealings with the physical world, but it is only in the world of social interaction that the objects about which they make inferences will purposely facilitate and hinder this inferential process.) The security that they justifiably feel in making inferences about the individual will vary, of course, depending on such factors as the amount of information they already possess about him, but no amount of such past evidence can entirely obviate the necessity of acting on the basis of inferences. As William I. Thomas suggested:

> It is also highly important for us to realize that we do not as a matter of fact lead our lives, make our decisions, and reach our goals in everyday life either statistically or scientifically. We live by inference. I am, let us say, your guest. You do not know, you cannot determine scientifically, that I will not steal your money or your spoons. But inferentially I will not, and inferentially you have me as a guest.[2]

Let us now turn from the others to the point of view of the individual who presents himself before them. He may wish them to think highly of him, or to think that he thinks highly of them, or to perceive how in fact he feels toward them, or to obtain no clearcut impression; he may wish to ensure sufficient harmony so that the interaction can be sustained, or to defraud, get rid of, confuse, mislead, antagonize, or insult them. Regardless of the particular objective which the individual has in mind and of his motive for having this objective, it will be in his interests to control the conduct of the others, especially their responsive treatment of him.[3] This control is achieved largely by influencing the definition of the situation which the others come to formulate, and he can influence this definition by expressing himself in such a way as to give them the kind of impression that will lead them to act voluntarily in accordance with his own plan. Thus, when an individual appears in the presence of others, there will usually be some reason for him to mobilize his activity so that it will convey an impression to others which it is in his interests to convey. Since a girl's dormitory mates will glean evidence of her popularity from the calls she receives on the phone, we can suspect

that some girls will arrange for calls to be made, and Willard Waller's finding
can be anticipated.

> It has been reported by many observers that a girl who is called to the tele-
> phone in the dormitories will often allow herself to be called several times, in
> order to give all the other girls ample opportunity to hear her paged.[4]

Of the two kinds of communication—expressions given and expressions
given off—this report will be primarily concerned with the latter, with the
more theatrical and contextual kind, the non-verbal, presumably unintentional kind, whether this communication be purposely engineered or not. As
an example of what we must try to examine, I would like to cite at length a
novelistic incident in which Preedy, a vacationing Englishman, makes his
first appearance on the beach of his summer hotel in Spain:

> But in any case he took care to avoid catching anyone's eye. First of all, he had
> to make it clear to those potential companions of his holiday that they were of
> no concern to him whatsoever. He stared through them, round them, over
> them—eyes lost in space. The beach might have been empty. If by chance a
> ball was thrown his way, he looked surprised; then let a smile of amusement
> lighten his face (Kindly Preedy), looked round dazed to see that there *were*
> people on the beach, tossed it back with a smile to himself and not a smile *at*
> the people, and then resumed carelessly his nonchalant survey of space.
>
> But it was time to institute a little parade, the parade of the Ideal Preedy.
> By devious handlings he gave any one who wanted to look a chance to see the
> title of the book—a Spanish translation of Homer, classic thus, but not daring,
> cosmopolitan too—and then gathered together his beachwrap and bag into a
> neat sand-resistant pile (Methodical and Sensible Preedy), rose slowly to
> stretch at ease his huge frame (Big-Cat Preedy), and tossed aside his sandals
> (Carefree Preedy, after all).
>
> The marriage of Preedy and the sea! There were alternative rituals. The
> first involved the stroll that turns into a run and a dive straight into the water,
> thereafter smoothing into a strong splashless crawl towards the horizon. But of
> course not really to the horizon. Quite suddenly he would turn on to his back
> and thrash great white splashes with his legs, somehow thus showing that he
> could have swum further had he wanted to, and then would stand up a quarter
> out of water for all to see who it was.
>
> The alternative course was simpler; it avoided the cold-water shock, and it
> avoided the risk of appearing too high-spirited. The point was to appear to be
> so used to the sea, the Mediterranean, and this particular beach, that one might
> as well be in the sea as out of it. It involved a slow stroll down and into the edge
> of the water—not even noticing his toes were wet, land and water all the same
> to *him!*—with his eyes up at the sky gravely surveying portents, invisible to
> others, of the weather (Local Fisherman Preedy).[5]

The novelist means us to see that Preedy is improperly concerned with the extensive impressions he feels his sheer bodily action is giving off to those around him. We can malign Preedy further by assuming that he has acted merely in order to give a particular impression, that this is a false impression, and that the others present receive either no impression at all, or worse still, the impression that Preedy is affectedly trying to cause them to receive. But the important point for us here is that the kind of impression Preedy thinks he is making is in fact the kind of impression that others correctly and incorrectly glean from someone in their midst.

I have said that when an individual appears before others his actions will influence the definition of the situation which they come to have. Sometimes the individual will act in a thoroughly calculating manner, expressing himself in a given way solely in order to give the kind of impression to others that is likely to evoke from them a specific response he is concerned to obtain. Sometimes the individual will be calculating in his activity but be relatively unaware that this is the case. Sometimes he will intentionally and consciously express himself in a particular way, but chiefly because the traditions of his group or social status require this kind of expression and not because of any particular response (other than vague acceptance or approval) that is likely to be evoked from those impressed by the expression. Sometimes the traditions of an individual's role will lead him to give a well-designed impression of a particular kind and yet he may be neither consciously nor unconsciously disposed to create such an impression. The others, in their turn, may be suitably impressed by the individual's efforts to convey something, or may misunderstand the situation and come to conclusions that are warranted neither by the individual's intent nor by the facts. In any case, in so far as the others act *as if* the individual had conveyed a particular impression, we may take a functional or pragmatic view and say that the individual has "effectively" projected a given definition of the situation and "effectively" fostered the understanding that a given state of affairs obtains.

There is one aspect of the others' response that bears special comment here. Knowing that the individual is likely to present himself in a light that is favorable to him, the others may divide what they witness into two parts: a part that is relatively easy for the individual to manipulate at will, being chiefly his verbal assertions, and a part in regard to which he seems to have little concern or control, being chiefly derived from the expressions he gives off. The others may then use what are considered to be the ungovernable aspects of his expressive behavior as a check upon the validity of what is conveyed by the governable aspects. In this a fundamental asymmetry is demonstrated in the communication process, the individual presumably being aware of only one stream of his communication, the witness of this stream and one other. For example, in Shetland Isle one crofter's wife, in serving native dishes to a visitor from the mainland of Britain, would listen with a polite smile to his polite claims of liking what he was eating; at the same time she would take note of the rapidity with which the visitor lifted his fork or spoon to his mouth, the eagerness with which he passed food into his mouth, and the gusto expressed in chewing the food, using these signs as a check on the stated feelings of the eater. The same woman, in order to discover what one acquaintance (A) "actually" thought of another acquaintance (B), would wait until B was in the presence of A but engaged in conversation with still another person (C). She would then covertly examine the facial expressions of A as he regarded B in conversation with C. Not being in conversation with B, and not being directly observed by him, A would sometimes relax usual constraints and tactful deceptions, and freely express what he was "actually" feeling about B. This Shetlander, in short, would observe the unobserved observer.

Now given the fact that others are likely to check up on the more controllable aspects of behavior by means of the less controllable, one can expect that sometimes the individual will try to exploit this very possibility, guiding the impression he makes through behavior felt to be reliably informing.[6] For example, in gaining admission to a tight social circle, the participant observer may not only wear an accepting look while listening to an informant, but may also be careful to wear the same look when observing the informant talking to others; observers of the observer will then not as easily discover where he actually stands. A specific illustration may be cited from Shetland Isle. When a neighbor dropped in to have a cup of tea, he would ordinarily wear at least a hint of an expectant warm smile as he passed through the door into the cottage. Since lack of physical obstructions outside the cottage and lack of light within it usually made it possible to observe the visitor unobserved as he approached the house, islanders sometimes took pleasure in watching the visitor drop whatever expression he was manifesting and replace it with a sociable one just before reaching the door. However, some visitors, in appreciating that this examination was occurring, would blindly adopt a social face a long distance from the house, thus ensuring the projection of a constant image.

This kind of control upon the part of the individual reinstates the symmetry of the communication process, and sets the stage for a kind of information game—a potentially infinite cycle of concealment, discovery, false revelation, and rediscovery. It should be added that since the others are likely to be relatively unsuspicious of the presumably unguided aspect of the individual's conduct, he can gain much by controlling it. The others of course may sense that the individual is manipulating the presumably spontaneous aspects of his behavior, and seek in this very act of manipulation some shading of conduct that the individual has not managed to control. This again provides a check upon the individual's behavior, this time his presumably uncalculated behavior, thus re-establishing the asymmetry of the communication process. Here I would like only to add the suggestion that the arts of piercing an individual's effort at calculated unintentionality seem better developed than our capacity to manipulate our own behavior, so that regardless of how many steps have occurred in the information game, the witness is likely to have the advantage over the actor, and the initial asymmetry of the communication process is likely to be retained.

When we allow that the individual projects a definition of the situation when he appears before others, we must also see that the others, however passive their role may seem to be, will themselves effectively project a definition of the situation by virtue of their response to the individual and by virtue of any lines of action they initiate to him. Ordinarily the definitions of the situation projected by the several different participants are sufficiently attuned to one another so that open contradiction will not occur. I do not mean that there will be the kind of consensus that arises when each individual present candidly expresses what he really feels and honestly agrees with the expressed feelings of the others present. This kind of harmony is an optimistic ideal and in any case not necessary for the smooth working of society. Rather, each participant is expected to suppress his immediate heartfelt feelings, conveying a view of the situation which he feels the others will be able to find at least temporarily acceptable. The maintenance of this surface of agreement, this veneer of consensus, is facilitated by each participant concealing his own wants behind statements which assert values to which everyone present feels obliged to give lip service. Further, there is usually a kind of division of definitional labor. Each participant is allowed to establish the tentative official ruling regarding matters which are vital to him but not immediately important to others, e.g., the rationalizations and justifications by which he accounts for his past activity. In exchange for this courtesy he remains silent or noncommittal on matters important to others but not immediately important to him. We have then a kind of interactional *modus vivendi*. Together, the participants contribute to a single over-all definition of the situation which involves not so much a real agreement as to what exists but rather a real agreement as to whose claims concerning what issues will be temporarily honored. Real agreement will also exist concerning the desirability of avoiding an open conflict of definitions of the situation.[7] I will refer to this level of agreement as a "working consensus." It is to be understood that the working consensus established in one interaction setting will be quite different in content from the working consensus established in a different type of setting. Thus, between two friends at lunch, a reciprocal show of affection, respect, and concern for the other is maintained. In service occupations, on the other hand, the specialist often maintains an image of disinterested involvement in the problem of the client, while the client responds with a show of respect for the competence and integrity of the specialist. Regardless of such differences in content, however, the general form of these working arrangements is the same.

In noting the tendency for a participant to accept the definitional claims made by the others present, we can appreciate the crucial importance of the information that the individual *initially* possesses or acquires concerning his fellow participants, for it is on the basis of this initial information that the individual starts to define the situation and starts to build up lines of responsive action. The individual's initial projection commits him to what he is proposing to be and requires him to drop all pretenses of being other things. As the interaction among the participants progresses, additions and modifications in this initial informational state will of course occur, but it is essential that these later developments be related without contradiction to, and even built up from, the initial positions taken by the several participants. It would seem that an individual can more easily make a choice as to what line of treatment to demand from and extend to the others present at the beginning of an encounter than he can alter the line of treatment that is being pursued once the interaction is under way.

In everyday life, of course, there is a clear understanding that first impressions are important. Thus, the work adjustment of those in service occupations will often hinge upon a capacity to seize and hold the initiative in the service relation, a capacity that will require subtle aggressiveness on the part of the server when he is of lower socio-economic status than his client. W. F. Whyte suggests the waitress as an example:

> The first point that stands out is that the waitress who bears up under pressure does not simply respond to her customers. She acts with some skill to control their behavior. The first question to ask when we look at the customer relationship is, "Does the waitress get the jump on the customer, or does the customer get the jump on the waitress?" The skilled waitress realizes the crucial nature of this question. . . .
>
> The skilled waitress tackles the customer with confidence and without hesitation. For example, she may find that a new customer has seated himself before she could clear off the dirty dishes and change the cloth. He is now leaning on the table studying the menu. She greets him, says, "May I change the cover, please?" and, without waiting for an answer, takes his menu away from him so that he moves back from the table, and she goes about her work. The relationship is handled politely but firmly, and there is never any question as to who is in charge.[8]

When the interaction that is initiated by "first impressions" is itself merely the initial interaction in an extended series of interactions involving the same participants, we speak of "getting off on the right foot" and feel that it is crucial that we do so. Thus, one learns that some teachers take the following view:

> You can't ever let them get the upper hand on you or you're through. So I start out tough. The first day I get a new class in, I let them know who's boss. . . . You've got to start off tough; then you can ease up as you go along. If you start out easy-going, when you try to be tough, they'll just look at you and laugh.[9]

Similarly, attendants in mental institutions may feel that if the new patient is sharply put in his place the first day on the ward and made to see who is boss, much future difficulty will be prevented.[10]

Given the fact that the individual effectively projects a definition of the situation when he enters the presence of others, we can assume that events may occur within the interaction which contradict, discredit, or otherwise throw doubt upon this projection. When these disruptive events occur, the interaction itself may come to a confused and embarrassed halt. Some of the assumptions upon which the responses of the participants had been predicted become untenable, and the participants find themselves lodged in an interaction for which the situation has been wrongly defined and is now no longer defined. At such moments the individual whose presentation has been discredited may feel ashamed while the others present may feel hostile, and all the participants may come to feel ill at ease, nonplussed, out of countenance, embarrassed, experiencing the kind of anomy that is generated when the minute social system of face-to-face interaction breaks down.

In stressing the fact that the initial definition of the situation projected by an individual tends to provide a plan for the cooperative activity that follows—in stressing this action point of view—we must not overlook the crucial fact that any projected definition of the situation also has a distinctive moral character. It is this moral character of projections that will chiefly concern us in this report. Society is organized on the principle that any individual who possesses certain social characteristics has a moral right to expect that others will value and treat him in an appropriate way. Connected with this principle is a second, namely that an individual who implicitly or explicitly signifies that he has certain social characteristics ought in fact to be what he claims he is. In consequence, when an individual projects a definition of the situation and thereby makes an implicit or explicit claim to be a person of a particular kind, he automatically exerts a moral demand upon the others, obliging them to value and treat him in the manner that persons of his kind have a right to expect. He also implicitly forgoes all claims to be things he does not appear to be[11] and hence forgoes the treatment that would be appropriate for such individuals. The others find, then, that the individual has informed them as to what is and as to what they *ought* to see as the "is."

One cannot judge the importance of definitional disruptions by the frequency with which they occur, for apparently they would occur more frequently were not constant precautions taken. We find that preventive practices are constantly employed to avoid these embarrassments and that corrective practices are constantly employed to compensate for discrediting occurrences that have not been successfully avoided. When the individual employs these strategies and tactics to protect his own projections, we may refer to them as "defensive practices"; when a participant employs them to save the definition of the situation projected by another, we speak of "protective practices" or "tact." Together, defensive and protective practices comprise the techniques employed to safeguard the impression fostered by an individual during his presence before others. It should be added that while we may be ready to see that no fostered impression would survive if defensive practices were not employed, we are less ready perhaps to see that few impressions could survive if those who received the impression did not exert tact in their reception of it.

In addition to the fact that precautions are taken to prevent disruption of projected definitions, we may also note that an intense interest in these disruptions comes to play a significant role in the social life of the group. Practical jokes and social games are played in which embarrassments which are to be taken unseriously are purposely engineered.[12] Fantasies are created in which devastating exposures occur. Anecdotes from the past—real, embroidered, or fictitious—are told and retold, detailing disruptions which occurred, almost occurred, or occurred and were admirably resolved. There seems to be no grouping which does not have a ready supply of these games, reveries, and cautionary tales, to be used as a source of humor, a catharsis for anxieties, and a sanction for inducing individuals to be modest in their claims and reasonable in their projected expectations. The individual may tell himself through dreams of getting into impossible positions. Families tell of the time a guest got his dates mixed and arrived when neither the house nor anyone in it was ready for him. Journalists tell of times when an all-too-meaningful misprint occurred, and the paper's assumption of objectivity or decorum was humorously discredited. Public servants tell of times a client ridiculously misunderstood form instructions, giving answers which implied an unanticipated and bizarre definition of the situation.[13] Seamen, whose home away from home is rigorously he-man, tell stories of coming back home and inadvertently asking mother to "pass the fucking butter."[14]

Diplomats tell of the time a near-sighted queen asked a republican ambassador about the health of his king.[15]

To summarize, then, I assume that when an individual appears before others he will have many motives for trying to control the impression they receive of the situation.

Notes

1. Gustav Ichheiser, "Misunderstandings in Human Relations," Supplement to *The American Journal of Sociology*, 55 (September, 1949):6–7.

2. Quoted in E. H. Volkart, editor, *Social Behavior and Personality, Contributions of W. I. Thomas to Theory and Social Research* (New York: Social Science Research Council, 1951), p. 5.

3. Here I owe much to an unpublished paper by Tom Burns of the University of Edinburgh. He presents the argument that in all interaction a basic underlying theme is the desire of each participant to guide and control the responses made by the others present. A similar argument has been advanced by Jay Haley in a recent unpublished paper, but in regard to a special kind of control, that having to do with defining the nature of the relationship of those involved in the interaction.

4. Willard Waller, "The Rating and Dating Complex," *American Sociological Review*, 2:730.

5. William Sansom, *A Contest of Ladies* (London: Hogarth, 1956), pp. 230–32.

6. The widely read and rather sound writings of Stephen Potter are concerned in part with signs that can be engineered to give a shrewd observer the apparently incidental cues he needs to discover concealed virtues the gamesman does not in fact possess.

7. An interaction can be purposely set up as a time and place for voicing differences in opinion, but in such cases participants must be careful to agree not to disagree on the proper tone of voice, vocabulary, and degree of seriousness in which all arguments are to be phrased, and upon the mutual respect which disagreeing participants must carefully continue to express toward one another. This debaters' or academic definition of the situation may also be invoked suddenly and judiciously as a way of translating a serious conflict of views into one that can be handled within a framework acceptable to all present.

8. W. F. Whyte, "When Workers and Customers Meet," Chap. VII, *Industry and Society*, ed. W. F. Whyte (New York: McGraw-Hill, 1946), pp. 132–33.

9. Teacher interview quoted by Howard S. Becker, "Social Class Variations in the Teacher-Pupil Relationship," *Journal of Educational Sociology*, 25:459.

10. Harold Taxel, "Authority Structure in a Mental Hospital Ward" (unpublished Master's thesis, Department of Sociology, University of Chicago, 1953).

11. This role of the witness in limiting what it is the individual can be has been stressed by Existentialists, who see it as a basic threat to individual freedom. See

Jean-Paul Sartre, *Being and Nothingness*, trans. by Hazel E. Barnes (New York: Philosophical Library, 1956), pp. 365 ff.

12. Erving Goffman, "Communication Conduct in an Island Community" (unpublished Ph.D. dissertation, Department of Sociology, University of Chicago, 1953), pp. 319–27.

13. Peter Blau, *Dynamics of Bureaucracy: A Study of Interpersonal Relationships in Two Government Agencies*, 2nd ed. (Chicago: University of Chicago Press, 1963).

14. Walter M. Beattie, Jr., "The Merchant Seaman" (unpublished M. A. Report, Department of Sociology, University of Chicago, 1950), p. 35.

15. Sir Frederick Ponsonby, *Recollections of Three Reigns* (New York: Dutton, 1952), p. 46.

PART
IV
Socialization and Gender

E ssential to our survival following birth is *socialization*—learning to become full-fledged members of a human group. As we saw in Part III, this learning involves such fundamental, taken-for-granted aspects of group life as ideas about health and morality, expressing emotions, and the many nuances of nonverbal communication. We saw that socialization involves learning rules (what we should and should not do under different circumstances) and values (what is considered good or bad, desirable or undesirable), as well as expectations about how we should present the self in different social settings.

The *agents of socialization* include our parents, brothers and sisters and other relatives, friends and neighbors, as well as clergy and schoolteachers. They also include people we do not know and never will know, such as clerks and shoppers who, by their very presence—and the expectations we know they have of us—influence our behavior in public settings, and thereby shape it for similar situations in the future. Through this process of socialization each of us develops a *personality,* the tendency to behave in nuanced, stylized, or individualistic ways, which distinguishes us from others.

Essential to our forming an identity is socialization into gender—that is, learning how to be masculine or feminine. The term *sex* refers to biological characteristics, while the term *gender* refers to what is expected of people because of those characteristics. We inherit our sex, but we learn our gender.

Although we come into this world with the biological equipment of a male or a female, these physical organs do not determine what we shall be like as a male or a female. Whether or not we defer to members of the opposite

147

sex, for example, is not an automatic result of our particular sexual equipment but is due to what we learn is proper for us because of the particular biological equipment we possess. This learning process is called *gender* or *sex role socialization*.

Our gender extends into almost every area of our lives, even into situations for which it may be quite irrelevant. For example, if we are grocery clerks, by means of our clothing, gestures, and the way we talk, we communicate to others that we are *male* or *female* clerks. Because gender cuts across most aspects of social life, sociologists refer to gender as a *master trait*.

Challenged for generations (the women's movement was active before our grandparents were born), the expectations attached to the sexes have undergone substantial modification in recent years. One can no longer safely assume particular behavior on the part of another simply because of that person's sex. Despite such changes, however, most Americans follow rather traditional lines as they socialize their children. Changes in something as basic as gender take place slowly, and male dominance remains a fact of social life.

What would we humans be like if we were untouched by culture? Although there is much speculation, no one knows the answer to this question, for any behavior or attitude that we examine is embedded within cultural learning. The closest we can come to answering the question is to observe those children who have received the least introduction to their culture—as Kingsley Davis does in the opening selection. Even isolated children, such as Anna and Isabelle, however, have been exposed to a culture, even though minimally. One really cannot think of humanity apart from culture, then, for culture shapes humanity.

In the past, occasional naked, wild-looking children were discovered living alone in the wilderness. They could not speak, walked and crawled on all fours, and pounced on small animals, devouring them raw while emitting guttural sounds. Such *feral* ("wild") *children* were thought to have been raised by animals and to be untouched by human culture. Documented cases of feral children do exist. In Cambodia, I visited a child whose parents had been shot by the Khmer Rouge. Months after being left alone to die in the jungle, villagers saw the baby in the arms of a female monkey. This female was shot and killed as she tried to flee, carrying the baby. One boy discovered in 1798 was even studied intensely by scientists. The study of feral children does not answer the question of what humans would be like if they were untouched by culture, for it is assumed that they have had at least some socialization from their parents. If it did, the answer certainly would not be encouraging—granted their lack of language, pouncing on and devouring small animals, and so on.

It is through our association with other humans, then, not some inborn instincts, that we learn what it means to be human. To provide a context for appreciating the deep implications of this fundamental aspect of life, this part opens with a classic article by Kingsley Davis, in which he relates the story of Anna. Essential to our becoming human is our socialization into gender, the primary focus of Part IV. Here we explore the question of how we learn gender, the sex roles we are socially destined to play. Memories of childhood may surface while reading my analysis of some of the processes by which boys are socialized into social dominance. Focusing on childhood, I examine experiences that direct boys into a world distinct from the female world, that often lead boys and men to think of themselves as superior, and that later make it difficult for men and women to communicate in depth and to maintain "significant relationships" with each other. Donna Eder continues this focus on children's experiences. The interactions of the girls she observed in middle school reveal another emphasis on superficiality, how appearance (or attractiveness) becomes an essential orientation of the self. Barrie Thorne and Zella Luria continue to place the sociological spotlight on the world of children, examining how schoolchildren separate their activities and friendships on the basis of sex and engage in forms of play that help to maintain male dominance in society. Deborah Tannen closes this Part with an analysis of how men and women express themselves. She highlights communication styles that not only hinder communication between men and women but which also may reflect underlying gender differences in orientations to social life.

Taken together, these articles help us to better understand how gender pervades our lives. They ought to provide considerable insight into your own socialization into gender—how you became masculine or feminine—and, once propelled into that role, how your ongoing experiences in society continue to influence your attitudes and behaviors.

13 Extreme Isolation

KINGSLEY DAVIS

What could the editor possibly mean by this article's heading in the table of contents: "Learning to be human"? Isn't it obvious that we humans are born human? Certainly this is true concerning our *biological* characteristics, that is, our possession of arms, legs, head, and torso, as well as our internal organs.

But to act like other people, to think the way others think—and perhaps even the ability to think—are *learned* characteristics. These are the result of years of exposure to people living in groups, especially the acquisition of language.

Just how much does biology contribute to what we are, and how much is due to social life? (Or, in Davis' terms, what are the relative contributions of the biogenic and the sociogenic factors?) Although this question has intrigued many, no one has yet been able to unravel its mystery. According to the findings reported here, however, the contributions of the social group reach much deeper and are of greater fundamental consequence than most of us imagine. Our speech, for example, helps shape our basic attitudes and orientations to life. As indicated in this article, the social group may even contribute characteristics that we ordinarily presume are biological, such as our ability to walk. Although this selection will not present any "final answers" to this age-old question of "nature versus nurture," it should stir up your sociological imagination.

EARLY IN 1940 THERE APPEARED . . . an account of a girl called Anna.[1] She had been deprived of normal contact and had received a minimum of human care for almost the whole of her first six years of life. At this time observations were not complete and the report had a tentative character. Now, however, the girl is dead, and with more information available,[2] it is possible to give a fuller and more definitive description of the case from a sociological point of view.

Anna's death, caused by hemorrhagic jaundice, occurred on August 6, 1942. Having been born on March 1 or 6,[3] 1932, she was approximately ten and a half years of age when she died. The previous report covered her development up to the age of almost eight years; the present one recapitulates the earlier period on the basis of new evidence and then covers the last two and a half years of her life.

Early History

The first few days and weeks of Anna's life were complicated by frequent changes of domicile. It will be recalled that she was an illegitimate child, the second such child born to her mother, and that her grandfather, a widowed farmer in whose house her mother lived, strongly disapproved of this new evidence of the mother's indiscretion. This fact led to the baby's being shifted about.

Two weeks after being born in a nurse's private home, Anna was brought to the family farm, but the grandfather's antagonism was so great that she was shortly taken to the house of one of her mother's friends. At this time a local minister became interested in her and took her to his house with an idea of possible adoption. He decided against adoption, however, when he discovered that she had vaginitis. The infant was then taken to a children's home in the nearest large city. This agency found that at the age of only three weeks she was already in a miserable condition, being "terribly galled and otherwise in very bad shape." It did not regard her as a likely subject for adoption but took her in for a while anyway, hoping to benefit her. After Anna had spent nearly eight weeks in this place, the agency notified her mother to come and get her. The mother responded by sending a man and his wife to the children's home with a view to their adopting Anna, but they made such a poor impression on the agency that permission was refused. Later the mother came herself and took the child out of the home and then gave her to this couple. It was in the home of this pair that a social worker found the girl a short time thereafter. The social worker went to the mother's home and pleaded with Anna's grandfather to allow the mother to bring the child home. In spite of threats, he refused. The child, by then more than four months old, was next taken to another children's home in a near-by town. A medical examination at this time revealed that she had impetigo, vaginitis, umbilical hernia, and a skin rash.

Anna remained in this second children's home for nearly three weeks, at the end of which time she was transferred to a private foster-home. Since, however, the grandfather would not, and the mother could not, pay for the child's care, she was finally taken back as a last resort to the grandfather's house (at the age of five and a half months). There she remained, kept on the second floor in an attic-like room because her mother hesitated to incur the grandfather's wrath by bringing her downstairs.

The mother, a sturdy woman weighing about 180 pounds, did a man's work on the farm. She engaged in heavy work such as milking cows and tending hogs and had little time for her children. Sometimes she went out at night, in which case Anna was left entirely without attention. Ordinarily, it seems, Anna received only enough care to keep her barely alive. She appears to have been seldom moved from one position to another. Her clothing and bedding were filthy. She apparently had no instruction, no friendly attention.

It is little wonder that, when finally found and removed from the room in the grandfather's house at the age of nearly six years, the child could not talk, walk, or do anything that showed intelligence. She was in an extremely emaciated and undernourished condition, with skeletonlike legs and a bloated abdomen. She had been fed on virtually nothing except cow's milk during the years under her mother's care.

Anna's condition when found, and her subsequent improvement, have been described in the previous report. It now remains to say what happened to her after that.

Later History

In 1939, nearly two years after being discovered, Anna had progressed, as previously reported, to the point where she could walk, understand simple commands, feed herself, achieve some neatness, remember people, etc. But she still did not speak, and, though she was much more like a normal infant of something over one year of age in mentality, she was far from normal for her age.

On August 30, 1939, she was taken to a private home for retarded children, leaving the county home where she had been for more than a year and a half. In her new setting she made some further progress, but not a great deal. In a report of an examination made November 6 of the same year, the head of the institution pictured the child as follows:

> Anna walks about aimlessly, makes periodic rhythmic motions of her hands, and, at intervals, makes guttural and sucking noises. She regards her hands as if she had seen them for the first time. It was impossible to hold her attention for more than a few seconds at a time—not because of distraction due to external stimuli but because of her inability to concentrate. She ignored the task in hand to gaze vacantly about the room. Speech is entirely lacking. Numerous unsuccessful attempts have been made with her in the hope of developing initial sounds. I do not believe that this failure is due to negativism or deafness but that she is not sufficiently developed to accept speech at this time. . . . The prognosis is not favorable. . . .

More than five months later, on April 25, 1940, a clinical psychologist, the late Professor Francis N. Maxfield, examined Anna and reported the following: large for her age; hearing "entirely normal"; vision apparently normal; able to climb stairs; speech in the "babbling stage" and "promise for developing intelligible speech later seems to be good." He said further that "on the Merrill–Palmer scale she made a mental score of 19 months. On the Vineland social maturity scale she made a score of 23 months.[4]

Professor Maxfield very sensibly pointed out that prognosis is difficult in such cases of isolation. "It is very difficult to take scores on tests standardized under average conditions of environment and experience," he wrote, "and interpret them in a case where environment and experience have been so unusual." With this warning he gave it as his opinion at that time that Anna would eventually "attain an adult mental level of six or seven years."[5]

The school for retarded children, on July 1, 1941, reported that Anna had reached 46 inches in height and weighed 60 pounds. She could bounce and catch a ball and was said to conform to group socialization, though as a follower rather than a leader. Toilet habits were firmly established. Food habits were normal, except that she still used a spoon as her sole implement. She could dress herself except for fastening her clothes. Most remarkable of all, she had finally begun to develop speech. She was characterized as being at about the two-year level in this regard. She could call attendants by name and bring in one when she was asked to. She had a few complete sentences to express her wants. The report concluded that there was nothing peculiar about her, except that she was feebleminded—"probably congenital in type."[6]

A final report from the school made on June 22, 1942, and evidently the last report before the girl's death, pictured only a slight advance over that given above. It said that Anna could follow directions, string beads, identify a few colors, build with blocks, and differentiate between attractive and unattractive pictures. She had a good sense of rhythm and loved a doll. She talked mainly in phrases but would repeat words and try to carry on a conversation. She was clean about clothing. She habitually washed her hands and brushed her teeth. She would try to help other children. She walked well and could run fairly well, though clumsily. Although easily excited, she had a pleasant disposition.

Interpretation

Such was Anna's condition just before her death. It may seem as if she had not made much progress, but one must remember the condition in which she had been found. One must recall that she had no glimmering of speech, absolutely no ability to walk, no sense of gesture, not the least capacity to feed herself even when the food was put in front of her, and no comprehension of cleanliness. She was so apathetic that it was hard to tell whether or not she could hear. And all this at the age of nearly six years. Compared with this condition, her capacities at the time of her death seem striking indeed, though they do not amount to much more than a two-and-a-half-year mental level. One conclusion therefore seems safe, namely, that her isolation prevented a considerable amount of mental development that was undoubtedly part of her capacity. Just what her original capacity was, of course, is hard to say; but her development after her period of confinement (including the ability to walk and run, to play, dress, fit into a social situation, and, above all, to speak) shows that she had at least this capacity—capacity that never could have been realized in her original condition of isolation.

A further question is this: What would she have been like if she had received a normal upbringing from the moment of birth? A definitive answer would have been impossible in any case, but even an approximate answer is made difficult by her early death. If one assumes, as was tentatively surmised in the previous report, that it is "almost impossible for any child to learn to speak, think, and act like a normal person after a long period of early isolation," it seems likely that Anna might have had a normal or near-normal capacity, genetically speaking. On the other hand, it was pointed out that Anna represented "a marginal case, [because] she was discovered before she had reached six years of age," an age "young enough to allow for some plasticity."[7] While admitting, then, that Anna's isolation *may* have been the major cause (and was certainly a minor cause) of her lack of rapid mental progress during the four and a half years following her rescue from neglect, it is necessary to entertain the hypothesis that she was congenitally deficient.

In connection with this hypothesis, one suggestive though by no means conclusive circumstance needs consideration, namely, the mentality of Anna's forebears. Information on this subject is easier to obtain, as one might guess, on the mother's than on the father's side. Anna's maternal grandmother, for example, is said to have been college educated and wished to have her children receive a good education, but her husband, Anna's stern grandfather, apparently a shrewd, hard-driving, calculating farmowner, was so penurious that her ambitions in this direction were thwarted. Under the circumstances her daughter (Anna's mother) managed, despite having to do hard work on the farm, to complete the eighth grade in a country school. Even so, however, the daughter was evidently not very smart. "A schoolmate of [Anna's mother] stated that she was retarded in school work; was very gullible at this age; and that her morals even at this time were discussed by other students." Two tests administered to her on March 4, 1938, when she was thirty-two years of age, showed that she was mentally deficient. On the Standard Revision of the Binet–Simon Scale her performance was equivalent to that of a child of eight years, giving her an I.Q. of 50 and indicating mental deficiency of "middle-grade moron type."[8]

As to the identity of Anna's father, the most persistent theory holds that he was an old man about seventy-four years of age at the time of the girl's birth. If he was the one, there is no indication of mental or other biological deficiency, whatever one may think of his morals. However, someone else may actually have been the father.

To sum up: Anna's heredity is the kind that *might* have given rise to innate mental deficiency, though not necessarily.

Comparison with Another Case

Perhaps more to the point than speculations about Anna's ancestry would be a case for comparison. If a child could be discovered who had been isolated about the same length of time as Anna but had achieved a much quicker recovery and a greater mental development, it would be a stronger indication that Anna was deficient to start with.

Such a case does exist. It is the case of a girl found at about the same time as Anna and under strikingly similar circumstances. A full description of the details of this case has not been published, but in addition to newspaper reports, an excellent preliminary account by a speech specialist, Dr. Marie K. Mason, who played an important role in the handling of the child, has appeared.[9] Also the late Dr. Francis N. Maxfield, clinical psychologist at Ohio State University, as was Dr. Mason, has written an as yet unpublished but penetrating analysis of the case.[10] Some of his observations have been included in Professor Zingg's book on feral man.[11] The following discussion is drawn mainly from these enlightening materials. The writer, through the kindness of Professors Mason and Maxfield, did have a chance to observe the girl in April, 1940, and to discuss the features of her case with them.

Born apparently one month later than Anna, the girl in question, who has been given the pseudonym Isabelle, was discovered in November, 1938, nine months after the discovery of Anna. At the time she was found she was approximately six and a half years of age. Like Anna, she was an illegitimate child and had been kept in seclusion for that reason. Her mother was a deafmute, having become so at the age of two, and it appears that she and Isabelle had spent most of their time together in a dark room shut off from the rest of the mother's family. As a result Isabelle had no chance to develop speech; when she communicated with her mother, it was by means of gestures. Lack of sunshine and inadequacy of diet had caused Isabelle to become rachitic. Her legs in particular were affected; they "were so bowed that as she stood erect the soles of her shoes came nearly flat together, and she got about with a skittering gait."[12] Her behavior toward strangers, especially men, was almost that of a wild animal, manifesting much fear and hostility.

In lieu of speech she made only a strong croaking sound. In many ways she acted like an infant. "She was apparently utterly unaware of relationships of any kind. When presented with a ball for the first time, she held it in the palm of her hand, then reached out and stroked my face with it. Such behavior is comparable to that of a child of six months."[13] At first it was even hard to tell whether or not she could hear, so unused were her senses. Many of her actions resembled those of deaf children.

It is small wonder that, once it was established that she could hear, specialists working with her believed her to be feeble-minded. Even on nonverbal tests her performance was so low as to promise little for the future. Her first score on the Stanford–Binet was 19 months, practically at the zero point of the scale. On the Vineland social maturity scale her first score was 39, representing an age level of two and a half years.[14] "The general impression was that she was wholly uneducable and that any attempt to teach her to speak, after so long a period of silence, would meet with failure."[15]

In spite of this interpretation, the individuals in charge of Isabelle launched a systematic and skillful program of training. It seemed hopeless at first. The approach had to be through pantomime and dramatization, suitable to an infant. It required one week of intensive effort before she even made her first attempt at vocalization. Gradually she began to respond, however, and, after the first hurdles had at last been overcome, a curious thing happened. She went through the usual stages of learning characteristic of the years from one to six not only in proper succession but far more rapidly than normal. In a little over two months after her first vocalization she was putting sentences together. Nine months after that she could identify words and sentences on the printed page, could write well, could add to ten, and could retell a story after hearing it. Seven months beyond this point she had a vocabulary of 1,500–2,000 words and was asking complicated questions. Starting from an educational level of between one and three years (depending on what aspect one considers), she had reached a normal level by the time she was eight and a half years old. In short, she covered in two years the stages of learning that ordinarily require six.[16] Or, to put it another way, her I.Q. trebled in a year and a half.[17] The speed with which she reached the normal level of mental development seems analogous to the recovery of body weight in a growing child after an illness, the recovery being achieved by an extra fast rate of growth for a period after the illness until normal weight for the given age is again attained.

When the writer saw Isabelle a year and a half after her discovery, she gave him the impression of being a very bright, cheerful, energetic little girl. She spoke well, walked and ran without trouble, and sang with gusto and accuracy. Today she is over fourteen years old and has passed the sixth grade in a public school. Her teachers say that she participates in all school activities as normally as other children. Though older than her classmates, she has fortunately not physically matured too far beyond their level.[18]

Clearly the history of Isabelle's development is different from that of Anna's. In both cases there was exceedingly low, or rather blank, intellectual level to begin with. In both cases it seemed that the girl might be congenitally feeble-minded. In both a considerably higher level was reached later on. But the Ohio girl achieved a normal mentality within two years, whereas Anna was still markedly inadequate at the end of four and half years. This difference in achievement may suggest that Anna had less initial capacity. But an alternative hypothesis is possible.

One should remember that Anna never received the prolonged and expert attention that Isabelle received. The result of such attention, in the case of the Ohio girl, was to give her speech at an early stage, and her subsequent rapid development seems to have been a consequence of that. "Until Isabelle's speech and language development, she had all the characteristics of a feeble-minded child." Had Anna, who, from the standpoint of psychometric tests and early history, closely resembled this girl at the start, been given a mastery of speech at an earlier point by intensive training, her subsequent development might have been much more rapid.[19]

The hypothesis that Anna began with a sharply inferior mental capacity is therefore not established. Even if she were deficient to start with, we have no way of knowing how much so. Under ordinary conditions she might have been a dull normal or, like her mother, a moron. Even after the blight of her isolation, if she had lived to maturity, she might have finally reached virtually the full level of her capacity, whatever it may have been. That her isolation did have a profound effect upon her mentality, there can be no doubt. This is proved by the substantial degree of change during the four and a half years following her rescue.

Consideration of Isabelle's case serves to show, as Anna's case does not clearly show, that isolation up to the age of six, with failure to acquire any form of speech and hence failure to grasp nearly the whole world of cultural meaning, does not preclude the subsequent acquisition of these. Indeed, there seems to be a process of accelerated recovery in which the child goes through the mental stages at a more rapid rate than would be the case in normal development. Just what would be the maximum age at which a person could remain isolated and still retain the capacity for full cultural acquisition is hard to say. Almost certainly it would not be as high as age fifteen; it might possibly be as low as age ten. Undoubtedly various individuals would differ considerably as to the exact age.

Anna's is not an ideal case for showing the effects of extreme isolation, partly because she was possibly deficient to begin with, partly because she did not receive the best training available, and partly because she did not live long enough. Nevertheless, her case is instructive when placed in the record with numerous other cases of extreme isolation. This and the previous article about her are meant to place her in the record. It is to be hoped that other cases will be described in the scientific literature as they are discovered (as unfortunately they will be), for only in these rare cases of extreme isolation is it possible "to observe *concretely separated* two factors in the development of human personality which are always otherwise only analytically separated, the biogenic and the sociogenic factors."[20]

Notes

1. Kingsley Davis, "Extreme Social Isolation of a Child," *American Journal of Sociology*, XLV (January, 1940), 554–65.
2. Sincere appreciation is due to the officials in the Department of Welfare, Commonwealth of Pennsylvania, for the kind cooperation in making available the records concerning Anna and discussing the case frankly with the writer. Helen C. Hubbell, Florentine Hackbusch, and Eleanor Mecklenburg were particularly helpful, as was Fanny L. Matchette. Without their aid neither of the reports on Anna could have been written.
3. The records are not clear as to which day.
4. Letter to one of the state officials in charge of the case.
5. *Ibid.*
6. Progress report of the school.
7. Davis, *op. cit.*, p. 564.
8. The facts set forth here as to Anna's ancestry are taken chiefly from a report of mental tests administered to Anna's mother by psychologists at a state hospital where she was taken for this purpose after the discovery of Anna's seclusion. This excellent report was not available to the writer when the previous paper on Anna was published.
9. Marie K. Mason, "Learning to Speak after Six and One-Half Years of Silence," *Journal of Speech Disorders*, VII (1942), 295–304.
10. Francis N. Maxfield, "What Happens When the Social Environment of a Child Approaches Zero." The writer is greatly indebted to Mrs. Maxfield and to Professor Horace B. English, a colleague of Professor Maxfield, for the privilege of seeing this manuscript and other materials collected on isolated and feral individuals.
11. J. A. L. Singh and Robert M. Zingg, *Wolf-Children and Feral Man* (New York: Harper & Bros., 1941), pp. 248–51.
12. Maxfield, unpublished manuscript cited above.
13. Mason, *op. cit.*, p. 299.
14. Maxfield, unpublished manuscript.
15. Mason, *op. cit.*, p. 299.

16. *Ibid.,* pp. 300–304.

17. Maxfield, unpublished manuscript.

18. Based on a personal letter from Dr. Mason to the writer, May 13, 1946.

19. This point is suggested in a personal letter from Dr. Mason to the writer, October 22, 1946.

20. Singh and Zingg, *op. cit.,* pp. xxi–xxii, in a foreword by the writer.

14 On Becoming Male: Reflections of a Sociologist on Childhood and Early Socialization

JAMES M. HENSLIN

Although relations between men and women are enveloped in social change, men still dominate our social institutions: law, politics, business, religion, education, the military, medicine, science, sports, and in many ways, even marriage and family. Despite far-reaching social change, women often find themselves in the more backstage, nurturing, and supportive roles—and those roles generally are supportive of the more dominant roles men play.

Why? Is this a consequence of genetic heritage—boys and girls being born with different predispositions? Or is it due to culture, because boys are socialized into dominance? While there is considerable debate among academics on this matter, sociologists side almost unanimously with the proponents of socialization. In this article, Henslin analyzes some of the socialization experiences that place boys in a distinctive social world and prepare them for dominance. This selection is an attempt to penetrate the taken-for-granted, behind-the-scenes aspects of socialization into masculine sexuality. Whether male or female, you might find it useful to contrast your experiences in growing up with those the author describes.

ACCORDING TO THE PREVAILING sociological perspective, our masculinity or femininity is not biologically determined. Although our biological or genetic inheritance gives each of us the sex organs of a male or female, how our "maleness" or "femaleness" is expressed depends on what we learn. Our masculinity or femininity, that is, what we are like as sexual beings—our orientations and how we behave as a male or a female—does not depend on biology but on social learning. It can be said that while our sex is part of our biological inheritance, our sexuality (or masculinity or femininity) is part of our social inheritance.

If this sociological position is correct—that culture, not anatomy, is our destiny—how do we become the "way we are"?[1] What factors shape or influence us into becoming masculine or feminine? If our behaviors do not come from our biology, how do we end up having behaviors that are typically associated with our sex? If they are learned, how do our behaviors, attitudes, and other basic orientations come to be felt by us as natural and essential to our identity? (And they are indeed essential to our identity.) In what ways is the process of "becoming" related to the social structure of society?

Not only would it take volumes to answer these questions fully, but it would also be impossible, since the answers are only now slowly being unraveled by researchers. In this short and rather informal article, I will be able to indicate only some of the basics underlying this foundational learning. I will focus exclusively on being socialized into masculinity, and will do this by reflecting on (1) my own experience in "becoming"; (2) my observations as a sociologist of the experiences of others; and (3) what others have shared with me concerning their own experiences. The reader should keep in mind that this article is meant to be neither definitive nor exhaustive, but is designed to depict general areas of male socialization and thereby to provide insight into the acquisition of masculinity in our culture.

In the Beginning . . .

Except for a few rare instances,[2] each of us arrives in this world with a clearly definable physical characteristic that sets us apart from about half the rest of the world. This characteristic makes a literal world of difference. Our parents become excited about whether we have been born with a penis or a vagina. They are usually either happy or disappointed about which organ we possess, seldom feeling neutral about the matter. They announce it to friends, relatives, and sometimes to complete strangers ("It's a boy!" "It's a girl!"). Regardless of how they feel about it, on the basis of our possessing a particular physical organ they purposely, but both consciously and subconsciously, separate us into two worlds. Wittingly and unwittingly, they thereby launch us onto a career that will encompass almost every aspect of our lives—one that will remain with us until death.

Colors, Clothing, and Toys

While it is not inherently more masculine or feminine than red, yellow, purple, orange, white, or black, the color blue is associated arbitrarily with infantile masculinity. After what is usually a proud realization that the neonate possesses a penis (which marks him as a member of the overlords of the universe), the inheritor of dominance is wrapped in blue. This color is merely an arbitrary choice, as originally any other would have done as well. But now that the association is made, no other will do. The announcing colors maintain their meaning for only a fairly short period, gradually becoming sexually neutralized.[3]

Our parents gently and sometimes not so gently push us onto a predetermined course. First they provide clothing designated appropriate to our masculine status. Even as infants our clothing displays sexual significance, and our parents are extremely careful that we never are clothed in either dresses or ruffles. For example, while our plastic panties are designed to keep mothers, fathers, and their furniture and friends dry, our parents make absolutely certain that ours are never pink with white ruffles. Even if our Mom had run out of all other plastic panties, she would rather stay home than take us out in public wearing ruffled pinkies. Mom would probably feel a twinge of guilt over such cross-dressing even in private.[4]

So both Mom and Dad are extremely cautious about our clothing. Generally plain, often simple, and usually sturdy, our clothing is designed to take the greater "rough and tumble" that they expect boys to give it. They also choose clothing that will help groom us into future adult roles; depending on the style of the period, they dress us in little sailor suits, miniature jogging togs, or two-piece suits with matching ties. Although at this early age we could care less about such things, and their significance appears irrelevant to us, our parents' concern is always present. If during a supermarket expedition even a stranger mistakes our sex, this agitates our parents, challenging their sacred responsibility to maintain the reality-ordering structure of the sex worlds. Such mistaken identification forces them to rethink their activities in proper sex typing, their deep obligation to make certain that their offspring is receiving the right start in life. They will either ascribe the mistake to the stupidity of the stranger or immediately forswear some particular piece of clothing.

Our parents' "gentle nudging" into masculinity does not overlook our toys. These represent both current activities thought gender appropriate and those symbolic of our future masculinity of courage, competition, daring—and of violence. We are given trucks, tanks, and guns. Although our mother might caution us about breaking them, it is readily apparent by her tone and facial expressions that she does not mean what she says. We can continue to bang them together roughly, and she merely looks at us—sometimes quite uncomprehendingly, and occasionally muttering something to the effect that boys will be boys. We somehow perceive her sense of confirmation and we bang them all the more, laughing gleefully, knowing that beneath our mom's grimaces and head-shaking lies approval.

Play and the Sexual Boundaries of Tolerance

We can make all sorts of expressive sounds as we play. We can shout, grunt, and groan on the kitchen floor or roll around in the sandbox. As she shoves us out the door, Mom always cautions us not to get dirty, but when we come in filthy her verbal and gestural disapproval is only mild. From holistic perception, of which by now we have become young masters, we have learned that no matter what Mom's words say, they do not represent the entirety of her feelings.

When we are "all dressed up" before going somewhere, or before company comes, Mom acts differently. We learn that at those times she means what she says about not getting dirty. If we do not want "fire in our pants," we'd better remain clean—at least for a while, for we also learn that after company has come and has had a glimpse of the neat and clean little boy (or, as they say, "the nice little gentleman" or the "fine young man"), we can go about our rough and tumble ways. Pushing, shouting, running, climbing, and other expressions of competition, glee, and freedom again become permissible. We learn that the appearance required at the beginning of a visit is quite unlike that which is passable at the end of the visit.

Our more boisterous and rougher play continues to help us learn the limits of our parents' tolerance. As we test those limits, somewhat to our dismay we occasionally find that we unwittingly have crossed beyond them. Through what is at times painful trial and error, we learn both the limits and how they vary with changed circumstance. We eventually learn those edges extremely well and know, for example, precisely how much more we can "get away with" when company comes than when only the immediate family is present, when Mom and Dad are tired or when they are arguing.

As highly rational beings, who are seldom adequately credited by adults for our keen cunning, we learn to calculate those boundaries exceedingly carefully. We eventually come to the point where we know precisely where the brink is—that one more word of back talk, one more quarrel with our brother, sister, or friend, even a small one, or even one more whine will move our parents from words to deeds, and their wrath will fall abruptly upon us. Depending on our parents' orientation to childrearing (or often simply upon their predilection of the moment, for at these times theory tends to fly out the window), this will result in either excruciating humiliation in front of our friends accompanied by horrible (though momentary) physical pain, or excruciating humiliation in front of our friends accompanied by the horrifying (and longer) deprivation of a privilege (which of course we know is really a "right" that is being withheld from us unjustifiably).

On Freedom and Being

As we calculate those boundaries of tolerance (or in the vernacular used by our parents and well understood by us, find out how much they can "stand"), we also learn something about our world vis-à-vis that of those strange female creatures who coinhabit our space. We learn that we can get dirtier, play rougher, speak louder, act more crudely, wander farther from home, stay away longer, and talk back more.

We see that girls live in a world foreign to ours. Theirs is quieter, neater, daintier, and in general more subdued. Sometimes our worlds touch, but then only momentarily. We learn, for example, that while little sisters might be all right to spend an occasional hour with on a rainy afternoon, they are, after all, "only girls." They cannot really enter our world, and we certainly do not want to become part of theirs, with its greater restrictions and fewer challenges. Occasionally, we even find ourselves delighting in this distinction as we taunt them about not being able to do something because it is "not for girls."

If we sometimes wonder about the reasons for the differences between our worlds, our curiosity quickly runs its course, for we know deep down that these distinctions are proper. They are *girls*, and, as our parents have told us repeatedly, we are NOT girls. We have internalized the appropriateness of our worlds; some things are right for us, others for them. Seldom are we sorry for the tighter reins placed on girls. We are just glad that we are not one of "them." We stick with "our own kind" and immensely enjoy our greater freedom. Rather than lose ourselves in philosophical reflections about the inequalities of this world (greatly beyond our mental capacities at this point anyway), we lose ourselves in exultation over our greater freedom and the good fortune that made us boys instead of girls.

That greater freedom becomes the most prized aspect of our existence. Before we are old enough to go to school (and later, during summer or weekends and any other nonschool days), when we awaken in the morning we can hardly wait to get our clothes on. Awaiting us is a world of adventure. If we are up before Mom, we can go outside and play in the yard. Before venturing beyond voice distance, however, we have to eat our "wholesome" breakfast, one that somehow (in mom's words) is helping to "make a man" out of us. After this man-producing breakfast, which might well consist of little more than cereal and juice, we are free to roam, to discover, to experience.

Certainly we have spatial and associational restrictions placed on us, but they are much more generous than those imposed on girls of our age. We know how many houses or blocks we can wander and whom we are allowed to see. But just as significant, we know how to go beyond that distance without getting caught and how to play with the "bad boys" and the "too big boys" without Mom ever being the wiser. So long as we are home within a certain time limit, despite verbal restrictions we really are free to come and go.

We do learn to accept limited responsibility in order to guard our freedom. We pester other mothers for the time or, learn that when both the big and little hands are at the top that it is noon, so we can make our brief appearance for lunch—and then quickly move back into the exciting world of boy activities. But we also learn to lie a lot, finding out that it is better to say anything plausible rather than to admit that we violated the boundaries and be "grounded," practically the worst form of punishment we can receive. Consequently, we learn to deny, to avoid, to deceive, to tell half-truths, and to involve ourselves in other sorts of subterfuge rather than to admit violations that might restrict our freedom of movement.

Our freedom is infinitely precious to us, for whether it is cops and robbers or space bandits, Spider Man or Darth Vader, ours is an imaginary world filled with daring and danger. Whether it is six-shooters with bullets or space missiles with laser disintegrators, we are always shooting or getting shot. There are always the good guys and the bad guys. Always there is a moral victory to be won. We are continuously running, shouting, hiding, and discovering. The world is filled with danger, with the inopportune and unexpected lurking just around the corner. As the enemy stalks us, the potential of sudden discovery and the sweet joys of being undetected or being the one who surprises the other are unsurpassable. Nothing in adulthood, despite its great allure, its challenges and victories yet to be experienced, will ever be greater than this intense bliss of innocence—and part of the joy of this period lies in our being entirely unaware of this savage fact of life.

. . . *And the Twain Shall Never Meet*

Seldom do we think about being masculine. Usually we are just being. The radical social differences that separate us from girls have not gone unnoticed, of course. Rather, these essential differences in life orientations not only have penetrated our consciousness but also have saturated our very beings. Our initial indifference to things male and female has turned to violent taste and distaste. We have learned our lessons so well that we sometimes end up teaching our own mothers lessons in gender. For example, we would rather be caught dead than to wear sissy clothing, and our tantrums will not cease until our mothers come to their senses and relent concerning putting something on us that we consider sissified.

We know there are two worlds, and we are grateful for the one we are in. Ours is superior. The evidence continually bombards us, and we exult in masculine privilege. We also protect our sexual boundaries from encroachment and erosion. The encroachment comes from tomboys who strive to become part of our world. We tolerate them—up to a point. But by excluding them from some activities, we let them know that there are irrevocable differences that forever separate us.

The erosion comes from sissies. Although we are not yet aware that we are reacting to a threat to our developing masculine identity, we do know that sissies make us uncomfortable. We come to dislike them intensely. To be a sissy is to be a traitor to one's very being. It is to be "like a girl," that which we are not—and that which we definitely never will be.

Sissies are to be either pitied or hated. While they are not girls, neither are they real boys. They look like us, but they bring shame on us because they do not represent anything we are. We are everything they are not. Consequently, we separate ourselves from them in the most direct manner possible. While we may be brutal, this breach is necessary, for we must define clearly the boundaries of our own existence—and one way that we know who we are is by knowing what we are not.

So we shame sissies. We make fun of anyone who is not the way he "ought" to be. If he hangs around the teacher or girls during recess instead of playing our rough and tumble games, if he will not play sports because he is afraid of getting dirty or being hurt, if he backs off from a fight, if he cries or whines, or even if he gets too many A's, we humiliate and ridicule him. We gather around him in a circle. We call him a sissy. We say, "Shame! Shame!" We call him gay, fag, and queer. We tell him he is a girl and not fit for us.

And as far as we are concerned, he never will be fit for us. He belongs to some strange status, not quite a girl and not quite a boy. Whatever he is, he certainly is not one of us. WE don't cry when we are punished or hurt. WE don't hang around girls. WE are proud of our average grades. WE play rough games. WE are not afraid of getting hurt. (Or if we are, we would never let it show.) WE are not afraid of sassing the teacher—or at least of calling the teacher names when his or her back is turned. We know who we are. We are boys.

The Puberty Shock

We never know, of course, how precarious our gender identity is. From birth we have been set apart from females, and during childhood we have severely separated ourselves both from females and from those who do not match our standards of masculinity. Our existence is well defined, our world solid. By the end of grade school, the pecking order is clear. For good or ill, each of us has been locked into a system of well-honed, peer-determined distinctions, our destiny determined by a heavily defended social order. Our masculine world seems secure, with distinct boundaries that clearly define "us" from "them." We know who we are, and we are cocky about it.

But then comes puberty, and overnight the world undergoes radical metamorphosis. Girls suddenly change. Right before our eyes the flat chests we have always taken for granted begin to protrude. Two little bumps magically appear, and while we are off playing our games, once in a while we cast quizzical glances in the direction of the girls. Witnessing a confusing, haunting change, we shrug off the dilemma and go back to our games.

Then the change hits us. We feel something happening within our own bodies. At first the feeling is vague, undefined. There is no form to it. We just know that something is different. Then we begin to feel strange stirrings within us. These stirrings come on abruptly, and that abruptness begins to shake everything loose in our secure world. Until this time our penis has never given us any particular trouble. It has just "been there," appended like a finger or toenail. It has been a fact of life, something that "we" had and "they" didn't. But now it literally springs to life, taking on an existence of its own and doing things that we once could not even imagine would ever take place. This sometimes creates embarrassment, and there are even times when, called to the blackboard to work out some problem, we must play dumb because of the bulge that we never willed.

It is a new game. The girls in our class are different. We are different. And never will we be the same.

We are forced into new concepts of masculinity. We find this upsetting, but fortunately we do not have to begin from scratch. We can build on our experiences, for mostly the change involves just one area of our lives, girls, and we are able to keep the rest intact. We can still swagger, curse, sweat, get dirty, and bloody ourselves in our games. While the girls still watch us admiringly from the sidelines as we "do our manly thing," we also now watch them more closely as they "do their womanly thing" and strut before us in tight sweaters and blouses.

While the girls still admire our toughness, a change is now demanded. At times we must show gentleness. We must be cleaner and watch our language more than before. We must even show consideration. These shifting boundaries are not easy to master, but we have the older, more experienced boys to count on—and they are more than willing to initiate us into this new world and, while doing so, to demonstrate their (always) greater knowledge and skills in traversing the social world, and in exhibiting their masculinity.

The Transition into Artificiality

It is with difficulty that we make the transition. A new sexuality is required, and radical change is easy for no one. We already have been fundamentally formed, and what we really learn at this point is to be more adept role-players. We behave one way when we are with the guys. This is the "natural" way, the way we feel. It is relaxed and easy. And we learn to act a different way while we are around girls. This form of presentation of self we find more contrived and artificial, for it requires greater politeness, consideration, and gentleness. In other words, it is contrary to what we have learned previously, to what we have become.

Consequently we hone our acting skills, the ability to put on expected performances. We always have been actors; it is just that we learned our earlier role at a more formative period, and, *having formed us*, this role now provides greater fit. Acting differently while we are around females is nothing new. We have been practicing this since we were at our mother's knee. But now the female expectations are more pressing as our worlds more frequently intersect. Although we become fairly skilled at meeting these expectations, they never become part of our being. Always they consist of superficial behaviors added onto what is truly and, by this time, "naturally" us.

This lesson in artificiality reinforces our many exercises in manipulation. We learn that to get what we want, whether that be an approving smile, a caress, a kiss, or more, we must meet the expectations of the one from whom we desire something. We are no strangers to this foundational fact of life, of course, but the masks we must wear in these more novel situations, our uncomfortable gestures and the requisite phrasing, make us awkward strangers to ourselves. We wonder why we are forced into situations that require such constant posturing.

But awkward or not (and as we become more proficient at the game, much of the initial discomfort leaves), we always come back for more. By now sports and games with the fellows are no longer enough. Girls seemingly hold the key to our happiness. They can withhold or grant as they see fit. And for favors to be granted, we must play this demanding intersexual game.

The Continuing Masculine World—and Marriage

Eventually, we become highly adept players in this intersexual game. We even come to savor our maturing manipulative abilities as the game offers highly stimulating psychological and physical payoffs. Our growing skills let us determine if a particular encounter will result in conquest, and thus calculate if it is worth the pursuit. To meet the challenge successfully provides yet another boost to our masculinity.

The hypocrisies and deceits that the game requires sometimes disturb us. We really want to be more honest than the game allows. But we do not know how to bring this about—and still succeed at the game *and* our masculinity.

Discomforts arising from the game, especially the intimate presence of the female world, must be relieved. Manly activities provide us refuge from this irritant, endeavors in which we men can truly understand one another, where we share a world of aspiration, conflict, and competition. Here we can laugh at the same things and talk the way we really feel with much less concern about the words we choose. We know that among men our interests, activities, and desires form an essential part of a shared, self-encapsulating world.

To continue to receive the rewards offered by females, on occasion we must leave our secure world of manliness momentarily to penetrate the conjoint world occupied by our feminine counterparts. But such leave-takings remain temporary, never a "real" part of us. Always awaiting are the "real" conversations that reflect the "real" world, that exciting realm whose challenging creativity, competition, and conflict help make life worth living.

And we are fortunate in having at our fingertips a socially constructed semi-imaginary masculine world, one we can summon at will to retreat into its beckoning confines. This world of televised football, baseball, basketball, wrestling, boxing, hockey, golf, soccer, and car racing is part of the domain of men. At least here is a world, manly and comfortable, that offers us refuge from that threatening feminine world, allowing us to withdraw from its suffocating demands of sharing and intimacy. This semi-imaginary world offers continual appeal because it summons up subconscious feelings from our childhood, adolescence, and, eventually as we grow older, early manhood.

Many of us would not deny that the characteristics we males learn or, if you prefer, the persons we tend to become, fail to provide an adequate basis for developing fulfilling intersexual relationships. But these characteristics, while underlying what is often the shallowness of our relationships with women, are indeed us. They are the logical consequence of our years of learning gender. We have become the image that our culture held out to us. Although willing participants in our social destiny, we are heirs of cultural divisions that long preceded our arrival on the social scene.

Some of us, only with great difficulty, have overcome our masculine socialization into intersexual superficiality and have developed relationships with wives and girlfriends that transcend the confines of those cultural dictates. But such relearning, painfully difficult, comes at a price, leaving in its wake much hurt and brokenness.

Hardly any aspect of this process of becoming a man in our society augurs well for marriage. The separateness of the world that we join at birth signals our journey into an intricate process whereby we become a specific type of being. Our world diverges in almost all aspects from the world of females. Not only do we look different, not only do we talk differently and act differently, but our fundamental thinking and orientations to life contrast sharply with theirs. This basic divergence is difficult for women to grasp and, when grasped, is often accompanied by a shudder of disbelief and distaste at the revelatory insight into such dissimilar reality. Yet we are expected to unite permanently with someone from this contradispositional world and, despite our essential differences, not only to share a life space but also to merge our goals, hopes, dreams, and aspirations.

Is it any wonder, then, that in the typical case men remain strangers to women, and women to men, with marriage a crucible of struggle?

Notes

1. The diversity of opinion among sociologists regarding the nature/nurture causes of behavioral differences of males and females is illustrated in *Society* magazine (September/October 1986:4–39). The connection between ideology and theoretical interpretation of data is especially apparent in this heated exchange. I also discuss this topic in my introductory textbooks: *Sociology: A Down-to-Earth Approach, Essentials of Sociology: A Down-to-Earth Approach,* and *Core Concepts of Sociology: A Down-to-Earth Approach,* all published by Allyn & Bacon of Boston.

2. Of about one in every 30,000 births, the sex of a baby is unclear. A genetic disorder called congenital adrenal hyperplasia results in the newborn having parts of both male and female genitals (*St. Louis Globe-Democrat,* March 10–11, 1979, p. 3D).

3. When people (almost exclusively women) are invited to a baby shower and the expectant mother has not yet given birth or has not had an ultrasound test to determine the baby's sex (or if they wish to take advantage of a sale and buy a gift in advance of the delivery), they find themselves in a quandary. The standard solution to this problem of not knowing the sex of the child (at least in the Midwest) is to purchase either clothing of yellow color or a "sex neutral" item.

4. Duly noted, of course, are the historical arbitrariness and relativity of the gender designation of clothing, with the meaning of ruffles and other stylistic variations depending on the historical period. Photos from the late 1800s, for example, show U.S. baby boys dressesd in lacey gowns or dresses.

15 On Becoming Female: Lessons Learned in School

DONNA EDER

In the previous article, we focused on how socialization puts boys on a distinct road in life. We saw how boys' experiences give them distinct orientations to the world, including what they feel they can reasonably expect out of life—and how those orientations become a divisive factor in marriage and other male–female relationships. In this article, we turn the focus on girls' experiences in peer groups, examining how peer groups vitally influence girls' orientations, even how they view the self.

The author of this article headed a research team that explored the social world of girls in middle school. This is a vital age, for at this point in life girls are developing a more precise sexual identity. Eder watched and listened as the girls interacted with one another, and as they interacted with boys, about whom they were ambivalent. Their statements, which disclose inner feelings, conflicts, rivalries, and jealousies, reveal the ongoing formation of a self. Note especially the role that peers play in the developing identity of the girls—and how the peer interactions focus on the superficialities of appearance. How do you think this emphasis on appearance and attractiveness becomes part of women's orientations to life and influences their interactions?

ATTRACTIVENESS has long been part of the construction of femininity. . . . Preoccupation [with appearance] among American women prevents them from focusing on more constructive aspects of themselves, such as who they are or what they are capable of accomplishing. It is becoming more and more clear that this is one of the main areas in which women are hindered by stereotypical notions of femininity.

At Woodview [Middle School], concerns about attractiveness were promoted primarily through the high-status activity of cheerleading. This focus

was most evident during the cheerleading tryouts. The teacher who organized the tryouts told the judges to keep [appearance] in mind as they selected the candidates.

> She also told them to pay attention to the person's weight, saying, "If you don't
> like the way they look, you wouldn't like them to stand in front of you."

This message conveys the essence of cheerleaders as adornments to a team as
well as promoters of team enthusiasm and support. The fact that cheerleaders are seen as team representatives makes their appearance salient in the
context of a culture that places a high value on female beauty. To be the best
representatives, they should be highly attractive as well as capable of pro-
moting school spirit.

Officially, appearance was included in the judging of cheerleaders under
the category of "sparkle." Ten of the fifty total points a candidate could obtain were allotted to this category, as the cheerleading coach explained to the
candidates during one of the practice sessions prior to the tryouts.

> At one point, Mrs. Tolson started to tell them what they were going to be
> judged on, saying they would get ten points for sparkle, which was their smile,
> personality, bubbliness, appearance, attractiveness—not that all cheerleaders
> had to be attractive, but it was important to have a clean appearance, not to be
> sloppy, have messy or greasy hair, because that doesn't look like a cheerleader.

Throughout the practice sessions girls were reminded to wear a clean, neat
outfit for tryouts and to have clean, neatly combed hair. This emphasis on
neatness continued despite the physical nature of this activity, which includes
cartwheels and backflips. It was important to have the skills to do these gym-
nastic routines, but it was equally important to find ways to maintain a neat,
feminine appearance throughout the performance. This again conveys the
message to girls that how they look is as important as what they do.

Another way in which cheerleading candidates were encouraged to enhance their looks was by remembering to smile. Smiling was considered an
important part of the cheerleading role—something that made you "look like
a cheerleader." Girls were encouraged to smile to cover up feelings that
might accompany their efforts, such as pain and concentration.

> When they were doing a stunt, she [the coach] said she wanted them to smile
> through the pain. Later on, when they were practicing the stunts in front of the
> eighth-graders, Karla [an eighth-grade cheerleader] continually reminded
> them to smile as they were working on their jumps. The way Karla put it was,
> "Smile the whole time."

The judges themselves evaluated the candidates' appearance during the decision-making process. Both neatness and cuteness were mentioned, as was the quality of their smiles. For example, one judge noted that the girl they were discussing had a cute smile. Another judge disagreed, indicating through imitation that the girl's smile was forced. This judge rated her more negatively than did the first one. Although weight was taken into account, one year some girls who were considered overweight were selected. The judges suggested that they be put on diets, preserving the idea that thinness is an important aspect of cheerleaders' appearance.

The high profile given to cheerleading means that traits that are valued in cheerleaders also have a greater impact on the school's informal peer culture.

Boys' Focus on Girls' Appearance in Peer Interaction

Many Woodview boys focused their evaluation of girls on their attractiveness. In fact, male interest in their bodies as being sexual and appealing could arouse the deepest level of appearance anxiety in girls. For example, one day a group of eighth-grade girls discussed a male ranking of female peers.

> Penny said that she had seen a list some boys had made which rated girls in the class. Karla was at the top, then Sara, then Peggy or Darlene. They said that they had told these guys, "Thanks a lot" for not including them on the list. Bonnie said, "Did you notice that all of those girls are early figure people?" indicating that the reason she thought they were rated highly was because they have a figure already. Then they pointed to Sara and said, "There she is. She's the one with the big hips. You can't miss her."

Informal rankings such as this remind girls that they are being evaluated on a daily basis, even when they haven't entered formal beauty contests or cheerleading tryouts.

Boys frequently referred to the physical appearance of girls they knew, both in their presence and when the girls were absent. For example, one day a boy announced at lunch, "Any girl who thinks she's beautiful, stand up." The appearance of someone's girlfriend was a typical topic of conversation, usually implying that some feature of hers was unattractive or that she was ugly in general. Even some of the prettiest girls in the school, cheerleaders and other high-status-group members, were criticized by boys for having ugly faces or deficient bodies.

The Role of Girls' Gossip

Even when girls are by themselves, their conversations are often dominated by cultural standards and male perspectives that highlight the importance of good looks. Girls themselves contribute to this, especially through gossip about the looks and dress of other girls. When we first told students we were interested in finding out what they did during their free time, some girls told us that mainly they talked about other girls. Given the frequency of this activity, many girls were constantly confronted with the topic of female appearance.

It was evident from the girls' comments that the continual focus on other girls' looks further added to their anxieties about their own appearance.

> There was an interesting discussion between Peggy and Lisa about the girl that Bob is taking to the dance. They talked about whether she was cute or not and ended up agreeing that she was a stack of bones. That generated some discussion about weight and Lisa said that she [Lisa] was fat. Peggy said that she wasn't. Then Wendy wondered if she was a stack of bones and Lisa told her that no, she was just right—that she wasn't skinny and she wasn't fat either. [Stephanie's notes]

While these girls got reassurance from their friends that they were neither too fat nor too thin, in most cases girls did not openly reveal their concerns and thus did not receive such assurance. Instead, many girls were likely to remain self-conscious and insecure about their body type and weight. Girls from lower-working-class backgrounds often couldn't afford to buy name-brand clothes and shoes, and their attire was often subject to criticism by girls who could afford nicer clothes. Comments about people's clothes were often made loudly enough for the targets to hear.

> As Lynn walked by they jeered at her and made fun of her. . . . One of these girls was going, "Oooh, look at those pants! Ohh, how could you wear those?" [Stephanie's notes]

At other times people were directly ridiculed.

> She also said that the cheerleaders made fun of people if they didn't wear Nike or Adidas shoes. They'd look at her and say, "Oh, where did you get your shoes?" She said that she just wears plain old tennis shoes. [Cathy's notes]

Besides being appraised on the basis of their attire, girls were also evaluated for their body weight and type. Girls who were particularly overweight were frequent targets of gossip, as in this extensive discussion of an isolate by several sixth-graders.

> A large part of what these girls did today was make fun of one girl, Gloria. One girl would say, "Here is the airplane; the pilot says, 'Will somebody please come up front,' and all of a sudden somebody walks up front," showing with her hands how the plane dives. Then somebody else says, "Or here's the plane flying," and she shows it flying lopsided with her hands. "Then Gloria walks over to the other side and it flips the other way." Or, "Here's the airplane and there's a weak spot in the middle, and Gloria walks down the aisle and she falls through." [Stephanie's notes]

This episode continued with other jokes about Gloria, including using her as a trampoline in gym class and how she could serve as a windblock for all of them at once.

It was not just overweight girls who were made fun of and evaluated, however. Girls who were too skinny were also criticized, as were girls who had large hips or large breasts. Girls have no control over most of these physical characteristics. Perhaps because of the extensive nature of this type of gossip, girls often try to increase their control over their weight by dieting, which leads, in more severe cases, to eating disorders such as anorexia and bulimia. Although this focus on body weight may seem obsessive, it makes sense in light of the frequency of body critiques in girls' evaluative talk and in the media.

Given the importance of good looks for gaining status among peers and avoiding negative evaluations, it is not surprising that girls devote so much attention to their appearance. Ironically, another relatively frequent theme of gossip was negatively judging others for putting too much emphasis on their looks. Girls seemed particularly critical of girls who tried to stand out in some manner, either by dressing in a unique fashion or by making themselves "too attractive" or "too sexy."

A group of sixth-graders spent much of one lunch period making fun of a popular girl for wearing a particularly unusual outfit to school.

> There was a long discussion throughout lunch about Jane, who I have been told before is the most popular girl in the sixth grade. Today she was wearing a khaki outfit, matching pants and a shirt—sort of a safari look. The first thing that got the conversation going was that Ilene started talking about a girl that had a "jungle suit" on. And Nicki, Jesse, and Kristy all sort of joined in with this conversation, and even Andrea played along with it for a while. They started out by saying that they'd seen her in the hall, given her the Tarzan yell, and she'd turned around and looked at them and they'd said, "Where'd you get

the jungle outfit?" And they wondered if she was going to give the Tarzan yell back. They started talking about it as though she was Tarzan's monkey, Chee-tah, and then the conversation sort of strayed from clothes and went to how she won the dog contest—how she's the number one dog of the school, which is the exact opposite since she's so popular. She does look older. She had her hair up, and had quite a bit of makeup on. [Stephanie's notes]

In another case, a group of eighth-grade girls was critical of a local beauty pageant contestant of high school age who visited the school to collect money for her campaign. In this case, they claimed that she used makeup to give a false image of beauty, and that underneath she was really ugly.

Eighth-Grade
PENNY: I'm not giving it to her.
CINDY: The only thing that makes her look anything is all the makeup and [unclear]
PENNY: She had a picture and she's standing there like this, she's going [Poses with one hand on her hip and one by her head]
CINDY: Her face is probably this skinny but it looks that big cuz of all the makeup she has on it.
PENNY: She's *ugly*, ugly, ugly! [In a low voice]
BONNIE: She looks like a cow.

This girl was criticized for her attempts to be "too attractive" and "too sexy." In her case, a flirtatious pose in one of her photographs was seen as evidence of trying to be too sexy.

These different themes of gossip add to the already confusing message girls receive about their appearance. On the one hand they are continually faced with media messages that emphasize the importance of using makeup and fashionable attire to enhance their attractiveness and their sexuality. If they do succeed in looking, acting, or dressing like the models they see in the media, however, they are likely to be accused of portraying false images or wanton sexuality. Furthermore, this practice of criticizing the objects of sexual gaze deflects criticism away from boys and men for viewing girls in this limited manner. Thus, girls blame each other for drawing sexual atten-tion to themselves rather than criticizing the social practices that promote a view of girls and women as sexual objects.

Attractiveness as an Increasing Concern for Girls

Appearance is already a salient concern among these students, and it is likely to increase in importance for many as they get older. The number of school-sponsored contests that emphasize attractiveness increases in high school as girls are selected for pompon teams, cheerleading, baton twirlers in marching bands, and so on. In most of these cases, girls choose to enter these contests, although sometimes this "choice" may be the result of maternal pressure. A more powerful form of school-sponsored competition is the selection of prom queens, homecoming queens, and attendants in which girls are annually evaluated on their attractiveness, often without ever volunteering to enter such competitions. Generally, school officials assume that every girl in the school wants to enter, which implies that all girls wish to be judged on the basis of their appearance. At the same time, diverse subcultures often develop within large high schools, some of which place less emphasis on stereotypical gender concerns such as appearance.

[Conclusion]

[These experiences] send girls a strong message that what they do and who they are is less important then how they look. Even girls in achievement roles, such as basketball team members, continue to receive messages about the importance of appearance. Such an emphasis prepares girls for adult careers and occupations where appearance continues to be an explicit or implicit basis for hiring and retaining employees. . . .

Girls and women continue to be viewed as sexual objects within the media as well as other arenas from cheerleading and pompon teams to swimsuit competitions. Increasingly, adult female models are portrayed as innocent and childlike in their sexual allure, while young girls are depicted as erotic and seductive. Since girls are cast as sexual objects at such an early age, they often internalize this image as a central aspect of their identity. It then becomes extraordinarily difficult for them to move beyond this self-image to develop a greater sense of their own erotic potential as well as their general creative life force. This denial contributes to such largely female maladies as anorexia and bulimia as well as a growing obsession with plastic surgery among adolescent girls.

Through objectification, women are denied their sense of totality. To be viewed primarily as a physical and sexual object is to experience denial of self as a whole person with thoughts, feelings, and actions. Women must struggle to overcome a perception of self as object rather than subject before they can begin the process of self-definition as total and complete human beings. Only then can they develop their unique interests and have a real impact on the world around them.

16 Sexuality and Gender in Children's Daily Worlds

BARRIE THORNE
ZELLA LURIA

In this selection, the researchers focus on children's play, examining its implications for relations between men and women. Their observations are likely to bring back many memories of your own childhood. You will also become aware that children's play is not simply play, but has serious sociological meaning—in this instance, the fierce maintenance of social boundaries between males and females.

To gather their data, Thorne and Luria studied fourth- and fifth-graders in four schools within three states. They found that the children usually are very careful to separate their friendships and activities on the basis of sex. Girls of this age are more concerned about "being nice," while the interests of boys center on sports and testing the limits of rules. The larger groups into which they band provide each boy a degree of protection and anonymity. The sociological significance of children's play is that both boys and girls are helping to socialize one another into primary adult gender roles, girls being more concerned with intimacy, emotions, and romance, and boys with independence and sexuality. These children are writing the "scripts" that they will follow as adults.

THE AMBIGUITIES OF "SEX"—a word used to refer to biological sex, to cultural gender, and also to sexuality—contain a series of complicated questions. Although our cultural understandings often merge these three domains, they can be separated analytically; their interrelationships lie at the core of the social organization of sex and gender. In this paper we focus on the domains of gender and sexuality as they are organized and experienced among elementary school children, especially nine- to eleven-year-olds. This analysis helps illuminate age-based variations and transitions in the organization of sexuality and gender.

We use "gender" to refer to cultural and social phenomena—divisions of labor, activity, and identity which are associated with but not fully determined by biological sex. The core of sexuality, as we use it here, is desire and arousal. Desire and arousal are shaped by and associated with socially learned activities and meanings which Gagnon and Simon (1973) call "sexual scripts." Sexual scripts—defining who does what, with whom, when, how, and what it means—are related to the adult society's view of gender (Miller and Simon, 1981). Nine- to eleven-year-old children are beginning the transition from the gender system of childhood to that of adolescence. They are largely defined (and define themselves) as children, but they are on the verge of sexual maturity, cultural adolescence, and a gender system organized around the institution of heterosexuality. Their experiences help illuminate complex and shifting relationships between sexuality and gender.

First we explore the segregated gender arrangements of middle childhood as contexts for learning adolescent and adult sexual scripts. We then turn from their separate worlds to relations *between* boys and girls, and examine how fourth- and fifth-grade children use sexual idioms to mark gender boundaries. Separate gender groups and ritualized, asymmetric relations between girls and boys lay the groundwork for the more overtly sexual scripts of adolescence.

The Daily Separation of Girls and Boys

Gender segregation—the separation of girls and boys in friendships and casual encounters—is central to daily life in elementary schools. A series of snapshots taken in varied school settings would reveal extensive spatial separation between girls and boys. When they choose seats, select companions for work or play, or arrange themselves in line, elementary school children frequently cluster into same-sex groups. At lunchtime, boys and girls often sit separately and talk matter-of-factly about "girls' tables" and "boys' tables." Playgrounds have gendered spaces: boys control some areas and activities, such as large playing fields and basketball courts; and girls control smaller enclaves like jungle-gym areas and concrete spaces for hopscotch or jump-rope. Extensive gender segregation in everyday encounters and in friendships has been found in many other studies of elementary- and middle-school children. Gender segregation in elementary and middle schools has been found to account for more segregation than race (Schofield, 1982).

Gender segregation is not total. Snapshots of school settings would also reveal some groups with a fairly even mix of boys and girls, especially in games like kickball, dodgeball, and handball, and in classroom and playground activities organized by adults. Some girls frequently play with boys, integrating their groups in a token way, and a few boys, especially in the lower grades, play with groups of girls. In general, there is more gender segregation when children are freer to construct their own activities.

Most of the research on gender and children's social relations emphasizes patterns of separation, contrasting the social organization and cultures of girls' groups with those of boys. In brief summary: Boys tend to interact in larger and more publicly visible groups; they more often play outdoors, and their activities take up more space than those of girls. Boys engage in more physically aggressive play and fighting; their social relations tend to be overtly hierarchical and competitive. Organized sports are both a central activity and a major metaphor among boys; they use a language of "teams" and "captains" even when not engaged in sports.

Girls more often interact in smaller groups or friendship pairs, organized in shifting alliances. Compared with boys, they more often engage in turn-taking activities like jump-rope and doing tricks on the bars, and they less often play organized sports. While boys use a rhetoric of contests and teams, girls describe their relations using language which stresses cooperation and "being nice." But the rhetorics of either group should not be taken for the full reality. Girls *do* engage in conflict, although it tends to take more indirect forms than the direct insults and challenges more often found in interactions among boys, and between girls and boys.

Interaction Among Boys

In daily patterns of talk and play, boys in all-male groups often build towards heightened and intense moments, moments one can describe in terms of group arousal with excited emotions. This especially happens when boys violate rules.

Dirty words are a focus of rules, and rule breaking, in elementary schools. Both girls and boys know dirty words, but flaunting of the words and risking punishment for their use was more frequent in boys' than in girls' groups in all the schools we studied. In the middle-class Massachusetts public school, both male and female teachers punished ballplayers for [their dirty words]. But teachers were not present after lunch and before school, when most group-directed play took place. A female paraprofessional, who alone managed almost 150 children on the playground, never intervened to stop bad language in play; the male gym teacher who occasionally appeared on the field at after-lunch recess always did. Boys resumed dirty talk immediately after he passed them. Dirty talk is a staple part of the repertoire of the boys' groups (also see Fine, 1980). Such talk defines their groups as, at least in part, outside the reach of the school's discipline.

Some of the dirty talk may be explicitly sexual, as it was in the Massachusetts public school when a group of five fifth-grade boys played a game called "Mad Lib" (also described in Luria, 1983). The game consisted of a paragraph (in this case, a section of a textbook discussing the U.S. Constitution) with key words deleted, to be filled in by the players. Making the paragraph absurd and violating rules to create excitement seemed to be the goal of the game. The boys clearly knew that their intentions were "dirty": They requested the field observer not to watch the game.

Sports, dirty words, and testing the limits are part of what boys teach boys how to do. The assumption seems to be: Dirty words, sports interest and knowledge, and transgression of politeness are closely connected.

RULE TRANSGRESSION: COMPARING GIRLS' AND BOYS' GROUPS

Rule transgression in *public* is exciting to boys in their groups. Boys' groups are attentive to potential consequences of transgression, but, compared with girls, groups of boys appear to be greater risk-takers. Adults tending and teaching children do not often undertake discipline of an entire boys' group; the adults might lose out and they cannot risk that. Girls are more likely to affirm the reasonableness of rules, and, when it occurs, rule-breaking by girls is smaller scale. This may be related to the smaller size of girls' groups and to adults' readiness to use rules on girls who seem to believe in them. It is dubious if an isolated pair of boys (a pair is the model size of girls' groups) could get away with the rule-breaking that characterizes the larger male group. A boy may not have power, but a boys' *group* does. Teachers avoid disciplining whole groups of boys, partly for fear of seeming unfair. Boys rarely identify those who proposed direct transgressions and, when confronted, they claim (singly), "I didn't start it; why should I be punished?"

Boys are visibly excited when they break rules together—they are flushed as they play, they wipe their hands on their jeans, some of them look guilty. The Mad Lib game described above not only violates rules, it also evokes sexual meanings within an all-male group. Arousal is not purely individual; in this case, it is shared by the group. . . . The audience for the excitement is the gender-segregated peer group, where each boy increases the excitement by adding still a "worse" word. All of this takes place in a game ("rules") context, and hence with anonymity despite the close-up contact of the game.

While we never observed girls playing a Mad Lib game of this sort, some of our female students recall playing the game in grade school but giving it up after being caught by teachers, or out of fear of being caught. Both boys and girls may acquire knowledge of the game, but boys repeatedly perform it because their gender groups give support for transgression.

These instances all suggest that boys experience a shared, arousing context for transgression, with sustained gender group support for rule-breaking. Girls' groups may engage in rule-breaking, but the gender group's support for repeated public transgression is far less certain. The smaller size of girls' gender groupings in comparison with those of boys, and girls' greater susceptibility to rules and social control by teachers, make girls' groups easier to control. Boys' larger groups give each transgressor a degree of anonymity. Anonymity—which means less probability of detection and punishment—enhances the contagious excitement of rule-breaking.

The higher rates of contagious excitement, transgression, and limit-testing in boys' groups means that when they are excited, boys are often "playing" to male audiences. The public nature of such excitement forges bonds among boys. This kind of bonding is also evident when boys play team sports, and when they act aggressively toward marginal or isolated boys. Such aggression is both physical and verbal (taunts like "sissy," "fag," or "mental"). Sharing a target of aggression may be another source of arousal for groups of boys.

THE TIE TO SEXUALITY IN MALES

When Gagnon and Simon (1973) argued that there are gender-differentiated sexual scripts in adolescence, they implied what our observations suggest: the gender arrangements and subcultures of middle childhood prepare the way for the sexual scripts of adolescence. Fifth- and sixth-grade boys share pornography, in the form of soft-core magazines like *Playboy* and *Penthouse,* with great care to avoid confiscation. Like the Mad Lib games with their forbidden content, soft-core magazines are also shared in all-male contexts, providing explicit knowledge about what is considered sexually arousing and about attitudes and fantasies. Since pornography is typically forbidden for children in both schools and families, this secret sharing occurs in a context of rule-breaking.

While many theorists since Freud have stressed the importance of boys loosening ties and identification with females (as mother surrogates), few theorists have questioned why "communally aroused" males do not uniformly bond sexually to other males. If the male groups of fifth and sixth grade are the forerunners of the "frankly" heterosexual gender groups of the junior and high school years, what keeps these early groups from open homosexual expression? Scripting in same-gender peer groups may, in fact, be more about gender than about sexual orientation. Boys, who will later view themselves as having homosexual or heterosexual preferences, are learning patterns of masculinity. The answer may also lie in the teaching of homophobia.

By the fourth grade, children, especially boys, have begun to use homophobic labels—"fag," "faggot," "queer"—as terms of insult, especially for marginal boys. They draw upon sexual allusions (often not fully understood, except for their negative and contaminating import) to reaffirm male hierarchies and patterns of exclusion. As "fag" talk increases, relaxed and cuddling patterns of touch decrease among boys. Kindergarten and first-grade boys touch one another frequently and with ease, with arms around shoulders, hugs, and holding hands. By fifth grade, touch among boys becomes more constrained, gradually shifting to mock violence and the use of poking, shoving, and ritual gestures like "give five" (flat hand slaps) to express bonding. The tough surface of boys' friendships is no longer like the gentle touching of girls in friendship.

Interaction Among Girls

In contrast with the larger, hierarchical organization of groups of boys, fourth- and fifth-grade girls more often organize themselves in pairs of "best friends" linked in shifting coalitions. These pairs are not "marriages"; the pattern is more one of dyads moving into triads, since girls often participate in two or more pairs at one time. This may result in quite complex social networks. Girls often talk about who is friends with or "likes" whom; they continually negotiate the parameters of friendships.

For example, in the California school, Chris, a fifth-grade girl, frequently said that Kathryn was her "best friend." Kathryn didn't proclaim the friendship as often; she also played and talked a lot with Judy. After watching Kathryn talk to Judy during a transition period in the classroom, Chris went over, took Kathryn aside, and said with an accusing tone, "You talk to Judy more than me." Kathryn responded defensively, "I talk to you as much as I talk to Judy."

In talking about their relationships with one another, girls use a language of "friends," "nice," and "mean." They talk about who is most and least "liked," which anticipates the concern about "popularity" found among junior high and high school girls (Eder, 1985). Since relationships sometimes break off, girls hedge bets by structuring networks of potential friends. The activity of constructing and breaking dyads is often carried out through talk with third parties. Some of these processes are evident in a sequence recorded in a Massachusetts school:

The fifth-grade girls, Flo and Pauline, spoke of themselves as "best friends," while Flo said she was "sort of friends" with Doris. When a lengthy illness kept Pauline out of school, Flo spent more time with Doris. One day Doris abruptly broke off her friendship with Flo and began criticizing her to other girls. Flo, who felt very badly, went around asking others in their network, "What did I do? Why is Doris being so mean? Why is she telling everyone not to play with me?"

On school playgrounds girls are less likely than boys to organize themselves into team sports. They more often engage in small-scale, turn-taking kinds of play. When they jump rope or play on the bars, they take turns performing and watching others perform in stylized movements which may involve considerable skill. Sometimes girls work out group choreographies, counting and jumping rope in unison, or swinging around the bars. In other synchronized body rituals, clusters of fifth- and sixth-grade girls practice cheerleading routines or dance steps. In interactions with one another, girls often use relaxed gestures of physical intimacy, moving bodies in harmony, coming close in space, and reciprocating cuddly touches. We should add that girls also poke and grab, pin one another from behind, and use hand-slap rituals like "giving five," although less frequently than boys.

In other gestures of intimacy, which one rarely sees among boys, girls stroke or comb their friends' hair. They notice and comment on one another's physical appearance such as haircuts or clothes. Best friends monitor one another's emotions. They share secrets and become mutually vulnerable through self-disclosure, with an implicit demand that the expression of one's inadequacy will induce the friend to disclose a related inadequacy. In contrast, disclosure of weakness among boys is far more likely to be exposed to others through joking or horsing around.

IMPLICATIONS FOR SEXUALITY

Compared with boys, girls are more focused on constructing intimacy and talking about one-to-one relationships. Their smaller and more personal groups provide less protective anonymity than the larger groups of boys. Bonding through mutual self-disclosure, especially through disclosure of vulnerability, and breaking off friendships by "acting mean," teach the creation, sustaining, and ending of emotionally intimate relations. Girls' preoccupation with who is friends with whom, and their monitoring of cues of "nice" and "mean," liking and disliking, teach them strategies for forming and leaving personal relationships. In their interactions girls show knowledge of motivational rules for dyads and insight into both outer and inner realities of social relationships. Occasionally, girls indicate that they see boys as lacking such "obvious" knowledge.

Girls' greater interest in verbally sorting out relationships was evident during an incident in the Massachusetts public school. The fifth-grade boys often insulted John, a socially isolated boy who was not good at sports. On one such occasion during gym class, Bill, a high status boy, angrily yelled "creep" and "mental" when John fumbled the ball. The teacher stopped the game and asked the class to discuss the incident. Both boys and girls vigorously talked about "words that kill," with Bill saying he was sorry for what he said, that he had lost control in the excitement of the game. The girls kept asking, "How could anyone do that?" The boys kept returning to, "When you get excited, you do things you don't mean." Both girls and boys understood and verbalized the dilemma, but after the group discussion the boys dropped the topic. The girls continued to converse, with one repeatedly asking, "How could Bill be so stupid? Didn't he know how he'd make John feel?"

When talking with one another, girls use dirty words much less often than boys do. The shared arousal and bonding among boys which we think occurs around public rule-breaking has as its counterpart the far less frequent giggling sessions of girls, usually in groups larger than three. The giggling often centers on carefully guarded topics, sometimes, although not always, about boys.

The sexually related discourse of girls focuses less on dirty words than on themes of romance. In the Michigan school, first- and second-grade girls often jumped rope to rhymes about romance. A favorite was, "Down in the Valley Where the Green Grass Grows," a saga of heterosexual romance which, with the name of the jumper and a boy of her choice filled in, concludes: ". . . along came Jason, and kissed her on the cheek . . . first comes love, then comes marriage, then along comes Cindy with a baby carriage." In the Michigan and California schools, fourth- and fifth-grade girls talked privately about crushes and about which boys were "cute," as shown in the following incident recorded in the lunchroom of the Michigan school:

> The girls and boys from one of the fourth-grade classes sat at separate tables. Three of the girls talked as they peered at a nearby table of fifth-grade boys, "Look behind you," one said. "Ooh," said the other two. "That boy's named Todd." "I know where my favorite guy is . . . there," another gestured with her head while her friends looked.

In the Massachusetts private school, fifth-grade girls plotted about how to get particular boy–girl pairs together.

As Gagnon and Simon (1973) have suggested, two strands of sexuality are differently emphasized among adolescent girls and boys. Girls emphasize and learn about the emotional and romantic before the explicitly sexual. The sequence for boys is the reverse; commitment to sexual acts precedes commitment to emotion-laden, intimate relationships and the rhetoric of romantic love. Dating and courtship, Gagnon suggests, are processes in which each sex teaches the other what each wants and expects. The exchange, as they point out, does not always go smoothly. Indeed, in heterosexual relationships among older adults, tension often persists between the scripts (and felt needs) of women and of men.

Children's Sexual Meanings and the Construction of Gender Arrangements

Girls and boys, who spend considerable time in gender-separate groups, learn different patterns of interaction which, we have argued, lay the groundwork for the sexual scripts of adolescence and adulthood. However, sexuality is not simply delayed until adolescence. Children engage in sexual practices—kissing, erotic forms of touch, masturbation, and sometimes intercourse. As school-based observers, we saw only a few overt sexual activities among children, mostly incidents of public, cross-gender kissing, surrounded by teasing, chasing, and laughter.

HETEROSEXUAL TEASING AND THE IMPORTANCE OF THIRD PARTIES

The special loading of sexual words and gestures makes them useful for accomplishing non-sexual purposes. Sexual idioms provide a major resource which children draw upon as they construct and maintain gender segregation. Through the years of elementary school, children use with increasing frequency heterosexual idioms—claims that a particular girl or boy "likes," "has a crush on," or is "goin' with" someone from the other gender group.

Children's language for heterosexual relationships consists of a very few, often repeated, and sticky words. In a context of teasing, the charge that a particular boy "likes" a particular girl (or vice versa) may be hurled like an insult. The difficulty children have in countering such accusations was evident in a conversation between the observer and a group of third-grade girls in the lunchroom at the Michigan school:

> Susan asked me what I was doing, and I said I was observing the things children do and play. Nicole volunteered, "I like running when boys chase all the girls. See Tim over there? Judy chases him all around the school. She likes him." Judy, sitting across the table, quickly responded, "I hate him. I like him for a friend." "Tim loves Judy," Nicole said in a loud, sing-song voice.

Sexual and romantic teasing marks social hierarchies. The most popular children and the pariahs—the lowest status, excluded children—are most frequently mentioned as targets of "liking." Linking someone with a pariah suggests shared contamination and is an especially vicious tease.

When a girl or boy publicly says that she or he "likes" someone or has a boyfriend or girlfriend, that person defines the romantic situation and is less susceptible to teasing than those targeted by someone else. Crushes may be secretly revealed to friends, a mark of intimacy, especially among girls. The entrusted may then go public with the secret ("Wendy likes John"), which may be experienced as betrayal, but which also may be a way of testing the romantic waters. Such leaks, like those of government officials, can be denied or acted upon by the original source of information.

Third parties—witnesses and kibbitzers—are central to the structure of heterosexual teasing. The teasing constructs dyads (very few of them actively "couples"), but within the control of larger gender groups. Several of the white fifth-graders in the Michigan and California schools and some of the black students in the Massachusetts schools occasionally went on dates, which were much discussed around the schools. Same-gender groups provide launching pads, staging grounds, and retreats for heterosexual couples, both real and imagined. Messengers and emissaries go between groups, indicating who likes whom and checking out romantic interest. By the time "couples" actually get together (if they do at all), the groups and their messengers have provided a network of constructed meanings, a kind of agenda for the pair. As we have argued, gender-divided peer groups sustain different meanings of the sexual. They also regulate heterosexual behavior by helping to define the emerging sexual scripts of adolescence (who "likes" whom, who might "go with" whom, what it means to be a couple).

HETEROSEXUALLY CHARGED RITUALS

Boundaries between boys and girls are also emphasized and maintained by heterosexually charged rituals like cross-sex chasing. Formal games of tag and informal episodes of chasing punctuate life on playgrounds. The informal episodes usually open with a provocation—taunts like "You can't get me!" or "Slobber monster!"; bodily pokes; or the grabbing of possessions like a hat or scarf. The person who is provoked may ignore the taunt or poke, handle it verbally ("Leave me alone!"), or respond by chasing. After a chasing sequence, which may end after a short run or a pummeling, the chaser and chased may switch roles.

Chasing has a gendered structure. When boys chase one another, they often end up wrestling or in mock fights. When girls chase girls, they less often wrestle one another to the ground. Unless organized as a formal game like "freeze tag," same-gender chasing goes unnamed and usually undiscussed. But children set apart cross-gender chasing with special names— "girls chase the boys"; "boys chase the girls"; "the chase"; "chasers"; "chase and kiss"; "kiss-chase"; "kissers and chasers"; "kiss or kill"—and with animated talk about the activity. The names vary by region and school, but inevitably contain both gender and sexual meanings.

When boys and girls chase one another, they become, by definition, separate teams. Gender terms override individual identities, especially for the other team: "Help, a girl's chasin' me!"; "C'mon Sarah, let's get that boy"; "Tony, help save me from the girls." Individuals may call for help from, or offer help to, others of their gender. In acts of treason they may also grab someone of their gender and turn them over to the opposing team, as when, in the Michigan school, Ryan grabbed Billy from behind, wrestled him to the ground, and then called, "Hey girls, get 'im."

Names like "chase and kiss" mark the sexual meanings of cross-gender chasing. The threat of kissing—most often girls threatening to kiss boys—is a ritualized form of provocation. Teachers and aides are often amused by this form of play among children in the lower grades. They are more perturbed by cross-gender chasing among fifth- and sixth-graders, perhaps because at those ages some girls "have their development" (breasts make sexual meanings seem more consequential), and because of the more elaborate patterns of touch and touch avoidance in chasing rituals among older children. The principal of one Michigan school forbade the sixth-graders from playing "pom-pom," a complicated chasing game, because it entailed "inappropriate touch."

Cross-gender chasing is sometimes structured around rituals of pollution, such as "cooties," where individuals or groups are treated as contaminating or "carrying germs." Children have rituals for transferring cooties (usually touching someone else and shouting "You've got cooties!"), for immunization (e.g., writing "CV" for "cootie vaccination" on their arms), and for eliminating cooties (e.g., saying "no gives" or using "cootie catchers" made of folded paper). Boys may transmit cooties, but cooties usually originate with girls. One version of cooties played in Michigan is called "girl stain." Although cooties is framed as play, the import may be serious. Female pariahs—the ultimate school untouchables by virtue of gender and some added stigma such as being overweight or from a very poor family—are sometimes called "cootie queens" or "cootie girls." Conversely, we have never heard or read about "cootie kings" or "cootie boys."

In these cross-gender rituals girls are defined as sexual. Boys sometimes threaten to kiss girls, but it is girls' kisses and touch which are deemed especially contaminating. Girls more often use the threat of kissing to tease boys and to make them run away, as in this example recorded among fourth-graders on the playground of the California school:

> Smiling and laughing, Lisa and Jill pulled a fourth-grade boy along by his hands, while a group of girls sitting on the jungle-gym called out, "Kiss him, kiss him." Grabbing at his hair, Lisa said to Jill, "Wanna kiss Jonathan?" Jonathan got away, and the girls chased after him. "Jill's gonna kiss your hair," Lisa yelled.

The use of kisses as a threat is double-edged, since the power comes from the threat of pollution. A girl who frequently uses this threat may be stigmatized as a "kisser."

Gender-marked rituals of teasing, chasing, and pollution heighten the boundaries between boys and girls. They also convey assumptions which get worked into later sexual scripts: (1) that girls and boys are members of distinctive, opposing, and sometimes antagonistic groups; (2) that cross-gender contact is potentially sexual and contaminating, fraught with both pleasure and danger; and (3) that girls are more sexually defined (and polluting) than boys.

Conclusion

Social scientists have often viewed the heterosexual dating rituals of adolescence—when girls and boys "finally" get together—as the concluding stage after the separate, presumably non-sexual, boys' and girls' groups that are so prevalent in childhood. We urge a closer look at the organization of sexuality and of gender in middle and late childhood. The gender-divided social worlds of children are not totally asexual. And same-gender groups have continuing import in the more overtly sexual scripts of adolescence and adulthood.

From an early age "the sexual" is prescriptively heterosexual and male homophobic. Children draw on sexual meanings to maintain gender segregation—to make cross-gender interaction risky and to mark and ritualize boundaries between "the boys" and "the girls." In their separate gender groups, girls and boys learn somewhat different patterns of bonding—boys sharing the arousal of group rule-breaking; girls emphasizing the construction of intimacy and themes of romance. Coming to adolescent sexual intimacy from different and asymmetric gender subcultures, girls and boys bring somewhat different needs, capacities, and types of knowledge.

17 "But What Do You Mean?" Women and Men in Conversation

DEBORAH TANNEN

We seldom realize how precarious social interaction is between men and women. For the most part, we manage to get our ideas across to one another with little difficulty. Sometimes, however, communication across gender lines leaves us headshakingly confused that "the other" could have said that, thought that, done that—giving us a glimmer that our worlds really are different. Sociologically, men and women represent distinct worlds of socialization—with all the differences this implies, from ideas about sex and love to the best ways to get ahead in life.

Are these statements exaggerations? Or are there really such fundamental differences in male/female communications? You be the judge, as you read Tannen's summary of how women and men communicate. Compare her analysis with your own experiences. You might also consider the implications of this analysis for problems that are experienced by couples "going together," as well as for difficulties between husbands and wives.

CONVERSATION IS A RITUAL. We say things that seem obviously the thing to say, without thinking of the literal meaning of our words, any more than we expect the question "How are you?" to call forth a detailed account of aches and pains.

Unfortunately, women and men often have different ideas about what's appropriate, different ways of speaking. Many of the conversational rituals common among women are designed to take the other person's feelings into account, while many of the conversational rituals common among men are designed to maintain the one-up position, or at least avoid appearing one-down. As a result, when men and women interact—especially at work—it's often women who are at the disadvantage. Because women are not trying to avoid the one-down position, that is unfortunately where they may end up.

Here are the biggest areas of miscommunication.

1. Apologies

Women are often told they apologize too much. The reason they're told to stop doing it is that, to many men, apologizing seems synonymous with putting oneself down. But there are many times when "I'm sorry" isn't self-deprecating, or even an apology; it's an automatic way of keeping both speakers on an equal footing. For example, a well-known columnist once interviewed me and gave me her phone number in case I needed to call her back. I misplaced the number and had to go through the newspaper's main switchboard. When our conversation was winding down and we'd both made ending-type remarks, I added "Oh, I almost forgot—I lost your direct number, can I get it again?" "Oh, I'm sorry," she came back instantly, even though she had done nothing wrong and *I* was the one who'd lost the number. But I understood she wasn't really apologizing; she was just automatically reassuring me she had no intention of denying me her number.

Even when "I'm sorry" *is* an apology, women often assume it will be the first step in a two-step ritual: I say "I'm sorry" and take half the blame, then you take the other half. At work, it might go something like this:

A. When you typed this letter, you missed this phrase I inserted.
B. Oh, I'm sorry. I'll fix it.
A. Well, I wrote it so small it was easy to miss.

When both parties share blame, it's a mutual face-saving device. But if one person, usually the woman, utters frequent apologies and the other doesn't, she ends up looking as if she's taking the blame for mishaps that aren't her fault. When she's only partially to blame, she looks entirely in the wrong.

I recently sat in on a meeting at an insurance company where the sole woman, Helen, said "I'm sorry" or "I apologize" repeatedly. At one point she said, "I'm thinking out loud. I apologize." Yet the meeting was intended to be an informal brain-storming session, and *everyone* was thinking out loud.

The reason Helen's apologies stood out was that she was the only person in the room making so many. And the reason I was concerned was that Helen felt the annual bonus she had received was unfair. When I interviewed her colleagues, they said that Helen was one of the best and most productive workers—yet she got one of the smallest bonuses. Although the problem might have been outright sexism, I suspect her speech style, which differs from that of her male colleagues, masks her competence.

Unfortunately, not apologizing can have its price too. Since so many women use ritual apologies, those who don't may be seen as hard-edged. What's important is to be aware of how often you say you're sorry (and why), and to monitor your speech based on the reaction you get.

2. *Criticism*

A woman who co-wrote a report with a male colleague was hurt when she read a rough draft to him and he leapt into a critical response—"Oh, that's too dry! You have to make it snappier!" She herself would have been more likely to say, "That's a really good start. Of course, you'll want to make it a little snappier when you revise."

Whether criticism is given straight or softened is a matter of convention. In general, women use more softeners. I noticed this difference when talking to an editor about an essay I'd written. While going over changes she wanted to make, she said, "There's one more thing. I know you may not agree with me. The reason I noticed the problem is that your other points are so lucid and elegant." She went on hedging for several more sentences until I put her out of her misery: "Do you want to cut that part?" I asked—and of course she did. But I appreciated her tentativeness. In contrast, another editor (a man) I once called summarily rejected my idea for an article by barking, "Call me when you have something new to say."

Those who are used to ways of talking that soften the impact of criticism may find it hard to deal with the right-between-the-eyes style. It has its own logic, however, and neither style is intrinsically better. People who prefer criticism given straight are operating on an assumption that feelings aren't involved. "Here's the dope. I know you're good; you can take it."

3. *Thank-Yous*

A woman manager I know starts meetings by thanking everyone for coming, even though it's clearly their job to do so. Her "thank-you" is simply a ritual.

A novelist received a fax from an assistant in her publisher's office; it contained suggested catalogue copy for her book. She immediately faxed him her suggested changes and said, "Thanks for running this by me," even though her contract gave her the right to approve all copy. When she thanked the assistant, she fully expected him to reciprocate: "Thanks for giving me such a quick response." Instead, he said, "You're welcome." Suddenly, rather than an equal exchange of pleasantries, she found herself positioned as the recipient of a favor. This made her feel like responding, "Thanks for nothing!"

Many women use "thanks" as an automatic conversation starter and closer; there's nothing literally to thank you for. Like many rituals typical of women's conversation, it depends on the goodwill of the other to restore the balance. When the other speaker doesn't reciprocate, a woman may feel like someone on a seesaw whose partner abandoned his end. Instead of balancing in the air, she has plopped to the ground, wondering how she got there.

4. Fighting

Many men expect the discussion of ideas to be a ritual fight—explored through verbal opposition. They state their ideas in the strongest possible terms, thinking that if there are weaknesses someone will point them out, and by trying to argue against those objections, they will see how well their ideas hold up.

Those who expect their own ideas to be challenged will respond to another's ideas by trying to poke holes and find weak links—as a way of *helping*. The logic is that when you are challenged you will rise to the occasion: Adrenaline makes your mind sharper, you get ideas and insights you would not have thought of without the spur of battle.

But many women take this approach as a personal attack. Worse, they find it impossible to do their best work in such a contentious environment. If you're not used to ritual fighting, you begin to hear criticism of your ideas as soon as they are formed. Rather than making you think more clearly, it makes you doubt what you know. When you state your ideas, you hedge in order to fend off potential attacks. Ironically, this is more likely to *invite* attack because it makes you look weak.

Although you may never enjoy verbal sparring, some women find it helpful to learn how to do it. An engineer who was the only woman among four men in a small company found that as soon as she learned to argue, she was accepted and taken seriously. A doctor attending a hospital staff meeting made a similar discovery. She was becoming more and more angry with a male colleague who'd loudly disagreed with a point she'd made. Her better judgment told her to hold her tongue, to avoid making an enemy of this powerful senior colleague. But finally she couldn't hold it any longer, and she rose to her feet and delivered an impassioned attack on his position. She sat down in a panic, certain she had permanently damaged her relationship with him. To her amazement, he came up to her afterward and said, "That was a great rebuttal. I'm really impressed. Let's go out for a beer after work and hash out our approaches to this problem."

5. Praise

A manager I'll call Lester had been on his new job six months when he heard that the women reporting to him were deeply dissatisfied. When he talked to them about it, their feelings erupted; two said they were on the verge of quitting because he didn't appreciate their work, and they didn't want to wait to be fired. Lester was dumbfounded: He believed they were doing a fine job. Surely, he thought, he had said nothing to give them the impression he didn't like their work. And indeed he hadn't. That was the problem. He had said *nothing*—and the women assumed he was following the adage "If you can't say something nice, don't say anything." He thought he was showing confidence in them by leaving them alone.

Men and women have different habits in regard to giving praise. For example, Deidre and her colleague William both gave presentations at a conference. Afterward, Deidre told William, "That was a great talk." He thanked her. Then she asked, "What did you think of mine?" and he gave her a lengthy and detailed critique. She found it uncomfortable to listen to his comments. But she assured herself that he meant well, and that his honesty was a signal that she, too, should be honest when he asked for a critique of his performance. As a matter of fact, she had noticed quite a few ways in which he could have improved his presentation. But she never got a chance to tell him because he never asked—and she felt put down. The worst part was that it seemed she had only herself to blame, since she *had* asked what he thought of her talk.

But had she really asked for his critique? The truth is, when she asked for his opinion, she was expecting a compliment, which she felt was more or less required following anyone's talk. When he responded with criticism, she figured, Oh, he's playing "Let's critique each other"—not a game she'd initiated, but one which she was willing to play. Had she realized he was going to criticize her and not ask her to reciprocate, she would never have asked in the first place.

It would be easy to assume that Deidre was insecure, whether she was fishing for a compliment or soliciting a critique. But she was simply talking automatically, performing one of the many conversational rituals that allow us to get through the day. William may have sincerely misunderstood Deidre's intention—or may have been unable to pass up a chance to one-up her when given the opportunity.

6. Complaints

"Troubles talk" can be a way to establish rapport with a colleague. You complain about a problem (which shows that you are just folks) and the other person responds with a similar problem (which puts you on equal footing).

But while such commiserating is common among women, men are likely to hear it as a request to solve the problem.

One woman told me she would frequently initiate what she thought would be pleasant complaint-airing sessions at work. She'd just talk about situations that bothered her just to talk about them, maybe to understand them better. But her male office mate would quickly tell her how she could improve the situation. This left her feeling condescended to and frustrated. She was delighted to see this very impasse in a section in my book *You Just Don't Understand,* and showed it to him. "Oh," he said, "I see the problem. How can we solve it?" Then they both laughed, because it had happened again: He short-circuited the detailed discussion she'd hoped for and cut to the chase of finding a solution.

Sometimes the consequences of complaining are more serious: A man might take a woman's lighthearted griping literally, and she can get a reputation as a chronic malcontent. Furthermore, she may be seen as not up to solving the problems that arise on the job.

7. Jokes

I heard a man call in to a talk show and say, "I've worked for two women and neither one had a sense of humor. You know, when you work with men, there's a lot of joking and teasing." The show's host and the guest (both women) took his comment at face value and assumed the women this man worked for were humorless. The guest said, "Isn't it sad that women don't feel comfortable enough with authority to see the humor?" The host said, "Maybe when more women are in authority roles, they'll be more comfortable with power." But although the women this man worked for *may* have taken themselves too seriously, it's just as likely that they each had a terrific sense of humor, but maybe the humor wasn't the type he was used to. They may have been like the woman who wrote to me: "When I'm with men, my wit or cleverness seems inappropriate (or lost!) so I don't bother. When I'm with my women friends, however, there's no hold on puns or cracks and my humor is fully appreciated."

The types of humor women and men tend to prefer differ. Research has shown that the most common form of humor among men is razzing, teasing, and mock-hostile attacks, while among women it's self-mocking. Women often mistake men's teasing as genuinely hostile. Men often mistake women's mock self-deprecation as truly putting themselves down.

Women have told me they were taken more seriously when they learned to joke the way the guys did. For example, a teacher who went to a national

conference with seven other teachers (mostly women) and a group of administrators (mostly men) was annoyed that the administrators always found reasons to leave boring seminars, while the teachers felt they had to stay and
take notes. One evening, when the group met at a bar in the hotel, the principal asked her how one such seminar had turned out. She retorted, "As soon
as you left, it got much better." He laughed out loud at her response. The
playful insult appealed to the men—but there was a trade-off. The women
seemed to back off from her after this. (Perhaps they were put off by her
using joking to align herself with the bosses.)

There is no "right" way to talk. When problems arise, the culprit may be
style differences—and *all* styles will at times fail with others who don't
share or understand them, just as English won't do you much good if you try
to speak to someone who knows only French. If you want to get your message
across, it's not a question of being "right"; it's a question of using language
that's shared—or at least understood.

PART V

Social Groups and Social Structure

No ONE IS ONLY A MEMBER of humanity in general; each of us is also a member of particular social groups. We live in a certain country and in a particular neighborhood. We belong to a family and are members of a gender and a racial–ethnic group. We have certain *peers*—like–minded people, often close to us in age—with whom we identify. Most of us work at a job and have friends, and many of us go to school or belong to churches, clubs, or other social organizations. The articles in this Part are meant to sensitize us to how social groups and social structure have far-reaching effects on our lives. Let's see what some of those effects are.

No fact of social life is more important than group membership. *To belong to a group is to yield to others the right to make certain decisions about our behavior, while assuming obligations to act according to the expectations of those others.* This is illustrated by a parent saying to a teenage daughter or son, "As long as you are living under my roof, you had better be home by midnight." In this instance, the parents are saying that as long as the daughter or son wants to remain a good-standing member of the social group known as the family, her or his behavior must conform to their expectations. So it is with *all* the groups to which we belong: By our membership and participation in them, we relinquish to others at least some control over our own lives.

Those memberships that come with our birth are called *involuntary memberships* or *associations*. These include our family and our gender and racial– ethnic groups. In contrast, those groups which we choose to join are called *voluntary memberships* or *associations*. The Boy and Girl Scouts, professional associations, church groups, clubs, friendship cliques, and work groups are examples. In certain instances, we willingly, sometimes even gladly, conform to the group's rules and expectations in order to become members. In all groups, we must modify some of our behaviors in order to remain members in good standing.

Not all memberships in voluntary associations involve the same degree of willingness to yield to others a measure of control over our lives. There even are groups, as in some jobs, where we can hardly bear to remain a member but feel that, under the circumstances, we cannot quit. Sociologists still use the term *voluntary association* to refer to such memberships. *Both* voluntary and involuntary memberships have deep effects on our lives, for our participation in a group, whether it is willing or unwilling, shapes not only our behaviors but also our ideas about life.

It is easy to see that social groups have far-reaching effects on our lives—for, as stressed in Part IV, we would not even be "human" without group membership. But what about the second term in the title of this Part? What does *social structure* mean? By this term, sociologists mean that the various social groups that make up our lives are not simply a random collection of components; rather, they are interrelated. The specific ways they are put together shapes them into a significant unit, one that surrounds us from birth.

I know that if any term in sociology sounds vague and irrelevant, it is *social structure*. This term, however, also refers to highly significant matters—for *the social organization that underlies your life determines your relationships with others.* To better see what this term means, we can note that "social structure" encompasses five "levels." As I summarize them, I shall go from the broadest to the narrowest level.

The first two levels are *inter*societal; that is, they refer to international relationships. *First,* on the broadest level, social structure refers to relationships among blocs (or groups) of nations. Examples are the West's dependence on the Middle East for much of its oil, and the domination of the poor, Least Industrialized Nations by the wealthy, Most Industrialized Nations. The *second* level, the next broadest, refers to relationships between particular nations, such as the extensive role that the United States plays in the Canadian economy. These first two levels—the international dimensions of social structure—sensitize us to relationships based on historical events as well as current balances of power and the division of resources among nations.

The next three levels are *intra*societal; that is, they refer to relationships *within* a society. The *first* level is quite broad. It refers to how the social institutions within a society are related to one another. This level sensitizes us to how political decisions affect the military, how economic booms and busts affect families, and the like. The *second,* a narrower level, refers to patterns among social groups, such as the relationship between McDonald's and other firms in the fast-food business. The *third,* the narrowest level, refers to how people are organized within a particular group—such as an individual's role as leader or follower. Another example is the parents' authority over their young children that empowers them to determine what the children eat, where they live, what schools they attend, and how they are to be disciplined.

This Part opens with an unusual focus, that of car selling. Helene Lawson, who interviewed men and women who sell cars, details how the socialization we stressed in Part IV shows up in distinct sales styles. (Another way of phrasing this is that gender is part of the social structure of the automobile industry—just as it is part of our own experience of social life, whatever corner of society we find ourselves in.) Kandi Stinson then analyzes the interaction of women in a weight loss group, noting that their behavior and orientations are so ritualized that they can be compared to a religion. In the next article, Mae Biggs and I analyze how nonsexuality is produced and sustained during pelvic examinations. Elliot Liebow then reports on his participant observation study of a shelter for homeless women. In the closing selection, William Thompson analyzes how morticians cope with the stigma that attaches to their work.

A DIGRESSION ON PARTICIPANT OBSERVATION

Because the articles in this Part—and many others in the book—are based on participant observation, it is useful to take a closer look at this research method. Lawson observed car salespeople at work (and also interviewed them). Stinson attended meetings at a local weight loss organization. Before Biggs went to graduate school in sociology, she worked for years as a gynecological nurse. Liebow, who became concerned about homeless people, spent time in their shelters and even loaned money to the homeless women. To do his research, Thompson observed undertakers at work and also interviewed them. As these researchers *participated* in the lives of the people they were studying, they systematically *observed* what was happening; hence the term *participant observation*.

To gather their data, participant observers sometimes place greater emphasis on observing people, at other times on participating in their lives. Lawson's focus was observation of the car salespeople, and she did little participation. In contrast, because Biggs didn't go to graduate school until after many years of work as a gynecological nurse, her emphasis was almost solely on participation. This is also the basis of Liebow's study of the homeless and Stinson's analysis of women dieters. Regardless of whether participation or observation receives the greater emphasis, when a researcher reports on personal observations of a social setting, the term *participant observation* is used to describe this method of studying social life. (The terms *field research, fieldwork, ethnographic research,* and *qualitative research* are also used to refer to this technique of studying people.)

Participant observation allows researchers to provide rich, detailed descriptions that, by retaining some of the "flavor" of the settings, bring the reader close to the events that occurred. Thus, in the article on the homeless you can sense the crushing despair of the women who stay at these shelters. Although participant observation lends itself to such rich, insightful descriptions, it is not the method, of course, but the author who does the communicating. We depend on an author's skills for learning what life is like in some group, even for gaining a sense of being there. Consequently, in article 23, in the next Part, the account of the experiment on conformity, although it is far from participant observation, you will feel the dilemma faced by the experimenter's victims.

As I stressed in my article on research methods in Part II, a chief concern of sociologists is to gather accurate information about the people they study. To do this, sociologists try to be objective, to leave their biases behind both when they gather data and as they interpret those data for books, articles, and other reports they write. A primary distinction between research methods is whether they are *quantitative* or *qualitative.* Participant observation is an example of a qualitative method, and is exploratory or descriptive. Quantitative methods, in contrast, place the emphasis on measuring precise differences between individuals and groups.

Through their training and experience, sociologists come to prefer some particular method of gathering data. They also associate with one another, both on the basis of the subject matter they are interested in *and* on the basis of the research methods they employ. Consequently, the qualitative and quantitative approaches to social research have become major identifiers among sociologists. Although sociologists have their preferences, and sometimes feel strongly that one approach is vastly superior, both qualitative and quantitative methods are valid means with which to gather data about social life.

In this book, the emphasis is on studies based on the qualitative approach. These selections impart the meanings and experiences of the groups being studied, sometimes even the "flavor" of being a member of these groups. This approach, in my biased opinion, best imparts the excitement of sociological discovery.

18 Attacking Nicely: Women Selling Cars

HELENE M. LAWSON

The articles in the preceding Part stressed how boys and girls experience childhood differently. These differences are not superficial, something that has little or no consequence for later life. We don't simply throw childhood experiences away, shoving them into the back of some closet, as we might do with a discarded toy. Rather, we carry these experiences with us for the rest of our lives. Our distinct socialization as boys or girls equips us with specific sets of attitudes, behaviors, and orientations. These become an essential part of how we view and approach the world, helping to set us on different paths in life's journey

The result is not that all women act one way and all men another. Sociologists don't make such a claim. Rather, they say that because of our socialization, women and men tend to show distinct approaches to life's tasks. These differences are often subtle, but they show up in almost everything we do. In Lawson's analysis of people who sell cars, some of these distinctions become apparent. None of these characteristics is inevitable, the unvarying consequence of biology, or socialization, or a combination thereof. As socialization changes, then, we can expect to see these behaviors—and even feelings—similarly change.

IN OUR SOCIETY car sales work goes against the norms of trust in human relations. Customers are aware that salespersons are trained in impression management techniques based on empathy to win confidence or on aggressive intimidation to overcome resistance to high prices (Oda 1983; Prus 1989). In addition, the car business is unstable; salesman and customers will probably never see each other again. This makes for transient relationships and an environment where the building of trust is problematic. In fact, throughout the whole social structure of sales interactions, there is little trust.

Researchers find that persons who enter this occupation cope with dishonesty, distrust, and immoral dealings in various ways. One way is to concentrate on monetary goals as a measure of success and status (Leidner

1991). A second way is to suppress reflections on the unethical tasks they perform (Oakes 1990). A third way is to claim innocence through apparent unawareness of illicit doings. A fourth way is to claim one was merely following orders. And lastly, workers blame the recipients or victims of their services for negative interactions (Hughes 1962).

Working under these conditions is especially problematic for women who have been socialized as mothers and care takers to be concerned with the needs of others and to maintain honesty in relations (Dinnerstein 1976; Mead 1934; Chodorow 1978; Gilligan 1982). Although few articles have been written about women's experience in the field of high commission sales, there is research on women in other high pressure, male-dominated fields such as management (Kanter 1977) and the military (Rustad 1984). These studies find that women take on stereotypical male or female roles to adapt to a structure in which they experience inherent role conflict (Turner 1990).

My research examines how women handle the conflict between their socialized roles and their adopted role of car salesperson. I will describe both how the women themselves change and how they are also changing the interactions within the workplace, shaping new definitions of what it is to be a car salesperson. This study, therefore, analyzes modes of personal adaption as well as modes of social change. To provide a framework for understanding these changes, I have identified a concept—adapting to an incompatible status through role making—as well as five categories of this concept, "Innocents," "Ladies," "Tough Guys," "Reformers," and "Retreaters." I use these categories to describe how women deal with co-workers and customers when they enter the field, and the changes that emerge as they progress along their career paths, from selling their first cars to becoming experienced salespersons. In an effort to explore the ways in which gender roles operate in the bartering and negotiations endemic to selling cars, the article focuses on saleswomen's initial values and attitudes toward co-workers and customers, the adaptations they make as they become more experienced, and finally, the ways in which some women change the dealership itself.

Data Collection and Sample

I collected the data for this study from in-depth interviews with and observations of 35 car saleswomen and 15 car salesmen at car agencies and restaurants in the Chicago metropolitan area, over a period of three years. The informants were recontacted at intervals in order to follow their career paths. In two instances, I became a customer out of necessity because I needed a car, buying automobiles from women who did not know I was doing research until after the purchases were completed. An additional male informant was a personal friend who began selling on a commission basis about the same time I started to do my research and who spoke with me about his progress on a daily basis.

How Women Come In

An examination of the work women did before beginning car sales shows that most had traditional women's careers, such as teaching, waitressing, social work, retail sales, and secretarial jobs. These occupations primarily involved service to others and paid low wages. Although ex-teachers complained that students were discipline problems, "little monsters" and "heathens," and ex-sales clerks and beauticians said customers were "pains in the ass," because they returned used merchandise or couldn't make up their minds about how they wanted their hair done, the women basically liked what they did in these jobs, especially the supportive relationships they had with co-workers. However, these women found it difficult to make a living and support families. Such women, with no previous sales experience, were usually encouraged to try car sales by male friends or family members who stressed the possibility of better pay. When they entered car sales, many assumed they would be able to make friends and establish good co-worker relations as they had done at their previous work. Nina commented:

> I used to cashier at a discount drug store, The pay was bad, but I got a real break on formula for the baby and make-up and stuff like that. Mostly, I stayed because the other saleswomen were terrific. We laughed a lot. . . . told each other our problems. When the store closed, I decided to try car sales. I figured, "What the hell. People like me. I shouldn't have a problem." And I was excited to work for commission.

The hours are very long in car sales and salesmen, for the most part, socialize during slow times, telling each other how well they are doing, commiserating over losses, telling jokes, or "kibitzing." To further cement friendships, many salesmen go drinking together after work. Most had been in car sales before so they knew others in the field. But even male novices to car sales said they were accepted by one clique or another. Newcomer women also attempted to befriend salesmen and socialize during slow times. They want to talk about a customer who gave them a hard time, family life, or even the weather. But when they approached the men, the women were usually rejected or harassed. Nina related:

When I would try to make conversation with other salesman they were very gross. They swear. They pat you on the butt like this. If I did well, the guys would say, "What do you need to sell a car, a bra?" If I was five minutes late, the boss would send me home. The guys would laugh. They made me an example.

Women who attempted to go to bars with salesmen after working hours developed a bad reputation. Evelyn observed:

You have to be careful. Women learn quick around here. You don't party. You don't hang out with the guys after work. Those who do are called "sluts" or "whores."

Co-worker relations between men and women were strained, and since there were usually only one or two saleswomen at most dealerships, women could not form their own cliques. Interactions between the two sexes remained an area of conflict, and probably will continue as such until there is a more equal balance between women and men car salespersons.

There are, however, more important areas than co-worker relations on which women must concentrate. If they are to succeed, saleswomen must interact well with customers. Yet, all 35 saleswomen remembered many initial contact experiences with male customers as upsetting and negative. These women agreed that most "older" men reacted in a rude, insulting manner when approached. Some openly refused to deal with women. Sara said these men "did not want to answer questions about their income or credit rating, or even discuss cars with a woman." Arlene said some "older men used foul language," or were so abrasive that saleswomen ended up "turning them over to a salesman." Because new saleswomen generally began work with no car sales experience, this rejection added to their self doubt and caused them to feel they needed to learn more about cars in order to sell them.

The car has traditionally been identified with men, and most saleswomen said they knew "little" about automobiles. They did not grow up fixing cars, talking about them with friends, or understanding how they operate. Therefore, at the beginning, many of the women said they thought it was most important to become technically knowledgeable about cars. Joyce had been in car sales for two months:

I think it is important to be able to talk to a customer about the vehicle—to understand how the engine works and what benefits the make has over others. I watch videos. I listen to other salesmen. I read all the pamphlets. I want to learn as much as I can.

To make matters more difficult, salespersons were not given much training. Newcomers were usually "thrown out on the floor" and had to figure out what to do on their own. Newcomers, men or women, had a hard time closing their first sales, because they lacked experience. Novices were generally hired by the type of dealership salespersons called "green pea stores." This is an agency which usually hires inexperienced salespersons and has managers close sales in the final stages of bargaining. Larry, a general manager, explained the social arrangements of these types of sales which function to shelter newcomers from the guilt and pressure of customer relations:

> They [management] try to keep new salespeople in the dark as far as gross cost on cars. They think it makes them more believable to customers. If the manager tells you, "no, you can't sell that car for this amount," for whatever reason, "this is the price you got to sell it for," you have to go out there, and that is what you do.

Ann, whose father owned a car dealership, said that even more experienced salespersons only got to see the front page of an invoice:

> There's an invoice that they [the dealership] can show you [the salesperson] and a customer can buy the car, usually for $100 over the invoice. But, you [the salesperson] will never see the back page which is all their profit. When they [the dealership] sell a car for invoice there is like about $1,200 usually in that figure. If you're talking Cadillac, it's more like $5,000.

Once newcomers in green pea stores had been at work a month or so, management expected them to begin to close on their own. Although salespersons were told by management at the beginning of their careers that making money for the dealership was paramount, the first steps most salespersons, men or women, took was to try to sell the customer a car close to the amount he or she wanted to pay. Generally this was lower than management would like, and meant a smaller commission for the salesperson. However, most women said pleasing the customer through a cheap price made them feel good because they felt they were helping someone.

> At the beginning I believed I didn't need to be greedy because there was a price I could sell at that would make everybody happy—the customer, my manager and myself. If you sell enough cars, you are going to make money anyway.

How Women Change

Yet, what women said about first sales in which they made high commissions show how their values were affected by their work. Fran discussed her new attitude:

I'll tell you about my first big sale because that one I remember very well. I was working for about a couple [of] weeks, and it was right after the auto show, and a young dentist came in with his wife, and he had his hands in his pockets jingling his money, and he goes, "I want to buy a Spider [Alfa Romeo]." I found out what the list price was and I wrote it down. I got a $5,000 deposit from him and he took his credit out and I knew nothing. I went into the boss and he almost died. So he goes, "Don't lose this one!" I sold that car way over cost and I didn't even know I was doing it. It was the most exciting thing I had ever done. When he [the customer] came in to pick up the car, he said, "I wanted that car so bad, and I guess I really got screwed." At the beginning I believed it was wrong to ask for too much money—that it was greedy. After that, I started going for the buck.

This sale was exciting for many reasons. It was unexpected, the manager was pleased, and the saleswoman made a large commission. But most of all, selling seemed so easy, as though it were done through luck or magic. Therefore, the saleswoman did not need to blame herself for "screwing" the customer. Events like this became a turning point in women's careers, when attitudes and values toward making lots of money at others' expense became fun.

And in order to sell themselves, women developed roles. They made tools of their personalities and gender traits in order to coerce customers into buying cars, distancing themselves from their potential disloyalty to the other in the relationship.

Innocents

Probably because the first high commission sale made by most newcomers was painless and negotiated in ignorance, many women continued on in the role of the Innocent. Innocents did not use crude language or insider argot. They employed dress and demeanor to portray their particular role. Denise, a younger woman, played school girl:

I've got a baby face and I do not pose a threat to anybody who walks in—young, old, seasoned buyer, first timer. I put people at ease. I don't scare anybody. I've sold many campers wearing sweats with sorority letters on the bottom. I have a face that will show people I'm honest.

Innocents continued to view their success as "luck" or "magic," both factors out of their control. They said that most customers would sell themselves a car if they [the saleswomen] said little. Innocents adapted through avoidance. They wore blinders so they did not see the dubious dealings going on around them and could deny being a party to the transactions. The woman who sold me my most recent car exemplified this orientation. She originally described the car as having been a manufacturer representative's car, a "brass hat." A week after I purchased the car, I dropped my pen and was feeling around underneath the front seat, when I felt a small plastic object. This turned out to be a key chain from a car rental agency in Florida. It had my car's identification number on it.

I called the rental agency and they verified that the car had indeed been theirs but they had recently sold it to Mazda. I do not think I would have bought this car if I had known it was previously used as a rental car. When I confronted Phyllis with the key chain, she replied:

> Is that true? I never asked too many questions. I know I saw literature on the car. . . . that it came from an auction. I know they buy when Mazda is having auctions. I thought is was a manufacturer rep's car.

Other experienced Innocents in my study told me when sales are slow they "dummy up" [use ignorance to sell cars], because customers believed that newcomers did not possess the ability to devise ways of cheating them. The greater trust in the saleswoman made the customers less resistant to her pitches.

Ladies

Women who wished to remain in the field, but were uncomfortable with the Innocent role, had several options. One was to become Ladies, taking on exaggerated feminine characteristics. Ladies said customers were more easily manipulated through forms of stereotypical feminine behavior than through aggressive "pushy" tactics. They cajoled and nurtured male customers in order to deter sexual harassment and to sell cars. Their work relationships became patterned to fit relationships men have experienced in families. Ann, a 52-year-old grandmother, described how she used the goodness of her maternal role to gain trust and respect from her customers: "I tell them, 'Look at these pictures on my desk. I am a mother. I am a grandmother. I wouldn't hurt you, now would I?'"

Ladies helped customers feel comfortable, served them coffee, listened with apparent interest to their problems and generally treated them with familial warmth and hospitality. Rita labeled this method of sales "attacking nicely":

> You have to be nice and talk to the [customers] and make them feel at home before you can sell them a car. It is usually easier to sell a car if you establish rapport. This guy and I got to talking, and he said something about playing the

accordion and we established a great rapport because I play the accordion. He still drops in to see me every now and then.

Ladies also attempted to manipulate male management and co-workers through these stereotypical feminine traits. I watched saleswomen sew buttons on managers' and co-workers' shirts, bring them home cooked food, and do clerical chores such as locating cars, or assisting with paperwork. These Ladies were still seen as outsiders, different from the group, and less than equal; but they had become non-threatening, like older sisters or mothers, and they were respected. Mary played big sister:

> Salesmen come to me for advice with their love life. They don't treat me like I'm one of the guys. They watch their mouths. They are very careful about talking dirty or swearing or anything like that. They treat me like a lady.

Tough Guys

Some women went directly from Innocents to Tough Guys, where they attempted to adapt the aggressive, competitive male model of sales. Generally these women said they took on this role because they were told to "toughen up or get out." To toughen up means to block feelings. To Tough Guys this was interpreted as being able to handle verbal abuse in order to become "one of the boys." Once Sheila became insensitive toward the use of profanity and sexual innuendos, she was allowed to join the men:

> At first I used to break down and cry and show them I was scared or frightened of them. Then they just kept on more. They teased me, called me a "bimbo" and asked me if it was that time of the month when I got depressed. At home, we never swore; we showed respect. I had to toughen up. Me, I'm just like one of the guys. They use profanity; I do too.

This woman not only accepted harassment; she had been socialized to use it against others. Most Tough Guys worked at high-volume dealerships they labeled "Revolving Door," "Beat 'Em Up," and "Slam Dunk 'Em" stores. Generally, women at these agencies had to make enough sales to meet a high quota and were continually worried about being fired. Therefore, they learned to "fight for the door" [grab persons who walk in the door before other salespersons got to them], and pushed hard on these would-be customers, often intimidating them in order to make quick sales. This style of selling resulted in many negative interactions which Tough Guys blamed on customers.

Innocents and Ladies labeled customers too, but Tough Guys were more extreme in their antagonism. Innocents viewed customers as "knowledgeable about cars," but "rude" or "disrespectful." Tough Guys put customers in an "out-group" as "enemies" who needed to be conquered. Respondents described what they did using argot that depicted a wrestling match between themselves and the customer where they "pinned customers down." Tough Guy language became progressively more violent and warlike. Women claimed to "put customers away," and "do 'em in." Carol blamed the customer for causing the dishonesty and animosity in car sales:

> Some customers really want our vehicle, but they come here to see if they can rip you off, and they will. They lie about the condition of their trade-ins. They bring a car that they just brought to the repair shop and the mechanic said it was going to cost $700 to fix the damage. That's why they want to trade it in. They lie about their credit ratings, and they say they can get cars at other dealerships for less. The people who come in here can afford bucks. Probably, the more money they have, the harder it is to get it away from them.

Tough Guys valued most what the customer gave them, not what they could do for the customer. Gina defined a "good" customer as one who gave her lots of money, and a "bad" customer as one who tried to bargain:

> We have wonderful people like Mr. Smith. What a wonderful guy. He brought his wife with him. She picked out the car. They added every accessory on it imaginable. The first price that I gave him he bought the car at. So the dealership made millions of dollars on it, and I made millions of dollars on it. But other people are always trying to chew you down. They're whiners, complainers. They deserve nothing and wouldn't be happy under any circumstance.

Yet, even when Tough Guys sold at high volume dealerships, blamed the customer for dishonesty in the business, sold more aggressively, and distanced themselves from concern for customer needs, male co-workers felt female Tough Guys were not equal to salesmen in their competitive attitudes. Frank, a manager, said:

> The women, they're more laid back. They don't have what it takes, the "killer instinct." People will buy under pressure. They feel intimidated. I have the killer instinct. My first four months I was here every day, 12 hours a day, because I didn't want to miss anything. I wanted to have the most numbers. I just wanted to win. I wanted to be on top, to get every walk-in. Competitiveness. Just about every guy here now has it. They hate to lose.

I found that more than a few of the women informants—Innocents, Ladies, Reformers as well as Tough Guys, had to change their family and social life drastically in order to fit into the male work world and make a living wage. Married and single women had to curtail their social activities. Younger women even lived at home with their parents because they could not find the time to keep up an apartment. Not unexpectedly, divorced women like Fran, who were responsible for the care of young children, had the hardest time dividing their loyalties between work and family:

> Before, when I was married, I worked part-time at home doing typing. I was there when Billy came home from school and we did lots of things together. Now, I can only spend Sunday and Wednesday with him. I have no time for myself, and it's hard. I need to help him with homework, do chores like grocery shop and laundry, go to the dentist—things like that. It is very hard.

Yet Tough Guys, even those who found car sales hard work, did not fight for change. They continued to try and fit into the male model of work.

Reformers

Reformers believed that women were intrinsically better at selling than men. They generally began as Ladies who were motivated to change the way work was structured because of how they felt about what they did, and the conflict this brought them. Most Reformers were in conflict over the imposed priorities and resultant interactions between themselves and their customers. They wanted to be more client centered. Many wanted a life style that did not divide work from home so drastically.

Ladies who turned to Reform usually began by distancing themselves from male co-workers. They stopped mothering and nurturing them. Reformers usually continued to relate to customers through the role of Lady. Betty felt that most salesmen were crass, ignorant, and dishonest, and therefore, befriending them was dangerous:

> I am not like salesmen. We [women] are not even in the same business as they are. I am an educated professional. I smile, and am polite to them [male co-workers], but it is best to tell them nothing. They try to steal your customers. They lie to management about you.

Reformers who led Reform were very concerned with building trust. For this reason they were willing to risk effort and time in interactions that might not result in a sale. They spent more time with customers who were not easily sold, might need more time to consider their purchase, or wanted to "kick the tires," leave and perhaps return later. Reformers like Evelyn said patience and understanding bring in referrals because previous customers remember you:

> I come on very soft, and I spend a lot of time with people. If I'm not going to be able to make money, I still treat people nice and spend time with them, because down the road, I might get some business.

Lorber (1984) and Lunneborg (1990) found similar patterns in their studies. Medical women scheduled longer appointments with fewer patients in order to devote more time and energy to answering questions and listening to concerns. And, women stockbrokers spent more time learning about client's particular needs rather than attempting to push them into pre-arranged high-profit packages.

In addition to spending time developing trust, Reformers, more than any other category of saleswomen, fought for the stability needed to develop a work environment which encouraged trust. This was in opposition to the male sales model which defined success as a move to a higher volume and more lucrative dealership or a dealership that sold more expensive cars. Most salesmen moved from dealership to dealership, depending on where the "grass was greener," i.e., what cars were hotter sellers that season, where they thought they could make higher commissions, or where they were promised a contract for salary plus commission. In contrast, Nina managed to remain at her dealership for six years, and defined success in terms of stability, trust, and ongoing customer relationships as well as money gained:

> I have been here six years. Right now I'm not making as much money because the business is slow and the cars aren't selling as well as in the past, but I have repeaters and referrals and I still make a good living. If I move to another place, that place may not do so well in the long run. My boss trusts me, and it is a good place to work.

The concept of "trust" between management and salespersons was seldom found in this field, where upper management sometimes replaced complete sales forces overnight. When Reformers managed to be more stable, distrust was minimized for customers. Clients could expect to get to know their car salespersons and form ongoing trusting relationships concerning service or future dealings, as they do with doctors, dentists, or other tradepersons.

Some Reformers were willing to make less money to find time for family. A few women even fought for and achieved part-time status. Ann was ecstatic:

> After 12 years, I finally got management to let me work part-time. Now I have time for my grandchildren; I can go shopping with my daughter, and see some friends. I have missed doing these things. I have been put on salary so I make less, but I'm doing okay. The owner knows my capabilities, and I have lots of steadies. They're willing to come in when I'm there.

Although Ann became a part-timer in 1990, she was fired six months later. Her boss complained she "did not fit with the team any longer" and had "lost her love for the work." She felt the real story was that "the car business is in a recession," and she was "fully vested" in a retirement program which was costing the dealership too much to keep her. Ann seemed very confused by the owner's singular disloyalty to her after 13 years because she made "good money" for the dealer over a long period of time, and her part-time pay was a relatively small salary of $100 a day. Yet, the mere fact that Reformers were continuing to demand and receive shorter hours, a concession rarely heard of in this field, changed the structure of the workplace and set important precedents.

Retreaters

Early on, many newcomers became disenchanted with car sales because they could find no role that allowed them to adapt to the changes they had to undergo to make a living at this work. Most Retreaters left the field because they felt the customer deserved better treatment—more honesty, lower prices, and less pressure to buy something he or she did not need. Retreaters could not distance themselves from their feelings, and did not "feel good" about what they had to do to build a career in car sales. Leah quit after a year:

> I told my manager I wanted to sell a lot of cars cheaper, and he screamed at me. I would say, "I'll sell a whole bunch for you, but I'm not going to make a whole lot of money on any one of them because I just couldn't do that, because I've got to shop with these people and live with them."

Mary, in the business for six months, was also leaving:

> I don't like the selling aspect of car sales. If you do well and you make your boss happy, you feel sick inside. I have a conscience. I am not the kind of individual who can gain your confidence and respect during the initial transaction of purchasing a car and then when it comes down to the dollars and cents, treat you like I never met you, which is to make the highest profit off of you. 90% of the men in this business have no conscience. When you purchase a car and come back, they'll start hiding. They pretend they don't know you for fear you're coming back to make a complaint, to address something that was not dealt with properly in the first place. I don't like approaching people and having that look come over their faces and having to overcome that objection of, "No, I'm not a crook," and "Yes, I'll sell you a car cheap," knowing I can't because if you sell a car cheap the boss will say, "What are you doing, giving my cars away? Do you want to work here long?"

The sales culture's firmly established response to these self-recriminations was to encourage the salesperson's estrangement from a higher conscience (Prus 1989; Oakes 1990). Saleswomen were told to "toughen up or get out." They were expected to confine their emotions to feeling good about making a lot of money. If women complained to their bosses about their guilty consciences, they suffered negative sanctions. Complaints about having to overcharge or pressure customers resulted in ridicule, taunts, or they were sent home for the day. Such women were told they were weak and could not "make it" in car sales. On the other hand, saleswomen were praised and rewarded for how much over-invoice they could sell a car. A really big sale was talked about throughout the area dealerships and the salesperson became a celebrity. This resulted in a lack of introspection on the part of many salespersons. They stopped reflecting about what they were doing and reasoned that this was the way things should be done in order to keep the dealer in business and to keep their jobs.

Male Roles Compared

Males also take on the Innocent, Tough Guy, Retreater, and even a "Mr. Nice Guy" role, which is comparable to that of the Lady, but my principal observation is that all men who remained in the field eventually became Tough Guys. For these men, this role was not as much of an act as it appeared to be for the women. It is a role representing the behavior expected of salesmen by their peers. It seems to be a natural consequence, in the heat of the sales arena, for men eventually to become hard boiled. Men said that they wanted to be tough.

When men or women enter the field, they are forced into the role of the Innocent. However, none of the men interviewed in this study were without previous sales experience. So the Innocent role for men appears to be transient. Unlike women, who would cultivate the role of innocence, men wanted to shed any such appellation as soon as possible.

The Tough Guy role for men seemed to be something that became part of their personality over time. In contrast, the roles for women often appeared to be masks to hide their true identities and feelings—feelings which were often quite disparate from those they chose to express.

The Retreater men and the Retreater women were quite similar when interviewed. They were people who were unable to feel comfortable meeting management's expectations. One of the men who left car sales went into consumer electronic sales at a bargain center, where the prices were fixed and haggling was absent. He, as did the women, wanted more respect in his sales interactions.

Discussion

Interactions between salespersons and customers are becoming more positive through the moderating effect of women in the sales force. Their continued introspection and gendered values have exerted a subtle but significant influence. Car saleswomen's definition of success seemed to include more factors than mere profit. Quality of life, both at work and in the home, [was] more important to them than mere gain. Reformers defined success to include a stable work environment where trust could be built, and a home life which could include a family. These gendered values, reflected in the classification scheme used in my work, show that sales tactics based on these ethics help women to remain reflective, as well as to build success. The linking between the Reformer and the Lady categories is an argument in favor of the idea that the expression of even stereotypical female behavior may exert a positive influence in improving relations in the workplace.

However, changes that did take place depended upon the strategies adopted by the women, and the philosophy of the dealership where they worked. Often changes were not permanent. Yet, the fact that Reformers were usually top-volume sellers made them enviable examples to men they worked with. They showed men that profit need not be sacrificed in order to obtain other rewards such as job stability, trustful relations with customers, and shorter work hours to accommodate family life. These rewards, often thought to be unobtainable, may lure men to emulate women's examples. Because women are increasingly entering male fields where humaneness in relations has been devalued, their ability to construct role models combining profit-making with concern for others needs future study.

19 Religion and Morality in Weight Loss Groups

KANDI M. STINSON

As you have seen in the previous readings, the expectations of our culture and of social groups affect us deeply. You have seen how our social or cultural frameworks affect ideas about hospitality, violence, masculinity, femininity, our use of space as we interact with others, our expressions of sympathy, our presentation of the self to others, and the style of our conversations. These—and our other expectations of what is the right way to do social life—are the result of our exposure to culture and of specific groups within our society.

In this reading, we examine another aspect of how deeply culture and society affect us. We aren't born with ideas of what a "good" body looks like any more than we are born with ideas about what makes a "good" gift. Our ideas of "good" bodies—just like our ideas of how we should use social space or of how we should talk to others or how we should express sympathy—are the result of being socialized into a particular society at a particular time in history. Evidently, women are much more likely than men to learn that their bodies need to be customized—made smaller and reshaped—for they join weight loss groups in far larger numbers than men. As Kandi Stinson analyzes in this article, these weight loss groups have characteristics similar to religion.

IN THE GROUP of women dieters that I studied, I was struck by how much their activities and views resemble those of a religion. In this article, I will use the metaphor of religion to analyze what I observed in this group: temptation, guilt, confession, sacrifice, ritual, and above all, good, evil, and morality.

The ever-present struggle between good and evil, or between the sacred and the profane, animates weight loss groups. The religious model is easily recognized in popular culture. A single individual is literally split into a good person, represented by an angel, complete with white gown and halo, and a bad person, represented by the devil, bedecked in horns and tail. With these characters perched on opposite shoulders of the person caught in the middle, the battle lines are drawn. All that is left is to wait to see which side emerges victorious. In the context of weight loss, the battle between good and evil is similarly played out.

One week the informational topic was "being your own best friend." Gail arrives home from work. Her place set for dinner, Gail is just sitting down to eat when the phone rings. She answers, and apparently it's someone from the office who needs Gail's help with a computer problem. She begins to talk him through the problem and at the same time begins to nibble on a cake that's sitting on the table. At the end of the phone conversation, the person tells Gail she can enjoy her dinner now and, looking down, she realizes that she has eaten nearly the entire cake. At this point, a member exclaimed, "Oh, my gosh, she ate the whole thing!" Amy turned to me and said quietly, "I've done that before." When Gail gets off the phone, she's very upset, chides herself for really blowing it, and obviously feels very guilty.

At this point in the video, another Gail appears, who represents the negative voice inside her. The negative Gail points out that since Gail ate almost the whole cake, she might as well go ahead and finish it. The positive Gail now makes an appearance, and tells her that she doesn't have to eat it; she can throw the rest out. Gail struggles with the two voices for a while, but eventually, realizing that the positive voice is the real Gail, she banishes the negative Gail. The video ends by displaying the slogan, "Be your own best friend."

The videotape is remarkable for several reasons. Consonant with the metaphor of the battle between good and evil, the character in the video is split into two separate, warring selves. Particularly significant is the meaning of good and bad. The bad self gives in to temptation and loses control. The good self not only maintains sufficient self-control to withstand temptation, but feels the appropriate guilt and remorse when self-control is lost. Ultimately, the solution to the ongoing battle is to remove the temptation.

Temptation

Like sex, food poses particular difficulties in the battle against evil. Being bad is equated with giving in to sensual pleasure, in this case, the sensual pleasure of food. To resist temptation you must deny yourself that pleasure.

Food is divided into good foods and bad foods. Bad food leads to the sins of overindulgence and loss of self-control. For group members, bad, or in this group's term, red-light foods, pose the greatest danger. Supposedly, red-light foods vary from one person to another, and the key is to know your weaknesses. In reality, there is a short list of common red-light foods. Chocolate leads the list, followed closely by alcohol and high-fat, salty foods like potato chips. The potential sinfulness of red-light foods extends to the situations in which they are often eaten, including parties, weddings, and holiday celebrations. In a world where good and evil do constant battle, temptation is everywhere, so it is no surprise that resisting temptation is a frequent topic of discussion in weight loss groups, particularly around holidays.

The Road to Righteousness: Sacrifice and Deprivation

The dieter who withstands temptation is willing and able to deprive herself of tempting, desirable foods. The association of dieting with deprivation is pervasive. According to popular understanding, if overeating causes weight gain, then food restriction causes weight loss. In the name of losing weight, you deprive yourself of pleasurable foods and experiences, but the sacrifice pays off, as pounds are lost.

Altering food or substituting a "better" food for the one that's desired is a commonplace response to the need to sacrifice, one that simultaneously minimizes the sense of deprivation. At the beginning of one meeting, Debbie had on an apron and she greeted the group by saying, "Hi, I'm from Gertie's Home Cooking Restaurant. We have fried chicken and everything homemade from scratch." Debbie asked the group how we would feel about being somewhere like that. Betty laughed and said, "I'd love every bite of it. I love that food! But really, I'd rather not be there if I had a choice." This led to a discussion of common substitutions that can be made to make food healthier. Debbie asked for substitutions for foods she had listed on the flip chart: sour cream, sausage, light cream, butter, sugar, and cooking oil. Members suggested yogurt, low-fat or nonfat products, or using less than was called for in a particular recipe. Debbie then told us to take out our trackers (forms on which members are to record the foods they eat), write down a food we would be cooking that week, and suggest substitutions we could make. She gave us a couple of minutes and then asked someone to share. Betty said she was making a rump roast for friends who were moving. She was going to cook it ahead, and then refrigerate it, so she could skim the fat off before using the broth for gravy.

When faced with the prospect of traditional home cooking, Betty's first response is that she would love it, but on second thought, she suggests that the best choice is to choose not to be at the restaurant in the first place, thus avoiding temptation. The subsequent group discussion reinforces this as a wise choice. Betty can choose to eat traditional home cooking if she wants, but it is best if she eats it at home, rather than in a restaurant, and only after she has altered it to make it a better choice. In either case, she is sacrificing (or giving up) something she wants.

Traditionally, sacrifice plays a central role in religion. In the Judeo-Christian tradition, the Bible is filled with stories of extraordinary sacrifice, including that of Abraham, who is willing to sacrifice his son, and of Jesus, who sacrifices his life. On a more mundane level, followers are often expected to sacrifice (or give up) certain activities in the name of religion. Tithing, whereby church members pledge a certain percentage of their income to the church, at times requires a considerable sacrifice. In many cases, religion involves sacrificing certain pleasurable activities, including food consumption. At times the sacrifice is restricted to specific time periods, as when Catholics were previously prohibited from eating meat on Fridays, or when Christians "give up" something for Lent. At other times, the proscription involves food that is not to be consumed at all, whether it be alcohol, beef, pork, or some other food. Given the strong cultural association between dieting and deprivation, it is not surprising that group members see sacrifice as a central component of their weight loss efforts.

Giving in to Temptation: Guilt

Given the discomfort of deprivation and almost endless temptation, there is plenty of guilt to go around. When Peggy finally lost two pounds after several unsuccessful weeks on the program, Debbie asked her what she had done differently. Peggy admitted that she had finally used her tracker to record everything she ate. Sheepishly, she said, "I'm embarrassed to admit it now, but this is the first time I've done it. . . . I could really see what I was eating and how I had been cheating before."

The prospect of getting caught cheating by others, and the resultant guilt, also came up in conversations. It is not coincidental that when the meeting topic was food secrets, the issue of hiding food from other people was a prominent theme. Linda began the discussion by telling members that she regularly snuck donuts from the break room at work so that co-workers would not see her eating them. When Linda asked members why they thought she acted that way, one member suggested that Linda probably felt "guilty or ashamed." Later in the discussion of food secrets, Linda said that for a while she let her daughter help her by writing what Linda ate in her food tracker. The problem was that Linda would purposely not tell her daughter everything she ate, with the predictable result that Linda ate more food than she should have eaten.

Although the organization formulates the rules and tries to socialize members into accepting them, it is not entirely successful. Ultimately the organization depends on members' cooperation. This is particularly evident in the case of exercise. The organization's official position is clear: successful weight loss requires both reformed eating habits and regular exercise. Members receive a number of written materials with suggestions and guidelines for incorporating exercise into weight loss efforts, and the weekly journals for recording food intake also contain space for recording exercise. Members are supposed to exercise for at least twenty minutes per day, and leaders encourage members to increase their activity levels. Leaders often suggest easy ways to become more physically active and reward those who do with stickers.

It is apparent from group discussions that a good number of members, if not the majority, do not exercise regularly. At the same time, members feel little guilt for not meeting the organizational expectation. I never witnessed a member confessing a failure to exercise; just the opposite. Members saw exercise as an extra for which they deserved special recognition. The matter-of-fact way in which members casually discussed their lack of exercise suggests that most simply did not share the organization's view of exercise as a requirement. Consequently, if you don't exercise, there's no need to feel guilty. Members resist the organization's efforts to formalize the expectation of regular exercise, and as a result it is virtually impossible to induce any significant degree of guilt for not exercising.

Confession and Forgiveness

When members do see the error of their ways and feel guilty after transgressions, meetings provide a forum for public confession. As members admit to the group the various ways they have cheated or broken rules, the meeting becomes a public confessional, with other members as witnesses. Leaders are particularly significant as they make their own confessions, solicit confessions from members, and model appropriate responses for members. Linda was an effective role model, as she regularly began discussions with stories of her own mistakes. Indeed, Linda frequently repeated her story about sneaking donuts from her co-workers. Similarly, Debbie often told her own story about eating nearly an entire cake at a family celebration.

As leaders make their own confessions, they promote similar sharing by members. The first time I heard Linda confess about the donuts, the discussion topic was "eating secrets," a personal and potentially embarrassing topic, particularly for people who do not know one another very well. Linda broke the ice, provided specific examples of the kinds of secrets she had in mind, and created a more comfortable and less threatening atmosphere in which members could confess their transgressions. At other times, leaders directly prompt confessions, as when Linda asked the group, "Has there ever been a time when you didn't do very well, or pay attention to what you ate all week, and then the day before coming to the meeting, not eat or drink anything?" Linda's question provoked laughter and heads nodding throughout the room, so apparently the practice is fairly common. In this case Linda explicitly identifies a specific transgression, and then allows members to confess as a group, rather than put an individual member on the spot. As previous weight-losers and current lifetime members of the group, leaders are especially well suited for modeling confession. Not coincidentally, leaders' confessions frequently take on the tone of evangelical preachers who publicly admit the error of their ways and then suggest that they have seen the light.

Confession fulfills a number of functions. First, new members are socialized into the group and its procedures as they listen to members confess. Second, public confession bonds the group together, as members reassert their commitment to group norms and thereby highlight and strengthen the moral boundaries surrounding the group. Third, group members are reinforced in their beliefs that there are good and bad ways of eating. In addition, public confession is a useful way to relieve stress for individual members. Traditionally, it is through confession that sinners receive forgiveness.

By confessing their sins to others, whether it is to a priest, the church, or the larger community, sinners publicly admit the error of their ways, and in return they receive absolution. Although members of the weight loss group do not literally receive forgiveness for their sins, nonetheless, a sort of forgiveness is experienced as members admit their transgressions to the group and simultaneously reaffirm their commitment to follow the rules in the future. When the meeting topic was food secrets, members were encouraged to confront and deal with their secrets, first by talking to themselves about what they were doing, and then by telling someone else. In addition, public confession is a useful way to relieve stress for individual members.

Confession is clearly useful both for individual members and for the group as a whole. But at the same time, the effects are more insidious: The good dieter not only accepts the group's teachings but continually examines herself for faults—and finds them. Confessing your sins provides relief from guilt, but it is temporary at best.

Removing Sin and Guilt Through Good Works

Just as in some religions, where sins can be removed, atoned, or made up for by doing good works, so it is in the weight loss group—but with a twist.

Food is divided into the good and the bad. Food that is healthy, that is, nutritionally sound, is good and acceptable, while food that leads to overindulgence and weight gain is bad and forbidden. In the language of group members, "red-light foods" signal temptation, danger, and sin. As members use group time to confess their sins, they frequently express guilt due to overeating. But at least as common, if not more so, is guilt over eating foods that they shouldn't have eaten.

Exercise can be viewed as punishment for overeating or for eating "bad" foods. Such sin is followed by guilt that literally can be worked off through the hard labor of exercise. Alternatively, exercise is the payment made for the right to sin. In a rather curious inversion of the sin-guilt-punishment-forgiveness cycle, members can use exercise to earn points to eat more food or to eat "red-light" foods. In both cases, exercise is directly tied to indulgence, either as the punishment exacted for past indulgence or as the ticket to future indulgence. Rarely do members or leaders talk about the health benefits of exercise independent of weight loss, and it is virtually unheard of to suggest that exercise can be pleasurable in and of itself.

Keeping Them in Line: Surveillance

In the face of nearly endless temptation, guilt and confession are not the only techniques used to keep members on the right track. The effectiveness of inducing guilt rests on another technique, continual surveillance. To the extent that members feel that they are being watched, they may be less likely to break the rules. About a month after I joined, Richard got out his stickers and ribbons and asked, "Does anyone get a ten-pound ribbon? Has anyone lost their first ten pounds?" As Richard was handing out ribbons, Amy turned to me and said, "You'll get that next week!" I immediately felt some pressure, knowing that someone else knew how close I was to losing ten pounds.

At other times members play more direct and active roles in surveillance. When I arrived one evening, Debbie asked Judy how she lost weight on vacation. Among other things, Judy said that she and her daughter "watched each other." And on numerous occasions Joyce spoke openly, freely, and critically about her friend Peggy and the problems she had sticking to the program.

Group surveillance is important, even if unintentional. Early one morning, a few months after I joined the group, I was out walking for exercise. As I crossed the street in front of a neighborhood elementary school, the crossing guard on duty looked at me, and then exclaimed, "Hey, I saw you at [the weight loss meeting] the other night!" On other occasions, I ran into members at restaurants or the grocery store, and I was immediately self-conscious about what I was eating or what I had in my grocery cart.

People outside the group also do a good deal of surveillance work. Significantly, Linda and Debbie's confessions involved attempts to avoid or subvert surveillance, most notably by hiding food or not eating in front of others. Members, too, frequently admit hiding food or tying to eat when no one else is around. At the very least, members feel as if their behavior is under public scrutiny, and several incidents suggest that this is not a figment of their imaginations. When Linda confessed that she hid donuts from her co-workers, she noted that since her colleagues knew she was a leader for a weight loss group, she felt self-conscious about eating donuts in front of them. She went on to ask members whether other people had ever made them self-conscious about what they were eating. This was an experience widely shared by members.

Aware that their eating habits are viewed and scrutinized by others, members become conscious of their own behavior and do a good deal of self-surveillance. Given the limitations of group surveillance and the potentially negative fall-out from surveillance by friends and family members, the organization relies heavily on members to monitor themselves. As most religious groups and parents come to find out, controlling members' behavior through external means is highly inefficient, not to mention difficult. Consequently religious groups and parents spend considerable time and energy instilling individual consciences in converts and children. If individuals watch themselves, the organization doesn't have to. Meticulously recording everything you eat takes on considerable importance in this regard. With repeated references to the tracker's importance in preventing and uncovering cheating, the food record is one strategy for carefully monitoring your own behavior. In effect, guilt can be self-induced, freeing the organization and leaders to provide mutual support and reinforcement.

Explaining the Inexplicable

In large part, religion functions to explain the inexplicable, to provide understanding of the mystery of life. Religion does this primarily by appealing to the transcendent mystery and power of God. People who are trying to lose weight also seek to explain the inexplicable. Weight gain is no mystery when members eat more than they think they should, indulge in high-calorie foods, or otherwise act in ways that can be expected to result in additional pounds. But at other times, weight gain is unexpected. Members do what they are supposed to do, eat what they are supposed to eat, but nevertheless do not lose weight—or, even worse, gain weight. In these situations, members desperately look for reasonable explanations for the unexpected gain.

Common responses to this question usually involve the body—first, its tendency to retain water, and second, the inconsistencies of body metabolism. Water retention is by far the most common explanation used for unexpected weight gain, but water retention itself is seen as having multiple causes. During my first week on the program, I lost about five pounds. After following the program for a second week, I was disappointed when I lost only one pound. Feeling that I had worked hard all week, I hoped to lose two or three more pounds. In some ways, the first week's rapid loss set me up for disappointment. Searching for possible explanations for the low loss, I wondered if I had eaten something I shouldn't have, possibly the cheese omelet I had for breakfast on Sunday. But I had charted it, probably generously, and even if I hadn't, it fell well within the week's optional calories. Then I noted the date, and wondered whether it could be water retention related to the menstrual cycle. Even though it was probably a little early, I assured myself that it was close enough to be the probable cause.

Besides the menstrual cycle, high sodium intake is often blamed for water retention and consequent weight gain. One evening, Debbie asked members what they had to share. Peggy said that she gained a pound, and was puzzled since she had done exactly what she had the week before. Peggy said that she drank a diet pop that day and wondered if that had anything to do with it. Joyce said, "Pop is high in sodium," and Debbie explained that sodium leads to water retention. The explanations for water retention go even further. Ruth said, "When it's hot and humid you retain water. Lots of people complained about their rings being tight."

As amusing as some of the explanations are, members take them quite seriously, as do leaders. To some extent, the explanations are accurate. Sodium intake, the menstrual cycle, and the weather all affect water retention, which in turn affects weight. At the same time, in at least some instances, water retention is not likely the sole or even the major explanation of lower than expected weight loss or unexpected weight gain. The explanations are useful not because they are necessarily *true*, but because they ultimately *make sense*, and thus help to make a seemingly irrational situation understandable. Believing that a can of diet soda can result in a one-pound weight gain is far more reassuring than feeling that your efforts have had no payoff whatsoever.

A second category of explanations for lower than expected weight losses involves the inconsistencies and mysteries of body metabolism. Some of these explanations involve the tendency of the body metabolism to slow down in response to deprivation. One week I lost a quarter pound, following

226 / *Kandi M. Stinson*

a loss of four pounds the previous week. When I expressed disappointment over the small loss, Donna said, "With the kind of loss you had last week, it's not unusual to have a smaller one the next week. Anyway, it's headed in the right direction." Donna's response was typical. On numerous occasions, receptionists helped members justify small losses by suggesting that the metabolism slows in response to a large loss.

Body metabolism does play a role in weight loss. But as in the case of the explanations involving water retention, the accuracy of the explanations is unimportant. The body and its workings are mysterious and pose difficulties and anxieties for the dieter, who is trying to control not only what she eats but her body's response to what is eaten. The explanations help relieve anxiety by trying to make some sense out of a perplexing situation. In members' discussions, the body is not reduced to sheer physiological matter that behaves in scientifically predictable ways. In contrast, the body is viewed as unpredictable and ultimately inexplicable.

Taboos

Occasionally, much to the amusement of everyone present, a member or leader would come across old organizational materials, sometimes from as many as thirty years ago, and share with the group various taboos, restrictions, or requirements. At one time, potatoes could only be eaten early in the day, and liver had to be eaten once a week. Although members found the stories funny, leaders used them to emphasize how much the program had changed and especially how much more freedom members now had to eat what they wanted. Taboos are associated with "the old days," and are presumably no longer necessary as we have become more enlightened.

At the same time, another taboo operates in the group and significantly affects group interaction: not sharing your body weight with others. Those few instances when individuals are forced to publicly announce their weight, such as when renewing a driver's license, are fraught with anxiety and embarrassment. When the information is potentially stigmatizing, individuals may use a number of techniques of information control in order to hide, obscure, or selectively reveal the stigmatizing condition. Since obesity is a visible stigma, the obese person is already discredited. At the same time, obese persons can conceal their exact weight, or at least control to whom and under what circumstances the information is revealed. Nonetheless, this can be very difficult, if not impossible. In weight loss groups, body weight is the central concern. Members may be publicly acknowledging that they are overweight, but this does not mean that they must openly divulge their weight. Indeed, weight loss groups may find it advantageous to allow members to conceal their weight, at least to some extent.

The "weigh-in" provides an excellent example of how the group balances its need to focus on weight and at the same time not violating this taboo. The few minutes prior to the meeting's official start, when members are weighed, are by far the most anxiety provoking in the meeting. The organization attempts to relieve tension by privatizing weigh-in to the extent possible. The scales were located at the very back of the meeting room, in three side-by-side cubicles, open in front, and separated only by thin, portable walls. Small windows were cut in the walls, so receptionists in adjoining cubicles could pass materials and tools, such as stamp pads, back and forth, and could easily talk to each other during weigh-in. The physical arrangement of the scales also contributed to the semblance of privacy. Unlike those in most physicians' offices or gyms, the part of the scale that showed body weight was turned backward. The numbers on the scale were hidden not only from people waiting in line but also from the person getting weighed. The only person who could observe the numbers was the receptionist. The numbers were further obscured by a paper sign hung on each scale that red "No Bare Feet on the Scale."

Weigh-in is a ritual, highly structured and predictable. After a member steps on the scale, the receptionist reads the scale and records the weight in the member's record. Although receptionists frequently say such things as "Down another one this week," or "Good job—you lost two pounds," I never observed a receptionist tell a member her actual weight. Rather, receptionists routinely write the weight in the record book, and then point to the weight with their pen. In order to find out their body weight, members have to read it in their books.

So ingrained was the ritual that I never asked a receptionist what I actually weighed. Rather, after sitting down, I checked my weight in my record book. The combination of ritualizing weigh-in and providing at least a bare minimum of privacy allowed members to get publicly weighed but retain some control over personal information.

Conclusion

As members and leaders talk about losing weight, they draw heavily on religious language and imagery. Good and evil, temptation, sin, guilt, and confession animate members' speech as they try to make sense of complex and ambivalent emotions surrounding food, the body, and weight loss.

Durkheim argued that the division of the world into the sacred and the profane is at the very core of religion. The concept captures the high degree of moralizing that characterizes these dieters' thinking about food, eating, obesity, and weight loss. The division of the world into the sacred and the profane deeply colors their everyday experiences and infuses their speech with notions of right and wrong, good and evil. Concomitantly, guilt is one of the most common states of people who are trying to lose weight.

In the United States, particularly in women's experiences, food intake is a central arena in which moral ideologies are played out. The fat body, associated with self-indulgence, losing self-control, and giving in to temptations of sensual pleasure represents the profane. The thin body is the outward sign that the mind has won its battle with the body. The thin body is redeemed: It represents restraint, control, and resisting temptation.

For Durkheim, community is at the core of all religion. In religion, community is defined, constructed, and experienced. Community is also constructed and reinforced in the weight loss group. As members share their frustrations and accomplishments, they make connections with one another. Even as a critical observer, I found it impossible not to be touched by Corinne's pride in losing enough weight to be able to help her young daughter learn to ride a bike, or by Lois's isolation due to extreme obesity, and her newfound freedom as she shed her oxygen tank and was able to leave her house.

The weight loss group is a supportive community, in some ways similar to a church. Not coincidentally, as churches build fellowship and community through sharing food, food is also at the center of the weight loss group's fellowship. A beverage table is set up for every meeting, and members commonly drink tea, both regular and decaffeinated coffee, or nonfat hot cocoa during the meeting. Occasionally members bring in food to share when they have tried a recipe for low-fat cookies or some other low-point dessert. And at times, the organization gives away food products as door prizes for members in attendance. More commonly, food is figuratively shared, as members exchange recipes, suggestions for accommodating restaurants, and other tricks of the weight loss trade. But while food sharing does occur, it is food restriction that unites members of the weight loss group.

20 Behavior in Pubic Places: The Sociology of the Vaginal Examination

JAMES M. HENSLIN
MAE A. BIGGS

All of us depend on others for the successful completion of the roles we play. In many ways, this makes cooperation the essence of social life (with due apologies to my conflict-theorist colleagues). Without teamwork, performances fall apart, people become disillusioned, jobs don't get done—and, ultimately, society is threatened. Accordingly, much of our socialization centers on learning to be good team players.

The work setting lends itself well to examining cooperative interaction and to seeing how people develop ways of handling differences—"working arrangements" that defuse threats to fragile social patterns. For example, instructors often accept from students excuses that they know do not match reality. For their part, students often accept publicly what instructors teach, even though they disagree privately with those interpretations. Not only is confrontation unpleasant, and therefore preferable to avoid, but also it is a threat to the continuity of interaction. Thus both instructors and students generally allow one another enough leeway to "get on with business" (which some might say is education, while others—more cynical—might say is the one earning a living and the other a degree).

One can gain much insight into the nature of society by trying to identify the implicit understandings that guide our interactions in everyday life. In this selection, Henslin and Biggs draw on Goffman's dramaturgical framework as they focus on the vaginal examination. Note the teamwork that is required to make the definition stick that nothing sexual is occurring.

GENITAL BEHAVIOR IS PROBLEMATIC for most of us. We are socialized at a very early age into society's dictates concerning the situations, circumstances, and purposes of allowable and unallowable genital exposure.

Our thanks to Erving Goffman for commenting on this paper while it was in manuscript form and for suggesting the title, a play on his book, *Behavior in Public Places*. Because the physicians in this study are men, the pronoun "he" is used.

After a U.S. female has been socialized into her society's expectations regarding the covering and privacy of specified areas of her body, especially her vagina, exposure of her pubic area becomes something that is problematic for her. Even for a woman who has overcome feelings of modesty and perhaps of shame at genital exposure in the presence of her sexual partner, the problem frequently recurs during the vaginal examination. Although her exposure is supposed to be nonsexual, the vaginal examination can be so threatening that for many women it not only punctures their feelings of modesty but it also threatens their self, their feelings of who they are.

Because emotions become associated with the genital area through the learning of meanings and taboos, the vaginal examination is an especially interesting process; it is an elaborately ritualized form of social interaction designed to desexualize the sexual organs. From a sociological point of view, what happens during such interaction? Since a (if not *the*) primary concern of the persons involved is that all the interaction be defined as nonsexual, with even the hint of sexuality to be avoided, what structural restraints on behavior operate? How does the patient cooperate in maintaining this definition of nonsexuality? In what ways are the roles of doctor, nurse, and patient performed such that each contributes to this definition?

This analysis is based on a sample of 12,000 to 14,000 vaginal examinations. Biggs served as an obstetrical nurse in hospital settings and as an office nurse for general practitioners for fourteen years, giving us access to this area of human behavior which ordinarily is not sociologically accessible. Based on these observations, we have divided the interaction of the vaginal examination into five major scenes. Let's examine what occurs as each of these scenes unfolds.

The setting for the vaginal examination may be divided into two areas (see Figure 20.1). Although there are no physical boundaries that demarcate the two areas, highly specific and ritualized interaction occurs in each. Area 1, where Scenes I and V are played, includes that portion of the "office-examination" room which is furnished with a desk and three chairs. Area 2, where Scenes II, III, and IV take place, contains an examination table, a swivel stool, a gooseneck lamp, a table for instruments, and a sink with a mirror above it.

Scene I: The Personalized Stage: The Patient as Person

The interaction flow of Scene I is as follows: (a) the doctor enters the "office-examination" room; (b) greets the patient; (c) sits down; (d) asks the

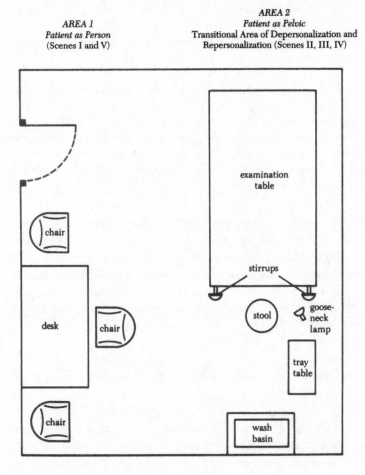

AREA 1
Patient as Person
(Scenes I and V)

AREA 2
Patient as Pelvic
Transitional Area of Depersonalization and
Repersonalization (Scenes II, III, IV)

Figure 20.1 The Doctor's Office—Examination Room

patient why she is there; (e) questions her on specifics; (f) decides on a course of action, specifically whether a pelvic examination is needed or not; (g) if he thinks a pelvic is needed, he signals the nurse on the intercom and says, "I want a pelvic in room (X)"; (h) he gets up and leaves the room.

During this scene, the patient is treated as a full person; that is, the courtesies of middle-class conversation are followed, and, in addition to gathering medical information, if the doctor knows the patient well he may intersperse his medical queries with questions about her personal life. The following interaction that occurred during Scene I demonstrates the doctor's treatment of his patient as a full person:

DOCTOR (upon entering the room): Hello, Joyce, I hear you're going to Southern Illinois University.
PATIENT: Yes, I am. I've been accepted, and I have to have my health record completed.

The doctor then seated himself at his desk and began filling out the health record that the patient gave him. He interspersed his questions concerning the record form with questions about the patient's teaching, about the area of study she was pursuing, about her children, their health and their schooling. He then said, "Well, we have to do this right. We'll do a pelvic on you." He then announced via the intercom, "I want to do a pelvic on Joyce in room 1." At that point he left the room.

This interaction sequence is typical of the interaction that occurs in Scene I between a doctor and a patient he knows well. When the doctor does not know the patient well, he does not include his patient's name, either her first or last name, in his announcement to the nurse that she should come into the room. In such a case, he simply says, "I want to do a pelvic in room 1," or, "Pelvic in room 1." The doctor then leaves the room, marking the end of the scene.

Scene II: The Depersonalized Stage: Transition from Person to Pelvic

When at the close of Scene I the doctor says, "Pelvic in room (X)," he is in effect announcing the coming transition of the person to a pelvic. The doctor's signal for the nurse to come in is, in fact, a signal that the nurse should now help the patient make the transition from a person to a pelvic. Additionally, it also serves as an announcement to the patient that she is about to undergo this metamorphosis.

The interaction flow which accomplishes the transition from person to pelvic is as follows: Upon entering the room, the nurse, without preliminaries, tells the patient, "The doctor wants to do a vaginal examination on you. Will you please remove your panties?" While the patient is undressing, the nurse prepares the props. She positions the stirrups of the examination table and arranges the glove, the lubricant, and the speculum (the instrument which, when inserted into the vagina, allows visual examination of the vaginal tract). She then removes the drape sheet from a drawer and directs the patient onto the table, covers the patient with the drape sheet, assists her in placing her feet into the stirrups, and positions her hips, putting her into the lithotomy position (lying on her back with knees flexed and out).

MEANING OF THE DOCTOR'S ABSENCE

The doctor's exiting just before this scene means that the patient will be undressing in his absence. This is not accidental. In many cases, the doctor may leave because another patient is waiting, but even if there are no waiting patients, the doctor always exits at the end of Scene I. His leaving means that he will not witness the patient undressing, thereby successfully removing any suggestion that a striptease is being performed, or that he is acting as a voyeur. From the patient's point of view, this greatly reduces embarrassment and other problems that would occur if she were to undress in front of the doctor. When the doctor returns, only a particularized portion of the woman's body will be exposed for the ensuing interaction. As we shall see, at that point the doctor is no longer dealing with a person, but he is, rather, facing a "pelvic."

THE PROBLEM OF UNDERCLOTHING

Undressing and nudity are problematic for the patient since she has been socialized into not undressing before strangers.[1] Almost without exception, when the woman undresses in Scene II, she turns away from the nurse and the door, even though the door is closed. She removes only her panties in the typical case, but a small number of patients also remove their shoes.

After the patient has removed her panties, she faces the problem of what to do with them. Underclothing does not have the same meaning as other items of clothing, such as a sweater, that can be casually draped around the body or strewn on furniture. Clothing is considered to be an extension of the self (Gross and Stone 1964), and clothing can represent the particular part of the body that it covers. In this case, this means that panties represent to women their "private area." Comments made by patients that illustrate the problematics of panty exposure include: "The doctor doesn't want to look at these," "I want to get rid of these before he comes in," and, "I don't want the doctor to see these old things."

Some patients seem to be at a loss in solving this problem and turn to the nurse for guidance, asking her what they should do with their underclothing. Most patients, however, do not ask for directions, but hide their panties in some way. The favorite hiding or covering seems to be in or under the purse.[2] Other women put their panties in the pocket of their coat or in the folds of a coat or sweater. Some cover them with a magazine, and others cover them with their own body on the examination table. It is rare that a woman leaves her panties exposed somewhere in the room.[3]

THE DRAPE SHEET

Another problematic area in the vaginal examination is what being undressed can signify. Disrobing for others frequently indicates preparation for sexual relations. Since sexuality is the very thing that this scene is oriented toward removing, a mechanism is put into effect to eliminate sexuality—the drape sheet. After the patient is seated on the table, the nurse places a drape sheet from just below her breasts (she still has her blouse on) to over her legs. Although the patient is draped by the sheet, when she is positioned on the table with her legs in the stirrups, her pubic region is exposed. Usually it is not necessary for the doctor even to raise a fold in the sheet in order to examine her genitals.

Since the drape sheet does not cover the genital area, but, rather, leaves it exposed, what is its purpose? The drape sheet depersonalizes the patient. It sets the pubic area apart, letting the doctor view the pubic area in isolation, separating the pubic area from the person. The pubic area or female genitalia becomes an object isolated from the rest of the body. Because of the drape sheet, the doctor, in his position on the low stool, does not see the patient's face. He no longer sees or needs to deal with a person, just the exposed genitalia marked off by the drape sheet. Yet, from the patient's point of view in her supine position, her genitals are covered! When *she* looks down at her body, she does not see exposed genitalia. The drape sheet effectively hides her pubic area *from herself* while exposing it to the doctor.

THIGH BEHAVIOR

U.S. girls are given early and continued socialization in "limb discipline," being taught at a very early age to keep their legs close together while they are sitting or while they are retrieving articles from the ground. They receive such instructions from their mothers as, "Keep your dress down," "Put your legs together," and "Nice girls don't let their panties show." Evidence of socialization into "acceptable" thigh behavior shows up in the vaginal examination while the women are positioned on the examination table and waiting for the doctor to arrive. They do not let their thighs fall outwards in a relaxed position, but they try to hold their upper or mid-thighs together until the doctor arrives. They do this even in cases where it is very difficult for them to do so, such as when the patient is in her late months of pregnancy.

Although the scene has been carefully orchestrated to desexualize the ensuing interaction, and although the patient is being depersonalized such that when the doctor returns he primarily has a pelvic to deal with and not a person, at this point in the interaction sequence the patient's "proper" thigh behavior shows that she is still holding onto her sexuality and "personality." Only later, when the doctor reenters the scene, will she consent fully to be desexualized and depersonalized and let her thighs fall outwards.

After the props are ready and the patient is positioned, the nurse announces to the doctor via intercom that the stage is set for the third scene, saying, "We're ready in room (X)."

Scene III: The Depersonalized Stage: The Person as Pelvic

FACE-TO-PUBIC INTERACTION

The interaction to this point, as well as the use of props, has been structured to project a singular definition of the situation—that of legitimate doctor–patient interaction and, specifically, the nonsexual examination of a woman's vaginal region by a man. To support this definition, team performance is vital (Goffman 1959:104). Although the previous interaction has been part of an ongoing team performance, it has been sequential, leading to the peak of the performance, the vaginal examination itself. At this time, the team begins its cooperative act, its skilled performance maintaining the legitimation of the examination. The doctor, while standing, places a disposable latex glove on his right hand, again symbolizing the depersonalized nature of the action: By using the glove, he is saying that he will not himself be actually touching the "private area," that the glove will serve as an insulator.[4] It is at this point that the doctor asks questions of the patient regarding such things as her bowels or bladder. Then, while he is still in this standing position, the nurse in synchronization actively joins the performance by squeezing a lubricant onto his outstretched gloved fingers, and the doctor inserts the index and middle fingers of his right hand into the patient's vagina while externally palpating (feeling) the uterus. He then withdraws his fingers from the vagina, seats himself on the stool, inserts a speculum, and while the nurse positions the gooseneck lamp behind him, he visually examines the cervix.

Prior to this third scene, the interaction has been dyadic only, consisting of nurse and patient in Scene II and doctor and patient in Scene I. In this scene, however, the interaction becomes triadic, with the doctor, nurse, and

patient simultaneously involved in the performance. The term triadic, however, does not even come close to accurately describing the role-playing of
this scene. Since the patient has essentially undergone a metamorphosis from
a person to an object—having been objectified or depersonalized—the focus
of the interaction is now on a specific part of her body. The positioning of
her legs, the use of the drape sheet, the shining of the light, and the doctor's
location on the stool have made the patient's pubic region the focus of interaction. This location of actors and arrangement and use of props also blocks
out the "talk lines" between the doctor and patient, physically obstructing
their exchange of glances. Interaction between the doctor and the patient is
no longer "face-to-face," being perhaps now more accurately described as
"face-to-pubic" interaction.

BREASTS AS NONSEXUAL OBJECTS

To project and maintain the definition of nonsexuality in the vaginal examination also requires the desexualization of the woman's breasts, since they
are attributed to have sexual meaning in our culture. When the breasts are to
be examined in conjunction with a vaginal examination, a rather interesting
ritual is employed. The goal of this ritual—like that of the vaginal ritual—is
to objectify the breasts by isolating them from the rest of the body, permitting the doctor to see the breasts apart from the person. In this ritual, after
the patient has removed her upper clothing, a towel is placed across her
breasts, and the drape sheet is then placed on top of the towel. Since the
towel in and of itself more than sufficiently covers the breasts, we can only
conclude that the purpose of the drape sheet is to enhance the definition of
nonsexual interaction. Additionally, the doctor first removes the sheet from
the breasts, exposing the towel. He then lifts the towel from *one* breast,
makes his examination, and *replaces* the towel over that breast. He then examines the other breast in exactly the same way, again replacing the towel
after the examination.

THE NURSE AS CHAPERONE

That the interaction in Scene III is triadic is not accidental, nor is it instrumentally necessary. It is, rather, designed to help desexualize the vaginal examination. Instrumentally, the nurse functions merely to lubricate the
doctor's fingers and to hand him the speculum. He obviously could do these
things himself. It becomes apparent, then, that doing these things is not the
purpose of the nurse's presence, that she plays an entirely different role in

this scene. That role is *chaperone,* the person assigned to be present in some traditional societies when an umarried man and woman come together in order to give assurance to interested persons that no sexual acts take place. Although the patient has been depersonalized, or at least this is the definition that the team has been attempting to project and maintain, the possibility exists that the vaginal examination can erupt into a sexual scene. Because of this possibility (or the potential accusation that sexual behavior has taken place), the nurse is always present. Interestingly, with contemporary sexual mores so vastly different from those of a century ago, this medical setting is one of the few remaining examples of the chaperone in our society.[5] It is a significant role, for it helps the performance to be initiated and to continue smoothly to its logical conclusion.

THE PATIENT AS A NONPERSON TEAM MEMBER

With this definition of objectification and desexualization, the patient represents a vagina disassociated from a person. She has been dramaturgically transformed for the duration of this scene into a nonperson (Goffman 1959:152).[6] This means that while he is seated and performing the vaginal examination, the doctor need not interact with the patient as a person; he no longer needs to carry on a conversation nor to maintain eye contact with her. Furthermore, this means that he now is permitted to carry on a "side conversation" with the person with whom he does maintain eye contact, his nurse. For example, during one examination the doctor looked up at the nurse and said: "Hank and I really caught some good-sized fish while we were on vacation. He really enjoyed himself." He then looked at his "work" and announced, "Cervix looks good; no inflammation—everything appears fine down here." Ordinarily, for middle-class interactions such ignoring of the presence of a third person would constitute a breach of etiquette, but *in this case there really isn't a third person present.* The patient has been "depersonalized," to such an extent that the rules of conversation have changed, and no breach of etiquette has taken place.[7]

Although she has been defined as an object, the patient is actually the third member of the team. Her assignment is to "play the role of an object"; that is, she contributes to the flow of the interaction by acting as an object and not as a person. Through studied alienation from the interaction, she demonstrates what is known as dramaturgical discipline (Goffman 1959:216–18). She studiously gazes at the ceiling or wall, only occasionally allowing herself the luxury (or is it the danger?) of fleeting eye contact with the nurse. Eye contact with the doctor, of course, is prevented by the position of her legs and the drape sheet.

After the doctor tells the patient to get dressed, he leaves the room, and the fourth scene is ready to unfold.

Scene IV: The Repersonalizing Stage: The Transition from Pelvic to Person

During this stage of the interaction the patient undergoes a demetamorphosis, dramaturgically changing from vaginal object to person. Immediately after the doctor leaves, the nurse assists the patient into a sitting position, and she gets off the table. The nurse then asks the patient if she would like to use a towel to cleanse her genital area, and about 80 percent of the patients accept the offer. In this scene, it is not uncommon for patients to make some statement concerning their relief that the examination is over. Statements such as "I'm glad that's over with" seem to indicate the patient's overt recognition of the changing scene, to acknowledge that she is now entering a different phase of the drama.

During this repersonalizing stage, the patient is concerned with regrooming and recostuming. Patients frequently ask if they look all right, and the common question "My dress isn't too wrinkled, is it?" appears to indicate the patient's awareness of and desire to be ready for the resumption of roles other than vaginal object. Her dress isn't too wrinkled for what? It must be that she is asking whether it is too wrinkled for (1) her resumption of the role of (patient as) person and (2) her resumption of nonpatient roles.

Modesty continues to operate during this scene, and it is interesting that patients who have just had their genital area thoroughly examined both visually and tactually by the doctor are concerned that this same man will see their underclothing. ("He won't be in before I get my underwear on, will he?") They are now desiring and preparing for the return to the feminine role. They apparently fear that the doctor will reenter the room as they literally have one foot in and one foot out of their panties. They want to have their personal front reestablished to their own satisfaction before the return of this man and the onset of the next scene. For this, they strive for the poise and composure that they deem fitting the person role for which they are now preparing, frequently using either their own pocket-mirror or the mirror above the sink to check their personal front.

During this transitional role, patients indicate by their comments to the nurse that they are again to be treated as persons. While they are dressing, they frequently speak about their medical problems, their aches and pains, their fight against gaining weight, or feelings about their pregnancy. In such ways they are reasserting the self and are indicating that they are again entering "personhood."

The patient who best illustrates awareness that she had undergone a process of repersonalization is the woman who, after putting on her panties, said, "There! Just like new again." She had indeed moved out of her temporary and uncomfortable role as object, and her reappearance as person matched her self-concept.

After the patient has recostumed and regroomed, the nurse directs the patient to a chair alongside the doctor's desk. She then announces via intercom to the doctor, "The patient is dressed," or, "The patient is waiting." It is significant that at this point the woman is referred to as "patient" in the announcement to the doctor and not as "pelvic" as she was at the end of the second scene. Sometimes the patient is also referred to by name in this announcement. The patient has completed her demetamorphosis at this point, and the nurse, by the way she refers to her, is officially announcing the transition.

The nurse then leaves the room, and her interaction with the patient ceases.

Scene V: The Repersonalized Stage: The Patient as Person Once Again

When the doctor makes his third entrance, the patient has again resumed the role of person and is interacted with on this basis. The doctor makes eye contact with her, speaks to her, and listens to her. During this fifth scene, the patient's whole personal front is visible. The doctor informs the patient of the results of her examination, he may prescribe medications, and, wherever indicated, he suggests further care. He also tells the patient whether or not she need see him again.

For us, the significance of the interaction of Scene V is that the patient is again allowed to interact *as a person within the role of patient.* The doctor allows time for questions that the patient might have about the results of the examination, and he also gives her the opportunity to ask about other medical problems that she might be experiencing.

Interaction between the doctor and patient terminates as the doctor gets up from his chair and moves toward the door.

Conclusion: Desexualization of the Sacred

In concluding this analysis, we shall briefly indicate that conceptualizing the vagina as a sacred object yields a perspective that appears to be of value in analyzing the vaginal examination. A sacred object is surrounded by rules protecting the object from being profaned, rules governing who may approach the "sacred," under what circumstances it may be approached, and what may and may not be done during such an approach (Durkheim 1965:51–59). If these rules are followed, the "sacred" will lose none of its "sacredness," but if they are violated, the sacred will be profaned.

Apart from the husband and significant others,[8] except in a medical setting and by the actors about whom we are speaking, no one else may approach the vagina other than the self and still have it retain its sacred character.[9] Because of this, the medical profession has taken great pains to establish a dramaturgical ritual that will ensure the continued sacredness of the vaginas of its female patients, one that will avoid even the imputation of taboo violation. Accordingly, by dramaturgically desexualizing the vagina by dissociating it from the person, and by elaborately defining it as just another organ of the body, this ritual of the vaginal examination allows the doctor to approach the sacred without profaning it or violating taboos. The vaginal examination is a fascinating example of how reality is socially constructed, in this instance of how physicians are able to handle a woman's vagina and yet maintain a definition of nonsexuality.

Notes

1. Undressing and nudity are problematic for many, but perhaps more for females than for males. Males are more likely to experience structured situations in which they undress and are nude before others, such as showering after high school physical education classes, while females in the same situation are often afforded a greater degree of privacy with, for example, private shower stalls in place of the mass showers of the males. This is not always the case, however, and Theresa France (private communication) reports that in her classes the girls also had communal showers.

2. From a psychiatric orientation this association of the panties with the purse is fascinating, given the Freudian interpretation that the purse signifies the female genitalia.

3. In some examination rooms, the problem of where to put the undergarments is solved by the provision of a special drawer for them located beneath the examination table.

4. It is true, of course, that the glove also serves instrumental purposes, such as protecting the physician from diseases that might be transmitted by means of digital–vaginal contact—and patients from diseases the physician might pass from one patient to another.

5. It is interesting to note that even the corpse of a female is defined as being in need of such chaperonage. Erving Goffman, on reading this paper in manuscript

form, commented that hospital etiquette dictates that "when a male attendant moves a female stiff from the room to the morgue he be accompanied by a female nurse."

6. Compare what Goffman (1959:104) has to say about secrets shared by team members. Remember that the patient in this interaction is not simply a member of the audience. She is also a team member, vitally interested in projecting and maintaining the definition of nonsexuality. Another reader of this paper, who wishes to remain anonymous, reports that during one of her pregnancies she had a handsome, young, and unmarried Hungarian doctor and that during vaginal examinations with him she would "concentrate on the instruments being used and the uncomfortableness of the situation" so as not to become sexually aroused.

7. While "playing the role" of an object, the patient is still able to hear verbal exchanges, of course, and she could enter the interaction if she so desired. As such, side comments between doctor and nurse must be limited. In certain other doctor-patient situations, however, the patient completely leaves the "person role," such as when the patient is anesthetized, which allows much freer banter among medical personnel. In delivery rooms of hospitals, for example, it is not uncommon for the obstetrician to comment while stitching the episiotomy, "She's like a new bride now," or, when putting in the final stitch, to say, "This is for the old man." Additionally, while medical students are stitching their first episiotomy, instructing doctors have been known to say, "It's not tight enough. Put one more in for the husband."

8. Some students have expressed their surprise and disapproval of this metaphor of genitalia being sacred. It certainly is the case that less "sacredness" is currently ascribed to the vagina than at earlier periods in our history, yet this depends a good deal on the individual's religion and age. To gain a culturally comparative perspective that reinforces this metaphor, consided "honor" killings in Islamic nations.

9. It is perhaps for this reason that prostitutes ordinarily lack respect: They have profaned the sacred. And in doing so, not only have they failed to limit vaginal access to culturally prescribed individuals, but they have added further violation by allowing vaginal access on a monetary basis. They have, in effect, sold the sacred.

Many obstetricians do not want prostitutes to be their patients. The greater incidence of diseases among prostitutes may be part of the reason for this, but so is their derided status.

21 The Lives of Homeless Women

ELLIOT LIEBOW

Can you imagine yourself being without a home? Think of what it must be like not to have a house or apartment, not to have your own bedroom or even one that you share with a sibling. You have no living room with a television, no kitchen with a refrigerator stocked with food that you can "raid" whenever you want. Night falls and you don't know where you will sleep. Day breaks, and you have no place to go, nothing to do—and no one who cares. Such is life for some people in our society—the discards of our new postindustrial or information age. As our communications technologies have advanced, the qualifications to participate successfully in the new world of work have become more demanding. The homeless, disqualified, have no place in our culturally mandated frenetic pursuit after material possessions.

Elliot Liebow, who had been diagnosed with incurable cancer, retired from his research position. He loved doing research, as he once told me, but he decided to spend his last days, which turned into years, doing things for others. He found himself working in a shelter for homeless women, where he was impressed with the ways that these women handled themselves in the midst of what is one of the most troubling and trying of human experiences. Liebow ended up doing more research, after all. This is his account.

THIS IS A PARTICIPANT OBSERVER study of single, homeless women in emergency shelters in a small city just outside Washington, D.C. In participant observation, the researcher tries to participate as fully as possible in the lives of the people being studied. Of course, there are obvious and severe limits to how well a man with a home and family can put himself in the place of homeless women. One simply goes where they go, gets to know them over time as best one can, and tries very hard to see the world from their perspective.

It is often said that, in participant observation studies, the researcher is the research instrument. So is it here. Everything reported about the women in this study has been selected by me and filtered through me, so it is important that I tell you something about myself and my prejudices as well as how this study came about. Indeed, I feel obliged to tell you more than is seemly and more than you may want to know, but these are things that the women themselves knew about me and that had an important if unknown influence on my relationship with them.

In a real sense, I backed into this study, which took shape, more or less, as I went along. In 1984, I learned that I had cancer and a very limited life expectancy. I did not want to spend my last months on the 12th floor of a government office building, so at 58 I retired on disability from my job of 20-some years as an anthropologist with the National Institute of Mental Health.

I looked well, felt well, and had a lot of time on my hands, so I became a volunteer at a soup kitchen that had recently opened. I worked there one night a week. In the early part of the evening, I helped served food or just sat around with the men and women who had come there, usually eating with them. In case of trouble, I tried to keep the peace. Later I went upstairs to "the counselor's office," where I met with people who needed assistance in getting shelter for the night. For the next hour or so, I called around to the various shelters in the county or in downtown Washington, D.C., trying to locate and reserve sleeping space for the men and women who needed it.

I enjoyed the work and the people at the soup kitchen, but this was only one night a week, so I became a volunteer at The Refuge, an emergency shelter for homeless women. This, too, was one night a week, from 6:30 to 10:00, and involved sleeping overnight twice a month. I picked this shelter because I had visited there briefly the year before and liked the feel of it. Here, along with three other volunteers, my job was to help prepare the food (usually just heat the main dishes and make a salad); help serve the food; distribute towels, soap, and other sundries on request; socialize with the women; keep order; and keep a daily log that included the names of all the women present and their time of arrival.

Almost immediately, I found myself enjoying the company of the women. I was awed by the enormous effort that most of them made to secure the most elementary necessities and decencies of life that the rest of us take for granted. And I was especially struck by their sense of humor, so at odds with any self-pity—the ability to step back and laugh at oneself, however wryly. One evening, soon after I started working at the shelter, several of us remained at the table to talk after finishing dinner. Pauline turned to me and said, in a stage whisper, making sure that Hilda would hear her, "Hilda has a Ph.D."

Hilda laughed. "No," she said, "I don't have a Ph.D., but I do have a bachelor's degree in biology." She paused, then began again. "You know," she said, "all my life I wanted to be an MD and now, at the age of 54, I finally made it. I'm a Manic Depressive."

Seduced by the courage and the humor of the women, and by the pleasure of their company, I started going to the shelter four and sometimes five days a week. (For the first two years, I also kept my one-night-a-week job with the soup kitchen.) Probably because it was something I was trained to do, or perhaps out of plain habit, I decided to take notes.

"Listen," I said at the dinner table one evening, after getting permission to do a study from the shelter director. "I want your permission to take notes. I want to go home at night and write down what I can remember about the things you say and do. Maybe I'll write a book about homeless women."

Most of the dozen or so women there nodded their heads or simply shrugged. All except Regina. Her acceptance was conditional. "Only if you promise not to publish before I do," she said. Believing that neither one of us, for different reasons, would ever publish anything in the future, I readily agreed.[1]

It is difficult to be precise about how I was perceived by the women. I am 6'1" and weigh about 175 pounds. I had a lot of white hair but was otherwise nondescript. I dressed casually, often in corduroy pants, shirt, and cardigan. The fact that I was Jewish did not seem to matter much one way or another so far as I could tell.

Most of the women probably liked having me around. Male companionship was generally in short supply and the women often made a fuss about the few male volunteers. I would guess that there were as many women who actively sought me out as there were women who avoided me. The fact that I had written a book that was available at the library (three or four women took the trouble to read it) enhanced my legitimacy in their eyes.[2]

Principally, I think, the women saw me as an important resource. I had money and a car, and by undertaking to write a book, I had made it my business to be with them. I routinely lent out $2, $5, $10, or even $20 on request to the handful who asked: I told them I had set aside a certain amount as a revolving fund and I could only keep lending money if they kept returning it. This worked fairly well.

There were a few women, of course, who would never be in a position to return the money, and this made for a problem. It would have been patronizing simply to make a gift of the money; they wanted to be borrowers, not beggars, and I was just as eager as they to avoid a demeaning panhandler/donor relationship. But I did not want them to be embarrassed or to avoid me simply because they couldn't repay a loan, nor did I want to shut them off from borrowing more. My solution was to reassure these women I had no immediate need for the money and could wait indefinitely for repayment.

Some of the women would perhaps characterize me as a friend, but I am not certain how deep or steadfast this sense of friendship might be. One day, Regina and I were talking about her upcoming trial about two months away. I had already agreed to accompany her to the courtroom and serve as an advisor, but Regina wanted further reassurance.

"You will be there, won't you?" she said.

As a way of noting the profundity that nothing in life is certain, I said, jokingly, "It's not up to me, it's up to The Man Upstairs."

"Well," she said, "if you die before the trial, you will ask one of your friends to help me, won't you?" I looked hard at her to see if she was joking, too. She wasn't. She was simply putting first things first.

One or two of the women did say something like "If you weren't married, would you give me a run for my money?" Neither "yes" nor "no" was a suitable response, but it usually sufficed for me to say (and mean), "I think you are a very nice person."

I tried to make myself available for driving people to Social Services, a job interview, a clinic or hospital, a cemetery, to someone's house, to another shelter, to help them move their belongings, or on other personal errands. With my consent, several women used my name as a personal reference for jobs or housing, and a few used my home as a mailing address for income tax refunds or other business.

Several of the women got to know my two daughters, both of whom came to The Refuge a few evenings each during the winters. One daughter was engaged to be married and her fiancé also came a few times. These visits helped strengthen my ties to those women who knew my daughters by face and name. They could ask me how my wife, Harriet, or Elisabeth and Jessica and Eric were doing, and my subsequent participation in discussions about family or child-rearing was much more personal and immediate as a result.

My association with the women was most intense during the winter of 1984–85, all of 1986, much of 1987, and the winter of 1987–88. Thereafter, I slackened off, partly for health reasons and partly because I had already collected more notes than I knew what to do with.[3] I continued to go to the shelters intermittently, and several of the women called me regularly at home. It was also at this time that I started playing around with the notes to see how I might eventually make sense of them.

In general, I have tried to avoid labeling any of the women as "mentally ill," "alcoholic," "drug addicted," or any other characterization that is commonly used to describe—or, worse, to explain—the homeless person. Judgments such as these are almost always made against a background of homelessness. If the same person were seen in another setting, the judgment might be altogether different. Like you, I know people who drink, people who do drugs, and bosses who have tantrums and treat their subordinates like dirt. They all have good jobs. Were they to become homeless, some of them would surely also become "alcoholics," "addicts," or "mentally ill." Similarly, if some of the homeless women who are now so labeled were to be magically transported to a more usual and acceptable setting, some of them—not all, of course—would shed their labels and take their places with the rest of us somewhere on the spectrum of normality.

The reader may be puzzled by the short shrift given here to mental illness. This was no oversight. I have no training as a mental health professional so it is not always clear to me who is mentally ill and who is not. There were always some women who acted crazy or whom most considered crazy, and the women themselves often agreed with the public at large that many homeless people are mentally ill.

From the beginning, however, I paid little attention to mental illness, partly because I had difficulty recognizing it, and partly for other reasons. Sometimes mental illness seemed to be "now-you-see-it, now-you-don't" phenomenon; some of the women were fine when their public assistance checks arrived, but became increasingly "symptomatic" as the month progressed and their money (security?) diminished, coming full circle when the next check arrived.[4] Others had good or bad days or weeks but with no obvious pattern or periodicity, although one woman linked her down period to her menstrual cycle. With a little patience on my part, almost all the women with mental or emotional problems were eventually and repeatedly accessible. Even on "bad" days, perhaps especially on "bad" days, these women sometimes said things that seemed to come, uncensored, from the depths of their emotional lives.

It seems to me that those women who may have been mentally ill (or alcoholic or drug addicted) by one or another standard were homeless for exactly the same proximal reason that everyone else was homeless: they had no place to live. Similarly, their greatest need of the moment was the same as everyone else's: to be assured of a safe, warm place to sleep at night, one or more hot meals a day, and the presence, if not the companionship, of fellow human beings. Given this perspective and my purposes, which and how many of the women were mentally ill was not a critical issue.

Whatever one's view of mental illness, it is probably true that the more one gets to know about a person, the easier it is to put oneself in that person's place or to understand his or her viewpoint, and the less reason one has for thinking of that person or treating that person as mentally ill.

This perspective—indeed, participant observation itself—raises the age-old problem of whether anyone can understand another or put oneself in another's place. Many thoughtful people believe that a sane person cannot know what it is to be crazy, that a white man cannot understand a black man, a Jew cannot see through the eyes of a Christian, a man through the eyes of a woman, and so forth in both directions. In an important sense, of course, and to a degree, this is certainly true; in another sense, and to a degree, it is surely false, because the logical extension of such a view is that no one can know another, that only John Jones can know John Jones, in which case social life would be impossible.

I do not mean that a man with a home and family can see and feel the world as homeless women see and feel it. I do mean, however, that it is reasonable and useful to try to do so. Trying to put oneself in the place of the other lies at the heart of the social contract and of social life itself. . .

In the early months, I sometimes tried to get Betty or one of the other women to see things as I saw them. One night Betty waited half an hour in back of the library for a bus that never came. She was convinced this was deliberate and personal abuse on the part of the Metro system. Metro was out to get her, she said. "But how did Metro know you were waiting for a bus at that time?" I asked. Betty shook her head in pity of me. "Well, Elliot, I was there on the street, right there in public, in the open! How could they not see me waiting for that damn bus?"

Fairly quickly, I learned not to argue with Betty but simply to relax and marvel at her end-of-the-month ingenuity. ("End-of-the-month" because that's when her public assistance money ran out and when she was most bitter at the way the world was treating her. At that time, a $10 or $20 loan could dramatically reduce or even eliminate her paranoid thoughts.) Once, when her food stamps had not come, even two days after Judy had received hers, Betty dryly observed that this was further proof that Richman County was trying to rid itself of homeless women. "They give Judy Tootie her food stamps so she'll eat herself to death [Judy weighed 300 pounds]. They won't give me mine so I'll starve to death." She got no argument from me. I had learned to go with the flow.

Sometimes I annoyed or even angered some of the women. When Louise told me that some of the women were following her around all day and harassing her, I asked her why they did these things. "You're just like the state's attorney," she said, "always asking for reasons. Whenever I tell him that someone assaulted me, he always asks me why they did it. People with criminal minds don't need a reason to do something. That's what makes them criminals."

. . . I think of Betty and Louise and many of the other women as friends. As a friend, I owe them friendship. Perhaps I also owe them something because I have so much and they have so little, but I do not feel under any special obligation to them as research subjects. Indeed, I do not think of them as "research subjects." Since they knew what I was trying to do and allowed me to do it, they could just as well be considered collaborators in what might fairly be seen as a cooperative enterprise.

Notes

1. Let the record show that now, some seven-plus years later, I have her permission to go ahead.

2. *Tally's Corner: A Study of Negro Streetcorner Men.*

3. For the same reason, I stopped taking life histories. After the women had known me for a few months, I took about 20 life histories on tape, often at the request of the women themselves and over a period of two years or so. Some of these lasted several hours over two or three sessions and I found myself accumulating more information than I could handle.

4. Many schizophrenics are completely lucid for long periods of time, and their thoughts and behavior are completely indistinguishable from those of normals. Even Bleuler . . . asserted that there were certain very important cognitive processes . . . that were frequently identical among schizophrenics and normals. "*In many important respects, then, an insane person may be completely sane*" (emphasis added). Morris Rosenberg, "A Symbolic Interactionist View of Psychosis," *Journal of Health and Social Behavior*, 25, no. 3 (September 1984), p. 291.

22 Handling the Stigma of Handling the Dead

WILLIAM E. THOMPSON

Life expectancy used to be short. As a result, at an early age people became acquainted personally with death. In 1900, the average American died by the age of 40, and children were likely to witness the death of one of their parents. Death seemed to hover over people, ready to intrude at any time. Consider a popular child's prayer from a few generations back. Each night as they went to bed, little Christian children, as young as two and three years, would kneel at their bedside, and say this prayer:

> Now I lay me down to sleep.
> I pray the Lord my soul to keep.
> If I should die before I wake,
> I pray the Lord my soul to take.

Death was also a family affair. Not only did people die at home, but also their mothers, wives, and sisters washed and dressed the body and the men made the coffin. Wakes (grieving ceremonies) were also held at home, with the body put on display in the "parlor," where family, friends, and neighbors "paid their last respects."

Today, in contrast, our life expectancy has almost doubled what it was in 1900, and we try to insulate ourselves from death. People die in hospitals, attended by strangers. Other strangers deliver the body to a funeral home. There, still more strangers prepare the body for burial by replacing its blood with embalming fluids. Afterward, these strangers dress the body in clothing selected by relatives, comb the hair, put makeup on the face, and place the body on display in a room reserved for this purpose (sometimes called "the eternal slumber room"). These strangers also transport the body in a special vehicle to the graveyard. Who are these "death specialists" who handle dead bodies, and how do they handle the stigma that comes from handling the dead? This is the focus of Thompson's article.

IN A COMPLEX, industrialized society a person's occupation or profession is central to his or her personal and social identity. As Pavalko (1988) pointed out, two strangers are quite ". . . likely to 'break the ice' by indicating the kind of work they do." As a result, individuals often made a number of initial judgments about others based on preconceived notions about particular occupations.

This study examines how morticians and funeral directors handle the stigma associated with their work. Historically, stigma has been attached to those responsible for caring for the dead, and the job typically was assigned to the lower classes (e.g., the Eta of Japan and the Untouchables in India), and in some cases, those who handled the dead were forbidden from touching the living.

Morticians and funeral directors are fully aware of the stigma associated with their work, so they continually strive to enhance their public image and promote their social credibility. They must work to shift the emphasis on their work from the dead to the living, and away from sales and toward service. As Aries (1976, 99) noted:

> In order to sell death, it had to be made friendly . . . since 1885 . . . [funeral directors have] presented themselves not as simple sellers of services, but as "doctors of grief" who have a mission . . . [which] consists in aiding the mourning survivors to return to normalcy.

Couched within the general theoretical framework of symbolic interactionism, there are a variety of symbolic and dramaturgical methods whereby morticians and funeral directors attempt to redefine their occupations and minimize and/or neutralize negative attitudes toward them and what they do.

Method

This study reflects over 2 years of qualitative fieldwork. Extensive ethnographic interviews were conducted with 19 morticians and funeral directors in four states: Kansas, Missouri, Oklahoma, and Texas. The funeral homes included both privately owned businesses and branches of large franchise operations.

Interviewees included people from different age groups, both sexes, and both whites and nonwhites. There were 16 males and 3 females interviewed for this study, ranging in age from 26 to 64 years.

The Stigma of Handling the Dead

Until [about 1900] in this country, people died at home and friends and family members prepared the bodies for burial (Lesy, 1987). As medical knowledge and technology progressed and became more specialized, more and more deaths occurred outside the home—usually in hospitals. Death became something to be handled by a select group of highly trained professionals—doctors, nurses, and hospital staff. As fewer people witnessed death firsthand, it became surrounded with more mystery, and physically handling the dead became the domain of only a few.

Members or friends of the family relinquished their role in preparing bodies for disposal to an *undertaker*, ". . . a special person who would 'undertake' responsibility for the care and burial of the dead" (Amos, 1983, 2). Most states began licensing embalmers around the end of the nineteenth century (Amos, 1983). These licensed embalmers were viewed as unusual, if not downright weird. They were not family members or friends of the deceased faced with the unsavory but necessary responsibility for disposing of a loved one's body, but strangers who *chose* to work with dead bodies—for compensation. Although most welcomed the opportunity to relinquish this chore they also viewed those who willingly assumed it with some skepticism and even disdain.

Sudnow (1967, 51–64) underscored the negative attitudes toward people who work with the dead in describing how those who work in a morgue, for example, are "death-tainted" and work very hard to rid themselves of the social stigma associated with their jobs. Morticians and funeral directors cannot escape from this "taint of death" and they must constantly work to "counteract the stigma" directed at them and their occupations.

Are morticians and funeral directors really that stigmatized? After all, they generally are well-known and respected members of their communities. In small communities and even many large cities, local funeral homes have been owned and operated by the same family for several generations. These people usually are members of civic organizations, have substantial incomes, and live in nice homes and drive nice automobiles. Most often they are viewed as successful business people. On the other hand, their work is surrounded by mystery, taboos, and stigma, and they often are viewed as cold, detached, and downright morbid for doing it. All the respondents in this study openly acknowledged that stigma was associated with their work. Some indicated that they thought the stigma primarily came from the "misconception" that they were "getting rich" off other people's grief; others believed it simply came from working with the dead. Clearly these two aspects of their work—handling the dead and profiting from death and grief—emerged as the two most stigmatizing features of the funeral industry according to respondents.

Managing Stigma

Erving Goffman wrote the most systematic analysis of how individuals manage a "spoiled" social identity in his classic work, *Stigma* (1963). He described several techniques, such as "passing," "dividing the social world," "mutual aid," "physical distance," "disclosure," and "covering," employed by the *discredited* and *discreditable* to manage information and conceal their stigmatizing attributes (41–104). Although these techniques work well for the physically scarred, blind, stammerers, bald, drug addicted, ex-convicts, and many other stigmatized categories of people, they are less likely to be used by morticians and funeral directors.

Except perhaps when on vacation, it is important for funeral directors to be known and recognized in their communities and to be associated with their work. Consequently, most of the morticians and funeral directors studied relied on other strategies for reducing the stigma associated with their work. Paramount among these strategies were: symbolic redefinition of their work, role distance, professionalism, emphasizing service, and enjoying socioeconomic status over occupational prestige. This was much less true for licensed embalmers who worked for funeral directors, especially in chain-owned funeral homes in large cities. In those cases the author found that many embalmers concealed their occupation from their neighbors and others with whom they were not intimately acquainted.

SYMBOLIC REDEFINITION

One of the ways in which morticians and funeral directors handle the stigma of their occupations is through symbolically negating as much of it as possible. Woods and Delisle (1978, 98) revealed how sympathy cards avoid the use of the terms "dead" and "death" by substituting less harsh words such as "loss," "time of sorrow," and "hour of sadness." This technique is also used by morticians and funeral directors to reduce the stigma associated with their work.

Words that are most closely associated with death are rarely used, and the most harsh terms are replaced with less ominous ones. The term *death* is almost never used by funeral directors; rather, they talk of "passing on," "meeting an untimely end," or "eternal slumber." There are no *corpses* or *dead bodies;* they are referred to as "remains" "the deceased," "loved one," or more frequently, by name (e.g., "Mr. Jones"). Use of the term *body* is almost uniformly avoided around the family. Viewing rooms (where the embalmed body is displayed in the casket) usually are given serene names such as "the sunset room," "the eternal slumber room," or, in one case, "the guest room." Thus, when friends or family arrive to view the body, they are likely to be told that "Mr. Jones is lying in repose in the eternal slumber room." This language contrasts sharply with that used by morticians and funeral directors in "backstage" areas (Goffman, 1959, 112) such as the embalming room where drowning victims often are called "floaters," burn victims are called "crispy critters," and others are simply referred to as "bodies" (Turner and Edgley, 1976).

All the respondents indicated that there was less stigma attached to the term *funeral director* than *mortician* or *embalmer*, underscoring the notion that much of the stigma they experienced was attached to physically handling the dead. Consequently, when asked what they do for a living, those who acknowledge that they are in the funeral business (several indicated that they often do not) referred to themselves as "funeral directors" even if all they did was the embalming. *Embalming* is referred to as "preservation" or "restoration," and in order to be licensed, one must have studied "mortuary arts" or "mortuary science." Embalming no longer takes place in an *embalming room*, but in a "preparation room," or in some cases the "operating room."

Coffins are now "caskets," which are transported in "funeral coaches" (not *hearses*) to their "final resting place" rather than to the *cemetery* or worse yet, *graveyard*, for their "interment" rather than *burial*. Thus, linguistically, the symbolic redefinition is complete, with death verbally redefined during every phase, and the stigma associated with it markedly reduced.

All the morticians and funeral directors in this study emphasized the importance of using the "appropriate" terms in referring to their work. Knowledge of the stigma attached to certain words was readily acknowledged, and all indicated that the earlier terminology was stigma-laden, especially the term "undertaker," which they believed conjured up negative images in the mind of the public. For example, a 29-year-old male funeral director indicated that his father still insisted on calling himself an "undertaker." "He just hasn't caught up with [modern times]," the son remarked. Interestingly, when asked why he did not refer to himself as an undertaker, he replied "It just sounds so old-fashioned [pause] plus, it sounds so morbid."

In addition to using language to symbolically redefine their occupations, funeral directors carefully attempt to shift the focus of their work away from the care of the dead (especially handling the body), and redefine it primarily in terms of caring for the living. The dead are deemphasized as most of the funeral ritual is orchestrated for the benefit of the friends and family of the deceased (Turner and Edgley, 1976). By redefining themselves as "grief therapists," or "bereavement counselors" their primary duties are associated with making funeral arrangements, directing the services, and consoling the family in their time of need.

ROLE DISTANCE

Because a person' sense of self is so strongly linked to occupation, it is common practice for people in undesirable or stigmatized occupations to practice role distance. Although the specific role-distancing techniques vary across different occupations and among different individuals within an occupation, they share the common function of allowing individuals to violate some of the role expectations associated with the occupation, and express their individuality within the confines of the occupational role. Although the funeral directors and morticians in this study used a variety of role-distancing techniques, three common patterns emerged: emotional detachment, humor, and countering the stereotype.

Emotional Detachment. One of the ways that morticians and funeral directors overcome their socialization regarding death taboos and the stigma associated with handling the dead is to detach themselves from the body of the work. Charmaz (1980) pointed out that a common technique used by coroners and funeral directors to minimize the stigma associated with death work is to routinize the work as much as possible. When embalming, morticians focus on the technical aspects of the job rather than thinking about the person they are working on. One mortician explained:

> When I'm in the preparation room I never think about who *who* I'm working on; I only think about what has to be done next. When I picked up the body, it was a person. When I get done, clean and dress the body, and place it in the casket, it becomes a person again. But in here it's just something to be worked on. I treat it like a mechanic treats an automobile engine—with respect, but there's no emotion involved. It's just a job that has to be done.

Another mortician described his emotional detachment in the embalming room:

> You can't think too much about this process [embalming], or it'll really get to you. For example, one time we brought in this little girl. She was about four years old—the same age as my youngest daughter at the time. She had been killed in a wreck; had gone through the windshield; was really a mess.
>
> At first, I wasn't sure I could do that one—all I could think of was my little girl. But when I got her in the prep room, my whole attitude changed. I know this probably sounds cold, and hard I guess, but suddenly I began to think of the challenge involved. This was gonna be an open-casket service, and while the body was in pretty good shape, the head and face were practically gone. This was gonna take a lot of reconstruction. Also, the veins are so small on children that you have to be a lot more careful.
>
> Anyway, I got so caught up in the job, that I totally forgot about working on a little girl. I was in the room with her about six hours when—[his wife] came in and reminded me that we had dinner plans that night. I washed up and went

out to dinner and had a great time. Later that night, I went right back to work on her without even thinking about it.

It wasn't until the next day when my wife was dressing the body, and I came in, and she was crying, that it hit me. I looked at the little girl, and I began crying. We both just stood there crying and hugging. My wife kept saying "I know this was tough for you," and "yesterday must have been tough." I felt sorta guilty, because I knew what she meant, and it should've been tough for me, real tough emotionally, but it wasn't. The only "tough" part had been the actual work, especially the reconstruction—I had totally cut off the emotional part.

It sometimes makes you wonder. Am I really just good at this, or am I losing something. I don't know. All I know is, if I'd thought about the little girl the way I did that next day, I never could have done her. It's just part of this job— you gotta just do what has to be done. If you think about it much, you'll never make it in this business.

Humor. Many funeral directors and morticians use humor to detach themselves emotionally from their work. The humor, of course, must be carefully hidden from friends and relatives of the deceased, and takes place in backstage areas such as the embalming room, or in professional group settings such as at funeral directors' conventions.

The humor varies from impromptu comments while working on the body to standard jokes told over and over again. Not unexpectedly, all the respondents indicated a strong distaste for necrophilia jokes. One respondent commented, "I can think of nothing less funny—the jokes are sick, and have done a lot of damage to the image of our profession."

Humor is an effective technique of diffusing the stigma associated with handling a dead body, however, and when more than one person is present in the embalming room, it is common for a certain amount of banter to take place, and jokes or comments are often made about the amount of body fat or the overendowment, or lack thereof, of certain body parts. For example, one mortician indicated that a common remark made about males with small genitalia is, "Well, at least he won't be missed."

• • •

As with any occupation, levels of humor varied among the respondents. During an interview one of the funeral directors spoke of some of the difficulties in advertising the business, indicating that because of attitudes toward death and the funeral business, he had to be sure that his newspaper advertisements did not offend anyone. He reached into his desk drawer and pulled out a pad with several "fake ads" written on it. They included:

"Shake and Bake Special—Cremation with No Embalming"
"Business Is Slow, Somebody's Gotta Go"
"Try Our Layaway Plan—Best in the Business"
"Count on Us, We'll Be the Last to Let You Down"
"People Are Dying to Use Our Services"
"Pay Now, Die Later"
"The Buck Really Does Stop Here"

He indicated that he and one of his friends had started making up these fake ads and slogans when they were doing their mortuary internships. Over the years, they occasionally corresponded by mail and saw each other at conventions, and they would always try to be one up on the other with the best ad. He said, "Hey, in this business, you have to look for your laughs where you can find them."

Countering the Stereotype. Morticians and funeral directors are painfully aware of the common negative stereotype of people in their occupations. The women in this study were much less concerned about the stereotype, perhaps because simply being female shattered the stereotype anyway. The men, however, not only acknowledged that they were well aware of the public's stereotypical image of them, but also indicated that they made every effort *not* to conform to it.

One funeral director, for instance, said:

> People think we're cold, unfriendly, and unfeeling. I always make it a point to be just the opposite. Naturally, when I'm dealing with a family I must be reserved and show the proper decorum, but when I am out socially, I always try to be very upbeat—very alive. No matter how tired I am, I try not to show it.

Another indicated that he absolutely never wore gray or black suits. Instead, he wore navy blue and usually with a small pinstripe. "I might be mistaken for the minister or a lawyer," he said, "but rarely for an undertaker."

The word "cold," which often is associated with death came up in a number of interviews. One funeral director was so concerned about the stereotype of being "cold," that he kept a handwarmer in the drawer of his desk. He said, "My hands tend to be cold and clammy. It's just a physical trait of mine, but there's no way that I'm going to shake someone's hand and let them walk away thinking how cold it was." Even on the warmest of days, he indicated that during services, he carried the handwarmer in his right-hand coat pocket so that he could warm his hand before shaking hands with or touching someone.

Although everyone interviewed indicated that he or she violated the public stereotype, each one expressed a feeling of being atypical. In other words, although they believed that they did not conform to the stereotype, they felt that many of their colleagues did. One funeral director was wearing jeans, a short-sleeved sweatshirt and a pair of running shoes during the interview. He had just finished mowing the lawn at the funeral home. "Look at me," he said, "Do I look like a funeral director? Hell, _____ [the funeral director across the street] wears a suit and tie to mow his grass!—or, at least he would if he didn't hire it done."

Others insisted that very few funeral directors conform to the public stereotype when out of public view, but feel compelled to conform to it when handling funeral arrangements, because it is an occupational role requirement. "I always try to be warm and upbeat," one remarked, "But, let's face it, when I'm working with a family, they're experiencing a lot of grief—I have to respect that, and act accordingly." Another indicated that he always lowered his voice when talking with family and friends of the deceased, and that it had become such a habit, that he found himself speaking softly almost all the time. "One of the occupational hazards, I guess," he remarked.

The importance of countering the negative stereotype was evident, when time after time, persons being interviewed would pause and ask "I'm not what you expected, am I?" or something similar. It seemed very important for them to be reassured that they did not fit the stereotype of funeral director or mortician.

PROFESSIONALISM

Another method used by morticians and funeral directors to reduce occupational stigma is to emphasize professionalism. Amos (1983, 3) described embalming as:

> . . . an example of a vocation in transition from an occupation to a profession. Until mid-nineteenth century, embalming was not considered a profession and this is still an issue debated in some circles today.

Most morticians readily admit that embalming is a very simple process and can be learned very easily. In all but two of the funeral homes studied, the interviewees admitted that people who were not licensed embalmers often helped with the embalming process. In one case, in which the funeral home was owned and operated by two brothers, one of the brothers was a licensed funeral director and licensed embalmer. The other brother had dropped out of high school and helped their father with the funeral business while his brother went to school to meet the educational requirements for licensure. The licensed brother said:

> By the time I got out of school and finished my apprenticeship, _____ [his brother] had been helping Dad embalm for over three years—and he was damned good at it. So when I joined the business, Dad thought it was best if I concentrated on handling the funeral arrangements and pre-service needs. After Dad died, I was the only licensed embalmer, so "officially" I do it all— all the embalming and the funeral arrangements. But, to tell you the truth, I only embalm every now and then when we have several to do, 'cause usually handles most of it. He's one of the best—I'd match him against any in the business.

Despite the relative simplicity of the embalming process and the open admission by morticians and funeral directors that "almost anyone could do it with a little practice," most states require licensure and certification for embalming. The four states represented in this study (Kansas, Oklahoma, Missouri, and Texas) have similar requirements for becoming a licensed certified embalmer. They include a minimum of 60 college hours with a core of general college courses (English, mathematics, social studies, etc.) plus 1 year of courses in the "mortuary sciences," or "mortuary arts." These consist of several courses in physiology and biology, and a 1-year apprenticeship under a licensed embalmer. To become a licensed funeral director requires the passing of a state board examination, which primarily requires a knowledge of state laws related to burial, cremation, disposal of the body, and insurance.

Although the general consensus among them was that an individual did not need a college education to become a good embalmer, they all stressed the importance of a college education for being a successful funeral director. Most thought that some basic courses in business, psychology, death and dying, and "bereavement counseling" were valuable preparation for the field. Also, most of the funeral directors were licensed insurance agents, which allowed them to sell burial policies.

Other evidence of the professionalization of the funeral industry includes state, regional, and national professional organizations that hold annual conventions and sponsor other professional activities; professional journals; state, regional, and national governing and regulating boards; and a professional code of ethics. Although the funeral industry is highly competitive, like most other professions, its members demonstrate a strong sense of cohesiveness and in-group identification.

One of the married couples in this study indicated that it was reassuring to attend national conventions where they met and interacted with other people in the funeral industry because it helps to "reassure us that we're not weird." The wife went on to say:

A lot of people ask us how we can stand to be in this business—especially because he does all of the embalming. They act like we must be strange or something. When we go to the conventions and meet with all of the other people there who are just like us—people who like helping other people—I feel normal again.

All these elements of professionalization—educational requirements, exams, boards, organizations, codes of ethics, and the rest—lend an air of credibility and dignity to the funeral business while diminishing the stigma associated with it. Although the requirements for licensure and certification are not highly exclusive, they still represent forms of boundary maintenance, and demand a certain level of commitment from those who enter the field. Thus, professionalization helped in the transition of the funeral business from a vocation that can be pursued by virtually anyone to a profession that can be entered only by those with the appropriate qualifications. As Pine (1975, 28) indicated:

Because professionalization is highly respected in American society, the word "profession" tends to be used as a symbol by occupations seeking to improve or enhance the lay public's conception of that occupation, and funeral directing is no exception. To some extent, this appears to be because the funeral director hopes to overcome the stigma of "doing death work."

"By claiming professional status, funeral directors claim prestige and simultaneously seek to minimize the stigma they experience for being death workers involved in 'dirty work.'"

THE SHROUD OF SERVICE

One of the most obvious ways in which morticians and funeral directors neutralize the stigma associated with their work is to wrap themselves in a "shroud of service." All the respondents emphasized their service role over all other aspects of their jobs. Although their services were not legally required in any of the four states included in this study, all the respondents insisted that people desperately needed them. As one funeral director summarized, "Service, that's what we're all about—we're there when people need us the most."

Unlike the humorous fantasy ads mentioned earlier, actual advertisements in the funeral industry focus on service. Typical ads for the companies in this study read:

"Our Family Serving Yours for Over 60 Years"
"Serving the Community for Four Generations"
"Thoughtful Service in Your Time of Need"

The emphasis on service, especially on "grief counseling" and "bereavement therapy," shifts the focus away from the two most stigmatizing elements of funeral work: the handling and preparation of the body, which already has been discussed at length; and retail sales, which are widely interpreted as profiting from other people's grief. Many of the funeral directors indicated that they believed the major reason for negative public feelings toward their occupation was not only that they handled dead bodies, but the fact that they made their living off the dead, or at least, off the grief of the living.

All admitted that much of their profit came from the sale of caskets and vaults, where markup is usually a minimum of 100%, and often 400–500%, but all played down this aspect of their work. The Federal Trade Commission requires that funeral directors provide their customers with itemized lists of all charges. The author was provided with price lists for all merchandise and services by all the funeral directors in this study. When asked to estimate the "average price" of one of their funerals, respondents' answers ranged from $3,000 to $4,000. Typically, the casket accounted for approximately half of the total expense. Respondents indicated that less than 5% of their business involved cremations, but that even then they often encouraged the purchase of a casket. One said, "A lot of people ask about cremation, because they think it's cheaper, but I usually sell them caskets even for cremation; then, if you add the cost of cremation and urn, cremation becomes more profitable than burial."

Despite this denial of the retail aspects of the job, trade journals provide numerous helpful hints on the best techniques for displaying and selling caskets, and great care is given to this process. In all the funeral homes visited, one person was charged with the primary responsibility for helping with "casket selection." In smaller family-operated funeral homes, this person usually was the funeral director's wife. In the large chain-owned companies, it was one of the "associate funeral directors." In either case, the person was a skilled salesperson.

Nevertheless, the sales pitch is wrapped in the shroud of service. During each interview, the author asked to be shown the "selection room," and to be treated as if he were there to select a casket for a loved one. All the funeral directors willingly complied, and most treated the author as if he actually were there to select a casket. Interestingly, most perceived this as an actual sales opportunity and mentioned their "pre-need selection service" and said that if the author had not already made such arrangements, they would gladly assist him with the process. The words "sell," "sales," "buy," and "purchase," were carefully avoided.

Also, although by law the price for each casket must be displayed separately, most funeral homes also displayed a "package price" that included the casket and "full services." If purchased separately, the casket was always more expensive than if it was included in the package of services. This gave the impression that a much more expensive casket could be purchased for less money if bought as part of a service package. It also implied that the services provided by the firm were of more value than the merchandise.

The funeral directors rationalized the high costs of merchandise and funerals by emphasizing that they were a small price to pay for the services performed. One insisted, "We don't sell merchandise, we sell service!" Another asked "What is peace of mind worth?" and another "How do you put a price on relieving grief?"

Another rationalization for the high prices was the amount involved in arranging and conducting funeral services. When asked about the negative aspects of their jobs, most emphasized the hard work and long hours involved. In fact, all but two of the interviewees said that they did not want their children to follow in their footsteps, because the work was largely misunderstood (stigmatized), too hard, the hours too long, and "the income not nearly as high as most people think."

In addition to emphasizing the service aspect of their work, funeral directors also tend to join a number of local philanthropic and service organizations (Pine, 1975, 49). Although many businessmen find that joining such organizations is advantageous for making contacts, Stephenson (1985, 223) contended that the small-town funeral director "may be able to counter the stigma of his or her occupation by being active in the community, thereby counteracting some of the negative images associated with the job of funeral directing."

SOCIOECONOMIC STATUS VERSUS OCCUPATIONAL PRESTIGE

It seems that what funeral directors lack in occupational prestige, they make up for in socioeconomic status. Although interviewees were very candid about the number of funerals they performed every year and the average costs per funeral, most were reluctant to disclose their annual incomes. One exception was a 37-year-old funeral home owner, funeral director, and licensed embalmer in a community of approximately 25,000 who indicated that in the previous year he had handled 211 funerals and had a gross income of just under $750,000. After deducting overhead (three licensed embalmers on staff, a receptionist, a gardener, a student employee, insurance costs, etc.), he estimated his net income to have been "close to $250,000." He quickly added, however, that he worked long hours, had his 5-day vacation cut to two (because of a "funeral call that he had to handle personally") and despite his relatively high income (probably one of the two or three highest incomes in the community), he felt morally, socially, and professionally obligated to hide his wealth in the community. "I have to walk a fine line," he said, "I can live in a nice home, drive a nice car, and wear nice suits, because people know that I am a successful businessman—but, I have to be careful not to flaunt it."

One of the ways he reconciles this dilemma was by enjoying "the finer things in life" outside the community. He owned a condominium in Vail where he took ski trips and kept his sports car. He also said that none of his friends or neighbors there knew that he was in the funeral business. In fact, when they inquired about his occupations he told them he was in insurance (which technically was true because he also was a licensed insurance agent who sold burial policies). When asked why he did not disclose his true occupational identity, he responded:

> When I tell people what I really do, they initially seem "put off," even repulsed. I have literally had people jerk their hands back during a handshake when somebody introduces me and then tells them what I do for a living. Later, many of them become very curious and ask a lot of questions. If you tell people you sell insurance, they usually let the subject drop.

Although almost all the funeral directors in this study lived what they characterized as fairly "conservative lifestyles," most also indicated that they enjoyed many of the material things that their jobs offered them. One couple rationalized their recent purchase of a very expensive sailboat (which both contended they "really couldn't afford"), by saying, "Hey, if anybody knows that you can't take it with you, it's us—we figured we might as well enjoy it while we can." Another commented, "Most of the people in this community would never want to do what I do, but most of them would like to have my income."

Summary and Conclusion

This study describes and analyzes how people in the funeral industry attempt to reduce and neutralize the stigma associated with their occupations. Morticians and funeral directors are particularly stigmatized, not only because they perform work that few others would be willing to do (preparing dead bodies for burial), but also because they profit from death. Consequently, members of the funeral industry consciously work at stigma reduction.

Paramount among their strategies are symbolically redefining their work. This especially involves avoiding all language that reminds their customer of death, the body, and retail sales; morticians and funeral directors emphasize the need for their professional services of relieving family grief and bereavement counseling. They also practice role distance, emphasize their professionalism, wrap themselves in a "shroud of service," and enjoy their relatively high socioeconomic status rather than lament their lower occupational prestige.

PART VI

Deviance and Social Control

F OR SOCIETY TO EXIST, people must be able to know what to expect of others. If they couldn't do this, the world would be in chaos. Because the behavior of humans is not controlled by instincts, people develop *norms* (standards, rules, or expectations) to provide regularity or patterns to social life. Norms provide a high degree of certainty in what, without them, would be a hopelessly disoriented world. If people followed their own inclinations and no one knew what to expect of others, we would have chaos. The confidence we can place in others is only relative, however, because not everyone follows all the rules all the time. In fact *deviance*, the violation of rules and expectations, is universal. All members of society violate some of the expectations that others have of them. In this sense, all of us are deviants.

Because in common usage the word *deviant* is equivalent to perverted, dirty, twisted, and nasty, to say that all of us are deviants may strike you as strange. It is important to stress that as used in sociology *deviance is not a term of negative judgment,* as it is when used by nonsociologists. To sociologists, *deviance* simply refers to activities that violate the expectations of others. This term is so broad that it includes both murder and lying. Unlike common usage, in sociology this term is neutral, passing judgment neither on the merit of the rules nor on those who violate them.

The norms that people develop to control one another cover a fascinating variety of human behavior. They include rules and expectations concerning our appearance, manner, and conduct.

1. *Appearance* (what we look like): the norms concerning clothing, makeup, hairstyle, and other such presentational aspects of our body, including its cleanliness and odors. These rules also cover the *social extensions of the*

self, those objects thought to represent the individual in some way, such as the person's home, car, and, often, even the individual's pet.

2. *Manner* (our style of doing things): people's expectations about how we will express ourselves, such as our facial expressions, gestures, and other body language. Manner includes *personal style* (gruff and direct-to-the-point; pleasant and charming), the expectations others have of us because of how we acted in the past. Manner also includes *group style*, expectations attached to us because of our membership in a social group (race–ethnic, gender, occupation, age, and so on—"the way those kind of people are").

3. *Conduct* (what we say, what we do): rules covering the rest of human behavior, specifying what we can and cannot do or say, as well as the circumstances that require or forbid that we say or do something. These include rules of *authority* (who has the right to give which order to whom), rules of *obligation* (who has the responsibility to do what for whom), and rules of *account giving* (what we are expected to say when we are asked for an explanation). Account-giving rules even specify the degree to which we are expected to be honest about some matter, to go into detail, or to avoid implicating others.

These everyday rules of appearance, manner, and conduct are sliced very fine. They specify the circumstances that apply, how we must phrase what we say, such as with how much respect or informality, even our facial expressions and eye contact when we say it. In other words, hardly a single aspect of our lives goes untouched by rules made by others—most of whom are long ago dead. *Social control* is a basic fact of social life, enveloping all of us in its pervasive net of expectations. This leaves none of us a free agent, able to do as we please.

Norms also follow social status. That is, they differ according to the social positions we occupy, especially those watershed identifiers of age, gender, occupation, and social class. For example, as you know, the rules of conduct, appearance, and manner differ for convicts, CEOs, students, children, old people, men, and women. Looking at this list, you can see that expectations (or rules) depend on reputation, prestige, wealth, occupation, age, and gender. In some instances, they also vary according to race–ethnicity.

The rules also change as we switch audiences. For example, as teenagers know so well, their parents' expectations usually aren't even close to what their friends expect of them. Similarly, we are expected to act one way when we are with members of our own age, gender, or racial–ethnic group, but differently when we are with others. Our everyday norms even dictate distinct clothing for different audiences (or as we are more likely to phrase it, for different occasions)—for a college classroom, for a formal dance, for the beach, and so on. In short, to change physical locations is to transform stages and audiences, bringing distinct expectations of how we are to present the self.

These complex expectations define *in* and define *out:* Those who conform to the norms are accorded the status of members-in-good-standing, while those who deviate from them are usually defined as outsiders of some sort. Often objects of suspicion, sometimes of derision and hostility, deviants are reacted to in a number of ways. They may be given more attention in order to bring them back into line, or they may be ostracized or kicked out of the group. For mild deviations, they may simply be stared at. People may also gossip about them, joke about them, divorce them, strike their names from guest lists, or demote or fire them. In more extreme cases of rule violations, the offender may be shunned or physically attacked. In the most extreme cases, they are tried and imprisoned—or even put to death.

This list of some of the social reactions to deviance indicates that people are extremely concerned with rule-following and rule-breaking behaviors. Challenging fundamental expectations about how social life is run, deviants are often seen as a threat to people's welfare. With such a stake in the conformity of others, then, people react to deviants—sharply and negatively if they consider the deviance threatening, but tolerantly and perhaps even with amusement if they believe it to be mild.

In Part VI, we examine both deviance and social control. The opening selection is a forceful reminder of the situational grounding of our morality. As Philip Meyer recounts Stanley Milgram's classic experiment, we come face-to-face with the power of social groups—they are so potent they can get us to participate in acts we know are evil. In the next selection, I tell the story of an airplane crash in the Andes—looking at how social control operated among the survivors, who ate their deceased friends and relatives. Then Ken Levi reports on his interviews with a hit man, examining how someone who participates in such extreme deviance explains his actions. William Chambliss then turns the focus on how community reactions to delinquents have far-reaching effects on their adult lives. Philip Zimbardo follows with a description of his intriguing experiment, in which he uncovered structural bases for the hostile relationships between prisoners and prison guards. David Rosenhan closes Part VI by exploring the intriguing question of whether or not we can tell the sane from the insane.

23 If Hitler Asked You to Electrocute a Stranger, Would You? Probably

PHILIP MEYER

Let's take the title of this selection seriously for a moment. Suppose that Hitler did ask you to electrocute a stranger, would you? "Of course, I wouldn't" is our immediate response. "*I* wouldn't even *hurt* a stranger just because someone asked me, much less electrocute the person."

Such an answer certainly seems reasonable, but unfortunately it may not be true. Consider two aspects of the power of groups over our lives. First, we all do things that we prefer not to—from going to work and taking tests when we really want to stay in bed to mowing the grass or doing the dishes when we want to watch television. Our roles and relationships require that we do them, and our own preferences become less important than fulfilling the expectations of others. Second, at least on occasion, most of us feel social pressures so strongly that we do things that conflict with our morals. Both these types of behavior are fascinating to sociologists, for they indicate how *social structure*—the way society is organized—shapes our lives.

But electrocute someone? Isn't that carrying the point a little too far? One would certainly think so. The experiments described by Meyer, however, indicate that people's positions in groups are so significant that even "nice, ordinary" people will harm strangers upon request. You may find the implications of authority and roles arising from these experiments disturbing. Many of us do.

IN THE BEGINNING, Stanley Milgram was worried about the Nazi problem. He doesn't worry much about the Nazis anymore. He worries about you and me, and perhaps, himself a little bit too.

Stanley Milgram is a social psychologist, and when he began his career at Yale University in 1960 he had a plan to prove, scientifically, that Germans are different. The Germans-are-different hypothesis had been used by historians, such as William L. Shirer, to explain the systematic destruction of the

Jews by the Third Reich. One madman could decide to destroy the Jews and
even create a master plan for getting it done. But to implement it on the scale
that Hitler did meant that thousands of other people had to go along with the
scheme and help to do the work. The Shirer thesis, which Milgram set out to
test, is that Germans have a basic character flaw which explains the whole
thing, and this flaw is a readiness to obey authority without question, no matter what outrageous acts the authority commands.

The appealing thing about this theory is that it makes those of us who
are not Germans feel better about the whole business. Obviously, you and I
are not Hitler, and it seems equally obvious that we would never do Hitler's
dirty work for him. But now, because of Stanley Milgram, we are compelled
to wonder. Milgram developed a laboratory experiment which provided a
systematic way to measure obedience. His plan was to try it out in New
Haven on Americans and then go to Germany and try it out on Germans. He
was strongly motivated by scientific curiosity, but there was also some moral
content in his decision to pursue this line of research, which was in turn colored by his own Jewish background. If he could show that Germans are more
obedient than Americans, he could then vary the conditions of the experiment and try to find out just what it is that makes some people more obedient than others. With this understanding, the world might, conceivably, be
just a little bit better.

But he never took his experiment to Germany. He never took it any farther than Bridgeport. The first finding, also the most unexpected and disturbing finding, was that we Americans are an obedient people: not blindly
obedient, and not blissfully obedient, just obedient. "I found so much obedience," says Milgram softly, a little sadly, "I hardly saw the need for taking
the experiment to Germany."

There is something of the theater director in Milgram, and his technique, which he learned from one of the old masters in experimental psychology, Solomon Asch, is to stage a play with every line rehearsed, every
prop carefully selected, and everybody an actor except one person. That one
person is the subject of the experiment. The subject, of course, does not
know he is in a play. He thinks he is in real life. The value of this technique
is that the experimenter, as though he were God, can change a prop here,
vary a line there, and see how the subject responds. Milgram eventually had
to change a lot of the script just to get people to stop obeying. They were
obeying so much, the experiment wasn't working—it was like trying to measure oven temperature with a freezer thermometer.

The experiment worked like this: If you were an innocent subject in
Milgram's melodrama, you read an ad in the newspaper or received one in
the mail asking for volunteers for an educational experiment. The job

would take about an hour and pay $4.50. So you make an appointment and go to an old Romanesque stone structure on High Street with the imposing name of The Yale Interaction Laboratory. It looks something like a broadcasting studio. Inside, you meet a young, crew-cut man in a laboratory coat who says he is Jack Williams, the experimenter. There is another citizen, fiftyish, Irish face, an accountant, a little overweight, and very mild and harmless looking. This other citizen seems nervous and plays with his hat while the two of you sit in chairs side by side and are told that the $4.50 checks are yours no matter what happens. Then you listen to Jack Williams explain the experiment.

It is about learning, says Jack Williams in a quiet, knowledgeable way. Science does not know much about the conditions under which people learn and this experiment is to find out about negative reinforcement. Negative reinforcement is getting punished when you do something wrong, as opposed to positive reinforcement which is getting rewarded when you do something right. The negative reinforcement in this case is electric shock. You notice a book on the table, titled, *The Teaching-Learning Process*, and you assume that this has something to do with the experiment.

Then Jack Williams takes two pieces of paper, puts them in a hat, and shakes them up. One piece of paper is supposed to say, "Teacher," and the other, "Learner." Draw one and you will see which you will be. The mild-looking accountant draws one, holds it close to his vest like a poker player, looks at it, and says, "Learner." You look at yours. It says, "Teacher." You do not know that the drawing is rigged, and both slips say "Teacher." The experimenter beckons to the mild-mannered "learner."

"Want to step right in here and have a seat, please?" he says. "You can leave your coat on the back of that chair . . . roll up your right sleeve, please. Now what I want to do is strap down your arms to avoid excessive movement on your part during the experiment. This electrode is connected to the shock generator in the next room.

"And this electrode paste," he says, squeezing some stuff out of a plastic bottle and putting it on the man's arm, "is to provide a good contact and to avoid a blister or burn. Are there any questions now before we go into the next room?"

You don't have any, but the strapped-in "learner" does.

"I do think I should say this," says the learner. "About two years ago, I was in the veterans' hospital . . . they detected a heart condition. Nothing serious, but as long as I'm having these shocks, how strong are they—how dangerous are they?"

Williams, the experimenter, shakes his head casually. "Oh, no," he says. "Although they may be painful, they're not dangerous. Anything else?"

Nothing else. And so you play the game. The game is for you to read a series of word pairs: for example, blue-girl, nice-day, fat-neck. When you finish the list, you read just the first word in each pair and then a multiple-choice list of four other words, including the second word of the pair. The learner, from his remote, strapped-in position, pushes one of four switches to indicate which of the four answers he thinks is the right one. If he gets it right, nothing happens and you go on to the next one. If he gets it wrong, you push a switch that buzzes and gives him an electric shock. And then you go on to the next word. You start with 15 volts and increase the number of volts by 15 for each wrong answer. The control board goes from 15 volts on one end to 450 volts on the other. So that you know what you are doing, you get a test-shock yourself, at 45 volts. It hurts. To further keep you aware of what you are doing to that man in there, the board has verbal descriptions of the shock levels, ranging from "Slight Shock" at the left-hand side, through "Intense Shock" in the middle, to "Danger: Severe Shock" toward the far right. Finally, at the very end, under 435- and 450-volt switches, there are three ambiguous X's. If, at any point, you hesitate, Mr. Williams calmly tells you to go on. If you still hesitate, he tells you again.

Except for some terrifying details, which will be explained in a moment, this is the experiment. The object is to find the shock level at which you disobey the experimenter and refuse to pull the switch.

When Stanley Milgram first wrote this script, he took it to 14 Yale psychology majors and asked them what they thought would happen. He put it this way: Out of one hundred persons in the teacher's predicament, how would their break-off points be distributed along the 15- to 450-volt scale? They thought a few would break off very early, most would quit someplace in the middle, and a few would go all the way to the end. The highest estimate of the number out of 100 who would go all the way to the end was three. Milgram then informally polled some of his fellow scholars in the psychology department. They agreed that very few would go to the end. Milgram thought so too.

"I'll tell you quite frankly," he says, "before I began this experiment, before any shock generator was built, I thought that most people would break off at 'Strong Shock' or 'Very Strong Shock.' You would get only a very, very small proportion of people going out to the end of the shock generator, and they would constitute a pathological fringe."

In his pilot experiments, Milgram used Yale students as subjects. Each of them pushed the shock switches, one by one, all the way to the end of the board.

So he rewrote the script to include some protests from the learner. At first, they were mild, gentlemanly, Yalie protests, but "it didn't seem to have as much effect as I thought it would or should," Milgram recalls. "So we had more violent protestation on the part of the person getting the shock. All of the time, of course, what we were trying to do was not to create a macabre situation, but simply to generate disobedience. And that was one of the first findings. This was not only a technical deficiency of the experiment, that we didn't get disobedience. It really was the first finding: that obedience would be much greater than we had assumed it would be and disobedience would be much more difficult than we had assumed."

As it turned out, the situation did become rather macabre. The only meaningful way to generate disobedience was to have the victim protest with great anguish, noise, and vehemence. The protests were tape-recorded so that all the teachers ordinarily would hear the same sounds and nuances, and they started with a grunt at 75 volts, proceeded through a "Hey, that really hurts," at 125 volts, got desperate with, "I can't stand the pain—don't do that," at 180 volts, reached complaints of heart trouble at 195, an agonized scream at 285, a refusal to answer at 315, and only heartrending, ominous silence after that.

Still, 65 percent of the subjects, 20- to 50-year-old American males, everyday, ordinary people, like you and me, obediently kept pushing those levers in the belief that they were shocking the mild-mannered learner, whose name was Mr. Wallace, and who was chosen for the role because of his innocent appearance, all the way up to 450 volts.

Milgram was not getting enough disobedience so that he had something he could measure. The next step was to vary the circumstances to see what would encourage or discourage obedience. There seemed very little left in the way of discouragement. The victim was already screaming at the top of his lungs and feigning a heart attack. So whatever new impediment to obedience reached the brain of the subject had to travel by some route other than the ear. Milgram thought of one.

He put the learner in the same room with the teacher. He stopped strapping the learner's hand down. He rewrote the script so that at 150 volts the learner took his hand off the shock plate and declared that he wanted out of experiment. He rewrote the script some more so that the experimenter then told the teacher to grasp the learner's hand and physically force it down on the plate to give Mr. Wallace his unwanted electric shock.

"I had the feeling that very few people would go on at that point, if any," Milgram says. "I thought that would be the limit of obedience that you would find in the laboratory."

It wasn't.

Although [years have] gone by, Milgram still remembers the first person to walk into the laboratory in the newly rewritten script. He was a construction worker, a very short man. "He was so small," says Milgram, "that when he sat on the chair in front of the shock generator, his feet didn't reach the floor. When the experimenter told him to push the victim's hand down and give the shock, he turned to the experimenter, and he turned to the victim, his elbow went up, he fell down on the hand of the victim, his feet kind of tugged to one side, and he said, 'Like this, boss?' Zzumph!"

The experiment was played out to its bitter end. Milgram tried it with 40 different subjects. And 30 percent of them obeyed the experimenter and kept on obeying.

"The protests of the victim were strong and vehement, he was screaming his guts out, he refused to participate, and you had to physically struggle with him in order to get his hand down on the shock generator," Milgram remembers. But 12 out of 40 did it.

Milgram took his experiment out of New Haven. Not to Germany, just 20 miles down the road to Bridgeport. Maybe, he reasoned, the people obeyed because of the prestigious setting of Yale University. If they couldn't trust a learning center that had been there for two centuries, whom could they trust? So he moved the experiment to an untrustworthy setting.

The new setting was a suite of three rooms in a run-down office building in Bridgeport. The only identification was a sign with a fictitious name: "Research Associates of Bridgeport." Questions about professional connections got only vague answers about "research for industry."

Obedience was less in Bridgeport. Forty-eight percent of the subjects stayed for the maximum shock, compared to 65 percent at Yale. But this was enough to prove that far more than Yale's prestige was behind the obedient behavior.

[Since the experiments] Stanley Milgram has been trying to figure out what makes ordinary American citizens so obedient. The most obvious answer—that people are mean, nasty, brutish, and sadistic—won't do. The subjects who gave the shocks to Mr. Wallace to the end of the board did not enjoy it. They groaned, protested, fidgeted, argued, and in some cases, were seized by fits of nervous, agitated giggling.

"They even try to get out of it," says Milgram, "but they are somehow engaged in something from which they cannot liberate themselves. They are locked into a structure, and they do not have the skills or inner resources to disengage themselves. . . ."

"The results, as seen and felt in the laboratory," he has written, "are disturbing. They raise the possibility that human nature, or more specifically the kind of character produced in American democratic society, cannot be counted on to insulate its citizens from brutality and inhumane treatment at the direction of malevolent authority. A substantial proportion of people do what they are told to do, irrespective of the content of the act and without limitation of conscience, so long as they perceive that the command comes from a legitimate authority. If, in this study, an anonymous experimenter can successfully command adults to subdue a 50-year-old man and force on him painful electric shocks against his protest, one can only wonder what government, with its vastly greater authority and prestige, can command of its subjects. . . ."

Stanley Milgram has his problems, too. He believes that in the laboratory situation, he would not have shocked Mr. Wallace. His professional critics reply that in his real-life situation he has done the equivalent. He has placed innocent and naive subjects under great emotional strain and pressure in selfish obedience to his quest for knowledge. When you raise this issue with Milgram, he has an answer ready. There is, he explains patiently, a critical difference between his naive subjects and the man in the electric chair. The man in the electric chair (in the mind of the naive subject) is helpless, strapped in. But the naive subject is free to go at any time.

Immediately after he offers this distinction, Milgram anticipates the objection.

"It's quite true," he says. "that this is almost a philosophic position, because we have learned that some people are psychologically incapable of disengaging themselves. But that doesn't relieve them of the moral responsibility."

The parallel is exquisite. "The tension problem was unexpected," says Milgram in his defense. But he went on anyway. The naive subjects didn't expect the screaming protests from the strapped-in learner. But they went on.

"I had to make a judgment," says Milgram. "I had to ask myself, was this harming the person or not? My judgment is that it was not. Even in the extreme cases, I wouldn't say that permanent damage results."

Sound familiar? "The shocks may be painful," the experimenter kept saying, "but they're not dangerous."

After the series of experiments was completed, Milgram sent a report of the results to his subjects and a questionnaire, asking whether they were glad or sorry to have been in the experiment. Eighty-three and seven-tenths percent said they were glad and only 1.3 percent were sorry; 15 percent were neither sorry nor glad. However, Milgram could not be sure at the time of the experiment that only 1.3 percent would be sorry.

Kurt Vonnegut, Jr., put one paragraph in the preface to *Mother Night*, in 1966, which pretty much says it for the people with their fingers on the shock-generator switches, for you and me, and maybe even for Milgram. "If I'd been born in Germany," Vonnegut said, "I suppose I would have *been* a

276 / Philip Meyer

Nazi, bopping Jews and gypsies and Poles around, leaving boots sticking out of snowbanks, warming myself with my sweetly virtuous insides. So it goes."

Just so. One thing that happened to Milgram back in New Haven during the days of the experiment was that he kept running into people he'd watched from behind the one-way glass. It gave him a funny feeling, seeing those people going about their everyday business in New Haven and knowing what they would do to Mr. Wallace if ordered to. Now that his research results are in and you've thought about it, you can get this funny feeling too. You don't need one-way glass. A glance in your own mirror may serve just as well.

24 Eating Your Friends Is the Hardest: The Survivors of the F-227

JAMES M. HENSLIN

A theme running through our previous readings is that each culture provides guidelines for how to view the world, even for how we determine right and wrong. The perspectives we learn envelop us much as a fish is enveloped by water. Almost all the world's cultures uphold the idea that it is wrong to eat human flesh. (Some exceptions do apply, such as warriors who used to eat the heart or kidneys of slain enemies in an attempt to acquire the source of their strength or courage.) Thus it is safe to say that nowhere in the world is there a culture whose members regularly consume people as food. Yet, in the unusual situation recounted here, this is precisely what these people did.

Note how, even in the midst of reluctantly committing acts that they themselves found repugnant—and ones they knew that the world condemns—this group developed norms to govern their behavior. This was crucial for these survivors, because group support, along with its attendant norms, is essential for maintaining sanity and a sense of a "good" self. At the conclusion of the article, Henslin shows how this event is more than simply an interesting story—that it represents the essence of social life.

LOCATED BETWEEN BRAZIL AND ARGENTINA, near Buenos Aires, is tiny Uruguay. On October 12, 1972, a propeller-driven Fairchild F-227 left Uruguay's capital, Montevideo, bound for Santiago, Chile—a distance of about 900 miles. On board were 15 members of an amateur rugby team from Uruguay, along with 25 of their relatives and friends. The pilots, from the Uruguayan Air Force, soon became concerned about turbulence over the Andes Mountains. Winds blowing in from the Pacific were colliding

The events related in this selection are based primarily on Read 1974, pages 26–39, 70, 81–91, 98, 101, 128, 136–139, 165, 168, 171, 199, and 218. Supplementary sources are "Cannibalism on the Cordillera," *Time*, January 8, 1973:27–28, and Benales, 1973.

with air currents coming from the opposite direction, creating a turbulence that could toss a plane around like a scrap of paper in a wind storm.

Since the threat was so great, the pilots decided to land in Mendoza, Argentina, where everyone spent the night. The next day, with the weather only slightly improved, the crew debated about turning back. Several of the rugby players taunted them, saying they were cowards. When the captain of a plane which had just flown over the Andes reported that the F-227 should be able to fly over the turbulence, the Fairchild's pilots decided to continue the trip. Once again airborne, the young passengers laughed about its being Friday the 13th as some threw a rugby ball around and others played cards. Many of them still in their teens, and all of them from Uruguay's upper class (two were nephews of the president of Uruguay), they were in high spirits.

Over the Andes the plane flew into a thick cloud, and the pilots had to fly by instrument. Amid the turbulence they hit an "air pocket," and the plane suddenly plunged 3,000 feet. When the passengers abruptly found themselves below the cloud, one young man turned to another and said, "Is it normal to fly so close?" He was referring to the mountainside just 10 feet off the right wing.

With a deafening roar, the right wing sheared off as it hit the side of the mountain. The wing whipped over the plane and knocked off the tail. The steward, the navigator, and three of the rugby players still strapped in their seats were blown out of the gaping hole. Then the left wing broke off and, like a toboggan going 200 miles an hour, the fuselage slid on its belly into a steep, snow-covered valley.

As night fell, the survivors huddled in the wreckage. At 12,000 feet the cold, especially at night, was brutal. There was little fuel, because not much wood is used in the construction of airplanes. They had almost no food—basically some chocolate that the passengers had bought on their overnight stay in Mendoza. There were a few bottles of wine, and the many cartons of cigarettes they had purchased at a duty-free shop.

The twenty-seven who survived the crash expected to be rescued quickly. At most, they thought, they would have to spend the night on the mountain top. Seventy days later, only sixteen remained alive.

The chocolate and wine didn't go very far, and provided little nourishment. The plane, off course by a hundred miles or so and painted white, was not only difficult to track, but virtually invisible against the valley's deep layer of snow: Search planes were unable to locate the wreckage.

As the days went by, the survivors' spirits seemed to be sucked into a hopeless pit. Hunger and starvation began to bear down on them. They felt cold all the time. They became weaker and had difficulty keeping their balance. Their skin became wrinkled, like that of old people. Although no one mentioned it, several of the young men began to realize that their only chance to survive was to eat the bodies of those who died in the crash. The corpses lay strewn in the snow around the plane, perfectly preserved by the bitter cold.

The thought of cutting into the flesh of their friends was too ghastly a prospect to put into words. Finally, however, Canessa, a medical student, brought up the matter with his friends. He asserted that the bodies were no longer people. The soul was gone, he said, and the body was simply meat—and essential to their survival. They were growing weaker, and they could not survive without food. And what food was there besides the corpses? "They are no more human beings than the dead flesh of the cattle we eat at home," he said.

Days later, the topic moved from furtive discussion in a small group to open deliberation among all the survivors. Inside the plane, arguing the matter, Canessa reiterated his position. His three closest friends supported him, adding, "We have a duty to survive. If we don't eat the bodies, it is a sin. We must do this not just for our own sakes but also for our families. In fact," they continued, "God wants us to survive, and He has provided these bodies so we can live." Some, however, just shook their heads, the thought too disturbing to even contemplate.

Serbino pushed the point. He said, "If I die, I want you to eat my body. I want you to use it." Some nodded in agreement. In an attempt to bring a little humor to the black discussion, he added, "If you don't, I'll come back and give you a swift kick in the butt." Some said that while they did not think it would be wrong to eat the bodies, they themselves could never do it. The arguments continued for hours.

Four of the young men went outside. Near the plane, the buttocks of a body protruded from the snow. No one spoke as they stared at it. Wordlessly, Canessa knelt and began to cut with the only instrument he had found, a piece of broken glass. The flesh was frozen solid, and he could cut only slivers the size of matchsticks. Canessa laid the pieces on the roof of the plane, and the young men went back inside. They said that the meat was drying in the sun. The others looked mutely at one another. No one made a move to leave the plane.

Canessa decided that he would have to be the first. Going outside, he picked up a sliver of meat. Staring at it, almost transfixed, he became as though paralyzed. He simply couldn't make his hand move to his mouth. Summoning every ounce of courage, he forced his hand upwards. While his stomach recoiled, he pushed the meat inside his mouth and forced himself to swallow. Later, Serbino took a piece. He tried to swallow, but the sliver hung halfway down his throat. Quickly grabbing some snow, he managed to wash it down. Canessa and Serbino were joined by others, who also ate.

The next morning, on the transistor radio they had struggled so hard to get working, their hearts plunged when they heard that the air force had called off the search. The survivors knew that this announcement almost sealed their fate. The only way out, if there was one, was on their own. They held a meeting and decided that the fittest should try to seek help—even though no one knew where to seek it. But none was strong enough to try. With the snow's crust breaking under every step, even to walk was exhausting. There was only one way to regain strength, and, without giving words to the thought, everyone knew what it was.

Canessa and Strauch went outside. The corpse was in the same position as before. They took a deep breath and began to hack meat off the bone. They laid the strips on the plane to thaw in the sun. The knowledge that no rescuers were looking for them encouraged others to join in eating the human flesh. They forced themselves to swallow—their consciences, seconded by their stomachs, accusing them of extreme wrongdoing. Still, they forced the flesh down, telling themselves over and over that there was no other way to survive.

Some, however, could not. Javier and Liliana Methol, husband and wife, though they longed to return to their children, could not eat human flesh. They said that the others could do as they liked, but perhaps God wanted them to choose to die.

The survivors began to organize. Canessa took charge of cutting up the bodies, while a group of the younger ones had the job of preventing the corpses from rotting by keeping them covered with snow. Another group had the task of seeing that the plane was kept in order. Even the weakest had a job to do: They were able to hold pieces of aluminum in the sun to melt snow for drinking water.

The first corpses they ate were those of the crew, strangers to them.

One day, when it was too cold to melt snow, they burned wooden Coca-Cola crates that they had found in the luggage compartment. After they had water, they roasted some meat over the embers. There was only enough heat to brown the pieces, but they found the flavor better-tasting, like beef, they said, but softer. Canessa said they should never do this again, for heat destroys proteins. "You have to eat it raw to get its full value," he argued. Rejecting his advice, the survivors cooked the meat when they had the chance, about once or twice a week. Daily, the recurring question was, "Are we cooking today?"

Liliana told Javier that after they got back home she wanted to have another baby. He agreed. As they looked at one another, though, they saw eyes sunken into their sockets and bones protruding from their cheeks. They knew there was no hope, unless. . . . Liliana and Javier shuddered as they picked up a piece of meat.

Some never could eat. Although the others argued with them, they never could overcome their feelings of revulsion. They continued to refuse, and so day by day grew weaker. Others, however, grew accustomed to what they were doing. They became able to cut meat from a body before everyone's eyes. They could even eat larger pieces, which they had to chew and taste.

As time went on, they developed a set of rules. They would not eat the women's bodies. No one had to eat. The meat would be rationed, and no one could eat more than his or her share. The three who were going to leave in search of help could eat more than the others. One corpse would always be finished before another would be started. (It was overlooked when those who had the disagreeable job of cutting the corpses ate a little as they cut.)

They refused to eat certain parts of the body—the lungs, the skin, the head, and the genitals.

There were some things they never could get used to, such as cutting up a close friend. When they dug a corpse out of the snow, it was preserved just as it had been at the moment of death. If the eyes had been open when the friend died, they were still open, now staring back at them. Everyone understood that no one had to eat a friend or relative.

Survival work became more organized. Those who could stomach it would cut large chunks from a body and pass them to another team, who would slice them with razor blades into smaller pieces. This was not as disagreeable a task, for, separated from the body, the meat was easier to deal with.

The sheets of fat from a body lay outside the rules. They were dried in the sun until a crust formed. Anyone could eat as much as they wished. But the fat wasn't as popular as the meat.

Also outside the rationing system were the pieces of the first carcasses they had cut up, before they developed the rules. Those pieces lay about the snow, and anyone who wanted could scavenge them. Some could never stomach the liver, others the heart or kidneys, and many could not eat the intestines of the dead. Three young men refused the red meat of the muscles.

The dead became part of their lives. One night, Inciarte reached up to get something from the hat rack and was startled when an icy hand brushed against his cheek. Apparently someone had sneaked it in as a late snack.

Constipation was an unexpected complication of their diet. As day after day went by without defecation, they began to worry that their insides would burst. Eventually they developed a sort of contest, wondering who would be the last hold-out. After 28 days, only two had not defecated. At 32, only one. Finally, on the 34th day, Bobby François joined the others.

The three who had been selected to go in search of rescuers had to solve the problem of preventing their feet from freezing. The skin of the dead provided the solution. By cutting an arm just above and below the elbow, and slowly pulling, the skin came away with its subcutaneous layers of fat. Sewing up the lower end made an insulated pair of socks.

Their bland diet became boring. As their bodies and minds cried out for variety, they began to seek new tastes. After eating the meat from a bone, they would crack it open and scoop out the marrow. Everyone liked the marrow. Some sought out the blood clots from around the heart. Others even ate parts of bodies that had started to rot. Many were revolted by this, but, as time went on, more of the survivors did the same.

Canessa, Parrado, and Vizintin were selected to go in search of help. Before they left, Parrado took aside a couple of friends and said that they might run short of food before help could arrive. "I prefer you don't," he whispered, "but I'll understand if you eat my mother and sister."

Ten days after the expeditionaries set out, they stumbled into a shepherd's hut. The news of their survival, long after they had been given up for dead, came as a shock to their friends and relatives. Those still waiting on the mountain were rescued by helicopter—just four days before Christmas.

Although the survivors felt a compulsive need to talk about what they had done, at first physicians and government officials kept the cannibalism a secret. When the news leaked out, however, it made headlines around the world. One survivor explained, "It was like a heart transplant. The dead sustained the living." Another said, "It was like holy communion. God gives us the body and blood of Christ in holy communion. God gave us these bodies and blood to eat."

All were Roman Catholics, and they asked forgiveness. The priests replied that they did not need forgiveness, for they had done nothing wrong. There was no soul in the bodies, the priests explained, and in extreme conditions, if there is no other way to survive, it is permissible to eat the dead. After consultation with relatives, it was decided to bury what was left of the dead at the crash site.

The young men, rejoining their families, became celebrities. They shunned the spotlight, however, banded together, and thought of themselves as special people. As persons who had survived the impossible, they felt that they had a unique purpose in life.

The world's reaction to the events in the Andes was shock and horror—mixed with fascination. As one Chilean paper asked in its headlines, "What would *you* have done?"

The Social Construction of Reality

I was going to let the story stop here, but I was told by a person very influential in my life that I really ought to make the sociology explicit. So let's see what sociological lessons we can derive from this tragedy in the Andes.

First, the main lesson, one from which the other points follow, comes from the symbolic interactionists, who stress that *our world is socially constructed.* By this, they mean that nothing contains built-in meanings. In other words, whatever meaning something has is arbitrary: We humans have given it a particular meaning, but we could just as well have given it a different meaning. *Second,* it is through a social process that we determine meanings; that is, people jointly decide on the meanings to assign events and objects. *Third,* because meanings (or what things symbolize to people) are arbitrary, people can change them. I am aware that these statements may sound extremely vague, but they should become clear as we look at how these survivors constructed their reality.

We might begin by asking what the meaning of a human body is. As with other aspects of life, a group can assign to a body any meaning that it wishes, for, by itself, a body has no meaning. These survivors did not begin to develop their definitions from scratch, however, for they brought to the Andes meanings that they had learned in their culture—basically that a body, while not a person, is still human, and must be treated with respect. A related meaning they had learned is that a human body is "not food." Such an understanding may seem natural to us because it matches our own cultural definitions—which obscures the arbitrary nature of the definition.

Fourth, when circumstances change, definitions can become outmoded—even definitions about fundamental aspects of life. *Fifth,* even though definitions no longer "work," changes in basic orientations do not come easily. *Sixth,* anyone who suggests such changes is likely to be seen as a threatening deviant. Shock, horror, or ridicule may be the reactions, and— for persons who persist on a disorienting course—shunning, ostracism, and violence may result. *Seventh,* the source of radical new ideas is extremely significant in determining whether or not they gain acceptance. *Eighth,* if an individual can drum up group support, then there exists a *social* basis for the new, competing definition. *Ninth,* if the group that offers the new definition can get enough others to accept it, then the common definition of reality will change. *Tenth,* changed circumstances make people more open to accepting new definitions of reality.

In this case, Canessa did not want to appear as a deviant, so he furtively proposed a new definition—entrusting it at first to only a few close friends. Even there, however, since it violated basic definitions acquired in early socialization, it was initially met with resistance. But the friends had high respect for Canessa, who had completed a year of medical school, and they were won over. This small group then proposed their new definition of human bodies to the larger group. Eventually, in the growing realization that death was imminent, this definition won out.

Eleventh, behavior follows definitions. That is, definitions of reality are not just abstract ideas; they also indicate the boundaries of what is allowable. We tend to do what our definitions allow. In this case, when the definition of human bodies changed, so did the survivors' behavior: The changed definition allowed them to eat human corpses.

Twelfth, definitions also follow behavior. That is, as people engage in an activity, they tend to develop ideas that lend support to what they are doing. In this instance, the eating of human flesh—especially since it was a group activity—reinforced the initial definition that had been held only tentatively, that the flesh was no longer human. Eventually, at least for many, the flesh indeed became meat—so much so that some people were even able to take a human hand to bed for a late-night snack.

Thirteenth, for their very survival, all groups must have norms. By allowing people to know what to expect in a given situation, norms provide a basic structure for people's relationships with one another. Without norms, anarchy and chaos would reign.

This principle also applies to groups that make deviance part of their activities. Although a superficial view from the outside may make such groups appear disorganized and without rules, they are in fact quite normative. Groups of outlaw motorcyclists, for example, share an elaborate set of rules about what they expect from one another, most of which, like those of other groups, are not in written form. In short, norms cover even deviant activities, for, without them, how can group members know what to expect of one another?

The Andes survivors developed a basic set of norms to provide order to their deviant activity. Some of those norms were:

1. No one had to violate his or her conscience. If someone did not wish to eat human flesh, no one would force them.
2. Some bodies were "off limits."
3. Meat was rationed, with a specified amount for each person:
   a. Fat was outside the rationing system, and
   b. Leftover parts from the first bodies were outside the rationing system.
4. Meat was distributed according to an orderly system, namely:
   a. Everyone who wished to could eat, and
   b. Designated parts of the body could be "wasted."

Fourteenth, human groups tend to stratify, that is, to sort themselves out on a basis of inequality, with some getting more of a group's resources, some less. A norm concerning eating human flesh that I did not mention above illustrates this principle: Those persons deemed most valuable to the group were allowed to eat more. These were persons who were going in search of rescue and those who performed the disagreeable task of cutting up the bodies. This unequal division of resources represents the formation of a basic system of social stratification.

Fifteenth, human groups tend to organize themselves. In this instance, the survivors did not just randomly cut away at the bodies, but specific tasks were assigned. Teamwork developed to coordinate tasks, with some individuals performing specialized jobs in making the meat edible. Even the weakest had a part to play. The incipient social stratification just mentioned is another example of organization, one that sociologists call the division of labor. *Sixteenth,* an essential part of the human tendency to organize is the emergence of leadership—to direct and coordinate the activities of others. In this case, Canessa stands out.

Seventeenth, people attempt to maintain a respectable sense of self. These survivors were conforming individuals in that they had accepted the norms of their society and were striving for a respectable place within it. They wanted to continue to think of themselves as good people. Yet, they had to make a decision about doing an activity that went beyond the bounds of what they looked at as normal—one they even knew that "everyone" defined as wrong.

Eighteenth, it is possible to maintain a "good" self-image and still engage in deviant activities. Because the essence of human society is the social construction of reality, so the key to the self also lies in how reality is defined. If you can redefine an activity to make it "not deviant," then it does not threaten your sense of a "good" self. In this present instance, the Andes survivors looked on eating human flesh as part of their "duty to survive." To do a duty is a good thing, and, accordingly, the acts required by it cannot be "bad." In fact, they must be "good." (The most infamous example of the use of this basic principle was Hitler's SS, who looked on killing Jews as necessary for the survival of the "Aryan" race and culture. They even termed the slaughter a "good" act and their participation in it as patriotic and self-sacrificing.)

This principle helps many people get through what otherwise would be excruciatingly painful nights—for they would toss sleeplessly owing to a gnawing conscience. Redefinition, by keeping one's sense of self intact, allows people to participate in a variety of acts condemned by society—even those disapproved by the self. For most people, redefinition involves much less dramatic acts than eating human flesh, such as a college student cheating on a test or a boss firing a worker.

Nineteenth, some people participate in deviant acts even though they remain unconvinced about such redefinitions. (Some do not even attempt to redefine them.) They may do so from a variety of motives—from what they consider "sheer necessity" to the desire to reach a future goal. Liliana and Javier, who decided that they wanted a baby, are an example. Such persons have greater difficulty adjusting to their acts than those who redefine them as "good." (Even the latter may have difficulty, for redefinitions may be only partial, especially in the face of competing definitions.)

Twentieth, people feel they must justify their actions to others. This process of justifying the self involves clothing definitions of reality in forms thought to be acceptable to others. In order for definitions to be accepted, they must be made to fit into the others' already-existing definitional framework. In this case, the survivors first justified their proposed actions by redefining the bodies as meat and by saying that they had a duty to survive. After their rescue—speaking to a Roman Catholic audience—they used the analogy of holy communion to justify their act.

Twenty-first, to gain institutional support is to secure a broad, solid base for one's definitions of reality. Then one no longer stands alone, which is to invite insanity, nor is one a member of a small group, which is to invite ridicule and may require cutting off oneself from the larger group. In this case, institutional support was provided by the Roman Catholic Church, which, while not accepting the survivors' analogy of cannibalism as communion, allowed them to avoid the label of sin by defining their actions as allowable under the circumstances.

Finally, note that these principles are fundamental to human life. They do not simply apply to the Andes survivors—or to deviants in general—but they underlie human society. For all of us, reality is socially constructed, and the story of the Andes survivors contains the essence of human society.

25 Becoming a Hit Man

KEN LEVI

There is no question that we all have deviant desires. If we probe our deeper recesses, we might even find a cesspool of feelings and impulses that we don't want to reveal to others or, at times, even to ourselves. No matter how we may suppress our desires for deviance, they remain nonetheless.

As you saw with the selection that opened this Part, even highly conforming people, those whose deviant desires are under high control, can do appalling things when the conditions are right. You read how obedience to authority can be so compelling that people will give electrical shocks to strangers. In the preceding article, you read about conforming people who ate human flesh. Again, the situation had to be right.

But killing strangers in cold blood? Methodically shooting men and women because someone offers money for their deaths? Who would do such a thing? And those who would, do they think of themselves as monsters, the way that we might think of them? On the contrary, as Levi shows, just as we have ways of neutralizing our deviance (telling a "white" lie or using the Internet to do a "little" cheating on a class paper), so hit men have ways of neutralizing their deeds. They, after all, just like us, have to live with themselves.

OUR KNOWLEDGE ABOUT deviance management is based primarily on behavior that is easily mitigated. The literature dwells on unwed fathers (Pfuhl, 1978), and childless mothers (Veevers, 1975), pilfering bread salesman (Ditton, 1977), and conniving shoe salesmen (Freidman, 1974), bridge pros (Holtz, 1975), and poker pros (Hayano, 1977), marijuana smokers (Langer, 1976), massage parlor prostitutes (Verlarde, 1975), and other minor offenders (see, for example, Berk, 1977; Farrell and Nelson, 1976; Gross, 1977). There is a dearth of deviance management articles on serious offenders, and no scholarly articles at all about one of the (legally) most serious offenders of all, the professional murderer. Drift may be possible for the minor offender exploiting society's *ambivalence* toward his relatively unserious behavior (Sykes and Matza, 1957). However, excuses for the more inexcusable forms of deviant behavior are, by definition, less easily come by, and the very serious offender may enter his career with few of the usual defenses.

This article will focus on ways that one type of serious offender, the professional hit man, neutralizes stigma in the early stages of his career. As we shall see, the social organization of the "profession" provides "neutralizers" which distance its members from the shameful aspects of their careers. But for the novice, without professional insulation, the problem is more acute. With very little outside help, he must negate his feelings, neutralize them, and adopt a "framework" (Goffman, 1974) appropriate to his chosen career. This process, called "reframing," is the main focus of the present article. Cognitively, the novice must *reframe his experience* in order to enter his profession.

The Social Organization of Murder

Murder, the unlawful killing of a person, is considered a serious criminal offense in the United States, and it is punished by extreme penalties. In addition, most Americans do not feel that the penalties are extreme enough (Reid, 1976:482). In overcoming the intense stigma associated with murder, the hit man lacks the supports available to more ordinary types of killers.

Some cultures allow special circumstances or sanction special organizations wherein people who kill are insulated from the taint of murder. Soldiers at war, or police in the line of duty, or citizens protecting their property operate under what are considered justifiable or excusable conditions. They receive so much informal support from the general public and from members of their own group that it may protect even a sadistic member from blame (Westley, 1966).

Subcultures (Wolfgang and Ferracuti, 1967), organizations (Maas, 1968), and gangs (Yablonsky, 1962) that unlawfully promote killing can at least provide their members with an "appeal to higher loyalties" (Sykes and Matza, 1957), if not a fully developed set of deviance justifying norms.

Individuals acting on their own, who kill in a spontaneous "irrational" outburst of violence can also mitigate the stigma of their behavior.

> I mean, people will go ape for one minute and shoot, but there are very few people who are capable of thinking about, planning, and then doing it [Joey, 1974:56].

Individuals who kill in a hot-blooded burst of passion can retrospectively draw comfort from the law which provides a lighter ban against killings performed without premeditation or malice or intent (Lester and Lester,

1975:35). At one extreme, the spontaneous killing may seem the result of a mental disease (Lester and Lester, 1975:39) or dissociative reaction (Tanay, 1972), and excused entirely as insanity.

But when an individual who generally shares society's ban against murder, is fully aware that his act of homicide is (1) unlawful, (2) self-serving, and (3) intentional, he does not have the usual defenses to fall back on. How does such an individual manage to *overcome his inhibitions* and *avoid serious damage to his self-image* (assuming that he does share society's ban)? This is the special dilemma of the professional hit man who hires himself out for murder.

Research Methods

Information for this article comes primarily from a series of intensive interviews with one self-styled "hit man." The interviews were spread over seven, tape-recorded sessions during a four-month period. The respondent was one of fifty prison inmates randomly sampled from a population of people convicted of murder in Metropolitan Detroit. The respondent told about an "accidental" killing, involving a drunken bar patron who badgered the respondent and finally forced his hand by pulling a knife on him. In court he claimed self-defense, but the witnesses at the bar claimed otherwise, so they sent him to prison. During the first two interview sessions, the respondent acted progressively ashamed of this particular killing, not on moral ground, but because of its "sloppiness" or "amateurishness." Finally, he indicated there was more he would like to say. So, I stopped the tape recorder. I asked him if he was a hit man. He said he was.

He had already been given certain guarantees, including no names in the interview, a private conference room, and a signed contract promising his anonymity. Now, as a further guarantee, we agreed to talk about him in the third person, as a fictitious character named "Pete," so that none of his statements would sound like a personal confession. With these assurances, future interviews were devoted to his career as a professional murderer, with particular emphasis on his entry into the career and his orientation toward his victims.

Was he reliable? Since we did not use names, I had no way of checking the veracity of the individual cases he reported. Nevertheless, I was able to compare his account of the hit man's career with information from other convicted murderers, with police experts, and with accounts from the available literature (Gage, 1972; Joey, 1974; Maas, 1968). Pete's information was generally supported by these other sources. As to his motive for submitting to the interview, it is hard to gauge. He apparently was ashamed of the one "accidental" killing that had landed him in prison, and he desired to set the record straight concerning what he deemed an illustrious career, now that he had arrived, as he said, at the end of it. Hit men pride themselves on not "falling" (going to jail) for murder, and Pete's incarceration hastened a decision to retire—that he had already been contemplating, anyway.

A question might arise about the ethics of researching self-confessed "hit men" and granting them anonymity. Legally, since Pete never mentioned specific names or specific dates or possible future crimes, there does not seem to be a problem. Morally, if confidentiality is a necessary condition to obtaining information about serious offenders, then we have to ask: Is it worth it? Pete insisted that he had retired from the profession. Therefore, there seems to be no "clear and imminent danger" that would justify the violation of confidentiality, in the terms set forth by the American Psychological Association (1978:40). On the other hand, the *possibility* of danger does exist, and future researchers will have to exercise their judgment.

Finally, hit men are hard to come by. Unlike more lawful killers, such as judges or night watchmen, and unlike run-of-the-mill murderers, the hit man (usually) takes infinite care to conceal his identity. Therefore, while it is regrettable that this paper has only one case to report on, and while it would be ideal to perform a comparative analysis on a number of hit men, it would be very difficult to obtain such a sample. Instead, Pete's responses will be compared to similar accounts from the available literature. While such a method can never produce verified findings, it can point to suggestive hypotheses.

The Social Organization of Professional Murder

There are two types of professional murderers: the organized and the independent. The killer who belongs to an organized syndicate does not usually get paid on a contract basis, and performs his job out of loyalty and obedience to the organization (Maas, 1968:81). The independent professional killer is a freelance agent who hires himself out for a fee (Pete). It is the career organization of the second type of killer that will be discussed.

The organized killer can mitigate his behavior through an "appeal to higher loyalties" (Sykes and Matza, 1957). He also can view his victim as an enemy of the group and then choose from a variety of techniques available for neutralizing an offense against an enemy (see, for example, Hirschi, 1969; Rogers and Buffalo, 1974). But the independent professional murderer lacks most of these defenses. Nevertheless, built into his role are certain structural features that help him avoid deviance ascription. These features include:

(1) *Contract.* A contract is an unwritten agreement to provide a sum of money to a second party who agrees, in return, to commit a designated murder (Joey, 1974:9). It is most often arranged over the phone, between people who have never had personal contact. And the victim, or "hit," is usually unknown to the killer (Gage, 1972:57; Joey, 1974:61–62). This arrangement is meant to protect both parties from the law. But it also helps the killer "deny the victim" (Sykes and Matza, 1957) by keeping him relatively anonymous.

In arranging the contract, the hired killer will try to find out the difficulty of the hit and how much the customer wants the killing done. According to Pete, these considerations determine his price. He does not ask about the motive for the killing, treating it as none of his concern. Now knowing the motive may hamper the killer from morally justifying his behavior, but it also enables him to further deny the victim by maintaining his distance and reserve. Finally, the contract is backed up by a further understanding.

> Like this guy who left here (prison) last summer, he was out two months before he got killed. Made a mistake somewhere. The way I heard it, he didn't finish filling a contract [Pete].

If the killer fails to live up to his part of the bargain, the penalties could be extreme (Gage, 1972:53; Joey, 1974:9). This has the ironic effect that after the contract is arranged, the killer can somewhat "deny responsibility" (Sykes and Matza, 1957), by pleading self-defense.

(2) *Reputation and Money.* Reputation is especially important in an area where killers are unknown to their customers, and where the less written, the better (Joey, 1974:58). Reputation, in turn, reflects how much money the hit man has commanded in the past.

> And that was the first time that I ever got 30 grand . . . it's based on his reputation. . . . Yeah, how good he really is. To be so-so, you get so-so money. If you're good, you get good money [Pete].

Pete, who could not recall the exact number of people he had killed, did, like other hit men, keep an accounting of his highest fees (Joey, 1974:58, 62). To him big money meant not only a way to earn a living, but also a way to maintain his professional reputation.

People who accept low fees can also find work as hired killers. Heroin addicts are the usual example. But, as Pete says, they often receive a bullet for their pains. It is believed that people who would kill for so little would also require little persuasion to make them talk to the police (Joey, 1974:63). This further reinforces the single-minded emphasis on making big money. As a result, killing is conceptualized as a "business" or as "just a job." Framing the hit in a normal businesslike context enables the hit man to deny wrongfulness, or "deny injury" (Sykes and Matza, 1957).

In addition to the economic motive, Pete and hit men discussed by other authors, refer to excitement, fun, game-playing, power, and impressing women as incentives for murder (Joey, 1974:81–82). However, none of these motives are mentioned by all sources. None are as necessary to the career as money. And, after a while, these other motives diminish and killing becomes only "just a job" (Joey, 1974:20). The primacy of the economic motive has been aptly expressed in the case of another deviant profession.

> Women who enjoy sex with their customers do not make good prostitutes, according to those who are acquainted with this institution first hand. Instead of thinking about the most effective way of making money at the job, they would be doing things for their own pleasure and enjoyment [Goode, 1974:342].

(3) *Skill.* Most of the hit man's training focuses on acquiring skill in the use of weapons.

> Then, he met these two guys, these two white guys . . . them two, them two was the best. And but they stayed around over there and they got together, and Pete told [them] that he really wanted to be good. He said, if [I] got to do something, I want to be good at it. So, they got together, showed him, showed him *how to shoot.* . . . And gradually, he became good. . . . Like he told me, like when he shoots somebody, he always goes for the head; he said, that's about the best shot. I mean, if you want him dead then and there. . . . And these two guys showed him, and to him, I mean, hey, I mean, he don't believe nobody could really outshoot these two guys, you know what I mean. *They know everything you want to know about guns, knives, and stuff like that* [Pete].

The hit man's reputation, and the amount of money he makes depends on his skill, his effective ability to serve as a means to someone else's ends. The result is a focus on technique.

> Like in anything you do, when you do it, you want to do it just right. . . . On your target and you hit it, how you feel: I hit it! I hit it! [Pete].

This focus on technique, on means, helps the hit man to "deny responsibility" and intent (Sykes and Matza, 1957). In frame-analytic terms, the hit man separates his morally responsible, or "principal" self from the rest of himself, and performs the killing mainly as a "strategist" (Goffman, 1974:523). In other words, he sees himself as a "hired gun." The saying, "If I didn't do it, they'd find someone else who would," reflects this narrowly technical orientation.

To sum up thus far, the contract, based as it is on the hit man's reputation for profit and skill, provides the hit man with opportunities for denying the victim, denying injury, and denying responsibility. But this is not enough. To point out the defenses of the professional hit man is one thing, but it is unlikely that the *novice* hit man would have a totally professional attitude so early in his career. The novice is at a point where he both lacks the conventional defense against the stigma of murder, *and* he has not yet fully acquired the exceptional defenses of the professional. How, then, does he cope?

The First Time: Negative Experience

Goffman defines "negative experience" as a feeling of disorientation.

> Expecting to take up a position in a well-framed realm, he finds that no particular frame is immediately applicable, or the frame that he thought was applicable no longer seems to be, or he cannot bind himself within the frame that does apparently apply. He loses command over the formulation of viable response. He flounders. Experience, the meld of what the current scene brings to him and what he brings to it—meant to settle into a form even while it is beginning, finds no form and is therefore no experience. Reality anomically flutters. He has a "negative experience"—negative in the sense that it takes its character from what it is not, and what it is not is an organized and organizationally affirmed response [1974:378–379].

Negative experience can occur when a person finds himself lapsing into an old understanding of the situation, only to suddenly awaken to the fact that it no longer applies. In this regard, we should expect negative experience to be a special problem for the novice. For example, the first time he killed a man for money, Pete supposedly became violently ill:

> When he [Pete], you know, hit the guy, when he shot the guy, the guy said, "You killed me" . . . something like that, cause he struck him all up here. And what he said, it was just, I mean, *the look right in the guy's eye,* you know. I mean he looked like: *why me?* Yeah? And he [Pete] couldn't shake that. Cause he remembered a time or two when he got cut, and all he wanted to do was get back and cut this guy that cut him. And this here. . . . No, he just could not shake it. And then he said that at night-time he'll start thinking about the guy: like he shouldn't have looked at him like that. . . . I mean actually [Pete] was sick. . . . He couldn't keep his food down, I mean, or nothing like that. . . . [It

lasted] I'd say about two months. . . . Like he said that he had feelings . . . that he never did kill nobody before [Pete].

Pete's account conforms to the definition of negative experience. He had never killed anyone for money before. It started when a member of the Detroit drug world had spotted Pete in a knife fight outside an inner city bar, was apparently impressed with the young man's style, and offered him fifty dollars to do a "job." Pete accepted. He wanted the money. But when the first hit came about, Pete of course knew that he was doing it for money, but yet his orientation was revenge. Thus, he stared his victim in the *face,* a characteristic gesture of people who kill enemies for revenge (Levi, 1975:190). Expecting to see defiance turn into a look of defeat, they attempt to gain "face" at the loser's expense.

But when Pete stared his victim in the face, he saw not an enemy, but an innocent man. He saw a look of: "Why me?" And this *discordant* image is what remained in his mind during the weeks and months to follow and made him sick. As Pete says, "He shouldn't have looked at him like that." The victim's look of innocence brought about what Goffman (1974:347) refers to as a "frame break":

> Given that the frame applied to an activity is expected to enable us to come to terms with all events in that activity (informing and regulating many of them), it is understandable that the unmanageable might occur, an occurrence which cannot be effectively ignored and to which the frame cannot be applied, with resulting bewilderment and chagrin on the part of the participants. In brief, a break can occur in the applicability of the frame, a break in its governance.

When such a frame break occurs, it produces negative experience. Pete's extremely uncomfortable disorientation may reflect the extreme dissonance between the revenge frame, that he expected to apply, and the unexpected look of innocence that he encountered and continued to recall.

Subsequent Time: Reframing the Hit

According to Goffman (1974:319), a structural feature of frames of experience is that they are divided into different "tracks" or types of information. These include, "a main track or story line and ancillary tracks of various kinds." The ancillary tracks are the directional track, the overlay track, the concealment tracks, and the disattend track. The disattend track contains the information that is perceived but supposed to be *ignored.* For example, the prostitute manages the distasteful necessity of having sex with "tricks" by remaining " absolutely . . . detached. Removed. Miles and miles away" (1974:344). The existence of different tracks allows an individual to define and redefine his experience by the strategic placement of information.

Sometimes, the individual receives outside help. For example, when Milgram in 1963 placed a barrier between people administering electric shocks, and the bogus "subjects" who were supposedly receiving the shocks, he made it easier for the shockers to "disattend" signs of human distress from their hapless victims. Surgeons provide another example. Having their patients completely covered, except for the part to be operated on, helps them work in a more impersonal manner. In both examples, certain crucial information is stored away in the "concealment track" (Goffman, 1974:218).

In other cases help can come from guides who direct the novice on what to experience and what to block out. Beginning marijuana smokers are cautioned to ignore feelings of nausea (Becker, 1953:240). On the other hand, novice hit men like Pete are reluctant to share their "experience" with anyone else. It would be a sign of weakness.

In still other cases, however, it is possible that the subject can do the reframing *on his own*. And this is what appears to have happened to Pete.

> And when the second one [the second hit] came up, [Pete] was still thinking about the first one. . . . Yeah, when he got ready to go, he was thinking about it. *Something changed.* I don't know how to put it right. Up to the moment that he killed the second guy now, he waited, you know. Going through his mind was the first guy he killed. He still seeing him, still see the *expression on his face.* Soon, the second guy walked up; I mean, it was like his mind just *blanked out* for a minute, everything just blanked out. . . . Next thing he know, he had killed the second guy. . . . *He knew what he was doing,* but what I mean, he just didn't have nothing on his mind. Everything was wiped out [Pete].

When the second victim approached, Pete says that he noticed the victim's approach, he was aware of the man's presence. But he noticed none of the victim's personal features. He did not see the victim's face or its expression. Thus, he did not see the very thing that gave him so much trouble the first time. It is as if Pete had *negatively conditioned* himself to avoid certain cues. Since he shot the victim in the head, it is probable that Pete saw him in one sense; this is not the same kind of experience as a "dissociative reaction," which has been likened to sleepwalking (Tanay, 1972). Pete says that, "he knew what he was doing." But he either did not pay attention to his victim's personal features at the time of the killing, or he blocked them out immediately afterward, so that now the only aspect of his victim he recalls is the victim's approach (if we are to believe him).

After that, Pete says that killing became *routine*. He learned to view his victims as "targets," rather than as people. Thus, he believes that the second experience is the crucial one, and that the disattendance of the victim's personal features made it so.

Support from other accounts of hit men is scant, due to a lack of data. Furthermore, not everything in Pete's account supports the "reframing" hypothesis. In talking about later killings, it is clear that he not only attends to his victims' personal features, on occasion, but he also derives a certain grim pleasure in doing so.

> [the victim was] a nice looking woman. . . . She started weeping, and [she cried], "I ain't did this, I ain't did that" . . . and [Pete] said that he shot her. Like it wasn't nothing . . . he didn't feel nothing. It was just money [Pete].

In a parallel story, Joey, the narrator of the *Killer*, also observes his victim in personal terms.

> [The victim] began to beg. He even went so far as to tell us where he had stashed his money. Finally, he realized there was absolutely nothing he could do. He sat there quietly. Then, he started crying. I didn't feel a thing for him [1974:56].

It may be that this evidence contradicts what I have said about reframing; but perhaps another interpretation is possible. Reframing may play a more crucial role in the original redefinition of an experience than in the continued maintenance of that redefinition. Once Pete has accustomed himself to viewing his victims as merely targets, as "just money," then it may be less threatening to look upon them as persons, once again. Once the "main story line" has been established, discordant information can be presented in the "overlay track" (Goffman, 1974:215), without doing too much damage. Indeed, this seems to be the point that both hit men are trying to make in the above excerpts.

The Heart of the Hit Man

For what I have been referring to as "disattendance" Pete used the term "heart," which he defined as a "coldness." When asked what he would look for in an aspiring hit man, Peter replied,

> See if he's got a whole lot of heart . . . you got to be cold . . . you got to build a coldness in yourself. It's not something that comes automatically. Cause, see, I don't care who he is, first, you've got feelings [Pete].

In contrast to this view, Joey (1974:56) said,

> There are three things you need to kill a man: the gun, the bullets, and the balls. A lot of people will point a gun at you, but they haven't got the courage to pull the trigger. It's as simple as that.

It may be that some are born with "heart," while others acquire it in the way I have described.

However, the "made rather than born" thesis does explain one perplexing feature of hit men and other "evil" men whose banality has sometimes seemed discordant. In other aspects of their lives they all seem perfectly capable of feeling ordinary human emotions. Their inhumanity, their coldness, seems narrowly restricted to their jobs. Pete, for example, talked about his "love" for little children. Eddie "The Hawk" Ruppolo meekly allowed his mistress to openly insult him in a public bar (Gage, 1972). And Joey (1974:55) has this to say about himself:

> Believe it or not, I'm a human being. I laugh at funny jokes. I love children around the house, and I can spend hours playing with my mutt.

All of these examples of human warmth indicate that the cold heart of the hit man may be less a characteristic of the killer's individual personality, than a feature of the professional framework of experience which the hit man has learned to adapt himself to, when he is on the job.

Discussion

This article is meant as a contribution to the study of deviance neutralization. The freelance hit man is an example of an individual who, relatively alone, must deal with a profound and unambiguous stigma in order to enter his career. Both Pete and Joey emphasize "heart" as a determining factor in becoming a professional. And Pete's experience, after the first hit, further indicates that the inhibitions against murder-for-money are real.

In this article "heart"—or the ability to adapt to a rationalized framework for killing—has been portrayed as the outcome of an initial process of reframing, in addition to other neutralization techniques established during the further stages of professionalization. As several theorists (see, for example, Becker, 1953; Douglas et al., 1977; Matza, 1969) have noted, people often enter into deviant acts first, and then develop rationales for their behavior later on. This was also the case with Pete, who began his career by first, (1) "being willing" (Matza, 1969), (2) encountering a frame break,

(3) undergoing negative experience, (4) being willing to try again (also known as "getting back on the horse"), (5) reframing the experience, and (6) having future, routine experiences wherein his professionalization increasingly enabled him to "deny the victim," "deny injury," and "deny responsibility." Through the process of reframing, the experience of victim-as-target emerged as the "main story line," and the experience of victim-as-person was downgraded from the main track to the disattend track to the overlay track. Ironically, the intensity of the negative experience seemed to make the process all the more successful. Thus, it may be possible for a person with "ordinary human feelings" to both pass through the novice stage, and to continue "normal relations" thereafter. The reframing hypothesis has implications for other people who knowingly perform stigmatized behaviors. It may be particularly useful in explaining a personal conversion experience that occurs despite the relative absence of deviant peer groups, deviant norms, extenuating circumstances, and neutralization rationales.

26 The Saints and the Roughnecks

WILLIAM J. CHAMBLISS

When people deviate from what is expected of them, other people react. But on what do their reactions depend? Do they depend simply on the nature of the deviance itself, or is more involved? If so, what sorts of things?

It is these fascinating questions that Chambliss examines in this study of two groups of delinquents in the same high school. He found that although both groups were involved in serious and repetitive delinquent acts, one was perceived as a group of saints, while the other was viewed as a bunch of roughnecks. After analyzing what influenced people's perceptions, and hence their reactions to the boys, Chambliss examines the far-reaching effects of those reactions. He indicates that in the case of the roughnecks, people's reactions helped lock the boys into behaviors that continued after high school, eventually leading to prison or to low-paying jobs. In contrast, social reactions to the saints helped to set them on a life course that meant not only staying out of prison but also entering well-paying positions of prestige.

EIGHT PROMISING YOUNG MEN—children of good, stable, white upper-middle-class families, active in school affairs, good pre-college students—were some of the most delinquent boys at Hanibal High School. While community residents knew that these boys occasionally sowed a few wild oats, they were totally unaware that sowing wild oats completely occupied the daily routine of these young men. The Saints were constantly occupied with truancy, drinking, wild driving, petty theft, and vandalism. Yet no one was officially arrested for any misdeed during the two years I observed them.

This record was particularly surprising in light of my observations during the same two years of another gang of Hanibal High School students, six lower-class white boys known as the Roughnecks. The Roughnecks were constantly in trouble with police and community even though their rate of delinquency was about equal with that of the Saints. What was the cause of this disparity? the result? The following consideration of the activities, social class, and community perceptions of both gangs may provide some answers.

299

The Saints from Monday to Friday

The Saints' principal daily concern was with getting out of school as early as possible. The boys managed to get out of school with minimum danger that they would be accused of playing hookey through an elaborate procedure for obtaining "legitimate" release from class. The most common procedure was for one boy to obtain the release of another by fabricating a meeting of some committee, program, or recognized club. Charles might raise his hand in his 9:00 chemistry class and ask to be excused—a euphemism for going to the bathroom. Charles would go to Ed's math class and inform the teacher that Ed was needed for a 9:30 rehearsal of the drama club play. The math teacher would recognize Ed and Charles as "good students" involved in numerous school activities and would permit Ed to leave at 9:30. Charles would return to his class, and Ed would go to Tom's English class to obtain his release. Tom would engineer Charles's escape. The strategy would continue until as many of the Saints as possible were freed. After a stealthy trip to the car (which had been parked in a strategic spot), the boys were off for a day of fun.

Over the two years I observed the Saints, this pattern was repeated nearly every day. There were variations on the theme, but in one form or another, the boys used this procedure for getting out of class and then off the school grounds. Rarely did all eight of the Saints manage to leave school at the same time. The average number avoiding school on the days I observed them was five.

Having escaped from the concrete corridors the boys usually went either to a pool hall on the other (lower-class) side of town or to a café in the suburbs. Both places were out of the way of people the boys were likely to know (family or school officials), and both provided a source of entertainment. The pool hall entertainment was the generally rough atmosphere, the occasional hustler, the sometimes drunk proprietor and, of course, the game of pool. The café's entertainment was provided by the owner. The boys would "accidentally" knock a glass on the floor or spill cola on the counter—not all the time, but enough to be sporting. They would also bend spoons, put salt in sugar bowls and generally tease whoever was working in the café. The owner had opened the café recently and was dependent on the boys' business which was, in fact, substantial since between the horsing around and the teasing they bought food and drinks.

The Saints on Weekends

On weekends the automobile was even more critical than during the week, for on weekends the Saints went to Big Town—a large city with a population of over a million 25 miles from Hanibal. Every Friday and Saturday night most of the Saints would meet between 8:00 and 8:30 and would go into Big Town. Big Town activities included drinking heavily in taverns or nightclubs, driving drunkenly through the streets, and committing acts of vandalism and playing pranks.

By midnight on Fridays and Saturdays the Saints were usually thoroughly high, and one or two of them were often so drunk they had to be carried to the cars. Then the boys drove around town, calling obscenities to women and girls; occasionally trying (unsuccessfully so far as I could tell) to pick girls up; and driving recklessly through red lights and at high speeds with their lights out. Occasionally they played "chicken." One boy would climb out the back window of the car and across the roof to the driver's side of the car while the car was moving at high speed (between 40 and 50 miles an hour); then the driver would move over and the boy who had just crawled across the car roof would take the driver's seat.

Searching for "fair game" for a prank was the boys' principal activity after they left the tavern. The boys would drive alongside a foot patrolman and ask directions to some street. If the policeman leaned on the car in the course of answering the question, the driver would speed away, causing him to lose his balance. The Saints were careful to play this prank only in an area where they were not going to spend much time and where they could quickly disappear around a corner to avoid having their license plate number taken.

Construction sites and road repair areas were the special province of the Saints' mischief. A soon-to-be-repaired hole in the road inevitably invited the Saints to remove lanterns and wooden barricades and put them in the car, leaving the hole unprotected. The boys would find a safe vantage point and wait for an unsuspecting motorist to drive into the hole. Often, though not always, the boys would go up to the motorist and commiserate with him about the dreadful way the city protected its citizenry.

Leaving the scene of the open hole and the motorist, the boys would then go searching for an appropriate place to erect the stolen barricade. An "appropriate place" was often a spot on a highway near a curve in the road where the barricade would not be seen by an oncoming motorist. The boys would wait to watch an unsuspecting motorist attempt to stop and (usually) crash into the wooden barricade. With saintly bearing the boys might offer help and understanding.

A stolen lantern might well find its way onto the back of a police car or hang from a street lamp. Once a lantern served as a prop for a reenactment of the "midnight ride of Paul Revere" until the "play," which was taking place at 2:00 A.M. in the center of a main street of Big Town, was interrupted by a police car several blocks away. The boys ran, leaving the lanterns on the street, and managed to avoid being apprehended.

Abandoned houses, especially if they were located in out-of-the-way places, were fair game for destruction and spontaneous vandalism. The boys would break windows, remove furniture to the yard and tear it apart, urinate on the walls, and scrawl obscenities inside.

Through all the pranks, drinking, and reckless driving the boys managed miraculously to avoid being stopped by police. Only twice in two years was I aware that they had been stopped by a Big Town policeman. Once was for speeding (which they did every time they drove whether they were drunk or sober), and the driver managed to convince the policeman that it was simply an error. The second time they were stopped they had just left a nightclub and were walking through an alley. Aaron stopped to urinate and the boys began making obscene remarks. A foot patrolman came into the alley, lectured the boys and sent them home. Before the boys got to the car one began talking in a loud voice again. The policeman, who had followed them down the alley, arrested this boy for disturbing the peace and took him to the police station where the other Saints gathered. After paying a $5.00 fine, and with the assurance that there would be no permanent record of the arrest, the boy was released.

The boys had a spirit of frivolity and fun about their escapades. They did not view what they were engaged in as "delinquency," though it surely was by any reasonable definition of that word. They simply viewed themselves as having a little fun and who, they would ask, was really hurt by it? The answer had to be no one, although this fact remains one of the most difficult things to explain about the gang's behavior. Unlikely though it seems, in two years of drinking, driving, carousing, and vandalism no one was seriously injured as a result of the Saints' activities.

The Saints in School

The Saints were highly successful in school. The average grade for the group was "B," with two of the boys having close to a straight "A" average. Almost all of the boys were popular and many of them held offices in the school. One of the boys was vice president of the student body one year. Six of the boys played on athletic teams.

At the end of their senior year, the student body selected ten seniors for special recognition as the "school wheels"; four of the ten were Saints. Teachers and school officials saw no problem with any of these boys and anticipated that they would all "make something of themselves."

How the boys managed to maintain this impression is surprising in view of their actual behavior in school. Their technique for covering truancy was so successful that teachers did not even realize that the boys were absent from school much of the time. Occasionally, of course, the system would backfire and then the boy was on his own. A boy who was caught would be most contrite, would plead guilty and ask for mercy. He inevitably got the mercy he sought.

Cheating on examinations was rampant, even to the point of orally communicating answers to exams as well as looking at one another's papers. Since none of the group studied, and since they were primarily dependent on one another for help, it is surprising that grades were so high. Teachers contributed to the deception in their admitted inclination to give these boys (and presumably others like them) the benefit of the doubt. When asked how the boys did in school, and when pressed on specific examinations, teachers might admit that they were disappointed in John's performance, but would quickly add that they "knew that he was capable of doing better," so John was given a higher grade than he had actually earned. How often this happened is impossible to know. During the time that I observed the group, I never saw any of the boys take homework home. Teachers may have been "understanding" very regularly.

One exception to the gang's generally good performance was Jerry, who had a "C" average in his junior year, experienced disaster the next year, and failed to graduate. Jerry had always been a little more nonchalant than the others about the liberties he took in school. Rather than wait for someone to come get him from class, he would offer his own excuse and leave. Although he probably did not miss any more class than most of the others in the group, he did not take the requisite pains to cover his absences. Jerry was the only Saint whom I ever heard talk back to a teacher. Although teachers often called him a "cut up" or a "smart kid," they never referred to him as a troublemaker or as a kid headed for trouble. It seems likely, then, that Jerry's failure his senior year and his mediocre performance his junior year were consequences of his not playing the game the proper way (possibly because he was disturbed by his parents' divorce). His teachers regarded him as "immature" and not quite ready to get out of high school.

The Police and the Saints

The local police saw the Saints as good boys who were among the leaders of the youth in the community. Rarely, the boys might be stopped in town for speeding or for running a stop sign. When this happened the boys were always polite, contrite, and pled for mercy. As in school, they received the mercy they asked for. None ever received a ticket or was taken into the precinct by the local police.

The situation in Big Town, where the boys engaged in most of their delinquency, was only slightly different. The police there did not know the boys at all, although occasionally the boys were stopped by a patrolman. Once they were caught taking a lantern from a construction site. Another time they were stopped for running a stop sign, and on several occasions they were stopped for speeding. Their behavior was as before: contrite, polite, and penitent. The urban police, like the local police, accepted their demeanor as sincere. More important, the urban police were convinced that these were good boys just out for a lark.

The Roughnecks

Hanibal townspeople never perceived the Saints' high level of delinquency. The Saints were good boys who just went in for an occasional prank. After all, they were well dressed, well mannered, and had nice cars. The Roughnecks were a different story. Although the two gangs of boys were the same age, and both groups engaged in an equal amount of wild-oat sowing, everyone agreed that the not-so-well-dressed, not-so-well-mannered, not-so-rich boys were heading for trouble. Townspeople would say, "You can see the gang members at the drugstore, night after night, leaning against the storefront (sometimes drunk) or slouching around inside buying cokes, reading magazines, and probably stealing old Mr. Wall blind. When they are outside and girls walk by, even respectable girls, these boys make suggestive remarks. Sometimes their remarks are downright lewd."

From the community's viewpoint, the real indication that these kids were in trouble was that they were constantly involved with the police. Some of them had been picked up for stealing, mostly small stuff, of course, "but still it's stealing small stuff that leads to big time crimes." "Too bad," people said. "Too bad that these boys couldn't behave like the other kids in town; stay out of trouble, be polite to adults, and look to their future."

The community's impression of the degrees to which this group of six boys (ranging in age from 16 to 19) engaged in delinquency was somewhat distorted. In some ways the gang was more delinquent than the community thought; in other ways they were less.

The fighting activities of the group were fairly readily and accurately perceived by almost everyone. At least once a month, the boys would get into some sort of fight, although most fights were scraps between members of the group or involved only one member of the group and some peripheral hanger-on. Only three times in the period of observation did the group fight together: once against a gang from across town, once against two blacks, and once against a group of boys from another school. For the first two fights the group went out "looking for trouble"—and they found it both times. The third fight followed a football game and began spontaneously with an argument on the football field between one of the Roughnecks and a member of the opposition's football team.

Jack has a particular propensity for fighting and was involved in most of the brawls. He was a prime mover of the escalation of arguments into fights.

More serious than fighting, had the community been aware of it, was theft. Although almost everyone was aware that the boys occasionally stole things, they did not realize the extent of the activity. Petty stealing was a frequent event for the Roughnecks. Sometimes they stole as a group and coordinated their efforts; other times they stole in pairs. Rarely did they steal alone.

The thefts ranged from very small things like paperback books, comics, and ballpoint pens to expensive items like watches. The nature of the thefts varied from time to time. The gang would go through a period of systematically lifting items from automobiles or school lockers. Types of thievery varied with the whim of the gang. Some forms of thievery were more profitable than others, but all thefts were for profit, not just thrills.

Roughnecks siphoned gasoline from cars as often as they had access to an automobile, which was not very often. Unlike the Saints, who owned their own cars, the Roughnecks would have to borrow their parents' cars, an event which occurred only eight or nine times a year. The boys claimed to have stolen cars for joy rides from time to time.

Ron committed the most serious of the group's offenses. With an unidentified associate the boy attempted to burglarize a gasoline station. Although this station had been robbed twice previously in the same month, Ron denied any involvement in either of the other thefts. When Ron and his accomplice approached the station, the owner was hiding in the bushes beside the station. He fired both barrels of a double-barreled shotgun at the boys. Ron was severely injured; the other boy ran away and was never caught. Though he remained in critical condition for several months, Ron finally recovered and served six months of the following year in reform school. Upon release from reform school, Ron was put back a grade in school, and began running around with a different gang of boys. The Roughnecks considered the new gang less delinquent than themselves, and during the following year Ron had no more trouble with the police.

The Roughnecks, then, engaged mainly in three types of delinquency: theft, drinking, and fighting. Although community members perceived that this gang of kids was delinquent, they mistakenly believed that their illegal activities were primarily drinking, fighting, and being a nuisance to passersby. Drinking was limited among the gang members, although it did occur, and theft was much more prevalent than anyone realized.

Drinking would doubtless have been more prevalent had the boys had ready access to liquor. Since they rarely had automobiles at their disposal, they could not travel very far, and the bars in town would not serve them. Most of the boys had little money, and this, too, inhibited their purchase of alcohol. Their major source of liquor was a local drunk who would buy them a fifth if they would give him enough extra to buy himself a pint of whiskey or a bottle of wine.

The community's perception of drinking as prevalent stemmed from the fact that it was the most obvious delinquency the boys engaged in. When one of the boys had been drinking, even a casual observer seeing him on the corner would suspect that he was high.

There was a high level of mutual distrust and dislike between the Roughnecks and the police. The boys felt very strongly that the police were unfair and corrupt. Some evidence existed that the boys were correct in their perception.

The main source of the boys' dislike for the police undoubtedly stemmed from the fact that the police would sporadically harass the group. From the standpoint of the boys, these acts of occasional enforcement of the law were whimsical and uncalled for. It made no sense to them, for example, that the police would come to the corner occasionally and threaten them with arrest for loitering when the night before the boys had been out siphoning gasoline from cars and the police had been nowhere in sight. To the boys, the police were stupid on the one hand, for not being where they should have been and catching the boys in a serious offense, and unfair on the other hand, for trumping up "loitering" charges against them.

From the viewpoint of the police, the situation was quite different. They knew, with all the confidence necessary to be a policeman, that these boys were engaged in criminal activities. They knew this partly from occasionally catching them, mostly from circumstantial evidence ("the boys were around when those tires were slashed"), and partly because the police shared the view of the community in general that this was a bad bunch of boys. The best the police could hope to do was to be sensitive to the fact that these boys were engaged in illegal acts and arrest them whenever there was some evidence that they had been involved. Whether or not the boys had in fact committed a particular act in a particular way was not especially important. The police had a broader view: their job was to stamp out these kids' crimes; the tactics were not as important as the end result.

Over the period that the group was under observation, each member was arrested at least once. Several of the boys were arrested a number of times and spent at least one night in jail. While most were never taken to court, two of the boys were sentenced to six months' incarceration in boys' schools.

The Roughnecks in School

The Roughnecks' behavior in school was not particularly disruptive. During school hours they did not all hang around together, but tended instead to spend most of their time with one or two other members of the gang who were their special buddies. Although every member of the gang attempted to avoid school as much as possible, they were not particularly successful and most of them attended school with surprising regularity. They considered school a burden—something to be gotten through with a minimum of conflict. If they were "bugged" by a particular teacher, it could lead to trouble. One of the boys, Al, once threatened to beat up a teacher and, according to the other boys, the teacher hid under a desk to escape him.

Teachers saw the boys the way the general community did, as heading for trouble, as being uninterested in making something of themselves. Some were also seen as being incapable of meeting the academic standards of the school. Most of the teachers expressed concern for this group of boys and were willing to pass them despite poor performance, in the belief that failing them would only aggravate the problem.

The group of boys had a grade point average just slightly above "C." No one in the group failed either grade, and no one had better than a "C" average. They were very consistent in their achievement or, at least, the teachers were consistent in their perception of the boys' achievement.

Two of the boys were good football players. Herb was acknowledged to be the best player in the school, and Jack was almost as good. Both boys were criticized for their failure to abide by training rules, for refusing to come to practice as often as they should, and for not playing their best during practice. What they lacked in sportsmanship they made up for in skill, apparently, and played every game no matter how poorly they had performed in practice or how many practice sessions they had missed.

Two Questions

Why did the community, the school, and the police react to the Saints as though they were good, upstanding, nondelinquent youths with bright futures but to the Roughnecks as though they were tough, young criminals who were headed for trouble? Why did the Roughnecks and the Saints in fact have quite different careers after high school—careers which, by and large, lived up to the expectations of the community?

The most obvious explanation for the differences in the community's and law enforcement agencies' reactions to the two gangs is that one group of boys was "more delinquent" than the other. Which group was more delinquent? The answer to this question will determine in part how we explain the differential responses to these groups by the members of the community and, particularly, by law enforcement and school officials.

In sheer number of illegal acts, the Saints were the more delinquent. They were truant from school for at least part of the day almost every day of the week. In addition, their drinking and vandalism occurred with surprising regularity. The Roughnecks, in contrast, engaged sporadically in delinquent episodes. While these episodes were frequent, they certainly did not occur on a daily or even a weekly basis.

The difference in frequency of offenses was probably caused by the Roughnecks' inability to obtain liquor and to manipulate legitimate excuses from school. Since the Roughnecks had less money than the Saints, and teachers carefully supervised their school activities, the Roughnecks' hearts may have been as black as the Saints', but their misdeeds were not nearly as frequent.

There are really no clear-cut criteria by which to measure qualitative differences in antisocial behavior. The most important dimension is generally referred to as the "seriousness" of the offenses.

If seriousness encompasses the relative economic costs of delinquent acts, then some assessment can be made. The Roughnecks probably stole an average of about $5.00 worth of goods a week. Some weeks the figure was considerably higher, but these times must be balanced against long periods when almost nothing was stolen.

The Saints were more continuously engaged in delinquency, but their acts were not for the most part costly to property. Only their vandalism and occasional theft of gasoline would so qualify. Perhaps once or twice a month they would siphon a tankful of gas. The other costly items were street signs, construction lanterns, and the like. All of these acts combined probably did not quite average $5.00 a week, partly because much of the stolen equipment was abandoned and presumably could be recovered. The difference in cost of stolen property between the two groups was trivial, but the Roughnecks probably had a slightly more expensive set of activities than did the Saints.

Another meaning of seriousness is the potential threat of physical harm to members of the community and to the boys themselves. The Roughnecks were more prone to physical violence; they not only welcomed an opportunity to fight; they went seeking it. In addition, they fought among themselves frequently. Although the fighting never included deadly weapons, it was still a menace, however minor, to the physical safety of those involved.

The Saints never fought. They avoided physical conflict both inside and outside the group. At the same time, though, the Saints frequently endangered their own and other people's lives. They did so almost every time they drove a car, especially if they had been drinking. Sober, their driving was risky; under the influence of alcohol it was horrendous. In addition, the Saints endangered the lives of others with their pranks. Street excavations left unmarked were a very serious hazard.

Evaluating the relative seriousness of the two gangs' activities is difficult. The community reacted as though the behavior of the Roughnecks was a problem, and they reacted as though the behavior of the Saints was not. But the members of the community were ignorant of the array of delinquent acts that characterized the Saints' behavior. Although concerned citizens were unaware of much of the Roughnecks' behavior as well, they were much better informed about the Roughnecks' involvement in delinquency than they were about the Saints'.

Visibility

Differential treatment of the two gangs resulted in part because one gang was infinitely more visible than the other. This differential visibility was a direct function of the economic standing of the families. The Saints had access to automobiles and were able to remove themselves from the sight of the community. In as routine a decision as to where to go to have a milkshake after school, the Saints stayed away from the mainstream of community life. Lacking transportation, the Roughnecks could not make it to the edge of town. The center of town was the only practical place for them to meet since their homes were scattered throughout the town and any noncentral meeting place put an undue hardship on some members. Through necessity the Roughnecks congregated in a crowded area where everyone in the community passed frequently, including teachers and law enforcement officers. They could easily see the Roughnecks hanging around the drugstore.

The Roughnecks, of course, made themselves even more visible by making remarks to passersby and by occasionally getting into fights on the corner. Meanwhile, just as regularly, the Saints were either at the café on one edge of town or in the pool hall at the other edge of town. Without any particular realization that they were making themselves inconspicuous, the Saints were able to hide their time-wasting. Not only were they removed from the mainstream of traffic, but they were almost always inside a building.

On their escapades the Saints were also relatively invisible, since they left Hanibal and traveled to Big Town. Here, too, they were mobile, roaming the city, rarely going to the same area twice.

Demeanor

To the notion of visibility must be added the difference in the responses of group members to outside intervention with their activities. If one of the Saints was confronted with an accusing policeman, even if he felt he was truly innocent of a wrongdoing, his demeanor was apologetic and penitent. A Roughneck's attitude was almost the polar opposite. When confronted with a threatening adult authority, even one who tried to be pleasant, the Roughneck's hostility and disdain were clearly observable. Sometimes he might attempt to put up a veneer of respect, but it was thin and was not accepted as sincere by the authority.

School was no different from the community at large. The Saints could manipulate the system by feigning compliance with the school norms. The availability of cars at school meant that once free from the immediate sight of the teacher, the boys could disappear rapidly. And this escape was well enough planned that no administrator or teacher was nearby when the boys left. A Roughneck who wished to escape for a few hours was in a bind. If it were possible to get free from class, downtown was still a mile away, and even if he arrived there, he was still very visible. Truancy for the Roughnecks meant almost certain detection, while the Saints enjoyed almost complete immunity from sanctions.

Bias

Community members were not aware of the transgressions of the Saints. Even if the Saints had been less discreet, their favorite delinquencies would have been perceived as less serious than those of the Roughnecks.

In the eyes of the police and school officials, a boy who drinks in an alley and stands intoxicated on the street corner is committing a more serious offense than is a boy who drinks to inebriation in a nightclub or a tavern and drives around afterwards in a car. Similarly, a boy who steals a wallet from a store will be viewed as having committed a more serious offense than a boy who steals a lantern from a construction site.

Perceptual bias also operates with respect to the demeanor of the boys in the two groups when they are confronted by adults. It is not simply that adults dislike the posture affected by boys of the Roughneck ilk; more important is the conviction that the posture adopted by the Roughnecks is an indication of their devotion and commitment to deviance as a way of life. The posture becomes a cue, just as the type of the offense is a cue, to the degree to which the known transgressions are indicators of the youths' potential for other problems.

Visibility, demeanor, and bias are surface variables which explain the day-to-day operations of the police. Why do these surface variables operate as they do? Why did the police choose to disregard the Saints' delinquencies while breathing down the backs of the Roughnecks?

The answer lies in the class structure of American society and the control of legal institutions by those at the top of the class structure. Obviously, no representative of the upper class drew up the operational chart for the police which led them to look in the ghettos and on street corners—which led them to see the demeanor of lower-class youth as troublesome and that of upper-middle-class youth as tolerable. Rather, the procedures simply developed from experience—experience with irate and influential upper-middle-class parents insisting that their son's vandalism was simply a prank and his drunkenness only a momentary "sowing of wild oats"—experience with cooperative or indifferent, powerless, lower-class parents who acquiesced to the law's definition of their son's behavior.

Adult Careers of the Saints and the Roughnecks

The community's confidence in the potential of the Saints and the Roughnecks apparently was justified. If anything, the community members underestimated the degree to which these youngsters would turn out "good" or "bad."

Seven of the eight members of the Saints went on to college immediately after high school. Five of the boys graduated from college in four years. The sixth one finished college after two years in the army, and the seventh spent four years in the air force before returning to college and receiving a B.A. degree. Of these seven college graduates, three went on for advanced degrees. One finished law school and is now active in state politics, one finished medical school and is practicing near Hanibal, and one boy is now working for a Ph.D. The other four college graduates entered submanagerial, managerial, or executive training positions with larger firms.

The only Saint who did not complete college was Jerry. Jerry had failed to graduate from high school with the other Saints. During his second senior year, after the other Saints had gone on to college, Jerry began to hang around with what several teachers described as a "rough crowd"—the gang that was heir apparent to the Roughnecks. At the end of his second senior year, when he did graduate from high school, Jerry took a job as a used-car salesman, got married, and quickly had a child. Although he made several abortive attempts to go to college by attending night school, when I last saw him (ten years after high school) Jerry was unemployed and had been living on unemployment for almost a year. His wife worked as a waitress.

Some of the Roughnecks have lived up to community expectations. A number of them were headed for trouble. A few were not.

Jack and Herb were the athletes among the Roughnecks, and their athletic prowess paid off handsomely. Both boys received unsolicited athletic scholarships to college. After Herb received his scholarship (near the end of his senior year), he apparently did an about-face. His demeanor became very similar to that of the Saints. Although he remained a member in good standing of the Roughnecks, he stopped participating in most activities and did not hang out on the corner as often.

Jack did not change. If anything, he became more prone to fighting. He even made excuses for accepting the scholarship. He told the other gang members that the school had guaranteed him a "C" average if he would come to play football—an idea that seems far-fetched, even in this day of highly competitive recruiting.

During the summer after graduation from high school, Jack attempted suicide by jumping from a tall building. The jump would certainly have killed most people trying it, but Jack survived. He entered college in the fall and played four years of football. He and Herb graduated in four years, and both are teaching and coaching in high schools. They are married and have stable families. If anything, Jack appears to have a more prestigious position in the community than does Herb, though both are well respected and secure in their positions.

Two of the boys never finished high school. Tommy left at the end of his junior year and went to another state. That summer he was arrested and placed on probation on a manslaughter charge. Three years later he was arrested for murder; he pleaded guilty to second degree murder and is serving a 30-year sentence in the state penitentiary.

Al, the other boy who did not finish high school, also left the state in his senior year. He is serving a life sentence in a state penitentiary for first degree murder.

Wes is a small-time gambler. He finished high school and "bummed around." After several years he made contact with a bookmaker who employed him as a runner. Later he acquired his own area and has been working it ever since. His position among the bookmakers is almost identical to the position he had in the gang; he is always around, but no one is really aware of him. He makes no trouble, and he does not get into any. Steady, reliable, capable of keeping his mouth closed, he plays the game by the rules, even though the game is an illegal one.

That leaves only Ron. Some of his former friends reported that they had heard he was "driving a truck up north," but no one could provide any concrete information.

Reinforcement

The community responded to the Roughnecks as boys in trouble, and the boys agreed with that perception. Their pattern of deviancy was reinforced, and breaking away from it became increasingly unlikely. Once the boys acquired an image of themselves as deviants, they selected new friends who affirmed that self-image. As that self-conception became more firmly entrenched, they also became willing to try new and more extreme deviances. With their growing alienation came freer expression of disrespect and hostility for representatives of the legitimate society. This disrespect increased the community's negativism, perpetuating the entire process of commitment to deviance. Lack of a commitment to deviance works the same way. In either case, the process will perpetuate itself unless some event (like a scholarship to college or a sudden failure) external to the established relationship intervenes. For two of the Roughnecks (Herb and Jack), receiving college athletic scholarships created new relations and culminated in a break with the established pattern of deviance. In the case of one of the Saints (Jerry), his parents' divorce and his failing to graduate from high school changed some of his other relations. Being held back in school for a year and losing his place among the Saints had sufficient impact on Jerry to alter his self-image and virtually to assure that he would not go on to college as his peers did. Although the experiments of life can rarely be reversed, it seems likely in view of the behavior of the other boys who did not enjoy this special treatment by the school that Jerry, too, would have "become something" had he graduated as anticipated. For Herb and Jack outside intervention worked to their advantage; for Jerry it was his undoing.

Selective perception and labeling—finding, processing, and punishing some kinds of criminality and not others—means that visible, poor, nonmobile, outspoken, undiplomatic "tough" kids will be noticed, whether their actions are seriously delinquent or not. Other kids, who have established a reputation for being bright (even though underachieving), disciplined, and involved in respectable activities, who are mobile and monied, will be invisible when they deviate from sanctioned activities. They'll sow their wild oats—perhaps even wider and thicker than their lower-class cohorts—but they won't be noticed. When it's time to leave adolescence most will follow the expected path, settling into the ways of the middle class, remembering fondly the delinquent but unnoticed fling of their youth. The Roughnecks and others like them may turn around, too. It is more likely that their noticeable deviance will have been so reinforced by police and community that their lives will be effectively channeled into careers consistent with their adolescent background.

27 The Pathology of Imprisonment

PHILIP G. ZIMBARDO

Why are our prisons such powder kegs? To most people, the answer is obvious—because of the kind of people who are locked up in prisons: They are criminals, antisocial, and disposed to violence. If not that, then they hate the guards, the food, or the restrictions of prison life (which is what they deserved in the first place!). Similarly, people have little difficulty explaining why prison guards are brutal: It is either the type of people with whom the guards must deal ("animals") or the type of people who are attracted to being prison guards in the first place ("sadistic types"). Such reasons are commonly cited to explain prison violence. It turns out, however, that more fundamental social processes are involved. As Zimbardo's remarkable experiment uncovered, the structuring of relationships within the prison lays the foundation for prison brutality and violence.

While reading this fascinating account, you may begin to think about how prisons could be improved in order to minimize violence. To reach such a goal, what changes would you suggest that we make in the social structure of prisons?

I was recently released from solitary confinement after being held therein for 37 months [months!]. A silent system was imposed upon me and to even whisper to the man in the next cell resulted in being beaten by guards, sprayed with chemical mace, blackjacked, stomped and thrown into a strip-cell naked to sleep on a concrete floor without bedding, covering, wash basin or even a toilet. The floor served as toilet and bed, and even there the silent system was enforced. To let a moan escape your lips because of the pain and discomfort . . . resulted in another beating. I spent not days, but months there during my 37 months in solitary. . . . I have filed every writ possible against the administrative acts of brutality. The state courts have all denied the petitions. Because of my refusal to let the things die down and forget all that happened during my 37 months in solitary . . . I am the most hated prisoner in [this] penitentiary, and called a "hard-core incorrigible."

Maybe I am an incorrigible, but if true, it's because I would rather die than to accept being treated as less than a

315

human being. I have never complained of my prison sentence as being unjustified except through legal means of appeals. I have never put a knife on a guard's throat and demanded my release. I know that thieves must be punished and I don't justify stealing, even though I am a thief myself. but now I don't think I will be a thief when I am released. No, I'm not rehabilitated. It's just that I no longer think of becoming wealthy by stealing. I now only think of killing—killing those who have beaten me and treated me as if I were a dog. I hope and pray for the sake of my own soul and future life of freedom that I am able to overcome the bitterness and hatred which eats daily at my soul, but I know to overcome it will not be easy.

THIS ELOQUENT PLEA FOR PRISON REFORM—for humane treatment of human beings, for the basic dignity that is the right of every American—came to me secretly in a letter from a prisoner who cannot be identified because he is still in a state correctional institution. He sent it to me because he read of an experiment I recently conducted at Stanford University. In an attempt to understand just what it means psychologically to be a prisoner or a prison guard, Craig Haney, Curt Banks, Dave Jaffe, and I created our own prison. We carefully screened over 70 volunteers who answered an ad in a Palo Alto city newspaper and ended up with about two dozen young men who were selected to be part of this study. They were mature, emotionally stable, normal, intelligent college students from middle-class homes throughout the United States and Canada. They appeared to represent the cream of the crop of this generation. None had any criminal record and all were relatively homogeneous on many dimensions initially.

Half were arbitrarily designated as prisoners by a flip of a coin, the others as guards. These were the roles they were to play in our simulated prison. The guards were made aware of the potential seriousness and danger of the situation and their own vulnerability. They made up their own formal rules for maintaining law, order, and respect, and were generally free to improvise new ones during their eight-hour, three-man shifts. The prisoners were unexpectedly picked up at their homes by a city policeman in a squad car, searched, handcuffed, fingerprinted, booked at the Palo Alto station house, and taken blindfolded to our jail. There they were stripped, deloused, put into a uniform, given a number, and put into a cell with two other prisoners where they expected to live for the next two weeks. The pay was good ($15 a day), and their motivation was to make money.

We observed and recorded on videotape the events that occurred in the prison, and we interviewed and tested the prisoners and guards at various points throughout the study. Some of the videotapes of the actual encounters between the prisoners and guards were seen on the NBC News feature "Chronolog" on November 26, 1971.

At the end of only six days we had to close down our mock prison because what we saw was frightening. It was no longer apparent to most of the subjects (or to us) where reality ended and their roles began. The majority had indeed become prisoners or guards, no longer able to clearly differentiate between role playing and self. There were dramatic changes in virtually every aspect of their behavior, thinking, and feeling. In less than a week the experience of imprisonment undid (temporarily) a lifetime of learning; human values were suspended, self-concepts were challenged, and the ugliest, most base, pathological side of human nature surfaced. We were horrified because we saw some boys (guards) treat others as if they were despicable animals, taking pleasure in cruelty, while other boys (prisoners) became servile, dehumanized robots who thought only of escape, of their own individual survival, and of their mounting hatred for the guards.

We had to release three prisoners in the first four days because they had such acute situational traumatic reactions as hysterical crying, confusion in thinking, and severe depression. Others begged to be paroled, and all but three were willing to forfeit all the money they had earned if they could be paroled. By then (the fifth day) they had been so programmed to think of themselves as prisoners that when their request for parole was denied, they returned docilely to their cells. Now, had they been thinking as college students acting in an oppressive experiment, they would have quit once they no longer wanted the $15 a day we used as our only incentive. However, the reality was not quitting an experiment but "being paroled by the parole board from the Stanford County Jail." By the last days, the earlier solidarity among the prisoners (systematically broken by the guards) dissolved into "each man for himself." Finally, when one of their fellows was put into solitary confinement (a small closet) for refusing to eat, the prisoners were given a choice by one of the guards: give up their blankets and the incorrigible prisoner would be let out, or keep their blankets and he would be kept in all night. They voted to keep their blankets and to abandon their brother.

About a third of the guards became tyrannical in their arbitrary use of power, in enjoying their control over other people. They were corrupted by the power of their roles and became quite inventive in their techniques of breaking the spirit of the prisoners and making them feel they were worthless. Some of the guards merely did their jobs as tough but fair correctional officers, and several were good guards from the prisoners' point of view since they did them small favors and were friendly. However, no good guards ever interfered with a command by any of the bad guards; they never intervened on the side of the prisoners, they never told the others to ease off because it was only an experiment, and they never even came to me as prison superintendent or experimenter in charge to complain. In part, they were good because the others were bad; they needed the others to help establish their own egos in a positive light. In a sense, the good guards perpetuated the prison more than the other guards because their own need to be liked prevented them from disobeying or violating the implicit guards' code. At the same time, the act of befriending the prisoners created a social reality which made the prisoners less likely to rebel.

By the end of the week the experiment had become a reality, as if it were a Pirandello play directed by Kafka that just keeps going after the audience has left. The consultant for our prison, Carlo Prescott, an exconvict with 16 years of imprisonment in California's jails, would get so depressed and furious each time he visited our prison, because of its psychological similarity to his experiences, that he would have to leave. A Catholic priest who was a former prison chaplain in Washington, D.C., talked to our prisoners after four days and said they were just like the other first-timers he had seen.

But in the end, I called off the experiment not because of the horror I saw out there in the prison yard, but because of the horror of realizing that *I* could have easily traded places with the most brutal guard or become the weakest prisoner full of hatred at being so powerless that I could not eat, sleep, or go to the toilet without permission of the authorities. *I* could have become Calley at My Lai, George Jackson at San Quentin, one of the men at Attica, or the prisoner quoted at the beginning of this article.

Individual behavior is largely under the control of social forces and environmental contingencies rather than personality traits, character, will power, or other empirically unvalidated constructs. Thus we create an illusion of freedom by attributing more internal control to ourselves, to the individual, than actually exists. We thus underestimate the power and pervasiveness of situational controls over behavior because: (a) they are often nonobvious and subtle, (b) we can often avoid entering situations where we might be so controlled, (c) we label as "weak" or "deviant" people in those situations who do behave differently from how we believed we would.

Each of us carries around in our heads a favorable self-image in which we are essentially just, fair, humane, and understanding. For example, we could not imagine inflicting pain on others without much provocation or hurting people who had done nothing to us, who in fact were even liked by us. However, there is a growing body of social psychological research which underscores the conclusion derived from this prison study. Many people, perhaps the majority, can be made to do almost anything when put into psychologically compelling situations—regardless of their morals, ethics, values, attitudes, beliefs, or personal convictions. My colleague, Stanley

Milgram, has shown that more than 60 percent of the population will deliver what they think is a series of painful electric shocks to another person even after the victim cries for mercy, begs them to stop, and then apparently passes out. The subjects complained that they did not want to inflict more pain but blindly obeyed the command of the authority figure (the experimenter) who said that they must go on. In my own research on violence, I have seen mild-mannered co-eds repeatedly give shocks (which they thought were causing pain) to another girl, a stranger whom they had rated very favorably, simply by being made to feel anonymous and put in a situation where they were expected to engage in this activity.

Observers of these and similar experimental situations never predict their outcomes and estimate that it is unlikely that they themselves would behave similarly. They can be so confident only when they are outside the situation. However, since the majority of people in these studies do act in nonrational, nonobvious ways, it follows that the majority of observers would also succumb to the social psychological forces in the situation.

With regard to prisons, we can state that the mere act of assigning labels to people and putting them into a situation where those labels acquire validity and meaning is sufficient to elicit pathological behavior. This pathology is not predictable from any available diagnostic indicators we have in the social sciences, and is extreme enough to modify in very significant ways fundamental attitudes and behavior. The prison situation, as presently arranged, is guaranteed to generate severe enough pathological reactions in both guards and prisoners as to debase their humanity, lower their feelings of self-worth, and make it difficult for them to be part of a society outside of their prison.

For years our national leaders have been pointing to the enemies of freedom, to the fascist or communist threat to the American way of life. In so doing they have overlooked the threat of social anarchy that is building within our own country without any outside agitation. As soon as a person comes to the realization that he is being imprisoned by his society or individuals in it, then, in the best American tradition, he demands liberty and rebels, accepting death as an alternative. The third alternative, however, is to allow oneself to become a good prisoner—docile, cooperative, uncomplaining, conforming in thought, and complying in deed.

Our prison authorities now point to the militant agitators who are still vaguely referred to as part of some communist plot, as the irresponsible, incorrigible troublemakers. They imply that there would be no trouble, riots, hostages, or deaths if it weren't for this small band of bad prisoners. In other words, then, everything would return to "normal" again in the life of our nation's prisons if they could break these men.

The riots in prison are coming from within—from within every man and woman who refuses to let the system turn them into an object, a number, a thing, or a no-thing. It is not communist-inspired, but inspired by the spirit of American freedom. No man wants to be enslaved. To be powerless, to be subject to the arbitrary exercise of power, to not be recognized as a human being is to be a slave.

To be a militant prisoner is to become aware that the physical jails are but more blatant extensions of the forms of social and psychological oppression experienced daily in the nation's ghettos. They are trying to awaken the conscience of the nation to the ways in which the American ideals are being perverted, apparently in the name of justice but actually under the banner of apathy, fear, and hatred. If we do not listen to the pleas of the prisoners at Attica to be treated like human beings, then we have all become brutalized by our priorities for property rights over human rights. The consequence will not only be more prison riots but a loss of all those ideals on which this country was founded.

The public should be aware that they own the prisons and that their business is failing. The 70 percent recidivism rate and the escalation in severity of crimes committed by graduates of our prisons are evidence that current prisons fail to rehabilitate the inmates in any positive way. Rather, they are breeding grounds for hatred of the establishment, a hatred that makes every citizen a target of violent assault. Prisons are a bad investment for us taxpayers. Until now we have not cared; we have turned over to wardens and prison authorities the unpleasant job of keeping people who threaten us out of our sight. Now we are shocked to learn that their management practices have failed to improve the product and instead turn petty thieves into murderers. We must insist upon new management or improved operating procedures.

The cloak of secrecy should be removed from the prisons. Prisoners claim they are brutalized by the guards; guards say it is a lie. Where is the impartial test of the truth in such a situation? Prison officials have forgotten that they work for us, that they are only public servants whose salaries are paid by our taxes. They act as if it is their prison, like a child with a toy he won't share. Neither lawyers, judges, the legislature, nor the public is allowed into prisons to ascertain the truth unless the visit is sanctioned by authorities and until all is prepared for their visit. I was shocked to learn that my request to join a congressional investigating committee's tour of San Quentin and Soledad was refused, as was that of the news media.

There should be an ombudsman in every prison, not under the pay or control of the prison authority, and responsible only to the courts, the state legislature, and the public. Such a person could report on violations of constitutional and human rights.

Guards must be given better training than they now receive for the difficult job society imposes upon them. To be a prison guard as now constituted is to be put in a situation of constant threat from within the prison, with no social recognition from the society at large. As was shown graphically at Attica, prison guards are also prisoners of the system who can be sacrificed to the demands of the public to be punitive and the needs of politicians to preserve an image. Social scientists and business administrators should be called upon to design and help carry out this training.

The relationship between the individual (who is sentenced by the courts to a prison term) and his community must be maintained. How can a prisoner return to a dynamically changing society that most of us cannot cope with after being out of it for a number of years? There should be more community involvement in these rehabilitation centers, more ties encouraged and promoted between the trainees and family and friends, more educational opportunities to prepare them for returning to their communities as more valuable members of it than they were before they left.

Finally, the main ingredient necessary to effect any change at all in prison reform, in the rehabilitation of a single prisoner, or even in the optimal development of a child is caring. Reform must start with people—especially people with power—caring about the well-being of others. Underneath the toughest, society-hating convict, rebel, or anarchist is a human being who wants his existence to be recognized by his fellows and who wants someone else to care about whether he lives or dies and to grieve if he lives imprisoned rather than lives free.

28 On Being Sane in Insane Places

DAVID L. ROSENHAN

On the one hand, it is not uncommon for people who violate *explicit* rules written into law to find themselves enmeshed in a formal system that involves passing judgment on their fitness to remain in society. As we saw in the preceding selection, removing people's freedom can thrust them into volatile situations. On the other hand, people who violate *implicit* rules (the assumptions about what characterizes "normal" people) also can find themselves caught up in a formal system that involves passing judgment on their fitness to remain in society. If found "guilty of insanity," they, too, are institutionalized—placed in the care of keepers who oversee almost all aspects of their lives.

The taken-for-granted assumption in institutionalizing people who violate implicit rules is that we are able to tell the sane from the insane. If we cannot do so, the practice itself would be insane! In that case, we would have to question psychiatry as a mechanism of social control. But what kind of question is this? Even most of us non-psychiatrists can tell the difference between who is sane and who is not, can't we? In a fascinating experiment, Rosenhan put to the test whether or not even psychiatrists can differentiate between the sane and the insane. As detailed in this account, the results contain a few surprises.

IF SANITY AND INSANITY EXIST . . . how shall we know them? The question is neither capricious nor itself insane. However much we may be personally convinced that we can tell the normal from the abnormal, the evidence is simply not compelling. It is commonplace, for example, to read about murder trials wherein eminent psychiatrists for the defense are contradicted by equally eminent psychiatrists for the prosecution on the matter of the defendant's sanity. More generally, there are a great deal of conflicting data on the reliability, utility, and meaning of such terms as "sanity," "insanity," "mental illness," and "schizophrenia."[1] Finally, as early as 1934, Benedict suggested that normality and abnormality are not universal.[2] What is viewed as normal in one culture may be seen as quite aberrant in another.

Thus, notions of normality and abnormality may not be quite as accurate as people believe they are.

To raise questions regarding normality and abnormality is in no way to question the fact that some behaviors are deviant or odd. Murder is deviant. So, too, are hallucinations. Nor does raising such questions deny the existence of the personal anguish that is often associated with "mental illness." Anxiety and depression exist. Psychological suffering exists. But normality and abnormality, sanity and insanity, and the diagnoses that flow from them may be less substantive than many believe them to be.

At its heart, the question of whether the sane can be distinguished from the insane (and whether degrees of insanity can be distinguished from each other) is a simple matter: Do the salient characteristics that lead to diagnoses reside in the patients themselves or in the environments and contexts in which observers find them? From Bleuler, through Kretschmer, through the formulators of the recently revised *Diagnostic and Statistical Manual* of the American Psychiatric Association, the belief has been strong that patients present symptoms, that those symptoms can be categorized, and, implicitly, that the sane are distinguishable from the insane. More recently, however, this belief has been questioned. Based in part on theoretical and anthropological considerations, but also on philosophical, legal, and therapeutic ones, the view has grown that psychological categorization of mental illness is useless at best and downright harmful, misleading, and pejorative at worst. Psychiatric diagnoses, in this view, are in the minds of the observers and are not valid summaries of characteristics displayed by the observed.[3,4,5]

Gains can be made in deciding which of these is more nearly accurate by getting normal people (that is, people who do not have, and have never suffered, symptoms of serious psychiatric disorders) admitted to psychiatric hospitals and then determining whether they were discovered to be sane and, if so, how. If the sanity of such pseudopatients were always detected, there would be *prima facie* evidence that a sane individual can be distinguished from the insane context in which he is found. Normality (and presumably abnormality) is distinct enough that it can be recognized wherever it occurs, for it is carried within the person. If, on the other hand, the sanity of the pseudopatients were never discovered, serious difficulties would arise for those who support traditional modes of psychiatric diagnosis. Given that the hospital staff was not incompetent, that the pseudopatient had been behaving as sanely as he had been outside of the hospital, and that it had never been previously suggested that he belonged in a psychiatric hospital, such an unlikely outcome would support the view that psychiatric diagnosis betrays little about the patient but much about the environment in which an observer finds him.

This article describes such an experiment. Eight sane people gained secret admission to twelve different hospitals.[6] Their diagnostic experiences constitute the data of the first part of this article; the remainder is devoted to a description of their experiences in psychiatric institutions. Too few psychiatrists and psychologists, even those who have worked in such hospitals, know what the experience is like. They rarely talk about it with former patients, perhaps because they distrust information coming from the previously insane. Those who have worked in psychiatric hospitals are likely to have adapted so thoroughly to the settings that they are insensitive to the impact of that experience. And while there have been occasional reports of researchers who submitted themselves to psychiatric hospitalization,[7] these researchers have commonly remained in the hospitals for short periods of time, often with the knowledge of the hospital staff. It is difficult to know the extent to which they were treated like patients or like research colleagues. Nevertheless, their reports about the inside of the psychiatric hospital have been valuable. This article extends those efforts.

Pseudopatients and Their Settings

The eight pseudopatients were a varied group. One was a psychology graduate student in his twenties. The remaining seven were older and "established." Among them were three psychologists, a pediatrician, a psychiatrist, a painter, and a housewife. Three pseudopatients were women, five were men. All of them employed pseudonyms, lest their alleged diagnoses embarrass them later. Those who were in mental health professions alleged another occupation in order to avoid the special attentions that might be accorded by staff, as a matter of courtesy or caution, to ailing colleagues.[8] With the exception of myself (I was the first pseudopatient and my presence was known to the hospital administrator and chief psychologist and, so far as I can tell, to them alone), the presence of pseudopatients and the nature of the research program were not known to the hospital staffs.[9]

The settings were similarly varied. In order to generalize the findings, admission into a variety of hospitals was sought. The twelve hospitals in the sample were located in five different states on the East and West coasts. Some were old and shabby; some were quite new. Some were research-oriented, others not. Some had good staff-patient ratios; others were quite understaffed. Only one was a strictly private hospital. All of the others were supported by state or federal funds, or in one instance, by university funds.

After calling the hospital for an appointment, the pseudopatient arrived at the admissions office complaining that he had been hearing voices. Asked what the voices said, he replied that they were often unclear, but as far as he could tell they said "empty," "hollow," and "thud." The voices were unfamiliar and were of the same sex as the pseudopatient. The choice of these symptoms was occasioned by their apparent similarity to existential symptoms. Such symptoms are alleged to arise from painful concerns about the perceived meaninglessness of one's life. It is as if the hallucinating person were saying, "My life is empty and hollow." The choice of these symptoms was also determined by the *absence* of a single report of existential psychoses in the literature.

Beyond alleging the symptoms and falsifying name, vocation, and employment, no further alterations of person, history, or circumstances were made. The significant events of the pseudopatient's life history were presented as they had actually occurred. Relationships with parents and siblings, with spouse and children, with people at work and in school, consistent with the aforementioned exceptions, were described as they were or had been. Frustrations and upsets were described along with joys and satisfactions. These facts are important to remember. If anything, they strongly biased the subsequent results in favor of detecting sanity, since none of their histories or current behaviors were seriously pathological in any way.

Immediately upon admission to the psychiatric ward, the pseudopatient ceased simulating *any* symptoms of abnormality. In some cases, there was a brief period of mild nervousness and anxiety, since none of the pseudopatients really believed that they would be admitted so easily. Indeed, their shared fear was that they would be immediately exposed as frauds and greatly embarrassed. Moreover, many of them had never visited a psychiatric ward; even those who had, nevertheless had some genuine fears about what might happen to them. Their nervousness, then, was quite appropriate to the novelty of the hospital setting, and it abated rapidly.

Apart from that short-lived nervousness, the pseudopatient behaved on the ward as he "normally" behaved. The pseudopatient spoke to patients and staff as he might ordinarily. Because there is uncommonly little to do on a psychiatric ward, he attempted to engage others in conversation. When asked by staff how he was feeling, he indicated that he was fine, that he no longer experienced symptoms. He responded to instructions from attendants, to calls for medication (which was not swallowed), and to dining-hall instructions. Beyond such activities as were available to him on the admissions ward, he spent his time writing down his observations about the ward, its patients, and the staff. Initially these notes were written "secretly," but as it soon became clear that no one much cared, they were subsequently written on standard tablets of paper in such public places as the dayroom. No secret was made of these activities.

The pseudopatient, very much as a true psychiatric patient, entered a hospital with no foreknowledge of when he would be discharged. Each was told that he would have to get out by his own devices, essentially by convincing the staff that he was sane. The psychological stresses associated with hospitalization were considerable, and all but one of the pseudopatients desired to be discharged almost immediately after being admitted. They were, therefore, motivated not only to behave sanely, but to be paragons of cooperation. That their behavior was in no way disruptive is confirmed by nursing reports, which have been obtained on most of the patients. These reports uniformly indicate that the patients were "friendly," "cooperative," and "exhibited no abnormal indications."

The Normal Are Not Detectably Sane

Despite their public "show" of sanity, the pseudopatients were never detected. Admitted, except in one case, with a diagnosis of schizophrenia,[10] each was discharged with a diagnosis of schizophrenia "in remission." The label "in remission" should in no way be dismissed as a formality, for at no time during any hospitalization had any question been raised about any pseudopatient's simulation. Nor are there any indications in the hospital records that the pseudopatient's status was suspect. Rather, the evidence is strong that, once labeled schizophrenic, the pseudopatient was stuck with that label. If the pseudopatient was to be discharged, he must naturally be "in remission"; but he was not sane, nor, in the institution's view, had he ever been sane.

The uniform failure to recognize sanity cannot be attributed to the quality of the hospitals, for, although there were considerable variations among them, several are considered excellent. Nor can it be alleged that there was simply not enough time to observe the pseudopatients. Length of hospitalization ranged from seven to fifty-two days, with an average of nineteen days. The pseudopatients were not, in fact, carefully observed, but this failure clearly speaks more to traditions within psychiatric hospitals than to lack of opportunity.

Finally, it cannot be said that the failure to recognize the pseudopatients' sanity was due to the fact that they were not behaving sanely. While there was clearly some tension present in all of them, their daily visitors could detect no serious behavioral consequences—nor, indeed, could other patients. It was quite common for the patients to "detect" the pseudopatients' sanity. During the first three hospitalizations, when accurate counts were kept, 35 of a total of 118 patients on the admissions ward voiced their suspicions, some vigorously. "You're not crazy. You're a journalist, or a professor [referring to the continual note-taking]. You're checking up on the hospital." While most of the patients were reassured by the pseudopatient's insistence that he had been sick before he came in but was fine now, some continued to believe that the pseudopatient was sane throughout his hospitalization.[11] The fact that the patients often recognized normality when staff did not raises important questions.

Failure to detect sanity during the course of hospitalization may be due to the fact that physicians operate with a strong bias toward what statisticians call the type 2 error. This is to say that physicians are more inclined to call a healthy person sick (a false positive, type 2) than a sick person healthy (a false negative, type 1). The reasons for this are not hard to find: It is clearly more dangerous to misdiagnose illness than health. Better to err on the side of caution, to suspect illness even among the healthy.

But what holds for medicine does not hold equally well for psychiatry. Medical illnesses, while unfortunate, are not commonly pejorative. Psychiatric diagnoses, on the contrary, carry with them personal, legal, and social stigmas.[12] It was therefore important to see whether the tendency toward diagnosing the sane insane could be reversed. The following experiment was arranged at a research and teaching hospital whose staff had heard these findings but doubted that such an error could occur in their hospital. The staff was informed that at some time during the following three months, one or more pseudopatients would attempt to be admitted into the psychiatric hospital. Each staff member was asked to rate each patient who presented himself at admissions or on the ward according to the likelihood that the patient was a pseudopatient. A 10-point scale was used, with a 1 and 2 reflecting high confidence that the patient was a pseudopatient.

Judgments were obtained on 193 patients who were admitted for psychiatric treatment. All staff who had had sustained contact with or primary responsibility for the patient—attendants, nurses, psychiatrists, physicians, and psychologists—were asked to make judgments. Forty-one patients were alleged, with high confidence, to be pseudopatients by at least one member of the staff. Twenty-three were considered suspect by at least one psychiatrist. Nineteen were suspected by one psychiatrist and one other staff member. Actually, no genuine pseudopatient (at least from my group) presented himself during this period.

The experiment is instructive. It indicates that the tendency to designate sane people as insane can be reversed when the stakes (in this case, prestige and diagnostic acumen) are high. But what can be said of the nineteen people who were suspected of being "sane" by one psychiatrist and another staff member? Were these people truly "sane," or was it rather the case that in the course of avoiding the type 2 error the staff tended to make more errors of the first sort—calling the crazy "sane"? There is no way of knowing. But one thing is certain: Any diagnostic process that lends itself so readily to massive errors of this sort cannot be a very reliable one.

The Stickiness of Psychodiagnostic Labels

Beyond the tendency to call the healthy sick—a tendency that accounts better for diagnostic behavior on admission than it does for such behavior after a lengthy period of exposure—the data speak to the massive role of labeling in psychiatric assessment. Having once been labeled schizophrenic, there is nothing the pseudopatient can do to overcome the tag. The tag profoundly colors others' perceptions of him and his behavior.

From one viewpoint, these data are hardly surprising, for it has long been known that elements are given meaning by the context in which they occur. Gestalt psychology made this point vigorously, and Asch[13] demonstrated that there are "central" personality traits (such as "warm" versus "cold") which are so powerful that they markedly color the meaning of other information in forming an impression of a given personality.[14] "Insane," "schizophrenic," "manic-depressive," and "crazy" are probably among the most powerful of such central traits. Once a person is designated abnormal, all of his other behaviors and characteristics are colored by that label. Indeed, that label is so powerful that many of the pseudopatients' normal behaviors were overlooked entirely or profoundly misinterpreted. Some examples may clarify this issue.

Earlier I indicated that there were no changes in the pseudopatient's personal history and current status behond those of name, employment, and, where necessary, vocation. Otherwise, a veridical description of personal history and circumstances was offered. Those circumstances were not psychotic. How were they made consonant with the diagnosis of psychosis? Or were those diagnoses modified in such a way as to bring them into accord with the circumstances of the pseudopatient's life, as described by him?

As far as I can determine, diagnoses were in no way affected by the relative health of the circumstances of a pseudopatient's life. Rather, the reverse occurred: The perception of his circumstances was shaped entirely by the diagnosis. A clear example of such translation is found in the case of a pseudopatient who had had a close relationship with his mother but was rather remote from his father during his early childhood. During adolescence and beyond, however, his father became a close friend, while his relationship with his mother cooled. His present relationship with his wife was characteristically close and warm. Apart from occasional angry exchanges, friction was minimal. The children had rarely been spanked. Surely there is nothing especially pathological about such a history. Indeed, many readers may see a similar pattern in their own experiences, with no markedly deleterious consequences. Observe, however, how such a history was translated in the psychopathological context, this from the case summary prepared after the patient was discharged.

> This white 39-year-old male . . . manifests a long history of considerable ambivalence in close relationships, which begins in early childhood. A warm relationship with his mother cools during adolescence. A distant relationship to his father is described as becoming very intense. Affective stability is absent. His attempts to control emotionality with his wife and children are punctuated by angry outbursts and, in the case of the children, spankings. And while he says that he has several good friends, one senses considerable ambivalence embedded in those relationships also. . . .

The facts of the case were unintentionally distorted by the staff to achieve consistency with a popular theory of the dynamics of schizophrenic reaction.[15] Nothing of an ambivalent nature had been described in relations with parents, spouse, or friends. To the extent that ambivalence could be inferred, it was probably not greater than is found in all human relationships. It is true the pseudopatient's relationships with his parents changed over time, but in the ordinary context that would hardly be remarkable—indeed, it might very well be expected. Clearly, the meaning ascribed to his verbalizations (that is, ambivalence, affective instability) was determined by the diagnosis: schizophrenia. An entirely different meaning would have been ascribed if it were known that the man was "normal."

All pseudopatients took extensive notes publicly. Under ordinary circumstances, such behavior would have raised questions in the minds of observers, as, in fact, it did among patients. Indeed, it seemed so certain that the notes would elicit suspicion that elaborate precautions were taken to remove them from the ward each day. But the precautions proved needless. The closest any staff member came to questioning these notes occurred when one pseudopatient asked his physician what kind of medication he was receiving and began to write down the response. "You needn't write it," he was told gently. "If you have trouble remembering, just ask me again."

If no questions were asked of the pseudopatients, how was their writing interpreted? Nursing records for three patients indicate that the writing was seen as an aspect of their pathological behavior. "Patient engages in writing behavior" was the daily nursing comment on one of the pseudopatients who was never questioned about his writing. Given that the patient is in the hospital, he must be psychologically disturbed. And given that he is disturbed, continuous writing must be a behavioral manifestation of that disturbance, perhaps a subset of the compulsive behaviors that are sometimes correlated with schizophrenia.

One tacit characteristic of psychiatric diagnosis is that it locates the sources of aberration within the individual and only rarely within the complex of stimuli that surrounds him. Consequently, behaviors that are stimulated by the environment are commonly misattributed to the patient's disorder. For example, one kindly nurse found a pseudopatient pacing the long hospital corridors. "Nervous, Mr. X?" she asked. "No, bored," he said.

The notes kept by pseudopatients are full of patient behaviors that were misinterpreted by well-intentioned staff. Often enough, a patient would go "berserk" because he had, wittingly or unwittingly, been mistreated by, say, an attendant. A nurse coming upon the scene would rarely inquire even cursorily into the environmental stimuli of the patient's behavior. Rather, she assumed that his upset derived from his pathology, not from his present interactions with other staff members. Occasionally, the staff might assume that the patient's family (especially when they had recently visited) or other patients had stimulated the outburst. But never were the staff found to assume that one of themselves or the structure of the hospital had anything to do with a patient's behavior. One psychiatrist pointed to a group of patients who were sitting outside the cafeteria entrance half an hour before lunchtime. To a group of young residents, he indicated that such behavior was characteristic of the oral-acquisitive nature of the syndrome. It seemed not to occur to him that there were very few things to anticipate in the psychiatric hospital besides eating.

A psychiatric label has a life and an influence of its own. Once the impression has been formed that the patient is schizophrenic, the expectation is that he will continue to be schizophrenic. When a sufficient amount of time has passed, during which the patient has done nothing bizarre, he is considered to be in remission and available for discharge. But the label endures beyond discharge, with the unconfirmed expectation that he will behave as a schizophrenic again. Such labels, conferred by mental health professionals, are as influential on the patient as they are on his relatives and friends, and it should not surprise anyone that the diagnosis acts on all of them as a self-fulfilling prophecy. Eventually, the patient himself accepts the diagnosis, with all of its surplus meanings and expectations, and behaves accordingly.[15]

The inferences to be made from these matters are quite simple. Much as Zigler and Phillips have demonstrated that there is enormous overlap in the symptoms presented by patients who have been variously diagnosed,[16] so there is enormous overlap in the behaviors of the sane and the insane. The sane are not "sane" all of the time. We lose our tempers "for no good reason." We are occasionally depressed or anxious, again for no good reason. And we may find it difficult to get along with one or another person—again for no reason that we can specify. Similarly, the insane are not always insane. Indeed, it was the impression of the pseudopatients while living with them that they were sane for long periods of time—that the bizarre behaviors upon which their diagnoses were allegedly predicated constituted only a small fraction of their total behavior. If it makes no sense to label ourselves permanently depressed on the basis of an occasional depression, then it takes better evidence than is presently available to label all patients insane or schizophrenic on the basis of bizarre behaviors or cognitions. It seems more useful, as Mischel[17] has pointed out, to limit our discussions to *behaviors*, the stimuli that provoke them, and their correlates.

It is not known why powerful impressions of personality traits, such as "crazy" or "insane," arise. Conceivably, when the origins of and stimuli that give rise to a behavior are remote or unknown, or when the behavior strikes us as immutable, trait labels regarding the *behavior* arise. When, on the other hand, the origins and stimuli are known and available, discourse is limited to the behavior itself. Thus, I may hallucinate because I am sleeping, or I may hallucinate because I have ingested a peculiar drug. These are termed sleep-induced hallucinations, or dreams, and drug-induced hallucinations, respectively. But when the stimuli to my hallucinations are unknown, that is called craziness, or schizophrenia—as if that inference were somehow as illuminating as the others. . . .

The Consequences of Labeling and Depersonalization

Whenever the ratio of what is known to what needs to be known approaches zero, we tend to invent "knowledge" and assume that we understand more than we actually do. We seem unable to acknowledge that we simply don't know. The needs for diagnosis and remediation of behavioral and emotional problems are enormous. But rather than acknowledge that we are just embarking on understanding, we continue to label patients "schizophrenic," "manic-depressive," and "insane," as if in those words we had captured the essence of understanding. The facts of the matter are that we have known for a long time that diagnoses are often not useful or reliable, but we have nevertheless continued to use them. We now know that we cannot distinguish insanity from sanity. It is depressing to consider how that information will be used.

Not merely depressing, but frightening. How many people, one wonders, are sane but not recognized as such in our psychiatric institutions? How many have been needlessly stripped of their privileges of citizenship, from the right to vote and drive to that of handling their own accounts? How many have feigned insanity in order to avoid the criminal consequences of their behavior, and, conversely, how many would rather stand trial than live interminably in a psychiatric hospital—but are wrongly thought to be mentally ill? How many have been stigmatized by well-intentioned, but nevertheless erroneous, diagnoses? On the last point, recall again that a "type 2 error" in psychiatric diagnosis does not have the same consequences it does in medical diagnosis. A diagnosis of cancer that has been found to be in error is cause for celebration. But psychiatric diagnoses are rarely found to be in error. The label sticks, a mark of inadequacy forever.

Notes

1. P. Ash, *J. Abnorm. Soc. Psychol. 44*, 272 (1949); A. T. Beck, *Amer. J. Psychiat. 119*, 210 (1962); A. T. Boisen, *Psychiatry 2*, 233 (1938); N. Kreitman, *J. Ment. Sci. 107*, 876 (1961); N. Kreitman, P. Sainsbury, J. Morrisey, J. Towers, J. Scrivener, *ibid.*, p. 887; H. O. Schmitt and C. P. Fonda, *J. Abnorm. Soc. Psychol. 52*, 262 (1956); W. Seeman, *J. Nerv. Ment. Dis. 118*, 541 (1953). For an analysis of these artifacts and summaries of the disputes, see J. Zubin, *Annu. Rev. Psychol. 18*, 373 (1967); L. Phillips and J. G. Draguns, *ibid. 22*, 447 (1971).

2. R. Benedict. *J. Gen. Psychol. 10*, 59 (1934).

3. See in this regard H. Becker, *Outsiders: Studies in the Sociology of Deviance* (New York: Free Press, 1963); B. M. Braginsky, D. D. Braginsky, K. Ring, *Methods of Madness: The Mental Hospital as a Last Resort* (New York: Holt, Rinehart & Winston, 1969); G. M. Crocetti and P. V. Lemkau, *Amer. Sociol. Rev. 30*, 577 (1965); E. Goffman, *Behavior in Public Places* (New York: Free Press, 1964); R. D. Laing, *The Divided Self: A Study of Sanity and Madness* (Chicago: Quadrangle, 1960); D. L. Phillips, *Amer. Sociol. Rev. 28*, 963 (1963); T. R. Sarbin, *Psychol. Today 6*, 18 (1972); E. Schur, *Amer J. Sociol. 75*, 309 (1969); T. Szasz, *Law, Liberty and Psychiatry* (New York: Macmillan, 1963); *The Myth of Mental Illness: Foundations of a Theory of Mental Illness* (New York: Hoeber Harper, 1963). For a critique of some of these views, see W. R. Gove, *Amer. Sociol. Rev. 35*, 873 (1970).

4. E. Goffman. *Asylums* (Garden City, NY: Doubleday, 1961).

5. T. J. Scheff, *Being Mentally Ill: A Sociological Theory* (Chicago: Aldine, 1966).

6. Data from a ninth pseudopatient are not incorporated in this report because, although his sanity went undetected, he falsified aspects of his personal history, including his marital status and parental relationships. His experimental behaviors therefore were not identical to those of the other pseudopatients.

7. A. Barry, *Bellevue Is a State of Mind* (New York: Harcourt Brace Jovanovich, 1971); I. Belknap, *Human Problems of a State Mental Hospital* (New York: McGraw-Hill, 1956); W. Caudill, F. C. Redlich, H. R. Gilmore, E. B. Brody, *Amer J. Orthopsychiat. 22*, 314 (1952); A. R. Goldman, R. H. Bohr, T. A. Steinberg, *Prof. Psychol. 1*, 427 (1970); unauthored, *Roche Report 1* (No. 13), 8 (1971).

8. Beyond the personal difficulties that the pseudopatient is likely to experience in the hospital, there are legal and social ones that, combined, require considerable attention before entry. For example, once admitted to a psychiatric institution, it is difficult, if not impossible, to be discharged on short notice, state law to the contrary notwithstanding. I was not sensitive to these difficulties at the outset of the project, nor to the personal and situational emergencies that can arise, but later a writ of habeas corpus was prepared for each of the entering pseudopatients and an attorney was kept "on call" during every hospitalization. I am grateful to John Kaplan and Robert Bartels for legal advice and assistance in these matters.

9. However distasteful such concealment is, it was a necessary first step to examining these questions. Without concealment, there would have been no way to know how valid these experiences were; nor was there any way of knowing whether whatever detections occurred were a tribute to the diagnostic acumen of the staff or to the hospital's rumor network. Obviously, since my concerns are general ones that cut across individual hospitals and staffs, I have respected their anonymity and have eliminated clues that might lead to their identification.

10. Interestingly, of the twelve admissions, eleven were diagnosed as schizophrenic and one, with the identical symptomatology, as manic-depressive psychosis. This diagnosis has a more favorable prognosis, and it was given by the only private hospital in our sample. On the relations between social class and psychiatric diagnosis, see A. B. Hollingshead and F. C. Redlich, *Social Class and Mental Illness: A Community Study* (New York: Wiley, 1958).

11. It is possible, of course, that patients have quite broad latitudes in diagnosis and therefore are inclined to call many people sane, even those whose behavior is patently aberrant. However, although we have no hard data on this matter, it was our distinct impression that this was not the case. In many instances, patients not only singled us out for attention, but came to imitate our behaviors and styles.

12. J. Cumming and E. Cumming, *Community Ment. Health 1*, 135 (1965); A. Farina and K. Ring. *J. Abnorm. Psychol. 70*, 47 (1965); H. E. Freeman and O. G. Simmons, *The Mental Patient Comes Home* (New York: Wiley, 1963); W. J. Johannsen, *Mental Hygiene 53*, 218 (1969); A. S. Linsky, *Soc. Psychiat. 5*, 166 (1970).

13. S. E. Asch, *J. Abnorm. Soc. Psychol. 41*, 258 (1946); *Social Psychology* (New York: Prentice-Hall, 1952).

14. See also, I. N. Mensh and J. Wishner, *J. Personality 16*, 188 (1947); J. Wishner, *Psychol. Rev. 67*, 96 (1960); J. S. Bruner and R. Tagiuri, in *Handbook of Social Psychology*, G. Lindzey, ed. (Cambridge, MA: Addison-Wesley, 1954), vol. 2, pp. 634–54; J. S. Bruner, D. Shapiro, R. Tagiuri, in *Person Perception and Interpersonal Behavior*, R. Tagiuri and L. Petrullo, eds. (Stanford, CA: Stanford Univ. Press, 1958), pp. 277–88.

15. For an example of a similar self-fulfilling prophecy, in this instance dealing with the "central" trait of intelligence, see R. Rosenthal and L. Jacobson, *Pygmalion in the Classroom* (New York: Holt, Rinehart & Winston, 1968).

16. E. Zigler and L. Phillips, *J. Abnorm. Soc. Psychol. 63,* 69 (1961). See also R. K. Freudenberg and J. P. Robertson, *A.M.A. Arch. Neurol. Psychiatr. 76,* 14 (1956).

17. W. Mischel, *Personality and Assessment* (New York: Wiley, 1968).

PART VII Social Inequality

ALL SOCIETIES, PAST AND PRESENT, are marked by inequalities of some sort. Some people are stronger, learn more quickly, are swifter, shoot weapons more accurately, or have more of *whatever is considered important in that particular society*. Other inequalities, whatever form they take, may appear more contrived—such as distinctions of social rank based on wealth. But whether based on biological characteristics, social skills, or material possessions, no system of dividing people into different groups is inevitable. Rather, each is arbitrary. Yet all societies rank their members, and whatever criteria they have chosen appear to them to be quite reasonable—and even natural.

The primary social division in small, tribal groups is drawn along the line of gender. Sorted into highly distinctive groupings, men and women in these societies engage in separate activities—ones deemed "appropriate" for each sex. Indeed, in these small groups gender usually represents a cleavage that cuts across most of social life. These peoples also draw finer distinctions along much more individualistic lines of personality, skills, and reputation. Of all human groups, hunting and gathering societies—where most activities revolve around subsistence and there is little or no material surplus—appear to have the least stratification. These societies apparently also have the least *gender typing*, or division of activities by sex.

Perhaps the primary significance of a group's hierarchies and statuses—no matter what form they may take in a particular society—is that they surround the individual with *boundaries*. Setting limits and circumscribing one's possibilities in life, these social divisions establish the framework of socialization. They launch children onto the social scene by presenting to them an already existing picture of what they ought to expect from life.

None of us escapes this fundamental fact of social life, which sociologists call *social inequality* and *social stratification*. No matter into which society we are born, then, each of us inherits some system of social

335

stratification. The boundaries and limits that come with social inequality have extensive consequences, for they envelop almost all aspects of our lives—our relationships with others, our behaviors, beliefs, and attitudes, our goals and aspirations, even our perception of the social world and of the self.

In analyzing the social inequality of contemporary society, sociologists focus on very large groupings of people. They call these groups *social classes,* which are determined by people's rankings on income, education, and occupation. The more income and education one has and the higher the prestige of one's work, the higher one's social class. Conversely, the lower one's income, education, and prestige of occupation, the lower one's social class.

On the basis of income, education, and occupation, one can divide Americans into three principle social classes: upper, middle, and lower. The *upper* are the very rich (several million dollars wouldn't even begin to buy your way in); the *middle*—primarily professionals, managers, executives, and other business people—is heavily rewarded with the material goods our society has to offer; and the *lower,* to understate the matter, receives the least.

Some sociologists add an upper and a lower to each of these divisions and say there are *six* social classes in the United States: an upper-upper and lower-upper, an upper-middle and lower-middle, and an upper-lower and lower-lower. Let's look at these.

Membership in the *upper-upper* (old capitalist) class is the most exclusive of all. It is accorded not only on the basis of huge wealth but also according to how long that money has been in the family—the longer the better. Somehow or other, it is difficult to make many millions of dollars while remaining scrupulously honest in business dealings. It appears that many people who have entered the monied classes have cut moral corners, at least here and there. This "taint" to the money disappears with time, however, and the later generations of Vanderbilts, Rockefellers, Mellons, DuPonts, Chryslers, Kennedys, Morgans, Nashes, and so on are considered to have "clean" money simply by virtue of the passage of time. They can be philanthropic as well as rich. They have attended the best private schools and universities, the male heirs probably have entered law, and they protect their vast fortunes and economic empires with far-flung political connections and contributions.

And the *lower-upper* (new capitalist) class? These people have money, but it is new, and therefore suspect. They lack "breeding" and proper social background. They have not gone to the right schools, and they cannot be depended on for adequate in-group loyalty. Unable themselves to make the leap into the upper-upper class, their hope for social supremacy lies in their children: If their children go to the right schools *and* marry into the upper-upper class, what has been denied the parents will be granted the children.

The *upper-middle* class consists primarily of people who have entered the professions or higher levels of management. They are doctors, professors, lawyers, dentists, pharmacists, and clergy. They are bank presidents and successful contractors and other business people. Their education is high, their income adequate for most of their needs.

The *lower-middle* class consists largely of lower-level managers, white-collar workers in the service industries, and the more highly paid and skilled blue-collar workers. Their education and income, as well as the prestige of their work, are lower than those of their upper-middle class counterparts.

The *upper-lower* class is also known as the *working class*. (Americans find this term much more agreeable than the term "lower," as "lower" brings negative things to mind, while "working" elicits more positive images.) This class consists primarily of blue-collar workers who work regularly, not seasonally, at their jobs. Their education is limited, and little prestige is attached to their work. With the changes in wages and lifestyles of recent years, however, it often is difficult to distinguish this class from the lower-middle class above it.

At the bottom of the ladder of social inequality is the *lower-lower* class. This is the social class that gets the worst of everything society has to offer. Its members have the least education and the least income, and often their work is scorned, because, as with sharecropping and other menial labor, it usually requires few skills, is "dirty," and is the type of work that most people try to avoid. The main difference between the lower-lower and the upper-lower classes is that the upper-lower class works the year round while the lower-lower class doesn't. Members of the lower-lower class live on welfare, handouts, and occasional work. They generally are considered the ne'er-do-wells of society.

To illustrate social class membership in U.S. society, let's look at the automotive industry. The Fords, for example, own and control a global manufacturing and financial empire whose net worth is truly staggering. Their vast accumulation of wealth, like their accrued power, is now several generations old. Their children attend elite schools, know how to spend money in the "right" way, and can be trusted to make their family and class interests paramount in life. They are without question members of the upper-upper class.

Next in line come top Ford executives, who direct the company. With stock options and bonuses, they earn several million dollars annually. Because they are new to wealth and power, however, they remain on the rung below, and are considered members of the lower-upper class.

A husband and wife who own a successful Ford agency are members of the upper-middle class. Their income clearly sets them apart from the majority of Americans, and they have an enviable reputation in the community. More than likely they also exert greater-than-average influence in community affairs, but find their capacity to wield power highly limited.

The sales staff, as well as those who work in the office, are members of the lower-middle class. Their income is less, their education is likely to be less, and people assign less prestige to their work than to that of the owners of the agency.

Mechanics who repair customers' cars would ordinarily be considered members of the upper-lower class. High union wages, however, have blurred this distinction, and they might more properly be classified as members of the lower-middle class. People who "detail" used cars (making them appear newer by washing and polishing them, painting their tires and floor mats, and so on) earn only minimum wage and are members of the upper-lower class.

Window washers and janitors who are hired to clean the agency during the busy season and then are laid off when business slacks off are members of the lower-lower class. (If they are year-round employees of the agency, they are members of the upper-lower class.) Their income is the least, as is their education, while the prestige accorded their work is also minimal.

It is significant to note that children are assigned the social class of their parents. For this reason, sociologists say we are born into a social class. Sociologists call this *ascribed membership* (compared with membership one earns or gains, which is called *achieved membership*). If a child of someone who "details" used cars for a living goes to college, works as a salesperson in the agency part-time and during vacations, and then eventually buys the agency, he or she experiences *upward social mobility.* The individual's new social class is said to be achieved membership. Conversely, if a child of the agency's owner becomes an alcoholic, fails to get through college, and takes a lower-status job, that person experiences *downward social mobility.* The resulting change in social class is also called *achieved* membership. (As you can see, "achieved" does not equal "achievement.")

You should note that this division into six social classes is not the only way that sociologists look at our social class system. In fact, sociologists have argued about this matter at length, and they have arrived at no single, standard, agreed-upon overview of the U.S. class system. Like others, this outline of classes is both arbitrary and useful, but it does not do justice to the nuances and complexities of our social class system.

One view within sociology (called *conflict* or *Marxist*) holds that to understand social inequality we need focus only on income. What is the *source* of a person's income? Know this, and you know the person's social class. There are those with money and those without money. The monied class owns the means of production—the factories and machinery and buildings—and lives off its investments. The other class exchanges its labor to produce more money for the wealthy owners. In short, the monied class (the *capitalists,* or owners) is in the controlling sector of society, while those who sell their labor (the *workers*) are controlled by them. With society divided into the haves and the have-nots, insist conflict theorists, it is misleading to pay attention to the fine distinctions among those with or without money.

Be that as it may (and this debate continues among sociologists), society certainly is stratified. And the sociological (and personal) significance of social inequality is that it determines our *life chances,* the probabilities as to the fate we may expect in life. It is obvious that not everyone has the same chances in life, and the single most significant factor in determining a person's life chances in our society is money. Simply put, if you have money, you can do a lot of things you can't do if you do not have money. And the more money you have, the more control over life you have, and the more likely you are to find life pleasant.

Beyond this obvious point, however, lies a connection between social inequality and life chances that is not so readily evident. It involves such things as one's chances of dying during infancy; being killed by accident, fire, or homicide; becoming a drug addict; getting arrested; ending up in prison; dropping out of school; beating your spouse (or getting beaten by your spouse); getting divorced; becoming disabled; or, in old age, having a meager life, plagued by illness and supported only by Social Security. All vary inversely with social class; that is, the lower people's social class, the higher the chances that these things will happen to them. Conversely, the higher their social class, the smaller the risk of these events taking place.

In this Part, we consider some of social inequality's major dimensions and emphasize its severe and lifelong effects. Our opening article on physical appearance may seem to hit only a light note, but Sidney Katz points to implications of attractiveness that, ordinarily lying beyond our perception, have deep consequences for our lives. The next article by Patricia Martin and Robert Hummer on fraternities and rape at first blush may seem strikingly out of place. Its implications go far beyond the specific setting and events, however, for its focus is gender inequality, the broadest and largest-scale social inequality of all. We then turn our focus on race–ethnicity, an aspect of inequality in U.S. society that pervades so much of social life. The experiences recounted by Clarence Page give us insight not only into the process of developing a racial identity but also into the consequences of that identity. Raphael Ezekiel then reports on his remarkable participant observation of groups that make hatred their reason for being. From here, we turn the focus on poverty, with Herbert Gans' claim that poverty is so functional for society that it can never be eliminated. Joan Morris and Michael Grimes then report on their research on the status inconsistency of middle-class adults who had been born into the working class. Stephen Higley concludes this Part with a focus on an understudied group, the wealthy and powerful upper class, or as it is sometimes called in sociology, the ruling class.

29 The Importance of Being Beautiful

SIDNEY KATZ

A chief characteristic of all societies is *social stratification,* a term that refers to a group's system of ranking. All of us find ourselves ranked according to a variety of dimensions, from our parents' social class when we are young to our own achievements, or lack thereof, when we grow older. Where we go to high school, if we attend college, and if so, where—make a difference in people's eyes. People rank us by our speech, by our walk, and even by things we own or display, from the car we drive to our hairstyles and the clothing we wear.

Central to much of the ranking done on a face-to-face level is attractiveness. Because of appearance, we judge others—and are judged by them. This type of ranking is ordinarily thought to have little consequence beyond such temporary, individual matters as whether or not we can get a date this weekend—personally significant and intense, yes, but probably of little long-term consequence. As Katz points out, however, rankings that are based on attractiveness have significant consequences for our lives.

UNLIKE MANY PEOPLE, I was neither shocked nor surprised when the national Israeli TV network fired a competent female broadcaster because she was not beautiful. I received the news with aplomb because I had just finished extensive research into "person perception" . . . the many ways in which physical attractiveness—or the lack of it—affects all aspects of your life.

Unless you're a 10—or close to it—most of you will respond to my findings with at least some feelings of frustration or perhaps disbelief. In a nutshell, you can't overestimate the importance of being beautiful. If you're beautiful, without effort you attract hordes of friends and lovers. You are given higher school grades than your smarter—but less appealing—classmates. You compete successfully for jobs against men or women who are better qualified but less alluring. Promotions and pay raises come your way more easily. You are able to go into a bank or store and cash a cheque with far less hassle than a plain Jane or John. And these are only a few of the many advantages enjoyed by those with a ravishing face and body.

"We were surprised to find that beauty had such powerful effects," confessed Karen Dion, a University of Toronto social psychologist who does person perception research. "Our findings also go against the cultural grain. People like to think that success depends on talent, intelligence, and hard work." But the scientific evidence is undeniable.

In large part, the beautiful person can attribute his or her idyllic life to a puzzling phenomenon that social scientists have dubbed the "halo effect." It defies human reason, but if you resemble Jane Fonda or Paul Newman [in their prime] it's assumed that you're more generous, trustworthy, sociable, modest, sensitive, interesting, and sexually responsive than the rest of us. Conversely, if you're somewhat physically unattractive, because of the "horns effect" you're stigmatized as being mean, sneaky, dishonest, antisocial, and a poor sport to boot.

The existence of the halo/horns effect has been established by several studies. One, by Dion, looked at perceptions of misbehavior in children.

Dion provided 243 female university students with identical detailed accounts of the misbehavior of a seven-year-old school child. She described how the youngster had pelted a sleeping dog with sharp stones until its leg bled. As the animal limped away, yelping in pain, the child continued the barrage of stones. The 243 women were asked to assess the seriousness of the child's offence and to give their impression of the child's normal behavior. Clipped to half of the reports were photos of seven-year-old boys or girls who had been rated "high" in physical attractiveness; the other half contained photos of youngsters of "low" attractiveness. "We found," said Dion, "that the opinions of the adults were markedly influenced by the appearance of the children."

One evaluator described the stone thrower, who in her report happened to be an angelic-looking little girl, in these glowing terms: "She appears to be a perfectly charming little girl, well mannered and basically unselfish. She plays well with everyone, but, like everyone else, a bad day may occur. . . . Her cruelty need not be taken too seriously." For the same offence, a homely girl evoked this comment from another evaluator: "I think this child would be quite bratty and would be a problem to teachers. She'd probably try to pick a fight with other children. . . . She would be a brat at home. All in all, she would be a real problem." The tendency throughout the 243 adult responses was to judge beautiful children as ordinarily well behaved and unlikely to engage in wanton cruelty in the future; the unbeautiful were viewed as being chronically antisocial, untrustworthy, and likely to commit similar transgressions again.

Dion found the implications of this study mind boggling. Every kid who was homely would be highly vulnerable in the classroom and elsewhere.

Prejudged by his or her appearance, a vicious cycle is set in motion. The teacher views the child as having negative traits and treats him accordingly; the child responds by conforming to the teacher's expectations. Dion thinks that adults must realize to what extent their opinion of a child can be biased by the child's appearance: "When there's a question of who started a classroom disturbance, who broke the vase—adults are more likely to identify the unattractive child as the culprit."

The same standards apply in judging adults. The beautiful are assumed innocent. John Jurens, a colorful private investigator, was once consulted by a small Toronto firm which employed 40 people. Ten thousand dollars' worth of merchandise had disappeared, and it was definitely an inside job. After an intensive investigation, which included the use of a lie detector, Jurens was certain he had caught the thief. She was 24 years old and gorgeous—a lithe princess with high cheekbones, green eyes and shining, long black hair. The employer dismissed Jurens's proof with the comment, "You've made a mistake. It just can't be her." Jurens commented sadly, "A lot of people refuse to believe that beautiful can be bad."

David Humphrey, a prominent Ontario criminal lawyer, observed, "If a beautiful woman is on trial, you practically have to show the judge and jury a movie of her committing the crime in order to get a conviction." Another experienced lawyer, Aubrey Golden, has found it difficult defending a man charged with assault or wife-beating if he's a brutish-looking hulk. By the same token, a rape victim who happens to be stocky is a less credible witness than a slender, good-looking woman.

The halo and horns effect often plays an important role in sentencing by courts. After spending 17 days observing cases heard in an Ontario traffic court, Joan Finegan, a graduate psychology student at the University of Western Ontario, concluded that pleasant and neat-looking defendants were fined an average of $6.31 less than those who were "messy." The same pro-beauty bias was found by a British investigator in a series of simulated court cases. Physically appealing defendants were given prison terms almost three years less than those meted out to unattractive ones for precisely the same offence.

Beauty—or the lack of it—influences a person's entire life. The halo and horns effect comes into play beginning with birth and continues throughout the various stages of life.

Early Life

The flawless, seraphlike infant is irresistible. It receives an inordinate amount of attention and love. The child is constantly picked up, cuddled, and cooed to. In contrast, the unattractive baby may suffer neglect and rejection, which can have enduring effects on its personality and mental health. "When a child is unappealing because he's been born with a visible physical defect," said Dr. Ian Munro, a specialist in reconstructive facial surgery at the Hospital for Sick Children in Toronto, "parents are sometimes reluctant to touch, fondle, or give their child the normal displays of affection."

Later, when the baby attends nursery school, the halo and horns effect is even more potent. "Nursery school teachers," observed Dr. Ellen Berscheid, a psychologist who has conducted extensive person perception research at the University of Minnesota, "often insist that all children are beautiful, yet they can, when they're asked, rank their pupils by appearance." Even more noteworthy, the children themselves, despite their tender years, "behave in accordance with the adult ranking."

One nursery school study by Berscheid and Dion revealed that unattractive kids were not as well liked by their peers as the attractive ones. They were accused of "fighting a lot," "hitting other students," and "yelling at the teacher." Furthermore, other students labeled them "fraidy cats." They needed help to complete their work. When asked to name the person in class who scared them the most, the children usually nominated an unattractive classmate.

At School

It's sad but true that grade school teachers tend to judge their pupils largely on the basis of their looks. Consider the provocative study conducted by two American psychologists, Elaine Walster and Margaret Clifford: Four hundred grade five teachers were asked to examine identical report cards. They itemized the student's grades in various subjects, his or her work habits, attendance record, and attitudes. There was only one difference. Half of the report cards had the photo of an attractive boy or girl attached to the upper right-hand corner; half, the photo of a less attractive child. The teachers were then asked a number of specific questions based on the information provided. They concluded that the beautiful children had higher IQs, were more likely to go to college, and had parents who were more interested in education.

Parents should be concerned about these results. Because of an inflated opinion of the beautiful child, the teacher can be expected to give him more than his share of friendliness, encouragement, and time. And, consequently, the beautiful one will blossom—at the expense of his not-so-beautiful classmates.

The College Years

The beautiful person reaps an even richer harvest when he or she attends college. In one test, 60 male undergraduates were handed a 700-word essay on the effects of televised violence on the behavior of children. The authors, they were told, were freshmen coeds, and the undergrads were asked to assign a grade to the essay and to give their impression of the writer's abilities. Half of the students received an essay that was excellently written; the other half were given an essay that was a mishmash of clichés, grammatical errors, and sloppy writing. One-third of the papers had attached to them the photo of the alleged author—a young woman of striking beauty. Another third contained the likeness of an unappealing woman, while the remaining third were submitted without a photograph. When the evaluations were tallied, it was found that the beautiful person was consistently awarded a higher mark for her essay than the unattractive one. The essays without photos attached were usually given average marks. The investigators, David Landy and Harold Sigall, psychologists at the University of Rochester at the time of the study, concluded, "If you are ugly, you are not discriminated against as long as your performance is impressive. However, should performance be below par, attractiveness matters: you may be able to get away with inferior work if you are beautiful."

Not surprisingly, college students also preferred beauty when grading the desirability of a date. In interviews 376 young men and 376 young women assured investigators that it was "vulgar" to judge people by their appearance. They then proceeded to list the human qualities that they really valued; intelligence, friendliness, sincerity, "soul," and warmth. Yet when these same people were interviewed after going out on a blind date that was arranged by a computer, it became apparent that they were blind to everything *but* the physical appearance of their partners. The more beautiful the partner, the more he or she was liked. Features such as exceptional personality, high intelligence, and shared interests hardly seemed to count at all. "We were surprised to find that a *man's* physical attractiveness was the largest determinant of how well he was liked by a woman," observed Elaine Walster, one of the psychologists who conducted the study.

In addition to giving top marks to their beautiful classmates as dates, college students also predict glittering futures for them. In one study by Dion, Berscheid, and Walster, the opinion was almost unanimous that the physically appealing would contract better marriages, make better husbands and wives, and lead more fulfilling social and career lives. This finding is all the more impressive, Dion explained, because "the unattractive people in our sample were by no means at the extremes of unattractiveness—they possessed only a minor flaw to their beauty."

Marriage

It's logical that a beautiful person's marriage should be idyllic. An alluring woman, say, might have a busier social life than her less appealing sisters and therefore have a better chance of meeting a compatible mate. She's also apt to be more sexually responsive. Good-looking women fall in love more often and have more sexual experiences than others. "And," observed Berscheid, "since in almost all areas of human endeavor practice makes perfect, it may well be that beautiful women are indeed sexually warmer simply because of experience."

One thing is certain: the power of beauty is such that the status of even a homely man skyrockets if he marries a dazzling woman. People discover positive qualities in him they never before noticed: self-confidence, likability, friendliness. Sigall and Landy refer to this phenomenon as "a generalized halo effect" and offer this explanation: "People viewing individuals who are romantically linked to an attractive person try to make sense of the association. In effect, they may ask themselves, 'Why is *she,* desirable as she appears to be, involved with him?' The observers may answer the question by attributing favorable qualities to him."

Careers

If you're a good-looking male over six feet tall, don't worry about succeeding at your career.

A study of university graduates by the *Wall Street Journal* revealed that well proportioned wage earners who were six-foot-two or taller earned 12 percent more than men under six feet. "For some reason," explained Ronald Burke, a York University psychologist and industrial consultant, "tall men are assumed to be dynamic, decisive, and powerful. In other words, born leaders." A Toronto consultant for Drake Personnel, one of the largest employment agencies in Canada, recalled trying to find a sales manager for an industrial firm. He sent four highly qualified candidates, only to have them all turned down. "The fifth guy I sent over was different," said the consultant. "He stood six-foot-four. He was promptly hired."

The well favored woman also has a distinct edge when it comes to getting a job she's after. "We send out three prospects to be interviewed, and it's almost always the most glamorous one that's hired," said Edith Geddes of the Personnel Centre, a Toronto agency that specializes in female place-ments. "We sometimes feel bad because the best qualified person is not cho-sen." Dr. Pam Ennis, a consultant to several large corporations, observed, "Look at the photos announcing promotions in the *Globe and Mail* business section. It's no accident that so many of the women happen to be attractive and sexy-looking." Ennis, an elegant woman herself, attributes at least part of her career success to good looks. Her photograph appears on the brochures she mails out to companies soliciting new clients. "About eight out of 10 company presidents give me an appointment," she said. "I'm sure that many of them are curious to see me in person. Beauty makes it easier to es-tablish rapport."

In an experiment designed to test the effect of stating or not stating an intent to change the listener's point of view, it was discovered that an attrac-tive woman was more persuasive than an unattractive woman. In one session, an attractive woman disguised her good looks. Her dress was ill-fitting, she wore no makeup on her oily skin, her hair was a tattered mess, and the trace of a moustache was etched on her upper lip. She attempted to persuade a classroom of men that a general education was superior to a specialized one. Her arguments, in large part, failed to change their points of view.

The same woman then made herself as alluring as possible. She wore chic, tight-fitting clothes and tasteful makeup, and sported a fashionable coiffeur. Using the identical argument, she had little difficulty in persuading a second group of men to share her enthusiasm for a general education.

Old Age

An elderly person's attractiveness influences the way in which he or she is treated in nursing homes and hospitals. Doctors and nurses give better care to the beautiful ones.

Lena Nordholm, an Australian behavioral scientist, presented 289 doc-tors, nurses, social workers, speech therapists, and physiotherapists with photos of eight attractive and unattractive men and women. They were asked to speculate about what kind of patients they would be. The good-lookers were judged to be more cooperative, better motivated, and more likely to improve than their less attractive counterparts. Pam Ennis, the consultant, commented, "Because the doctor feels that beautiful patients are more likely to respond to his treatment, he'll give them more time and attention."

In the myths that shape modern civilization, beauty is equated with success. It has been that way since time began. In most of literature, the heroines are beautiful. Leo Tolstoy wrote, "It is amazing how complete is the delusion that beauty is goodness."

We like to think we have moved beyond the era when the most desirable woman was the beauty queen, but we haven't. Every day we make assumptions about the personality of the bank teller, the delivery man, or the waitress by their looks. The way in which we attribute good and bad characteristics still has very little to do with fact. People seldom look beyond a pleasing facade, a superficial attractiveness. But the professors of person perception are not discouraged by this. They want to educate us. Perhaps by arming us with the knowledge and awareness of why we discriminate against the unattractive, we'll learn how to prevent this unwitting bigotry. Just maybe, we can change human nature.

30 Fraternities and Rape on Campus

PATRICIA YANCEY MARTIN
ROBERT A. HUMMER

College certainly is a varied experience: challenging, with its many assignments, higher academic standards, and new vocabularies; frustrating, when concepts don't seem to sink in and instructors demand too much; fulfilling, with the satisfactions that come from forming new friendships and a sense of accomplishment as courses are passed and new ideas mastered; and, at the end, threatening, when the world of work and careers looms and, by comparison, college life suddenly appears so comfortable, almost serene.

On many campuses, fraternities are part of college life, a welcome respite from onerous classroom demands. They provide friendships, fun, diversion, sometimes even a test or paper to help pass a particularly grueling course. In some cases, bonds are formed that become significant for successful careers. There is a darker side to fraternities, however, a stress on hypermasculinity and calculated exploitation that destroys people. It is this dark side of fraternities that Martin and Hummer explore.

MANY RAPES, FAR MORE THAN COME to the public's attention, occur in fraternity houses on college and university campuses. . . .

The study reported here examined dynamics associated with the social construction of fraternity life, with a focus on processes that foster the use of coercion, including rape, in fraternity men's relations with women. We make no claims that all fraternities are "bad" or that all fraternity men are rapists. Our observations indicated, however, that rape is especially probable in fraternities because of the kinds of organizations they are, the kinds of members they have, the practices their members engage in, and a virtual absence of university or community oversight. . . . We conclude that unless fraternities change in fundamental ways, little improvement can be expected.

350 / *Patricia Yancey Martin and Robert A. Hummer*

Methodology

We developed a conceptual framework from an initial case study of an alleged gang rape at Florida State University that involved four fraternity men and an eighteen-year-old coed. The group rape took place on the third floor of a fraternity house and ended with the "dumping" of the woman in the hallway of a neighboring fraternity house. According to newspaper accounts, the victim's blood-alcohol concentration, when she was discovered, was .349 percent, more than three times the legal limit for automobile driving and an almost lethal amount. One law enforcement officer reported that sexual intercourse occurred during the time the victim was unconscious. When the victim was found, she was comatose and had suffered multiple scratches and abrasions. Crude words and a fraternity symbol had been written on her thighs. When law enforcement officials tried to investigate the case, fraternity members refused to cooperate. This led, eventually, to a five-year ban of the fraternity from campus by the university and by the fraternity's national organization.

In trying to understand how such an event could have occurred, and how a group of over 150 members (exact figures are unknown because the fraternity refused to provide a membership roster) could hold rank, deny knowledge of the event, and allegedly lie to a grand jury, we analyzed newspaper articles about the case and conducted open-ended interviews with a variety of respondents about the case and about the fraternities, rapes, alcohol use, gender relations, and sexual activities on campus. Our data included over 100 newspaper articles on the initial gang rape case; open-ended interviews with Greek (social fraternity and sorority) and non-Greek (independent) students (N = 20); university administrators (N = 8, five men, three women); and alumni advisers to Greek organizations (N = 6). Open-ended interviews were held also with judges, public and private defense attorneys, victim advocates, and state prosecutors regarding the processing of sexual assault cases. . . .

Fraternities and the Social Construction of Men and Masculinity

Our research indicated that fraternities are vitally concerned—more than with anything else—with masculinity. They work hard to create a macho image and context and try to avoid any suggestion of "wimpishness," effeminacy, and homosexuality. Valued members display, or are willing to go along with, a narrow conception of masculinity that stresses competition, athleticism, dominance, winning, conflict, wealth, material possessions, willingness to drink alcohol, and sexual prowess vis-à-vis women.

VALUED QUALITIES OF MEMBERS

When fraternity members talked about the kind of pledges they prefer, a litany of stereotypical and narrowly masculine attributes and behaviors was recited and feminine or woman-associated qualities and behaviors were expressly denounced. Fraternities seek men who are "athletic," "big guys," good in intramural competition, "who can talk college sports." Males "who are willing to drink alcohol," "who drink socially," or "who can hold their liquor" are sought. Alcohol and activities associated with the recreational use of alcohol are cornerstones of fraternity social life. Non-drinkers are viewed with skepticism and rarely selected for membership.

Fraternities try to avoid "geeks," nerds, and men said to give the fraternity a "wimpy" or "gay" reputation. Art, music, and humanities majors, majors in traditional women's fields (nursing, home economics, social work, education), men with long hair, and those whose appearance or dress violate current norms are rejected. Clean-cut, handsome men who dress well (are clean, neat, conforming, fashionable) are preferred. . . .

One fraternity man, a senior, said his fraternity recruited "some big guys, very athletic" over a two-year period to help overcome its image of wimpiness. His fraternity had won the interfraternity competition for highest grade-point average several years running but was looked down on as "wimpy, dancy, even gay." With their bigger, more athletic recruits, "our reputation improved; we're a much more recognized fraternity now." Thus a fraternity's reputation and status depend on members' possession of stereotypically masculine traits. Good grades, campus leadership, and community service are "nice" but masculinity dominance—for example, in athletic events, physical size of members, athleticism of members—counts most.

One fraternity man, a junior, said: "We watch a guy [a potential pledge] talk to women . . . we want guys who can relate to girls." Assessing a pledge's ability to talk to women is, in part, a preoccupation with homosexuality and a conscious avoidance of men who seem to have effeminate manners or qualities. If a member is suspected of being gay, he is ostracized and informally drummed out of the fraternity. A fraternity with a reputation as wimpy or tolerant of gays is ridiculed and shunned by other fraternities. . . .

THE STATUS AND NORMS OF PLEDGESHIP

A pledge (sometimes called an associate member) is a new recruit who occupies a trial membership status for a specific period of time. The pledge period (typically ranging from ten to fifteen weeks) gives fraternity brothers an opportunity to assess and socialize new recruits. Pledges evaluate the fraternity also and decide if they want to become brothers. The socialization experience is structured partly through assignment of a Big Brother to each pledge. Big Brothers are expected to teach pledges how to become a brother and to support them as they progress through the trial membership period. Some pledges are repelled by the pledging experience, which can entail physical abuse; harsh discipline; and demands to be subordinate, follow orders, and engage in demeaning routines and activities, similar to those used by the military to "make men out of boys" during boot camp.

. . . One fraternity pledge who quit the fraternity he had pledged described an experience during pledgeship as follows:

> This one guy was always picking on me. No matter what I did, I was wrong. One night after dinner, he and two other guys called me and two other pledges into the chapter room. He said, "Here, X, hold this twenty-five-pound bag of ice at arm's length 'til I tell you to stop." I did it even though my arms and hands were killing me. When I asked if I could stop, he grabbed me around the throat and lifted me off the floor. I thought he would choke me to death. He cussed me and called me all kinds of names. He took one of my fingers and twisted it until it nearly broke. . . . I stayed in the fraternity for a few more days, but then I decided to quit. I hated it. Those guys are sick. They like seeing you suffer.

Fraternities' emphasis on toughness, withstanding pain and humiliation, obedience to superiors, and using physical force to obtain compliance contributes to an interpersonal style that de-emphasizes caring and sensitivity but fosters intragroup trust and loyalty. If the least macho or most critical pledges drop out, those who remain may be more receptive to, and influenced by, masculinist values and practices that encourage the use of force in sexual relations with women and the covering up of such behavior.

NORMS AND DYNAMICS OF BROTHERHOOD

Brother is the status occupied by fraternity men to indicate their relations to each other and their membership in a particular fraternity organization or group. Brother is a male-specific status; only males can become brothers, although women can become "Little Sisters," a form of pseudomembership. "Becoming a brother" is a rite of passage that follows the consistent and often lengthy display by pledges of appropriately masculine qualities and behaviors. Brothers have a quasi-familial relationship with each other, are normatively said to share bonds of closeness and support, and are sharply set off from nonmembers. Brotherhood is a loosely defined term used to represent the bonds that develop among fraternity members and the obligations and expectations incumbent upon them. . . .

Some of our respondents talked about brotherhood in almost reverential terms, viewing it as the most valuable benefit of fraternity membership. One senior, a business-school major who had been affiliated with a fairly high-status fraternity throughout four years on campus, said:

> Brotherhood spurs friendship for life, which I consider its best aspect, although I didn't see it that way when I joined. Brotherhood bonds and unites. It instills values of caring about one another, caring about community, caring about ourselves. The values and bonds [of brotherhood] continually develop over the four years [in college] while normal friendships come and go.

Despite this idealization, most aspects of fraternity practice and conception are more mundane. Brotherhood often plays itself out as an overriding concern with masculinity and, by extension, femininity. As a consequence, fraternities comprise collectivities of highly masculinized men with attitudinal qualities and behavioral norms that predispose them to sexual coercion of women. The norms of masculinity are complemented by conceptions of women and femininity that are equally distorted and stereotyped and that may enhance the probability of women's exploitation.

PRACTICES OF BROTHERHOOD

Practices associated with fraternity brotherhood that contribute to the sexual coercion of women include a preoccupation with loyalty, group protection and secrecy, use of alcohol as a weapon, and involvement in violence and physical force. . . .

Loyalty, Group Protection, and Secrecy.   Loyalty is a fraternity preoccupation. Members are reminded constantly to be loyal to the fraternity and to their brothers. Among other ways, loyalty is played out in the practices of group protection and secrecy. The fraternity must be shielded from criticism. Members are admonished to avoid getting the fraternity in trouble and to bring all problems "to the chapter" (local branch of a national social fraternity) rather than to outsiders. Fraternities try to protect themselves from close scrutiny and criticism by the Interfraternity Council (a quasi-governing body composed of representatives from all social fraternities on campus), their fraternity's national office, university officials, law enforcement, the media, and the public. Protection of the fraternity often takes precedence over what is procedurally, ethically, or legally correct. Numerous examples were related to us of fraternity brothers' lying to outsiders to "protect the fraternity."

Group protection was observed in the alleged gang rape case with which we began our study. Except for one brother, a rapist who turned state's evidence, the entire remaining fraternity membership was accused by university and criminal justice officials of lying to protect the fraternity. Members consistently failed to cooperate even though the alleged crimes were felonies, involved only four men (two of whom were not even members of the local chapter), and the victim of the crime nearly died. According to a grand jury's findings, fraternity officers repeatedly broke appointments with law enforcement officials, refused to provide police with a list of members, and refused to cooperate with police and prosecutors investigating the case.

Secrecy, a priority value and practice in fraternities . . . is a boundary-maintaining mechanism, demarcating in-group from out-group, us from them. Secret rituals, handshakes, and mottos are revealed to pledge brothers as they are initiated into full brotherhood. Since only brothers are supposed to know a fraternity's secrets, such knowledge affirms membership in the fraternity and separates a brother from others. Extending secrecy tactics from protection of private knowledge to protection of the fraternity from criticism is a predictable development. Our interviews indicated that individual members knew the difference between right and wrong, but fraternity norms that emphasize loyalty, group protection, and secrecy often overrode standards of ethical correctness.

Alcohol as Weapon.   Alcohol use by fraternity men is normative. They use it on weekdays to relax after class and on weekends to "get drunk," "get crazy," and "get laid." The use of alcohol to obtain sex from women is pervasive—in other words, it is used as a weapon against sexual reluctance. According to several fraternity men whom we interviewed, alcohol is the major tool used to gain sexual mastery over women. . . . One fraternity man, a twenty-one-year-old senior, [said:] ". . . You have to buy them drinks or find out if she's drunk enough. . . ."

A similar strategy is used collectively. A fraternity man said that at parties with Little Sisters: "We provide them with 'hunch punch' and things get wild. We get them drunk and most of the guys end up with one." "Hunch punch" he said, "is a girls' drink made up of overproof alcohol and powdered Kool-Aid, no water or anything, just ice. It's very strong. Two cups will do a number on a female." He had plans in the next academic term to surreptitiously give hunch punch to women in a "prim and proper" sorority because "having sex with prim and proper sorority girls is definitely a goal." These women are a challenge because they "won't openly consume alcohol and won't get openly drunk as hell." Their sororities have "standards committees" that forbid heavy drinking and easy sex.

In the gang rape case, our sources said that many fraternity men on campus believed the victim had a drinking problem and was thus an "easy make." According to newspaper accounts, she had been drinking alcohol on the evening she was raped; the lead assailant is alleged to have given her a bottle of wine after she arrived at his fraternity house. Portions of the rape occurred in a shower, and the victim was reportedly so drunk that her assailants had difficulty holding her in a standing position. While raping her, her assailants repeatedly told her they were members of another fraternity under the apparent belief that she was too drunk to know the difference. Of course, if she was too drunk to know who they were, she was too drunk to consent to sex.

One respondent told us that gang rapes are wrong and can get one expelled, but he seemed to see nothing wrong in sexual coercion one-on-one. He seemed unaware that the use of alcohol to obtain sex from a woman is grounds for a claim that a rape occurred. Few women on campus (who also may not know these grounds) report date rapes, however; so the odds of detection and punishment are slim for fraternity men who use alcohol for "seduction" purposes.

Violence and Physical Force. Fraternity men have a history of violence. Their record of hazing, fighting, property destruction, and rape has caused them problems with insurance companies. Two university officials told us that fraternities "are the third riskiest property to insure behind toxic waste dumps and amusement parks." . . .

Fraternities' Commodification of Women

In claiming that women are treated by fraternities as commodities, we mean that fraternities knowingly, and intentionally, *use* women for their benefit. Fraternities use women as bait for new members, as servers of brothers' needs, and as sexual prey.

Women as Bait. Fashionably attractive women help a fraternity attract new members. As one fraternity man, a junior, said, "They are good bait." Beautiful, sociable women are believed to impress the right kind of pledges and give the impression that the fraternity can deliver this type of woman to its members. Photographs of shapely, attractive coeds are printed in fraternity brochures and videotapes that are distributed and shown to potential pledges. The women pictured are often dressed in bikinis, at the beach, and are pictured hugging the brothers of the fraternity. One university official says such recruitment materials give the message: "Hey, they're here for you, you can have whatever you want," and, "we have the best-looking women. Join us and you can have them, too." Another commented: "Something's wrong when males join an all-male organization as the best place to meet women. It's so illogical."

Fraternities compete in promising access to beautiful women. One fraternity man, a senior, commented that "the attraction of girls [i.e., a fraternity's success in attracting women] is a big status symbol for fraternities." One university official commented that the use of women as a recruiting tool is so well entrenched that fraternities that might be willing to forgo it say they cannot afford to unless other fraternities do so as well. One fraternity man said, "Look, if we don't have Little Sisters, the fraternities that do will get all the good pledges." Another said, "We won't have as good a rush [the period during which new members are assessed and selected] if we don't have these women around."

In displaying good-looking, attractive, skimpily dressed, nubile women to potential members, fraternities implicitly, and sometimes explicitly, promise sexual access to women. One fraternity man commented that "part of what being in a fraternity is all about is the sex" and explained how his fraternity uses Little Sisters to recruit new members:

> We'll tell the sweetheart [the fraternity's term for Little Sister], "You're gorgeous; you can get him." We'll tell her to fake a scam and she'll go hang all over him during a rush party, kiss him, and he thinks he's done wonderful and wants to join. The girls think it's great too. It's flattering for them.

Women as Servers.   The use of women as servers is exemplified in the Little Sister program. Little Sisters are undergraduate women who are rushed and selected in a manner parallel to the recruitment of fraternity men. They are affiliated with the fraternity in a formal but unofficial way and are able, indeed required, to wear the fraternity's Greek letters. Little Sisters are not full-fledged fraternity members, however, and fraternity national offices and most universities do not register or regulate them. Each fraternity has an officer called Little Sister Chairman who oversees their organization and activities. The Little Sisters elect officers among themselves, pay monthly dues to the fraternity, and have well-defined roles. Their dues are used to pay for the fraternity's social events, and Little Sisters are expected to attend and hostess fraternity parties and hang around the house to make it a "nice place to be." One fraternity man, a senior, described Little Sisters this way: "They are very social girls, willing to join in, be affiliated with the group, devoted to the fraternity." Another member, a sophomore, said: "Their sole purpose is social—attend parties, attract new members, and 'take care' of the guys." . . .

Women as Sexual Prey.   Little Sisters are a sexual utility. Many Little Sisters do not belong to sororities and lack peer support for refraining from unwanted sexual relations. One fraternity man (whose fraternity has 65 members and 85 Little Sisters) told us they had recruited "wholesale" in the prior year to "get lots of new women." The structural access to women that the Little Sister program provides and the absence of normative supports for refusing fraternity members' sexual advances may make women in this program particularly susceptible to coerced sexual encounters with fraternity men.

Access to women for sexual gratification is a presumed benefit of fraternity membership, promised in recruitment materials and strategies, and through brothers' conversations with new recruits. One fraternity man said: "We always tell the guys that you get sex all the time, there's always new girls. . . . After I became a Greek, I found out I could be with females at will." A university official told us that, based on his observations, "no one [i.e., fraternity men] on this campus wants to have 'relationships.' They just want to have fun [i.e., sex]." Fraternity men plan and execute strategies aimed at obtaining sexual gratification, and this occurs at both individual and collective levels.

Individual strategies include getting a woman drunk and spending a great deal of money on her. As for collective strategies, most of our undergraduate inteviewees agreed that fraternity parties often culminate in sex and that this outcome is planned. One fraternity man said fraternity parties often involve sex and nudity and can "turn into orgies." Orgies may be planned in advance, such as the Bowery Ball party held by one fraternity. A former fraternity member said of this party:

> The entire idea behind this is sex. Both men and women come to the party wearing little or nothing. There are pornographic pinups on the walls and usually porno movies playing on the TV. The music carries sexual overtones. . . . They just get schnockered [drunk] and, in most cases, they also get laid.

When asked about the women who come to such a party, he said: "Some Little Sisters just won't go. . . . The girls who do are looking for a good time, girls who don't know what it is, things like that."

Other respondents denied that fraternity parties are orgies but said that sex is always talked about among the brothers and they all know "who each other is doing it with." One member said that most of the time, guys have sex with their girlfriends "but with socials, girlfriends aren't allowed to come and it's their [members'] big chance [to have sex with other women]." The use of alcohol to help them get women into bed is a routine strategy at fraternity parties.

Conclusion

In general, our research indicated that the organization and membership of fraternities contribute heavily to coercive and often violent sex. Fraternity houses are occupied by same-sex (all men) and same-age (late teens, early twenties) peers whose maturity and judgment are often less than ideal. Yet fraternity houses are private dwellings that are mostly off-limits to, and away from scrutiny of, university and community representatives, with the result that fraternity house events seldom come to the attention of outsiders. Practices associated with the social construction of fraternity brotherhood emphasize a macho conception of men and masculinity, a narrow, stereotyped conception of women and femininity, and the treatment of women as commodities. Other practices contributing to coercive sexual relations and the cover-up of rapes include excessive alcohol use, competitiveness, and normative support for deviance and secrecy.

Some fraternity practices exacerbate others. Brotherhood norms require "sticking together" regardless of right or wrong; thus rape episodes are unlikely to be stopped or reported to outsiders, even when witnesses disapprove. The ability to use alcohol without scrutiny by authorities and alcohol's frequent association with violence, including sexual coercion, facilitate rape in fraternity houses. Fraternity norms that emphasize the value of maleness and masculinity over femaleness and femininity and that elevate the status of men and lower the status of women in members' eyes undermine perceptions and treatment of women as persons who deserve consideration and care. . . .

Our research led us to conclude that fraternity norms and practices influence members to view the sexual coercion of women, which is a felony crime, as sport, a contest, or a game. This sport is played not between men and women but between men and men. Women are the pawns or prey in the interfraternity rivalry game; they prove that a fraternity is successful or prestigious. The use of women in this way encourages fraternity men to see women as objects and sexual coercion as sport. Today's societal norms support young women's right to engage in sex at their discretion, and coercion is unnecessary in a mutually desired encounter. However, nubile young women say they prefer to be "in a relationship" to have sex while young men say they prefer to "get laid" without a commitment. In a fraternity context, getting sex without giving emotionally demonstrates "cool" masculinity. More important, it poses no threat to the bonding and loyalty of the fraternity brotherhood.

Unless fraternities' composition, goals, structures, and practices change in fundamental ways, women on campus will continue to be sexual prey for fraternity men. As all-male enclaves dedicated to opposing faculty and administration and to cementing in-group ties (i.e., fraternity members eschew any hint of homosexuality), their version of masculinity transforms women, and men with womanly characteristics, into the out-group. "Womanly men" are ostracized; feminine women are used to demonstrate members' masculinity. A case for or against fraternities cannot be made by studying individual members. The fraternity qua group and organization is at issue. Located on campus along with many vulnerable women, embedded in a sexist society, and caught up in masculinist goals, practices, and values, fraternities' violation of women—including forcible rape—should come as no surprise.

31 Showing My Color

CLARENCE PAGE

As you know, the circumstances that we inherit at birth (sometimes called *social capital*) affect what happens to us in life. Some of us are born poor, others rich, and most of us in between. Some of us are born to single mothers, others to married parents; some to parents who are college graduates, others to parents who have not finished high school. Even our geography (South, West, rural, urban) sets up background factors that play a significant role in our orientations to life. Sociologists use the term *life chances* to refer to how the background factors that surround our birth affect our fate in life.

In the United States, race–ethnicity is a major divide. It opens and closes doors of opportunity and privilege. It is a primary source of identity, uniting us with some people, while separating us from others. Although race–ethnicity becomes a vital part of our identity, as with other concepts, we are not born with an awareness of race or ethnicity. These we learn from others around us, which can be a jarring experience. In this selection, Page, a journalist, recounts how he learned that he was a black in a white society. He also shares examples of what this has meant for his life.

RACE HAS LONG HAD A RUDE PRESENCE in my life. While visiting relatives in Alabama as a child in the 1950s, I first saw water fountains marked "white" and "colored." I vaguely recall being excited. I rushed over to the one marked "colored" and turned it on, only to find, to my deep disappointment, that the water came out clear, just like the water back home in Ohio.

"Segregation," my dad said. I'd never heard the word before. My southern-born parents explained that it was something the white folks "down home" practiced. Some "home." Yet unpleasant experiences in the North already had taught me a more genteel, yet no less limiting, version.

"There are places white people don't want colored to go," my elders told me in their soft southern accents, "and white people make the rules."

We had plenty of segregation like that in the North. We just didn't have the signs, which made it cheaper and easier to deny. We could look out of my schoolhouse window to see a public swimming pool closed to nonwhites. We had to go across town to the separate-but-equal "pool for colored." The steel mill that was our town's biggest employer held separate picnics for colored and white employees, which seemed to be just fine with the employees. Everyone had a good time, separately and unequally. I think the colored folks, who today would be called the "black community," were just happy to have something to call their own.

When I was about six years old, I saw a television commercial for an amusement park near the southern Ohio factory town where I grew up.

I chose to go. I told my parents. They looked at each other sadly and informed me that "little colored kids can't go there." I was crushed.

"I wish I was white," I told my parents.

"No, you don't!" Mom snapped. She gave me a look terrible enough to persuade me instantly that no, I didn't.

"Well, maybe for a few minutes, anyway?" I asked. "Just long enough for me to get past the front gate?" Then I could show them, I thought. I remember I wanted to show them what a terrific kid I was. I felt sorry for the little white children who would be deprived of getting to know me.

Throughout our childhood years, my friendships with white schoolchildren (and with Pancho from the only Latino family in the neighborhood) proceeded without interruption. Except for the occasional tiff over some injudicious use of the N-word or some other slur we had picked up from our elders, we played in each other's backyards as congenially as Spanky, Buckwheat, and the rest of the gang on the old Hal Roach *Our Gang* comedies we used to watch on television.

Yet it quickly became apparent to me that my white friends were growing up in a different reality from the one to which I was accustomed. I could tell from the way one white friend happily discussed his weekend at LeSourdesville Lake that he did not have a clue of my reality.

"Have you been?" he asked.

"Colored can't go there," I said, somewhat astonished that he had not noticed.

"Oh, that can't be," he said.

For a moment, I perked up, wondering if the park's policy had changed. "Have you seen any colored people there?" I asked.

My white friend thought for a moment, then realized that he had not. He expressed surprise. I was surprised that he was surprised.

By the time I reached high school in the early 1960s, LeSourdesville Lake would relax its racial prohibitions. But the lessons of it stuck with me. It taught me how easily white people could ignore the segregation problem because, from their vantage point, it was not necessarily a problem. It was not necessarily an advantage to them, either, although some undoubtedly

362 / Clarence Page

thought so. White people of low income, high insecurity, or fragile ego could always say that, no matter how badly off they felt, at least they were not black. Segregation helped them uphold and maintain this illusion of superiority. Even those white people who considered themselves to have a well-developed sense of social conscience could easily rationalize segregation as something that was good for both races. We played unwittingly into this illusion, I thought, when my friends and I began junior high school and, suddenly thrust into the edgy, high hormonal world of adolescence, quickly gravitated into social cliques according to tastes and race.

It became even more apparent to me that my white friends and I were growing up in *parallel realities,* not unlike the parallel universes described in the science fiction novels and comic books I adored—or the "parallel realities" experienced by Serbs, Bosnians, and Croatians as described years later by feminist writer Slavenka Drakulic in *The Balkan Express.* Even as the evil walls of legal segregation were tumbling down, thanks to the hard-fought struggles of the civil rights movement, it occurred to me that my reality might never be quite the same as that experienced by my white friends. We were doomed, I felt, to dwell in our parallel realities. Separated by thick walls of prejudice, we would view each other through windows of stained-glass perceptions, colored by our personal experiences. My parents had taught me well.

"Don't be showin' yo' color," my parents would admonish me in my youth, before we would go out in public, especially among white folks. The phrase had special meaning in Negro conversations. Imbued with many subtle meanings and nuances, the showing of one's "color" could be an expression of chastisement or warning, admonishment or adulation, satire or self-hatred, anger or celebration. It could mean acting out or showing anger in a loud and uncivilized way.

Its cultural origins could be traced to the Africa-rooted tradition of "signifying," a form of witty, deliberately provocative, occasionally combative word play. The thrill of the game comes from taking one's opponent close to the edge of tolerable insult. Few subjects—except perhaps sex itself—could be a more sensitive matter between black people than talk about someone else's "color." The showing of one's "color" then, connoted the display of the very worst stereotypes anyone ever dreamed up about how black people behaved. "White people are not really white," James Baldwin wrote in 1961, "but colored people can sometimes be extremely colored."

Sometimes you can still hear black people say in the heat of frustration, "I almost showed my color today," which is a way of saying they almost lost their "cool," "dropped the mask," or "went off." Losing one's cool can be a capital offense by black standards, for it shows weakness in a world in which spiritual rigor is one of the few things we can call our own. Those who keep their cool repress their "color." It is cool, in other words, to be colorless.

Showing My Color (the title of the book from which this reading is taken) emerged from my fuming discontent with the current fashions of *racial denial*, steadfast repudiations of the difference race continues to make in American life. Old liberals, particularly white liberals who have become new conservatives, charge that racial pride and color consciousness threaten to "Balkanize" American life, as if it ever was a model of unity. Many demand that we "get past race." But denials of a cancer, no matter how vigorous they may be, will not make the malignancy go away.

No less august a voice than the Supreme Court's conservative majority has taken to arguing in the 1990s for a "color-blind" approach to civil rights law, the area of American society in which color and gender consciousness have made the most dramatic improvement in equalizing opportunities.

The words of the Reverend Martin Luther King, Jr., have been perverted to support this view. Most frequently quoted is his oft-stated dream of the day when everyone would "not be judged by the color of their skin but by the content of their character." I would argue that King never intended for us to forget *all* about color. Even in his historic "I Have a Dream" speech, from which this line most often is lifted, he also pressed the less-often quoted but piquantly salient point about "the promissory note" America gave freed slaves, which, when they presented it, was returned to them marked "insufficient funds."

• • •

I would argue that too much has been made of the virtue of "color blindness." I don't want Americans to be blind to my color as long as color continues to make a profound difference in determining life chances and opportunities. Nor do I wish to see so significant a part of my identity denied. "Ethnic differences are the very essence of cultural diversity and national creativity," black social critic Albert Murray wrote in *The Omni-Americans* (1970). "The problem is not the existence of ethnic differences, as is so often assumed, but the intrusion of such differences into areas where they do not belong."

Where, then *do* they belong? Diversity is enriching, but race intrudes rudely on the individual's attempts to define his or her own identity. I used to be "colored." Then I was "Negro." Then I became "black." Then I became "African-American." Today I am a "person of color." In three decades, I have been transformed from a "colored person" to a "person of color." Are you keeping up with me?

Changes in what we black people call ourselves are quite annoying to some white people, which is its own reward to some black people. But if white people are confused, so are quite a few black people. There is no one way to be black. We are a diverse people amid a nation of diverse people. Some black people are nationalists who don't want anything to do with white people. Some black people are assimilationists who don't want anything to do with other black people. Some black people are integrationists who move in and out of various groups with remarkable ease. Some of us can be any of the three at any given time, depending on when you happen to run into us.

Growing up as part of a minority can expose the individual to horrible bouts of identity confusion. I used to think of myself as something of a *transracial man,* a figure no less frustrated than a transsexual who feels trapped in the body of something unfamiliar and inappropriate to his or her inner self.

These bouts were most torturous during adolescence, the period of life when, trembling with the shock of nascent independence from the ways of one's elders, the budding individual stitches together the fragile garments of an identity to be worn into adulthood. Stuttering and uncooperative motor skills left me severely challenged in dancing, basket shooting, and various social applications; I felt woefully inadequate to the task of being "popular" in the hot centers of black social activity at my integrated high school and college. "Are you black?" an arbiter of campus militancy demanded one day, when he "caught" me dining too many times with white friends. I had the skin pass, sure enough, but my inclinations fell well short of his standards. But I was not satisfied with the standards of his counterparts in the white world, either. If I was not "black" enough to please some blacks, I would never be "white" enough to please all whites.

Times have changed. Choices abound for black people, if we can afford them. Black people can now go anywhere they choose, as long as they can pay the bill when they get there. If anyone tries to stop them or any other minorities just because of their color, the full weight of the federal government will step in on the side of the minorities. I thank God and the hard-won gains of the civil rights revolution for my ability to have more choices. But the old rules of race have been replaced in many ways by new ones.

• • •

Today, I live a well-integrated life in the suburbs [of Montgomery County, Maryland, outside Washington, D.C.]. Black folks still tell me how to be "black" when I stray from the racial party lines, while white folks tell me how to be "color-blind." I still feel as frustrated in my attempts to transcend race as a reluctant lemming must feel while being rushed over the brink by its herd. But I find I have plenty of company in my frustration. Integration has not been a simple task for upwardly mobile African-Americans, especially for those of us who happen also to be parents.

A few years ago, after talking to black friends who were raising teenage boys, I realized that I was about to face dilemmas not unlike those my parents faced. My son was turning three years old. Everyone was telling me that he was quite cute, and because he was the spitting image of his dad, I was the last to argue.

But it occurred to me that in another decade he would be not three but thirteen. If all goes well, somewhere along the way he is going to turn almost overnight from someone who is perceived as cute and innocent into someone who is perceived as a menace, the most feared creature on America's urban streets today, a *young black male*. Before he, like me when I was barred from a childhood amusement park, would have a chance to let others get to know him, he would be judged not by the content of his character, but by the color of his skin. . . .

• • •

My mom is gone now, after helping set me up with the sort of education that has freed me to make choices. I have chosen to move my father to a nice, predominantly white, antiseptically tidy retirement village near me in Maryland with large golf courses and swimming pools. It is the sort of place he might have scrubbed floors in but certainly not have lived in back in the old days. It has taken him a while to get used to having so many well-off white people behaving so nicely and neighborly to him, but he has made the adjustment well.

Still the ugly specter of racism does not easily vanish. He and the other hundred or so African-American residents decided to form a social club like the other ethnically or religiously based social clubs in the village. One night during their meeting in the main social room, someone scrawled *KKK* on little sheets of paper and slipped them under the windshields of some of their cars in the parking lot. "We think maybe some of the white people wanted the blacks to socialize with the whites, not in a separate group," one lady of the club told me. If so, they showed an unusual method for extending the arms of brotherhood.

I live in a community that worships diversity like a state religion, although individuals sometimes get tripped up by it. The excellent Spanish "immersion" program that one of the county's "magnet" schools installed to encourage middle-class parents to stay put has itself become a cover for "white flight" by disgruntled white parents. Many of them, despite a lack of empirical evidence, perceive the school's regular English program as inferior, simply because it is 90 percent minority and mostly composed of children who come from a less-fortunate socioeconomic background. So the Spanish immersion classes designed to encourage diversity have become almost exclusively white and Asian America, while the English classes have become almost exclusively—irony of ironies—black and Latino, with many of the children learning English as a second language. Statistically, the school is "diverse" and "integrated." In reality, its student body is divided by an indelible wall, separate but supposedly equal. . . .

Despite all these color-conscious efforts to educate the country's children in a color-blind ideal of racial equality, many of our children seem to be catching on to race codes anyway, although with a twist suitable to the hip-hop generation. One local junior high school teacher, when he heard his black students referring to themselves as "bad," had the facts of racial life explained to him like this: They were not talking about the "bad means good" slang popularized by Michael Jackson's *Bad* album. They meant "bad" in the sense of misbehaving and poorly motivated. The black kids are "bad," the students explained, and the white kids are "good." The Asian kids are "like white," and the Latino kids "try to be bad, like the blacks." Anyone who tried to break out of those stereotypes was trying to break the code, meaning that a black or Latino who tried to make good grades was "trying to be white."

It is enough, as Marvin Gaye famously sang, to make you want to holler and throw up both your hands. Yet my neighbors and I hate to complain too loudly because, unlike other critics you may read or hear about, we happen to be a liberal community that not only believes in the dream of integration and true diversity, but actually is trying to live it. . . .

We see icons of black success—Colin Powell, Douglas Wilder, Bill Cosby, Oprah Winfrey, Bryant Gumbel, the two Michaels: Jordan and Jackson—not only accepted but adored by whites in ways far removed from the arm's-length way white America regarded Jackie Robinson, Willie Mays, Lena Horne, and Marian Anderson.

Yet, although the media show happy images of blacks, whites, Asians, and Hispanics getting along, amicably consuming the good life, a fog of false contentment conceals menacing fissures cracking the national racial landscape.

Despite the growth of the black middle class, most blacks and whites live largely separate lives. School integration actually peaked in 1967, according to a Harvard study, and has declined ever since. Economic segregation has proceeded without interruption, distancing poor blacks not only from whites but also from upwardly mobile blacks, making the isolation and misery of poor blacks worse. One out of every two black children lives below the poverty line, compared to one out of every seven white children. Black infants in America die at twice the rate of white infants. A record-setting million inmates crowd the nation's prisons, half of them black. The black out-of-wedlock birth rate has grown from about 25 percent in 1965 to more than 60 percent (more than 90 percent in the South Bronx and other areas of concentrated black poverty). . . .

The decline of industrial America, along with low-skill, high-pay jobs, has left much of black America split in two along lines of class, culture, opportunity and hope. The "prepared" join the new black middle class, which grew rapidly in the 1970s and early 1980s. The unprepared populate a new culture, directly opposed not only to the predominantly white mainstream, but also to any blacks who aspire to practice the values of hard work, good English, and family loyalty that would help them to join the white mainstream. The results of this spiritual decline, along with economic decline, have been devastating. Although more black women go to college than ever before, it has become a commonplace to refer to young black males as an endangered species. New anti-black stereotypes replace the old. Prosperous, well-dressed African Americans still complain of suffering indignities when they try to hail a taxicab. The fact that the taxi that just passed them by was driven by a black cabby, native born or immigrant, makes no difference. . . .

Behind our questions of race lurk larger questions of identity, our sense of who we are, where we belong, and where we are going. Our sense of place and peoplehood within groups is a perpetual challenge in some lives, particularly lives in America, a land where identity bubbles quite often out of nothing more than a weird alchemy of history and choice. "When I discover who I am, I'll be free," Ralph Ellison once wrote.

I reject the melting pot metaphor. People don't melt. Americans prove it on their ethnic holidays, in the ways they dance, in the ways they sing, in the culturally connected ways they worship. Displaced people long to celebrate their ethnic roots many generations and intermarriages after their ancestors arrived in their new land. Irish-American celebrations of St. Patrick's Day in Boston, Chicago, and New York City are far more lavish than anything seen on that day in Dublin or Belfast. Mexican-American celebrations of Cinco de Mayo, the Fifth of May, are far more lavish in Los Angeles and San Antonio than anything seen that day in Mexico City. It is as if holidays give us permission to expose our former selves as we imagine them to be. Americans of European descent love to show their ethnic cultural backgrounds. Why do they get nervous only when black people show their love for theirs? Is it that black people on such occasions suddenly remind white people of vulnerabilities black people feel quite routinely as a minority in a majority white society? Is it that white people, by and large, do not like this feeling, that they want nothing more than to cleanse themselves of it and make sure that it does not come bubbling up again? Attempts by Americans to claim some ephemeral, all-inclusive "all-American" identity reminds me of Samuel Johnson's observation: "Sir, a man may be so much of everything, that he is nothing of anything."

Instead of the melting pot metaphor, I prefer the mulligan stew, a concoction my parents tell me they used to fix during the Great Depression, when there was not a lot of food around the house and they "made do" with whatever meats, vegetables, and spices they had on hand. Everything went into the pot and was stirred up, but the pieces didn't melt. Peas were easily distinguished from carrots or potatoes. Each maintained its distinctive character. Yet each loaned its special flavor to the whole, and each absorbed some of the flavor from the others. That flavor, always unique, always changing, is the beauty of America to me, even when the pot occasionally boils over. . . .

African Americans are as diverse as other Americans. Some become nationalistic and ethnocentric. Others become pluralistic or multicultural, fitting their black identity into a comfortable niche among other aspects of themselves and their daily lives. Whichever they choose, a comfortable identity serves to provide not only a sense of belonging and protection for the individual against the abuses of racism, but also, ultimately, a sturdy foundation from which the individual can interact effectively with other people, cultures, and situations beyond the world of blackness.

"Identity would seem to be the garment with which one covers the nakedness of the self," James Baldwin wrote in *The Devil Finds Work,* "in which case, it is best that the garment be loose, a little like the robes of the desert, through which one's nakedness can always be felt, and, sometimes, discerned. This trust in one's nakedness is all that gives one the power to change one's robes."

The cloak of proud black identity has provided a therapeutical warmth for my naked self after the chilly cocoon of inferiority imposed early in my life by a white-exalting society. But it is best worn loosely, lest it become as constricting and isolating for the famished individual soul as the garment it replaced.

The ancestral desire of my ethnic people to be "just American" resonates in me. But I cannot forget how persistently the rudeness of race continues to intrude between me and that dream. I can defy it, but I cannot deny it. . . .

32 The Racist Mind

RAPHAEL EZEKIEL

Racism has declined considerably in the United States, so much so that it is difficult to recognize the past. There was a time when Klansmen rode through black neighborhoods, burning and killing with impunity. The mere accusation that a black man had raped a white woman was sufficient for the man to be lynched by an angry mob of whites. Ads for employment used to say, "No colored need apply." Blacks, if allowed at all, were confined to the balconies of movie theaters. There were separate schools, separate restrooms, and separate drinking fountains.

Times have so changed that this description seems to be that of some mythical past. Yet, the racial-ethnic integration of today's society is far from complete. We can assume that the time will come when the urban ghetto, with all of its ills and the fears it brings to the middle class (both minority and white), as well as our almost all-black urban schools, will also be part of someone's mythical past.

Racism, though diminished, has not disappeared, as was noted in article 6 on hiring ex-convicts. And there still are people who hate others because they look different. Racial hatred knows no color. It marks not only some whites, but also some blacks and some members of other minority groups. In this reading, Ezekiel reports on his observations and interviews with groups of white racists. No matter what your race-ethnicity, this thought-provoking selection by Ezekiel should give you insight into hate-centered groups, as well as help you attain greater self-understanding.

WE DO NOT KNOW, the old joke says, who discovered water, but we do know that it was not a fish. Just so, in a society in which white folk predominate and are seldom challenged in everyday life, white Americans have little conscious awareness of being white or of what that might mean. Only challenge or crisis makes this categorization relevant. The militant white racist movement is composed of people who permanently feel in crisis.

The militant white racists look at a world in which white Americans and nonwhite Americans are treated differently in almost every interaction; they infer that race is a powerful biological construct that identifies essences. (They are unfamiliar with modern genetic research, which has found that "race" identifies only trivial aspects of human genetic variation.) They look

369

at a world in which almost all positions of power are held by men who are white; they infer that whites (and men) have a nature that is superior. The *boss*, the person one must worry about, is white. Everyday experience tells the militant white racist that race is basic and that white is good.

Because most white Americans, *at some level*, share these perceptions, the potential exists at all times for the militant movement to expand its influence. The militant movement keeps these ideas fresh and strong, persistently reinjecting them into the social discourse, ensuring that people stay vulnerable to interested parties who wish to use racism to capture public allegiance.

We in the general European-American public share many beliefs with the militant white racists, but we are not identical to them—it is *not* that "we have met the enemy, and he is us." We whites believe many things; we believe most of them in a dull and muddled and jumbled fashion; many of our beliefs are contradictory. The militant movement takes one of the many jumbled belief sets in our heads and preserves it in sharpened, intense form, adding to it a sense that life is struggle, that the fundamental issue between humans is power, that the world divides into Good and Evil, and that Good and Evil must fight to the death. And that events usually have hidden causes.

Because the movement rests partly on beliefs that *are* a part of us white Americans, but a part that we do not acknowledge and do not deal with, it has enjoyed an extraordinarily long life; it is regenerated again and again, taking new forms as circumstances change. The situation is going to become worse. Our national economy is grinding through brutal transformation: An enormous number of people can have no confidence that their jobs, wage levels, health care, or pensions are safe. They face *erosion* of their positions. Their fears will become only more acute as the swelling populations of the underdeveloped nations try to save themselves through mass migration. These highly predictable changes are going to make white Americans more and more vulnerable to a movement whose ideas are already a part of their inner life.

• • •

For a decade I interviewed followers and leaders in the militant white racist movement, the white supremacist movement, and have observed some of their rallies and get-togethers. I dealt openly and honestly with these people, making it clear that I am Jewish, a leftist opposed to racism, a professor at the University of Michigan.

• • •

We drove through town toward the mountain, to a huge meadow at its foot. I saw little knots of men by small fires. We walked to a fire and met Dave Holland, a young leader who was organizing the rally, and two of his lieutenants. I walked across to four young men who leaned on a truck. They were hesitant and careful, but soon got interested in talking. I talked at length with two of them. They were friends, trying to keep a North Carolina Klan alive after the arrest of its leader, worried about how to do that work without seeming to try to take over the group. Both were twenty-two years old; both came from blue-collar families. They believed in the Aryan Jesus, the Aryan Israelites.

Men were setting up their sleeping bags around the fires. People had driven in from a distance. It felt like a camping trip, a kids' gang.

Later I talked more with Venable [one of the main leaders] at the house, wrote some field notes in my motel room, and slept.

Saturday morning was cold with light rain. I had breakfasted with my former student, who wanted to join me in a brief morning reconnaissance. Raised in Chicago, Jewish, very thoughtful and very bright, Judy has lived in the South for some time, and I value her reactions. Back at the rally field we saw flags snapping in the wind: Masses of Reb flags lined the great stage that had been erected at the far edge of the meadow; flags flew from many of the dozens of vans and trucks that had by now accumulated—there were rattlesnake DON'T TREAD ON ME flags, Nazi battle flags with swastikas, and many more Reb flags.

We walked through the meadow. Additional vehicles arrived steadily. At four or five places, wooden booths set up beneath tents held books, buttons, and stickers for sale—WHITE BY BIRTH, SOUTHERN BY THE GRACE OF GOD, PRAISE GOD FOR AIDS. Judy chatted with an older woman who talked of her own childhood in Michigan's Upper Peninsula. I listened to the conversations; I looked at the mass of Confederate flags up at the speaker stand—the racists had taken over the handsome symbol. I listened to the lively country-western music coming over the loudspeaker. I started to be able to understand the words in the lyrics: Again and again the lyrics used the word "nigger." They had their own music, their own songs, and they were getting joy by being able to say "nigger" out loud.

I drove Judy back to the city. She talked about her work in nearby towns with country people. They are independent, she said; they are warm when they have accepted you; they are cautious, defensive, and secretive, afraid of being patronized by city people. This crowd at the rally ground had seemed familiar to her. My own mood was dark. I was getting a headache and feeling the strain: It is important for my goal to let a real sense of the stranger come into me, not to block it or distort it. At the same time I need to keep my own sense of myself. It would be less effort just to reject the stranger. But I would gain no understanding.

I thanked Judy and ate lunch. Wool socks made my feet warmer and I was happier. I returned to the rally field. The rain was lightening. Knots of men spread across the meadow.

[One of the men] stared at me. "I have no use for a Jew. Keep Hitler's dream alive: Kill a Jew."

He was trying to provoke me.

He said again that he had no use for a Jew.

I said, "Well, that's you."

I had already told him I was studying the movement; I now said, truthfully, that I would like to hear more about what he was saying—that this wasn't the time or place, but if it were, I would want to hear more about this.

He said, "If it were the time and the place, I would *show* you."

"That's you," I said in a level voice. I walked off.

I realize now, some years later and after much more interaction, that I must have been conspicuous since my first appearance. I had felt rather casual, strolling among the folk, nodding and saying "howdy" now and then. I was dressed in no particular manner. I had supposed I seemed out of place, but not especially noteworthy. I much misunderstood, I now can see the amount of fear in which these people live, and their belief that a Jewish power base was out to endanger them. There had undoubtedly been bits of gossip following me all morning and afternoon as I walked about. A strange few hours, harmless, deeply frightening, and deeply educational, followed.

As I experienced it, tentacles of hostility seemed to snake out from the encounter, seemed to spread through the meadow the rest of the afternoon. I was talking first with the North Carolina men, and someone called across from an enclosure, "He's a Jew!" As I walked about the meadow, I picked up pieces of conversation: "Jew," "Jewboy." There were periodic catcalls. As I passed near a row of parked vehicles, one of the Klansmen hidden in a van called over a speaker system in a metallic, loud, and nasty voice, "*Yeah,* just move your niggerized self along, Jewboy! Just *move along.*" More catcalls; more frozen stares as I passed; more hard, hostile faces.

I talked then a long time with the men from North Carolina about Jews: What was the deal? I heard deep enmity. The Klan was profoundly anti-Semitic. I left that little group and continued to walk about; the catcalls followed, the nasty stares.

I stood near a tent, quietly. I was not willing to be driven away. More catcalls came. I understood: I would not be safe here if it were dark: If someone moved to hurt me, no one would stop him.

I had been defined. I was not "Rafe," not Raphael Ezekiel; I was not the individual my friends knew, my students knew, I knew. I was Alien, stripped of my particular history.

I was Jew.

It was incredibly lonesome.

I wandered quietly along the meadow, tasting the strange sense of isolation. People were stirring, thinking about getting ready for their parade. Venable arrived and we talked a moment; then he reached into the car for his robe and pulled it over his street clothes. Other old men followed suit. Soon men all over the meadow were pulling folded robes from the cabs of their trucks—robes of all designs, all manner of trim on the sleeves, one even reading KLAN BOAT SQUAD. Dressed now, the men—there may have been one or two women on the grounds—drove off, headed to a nearby schoolyard.

• • •

The ready pool of whites who will respond to the racist signal has posed an enticement. This population, always hungry for activity—or for the talk of activity—that promises dignity and meaning to lives that are working poorly in a highly competitive world, constitutes an alluring prize. The people are needy, and they respond quickly to the signal flag of race.

Much as I don't want to believe it, [the racist] movement brings a sense of meaning—at least for a while—to some of the discontented. To struggle in a cause that transcends the individual lends meaning to a life, no matter how ill-founded or narrowing the cause. For young men in the neo-Nazi group that I had studied in Detroit, membership was an alternative to atomization and drift; within the group they worked for a cause and took direct risks in the company of comrades. Similarly, many people derive a degree of self-confidence and dignity from the suggestion that they are engaged in a heroic struggle for the sake of a larger entity, the reborn family of Whites.

Having accepted a people particularly predisposed to racism as their base, the trap for the leaders is quite real. To animate this base, the leaders must put most of their energy into a particular kind of theater. The movement lives on demonstrations, rallies, and counterallies; on marches and countermarches; on rabid speeches at twilight; on cross-burnings with Gothic ritual by moonlight.

By their nature those actions guarantee failure and bear little relation to the issues of these lives. When interviewing the young neo-Nazis in Detroit, I have often found myself driving with them past the closed factories, the idled plants of our shrinking manufacturing base. The fewer and fewer plants that remain can demand better educated and more highly skilled workers. These fatherless Nazi youths, these high-school dropouts, will find little place in the emerging economy. Enacting the charade of white struggle only buys a wasteful time-out. The current economy has little use for overt racist drama; labor is surplus; a permanently underemployed white underclass is taking its place alongside the permanent black underclass. The struggle over race merely diverts youth from confronting the real issues of their lives. Not many seats are left on the train, and the train is leaving the station.

Stirred for a time by the emotions, but soon finding that nothing has changed in their lives, many waves of membership will pass through these movements. The symbols that are used by the movements touch them; the

374 / *Raphael Ezekiel*

ape-beast, the Serpent, reflect deep human fears. But eventually the symbols lose their power, as the individual asks, *What is happening to my life?*

The weary cycle drains even the organizer. Butler [one of the leaders] ponders what it means to have accomplished nothing. Miles alludes to his own weariness. "What is he to do, though?" he asks. He has done this all his life. His wife is annoyed that he talks this way when he speaks with me. "You make him talk about things he doesn't think about normally," Dot charges.

• • •

I am concerned. At home, next to my typewriter, I keep a photo that was reproduced in *The New York Times* in 1980. The photo shows a ten-year-old boy and his eight-year-old brother. They are in coats and caps. A woman holding an infant stands in the background. Six-pointed stars are sewn to the coats of one of the boys and the woman. An officer of the SS snapped this photo of Selig Jacob and Zrilu Jacob minutes after they had arrived at Auschwitz, moments before they were marched into the gas chamber. In the photo, Selig's eyes are fixed. Zrilu's are puzzled, his mouth is twisted, he is near tears. The boys cannot tell what is happening. They are uncertain and frightened.

Their sister, who somehow survived Auschwitz, came upon the photo in an SS barracks the day after liberation.

This photo is my talisman; it reminds me why I study racism.

For four years I conducted interviews with black men and women on a terribly poor corner in Detroit. My respondents were all migrants from Alabama and Mississippi. Almost every one had stories of relatives or townspeople who had been tortured and killed by hooded men in the night.

The Klan, across time, has been a nesting ground for murder, whatever else it has been. Members of the Order did kill, as well as rob.

• • •

Organized white racism is about a mood—lonely resentment—and several ideas—white specialness, the biological significance of "race," and the primacy of power in human relations. These ideas and the feeling of being cheated (not unique to racists) are powerfully motivating in the absence of ideas that might lead to more positive action. People will find some way to make their lives meaningful, and if nothing richer is at hand, racism (or religious fanaticism or nationalism or gang membership) will do. The appeal of white racist ideologies reflects the absence of competing sets of thought, emotion, and experience, competing faiths that say "This is how the world is constructed" and "This is how you can become a person who matters and whose life matters."

Formal and informal education about racism tend to undervalue the importance of experience. You can't sell people a new idea backed only by your authority. You have to have respect for the lives the people have led to this point and begin with them there; their experiences have led them to their assumptions and conceptions. As you identify and legitimate those experiences, you can help people identify their own primary needs in society. Then they can begin to imagine other people as having parallel needs. You can begin to think together about what each of you needs in the world in order to get along, and you can begin to think together about what others need. Education about racism should be education about personal identity; we have to begin with our own lives. We must begin with respect for the lives of one another.

I've often encountered a related problem in courses I've taught. Students often want to say, "I am color blind; I don't see black and white." This is a way to say "I am a good girl/boy" in a subculture where racism is not chic. Students feel a push to declare their non-racism. The words used come from a misconception that racism is a thing out there in the environment that one could pick up or reject. The students don't understand. Racism is a way of perceiving the world and a way of thinking. To a certain degree it is part of everyone who lives in a racist society. Imagine growing up next to a cement factory, and imagine the cement dust inevitably becoming a part of your body. As we grow up within a society that is saturated in white racism, year after year we pass through interactions in which white racist conceptions are an unspoken subtext. We make lives in institutions in which this is true. We cannot live from day to day without absorbing a certain amount of white racism into our thoughts. (We similarly absorb homophobia and sexism.) It is foolish to say, "I am not racist." Part of one's mind (if one is white and perhaps if one is a person of color) has necessarily absorbed racist ways of thinking. It is important to discover the subtle ways our culture's racism has affected our thinking: to identify those habits of thought and learn how to keep them from influencing us. We can get tripped up by ideas we don't allow ourselves to acknowledge.

In one of his songs, Leadbelly tells us how to deal with the blues: When you wake up in the morning with the blues, you got to say "Good morning, blues," you got to sit down and talk with your blues, got to get to know them, got to talk it over. Whites (and maybe sometimes people of color) have to get well acquainted with the subtext of racism in our lives. Not in order to feel guilty, but in order to be sure the way we act more accurately reflects our intentions.

It doesn't matter whether or not you or I can call ourselves good folk. Our actions are what matter. Real people get hurt badly in our society by poverty and racism. We can alter the institutions that do the damage. We need to be fully conscious of our influences; we need to know ourselves. The militant racists let us see the racist parts of our souls with few filters; we should observe and learn.

33 The Uses of Poverty: The Poor Pay All

HERBERT J. GANS

Some people think that poverty simply means having to tighten your belt, but the meaning of poverty goes much deeper than this. Sociologists have documented that the poor confront social conditions so damaging that their marriages are more likely to break up, they are sicker than others, their children are more likely to drop out of school and get in trouble with the law, they are more likely to commit and to be victimized by violent crime. On average, they also die younger than most. It is difficult to romanticize poverty when one knows what its true conditions are.

In this selection, Gans does not document the degradation of the poor (although this is intrinsically present in his analysis), nor their failing health or troubled lives. Nor is his article a plea for social reform. Rather, from the observation that the poor are always present in society, he concludes that this is because the poor perform vital services (functions) for society. (An essential assumption of *functionalism,* one of the theoretical perspectives in sociology, is that conditions persist in society only if they benefit—perform functions for—society or some of its parts.) In this selection, then, the author tries to identify those functions.

Do you think the author has overlooked any "functions" of the poor? If his analysis, which many find startling, is not correct, what alternative explanation could you propose?

SOME YEARS AGO ROBERT K. MERTON applied the notion of functional analysis to explain the continuing though maligned existence of the urban political machine: If it continued to exist, perhaps it fulfilled latent—unintended or unrecognized—positive functions. Clearly it did. Merton pointed out how the political machine provided central authority to get things done when a decentralized local government could not act, humanized the services of the impersonal bureaucracy for fearful citizens, offered concrete help (rather than abstract law or justice) to the poor, and otherwise performed services needed or demanded by many people but considered unconventional or even illegal by formal public agencies.

Today, poverty is more maligned than the political machine ever was; yet it, too, is a persistent social phenomenon. Consequently, there may be some merit in applying functional analysis to poverty, in asking whether it also has positive functions that explain its persistence.

Merton defined functions as "those observed consequences [of a phenomenon] which make for the adaptation or adjustment of a given [social] system." I shall use a slightly different definition; instead of identifying functions for an entire social system, I shall identify them for the interest groups, socio-economic classes, and other population aggregates with shared values that "inhabit" a social system. I suspect that in a modern heterogeneous society, few phenomena are functional or dysfunctional for the society as a whole, and that most result in benefits to some groups and costs to others. Nor are any phenomena indispensable; in most instances, one can suggest what Merton calls "functional alternatives" or equivalents for them, i.e., other social patterns or policies that achieve the same positive functions but avoid the dysfunction. (In the following discussion, positive functions will be abbreviated as functions and negative functions as dysfunctions. Functions and dysfunctions, in the planner's terminology, will be described as benefits and costs.)

Associating poverty with positive functions seems at first glance to be unimaginable. Of course, the slumlord and the loan shark are commonly known to profit from the existence of poverty, but they are viewed as evil men, so their activities are classified among the dysfunctions of poverty. However, what is less often recognized, at least by the conventional wisdom, is that poverty also makes possible the existence or expansion of respectable professions and occupations, for example, penology, criminology, social work, and public health. More recently, the poor have provided jobs for professional and para-professional "poverty warriors," and for journalists and social scientists, this author included, who have supplied the information demanded by the revival of public interest in poverty.

Clearly, then, poverty and the poor may well satisfy a number of positive functions for many nonpoor groups in American society. I shall describe 13 such functions—economic, social, and political—that seem to me most significant.

The Functions of Poverty

First, the existence of poverty ensures that society's "dirty work" will be done. Every society has such work: physically dirty or dangerous, temporary, dead-end and underpaid, undignified, and menial jobs. Society can fill these jobs by paying higher wages than for "clean" work, or it can force people who have no other choice to do the dirty work—and at low wages. In America, poverty functions to provide a low-wage labor pool that is willing—or, rather, unable to be *un*willing—to perform dirty work at low cost. Indeed, this function of the poor is so important that in some Southern states, welfare payments have been cut off during the summer months when the poor are needed to work in the fields. Moreover, much of the debate about the Negative Income Tax and the Family Assistance Plan has concerned their impact on the work incentive, by which is actually meant the incentive of the poor to do the needed dirty work if the wages therefrom are no larger than the income grant. Many economic activities that involve dirty work depend on the poor for their existence: restaurants, hospitals, parts of the garment industry, and "truck farming," among others, could not persist in their present form without the poor.

Second, because the poor are required to work at low wages, they subsidize a variety of economic activities that benefit the affluent. For example, domestics subsidize the upper-middle and upper classes, making life easier for their employers and freeing affluent women for a variety of professional, cultural, civic, and partying activities. Similarly, because the poor pay a higher proportion of their income in property and sales taxes, among others, they subsidize many state and local governmental services that benefit more affluent groups. In addition, the poor support innovation in medical practice as patients in teaching and research hospitals and as guinea pigs in medical experiments.

Third, poverty creates jobs for a number of occupations and professions that serve or "service" the poor, or protect the rest of society from them. As already noted, penology would be minuscule without the poor, as would the police. Other activities and groups that flourish because of the existence of poverty are the numbers game, the sale of heroin and cheap wines and liquors, pentecostal ministers, faith healers, prostitutes, pawn shops, and the peacetime army, which recruits its enlisted men mainly from among the poor.

Fourth, the poor buy goods others do not want and thus prolong the economic usefulness of such goods—day-old bread, fruit and vegetables that would otherwise have to be thrown out, secondhand clothes, and deteriorating automobiles and buildings. They also provide incomes for doctors, lawyers, teachers, and others who are too old, poorly trained, or incompetent to attract more affluent clients.

In addition to economic functions, the poor perform a number of social functions.

Fifth, the poor can be identified and punished as alleged or real deviants in order to uphold the legitimacy of conventional norms. To justify the desirability of hard work, thrift, honesty, and monogamy, for example, the defenders of these norms must be able to find people who can be accused of being lazy, spendthrift, dishonest, and promiscuous. Although there is some evidence that the poor are about as moral and law-abiding as anyone else, they are more likely than middle-class transgressors to be caught and punished when they participate in deviant acts. Moreover, they lack the political and cultural power to correct the stereotypes that other people hold of them and thus continue to be thought of as lazy, spendthrift, etc., by those who need living proof that moral deviance does not pay.

Sixth, and conversely, the poor offer vicarious participation to the rest of the population in the uninhibited sexual, alcoholic, and narcotic behavior in which they are alleged to participate and which, being freed from the constraints of affluence, they are often thought to enjoy more than the middle classes. Thus many people, some social scientists included, believe that the poor not only are more given to uninhibited behavior (which may be true, although it is often motivated by despair more than by lack of inhibition) but derive more pleasure from it than affluent people (which research by Lee Rainwater, Walter Miller, and others shows to be patently untrue). However, whether the poor actually have more sex and enjoy it more is irrelevant; so long as middle-class people believe this to be true, they can participate in it vicariously when instances are reported in factual or fictional form.

Seventh, the poor also serve a direct cultural function when culture created by or for them is adopted by the more affluent. The rich often collect artifacts from extinct folk cultures of poor people; and almost all Americans listen to the blues, Negro spirituals, and country music, which originated among the Southern poor. Recently they have enjoyed the rock styles that were born, like the Beatles, in the slums; and in the last year, poetry written by ghetto children has become popular in literary circles. The poor also serve as culture heroes, particularly, of course, to the left; but the hobo, the cowboy, the hipster, and the mythical prostitute with a heart of gold have performed this function for a variety of groups.

Eighth, poverty helps to guarantee the status of those who are not poor. In every hierarchical society someone has to be at the bottom; but in American society, in which social mobility is an important goal for many and people need to know where they stand, the poor function as a reliable and relatively permanent measuring rod for status comparisons. This is particularly true for the working class, whose politics is influenced by the need to maintain status distinctions between themselves and the poor, much as the aristocracy must find ways of distinguishing itself from the *nouveaux riches.*

Ninth, the poor also aid the upward mobility of groups just above them in the class hierarchy. Thus a goodly number of Americans have entered the middle class through the profits earned from the provision of goods and services in the slums, including illegal or nonrespectable ones that upper-class and upper-middle-class businessmen shun because of their low prestige. As a result, members of almost every immigrant group have financed their upward mobility by providing slum housing, entertainment, gambling, narcotics, etc., to later arrivals—most recently to blacks and Puerto Ricans.

Tenth, the poor help to keep the aristocracy busy, thus justifying its continued existence. "Society" uses the poor as clients of settlement houses and beneficiaries of charity affairs; indeed, the aristocracy must have the poor to demonstrate its superiority over other elites who devote themselves to earning money.

Eleventh, the poor, being powerless, can be made to absorb the costs of change and growth in American society. During the nineteenth century, they did the backbreaking work that built the cities; today, they are pushed out of their neighborhoods to make room for "progress." Urban renewal projects to hold middle-class taxpayers in the city and expressways to enable suburbanites to commute downtown have typically been located in poor neighborhoods, since no other group will allow itself to be displaced. For the same reason, universities, hospitals, and civic centers also expand into land occupied by the poor. The major costs of the industrialization of agriculture have been borne by the poor, who are pushed off the land without recompense; and they have paid a large share of the human cost of the growth of American power overseas, for they have provided many of the foot soldiers for Vietnam and other wars.

Twelfth, the poor facilitate and stabilize the American political process. Because they vote and participate in politics less than other groups, the political system is often free to ignore them. Moreover, since they can rarely support Republicans, they often provide the Democrats with a captive constituency that has no other place to go. As a result, the Democrats can count on their votes, and be more responsive to voters—for example, the white working class—who might otherwise switch to the Republicans.

Thirteenth, the role of the poor in upholding conventional norms (see the *fifth* point, above) also has a significant political function. An economy based on the ideology of laissez-faire requires a deprived population that is allegedly unwilling to work or that can be considered inferior because it must accept charity or welfare in order to survive. Not only does the alleged moral deviancy of the poor reduce the moral pressure on the present political economy to eliminate poverty, but socialist alternatives can be made to look quite unattractive if those who will benefit most from them can be described as lazy, spendthrift, dishonest, and promiscuous.

The Alternatives

I have described 13 of the more important functions that poverty and the poor satisfy in American society, enough to support the functionalist thesis that poverty, like any other social phenomenon, survives in part because it is useful to society or some of its parts. This analysis is not intended to suggest that because it is often functional, poverty *should* exist, or that it *must* exist. For one thing, poverty has many more dysfunctions than functions; for another, it is possible to suggest functional alternatives.

For example, society's dirty work could be done without poverty, either by automation or by paying "dirty workers" decent wages. Nor is it necessary for the poor to subsidize the many activities they support through their low-wage jobs. This would, however, drive up the costs of these activities, which would result in higher prices to their customers and clients. Similarly, many of the professionals who flourish because of the poor could be given other roles. Social workers could provide counseling to the affluent, as they prefer to do anyway; and the police could devote themselves to traffic and organized crime. Other roles would have to be found for badly trained or incompetent professionals now relegated to serving the poor, and someone else would have to pay their salaries. Fewer penologists would be employable, however. And pentecostal religion could probably not survive without the poor—nor would parts of the second- and third-hand-goods market. And in many cities, "used" housing that no one else wants would then have to be torn down at public expense.

Alternatives for the cultural functions of the poor could be found more easily and cheaply. Indeed, entertainers and adolescents are already serving as the deviants needed to uphold traditional morality and as devotees of orgies to "staff" the fantasies of vicarious participation.

The status functions of the poor are another matter. In a hierarchical society, some people must be defined as inferior to everyone else with respect to a variety of attributes, but they need not be poor in the absolute sense. One could conceive of a society in which the "lower class," though last in the pecking order, received 75 percent of the median income, rather than 15–40 percent, as is now the case. Needless to say, this would require considerable income redistribution.

The contribution the poor make to the upward mobility of the groups that provide them with goods and services could also be maintained without the poor's having such low incomes. However, it is true that if the poor were more affluent, they would have access to enough capital to take over the provider role, thus competing with, and perhaps rejecting, the "outsiders." (Indeed, owing in part to antipoverty programs, this is already happening in a number of ghettos, where white storeowners are being replaced by blacks.) Similarly, if the poor were more affluent, they would make less willing clients for upper-class philanthropy, although some would still use settlement houses to achieve upward mobility, as they do now. Thus "Society" could continue to run its philanthropic activities.

The political functions of the poor would be more difficult to replace. With increased affluence the poor would probably obtain more political power and be more active politically. With higher incomes and more political power, the poor would be likely to resist paying the costs of growth and change. Of course, it is possible to imagine urban renewal and highway projects that properly reimbursed the displaced people, but such projects would then become considerably more expensive, and many might never be built. This, in turn, would reduce the comfort and convenience of those who now benefit from urban renewal and expressways.

In sum, then, many of the functions served by the poor could be replaced if poverty were eliminated, but almost always at higher costs to others, particularly more affluent others. Consequently, a functional analysis must conclude that poverty persists not only because it fulfills a number of positive functions but also because many of the functional alternatives to poverty would be quite dysfunctional for the affluent members of society. A functional analysis thus ultimately arrives at much the same conclusion as radical sociology, except that radical thinkers treat as manifest what I describe as latent: that social phenomena that are functional for affluent or powerful groups and dysfunctional for poor or powerless ones persist; that when the elimination of such phenomena through functional alternatives would generate dysfunctions for the affluent or powerful, they will continue to persist; and that phenomena like poverty can be eliminated only when they become dysfunctional for the affluent or powerful, or when the powerless can obtain enough power to change society.

Postscript*

Over the years, this article has been interpreted as either a direct attack on functionalism or a tongue-in-cheek satirical comment on it. Neither interpretation is true. I wrote the article for two reasons. First and foremost, I wanted to point out that there are, unfortunately, positive functions of poverty which have to be dealt with by antipoverty policy. Second, I was trying to show that functionalism is not the inherently conservative approach for which it has often been criticized, but that it can be employed in liberal and radical analyses.

* Written for this book.

34 Moving Up from the Working Class

JOAN M. MORRIS

MICHAEL D. GRIMES

Many of us want desperately to get ahead in life. So that we can go to college and achieve our goals, some of our parents work two jobs and go without luxuries. Some even do without necessities, as my own mother did when she put off dental care until I completed college. To be upwardly mobile, it is essential that we be future oriented. So we, too, work hard, sacrifice pleasures, and postpone gratifications in order to achieve goals and reach farther in life than our parents did.

Most students from working-class homes who are striving to better their situation in life become discouraged at the many obstacles in their paths. Many give up, substituting less lofty goals for those that originally formed the substance of their dreams. Despite what sociologists call a "deficit of cultural capital," through determined hard work, native ability, and perseverance some members of the working class manage to attain social mobility. In this selection, Morris and Grimes analyze people who have made this jump in social class, in this case people who became sociologists.

THE FOCUS OF THIS PAPER is on the childhood socialization of sociologists from working-class backgrounds—people who have, by most standards, "made something" of themselves, but not necessarily in the ways their parents intended. In fact, as will be demonstrated below, for many of them, their successes have been accomplished despite what they were taught about what it means to be successful during their childhoods; their successes have also sometimes come at the expense of the approval and acceptance of their families and childhood peers. The data for the paper come from a larger study that addresses events throughout the life courses and careers of forty-five sociologists from working-class backgrounds. Each participant who volunteered to be part of the study was asked to contribute three things: responses to a set of open-ended questions; responses to a questionnaire; and a curriculum vitae.

The major thesis of this paper is that early socialization within a class culture has deep and abiding effects. More specifically, when individuals are socialized within a working-class family environment, they can expect to experience "culture shock" when they achieve upward mobility that takes them out of their class of origin and into the foreign terrain of middle-class culture. And, to the extent that gender and race or ethnicity manifest themselves in ways that are distinctively class oriented, the effects of this "shock" are magnified for women, for people of color, and for the members of ethnic minorities. The present analysis focuses its attention on the impacts of early socialization within working-class culture, how these experiences have influenced the careers of academics from working-class backgrounds, and the unique effects that result for women and for the members of racial and ethnic minorities from working-class backgrounds.

Learning What "Feels Right"

The first and most enduring exposure to culture occurs during childhood socialization. A number of analysts have concluded that the class location of parents is one of the most important influences on the socialization experiences of children (Kohn and Schooler 1983; Bourdieu 1984, 1986; Coleman 1990; Lareau 1989) because the parents' class location is directly linked to the nature of the resources that a family possesses and makes available to its children.

Parents may pass a variety of resources down to their children, including a range of explicit but also implicit goods, not the least of which is the cultural knowledge associated with their social class. Wright defines social class as based on three dimensions, each a type of power that is indicative of where one stands in the class structure. The three (property, skills/credentials, and organizational control) combine to produce a class system in which the hierarchy is defined according to power over oneself and others (see Wright 1985). The working-class, in Wright's model, have least power over the three dimensions, i.e., they do not own the means of production; they possess few credentials; and they have little decision-making power over their work or the work of others. Kohn and Schooler (1983) and others have found that the power relations present in one's job carry over into the home. Families who command few of the resources valued in the work world cannot help also including a sense of powerlessness in the resources they pass down to their children.

Bourdieu (1984, 1986) refers to family resources as the total volume of "capital" available for expropriation by a child. He argues that capital assumes three forms: economic, cultural, and social. *Economic capital* refers to material wealth or economic power, a form of capital "which is immediately or directly convertible into money and may be institutionalized in the form of property rights" (Bourdieu 1986:243). *Cultural capital* refers to a broad range of knowledge about the world within which an individual lives. This form of capital is important because it is "convertible, in certain situations, into economic capital and may be institutionalized in the form of educational qualifications (Bourdieu 1986:243). *Social capital* refers to the network of social connections (a social network) that can be effectively mobilized by the family for its use. It, too, can be converted into economic capital under certain circumstances. Bourdieu argues that social classes can be placed on a continuum (or a set of continua) according to the level of economic or material wealth it controls, the cultural capital it possesses, and the potential benefits of its social contacts.

We asked the participants in our study to describe the cultural environment in their homes while growing up. Based on their responses, we developed a coding scheme that contained a total of eighteen indicators of cultural activities. This list included such things as: (the presence of) books, newspapers, magazines in the home; listening to music (and the type of music); visits to museums and libraries; attending movies; going to plays and concerts; taking music or dance lessons; television viewing, etc. Following Bourdieu's (1984) distinction between "high" and "low" cultural activities, we then selected a sub-set of these activities that served as a kind of index of "high" culture. This group of activities included such things as listening to classical music, taking music/dance lessons, visits to museums, attending plays and concerts, and engaging in intellectual discussions with parents or older siblings.

Our results show that a full two-thirds of our respondents had experienced *none* of these activities during their childhoods. Only two out of ten had experienced one of them; and no respondent had experienced more than three of them. In terms of gender, female respondents were no more likely to have experienced these activities than were our male respondents (though the one respondent who experienced three of them was a woman). Without identical data on this subject from a group of academics from middle-class backgrounds with which to compare findings, it is difficult to place them in a meaningful context. What we can say, however, is that these data contrast sharply with the levels of exposure to "high" culture enjoyed by our own children and those of most of our colleagues. They are also consistent with Bourdieu's (1984) conclusion that the exposure to "high" culture is directly related to the family's position in the class structure. . . .

As the work of Bourdieu, Coleman, and others makes clear, socialization in working-class homes is, in many ways, different from socialization in middle-class or upper middle-class homes. This goes beyond the level of material consumption (economic capital) the family is able to enjoy. In comparison to middle-class children, working-class children are taught a different set of values and are, themselves, valued differently. As has been well established (Kohn and Schooler 1983; Coleman 1990; Parcel and Menaghan 1994), the socialization of working-class children is heavily influenced by the occupational experiences of their parents. Parents tend to re-create components of their work environments at home; e.g., when parents work in jobs that provide little opportunity for autonomy and independent thought, they are likely to encourage their children to conform rather than to think independently. Despite the fact that most parents stress "independence" in their children; it is what they mean by it that differs. While middle-class parents may be more interested in creativity and self-determination, the primary concern of working-class parents is that their children be able to support themselves, i.e., to do a "day's work for a day's pay" and to avoid appearing weak by asking for help.

Economic Capital

The U.S. working-class is a heterogeneous group in its range of material circumstances and our respondents' childhood homes were not exceptional in that regard. About one-third of respondents reported no material deprivation during their childhoods (16 respondents); another third reported they did feel a sense of material deprivation as children (15 respondents); and the remainder fell between these two extremes, reporting various experiences of relative deprivation.

The following examples are typical of those who commented on their recognition of socioeconomic differences and their disadvantaged status:

> "I became aware of income differences (which is not to say class differences) around the fifth grade. Another child in my class asked me why I wore the same thing to school every day."

> "I felt materially deprived after my father died. As the years after went by we became poorer and poorer. By high school, I was wearing old (my mother's) clothes, my middle brother would complain about not being able to buy new clothes. My older brother and mother would fight constantly about his giving more money to the household. The meals became smaller, but always attractively prepared."

The example below describes the sense of relative deprivation that one woman remembered feeling when she compared herself to her childhood peers:

> "I was quite aware of the fact that other Jewish families often went on summer vacation . . . we never did. My father had overtime, a concept unknown to my friends, their fathers worked 9 to 5. Also, when I was in elementary school and

my mother went back to work, I had to go to summer day camp. I could not go to the day camp associated with the Jewish Community Center (JCC), but had to go to Girl Scouts Camp, because it cost less. . . . We only got one present on Hanukkah, not eight. I had hand-me-down clothes, not full priced clothing from department stores."

Cultural Capital

The participants in this study provided a wealth of evidence in support of Bourdieu's statement that cultural capital is "determinant in the reproduction of social structure" (1986:254). Yet, the fact that they have failed to reproduce the class structure within which they were raised raises an important point. Cultural capital is based on values, knowledge, and meaning. The autobiographical accounts provided by our respondents show how the social structure is reinforced and usually reproduced, often in subtle, nonobvious ways by the transmission of working-class culture. Parental encouragement and expectations are perhaps the most influential.

Encouragement and Expectations

The majority of respondents to our study reported that their parents encouraged them in their early educations. This is consistent with Lareau's (1989) findings that both working-class and middle-class parents prepare their children for school. The main difference, however, is that working-class parents tend to leave education to the "professionals" (teachers, guidance counselors, etc.) while middle-class parents stay more involved with their children's education throughout their school years. Working-class parents often see education as the route to a better job. One respondent wrote:

> "My parents were both committed to our gaining an education so we could have 'sit-down' jobs performing 'clean' work."

To many, however, parental encouragement to "do well" in school meant to follow the rules, keep out of trouble, etc. To many working-class parents, a "good" report card was equivalent to a satisfactory evaluation at work. Getting good grades was an outward sign that you were able to fit into a system and accomplish what was expected. One respondent referred to his father's efforts to teach him "industrial discipline" in the following way:

> "He explained that I would always have a 'boss,' and that I would have to obey authority without question or reason."

And in a similar vein, a respondent talks about her parents' concern that she "do well" in school:

". . . this urgent need for conformity could be attributed in part to the working-class attitudes toward work. For the types of work that everyone did and that I was expected to do when I was grown, it was very necessary that one develop the 'proper' attitude toward authority."

Education was perhaps more important in minority families. Several African American respondents commented on their families' exceptional encouragement of education—encouragement at a level that was somewhat unusual for white working-class children. For example:

"My parents, grandparents and other relatives encouraged me during the years of my early education. My maternal grandmother, with whom I spent a great deal of time when I was very young, remembered the days when it was illegal to teach blacks to read. Therefore, she was able to impress upon us the value of education. My parents were always supportive as well."

"I was an only child and the center of a great deal of attention and favor. I was sheltered from the streets, continually watched and not allowed to play with many of the kids in the neighborhood and was sent back to the South during the summer, a not uncommon pattern of Black Southerners. In many ways, my mother and our family always had high expectations for behavior since it was one of the ways to separate us from 'low class' people."

Pursuit of the "American Dream"

Respondents often gave accounts of parental support that were couched in the ideology of the dominant culture—the idea that one's achievements are only limited by individual ability, willingness to work, etc. In the case of childhood socialization into the working-class, this ideology is inherently contradictory. That is, the belief that individuals can "make something of themselves," and in fact, that *anyone* can make *anything* of themselves that they wish, suggests an open system, a meritocracy. However, any system within which merit would determine success would have to be based on equal access to resources, information being the most important. Working-class kids simply do not "see" the same career opportunities that middle-class kids see. Part of this is due to limited information about what is available and what the requirements are for seeking it. But some, and perhaps this is the larger issue, is due to limited aspirations. The following is a good example:

". . . Being a white, working class male in a stable household made me secure and comfortable. I believed in the "American Dream" which meant that I could do or be almost anything I wanted. That I didn't aspire to be a professional or manager was like not thinking that I could fly, it wasn't a possibility. I figured I was going to do some type of blue-collar work, get married, have children, and own my own house."

All children develop their career aspirations within a class-specific culture. The fact that proportionately fewer children attend college at each lower level of the socioeconomic hierarchy is no accident—and it is not entirely due to affordability factors. One of the major places in which the class system is institutionalized is the family. The family's location in the class system, in turn, determines the location and content of early educational experiences, and has a huge effect on the make-up and orientation of peer groups. Values, expectations, and aspirations are formed and reinforced through interaction with family, friends, and teachers. Thus the social-psychological effects of early socialization have deep and enduring effects on individuals' lives. The following examples illustrate some of this.

". . . I was never encouraged to think about college (by teachers) and I was even discouraged from attending college by family and friends. Their attitudes have been developed by class background. The impact was that I got a terribly late start in completing my first college class (age 24).

"None of my teachers were influential in directing my path towards higher education before I dropped out of school. In fact, just the opposite. In the 9th grade, we were tested with a battery of tests. My homeroom teacher, an English teacher whom I was crazy about, informed my mother that I was a B student and was not college material. This was ironic because two years later, while I was pregnant, I undertook testing by (a federal agency . . . my mother made me do it) and they told me that I was almost a genius. I remember her words as we were leaving the building . . . she looked at my stomach and said, 'some genius.'"

Inherent Contradictions in Parental Encouragement

Most respondents reported that their parents were interested in seeing their children "do better" than they had done. These interests were usually stated in general terms such as the following:

"Both my parents had strong upwardly mobile ambitions for themselves, but especially for their children; they strove always to "get ahead" to improve their economic condition and achieve some mobility."

Such generalized "encouragement" constitutes another contradiction to a common theme in these essays. This is something David Hale reported in his 1984 book, *America's Working Man*, the definition of manual work as the only real work, with intellectual or managerial work dismissed as not really work at all. By this definition, nonmanual workers are shamming, getting by, often not knowing what they are doing, and existing at the expense of the real workers. In response to a question concerning their parents' feelings about their work and its relative status and importance in society, the respondents repeatedly echoed this theme. One respondent said his father made a distinction between himself and those at higher levels of the socio-economic hierarchy by referring to himself as ". . . someone who actually works for a living." Another referred to his father's "canned phrases," most of which he has forgotten but which implied that the "working man was always getting the shaft." Other examples follow.

". . . he was hostile to the 'big shots' who worked in the plant office . . ."

". . . she felt that her work was very necessary—what would all those middle-class and rich women do without people like my mother to alter and mend their clothing?—was her line. She frequently compared herself invidiously to her customers, commented that they didn't know how to thread a needle."

"Both parents felt their work was important. My dad believed the working man did the real work while managers and engineers/architects did not generally know what they were doing."

"My father would boast about how smart he was and how stupid his bosses were, I think to elevate the importance of his job."

Social Capital

Bourdieu's third form of capital is social capital, the potential to mobilize resources to one's advantage through social ties. The clearest case of a shortage of social capital expressed by our respondents concerned access to higher education. Academics from working-class backgrounds often lack the information they need to achieve upward mobility, but this is, in large part, due to their limited access to a network of social ties with people who know the answers to their questions. For the members of working-class families who achieve mobility into professional positions, not only is it unclear how to map out a career path, but the options themselves are often as hidden as the means for finding out how to learn about them. The autobiographical essays written for this study contain numerous examples of individuals' uncertainty about the answers to important questions, but more than that, they convey the retrospective recognition that they were as ignorant about the appropriate questions to be asked as they were of whom to ask them. One respondent gave the following account of her entry into college:

> "It is at this point that I became aware that both my economic and social origins provided a huge impediment to my undergraduate studies. I became aware of class for really the first time. No one was able to help me find financial aid, fill out application forms, apply for scholarships, etc. No one read my scholarship essays. No one took me to the University to check it out. No one helped me to find an apartment. Even if it had entered my parents thoughts, no one knew how to help me. I missed out on a huge chunk of financial aid because I missed the relevant deadlines. Every summer for the first three years of school, I lost 10–15 pounds for lack of food, really. I was even too stupid to apply for food stamps."

Another essayist talks about the influence of growing up in a Jewish home. Though her family was "clearly working-class," most of her parents' friends were middle-class. For her, the intersection of ethnicity and social class was somewhat positive, i.e., the influence of the Jewish subculture offset some of the limitations of working-class subculture. She attributes her parents' encouragement for her education to her ethnicity. In her words, "To them, education was the most meaningful aspect of one's life." Still, she identifies class background as an impediment to higher education:

> "In some ways my class background was an impediment to higher education, in other ways it was not. I was not aware of many options. My parents did not know much of the college scene and guidance counselors at my high school were not well versed."

The Relevance of 'Social Class' as an Issue

The popular mythology in this country is that we live in a classless society or that, since most of us are located within an amorphous middle, social class has few consequences. The study's participants reported similar attitudes for their parents. Though 81 percent of the respondents said their parents were aware of different class locations (most stated that their parents did not speak of *class* per se, but apparently recognized the existence of hierarchical arrangements in society) and of their places within the structure, nearly half said their parents saw few to no consequences for themselves. Many reported that their parents believed that most others were similar to themselves. The following examples are typical.

"My parents, to this day, have absolutely no awareness of class and the influences of class on their place in society. As far as they are concerned, everyone is the same as them and if you are different from them, well, there is something wrong with you."

"My parents were not significantly aware of class positions in any manner that made this clear to the children. Further, in the community we lived there were few rich people and all classes in the community participated in the same institutions (churches, schools) and lived in the same general areas. There were few families to compare one's self to and identify these as 'rich' or 'poor.'"

Given the pervasiveness of the dominant American ideology, it is no wonder that most of our respondents reported that their parents believed in the importance of individual achievement and self-motivation. Few respondents reported that their parents recognized any sort of systematic discrimination based on socioeconomic status or social class. In fact, in some cases, there was a certain kind of pride associated with belonging to the working-class. The following is a good example of this.

". . . I should add that being working-class in (my hometown) carried with it no shame. You were proud to be working-class. You felt yourself to be strong and to be part of a strong breed, i.e., northern working-class. (My hometown) was built on the labor of the skilled working-class and my father was part of that class."

Weighing the Effects of Race, Gender, and Class

The effects of racial and ethnic prejudice and discrimination cross both class and gender lines. Having the experience of racial discrimination adds an important element to the equation and modifies the experience of growing up working-class. One such modification is illustrated in the following quote from an Hispanic respondent as he explains how his father instilled suspicion of the white middle-class.

"They spoke of class only in economic terms and saw the system as 'haves' versus the 'have-nots.' My Dad often told me to always watch a smiling white guy because they all cheat. He saw the haves as crooked but said he would never steal as 'most whites who are rich do.'"

The effects of the intersection of gender and class are the focus of Barker's (1995) paper. She defines gender as carrying implied limitations within its labels (e.g., men are "naturally" smarter than women, etc.). The negative connotations associated with femininity that are present for all academics are added to the disadvantage of class background for women from working-class families. This, coupled with the expectations that women face from working-class families (i.e., that she "owes" it to her family to remain connected and supportive) generate different results for academic women from working-class backgrounds than it does for similar men. The bottom line is that these factors combine to produce a climate within which women from working-class backgrounds find it especially challenging to perform the necessary requirements to gain entry and acquire legitimacy within primarily upper middle-class, male-dominated institutions of higher learning.

The early-childhood socialization experiences of the women in our study lend support to this. The first example illustrates the implicit preference for males in working-class families:

> "Since I was the oldest child (and only child for about nine years), I participated in ALL business and farm work: milking, field work . . . dressing turkeys, gathering and sorting and packing fruits and vegetables for sale on the routes, helping with books and often responsible for checks . . . My father often said that he had wished for a boy as his first child, but that I was [as] good as any boy would have been!"

The following is a typical scenario for girls in working-class families:

> "I was expected, as the oldest girl child, to baby-sit the younger children, clean house every week, do dishes, cook, help can food, mow the lawn, rake the leaves. Since I was a girl, it did not matter that I was in high school sports and held a part-time job, I was still expected to do my work around the house on top of everything else."

In addition to the expectation that girls will take on a larger share of domestic responsibilities, there are expectations that girls will pursue particular occupational paths. Note the following example:

> ". . . I was told that my options were nurse, teacher, nun, mommy, or secretary, and since I would ultimately be 'just' a mommy anyway, any of the others would do (except nun of course!). One distant cousin was held out as an ideal to emulate; her secretarial job was within an airline, so she got to travel—it was thought that might satisfy my craving for something more/else. There were also strong messages to never move far away (2 hours distant was considered very far), since family, relatives, etc., were the most important thing. Two of my cousins were offered complete athletic scholarships one state (about 3 hours) away, and my aunt and uncle made them turn them down because they didn't want them to move away from home. When I finally left home to go to graduate school, I felt guilty as hell!"

The effects of gender thus intensify the difficulty for women in leaving their working-class origins. Girls in working-class families are instilled with similar levels of (limited) class culture as their male peers but with the added expectations that accompany socialization into working-class womanhood.

Conclusion: Caught in the Middle

In this paper, we have begun to explore the childhood recollections of a group of sociologists from working-class backgrounds. These individuals were socialized to assume a place within the working-class and many have experienced a particular kind of angst alongside their upward class mobility. They have experienced a form of culture shock not unlike that experienced by travelers in a foreign land. Similar to Ryan and Sackrey's metaphor of "strangers in paradise," these respondents have described how their successes have often been accompanied by ambivalence and uncertainty. In the process of "making something" of themselves, they have moved into an ambiguous "middle," no longer working-class but not comfortably middle-class either.

In a myriad of subtle ways, working-class culture prepares the next generation of workers to voluntarily assume their positions in the hierarchy (Willis 1977). Culture offers meaning; it provides the process for internalizing the social structure and coming to see the status quo as natural, something that "feels right." Since a large part of the content of working-class culture is antithetical to scholarly pursuit, having grown up in an environment that assumes the "naturalness" of working-class values presents a conflict for intellectuals from such backgrounds. The conflict is, for many, deep and aching, lingering long after they have become, objectively, members of the middle-class. Socialization within a class culture is perhaps not as "determinant in the reproduction of the social structure" as Bourdieu implied (1983:253). It is possible to achieve upward mobility in this society; the lives of professional sociologists from working-class backgrounds attest to that. It is much more difficult, however, to "become" middle-class—to experience middle-class existence in a way that "feels right." It is this lingering difficulty that academics from working-class backgrounds experience as a feeling of being "caught in the middle."

35 The U.S. Upper Class

STEPHEN HIGLEY

Social inequality is a fact of life in all societies. Some people receive more of their society's goods and services, others far less. This is the way it has been in every known society of the past, is now, and—people's hopes to the contrary notwithstanding—likely always will be.

As much as many of us would wish it different, our own society is no exception. We, too, are marked by vast divisions, especially of wealth and power. Because the poor are the most accessible, research on social inequality usually focuses on them. In this selection, in contrast, Higley examines the life situation of the rich. You might ask yourself in what ways your own life would be different if you had been born into one of the families on which this article focuses. Obviously, your material circumstances would be different, but the distinctions of wealth and power go far beyond this obvious matter. They vitally affect our ideas of the world—and of our place in it.

FROM A CLASS PERSPECTIVE, the American upper class exhibits a class solidarity derived from the group awareness that they share a common fate. They consider one another equals, and their voting behavior in support of the Republican Party and their charitable efforts are the most obvious manifestations of their ability for joint action in the pursuit of common interests.

Those who are listed in the *Social Register* are chosen primarily for the style of life (and, implicitly, the system of values) they exhibit. The main purpose of the *Social Register* is to restrict social intercourse for the members by acting as a ready reference as to who is "in" and who is "out" of proper society. Although it is hard to confirm (because of the *Social Register's* policy of not responding to inquiries), the *Social Register* strives to "confine normal marriage to within the status circle" by requiring members who marry outside the *Register* to resubmit themselves and their bride or groom for membership. And the *Social Register* is but one element of the upper class's complete system of socialization. The American upper class has attempted to separate itself socially from the *hoi polloi* literally from birth to death—from favored maternity hospitals and attending physicians to specific retirement homes such as Dunwoody Village in Newtown Square, Pennsylvania, and Cathedral Village in Washington, D.C. . . . Between birth and retirement is a full array of socializing institutions: prep schools, Ivy League schools, debutante balls, and metropolitan clubs, to name a few.

The upper-class families listed in the *Social Register* are direct descendants of the men who made great fortunes during the Gilded Age (1870–1910). . . . The short-term and long-term economic success of the upper class is fundamentally important to maintaining the style of life that differentiates the upper class from the other classes in society. Once a family no longer has the economic resources to give its members the advantages that money can buy in the United States, the fall from social grace is swift and sure. The family that is reduced to "shabby gentility" is an often-used literary device that underlines the importance of liquid assets to continued good standing in American society.

The men and women who defined late-nineteenth- and early-twentieth-century American upper-class society were overwhelmingly white, Anglo-Saxon, and Protestant. As the personal, ethnic, and religious characteristics were unofficially codified, social and generational seasoning became equally important for acceptance into upper-class society. No amount of improperly socialized new money could buy its way into "proper" upper-class society. . . .

If one subscribes to the Weberian theory that status is ultimately dependent on economic control and wealth, there are clear implications that the influence of white, Anglo-Saxon Protestants will inevitably decline in the twenty-first century. Although "WASP" and "upper class" have been synonymous in the past, it is apparent that the ethnic definition of upper class will be transformed and redefined in the future.

The transformation, or de-WASPing, of the upper class that is now taking place in the United States is not easily evident to the casual observer. The status order will eventually reflect the economic order, although there are a multitude of cultural bulwarks that make the change slower and more subtle than [some] anticipate. There is a powerful WASP cultural inertia in the United States, and it will take decades to effect changes in the way Americans define themselves culturally. WASP culture is essentially derivative of the English nobility, and to this day, Anglophilia continues to pervade the American upper class. Because the upper class provides a value and consumptive role model for the American upper-middle class, upper-class values are in turn transmitted to the rest of American society—the upper-middle class being relatively large and visible to the rest of society. . . .

The Elements of Upper-Class Cohesion

The American upper class has a large number of institutions and associational arrangement that have made it possible for members to pass through life with very little significant contact with other social classes. This section reviews the most important of these institutions: private boarding schools (prep schools), colleges, metropolitan and country clubs, and the Episcopal and Presbyterian churches. The role of debutante balls, service organizations, and charitable organizations as contributing factors in maintaining upper-class cohesion will also be explored. Finally, an in-depth look at the *Social Register* will examine the role of neighborhood and community in upper-class cohesiveness.

PRIVATE PREPARATORY SCHOOLS

Of all of the institutions that inculcate upper-class values, private preparatory schools may have the greatest role (Cookson and Persell 1985, 13–30). The role of private education begins with upper-class day schools. Baltzell, in his examination of the role of education, termed the local institutions *provincial family surrogates* in that their outlooks were local in nature (Baltzell 1958, 292–300). Baltzell chronicles the changing role and fortunes of the Protestant Episcopal Academy, the first educator of large numbers of Philadelphia's young male upper class. The Episcopal Academy was founded in 1785 and began catering consciously to the upper class in 1846. The institution's move in 1921 to the suburban Main Line in pursuit of its clientele maintained its primacy in Philadelphia. The Episcopal Academy was not without competitors, however; other day schools were Haverford, Penn Charter, and Chestnut Hill. There were also day schools (such as Springside, Shipley, and Agnes Irwin) for upper-class girls in Philadelphia that served the same socializing functions as the boys' schools (Baltzell 1958, 300–301).

The day schools' popularity began to wane in the second half of the nineteenth century as boarding schools became the preferred method of educating young upper-class men and women. Boarding schools made it possible to completely control the social and educational environment of the students (Cookson and Persell 1985, 31–48). Parents could be assured that their child would be raised away from the distractions of the large cities and their hordes of newly arrived aliens. The prep schools were staffed with teachers who could be relied on to transmit the values of the upper class. The WASP ethic of civility, honesty, principle, and service was imparted within a totally structured environment. The schools, particularly the Episcopalian schools, were modeled after the public schools of England, complete with "forms" for grades and "headmasters" for principals.

The day schools increasingly turned to the nouveau riche to fill the slots left by the defections of some of their constituency. In his 1980 article, "The Rise of American Boarding Schools and the Development of a National Upper Class," Levine writes that the original purpose of the schools was to protect the "old guard" of the upper class from the arrivistes, [the "newly arrived"—people who only recently became rich] with their newly minted family fortunes created during the last quarter of the nineteenth century. He theorizes that New England led the way in the creation of boarding schools as the Boston Brahmins reacted to their imminent social eclipse by the much larger fortunes the Gilded Age was producing. The elites of cities such as New York and Philadelphia were able to participate in the industrialization of America, whereas the Boston Brahmins, whose fortunes were grounded largely in the trade from the Far East, were not as effective in gaining a share of the new wealth. The boarding schools were but one of a series of institutions founded during this era to create social distance between old money and new money. Country clubs and metropolitan clubs were other examples. It was also during this time that books such as the *Social Register* and various blue books were published to provide a scorecard as to who was in and who was out of proper society.

More important than the social distancing function prep schools provide is the common socializing force they exert on young men and women of the upper class. C. Wright Mills felt that prep schools were an essential element in the calculus of preserving privilege. He wrote:

> As a selection and training place of the upper classes, both old and new, the private school is a unifying influence, a force for the nationalization of the upper classes. The less important the pedigreed family becomes in the careful transmission of moral and cultural traits, the more important the private school—rather than the upper-class family—as the most important agency for transmitting the traditions of the upper social classes and regulating the new admission of wealth and talent. It is the characterizing point in the upper-class experience. (Mills 1956, 64–65)

Although upper-class schools were originally conceived to buffer the old guard from the nouveau riche, the need to infuse the upper class with new talent and money and the need to socialize the parvenus into the minutiae of upper-class culture led to the acceptance of some newly moneyed families. As sociologist Randall Collins notes, "Schools primarily teach vocabulary and inflection, styles of dress, aesthetic tastes, values and manners" (Collins 1971, 101). Levine's 1980 study found that, in general, it took one generation to socialize upper-class fortunes. The sons of fathers who acquired large fortunes in the early twentieth century often placed their children in the most prestigious boarding schools. The fathers were not above building a new library or classroom building to ensure their son's entrance. In most cases, the sons went on to Ivy League schools and became members of the upper-class secret societies and eating clubs. They were also likely to be listed in the *Social Register*. Gaining membership in upper-class secret societies and eating clubs would not present a problem because sponsorship would come easily from former schoolmates who were already members of the clubs.

Although there were literally hundreds of schools founded in the Gilded Age, a hierarchy of preferred schools quickly developed. At the top of the list in terms of prestige are the five Episcopalian boarding schools known collectively as St. Grottlesex (St. Paul's, St. Mark's, St. George's, Groton, and Middlesex). St. Paul's is often held up as the quintessential upper-class school (Domhoff 1983). Located in Concord, New Hampshire, it has a campus of eighty buildings (for six hundred students) and is situated on two thousand acres of woods and open land. In 1981, the student-faculty ratio was 6.3 to 1 and the average class size was twelve.

The second group of prestigious prep schools is represented by Choate, Hotchkiss, and Kent—nondenominational schools that were founded specifically to cater to the burgeoning market for private, exclusive education at the turn of the century.

The two oldest schools are usually put in a class by themselves. The Phillips Academy (commonly called Andover) and the Phillips Exeter Academy were founded originally to provide secondary education for a large array of students before the advent of the public school system. With the growth of the public school systems, Andover and Exeter became oriented strictly to preparing students for college. Both schools are larger and less aristocratic and have higher academic standards than the other boarding schools mentioned (Cookson and Persell 1985, 38).

In summary, boarding schools offered a place where the upper class could rest assured that class-supportive values would be instilled in their young. Their children would be exposed to only those nouveau riche children who were "acceptable" and to none of the perceived evils of the city. They would make valuable social and business friendships that would be nourished in college and in the world of private clubs during their adult lives.

AN UPPER-CLASS COLLEGE EDUCATION

Just as there are preferred upper-class boarding schools to attend, there are preferred universities for young men and women of the upper class. The three universities that are considered most desirable by upper class parents are Harvard, Yale, and Princeton. These three are followed by any other schools in the Ivy League (Brown University has become increasingly popular among students) or any number of small prestigious schools located primarily in New England (for example, Williams, Amherst, or Trinity). If an upper-class family lives in a state with an academically prestigious public university, such as Wisconsin, Michigan, or California, it is increasingly considered appropriate to attend those universities. In addition, there are selected private regional universities that are considered acceptable as one's first choice. Examples of these schools are Duke, Stanford, and Northwestern.

FRATERNITIES AND EATING CLUBS

Once a young man has been accepted at Harvard, Princeton, or Yale, he is confronted with a large university that is dominated in numbers, if not tone, by members of other social classes. The solution to the problem of having to mix with the upper-middle class (or worse) is a system of private clubs similar to the fraternities and sororities found on many American campuses. The system of private clubs is best described in the words of Baltzell:

> An intricate system of exclusive clubs, like the fraternities on less rarefied American campuses, serve to insulate the members of the upper class from the rest of the students at Harvard, Princeton, and Yale. There are virtually "two nations" at Harvard. The private-school boys, with their accents, final clubs, and Boston debutante parties—about one-fifth of the student body—stand aloof and apart from the ambitious, talented, and less polished boys who come to Cambridge each year from public schools over the nation. (Baltzell 1958, 329–330)

The private eating clubs of Princeton were formed in the years following Woodrow Wilson's 1906 ban on fraternities. Juniors and Seniors joined eating clubs that had a "pecking order" based on social status. Upper-class young men usually joined the Ivy Club or the Cottage Club. The exclusivity of the eating clubs ended in the 1960s when the university compelled the clubs to accept all who had applied but had not been accepted.

At Harvard, Porcellian is the club of the most prestigious boarding schools such as St. Paul's and Groton. Other social clubs that are notable but of slightly less status are A.D., Fly, Spee, Delphic, and Owl. Porcellian's counterpart at Yale is the Fence Club. As at Harvard, there are a host of slightly prestigious clubs to join. Perhaps the senior societies are even more important than the social clubs at Yale. The two most important are the elite and meritorious Skull and Bones Club (of which former President George

Bush is a member) and the more socially exclusive Scroll and Key Club. The purpose of these clubs is to build class solidarity and personal alliances that will be translated into lifetime friendships and business relationships at graduation (Baltzell 1958, 330–334).

At each critical juncture of a young person's life, the upper class has developed a series of supporting institutions to link individuals with a shared outlook and value system. By carefully molding young upper-class people into the established value system, the upper class assures its own continuity.

THE UPPER-CLASS WORLD OF PRIVATE CLUBS

On graduation, young men and women begin their careers with yet another array of private clubs that will act as an extended class-oriented family. One can differentiate between two types of private clubs, the metropolitan dining clubs and the more familiar suburban country clubs. Baltzell maintains that the metropolitan clubs are much more important than country clubs in terms of the social ascription of status.

Unlike the American middle classes, and resembling the lower classes, in fact, the Philadelphia upper class is largely male dominated and patriarchal. The social standing of the male family head, the best index of which is his metropolitan club affiliation, usually determines the social position of the family as a whole (Baltzell 1958, 336).

The first American metropolitan club, following the British experience with such clubs, grew out of an informal gathering of the leading citizens to discuss daily affairs over coffee. In the days before reliable newspapers, it was a way to pass on news and keep informed of current events. The first club formed in the United States was the Philadelphia Club in 1835. It was closely followed by the Union Club of New York City, which was founded in 1836 (Baltzell 1958, 335–363). The metropolitan club subculture, with its distinctive mores and value rituals, was perceptively outlined by Wecter:

> The social club in America has done a great deal to keep alive the gentleman in the courtly sense. Here is a peculiar asylum from the Pandemonium of commerce, the bumptiousness of democracy, and the feminism of his own household. Here he is technically invisible from the critical female eye—a state of bliss reflected in the convention that a gentleman never bows to a lady from a club window and does not, according to best form, discuss ladies there. The club is the Great Good Place with its comfortable and slightly shabby leather chairs, the pleasant malt-like effluvium of its bar, the newspaper room with a club servant to repair quickly the symptoms of disarray, the catholicity of magazines from highbrows to *La Vie Parisienne* which in less stately company

would seem a trifle sophomoric, the abundant newspaper, the good cigars and hearty carnivorous menus. . . .

With what Henry James called "a certain light of fine old gentlemenly prejudice to guide it," the preeminently social club welcomes the serious frivolity of horses, hounds, foxes, and boats, but not the effeminate frivolity of aestheticism. Pedantry is also frowned upon; except for the *Social Register,* the *World Almanac,* and *Lloyd's Register of American Yachts,* not a volume in the club library has been taken down since the cross-word puzzle craze. It is comforting to think that one's sons and grandsons will sit in these same chairs, and firelight will flicker on the same steel engravings and oil portraits of past presidents—and though the stars may wheel in their courses and crowned heads totter to the guillotine, this little world will remain, so long as first mortgages and government bonds endure. (Wecter 1937, 253–255)

This evocative description of metropolitan clubs was written in 1937 and is dated in some details but still accurate in its main thrust.

There have been several recent legal challenges to the all-male membership policies of metropolitan clubs. The Supreme Court has ruled against the males-only policies of the clubs. The main argument made by female complainants was that women are excluded from important business transactions that are discussed in the clubs. Aldrich maintains that the women's victory will be mainly Pyrrhic because it is considered extremely bad form to discuss business in metropolitan clubs (Aldrich 1988, 122–123). However, Aldrich does not address the valuable alliances made in leisure that lead to business deals later, outside the confines of the club.

The suburban country club is less important than the metropolitan club, but it is significant in that the entire family are members and there are facilities and activities for all. The first American country club was established in 1882 in Brookline, Massachusetts; it is simply called The Country Club. These clubs are most frequently associated with golf, but they may include facilities for swimming, tennis, and, in some cases, polo. Americans are familiar with suburban country clubs, which have been enthusiastically established by the upper-middle class throughout the country.

As in the case of the metropolitan clubs, there is a status hierarchy among the country clubs. Because of the relatively small number of upper-class families, upper-class country clubs make up only a small portion of the private equity country clubs in the United States.

Yacht clubs are also an integral part of upper-class social life. Again, only a select few of the yacht clubs in America are favored by the American upper class. Similarly, there are a large number of historically oriented clubs, such as the well-known Daughters of the American Revolution and more obscure clubs such as the American Association of the Sovereign Military Order of Malta.

RELIGION AND THE UPPER CLASS

Observers of the American scene have long commented on the status differentiation of Protestant denominations. The upper class has had a long association with the Protestant Episcopal Church and to a lesser degree with the Presbyterian Church. The Episcopalian connection is a logical extension of the Anglophilia of the American upper class because the church has a number of characteristics that make it attractive to upper-class men and women. The richness of the church's ritual, the classic traditionalism of most Episcopalian architecture, and the sophisticated, urbane, and intellectual nature of its leaders have great appeal to the upper class (Cookson and Persell 1985, 44–48). The Episcopalian Church was very close to an established church for some parts of colonial America and was, in fact, the established church of the state of Virginia until 1786. Although the church suffered during and immediately following the Revolutionary War because of its close association with England and her Loyalists, it quickly recovered its status as a church of the educated elite in the postwar period.

Baltzell confirmed the alliance statistically by analyzing the church membership of those people in the upper class who were in both the 1940 edition of *Who's Who in America* and the 1940 Philadelphia *Social Register*. *Who's Who's* listing of church membership enabled Baltzell to determine religious affiliation for 226 upper-class heads of households. Although 35 percent did not acknowledge a church membership, 42 percent were affiliated with the Episcopalian Church (compared with 1.0 percent of the total U.S. population). An additional 13 percent of those in *Who's Who* listed the Presbyterian Church as their place of worship (compared to 1.2 percent of the general population). Because of the general privacy of religious information, it is difficult to verify Baltzell's findings. However, it is fair to say that the subjective information on the relationship is indeed overwhelming. Of course, not all Episcopalians are upper class. The actual number of upper-class families within the church is small compared to the total membership of Episcopalian churches; however, the church carries the distinctive imprint of upper-class support, philanthropy, and values.

DEBUTANTE BALLS

The debutante season consists of a series of parties, teas, and dances held by upper-class families to formally announce the arrival and availability of their daughters for suitable matrimonial partners. Each major city holds a grand ball that is the highlight of the season. Debutante "coming-out" parties are yet another means of reinforcing class solidarity because the young women and men who participate are carefully screened to ensure upper-class exclusivity.

Because upper-class endogamy is highly valued, the debutante season is a formal process, the sole purpose of which is to encourage and create upper-class familial unions. Although there is often a philanthropic cause behind the tens of thousands of dollars spent for each coming out, none of the participants are under any illusion as to the real purpose behind the festivities. The debutante season strengthens the bonds of intermetropolitan upper-class social relationships just as shared summer resort holidays strengthen intermetropolitan alliances.

THE SOCIAL REGISTER

Before the Civil War, "society" in most large American cities, including New York City, was small enough that members of the upper class knew each other informally. Invitations to balls and other "serious" social events were handled either by personal secretaries or by the hostess herself. There were also self-appointed social arbiters whose dictates could help the unsure hostess in determining who was "in" and who was "out" of society.

The role of individual society kingmakers would soon be eclipsed with the appearance of the first *Social Register* in 1886. Hundreds of new fortunes were being made (and lost) during the last two decades of the nineteenth century, and a book was needed to take the place of personal knowledge as to a family's acceptability in polite society.

The first edition of the *Social Register* was a listing of society in Newport, Rhode Island. The next year, 1887, saw the first appearance of the New York City edition. It has been published continuously ever since that date. The *Social Register* was not the first of its kind; there were many books that purported to list society in the 1880s. The secret of success for the founder, Louis Keller, was the quality of his list and his refusal to clutter the book with advertisements for wine merchants, dressmakers, and the like.

Another component of Keller's success was a strict code of secrecy that has been conscientiously maintained to the present. The all-enveloping veil of secrecy has given the book a mystique that has made it all the more alluring to those who aspire to join. The aura of exclusivity is enhanced by the *Social Register's* policy of rarely speaking to the press or publicly commenting on itself in any way.

Keller incorporated his idea as the Social Register Association; new editions quickly followed the New York City volume in Philadelphia and Boston (1890), Baltimore (1892), Chicago (1893), Washington, D.C. (1903), St. Louis and Buffalo (1903), Pittsburgh (1904), San Francisco (1906), and Cleveland and Cincinnati-Dayton (1910). At its height in the 1920s, there were 24 volumes. Many of these editions failed during the Great Depression because of the lack of a large and sophisticated industrial elite and/or insufficient interest on the part of the local population. This would explain the absence of a large number of *Social Register* families from Detroit, a city that made its fortune in the 1920s, and the three post–World War II growth centers of Dallas, Houston, and Los Angeles. The families that dominate the *Social Register* were created during the Gilded Age, and the sunbelt families would have to wait for their generational acculturation into upper-class mores.

The *Social Register* has remained the only social listing for the thirteen cities listed above since 1939. In 1977, the twelve editions were combined into one large book—a reflection of the national solidarity of the upper class and also of cost considerations (Birmingham 1978). The *Social Register* has subsequently become an address and telephone book for the American upper class. Along with this basic information, the *Register* also lists which boarding school and which university members attended, the year in which he or she graduated, and their club memberships. Members may also list their children and the schools they are attending or their current addresses. It has several useful appendices: "Married Maidens," a listing of the maiden names of the wives (very helpful in a divorce-prone culture), and "Dilatory Domiciles," for those who are late in returning their annual questionnaires. There is also a separate volume published each summer called the *Summer Social Register*. The summer edition lists summer homes and also has a yacht registry that lists the home port, tonnage, and year built for each yacht. As the upper class has added winter homes in the post–World War II period, they have tended to list those addresses in the main *Social Register*.

Getting into the *Social Register* and being dropped from the book have been subjects of endless speculation among the upper class and among gossip columnists. The best term to describe the process is *idiosyncratic*. There are three methods for obtaining membership. The most likely way to get in is to be born into it. The second is to marry into a listed family. However, a new bride or groom who is not in the *Register* must submit a new application to be accepted or rejected (without comment) by the "advisory committee." (The makeup of the committee has been the subject of much speculation, and some have questioned if there really is one.) The third way to gain a listing in the *Social Register* is to apply for membership. The prospective member fills out an application and if it passes initial review, he or she must then supply the committee with four or five recommendations from current listees. The application then goes to the advisory committee and the applicant is either accepted or rejected without comment. It is believed that the number that gain membership through this process is extremely limited (Winfrey 1980).

Even the ownership of the *Social Register* is veiled in mystery. When Keller died in 1924, he left the Association to several heirs. It was purchased by Malcolm Forbes in 1977 and remained in his family after his death in 1989, but who actually owns it is not known.

The reasons why members are dropped from the *Social Register* has also been the subject of much musing. Perhaps the surest way to guarantee elimination is to publicly disparage the *Social Register* or to be publicly disgraced. As long as one's personal foibles do not become public knowledge, one seems to be immune from being dropped. Another way to be banished is to marry an entertainer—one of the many groups of people who are *personae non gratae* in the *Social Register*.

The largest groups that are systematically excluded from the *Social Register* are Jews, African Americans, and Asian Americans. Although there are one known Black and several Jewish members, the *Social Register* remains a compendium that is overwhelming white, Anglo-Saxon, and Protestant American (*Newsday,* December 12, 1984, 10–11). A small percentage of the listees have French and Dutch surnames, but it is a challenge to find German, Scandinavian, or southern European surnames anywhere in the *Social Register*.

There are members of the upper class who have asked to have their names removed from the *Social Register* because of the *Register*'s discriminatory practices. Alfred Gwynne Vanderbilt and "Jock" Whitney were among the notable society people who asked to be deleted. It is politically astute for politicians to request that their names be deleted. George Bush had his name deleted before he received his complimentary listings as vice president and president. Former presidents and the chief justice of the Supreme Court are also given complimentary listings. There are many retired senators who are listed once it is "safe" to be associated with an organization that is so blatant in its discrimination.

[Summary]

The upper class has a distinct set of institutions that provide social and physical separation from the rest of society, and these institutions inculcate an intricate set of values and beliefs in both young and old. They affirm cultural and group solidarity within the upper class and clearly delineate class boundaries.

PART VIII   Social Institutions

AT FIRST GLANCE, the term *social institution* appears far removed from everyday life. But in fact this term refers to concrete and highly relevant realities that affect our lives profoundly. Parents and their children, the basic family unit, constitute a social institution. So does the church, with its sacred books, clergy, and worship; and the law, with its police, lawyers, judges, courts, and prisons. Social institution also means politics—running the full gamut of the U.S. political process, from campaign lies told with a straight face to the official acts of Congress, the president, and his cabinet. Too, social institution means the economic order, with new plants opening and old ones closing, working for a living, or drawing unemployment or welfare or a pension. Schools, colleges, and universities—places where people are socialized (as sociologists phrase the matter) or where they go to learn (as most other people put it)—also are examples of a social institution. This term also refers to science, with its test tubes and experiments, interviewers and questionnaires. It means doctors and nurses and hospitals, as well as the patients they treat, and the Medicare and Blue Cross and Blue Shield that people struggle to pay for in order to keep the U.S. medical enterprise from destroying their present and future finances. Social institution also means the military, with its generals and privates and tanks and planes, and the whole war game for training people in the business of death. Far from being removed from life, then, social institution means all these vital aspects of life in society—and more.

To understand social life, it is necessary to understand the institutions of a society. It is not enough to understand what people do when they are in one another's presence. These interactions certainly are significant, but they form only part of the picture. The sociological (and personal) significance of social institutions is that *they provide the structure within which we live our lives.*

The characteristics of a society's institutions, in fact, dictate much of our interaction in everyday life. For example, because of the way our economic order is arranged, a common pattern is to work 8 hours a day, to be off

16, and to repeat this pattern five days a week. There is nothing natural about this pattern. Its regularity is but an arbitrarily imposed temporal arrangement for work, leisure, and personal concerns. Yet this one aspect of a single social institution has far-reaching consequences for how we deal with our family and friends, how we meet our personal needs and nonwork obligations, and indeed on how we view time and even life itself.

Each social institution has similarly far-reaching effects on our lives and viewpoints. By shaping our society as a whole and establishing the context in which we live, these institutions give form to almost everything that is of concern to us. We can say, in fact, that if the social institutions of our society were different, we would be different people. We certainly could not be the same, for our ideas and attitudes and other orientations to the physical and social worlds would be changed.

Sociologists classify social institutions as primary and secondary. The *primary* U.S. social institutions are the economy, the political system, and the military establishment. According to conflict theory, these three social institutions dominate our society. Their top leaders make the major decisions that have the greatest impact on our society, and thereby on our own lives. With the United States so dominant in world affairs, these three social institutions are far-reaching, not only for our society but also for the rest of the world.

The *secondary* social institutions are the others: family, education, religion, sports, medicine, law, science, and the mass media. As the name implies, they are secondary in power, and, as conflict theorists stress, these secondary social institutions exist to serve the primary ones. According to conflict theory, the family produces workers (for the economy), voters and taxpayers (for the political system), and soldiers (for the military); education socializes children (and adults) into values that support the current social class arrangement and trains workers to serve the ruling elite; the religious institution instills patriotism and acceptance of the current arrangement of power; sports take people's minds off social issues so they remain compliant workers; the medical institution patches workers up so they can continue to work; the law keeps the poor under its yoke so they don't rebel and upset current power arrangements; science produces knowledge that allows capitalists to exploit nature and produce wealth; and the mass media create desire for goods produced by the capitalist class so this elite can become even wealthier.

To lead off this Part, Barbara Ehrenreich places the focus on economics, sharing her experiences as she attempted to live on a minimum wage. Stephanie Coontz then challenges our thinking by documenting how American family life in the past was quite unlike our mythical images. Robbie

Davis–Floyd follows with an analysis of how U.S. medicine has produced a distinctive "American way" of giving birth. Harry Gracey then uses the conflict perspective to analyze kindergarten, viewing it as a means by which children learn to become conformists so they can take a "proper" place in life. Focusing on religion, Marvin Harris uses a functionalist lens to analyze the role of sacred cows in India. Jennifer Hunt's inside report of police violence allows us to peer behind the scenes of the legal institution. The final article in this Part, which focuses on the military, allows us to continue to look behind closed doors. As Gwynne Dyer analyzes boot camp, we are able to see how the Marines successfully turn civilians into soldiers.

36 Nickel and Dimed

BARBARA EHRENREICH

Middle-class people have a difficult time understanding what life is like for the poor. Most people in the middle class enjoy health insurance, paid vacations, and sick leave. They drive late model cars and have credit cards, bank accounts, and closets full of clothing. If oranges go up fifty cents a pound, or if the price of milk increases by a dollar a gallon, they might grumble, but it is an inconvenience, not a disaster. For the poor, in contrast, such price increases are not trivial matters, and they can force the poor to go without oranges and milk.

From their upper-middle-class vantage point in life, Ehrenreich and her editor were discussing what it must be like to live on a minimum wage. As they were relaxing over their $30 lunch at an upscale French restaurant, they wondered about the "unfortunate" people—those lower than themselves on the social class ladder. "How are those people who have come off the welfare rolls getting along?" they asked one another as they sipped fine wine charged to an expense account. When Ehrenreich said, "Someone should find out," her editor looked at her and said, "You should do it." She didn't expect her life to change so abruptly, but she took him up on the challenge. This selection describes some of her experiences.

AT THE BEGINNING of June 1998 I leave behind everything that normally soothes the ego and sustains the body—home, career, companion, reputation, ATM card—for a plunge into the low-wage workforce. There I become another, occupationally much diminished "Barbara Ehrenreich"—depicted on job-application forms as a divorced homemaker whose sole work experience consists of housekeeping in a few private homes. I am terrified, at the beginning, of being unmasked for what I am: a middle-class journalist setting out to explore the world that welfare mothers are entering, at the rate of approximately 50,000 a month, as welfare reform kicks in. Happily, though, my fears turn out to be entirely unwarranted during a month of poverty and toil, my name goes unnoticed and for the most part unuttered. In this parallel universe where my father never got out of the mines and I never got through college, I am "baby," "honey," "blondie," and most commonly, "girl."

My first task is to find a place to live. I figure that if I can earn $7 an hour—which, from the want ads, seems doable—I can afford to spend $500 on rent, or maybe, with severe economies, $600. In the Key West area, where

411

I live, this pretty much confines me to flophouses and trailer homes—like the one, a pleasing fifteen-minute drive from town, that has no air-conditioning, no screens, no fans, no television, and, by way of diversion, only the challenge of evading the landlord's Doberman pinscher. The big problem with this place, though, is the rent, which at $675 a month is well beyond my reach. All right, Key West is expensive. But so is New York City, or the Bay Area, or Jackson Hole, or Telluride, or Boston, or any other place where tourists and the wealthy compete for living space with the people who clean their toilets and fry their hash browns. Still, it is a shock to realize that "trailer trash" has become, for me, a demographic category to aspire to.

So I decide to make the common trade-off between affordability and convenience, and go for a $500-a-month efficiency thirty miles up a two-lane highway from the employment opportunities of Key West, meaning forty-five minutes if there's no road construction and I don't get caught behind some sun-dazed Canadian tourists. I hate the drive, along a roadside studded with white crosses commemorating the more effective head-on collisions, but it's a sweet little place—a cabin, more or less, set in the swampy back yard of the converted mobile home where my landlord, an affable TV repairman, lives with his bartender girlfriend. Anthropologically speaking, a bustling trailer park would be preferable, but here I have a gleaming white floor and a firm mattress, and the few resident bugs are easily vanquished.

But is it really possible to make a living on the kinds of jobs currently available to unskilled people? Mathematically, the answer is no, as can be shown by taking $6 to $7 an hour, perhaps subtracting a dollar or two an hour for child care, multiplying by 160 hours a month, and comparing the result to the prevailing rents. According to the National Coalition for the Homeless, for example, in 1998 it took, on average nationwide, an hourly wage of $8.89 to afford a one-bedroom apartment and the Preamble Center for Public Policy estimates that the odds against a typical welfare recipient's landing a job at such a "living wage" are about 97 to 1. If these numbers are right, low-wage work is not a solution to poverty and possibly not even to homelessness.

It may seem excess to put this proposition to an experimental test. As certain family members keep unhelpfully reminding me, the viability of low-wage work could be tested, after a fashion, without ever leaving my study. I could just pay myself $7 an hour for eight hours a day, charge myself for room and board and total up the numbers after a month. Why leave the people and work that I love? But I am an experimental scientist by training. In that business, you don't just sit at a desk and theorize; you plunge into the everyday chaos of nature, where surprises lurk in the most mundane measurements.

On the morning of my first full day of job searching, I take a red pen to the want ads, which are suspiciously numerous. Everyone in Key West's booming "hospitality industry" seems to be looking for someone like me—trainable, flexible, and with suitably humble expectations as to pay. I decide on two rules: One, I cannot use any skills derived from my education or usual work—not that there are a lot of want ads for satirical essayists anyway. Two, I have to take the best-paid job that is offered me and of course do my best to hold it[.]

So I put on what I take to be a respectful-looking outfit of ironed Bermuda shorts and scooped-neck T-shirt and set out for a tour of the local hotels and supermarkets. Best Western, Econo Lodge, and HoJo's all let me fill out application forms, and these are, to my relief, interested in little more than whether I am a legal resident of the United States and have committed any felonies.

I lunch at Wendy's, where $4.99 gets you unlimited refills at the Mexican part of the Superbar, a comforting surfeit of refried beans and "cheese sauce." A teenage employee, seeing me studying the want ads, kindly offers me an application form, which I fill out, though here, too, the pay is just $6 and change an hour. Then it's off for a round of the locally owned inns and guesthouses. At "The Palms," let's call it, a bouncy manager actually takes me around to see the rooms and meet the existing housekeepers, who, I note with satisfaction, look pretty much like me—faded ex-hippie types in shorts with long hair pulled back in braids. Mostly, though, no one speaks to me or even looks at me except to proffer an application form. At my last stop, a palatial B&B, I wait twenty minutes to meet "Max," only to be told that there are no jobs now but there should be one soon, since "nobody lasts more than a couple weeks."

Three days go by like this, and, to my chagrin, no one out of the approximately twenty places I've applied calls me for an interview. I had been vain enough to worry about coming across as too educated for the jobs I sought, but no one even seems interested in finding out how overqualified I am. Only later will I realize that the want ads are not a reliable measure of the actual jobs available at any particular time. They are, as I should have guessed from Max's comment, the employers' insurance policy against turnover of the low-wage work force. Most of the big hotels run ads almost continually, just to build a supply of applicants to replace the current workers as they drift away or are fired, so finding a job is just a matter of being at the right place at the right time, and flexible enough to take whatever is being offered that day. This finally happens to me at one of the big discount hotel chains, where I go, as usual, for housekeeping and am sent, instead, to try out as a waitress at the attached "family restaurant," a dismal spot with a counter and about thirty tables that looks out on a parking garage and features such tempting fare as "Polish [sic] sausage and BBQ sauce" on 95-degree days. Philip, the dapper young West Indian who introduces himself as the manager, inter-views me with about as much enthusiasm as if he were a clerk processing me for Medicare, the principal questions being what shifts can I work and when can I start. I mutter something about being woefully out of practice as a waitress, but he's already on to the uniform: I'm to show up tomorrow wear-ing black slacks and black shoes; he'll provide the rust-colored polo shirt with HEARTHSIDE embroidered on it, though I might want to wear my own shirt to get to work, ha ha. At the word "tomorrow," something between fear and indignation rises in my chest. I want to say, "Thank you for your time, sir, but this is just an experiment, you know, not my actual life."

So begins my career at the Hearthside, I shall call it, one small profit center within a global discount hotel chain, where for two weeks I work from 2:00 til 10:00 P.M. for $2.43 an hour plus tips. For the next eight hours, I run after the agile Gail, absorbing bits of instruction along with fragments of personal tragedy. All food must be trayed, and the reason she's so tired today is that she woke up in a cold sweat thinking of her boyfriend, who killed himself recently in an upstate prison. No refills on lemonade. And the reason he was in prison is that a few DUIs caught up with him, that's all, could have happened to anyone. Carry the creamers to the table in a monkey bowl, never in your hand. And after he was gone she spent several months living in her truck, peeing in a plastic pee bottle and reading by candlelight at night, but you can't live in a truck in the summer, since you need to have the win-dows down, which means anything can get in, from mosquitoes on up.

At least Gail puts to rest any fears I had of appearing overqualified. From the first day on, I find that of all the things I have left behind, such as home and identity, what I miss the most is competence. Not that I have ever felt utterly competent in the writing business, in which one day's success au-gurs nothing at all for the next. But in my writing life, I at least have some notion of procedure: do the research, make the outline, rough out a draft, etc. As a server, though, I am beset by requests like bees: more iced tea here, ketchup over there, a to-go box for table fourteen, and where are the high chairs, anyway? Of the twenty-seven tables, up to six are usually mine at any time, though on slow afternoons or if Gail is off, I sometimes have the whole place to myself. There is the touch-screen computer-ordering system to mas-ter, which is, I suppose, meant to minimize server-cook contact, but in prac-tice requires constant verbal fine-tuning: "That's gravy on the mashed, okay? None on the meatloaf," and so forth—while the cook scowls as if I were in-venting these refinements just to torment him. Plus, something I had forgot-ten in the years since I was eighteen: about a third of a server's job is "side work" that's invisible to customers—sweeping, scrubbing, slicing, refilling, and restocking. If it isn't all done, every little bit of it, you're going to face the 6:00 P.M. dinner rush defenseless and probably go down in flames. I screw up dozens of times at the beginning, sustained in my shame entirely by Gail's support—"It's okay, baby, everyone does that sometime"—because, to my total surprise and despite the scientific detachment I am doing my best to maintain, I care.

After a few days at the Hearthside, I feel the service ethic kick in like a shot of oxytocin, the nurturance hormone. The plurality of my customers are hard-working locals—truck drivers, construction workers, even housekeepers from the attached hotel—and I want them to have the closest to a "fine dining' experience that the grubby circumstances will allow. No "you guys" for me; everyone over twelve is "sir" or "ma'am." I ply them with iced tea and coffee refills; I return, mid-meal, to inquire how everything is; I doll up their salads with chopped raw mushrooms, summer squash slices, or whatever bits of produce I can find that have survived their sojourn in the cold-storage room mold-free.

• • •

Ten days into it, this is beginning to look like a livable lifestyle. I like Gail, who is "looking at fifty" but moves so fast she can alight in one place and then another without apparently being anywhere between them. I clown around with Lionel, the teenage Haitian busboy, and catch a few fragments of conversation with Joan, the svelte fortyish hostess and militant feminist who is the only one of us who dares to tell Jack to shut up. I even warm up to Jack when, on a low night and to make up for a particularly unwarranted attack on my abilities, or so I imagine, he tells me about his glory days as a young man at "coronary school"—or do you say "culinary"?—in Brooklyn, where he dated a knock-out Puerto Rican chick and learned everything there is to know about food. I finish up at 10:00 or 10:30, depending on how much side work I've been able to get done during the shift, and cruise home[.] ° ° ° To bed by 1:30 or 2:00, up at 9:00 or 10:00, read for an hour while my uniform whirls around in the landlord's washing machine, and then it's another eight hours spent following Mao's central instruction, as laid out in the Little Red Book, which was: Serve the people.

I could drift along like this, in some dreamy proletarian idyll, except for two things. One is management. If I have kept this subject on the margins thus far it is because I still flinch to think that I spent all those weeks under the surveillance of men (and later women) whose job it was to monitor my behavior for signs of sloth, theft, drug abuse, or worse.

Managers can sit—for hours at a time if they want—but it's their job to see that no one else ever does, even when there's nothing to do, and this is why, for servers, slow times can be as exhausting as rushes. You start dragging out each little chore, because if the manager on duty catches you in an idle moment, he will give you something far nastier to do. So I wipe, I clean, I consolidate ketchup bottles and recheck the cheesecake supply, even tour the tables to make sure the customer evaluation forms are all standing perkily in their places—wondering all the time how many calories I burn in these strictly theatrical exercises. When, on a particularly dead afternoon, Stu finds me glancing at a *USA Today* a customer has left behind, he assigns me to vacuum the entire floor with the broken vacuum cleaner that has a handle only two feet long, and the only way to do that without incurring orthopedic damage is to proceed from spot to spot on your knees.

The other problem, in addition to the less-than-nurturing management style, is that this job shows no sign of being financially viable. You might imagine, from a comfortable distance, that people who live, year in and year out, on $6 to $10 an hour have discovered some survival stratagems unknown to the middle class. But no. It's not hard to get my co-workers to talk about their living situations, because housing, in almost every case, is the principal source of disruption in their lives, the first thing they fill you in on when they arrive for their shifts. After a week, I have compiled the following survey:

- Gail is sharing a room in a well-known downtown flophouse for which she and a roommate pay about $250 a week. Her roommate, a male friend, has begun hitting on her, driving her nuts, but the rent would be impossible alone.
- Claude, the Haitian cook, is desperate to get out of the two-room apartment he shares with his girlfriend and two other, unrelated, people. As far as I can determine, the other Haitian men (most of whom only speak Creole) live in similarly crowded situations.
- Annette, a twenty-year-old server who is six months pregnant and has been abandoned by her boyfriend, lives with her mother, a postal clerk.
- Marianne and her boyfriend are paying $170 a week for a one-person trailer.
- Jack, who is, at $10 an hour, the wealthiest of us, lives in the trailer he owns, paying only the $400-a-month lot fee.
- The other white cook, Andy, lives on his dry-docked boat, which, as far as I can tell from his living descriptions, can't be more than twenty feet long. He offers to take me out on it, once it's repaired, but the offer comes with inquiries as to my marital status, so I do not follow up on it.
- Tina and her husband are paying $60 a night for a double room in a Days Inn. This is because they have no car and the Days Inn is within walking distance of the Hearthside. When Marianne, one of the breakfast servers, is tossed out of her trailer for subletting (which is

against the trailer-park rules), she leaves her boyfriend and moves in with Tina and her husband.

- Joan, who has fooled me with her numerous and tasteful outfits (hostesses wear their own clothes), lives in a van she parks behind a shopping center at night and showers in Tina's motel room. The clothes are from thrift shops.

It strikes me, in my middle-class solipsism, that there is gross improvidence in some of these arrangements. When Gail and I are wrapping silverware in napkins—the only task for which we are permitted to sit—she tells me she is thinking of escaping from her roommate by moving into the Days Inn herself. I am astounded: How can she even think of paying between $40 and $60 a day? But if I was afraid of sounding like a social worker, I come out just sounding like a fool. She squints at me in disbelief, "And where am I supposed to get a month's rent and a month's deposit for an apartment?" I'd been feeling pretty smug about my $500 efficiency, but of course it was made possible only by the $1,300 I had allotted myself for start-up costs when I began my low-wage life: $1,000 for the first month's rent and deposit, $100 for initial groceries and cash in my pocket, $200 stuffed away for emergencies. In poverty, as in certain propositions in physics, starting conditions are everything.

There are no secret economies that nourish the poor; on the contrary, there are a host of special costs. If you can't put up the two months' rent you need to secure an apartment, you end up paying through the nose for a room by the week. If you have only a room, with a hot plate at best, you can't save by cooking up huge lentil stews that can be frozen for the week ahead. You eat fast food, or the hot dogs and styrofoam cups of soup that can be microwaved in a convenience store. If you have no money for health insurance—and the Hearthside's niggardly plan kicks in only after three months—you go without routine care or prescription drugs and end up paying the price.

• • •

My own situation, when I sit down to assess it after two weeks of work, would not be much better if this were my actual life. The seductive thing about waitressing is that you don't have to wait for payday to feel a few bills in your pocket, and my tips usually cover meals and gas, plus something left over to stuff into the kitchen drawer I use as a bank. But as the tourist business slows in the summer heat, I sometimes leave work with only $20 in tips (the gross is higher, but servers share about 15 percent of their tips with the bus boys and bartenders). With wages included, this amounts to about the minimum wage of $5.15 an hour. Although the sum in the drawer is piling up, at the present rate of accumulation it will be more than a hundred dollars short of my rent when the end of the month comes around. Nor can I see any expenses to cut. True, I haven't gone the lentil-stew route yet, but that's because I don't have a large cooking pot, pot holders, or a ladle to stir with (which cost about $30 at Kmart, less at thrift stores), not to mention onions, carrots, and the indispensable bay leaf. I do make my lunch almost every day—usually some slow-burning, high-protein combo like frozen chicken patties with melted cheese on top and canned pinto beans on the side. Dinner is at the Hearthside, which offers its employees a choice of BLT, fish sandwich, or hamburger for only $2. The burger lasts longest, especially if it's heaped with gut-puckering jalapenos, but by midnight my stomach is growling again.

So unless I want to start using my car as a residence, I have to find a second, or alternative, job. Jerry's, which is part of a well-known national family restaurant chain and physically attached here to another budget hotel chain, is ready to use me at once. The prospect is both exciting and terrifying, because, with about the same number of tables and counter seats, Jerry's attracts three or four times the volume of customers as the gloomy old Hearthside.

Picture a fat person's hell, and I don't mean a place with no food. Instead there is everything you might eat if eating had no bodily consequences— cheese fries, chicken-fried steaks, fudge-laden desserts—only here every bite must be paid for, one way or another, in human discomfort. The kitchen is a cavern, a stomach leading to the lower intestine that is the garbage and dishwashing area, from which issue bizarre smells combining the edible and the offal: creamy carrion, pizza barf, and that unique and enigmatic Jerry's scent—citrus fart. The floor is slick with spills, forcing us to walk through the kitchen with tiny steps[.] ° ° ° Put your hand down on any counter and you risk being stuck to it by the film of ancient syrup spills, and this is unfortunate, because hands are utensils here, used for scooping up lettuce onto salad plates, lifting out pie slices, and even moving hash browns from one plate to another. The regulation poster in the single unisex restroom admonishes us to wash our hands thoroughly and even offers instructions for doing so, but there is always some vital substance missing—soap, paper towels, toilet paper—and I never find all three at once. You learn to stuff your pockets with napkins before going in there, and too bad about the customers, who must eat, though they don't realize this, almost literally out of our hands.

I start out with the beautiful, heroic idea of handling the two jobs at once, and for two days I almost do it: the breakfast/lunch shift at Jerry's, which goes till 2:00, arriving at the Hearthside at 2:10, and attempting to hold out until 10:00. In the ten minutes between jobs, I pick up a spicy chicken sandwich at the Wendy's drive-through window, gobble it down in the car, and change from khaki slacks to black, from Hawaiian to rust polo. There is a problem, though. When during the 3:00 to 4:00 P.M. dead time I finally sit down to wrap silver, my flesh seems to bond to the seat. I try to refuel with a purloined cup of soup, as I've seen Gail and Joan do dozens of times, but a manager catches me and hisses "No eating!" though there's not a customer around to be offended by the sight of food making contact with a server's lips.

I make friends, over time, with the other "girls" who work my shift: Nita, the tattooed twenty-something who taunts us by going around saying brightly, "Have we started making money yet?" Ellen, whose teenage son cooks on the graveyard shift and who once managed a restaurant in Massachusetts but won't try out for management here because she prefers being a "common worker" and not "ordering people around." Easy-going fiftyish Lucy, with the raucous laugh, who limps toward the end of the shift because of something that has gone wrong with her leg, the exact nature of which cannot be determined without health insurance. We talk about the usual girl things—men, children, and the sinister allure of Jerry's chocolate peanut-butter cream pie—though no one, I notice, every brings up anything potentially expensive, like shopping or movies. As at the Hearthside, the only recreation ever referred to is partying, which requires little more than some beer, a joint, and a few close friends. Still, no one here is homeless, or cops to it anyway, thanks usually to a working husband or boyfriend. All in all, we form a reliable mutual-support group: If one of us is feeling sick or overwhelmed, another one will "bev" a table or even carry trays for her. If one of us is off sneaking a cigarette or a pee, the others will do their best to conceal her absence from the enforcers of corporate rationality.

I make the decision to move closer to Key West. First, because of the drive. Second and third, also because of the drive: gas is eating up $4 to $5 a day, and although Jerry's is as high-volume as you can get, the tips average only 10 percent, and not just for a newbie like me. Between the base pay of $2.15 an hour and the obligation to share tips with the busboys and dishwashers, we're averaging only about $7.50 an hour. Then there is the $30 I had to spend on the regulation tan slacks worn by Jerry's servers—a setback it could take weeks to absorb. (I had combed the town's two downscale department stores hoping for something cheaper but decided in the end that these marked-down Dockers, originally $49, were more likely to survive a daily washing.) Of my fellow servers, everyone who lacks a working husband or boyfriend seems to have a second job: Nita does something at a computer eight hours a day; another welds. Without the forty-five minute commute, I can picture myself working two jobs and having the time to shower between them.

So I take the $500 deposit I have coming from my landlord, the $400 I have earned toward the next month's rent, plus the $200 reserved for emergencies, and use the $1,100 to pay the rent and deposit on trailer number 46 in the Overseas Trailer Park, a mile from the cluster of budget hotels that constitute Key West's version of an industrial park. Number 46 is about eight feet in width and shaped like a barbell inside, with a narrow region—because of the sink and the stove—separating the bedroom from what might optimistically be called the "living" area, with its two-person table and half-sized couch. The bathroom is so small my knees rub against the shower stall when I sit on the toilet, and you can't just leap out of the bed, you have to climb down to the foot of it in order to find a patch of floor space to stand on. Outside, I am within a few yards of a liquor store, a bar that advertises "free beer tomorrow," a convenience store, and a Burger King—but no supermarket or, alas, laundromat. By reputation, the Overseas park is a net of crime and crack, and I am hoping at least for some vibrant, multicultural street life. But desolation rules night and day, except for a thin stream of pedestrian traffic heading for their jobs at the Sheraton or 7-Eleven. There are not exactly people here but what amounts to canned labor, being preserved from the heat between shifts.

When my month-long plunge into poverty is almost over, I finally land my dream job—housekeeping. I do this by walking into the personnel office of the only place I figure I might have some credibility, the hotel attached to Jerry's, and confiding urgently that I have to have a second job if I am to pay my rent and, no, it couldn't be front-desk clerk. "All right," the personnel lady fairly spits, "So it's housekeeping," and she marches me back to meet Maria, the housekeeping manager, a tiny, frenetic Hispanic woman who greets me as "babe" and hands me a pamphlet emphasizing the need for a positive attitude. The hours are nine in the morning til whenever, the pay is $6.10 an hour, and there's one week of vacation a year. I don't have to ask about health insurance once I meet Carlotta, the middle-aged African-American woman who will be training me. Carla, as she tells me to call her, is missing all of her top front teeth.

On that first day of housekeeping and last day of my entire project—although I don't yet know it's the last—Carla is in a foul mood. We have been given nineteen rooms to clean, most of them "checkouts," as opposed to "stayovers," that require the whole enchilada of bed-stripping, vacuuming, and bathroom-scrubbing. For four hours without a break I strip and remake beds, taking about four and half minutes per queen-sized bed, which I could get down to three if there were any reason to. We try to avoid vacuuming by picking up the larger specks by hand, but often there is nothing to do but drag the monstrous vacuum cleaner—it weighs about thirty pounds—off our cart and try to wrestle it around the floor. Sometimes Carla hands me the squirt bottle of "BAM" (an acronym for something that begins, ominously, with "butyric"; the rest has been worn off the label) and lets me do the bathrooms. No service ethic challenges me here to new heights of performance. I just concentrate on removing the pubic hairs from the bathtubs, or at least the dark ones that I can see.

I had looked forward to the breaking-and-entering aspect of cleaning the stay-overs, the chance to examine the secret, physical existence of strangers. But the contents of the rooms are always banal and surprisingly neat—zipped up shaving kits, shoes lined up against the wall (there are no closets), flyers for snorkeling trips, maybe an empty wine bottle or two. It is the TV that keeps us going, from *Jerry* to *Sally* to *Hawaii Five-O* and then on to the soaps. If there's something especially arresting, like "Won't Take No for an Answer" on *Jerry,* we sit down on the edge of a bed and giggle for a moment as if this were a pajama party instead of a terminally dead-end job. The soaps are the best, and Carla turns the volume up full blast so that she won't miss anything from the bathroom or while the vacuum is on. In room 503, Marcia confronts Jeff about Lauren. In 505, Lauren taunts poor cuckolded Marcia. In 511, Helen offers Amanda $10,000 to stop seeing Eric, prompting Carla to emerge from the bathroom to study Amanda's troubled face. "You take it, girl," she advises. "I would for sure."

The tourists' rooms that we clean and, beyond them, the far more expensively appointed interiors in the soaps, begin after a while to merge. We have entered a better world—a world of comfort where every day is a day off, waiting to be filled up with sexual intrigue. We, however, are only gatecrashers in this fantasy, forced to pay for our presence with backaches and perpetual thirst. The mirrors, and there are far too many of them in hotel rooms, contain the kind of person you would normally find pushing a shopping cart down a city street—bedraggled, dressed in a damp hotel polo shirt two sizes too large, and with sweat dribbling down her chin like drool. I am enormously relieved when Carla announces a half-hour meal break, but my appetite fades when I see that the bag of hot-dog rolls she has been carrying around on our cart is not trash salvaged from a checkout but what she has brought for her lunch.

When I request permission to leave at about 3:30, another housekeeper warns me that no one has so far succeeded in combining housekeeping at the hotel with serving at Jerry's: "Some kid did it once for five days, and you're no kid." With that helpful information in mind, I rush back to number 46, down four Advils (the name brand this time), shower, stooping to fit into the stall, and attempt to compose myself for the oncoming shift. So much for what Marx terms the "reproduction of labor power," meaning the things a worker has to do just so she'll be ready to work again. The only unforeseen obstacle to the smooth transition from job to job is that my tan Jerry's slacks, which had looked reasonably clean by 40-watt bulb last night when I hand-washed my Hawaiian shirt, prove by daylight to be mottled with ketchup and ranch-dressing stains. I spend most of my hour-long break between jobs attempting to remove the edible portions with a sponge and then drying the slacks over the hood of my car in the sun.

I can do this two-job thing, is my theory, if I can drink enough caffeine. At eight, Ellen and I grab a snack together standing at the mephitic end of the kitchen counter, but I can only manage two or three mozzarella sticks and lunch had been a mere handful of McNuggets. I am not tired at all, I assure myself, though it may be that there is simply no more "I" left to do the tiredness monitoring. What I would see, if I were more alert to the situation, is that the forces of destruction are already massing against me.

Then it comes, the perfect storm. Four of my tables fill up at once. Four tables is nothing for me now, but only so long as they are obligingly staggered. As I bev table 27, tables 25, 28, and 24 are watching enviously. As I bev 25, 24 glowers because their bevs haven't even been ordered. Twenty-eight is four yuppyish types, meaning everything on the side and agonizing instructions as to the chicken Caesars. Twenty-five is a middle-aged black couple, who complain, with some justice, that the iced tea isn't fresh and the tabletop is sticky. But table 24 is the meteorological event of the century: ten British tourists who seem to have made the decision to absorb the American experience entirely by mouth. Here everyone has at least two drinks—iced tea and milk shake, Michelob and water (with lemon slice, please)—and a huge promiscuous orgy of breakfast specials, mozz sticks, chicken strips, quesadillas, burgers with cheese and without, sides of hash browns with cheddar, with onions, with gravy, seasoned fries, plain fries, banana splits. Poor me! Because when I arrive with their first tray of food—after three prior trips just to refill bevs—Princess Di refuses to eat her chicken strips with her pancake-and-sausage special, since, as she now reveals, the strips were meant to be an appetizer. Maybe the others would have accepted their meals, but Di, who is deep into her third Michelob, insists that everything else go back while they work on their "starters." Meanwhile, the yuppies are waving me down for more decaf and the black couple looks ready to summon the NAACP.

Much of what happened next is lost in the fog of war. The little printer on the counter in front of him is spewing out orders faster than he can rip them off, much less produce the meals. Even the invincible Ellen is ashen from stress. I bring table 24 their reheated main courses, which they immediately reject as either too cold or fossilized by the microwave. When I return to the kitchen with their trays (three trays in three trips), Joy confronts me with arms akimbo: "What is this?" She means the food—the plates of rejected pancakes, hash browns in assorted flavors, toasts, burgers, sausages, eggs. "Uh, scrambled with cheddar." I try, "and that's . . ." "NO," she screams in my face. "Is it a traditional, a super-scramble, an eye-opener?" I pretend to study my check for a clue, but entropy has been up to its tricks, not only on the plates but in my head, and I have to admit that the original order is beyond reconstruction. "You don't know an eye-opener from a traditional?" she demands in outrage.

I leave. I don't walk out, I just leave. I don't finish my side work or pick up my credit-card tips, if any, at the cash register or, of course, ask Joy's permission to go. And the surprising thing is that you can walk out without permission, that the door opens, that the thick tropical night air parts to let me pass, that my car is still parked where I left it. There is no vindication in this exit, just an overwhelming, dark sense of failure pressing down on me and the entire parking lot. I had gone into this venture in the spirit of science, to test a mathematical proposition, but somewhere along the line, in the tunnel vision imposed by long shifts and relentless concentration, it became a test of myself, and clearly I have failed.

In one month, I had earned approximately $1,040 and spent $517 on food, gas, toiletries, laundry, phone, and utilities. If I had remained in my $500 efficiency, I would have been able to pay the rent and have $22 left over (which is $78 less than the cash I had in my pocket at the start of the month). During this time I bought no clothing except for the required slacks and no prescription drugs or medical care (I did finally buy some vitamin B to compensate for the lack of vegetables in my diet). Perhaps I could have saved a little on food if I had gotten to a supermarket more often, instead of convenience stores, but it should be noted that I lost almost four pounds in four weeks, on a diet weighted heavily toward burgers and fries.

How former welfare recipients and single mothers will (and do) survive in the low-wage workforce, I cannot imagine. Maybe they will figure out how to condense their lives—including child-raising, laundry, romance, and meals—into the couple of hours between full-time jobs. Maybe they will take up residence in their vehicles, if they have one. All I know is that I couldn't hold two jobs and I couldn't make enough money to live on with one. And I had advantages unthinkable to many of the long-term poor—health, stamina, a working car, and no children to care for and support. Certainly nothing in my experience contradicts the conclusion of Kathryn Edin and Laura Lein, in their book *Making Ends Meet: How Single Mothers Survive Welfare and Low-Wage Work*, that low-wage work actually involves more hardship and deprivation than life at the mercy of the welfare state. In the coming months and years, economic conditions for the working poor are bound to worsen, even without the almost inevitable recession. As mentioned earlier, the influx of former welfare recipients into the low-skilled workforce will have a depressing effect on both wages and the number of jobs available. A general economic downturn will only enhance these effects, and the working poor will of course be facing it without the slight, but nonetheless often saving, protection of welfare as a backup.

The thinking behind welfare reform was that even the humblest jobs are morally uplifting and psychologically buoying. In reality they are likely to be fraught with insult and stress. But I did discover one redeeming feature of the most abject low-wage work—the camaraderie of people who are, in almost all cases, far too smart and funny and caring for the work they do and the wages they're paid. The hope, of course, is that someday these people will come to know what they're worth, and take appropriate action.

37 The American Family

STEPHANIE COONTZ

"Marriage and family are going to hell in a handbasket." From time to time, I hear statements like this. Although I may not be sure how marriage and family got in a handbasket, the meaning of this statement is clear: Gloom and doom. Frustration and anxiety. Things are getting worse fast. Husbands and wives are fighting, and as they tear at each other, marriages are falling apart and kids are neglected. The divorce court is filled to capacity, and families are filled with abuse. The situation is so dire that young people are postponing the day they marry longer than at any previous period in our history. When they do marry, they are "trying it out"—usually after they have tested the relationship by "trying" cohabitation.

Not long ago, in contrast, marriages were happy, and family life for both spouses and children was fulfilling. Members of the family shared goals and worked together in harmony. Parents spent more time with each other and with their children. Ah, if only we could go back to those idyllic times and have marriage and family life like that again. So goes the reasoning—its assumptions usually unquestioned. But were marriage and family life in the past so happy and satisfying? As Coontz points out in this selection, such reconstructions of the past are based not on fact but on myth, on some common but mistaken assumptions of the way things used to be.

. . . [M]any observers fear for the future of America's families. Our divorce rate is the highest in the world, and the percentage of unmarried women is significantly higher than in 1960. Educated women are having fewer babies, while immigrant children flood the schools, demanding to be taught in their native language. Harvard University reports that only 4 percent of its applicants can write a proper sentence.

There's an epidemic of sexually transmitted diseases among men. Many streets in urban neighborhoods are littered with cocaine vials. Youths call heroin "happy dust." Even in small towns, people have easy access to addictive drugs, and drug abuse by middle-class wives is skyrocketing. Police see 16-year-old killers, 12-year-old prostitutes, and gang members as young as 11.

America today? No, America at the end of the 1890s.

The litany of complaints may sound familiar, but the truth is that many things were worse a [hundred years ago] than they are today. Then, thousands of children worked full-time in mines, mills, and sweatshops. Most workers labored 10 hours a day, often six days a week, which left them little time or energy for family life. Race riots were more frequent and more deadly than those experienced by recent generations. Women couldn't vote, and their wages were so low that many turned to prostitution.

In 1890 a white child had one chance in three of losing a brother or sister before age 15, and a black child had a fifty-fifty chance of seeing a sibling die. Children's-aid groups reported widespread abuse and neglect by parents. Men who deserted or divorced their wives rarely paid child support. And only 6 percent of the children graduated from high school, compared with 88 percent today.

Why do so many people think American families are facing worse problems now than in the past? Partly it's because we compare [today's] complex and diverse families with the seemingly more standard-issue ones of the 1950s, a unique decade when every long-term trend of the 20th century was temporarily reversed. In the 1950s, for the first time in 100 years, the divorce rate fell while marriage and fertility rates soared, creating a boom in nuclear-family living. The percentage of foreign-born individuals in the country decreased. And the debates over social and cultural issues that had divided Americans for 150 years were silenced, suggesting a national consensus on family values and norms.

Some nostalgia for the 1950s is understandable: Life looked pretty good in comparison with the hardship of the Great Depression and World War II. The GI Bill gave a generation of young fathers a college education and a subsidized mortgage on a new house. For the first time, a majority of men could support a family and buy a home without pooling their earnings with those of other family members. Many Americans built a stable family life on these foundations.

But much nostalgia for the 1950s is a result of selective amnesia—the same process that makes childhood memories of summer vacations grow sunnier with each passing year. The superficial sameness of 1950s family life was achieved through censorship, coercion, and discrimination. People with unconventional beliefs faced governmental investigation and arbitrary firings. African Americans and Mexican Americans were prevented from voting in some states by literacy tests that were not administered to whites. Individuals who didn't follow the rigid gender and sexual rules of the day were ostracized.

Leave It to Beaver did not reflect the real-life experience of most American families. While many moved into the middle class during the 1950s, poverty remained more widespread than in the worst of our last three recessions. More children went hungry, and poverty rates for the elderly were more than twice as high as today's.

Even in the white middle class, not every woman was as serenely happy with her lot as June Cleaver was on TV. Housewives of the 1950s may have been less rushed than today's working mothers, but they were more likely to suffer anxiety and depression. In many states, women couldn't serve on juries or get loans or credit cards in their own names.

And not every kid was as wholesome as Beaver Cleaver, whose mischievous antics could be handled by Dad at the dinner table. In 1955 alone, Congress discussed 200 bills aimed at curbing juvenile delinquency. Three years later, LIFE reported that urban teachers were being terrorized by their students. The drugs that were so freely available in 1900 had been outlawed, but many children grew up in families ravaged by alcohol and barbiturate abuse.

Rates of unwed childbearing tripled between 1940 and 1958, but most Americans didn't notice because unwed mothers generally left town, gave their babies up for adoption and returned home as if nothing had happened. Troubled youths were encouraged to drop out of high school. Mentally handicapped children were warehoused in institutions like the Home for Idiotic and Imbecilic Children in Kansas, where a woman whose sister had lived there for most of the 1950s once took me. Wives routinely told pollsters that being disparaged or ignored by their husbands was a normal part of a happier than-average marriage.

Denial extended to other areas of life as well. In the early 1900s, doctors refused to believe that the cases of gonorrhea and syphilis they saw in young girls could have been caused by sexual abuse. Instead, they reasoned, girls could get these diseases from toilet seats, a myth that terrified generations of mothers and daughters. In the 1950s, psychiatrists dismissed incest reports as Oedipal fantasies on the part of children.

Spousal rape was legal throughout the period and wife beating was not taken seriously by authorities. Much of what we now label child abuse was accepted as a normal part of parental discipline. Physicians saw no reason to question parents who claimed that their child's broken bones had been caused by a fall from a tree.

American Mirror

Muncie, Ind. (pop. 67,476), calls itself America's Hometown. But to generations of sociologists it is better known as America's Middle-town—the most studied place in the 20th century American land-scape. "Muncie has nothing extraordinary about it," says University of Virginia professor Theodore Caplow, which is why, for the past 75 years, researchers have gone there to observe the typical American family. Muncie's averageness first drew sociologists Robert and Helen Lynd in 1924. They returned in 1935 (their follow-up study was fea-tured in a LIFE photo essay by Margaret Bourke-White). And in 1976, armed with the Lynds' original questionnaire, Caplow launched yet another survey of the town's citizens.

Caplow discovered that family life in Muncie was much healthier in the 1970s than in the 1920s. Not only were husbands and wives com-municating more, but unlike married couples in the 1920s, they were also shopping, eating out, exercising, and going to movies and concerts together. More than 90 percent of Muncie's couples characterized their marriages as "happy" or "very happy." In 1929 the Lynds had de-scribed partnerships of a drearier kind, "marked by sober accommoda-tion of each partner to his share in the joint undertaking of children, paying off the mortgage and generally 'getting on.'"

Caplow's five-year study, which inspired a six-part PBS series, found that even though more moms were working outside the home, two thirds of them spent at least two hours a day with their children; in 1924 fewer than half did. In 1924 most children expected their mothers to be good cooks and housekeepers, and wanted their fathers to spend time with them and respect their opinions. Fifty years later, expectations of fathers were unchanged, but children wanted the same—time and respect—from their mothers.

—Sora Song

There are plenty of stresses in modern family life, but one reason they seem worse is that we no longer sweep them under the rug. Another is that we have higher expectations of parenting and marriage. That's a good thing. We're right to be concerned about inattentive parents, conflicted marriages, antisocial values, teen violence, and child abuse. But we need to realize that many of our worries reflect how much better we *want* to be, not how much better we *used* to be.

Fathers in intact families are spending more time with their children than at any other point in the past 100 years. Although the number of hours the average woman spends at home with her children has declined since the early 1900s, there has been a decrease in the number of children per family and an increase in individual attention to each child. As a result, mothers today, including working moms, spend almost twice as much time with each child as mothers did in the 1920s. People who raised children in the 1940s and 1950s typically report that their own adult children and grandchildren communicate far better with their kids and spend more time helping with homework than they did—even as they complain that other parents today are doing a worse job than in the past.

Despite the rise in youth violence from the 1960s to the early 1990s, America's children are also safer now than they've ever been. An infant was four times more likely to die in the 1950s than today. A parent then was three times more likely than a modern one to preside at the funeral of a child under the age of 15, and 27 percent more likely to lose an older teen to death.

If we look back over the last millennium, we can see that families have always been diverse and in flux. In each period, families have solved one set of problems only to face a new array of challenges. What works for a family in one economic and cultural setting doesn't work for a family in another. What's helpful at one stage of a family's life may be destructive at the next stage. If there is one lesson to be drawn from the last millennium of family history, it's that families are always having to play catch-up with a changing world.

Take the issue of working mothers. Families in which mothers spend as much time earning a living as they do raising children are nothing new. They were the norm throughout most of the last two millennia. In the 19th century, married women in the United States began a withdrawal from the workforce, but for most families this was made possible only by sending their children out to work instead. When child labor was abolished, married women began reentering the workforce in ever large numbers.

For a few decades, the decline in child labor was greater than the growth of women's employment. The result was an aberration: the male-breadwinner family. In the 1920s, for the first time, a bare majority of American children grew up in families where the husband provided all the income, the wife stayed home full-time, and they and their siblings went to school instead of work. During the 1950s, almost two thirds of children grew up in such families, an all-time high. Yet that same decade saw an acceleration of workforce participation by wives and mothers that soon made the dual-earner family the norm, a trend not likely to be reversed in the next century.

What's new is not that women make half their families' living, but that for the first time they have substantial control over their own income, along with the social freedom to remain single or to leave an unsatisfactory marriage. Also new is the declining proportion of their lives that people devote to rearing children, both because they have fewer kids and because they are living longer. Until about 1940, the typical marriage was broken by the death of one partner within a few years after the last child left home. Today, couples can look forward to spending more than two decades together after the children leave.

The growing length of time partners spend with only each other for company has made many individuals less willing to put up with an unhappy marriage, while women's economic independence makes it less essential for them to do so. It is no wonder that divorce has risen steadily since 1900. Disregarding a spurt in 1946, a dip in the 1950s, and another peak around 1980, the divorce rate is just where you'd expect to find it, based on the rate of increase from 1900 to 1950. Today, 40 percent of all marriages will end in divorce before a couple's 40th anniversary. Yet despite this high divorce rate, expanded life expectancies mean that more couples are reaching that anniversary than ever before.

Families and individuals in contemporary America have more life choices than in the past. That makes it easier for some to consider dangerous or unpopular options. But it also makes success easier for many families that never would have had a chance before—interracial, gay or lesbian, and single mother families, for example. And it expands horizons for most families.

Women's new options are good not just for themselves but for their children. While some people say that women who choose to work are selfish, it turns out that maternal self-sacrifice is not good for children. Kids do better when their mothers are happy with their lives, whether their satisfaction comes from being a full-time homemaker or from having a job.

Largely because of women's new roles at work, men are doing more at home. Although most men still do less housework than their wives, the gap has been halved since the 1960s. Today, 49 percent of couples say they share childcare equally, compared with 25 percent of 1985.

Men's greater involvement at home is good for their relationships with their parents, and also good for their children. Hands-on fathers make better parents than men who let their wives do all the nurturing and childcare: They raise sons who are more expressive and daughters who are more likely to do well in school, especially in math and science.

In 1900, life expectancy was 47 years, and only 4 percent of the population was 65 or older. Today, life expectancy is 76 years, and by 2025, about 20 percent of Americans will be 65 or older. For the first time, a generation of adults must plan for the needs of both their parents and their children. Most Americans are responding with remarkable grace. One in four households gives the equivalent of a full day a week or more in unpaid care to an aging relative, and more than half say they expect to do so in the next 10 years. Older people are less likely to be impoverished or incapacitated by illness than in the past, and they have more opportunity to develop a relationship with their grandchildren.

Even some of the choices that worry us the most are turning out to be manageable. Divorce rates are likely to remain high, but more non-custodial parents are staying in touch with their children. Child-support receipts are up. And a lower proportion of kids from divorced families are exhibiting problems than in earlier decades. Step-families are learning to maximize children's access to supportive adults rather than cutting them off from one side of the family.

Out-of-wedlock births are also high, however, and this will probably continue because the age of first marriage for women has risen to an all-time high of 25, almost five years above what it was in the 1950s. Women who marry at an older age are less likely to divorce, but they have more years when they are at risk—or at choice—for a nonmarital birth.

Nevertheless, births to teenagers has fallen from 50 percent of all nonmarital births in the late 1970s to just 30 percent today. A growing proportion of women who have a nonmarital birth are in their twenties and thirties and usually have more economic and educational resources than unwed mothers of the past. While two involved parents are generally better than one, a mother's personal maturity, along with her educational and economic status, is a better predictor of how well her child will turn out than her marital status. We should no longer assume that children raised by single parents face debilitating disadvantages.

As we begin to understand the range of sizes, shapes, and colors that today's families come in, we find that the differences *within* family types are more important than the differences *between* them. No particular family form guarantees success, and no particular form is doomed to fail. How a family functions on the inside is more important than how it looks from the outside.

The biggest problem facing most families is not that our families have changed too much but that our institutions have changed too little. America's work policies are 50 years out of date, designed for a time when most moms weren't in the workforce and most dads didn't understand the joys of being involved in childcare. Our school schedules are 150 years out of date, designed for a time when kids needed to be home to help with the milking and haying. And many political leaders feel they have to decide whether to help parents stay home longer with their kids or invest in better childcare, preschool, and afterschool programs, when most industrialized nations have long since learned it's possible to do both.

So America's social institutions have some bugs to iron out. But for the most part, our families are ready.

38 Giving Birth the American Way

ROBBIE E. DAVIS-FLOYD

Social institutions dominate our lives. Our family gives us our fundamental orientations to life, with this basic socialization process being shared with schools and, for many, also with religion. If we were to pick a single social institution as the one that dominates society and, along with it, our own lives, it would be economics. Because we have to work to make a living, we make our lives conform to the demands of this social institution: choosing college, courses, and a major that help us prepare for a career; meeting the rhythms and routines of work schedules; and performing the tasks required to get a paycheck. In this selection, we turn the emphasis on how social institutions have even taken over and modified what not long ago was considered a natural process in human life: giving birth.

Davis-Floyd, an anthropologist who specializes in research on birthing customs, examines what she calls "the American way of giving birth." Although many people take "the American way of giving birth" for granted, are all those medical devices really necessary? Why has giving birth so changed that no longer is it considered a natural event but, rather, has become something that depends on technology for it to be successful? What are the effects of the "technological ritual" that now enshrouds childbirth? Davis-Floyd grapples with these issues in this reading.

ALTHOUGH THE ARRAY OF NEW TECHNOLOGIES that alter the nature of human reproduction is exponentially increasing, childbirth is still a gendered phenomenon. Because only women have babies, the way society treats pregnancy and childbirth reveals a great deal about the way that society treats women. The experience of childbirth is unique for every woman, and yet in the United States childbirth is treated in a highly standardized way. No matter how long or short, how easy or hard their labors, the vast majority of American women are hooked up to an electronic fetal monitor and an IV (intravenously administered fluids and/or medication), are encouraged to use pain-relieving drugs, receive an episiotomy (a surgical incision in the vagina to widen the birth outlet in order to prevent tearing) at the moment of birth, and are separated from their babies shortly after birth. Most women also receive doses of the synthetic hormone pitocin to speed their labors, and they give birth flat on their backs. Nearly one-quarter of babies are delivered by Cesarean section.

Many Americans, including most of the doctors and nurses who attend birth, view these procedures as medical necessities. Yet anthropologists describe other, less technological ways to give birth. For example, the Mayan Indians of Highland Chiapas hold onto a rope while squatting for birth, a position that is far more beneficial than the flat-on-your-back-with-your-feet-in-stirrups (lithotomy) position. Mothers in many low-technology cultures give birth sitting, squatting, semi-reclining in their hammocks, or on their hands and knees, and are nurtured through the pain of labor by experienced midwives and supportive female relatives. What then might explain the standardization and technical elaboration of the American birthing process?

One answer [is] that in many societies around the world, major life transitions are ritualized. These cultural rites of passage make it appear that society itself effects the transformation of the individual. Could this explain the standardization of American birth? I believe the answer is yes.

I came to this conclusion as a result of interviewing over 100 mothers, as well as many of the obstetricians, nurses, childbirth educators, and midwives who attended them.[1] While poring over my interviews, I began to understand that the forces shaping American hospital birth are invisible to us because they stem from the conceptual foundations of our society. I realized that American society's deepest beliefs center on science, technology, patriarchy, and the institutions that control and disseminate them, and that there could be no better transmitter of these core values and beliefs than the hospital procedures so salient in American birth. Through these procedures, American women are repeatedly told, in dozens of visible and invisible ways, that their bodies are defective machines incapable of giving birth without the assistance of these other, male-created, more perfect machines.

Rites of Passage

A *ritual* is a patterned, repetitive, and symbolic enactment of a cultural belief or value; its primary purpose is alignment of the belief system of the individual with that of society. A *rite of passage* is a series of rituals that move individuals from one social state or status to another as, for example, from girlhood to womanhood, boyhood to manhood, or from the womb to the world of culture. Rites of passage transform both society's perception of individuals and individuals' perceptions of themselves.

Rites of passage generally consist of three stages, originally outlined by van Gennep: (1) *separation* of the individuals from their preceding social state; (2) a period of *transition* in which they are neither one thing nor the other; and (3) an *integration* phase, in which, through rites of incorporation, they are absorbed into their new social state. In the year-long pregnancy/childbirth rite of passage in American society, the separation phase begins with the woman's first awareness of pregnancy; the transition stage lasts until several days after the birth; and the integration phase ends gradually in the newborn's first few months of life, when the new mother begins to feel that, as one woman put it, she is "mainstreaming it again."

Victor Turner, an anthropologist famous for his writings on ritual, pointed out that the most important feature of all rites of passage is that they place their participants in a transitional realm that has few of the attributes of the past or coming state. Existing in such a non-ordinary realm, he argues, facilitates the gradual opening of the initiates to profound interior change. In many initiation rites involving major transitions into new social roles (such as military basic training), ritualized physical and mental hardships serve to break down initiates' belief systems, leaving them open to new learning and the construction of new cognitive categories.

Birth is an ideal candidate for ritualization of this sort, and is, in fact, used in many societies as a model for structuring other rites of passage. By making the naturally transformative process of birth into a cultural rite of passage, a society can ensure that its basic values will be transmitted to the three new members born out of the birth process: the new baby, the woman reborn into the new social role of mother, and the man reborn as father. The new mother especially must be clear about these values, as she is generally the one primarily responsible for teaching them to her children, who will be society's new members and the guarantors of its future.

The Characteristics of Ritual

Some primary characteristics of ritual are particularly relevant to understanding how the initiatory process of cognitive restructuring is accomplished in hospital birth. We will examine each of these characteristics in order to understand (1) how ritual works; (2) how the natural process of childbirth is transformed in the United States into a cultural rite of passage; and (3) how that transformation works to cement the patriarchal status quo.

SYMBOLISM

Above all else, ritual is symbolic. Ritual works by sending messages in the form of symbols to those who perform and those who observe it. A *symbol* is an object, idea, or action that is loaded with cultural meaning. The left hemisphere of the human brain decodes and analyzes straightforward verbal messages, enabling the recipient to either accept or reject their content. Complex ritual symbols, on the other hand, are received by the right hemisphere of the brain, where they are interpreted holistically. Instead of being analyzed intellectually, a symbol's message will be *felt* through the body and the emotions. Thus, even though recipients may be unaware of incorporating the symbol's message, its ultimate effect may be extremely powerful.

Routine obstetric procedures are highly symbolic. For example, to be seated in a wheelchair upon entering the hospital, as many laboring women are, is to receive through their bodies the symbolic message that they are disabled; to then be put to bed is to receive the symbolic message that they are sick. Although no one pronounces, "You are disabled; you are sick," such graphic demonstrations of disability and illness can be far more powerful than words. Suzanne Sampson told me:

> I can remember just almost being in tears by the way they would wheel you in. I would come into the hospital on top of this, breathing, you know, all in control. And they slap you in a wheelchair! It made me suddenly feel like maybe I wasn't in control any more.

The intravenous drips commonly attached to the hands or arms of birthing women make a powerful symbolic statement: They are umbilical cords to the hospital. The cord connecting her body to the fluid-filled bottle places the woman in the same relation to the hospital as the baby in her womb is to her. By making her dependent on the institution for her life, the IV conveys to her one of the most profound messages of her initiation experience: In American society, we are all dependent on institutions for our lives. The message is even more compelling in her case, for *she* is the real giver of life. Society and its institutions cannot exist unless women give birth, yet the birthing woman in the hospital is shown, not that she gives life, but rather that the institution does.

A COGNITIVE MATRIX

A *matrix* (from the Latin *mater,* mother), like a womb, is something from within which something else comes. Rituals are not arbitrary; they come from within the belief system of a group. Their primary purpose is to enact, and thereby, to transmit that belief system into the emotions, minds, and bodies of their participants. Thus, analysis of a culture's rituals can lead to a profound understanding of its belief system.

Analysis of the rituals of hospital birth reveals their cognitive matrix to be the *technocractic model* of reality which forms the philosophical basis of both Western biomedicine and American society. Its early forms were originally developed in the 1600s by Descartes, Bacon, and Hobbes, among others. This model assumes that the universe is mechanistic, following predictable laws that the enlightened can discover through science and manipulate through technology, in order to decrease their dependence on nature. In this model, the human body is viewed as a machine that can be taken apart and put back together to ensure proper functioning. In the seventeenth century, the practical utility of this body-as-machine metaphor lay in its separation of body, mind, and soul. The soul could be left to religion, the mind to the philosophers, and the body could be opened up to scientific investigation.

The dominant religious belief systems of Western Europe at that time held that women were inferior to men—closer to nature and feebler both in body and intellect. Consequently, the men who developed the idea of the body-as-machine also firmly established the male body as the prototype of this machine. Insofar as it deviated from the male standard, the female body was regarded as abnormal, inherently defective, and dangerously under the influence of nature.

The metaphor of the body-as-machine and the related image of the female body as a defective machine eventually formed the philosophical foundations of modern obstetrics. Wide cultural acceptance of these metaphors accompanied the demise of the midwife and the rise of the male-attended, mechanically manipulated birth. Obstetrics was thus enjoined by its own conceptual origins to develop tools and technologies for the manipulation and improvement of the inherently defective, and therefore anomalous and dangerous, process of birth.

The rising science of obstetrics ultimately accomplished this goal by adopting the model of the assembly-line production of goods as its template for hospital birth. Accordingly, a woman's reproductive tract came to be treated like a birthing machine by skilled technicians working under semi-flexible timetables to meet production and quality control demands. As one fourth-year resident observed:

> We shave 'em, we prep 'em, we hook 'em up to the IV and administer sedation. We deliver the baby, it goes to the nursery, and the mother goes to her room. There's no room for niceties around here. We just move 'em right on through. It's hard not to see it like an assembly line.

REPETITION AND REDUNDANCY

Ritual is marked by repetition and redundancy. For maximum effectiveness, a ritual concentrates on sending one basic set of messages, repeating it over and over again in different forms. Hospital birth takes place in a series of ritual procedures, many of which convey the same message in different forms. The open and exposing hospital gown, the ID bracelet, the intravenous fluid, the bed in which she is placed—all these convey to the laboring woman that she is dependent on the institution.

She is also reminded in myriad ways of the potential defectiveness of her birthing machine. These include periodic and sometimes continuous electronic monitoring of that machine, frequent manual examinations of her cervix to make sure that it is dilating on schedule, and, if it isn't, administration of the synthetic hormone pitocin to speed up labor so that birth can take place within the required 26 hours.[2] All three of these procedures convey the same messages over and over: *Time is important, you must produce on time, and you cannot do that without technological assistance because your machine is defective.* In the technocracy, we supervalue time. It is only fitting that messages about time's importance should be repeatedly conveyed during the births of new social members.

COGNITIVE REDUCTION

Ritual utilizes specific techniques, such as rhythmic repetition to reduce all participants to the same narrower level of cognitive functioning. This low level involves thinking in either/or patterns that do not allow for consideration of options or alternative views.

Four techniques are often employed by ritual to accomplish this end. One is the *repetition* already discussed above. A second is *hazing,* which is familiar to undergraduates who undergo fraternity initiation rites but is also part of rites of passage all over the world. A third is *strange-making*—making the commonplace appear strange by juxtaposing it with the unfamiliar. Fourth is *symbolic inversion*—metaphorically turning things upside-down and inside-out to generate, in a phrase coined by Roger Abrahams (1973), "The power attendant upon confusion."

For example, in the rite of passage of military basic training, the initiate's normal patterns of action and thought are turned topsy-turvy. He is made strange to himself: His head is shaved, so that he does not even recognize himself in the mirror. He must give up his clothes, those expressions of his past individual identity and personality, and put on a uniform identical to that of the other initiates. Constant and apparently meaningless hazing, such as orders to dig six ditches and then fill them in, further breaks down his cognitive structure. Then through repetitive and highly symbolic rituals, such as sleeping with his rifle, the basic values, beliefs, and practices of the Marines are incorporated into his body and his mind.

In medical school and again in residency, the same ritual techniques that transform a youth into a Marine are employed to transform college students into physicians. Reduced from the high status of graduate to the lowly status of first-year medical student, initiates are subjected to hazing techniques of rote memorization of endless facts and formulas, absurdly long hours of work, and intellectual and sensory overload. As one physician explained:

> You go through, in a six-week course, a thousand-page book. You have pop quizzes in two or three courses every day the first year. We'd get up around 6, attend classes till 5, go home and eat, then head back to school and be in anatomy lab working with a cadaver, or something, until 1 or 2 in the morning, and then go home and get a couple of hours sleep, and then go out again.

Subjected to such a process, medical students often gradually lose any broadminded goals of "helping humanity" they had upon entering medical school. A successful rite of passage produces new professional values structured in accordance with the technocractic and scientific values of the dominant medical system. The emotional impact of this cognitive narrowing is aptly summarized by a former resident:

> Most of us went into medical school with pretty humanitarian ideals. I know I did. But the whole process of medical education makes you inhuman . . . you forget about the rest of life. By the time you get to residency, you end up not caring about anything beyond the latest techniques and most sophisticated tests.

Likewise, the birthing woman is socialized by ritual techniques of cognitive reduction. She is made strange to herself by being dressed in a hospital gown, tagged with an ID bracelet, and by the shaving or clipping of her pubic hair, which symbolically de-sexualizes the lower portion of her body, returning it to a conceptual state of childishness. (In many cultures, sexuality and hair are symbolically linked.) Labor itself is painful, and is often rendered more so by the hazing technique of frequent and very painful insertion of someone's fingers into her vagina to see how far her cervix has dilated. This technique also functions as a strange-making device. Since almost any nurse or resident in need of practice may check her cervix, the birthing woman's most private parts are symbolically inverted into institutional property. One respondent's obstetrician observed, "It's a wonder you didn't get an infection, with so many people sticking their hands inside of you."

ORDER, FORMALITY, AND A SENSE OF INEVITABILITY

Its exaggerated and precise order and formality set ritual apart from other modes of social interaction, enabling it to establish an atmosphere that feels both inevitable and inviolate. To perform a series of rituals is to feel oneself locking onto a set of "cosmic gears" that will safely crank the individual through danger to safety. For example, Trobriand sea fishermen described by anthropologist Bronislaw Malinowski (1954) regularly performed an elaborate series of rituals on the beach before embarking. The fishermen believed that these rituals, when carried out with precision, would obligate the gods of the sea to do their part to bring the fishermen safely home. Likewise, obstetricians, and many birthing women, feel that correct performance of standardized procedures ought to result in a healthy baby. Such rituals generate in humans a sense of confidence that makes it easier to face the challenge and caprice of nature.

However, once those "cosmic gears" have been set into motion, there is often no stopping them. The very inevitability of hospital procedures makes them almost antithetical to the possibility of normal, natural birth. A "cascade of intervention" occurs when one obstetric procedure alters the natural birthing process, causing complications, and so inexorably "necessitates" the next procedure, and the next.

Many of the women in my study experienced such a "cascade" when they received some form of pain relief, such as an epidural, which slowed their labor. Then pitocin was administered through the IV to speed up the labor, but pitocin very suddenly induced longer and stronger contractions. Unprepared for the additional pain, the women asked for more pain relief, which ultimately necessitated more pitocin. Pitocin-induced contractions, together with the fact that the mother must lie flat on her back because of the electronic monitor belts strapped around her stomach, can cause the supply of blood and oxygen to the fetus to drop, affecting the fetal heart rate. In response to the "distress" registered on the fetal monitor, an emergency Cesarean is performed.

COGNITIVE TRANSFORMATION

The goal of most initiatory rites of passage is cognitive transformation. It occurs when the symbolic messages of ritual fuse with individual emotion and belief.

Cognitive transformation of the initiate occurs when reality as presented by the technocratic model, and reality as the initiate perceives it, become one and the same. This process is gradual. Routine obstetric procedures cumulatively map the technocratic model of birth onto the birthing woman's perceptions of her labor experience. They align her belief system with that of society.

Take the way many mothers come to think about the electronic fetal monitor, for example. The monitor is a machine that uses ultrasound to measure the strength of the mother's contractions and the rate of the baby's heartbeat through electrodes belted onto the mother's abdomen. This machine has become the symbol of high technology hospital birth. Observers and participants alike report that the monitor, once attached, becomes the focal point of the labor.[3] Nurses, physicians, husbands, and even the mother herself become visually and conceptually glued to the machine, which then shapes their perceptions and interpretations of the birth process. Diana Crosse described her experience this way:

> As soon as I got hooked up to the monitor, all everyone did was stare at it. The nurses didn't even look at me anymore when they came into the room—they went straight to the monitor. I got the weirdest feeling that *it* was having the baby, not me.

Consider the visual and kinesthetic images that the laboring woman experiences—herself in bed, in a hospital gown, staring up at an IV pole, bag, and cord, and down at a steel bed and a huge belt encircling her waist. Her entire sensory field conveys one overwhelming message about our culture's deepest values and beliefs: Technology is supreme, and the individual is utterly dependent upon it.

Internalizing the technocratic model, women come to accept the notion that the female body is inherently defective. This notion then shapes their perceptions of the labor experience, as exemplified by Merry Simpson's story:

> It seemed as though my uterus had suddenly tired! When the nurses in attendance noted a contraction building on the recorder, they instructed me to begin pushing, not waiting for the urge to push, so that by the time the *urge* pervaded, I invariably had no strength remaining but was left gasping and dizzy. . . . I felt suddenly depressed by the fact that labor, which had progressed so uneventfully up to this point, had now become unproductive.

Note that she does not say "The nurses had me pushing too soon," but "My uterus had tired," and labor had "become unproductive." These responses reflect her internalization of the technocratic tenet that when something goes wrong, it is her body's fault.

AFFECTIVITY AND INTENSIFICATION

Rituals tend to intensify toward a climax. Behavioral psychologists have long understood that people are far more likely to remember, and to absorb lessons from, those events that carry an emotional charge. The order and stylization of ritual, combined with its rhythmic repetitiveness and the intensification of its messages, methodically create just the sort of highly charged emotional atmosphere that works to ensure long-term learning.

As the moment of birth approaches, the number of ritual procedures performed upon the woman will intensify toward the climax of birth, whether or not her condition warrants such intervention. For example, once the woman's cervix reaches full dilation (10 cm), the nursing staff immediately begins to exhort the woman to push with each contraction, whether or not she actually feels the urge to push. When delivery is imminent, the woman must be transported, often with a great deal of drama and haste, down the hall to the delivery room. Lest the baby be born *en route,* the laboring woman is then exhorted, with equal vigor, *not* to push. Such commands constitute a complete denial of the natural rhythms of the woman's body. They signal that her labor is a mechanical event and that she is subordinate to the institution's expectations and schedule. Similar high drama will pervade the rest of her birthing experience.

PRESERVATION OF THE STATUS QUO

A major function of ritual is cultural preservation. Through explicit enactment of a culture's belief system, ritual works both to preserve and to transmit the culture. Preserving the culture includes perpetuating its power structure, so it is usually the case that those in positions of power will have unique control over ritual performance. They will utilize the effectiveness of ritual to reinforce both their own importance and the importance of the belief and value system that legitimizes their positions.

Despite tremendous advances in equality for women, the United States is still a patriarchy. It is no cultural accident that 99 percent of American women give birth in hospitals, where only physicians, most of whom are male, have final authority over the performance of birth rituals—an authority that reinforces the cultural privileging of patriarchy for both mothers and their medical attendants.

Nowhere is this reality more visible than in the lithotomy position. Despite years of effort on the part of childbirth activists, including many obstetricians, the majority of American women still give birth lying flat on their backs. This position is physiologically dysfunctional. It compresses major blood vessels, lowering the mother's circulation and thus the baby's oxygen supply. It increases the need for forceps because it both narrows the pelvic outlet and ensures that the baby, who must follow the curve of the birth canal, quite literally will be born heading upward, against gravity. This lithotomy position completes the process of symbolic inversion that has been in motion ever since the woman was put into that "upside-down" hospital gown. Her normal bodily patterns are turned, quite literally, upside-down—her legs are in the air, her vagina totally exposed. As the ultimate symbolic inversion, it is ritually appropriate that this position be reserved for the peak transformational moments of the initiation experience—the birth itself. The doctor—society's official representative—stands in control not at the mother's head or at her side, but at her bottom, where the baby's head is beginning to emerge.

Structurally speaking, this puts the woman's vagina where her head should be. Such total inversion is perfectly appropriate from a social perspective, as the technocratic model promises us that eventually we will be able to grow babies in machines—that is, have them with our cultural heads instead of our natural bottoms. In our culture, "up" is good and "down" is bad, so the babies born of science and technology must be delivered "up" toward the positively valued cultural world, instead of down toward the negatively valued natural world. Interactionally, the obstetrician is "up" and the birthing woman is "down," an inversion that speaks eloquently to her of her powerlessness and of the power of society at the supreme moment of her own individual transformation.

The episiotomy performed by the obstetrician just before birth also powerfully enacts the status quo in American society. This procedure, performed on over 90 percent of first-time mothers as they give birth, expresses the value and importance of one of our technocratic society's most fundamental markers—the straight line. Through episiotomies, physicians can deconstruct the vagina (stretchy, flexible, part-circular and part-formless, feminine, creative, sexual, non-linear), then reconstruct it in accordance with our cultural belief and value system. Doctors are taught (incorrectly) that straight cuts heal faster than the small jagged tears that sometimes occur during birth. They learn that straight cuts will prevent such tears, but in fact, episiotomies often cause severe tearing that would not otherwise occur (Klein 1992; Shiono et al. 1990; Thorp and Bowes 1989; Wilcox et al. 1989[4]). These teachings dramatize our Western belief in the superiority of culture over nature. Because it virtually does not exist in nature, the line is most useful in aiding us in our constant conceptual efforts to separate ourselves from nature.

Moreover, since surgery constitutes the ultimate form of manipulation of the human body-machine, it is the most highly valued form of medicine. Routinizing the episiotomy, and increasingly, the Cesarean section, has served both to legitimize and to raise the status of obstetrics as a profession, by ensuring that childbirth will be not a natural but a surgical procedure.

EFFECTING SOCIAL CHANGE

Nine percent of my interviewees entered the hospital determined to avoid technocratic rituals in order to have "completely natural childbirth," yet ended up with highly technocratic births. These nine women experienced extreme cognitive dissonance between their previously held self-images and those internalized in the hospital. Most of them suffered severe emotional wounding and short-term post-partum depression as a result.

But 15 percent did achieve their goal of natural childbirth, thereby avoiding conceptual fusion with the technocratic model. These women were personally empowered by their birth experiences. They tended to view technology as a resource that they could choose to utilize or ignore, and often consciously subverted their socialization process by replacing technocratic symbols with self-empowering alternatives. For example, they wore their own clothes and ate their own food, rejecting the hospital gown and the IV. They walked the halls instead of going to bed. They chose perineal massage instead of episiotomy, and gave birth like "primitives," sitting up, squatting, or on their hands and knees. One of them, confronted with the wheelchair, said "I don't need this," and used it as a luggage cart. This rejection of customary ritual elements is an exceptionally powerful way to induce change, as it takes advantage of an already charged and dramatic situation.

The conceptual hegemony of the technocratic model in the hospital [has been] challenged by the natural childbirth movement which these 24 women represent. Birth activists succeeded in getting hospitals to allow fathers into labor and delivery rooms, mothers to birth consciously (without being put to sleep), and mothers and babies to room together after birth. They fought for women to have the right to birth without drugs or interventions, to walk around or even be in water during labor (in some hospitals, Jacuzzis were installed).

Six of my interviewees (6 percent) rejected the technocratic model altogether. They chose to give birth at home under an alternative paradigm, the *holistic model*. This model stresses the organicity and trustworthiness of the female body, the natural rhythmicity of labor, the integrity of the family, and self-responsibility. These homebirthers see the safety of the baby and the emotional needs of the mother as one. The safest birth for the baby will be the one that provides the most nurturing environment for the mother.[5] Said Ryla,

> I got criticized for choosing a home birth, for not considering the safety of the baby. But that's exactly what I was considering! How could it possibly serve my baby for me to give birth in a place that causes my whole body to tense up in anxiety as soon as I walk in the door?

Although homebirthers constitute only about 2 percent of the American birthing population, their conceptual importance is tremendous, as through the alternative rituals of giving birth at home, they enact—and thus guarantee the existence of—a paradigm of pregnancy and birth based on the value of connection, just as the technocratic model is based on the principle of separation.

Conclusion

The technocratic and holistic models represent opposite ends of a spectrum of beliefs about birth and about cultural life. Their differences are mirrored on a wider scale by the ideological conflicts between biomedicine and holistic healing, and between industrialists and ecological activists. These groups are engaged in a core value struggle over the future—a struggle clearly visible in the profound differences in the rituals they daily enact.

Women have made great strides in attaining equality with men on many cultural fronts. Yet, as I noted at the beginning, the cultural treatment of birth is one of the most revealing indicators about the status of women in a given society. In the United States, through their ritual transformation during birth, women learn profound lessons about the weakness and defectiveness of their bodies and the power of technology. In this way, every day in hospitals all over the country, women's status as subordinate is subtly reinforced, as is the patriarchal nature of the technocracy.

Notes

1. The full results of this study appear in Davis-Floyd 1992.

2. In Holland, by way of contrast, most births are attended by midwives who recognize that individual labors have individual rhythms. They can stop and start; can take a few hours or several days. If labor slows, the midwives encourage the woman to eat to keep up her strength, and then to sleep until contractions pick up again (Beatriz Smulders, Personal Communication, 1994; Jordan 1993).

3. As is true for most of the procedures interpreted here as rituals, there is no scientific justification for the routine use of the electronic fetal monitor: Numerous large-scale studies have shown no improvement in outcome (Leveno et al. 1986; Prentice and Lind 1987; Sandmire 1990; Shy et al. 1990). What these studies do show is that a dramatic increase in the rate of Cesarean section accompanies routine electronic monitoring. Most commonly, this increase is due both to the occasional malfunctioning of the machine, which sometimes registers fetal distress when there

is none, and to the tendency of hospital staff to overreact to fluctuations on the monitor strip.

4. See Goer 1995:274–284 for summaries and interpretations of these studies and others concerning electronic fetal monitoring.

5. For summaries of studies that demonstrate the safety of planned, midwife-attended home birth relative to hospital birth, see Davis-Floyd 1992, Chapter 4, and Goer 1995.

39 Kindergarten as Academic Boot Camp

HARRY L. GRACEY

As we have seen in the preceding Parts, each society (and each group) maintains a vital interest in making its members conform to expectations. A major social institution for which conformity is a primary goal is education. Educators want to graduate people who are acceptable to the community, not only in terms of marketable skills but also in terms of their ideas, attitudes, and behaviors. Whether it be grade school, high school, or college, educational administrators want instructors to teach standard ideas and facts, to steer clear of radical politics, and to not stir up trouble in the school or community. *Then* the social institution can go about its business—and that business, when you probe beneath official utterances and uncover the *hidden curriculum,* is producing conformists who fit well in society.

Although Gracey's focus is kindergarten, this article was chosen to represent the educational institution because it focuses on this essential nature of education, training in conformity. The primary goal of kindergarten is to teach children to be students—so they can participate in conformity. If this is what education really is about, where are intellectual stimulation, the excitement of discovery, and creativity—long associated in the public mind with education? The answer is that they may occur so long as they are noncontroversial. In other words, even discovery and creativity are expected to reflect the conformist nature of the educational institution.

Based on your own extensive experiences with education, how do you react to the idea that the essence of the educational institution is training into conformity?

EDUCATION MUST BE CONSIDERED one of the major institutions of social life today. Along with the family and organized religion, however, it is a "secondary institution," one in which people are prepared for life in society as it is presently organized. The main dimensions of modern life, that is, the nature of society as a whole, are determined principally by the "primary institutions," which today are the economy, the political system, and the military establishment. Education has been defined by sociologists, classical and contemporary, as an institution which serves society by socializing people into it through a formalized, standardized procedure. At the beginning of the last century Emile Durkheim told student teachers at the University of Paris that education "consists of a methodical socialization of the younger generation." He went on to add:

> It is the influence exercised by adult generations on those that are not ready for social life. Its object is to arouse and to develop in the child a certain number of physical, intellectual, and moral states that are demanded of him by the political society as a whole and by the special milieu for which he is specifically destined. . . . To the egotistic and asocial being that has just been born, [society] must, as rapidly as possible, add another, capable of leading a moral and social life. Such is the work of education.[1]

The education process, Durkheim said, "is above all the means by which society perpetually recreates the conditions of its very existence."[2] The contemporary educational sociologist Wilbur Brookover offers a similar formulation in his recent textbook definition of education:

> Actually, therefore, in the broadest sense education is synonymous with socialization. It includes any social behavior that assists in the induction of the child into membership in the society or any behavior by which the society perpetuates itself through the next generation.[3]

The educational institution is, then, one of the ways in which society is perpetuated through the systematic socialization of the young, while the nature of the society which is being perpetuated—its organization and operation, its values, beliefs, and ways of living—are determined by the primary institutions. The educational system, like other secondary institutions, *serves* the society which is *created* by the operation of the economy, the political system, and the military establishment.

Schools, the social organizations of the educational institution, are today for the most part large bureaucracies run by specially trained and certified people. There are few places left in modern societies where formal teaching and learning are carried on in small, isolated groups, like the rural, one-room schoolhouses of [the 1800s]. Schools are large, formal organizations which tend to be parts of larger organizations, local community School Districts. These School Districts are bureaucratically organized and their operations are supervised by state and local governments. In this context, as Brookover says:

> The term education is used . . . to refer to a system of schools, in which specif-
> ically designated persons are expected to teach children and youth certain
> types of acceptable behavior. The school system becomes a . . . unit in the total
> social structure and is recognized by the members of the society as a separate
> social institution. Within this structure a portion of the total socialization pro-
> cess occurs.[4]

Education is the part of the socialization process which takes place in
the schools; and these are, more and more today, bureaucracies within
bureaucracies.

Kindergarten is generally conceived by educators as a year of preparation for school. It is thought of as a year in which small children, five or six
years old, are prepared socially and emotionally for the academic learning
which will take place over the next twelve years. It is expected that a foundation of behavior and attitudes will be laid in kindergarten on which the
children can acquire the skills and knowledge they will be taught in the
grades. A booklet prepared for parents by the staff of a suburban New York
school system says that the kindergarten experience will stimulate the
child's desire to learn and cultivate the skills he will need for learning in the
rest of his school career. It claims that the child will find opportunities for
physical growth, for satisfying his "need for self-expression," acquire some
knowledge, and provide opportunities for creative activity. It concludes,
"The most important benefit that your five-year-old will receive from
kindergarten is the opportunity to live and grow happily and purposefully
with others in a small society." The kindergarten teachers in one of the elementary schools in this community, one we shall call the Wilbur Wright
School, said their goals were to see that the children "grew" in all ways: physically, of course, emotionally, socially, and academically. They said they
wanted children to like school as a result of their kindergarten experiences
and that they wanted them to learn to get along with others.

None of these goals, however, is unique to kindergarten; each of them is
held to some extent by teachers in the other six grades at Wright School. And
growth would occur, but differently, even if the child did not attend school.
The children already know how to get along with others, in their families and
their play groups. The unique job of the kindergarten in the educational division of labor seems rather to be teaching children the student role. The
student role is the repertoire of behavior and attitudes regarded by educators as appropriate to children in school. Observation in the kindergartens of
the Wilbur Wright School revealed a great variety of activities through
which children are shown and then drilled in the behavior and attitudes defined as appropriate for school and thereby induced to learn the role of student. Observations of the kindergartens and interviews with the teachers

both pointed to the teaching and learning of classroom routines as the main element of the student role. The teachers expended most of their efforts, for the first half of the year at least, in training the children to follow the routines which teachers created. The children were, in a very real sense, *drilled* in tasks and activities created by the teachers for their own purposes and beginning and ending quite arbitrarily (from the child's point of view) at the command of the teacher. One teacher remarked that she hated September, because during the first month "everything has to be done rigidly, and repeatedly, until they know exactly what they're supposed to do." However, "by January," she said, "they know exactly what to do [during the day] and I don't have to be after them all the time." Classroom routines were introduced gradually from the beginning of the year in all the kindergartens, and the children were drilled in them as long as was necessary to achieve regular compliance. By the end of the school year, the successful kindergarten teacher has a well-organized group of children. They follow classroom routines automatically, having learned all the command signals and the expected responses to them. They have, in our terms, learned the student role. The following observation shows one such classroom operating at optimum organization on an afternoon late in May. It is the class of an experienced and respected kindergarten teacher.

An Afternoon in Kindergarten

At about 12:20 in the afternoon on a day in the last week of May, Edith Kerr leaves the teachers' room where she has been having lunch and walks to her classroom at the far end of the primary wing of Wright School. A group of five- and six-year-olds peers at her through the glass doors leading from the hall cloakroom to the play area outside. Entering her room, she straightens some material in the "book corner" of the room, arranges music on the piano, takes colored paper from her closet and places it on one of the shelves under the window. Her room is divided into a number of activity areas through the arrangement of furniture and play equipment. Two easels and a paint table near the door create a kind of passageway inside the room. A wedge-shaped area just inside the front door is made into a teacher's area by the placing of "her" things there: her desk, file, and piano. To the left is the book corner, marked off from the rest of the room by a puppet stage and a movable chalkboard. In it are a display rack of picture books, a record player, and a stack of children's records. To the right of the entrance are the sink and clean-up area. Four large round tables with six chairs at each for the children are placed near the walls about halfway down the length of the room, two on each side, leaving a large open area in the center for group games, block building, and toy truck driving. Windows stretch down the length of both walls, starting about three feet from the floor and extending almost to the high ceilings. Under the windows are long shelves on which are kept all the toys, games, blocks, paper, paints, and other equipment of the kindergarten. The left rear corner of the room is a play store with shelves, merchandise, and cash register; the right rear corner is a play kitchen with stove, sink, ironing board, and bassinette with baby dolls in it. This area is partly shielded from the rest of the room by a large standing display rack for posters and children's art work. A sandbox is found against the back wall between these two areas. The room is light, brightly colored, and filled with things adults feel five- and six-year-olds will find interesting and pleasing.

At 12:25 Edith opens the outside door and admits the waiting children. They hang their sweaters on hooks outside the door and then go to the center of the room and arrange themselves in a semi-circle on the floor, facing the teacher's chair, which she has placed in the center of the floor. Edith follows them in and sits in her chair checking attendance while waiting for the bell to ring. When she has finished attendance, which she takes by sight, she asks the children what the date is, what day and month it is, how many children are enrolled in the class, how many are present, and how many are absent.

The bell rings at 12:30 and the teacher puts away her attendance book. She introduces a visitor, who is sitting against the wall taking notes, as someone who wants to learn about schools and children. She then goes to the back of the room and takes down a large chart labeled "Helping Hands." Bringing it to the center of the room, she tells the children it is time to change jobs. Each child is assigned some task on the chart by placing his name, lettered on a paper "hand," next to a picture signifying the task—e.g., a broom, a blackboard, a milk bottle, a flag, and a Bible. She asks the children who wants each of the jobs and rearranges their "hands" accordingly. Returning to her chair, Edith announces, "One person should tell us what happened to Mark." A girl raises her hand, and when called on says, "Mark fell and hit his head and had to go to the hospital." The teacher adds that Mark's mother had written saying he was in the hospital.

During this time the children have been interacting among themselves, in their semi-circle. Children have whispered to their neighbors, poked one another, made general comments to the group, waved to friends on the other side of the circle. None of this has been disruptive, and the teacher has ignored it for the most part. The children seem to know just how much of each kind of interaction is permitted—they may greet in a soft voice someone who sits next to them, for example, but may not shout greetings to a friend who sits across the circle, so they confine themselves to waving and remain well within understood limits.

At 12:35 two children arrive. Edith asks them why they are late and then sends them to join the circle on the floor. The other children vie with each other to tell the newcomers what happened to Mark. When this leads to a general disorder Edith asks, "Who has serious time?" The children become quiet and a girl raises her hand. Edith nods and the child gets a Bible and hands it to Edith. She reads the Twenty-third Psalm while the children sit quietly. Edith helps the child in charge begin reciting the Lord's Prayer; the other children follow along for the first unit of sounds, and then trail off as Edith finishes for them. Everyone stands and faces the American flag hung to the right of the door. Edith leads the pledge to the flag, with the children again following the familiar sounds as far as they remember them. Edith then asks the girl in charge what song she wants and the child replies, "My Country." Edith goes to the piano and plays "America," singing as the children follow her words.

Edith returns to her chair in the center of the room and the children sit again in the semi-circle on the floor. It is 12:40 when she tells the children, "Let's have boys' sharing time first." She calls the name of the first boy sitting on the end of the circle, and he comes up to her with a toy helicopter. He turns and holds it up for the other children to see. He says, "It's a helicopter." Edith asks, "What is it used for?" and he replies, "For the army. Carry men. For the war." Other children join in, "For shooting submarines." "To bring back men from space when they are in the ocean." Edith sends the boy back to the circle and asks the next boy if he has something. He replies "No" and she passes on to the next. He says "Yes" and brings a bird's nest to her. He holds it for the class to see, and the teacher asks, "What kind of bird made the nest?" The boy replies, "My friend says a rain bird made it." Edith asks what the nest is made of and different children reply, "mud," "leaves," and "sticks." There is also a bit of moss woven into the nest, and Edith tries to describe it to the children. They, however, are more interested in seeing if anything is inside it, and Edith lets the boy carry it around the semi-circle showing the children its insides. Edith tells the children of some baby robins in a nest in her yard, and some of the children tell about baby birds they have seen. Some children are asking about a small object in the nest which they say looks like an egg, but all have seen the nest now and Edith calls on the next boy. A number of children say, "I know what Michael has, but I'm not telling." Michael brings a book to the teacher and then goes back to his place in the circle of children. Edith reads the last page of the book to the class. Some children tell of books which they have at home. Edith calls the next boy, and three children call out, "I know what David has." "He always has the same thing." "It's a bang-bang." David goes to his table and gets a box which he brings to Edith. He opens it and shows the teacher a scale-model of an old-fashioned dueling pistol. When David does not turn around to the class, Edith tells him, "Show it to the children" and he does. One child says, "Mr. Johnson [the principal] said no guns." Edith replies, "Yes, how many of you know that?" Most of the children in the circle raise their hands. She continues, "That you aren't supposed to bring guns to school?" She calls the next boy on the circle and he brings two large toy soldiers to her which the children enthusiastically identify as being from "Babes in Toyland." The next boy brings an American flag to Edith and shows it to the class. She asks him what the stars and stripes stand for and admonishes him to treat it carefully. "Why should you treat it carefully?" she asks the boy. "Because it's our flag," he replies. She congratulates him, saying, "That's right."

"Show and Tell" lasted twenty minutes and during the last ten one girl in particular announced that she knew what each child called upon had to show. Edith asked her to be quiet each time she spoke out, but she was not content, continuing to offer her comment at each "show." Four children from other classes had come into the room to bring something from another teacher or to ask for something from Edith. Those with requests were asked to return later if the item wasn't readily available.

Edith now asks if any of the children told their mothers about their trip to the local zoo the previous day. Many children raise their hands. As Edith calls on them, they tell what they liked in the zoo. Some children cannot wait to be called on, and they call out things to the teacher, who asks them to be quiet. After a few of the animals are mentioned, one child says, "I liked the spooky house," and the others chime in to agree with him, some pantomiming fear and horror. Edith is puzzled, and asks what this was. When half the children try to tell her at once, she raises her hand for quiet, then calls on individual children. One says, "The house with nobody in it"; another, "The dark little house." Edith asks where it was in the zoo, but the children cannot describe its location in any way which she can understand. Edith makes some jokes but they involve adult abstractions which the children cannot grasp. The children have become quite noisy now, speaking out to make both relevant and irrelevant comments, and three little girls have become particularly assertive.

Edith gets up from her seat at 1:10 and goes to the book corner, where she puts a record on the player. As it begins a story about the trip to the zoo, she returns to the circle and asks the children to go sit at the tables. She divides them among the tables in such a way as to indicate that they don't have regular seats. When the children are all seated at the four tables, five or six to a table, the teacher asks, "Who wants to be the first one?" One of the noisy girls comes to the center of the room. The voice on the record is giving directions for imitating an ostrich and the girl follows them, walking around the center of the room holding her ankles with her hands. Edith replays the record, and all the children, table by table, imitate ostriches down the center of the room and back. Edith removes her shoes and shows that she can be an ostrich too. This is apparently a familiar game, for a number of children are calling out, "Can we have the crab?" Edith asks one of the children to do a crab "so we can all remember how," and then plays the part of the record with music for imitating crabs by. The children from the first table line up across the room, hands and feet on the floor and faces pointing toward the ceiling. After they have "walked" down the room and back in this posture they sit at their table and the children of the next table play "crab." The children love this; they run from their tables, dance about on the floor waiting for their turns, and are generally exuberant. Children ask for the "inch worm," and the game is played again with the children squirming down the floor. As a conclusion Edith shows them a new animal imitation, the "lame dog." The children all hobble down the floor on three "legs," table by table to the accompaniment of the record.

At 1:30 Edith has the children line up in the center of the room: she says, "Table one, line up in front of me," and children ask, "What are we going to do?" Then she moves a few steps to the side and says, "Table two over here; line up next to table one," and more children ask, "What for?" She does this for table three and table four, and each time the children ask, "Why, what are we going to do?" When the children are lined up in four lines of five each, spaced so that they are not touching one another, Edith puts on a new record and leads the class in calisthenics, to the accompaniment of the record. The children just jump around every which way in their places instead of doing the exercises, and by the time the record is finished, Edith, the only one following it, seems exhausted. She is apparently adopting the President's new "Physical Fitness" program for her classroom.

At 1:35 Edith pulls her chair to the easels and calls the children to sit on the floor in front of her, table by table. When they are all seated she asks, "What are you going to do for worktime today?" Different children raise their hands and tell Edith what they are going to draw. Most are going to make pictures of animals they saw in the zoo. Edith asks if they want to make pictures to send to Mark in the hospital, and the children agree to this. Edith gives drawing paper to the children, calling them to her one by one. After getting a piece of paper, the children go to the crayon box on the right-hand shelves, select a number of colors, and go to the tables, where they begin drawing. Edith is again trying to quiet the perpetually talking girls. She keeps two of them standing by her so they won't disrupt the others. She asks them, "Why do you feel you have to talk all the time?" and then scolds them for not listening to her. Then she sends them to their tables to draw.

Most of the children are drawing at their tables, sitting or kneeling in their chairs. They are all working very industriously and, engrossed in their work, very quietly. Three girls have chosen to paint at the easels, and having donned their smocks, they are busily mixing colors and intently applying them to their pictures. If the children at the tables are primitives and neo-realists in their animal depictions, these girls at the easels are the class abstract-expressionists, with their broad-stroked, colorful paintings.

Edith asks of the children generally, "What color should I make the cover of Mark's book?" Brown and green are suggested by some children "because Mark likes them." The other children are puzzled as to just what is going on and ask, "What book?" or "What does she mean?" Edith explains what she thought was clear to them already, that they are all going to put their pictures together in a "book" to be sent to Mark. She goes to a small table in the play-kitchen corner and tells the children to bring her their pictures when they are finished and she will write their message for Mark on them.

By 1:50 most children have finished their pictures and given them to Edith. She talks with some of them as she ties the bundle of pictures together—answering questions, listening, carrying on conversations. The children are playing in various parts of the room with toys, games, and blocks which they have taken off the shelves. They also move from table to table examining each other's pictures, offering compliments and suggestions. Three girls at a table are cutting up colored paper for a collage. Another girl is walking about the room in a pair of high heels with a woman's purse over her arm. Three boys are playing in the center of the room with the large block set, with which they are building walk-ways and walking on them. Edith is very much concerned about their safety and comes over a number of times to fuss over them. Two or three other boys are pushing trucks around the center of the room, and mild altercations occur when they drive through the block constructions. Some boys and girls are playing at the toy store, two girls are serving "tea" in the play kitchen, and one is washing a doll baby. Two boys have elected to clean the room, and with large sponges they wash the movable blackboard, the puppet stage, and then begin on the tables. They run into resistance from the children who are working with construction toys on the tables and do not want to dismantle their structures. The class is like a room full of bees, each intent on pursuing some activity, occasionally bumping into one another, but just veering off in another direction without serious altercation. At 2:05 the custodian arrives pushing a cart loaded with half-pint milk containers. He places a tray of cartons on the counter next to the sink, then leaves. His coming and going is unnoticed in the room (as, incidentally, is the presence of the observer, who is completely ignored by the children for the entire afternoon).

At 2:15 Edith walks to the entrance of the room, switches off the lights, and sits at the piano and plays. The children begin spontaneously singing the song, which is "Clean up, clean up. Everybody clean up." Edith walks around the room supervising the clean-up. Some children put their toys, the blocks, puzzles, games, and so on back on their shelves under the windows. The children making a collage keep right on working. A child from another class comes in to borrow the 45-rpm adaptor for the record player. At more urging from Edith the rest of the children shelve their toys and work. The children are sitting around their tables now, and Edith asks, "What record would you like to hear while you have your milk?" There is some confusion and no general consensus, so Edith drops the subject and begins to call the children, table by table, to come get their milk. "Table one," she says, and the five children come to the sink, wash their hands and dry them, pick up a carton of milk and a straw, and take it back to their table. Two talking girls wander about the room interfering with the children getting their milk and Edith calls out to them to "settle down." As the children sit, many of them call out to Edith the name of the record they want to hear. When all the children are seated at tables with milk, Edith plays one of these records called "Bozo and the Birds" and shows the children pictures in a book which go with the record. The record recites, and the book shows the adventures of a clown, Bozo, as he walks through a woods meeting many different kinds of birds who, of course, display the characteristics of many kinds of people or, more accurately, different stereotypes. As children finish their milk, they take blankets or pads from the shelves under the windows and lie on them in the center of the room, where Edith sits on her chair showing the pictures. By 2:30 half the class is lying on the floor on their blankets, the record is still playing, and the teacher is turning the pages of the book. The child who came in previously returns the 45-rpm adaptor, and one of the kindergartners tells Edith what the boy's name is and where he lives.

The record ends at 2:40. Edith says, "Children, down on your blankets." All the class is lying on blankets now. Edith refuses to answer the various questions individual children put to her because, she tells them, "it's rest time now." Instead she talks very softly about what they will do tomorrow. They are going to work with clay, she says. The children lie quietly and listen. One of the boys raises his hand and when called on tells Edith, "The animals in the zoo looked so hungry yesterday." Edith asks the children what they think about this and a number try to volunteer opinions, but Edith accepts only those offered in a "rest-time tone," that is, softly and quietly. After a brief discussion of animal feeding, Edith calls the names of the two children on milk detail and has them collect empty milk cartons from the tables and return them to the tray. She asks the two children on clean-up detail to clean up the room. Then she gets up from her chair and goes to the door to turn on the lights. At this signal, the children all get up from the floor and return their blankets and pads to the shelf. It is raining (the reason for no outside play this afternoon) and cars driven by mothers clog the school drive and line up along the street. One of the talkative little girls comes over to Edith and pointing out the window says, "Mrs. Kerr, see my mother in the new Cadillac?"

At 2:50 Edith sits at the piano and plays. The children sit on the floor in the center of the room and sing. They have a repertoire of songs about animals, including one in which each child sings a refrain alone. They know these by heart and sing along through the ringing of the 2:55 bell. When the song is finished, Edith gets up and coming to the group says, "Okay, rhyming words to get your coats today." The children raise their hands and as Edith calls on them, they tell her two rhyming words, after which they are allowed to go into the hall to get their coats and sweaters. They return to the room with these and sit at their tables. At 2:59 Edith says, "When you have your coats on, you may line up at the door." Half of the children go to the door and stand in a long line. When the three o'clock bell rings, Edith returns to the piano and plays. The children sing a song called "Goodbye," after which Edith sends them out.

Training for Learning and for Life

The day in kindergarten at Wright School illustrates both the content of the student role as it has been learned by these children and the processes by which the teacher has brought about this learning, or, "taught" them the student role. The children have learned to go through routines and to follow orders with unquestioning obedience, even when these make no sense to them. They have been disciplined to do as they are told by an authoritative person without significant protest. Edith has developed this discipline in the children by creating and enforcing a rigid social structure in the classroom through which she effectively controls the behavior of most of the children for most of the school day. The "living with others in a small society" which the school pamphlet tells parents is the most important thing the children will learn in kindergarten can be seen now in its operational meaning, which is learning to live by the routines imposed by the school. This learning appears to be the principal content of the student role.

Children who submit to school-imposed discipline and come to identify with it, so that being a "good student" comes to be an important part of their developing identities, *become* the good students by the school's definitions. Those who submit to the routines of the school but do not come to identify with them will be adequate students who find the more important part of their identities elsewhere, such as in the play group outside school. Children who refuse to submit to the school routines are rebels, who become known as "bad students" and often "problem children" in the school, for they do not learn the academic curriculum and their behavior is often disruptive in the classroom. Today schools engage clinical psychologists in part to help teachers deal with such children.

In looking at Edith's kindergarten at Wright School, it is interesting to ask how the children learn this role of student—come to accept school-imposed routines—and what, exactly, it involves in terms of behavior and attitudes. The most prominent features of the classroom are its physical and social structures. The room is carefully furnished and arranged in ways adults feel will interest children. The play store and play kitchen in the back of the room, for example, imply that children are interested in mimicking these activities of the adult world. The only space left for the children to create something of their own is the empty center of the room, and the materials at their disposal are the blocks, whose use causes anxiety on the part of the teacher. The room, being carefully organized physically by the adults, leaves little room for the creation of physical organization on the part of the children.

The social structure created by Edith is a far more powerful and subtle force for fitting the children to the student role. This structure is established by the very rigid and tightly controlled set of rituals and routines through which the children are put during the day. There is first the rigid "locating procedure" in which the children are asked to find themselves in terms of the month, date, day of the week, and the number of the class who are present and absent. This puts them solidly in the real world as defined by adults. The day is then divided into six periods whose activities are for the most part determined by the teacher. In Edith's kindergarten the children went through Serious Time, which opens the school day, Sharing Time, Play Time (which in clear weather would be spent outside), Work Time, Clean-up Time, after which they have their milk, and Rest Time, after which they go home. The teacher has programmed activities for each of these Times.

Occasionally the class is allowed limited discretion to choose between proffered activities, such as stories or records, but original ideas for activities are never solicited from them. Opportunity for free individual action is open only once in the day, during the part of Work Time left after the general class assignment has been completed (on the day reported the class assignment was drawing animal pictures for the absent Mark). Spontaneous interests or observations from the children are never developed by the teacher. It seems that her schedule just does not allow room for developing such unplanned events. During Sharing Time, for example, the child who brought a bird's nest told Edith, in reply to her question of what kind of bird made it, "My friend says it's a rain bird." Edith does not think to ask about this bird, probably because the answer is "childish," that is, not given in accepted adult categories of birds. The children then express great interest in an object in the nest, but the teacher ignores this interest, probably because the object is uninteresting to her. The soldiers from "Babes in Toyland" strike a responsive note in the children, but this is not used for a discussion of any kind. The soldiers are treated in the same way as objects which bring little interest from the children. Finally, at the end of Sharing Time the child-world of perception literally erupts in the class with the recollection of "the spooky house" at the zoo. Apparently this made more of an impression on the children than did any of the animals, but Edith is unable to make any sense of it for herself. The tightly imposed order of the class begins to break down as the children discover a universe of discourse of their own and begin talking excitedly with one another. The teacher is effectively excluded from this child's world of perception and for a moment she fails to dominate the classroom situation. She reasserts control, however, by taking the children to the next activity she has planned for the day. It seems never to have occurred to Edith that there might be a meaningful learning experience for the children in re-creating the "spooky house" in the classroom. It seems fair to say that this would have offered an exercise in spontaneous self-expression and an opportunity for real creativity on the part of the children. Instead, they are taken through a canned animal imitation procedure, an activity which they apparently enjoy, but which is also imposed upon them rather than created by them.

While children's perceptions of the world and opportunities for genuine spontaneity and creativity are being systematically eliminated from the kindergarten, unquestioned obedience to authority and rote learning of meaningless material are being encouraged. When the children are called to line up in the center of the room they ask "Why?" and "What for?" as they are in the very process of complying. They have learned to go smoothly through a programmed day, regardless of whether parts of the program make any sense to them or not. Here the student role involves what might be called "doing what you're told and never mind why." Activities which might "make sense" to the children are effectively ruled out, and they are forced or induced to participate in activities which may be "senseless," such as calisthenics.

At the same time the children are being taught by rote meaningless sounds in the ritual oaths and songs, such as the Lord's Prayer, the Pledge to the Flag, and "America." As they go through the grades children learn more and more of the sounds of these ritual oaths, but the fact that they have often learned meaningless sounds rather than meaningful statements is shown when they are asked to write these out in the sixth grade; they write them as groups of sounds rather than as a series of words, according to the sixth grade teachers at Wright School. Probably much learning in the elementary grades is of this character, that is, having no intrinsic meaning to the children, but rather being tasks inexplicably required of them by authoritative adults. Listening to sixth grade children read social studies reports, for example, in which they have copied material from encyclopedias about a particular country, an observer often gets the feeling that he is watching an activity which has no intrinsic meaning for the child. The child who reads, "Switzerland grows wheat and cows and grass and makes a lot of cheese" knows the dictionary meaning of each of these words but may very well have no conception at all of this "thing" called Switzerland. He is simply carrying out a task assigned by the teacher *because* it is assigned, and this may be its only "meaning" for him.

Another type of learning which takes place in kindergarten is seen in children who take advantage of the "holes" in the adult social structure to create activities of their own, during Work Time or out-of-doors during Play Time. Here the children are learning to carve out a small world of their own within the world created by adults. They very quickly learn that if they keep within permissible limits of noise and action they can play much as they please. Small groups of children formed during the year in Edith's kindergarten who played together at these times, developing semi-independent little groups in which they created their own worlds in the interstices of the adult-imposed physical and social world. These groups remind the sociological observer very much of the so-called "informal groups" which adults develop in factories and offices of large bureaucracies.[5] Here, too, within authoritatively imposed social organizations people find "holes" to create little subworlds which support informal, friendly, unofficial behavior. Forming and participating in such groups seems to be as much part of the student role as it is of the role of bureaucrat.

The kindergarten has been conceived of here as the year in which children are prepared for their schooling by learning the role of student. In the classrooms of the rest of the school grades, the children will be asked to submit to systems and routines imposed by the teachers and the curriculum. The days will be much like those of kindergarten, except that academic subjects will be substituted for the activities of the kindergarten. Once out of the school system, young adults will more than likely find themselves working in large-scale bureaucratic organizations, perhaps on the assembly line in the factory, perhaps in the paper routines of the white collar occupations, where they will be required to submit to rigid routines imposed by "the company" which may make little sense to them. Those who can operate well in this situation will be successful bureaucratic functionaries. Kindergarten, therefore, can be seen as preparing children not only for participation in the bureaucratic organization of large modern school systems, but also for the large-scale occupational bureaucracies of modern society.

Notes

1. Emile Durkheim, *Sociology and Education* (New York: The Free Press, 1956), pp.|nb|71–72.

2. *Ibid.*, p.|nb|123.

3. Wilbur Brookover, *The Sociology of Education* (New York: American Book Company, 1957), p.|nb|4.

4. *Ibid.*, p.|nb|6.

5. See, for example, Peter M. Blau, *Bureaucracy in Modern Society* (New York: Random House, 1956), Chapter 3.

40 India's Sacred Cow

MARVIN HARRIS

Although its form varies widely from one culture to another, religion is one of humanity's fundamental social institutions. A generation or so ago, some "experts" predicted that with the increasing dominance of science and the secularization of U.S. culture religion would fade quietly into the background. On the contrary, religion is as vital for Americans today as it was in the past. Church membership is even much higher now than when the country was founded. Tens of millions of Americans seek comfort and guidance in religion, looking to religion for answers to many of the perplexing questions that social life poses and that science cannot answer.

Like the other social institutions, religion is interconnected with the other parts of society. It sometimes is difficult to recognize these interconnections when we refer to our own religion, for we tend to focus on its smaller aspects, such as our own congregation, synagogue, or mosque. It often is easier to see this point, however, when we look at unfamiliar religions, those whose practices are far removed from our experiences. There, since we are not immersed in taken-for-granted assumptions, we may be prompted to ask basic questions. For example, why are cows allowed to wander India's city streets and country roads? Why don't deprived and hungry Indians eat them? Essential interconnections between religion and culture become evident as Harris analyzes such questions.

NEWS PHOTOGRAPHS that came out of India during the famine of the late 1960s showed starving people stretching out bony hands to beg for food while sacred cattle strolled behind undisturbed. The Hindu, it seems, would rather starve to death than eat his cow or even deprive it of food. The cattle appear to browse unhindered through urban markets eating an orange here, a mango there, competing with people for meager supplies of food.

By Western standards, spiritual values seem more important to Indians than life itself. Specialists in food habits around the world like Fred Simons at the University of California at Davis consider Hinduism an irrational ideology that compels people to overlook abundant, nutritious foods for scarcer, less healthful foods.

461

What seems to be an absurd devotion to the mother cow pervades Indian life. Indian wall calendars portray beautiful young women with bodies of fat white cows, often with milk jetting from their teats into sacred shrines.

Cow worship even carries over into politics. In 1966 a crowd of 120,000 people, led by holy men, demonstrated in front of the Indian House of Parliament in support of the All-Party Cow Protection Campaign Committee. In Nepal, the only contemporary Hindu kingdom, cow slaughter is severely punished. As one story goes, the car driven by an official of a United States agency struck and killed a cow. In order to avoid the international incident that would have occurred when the official was arrested for murder, the Nepalese magistrate concluded that the cow had committed suicide.

Many Indians agree with Western assessments of the Hindu reverence for their cattle, the zebu, or *Bos indicus,* a large-humped species prevalent in Asia and Africa. M.N. Srinivas, an Indian anthropologist, states: "Orthodox Hindu opinion regards the killing of cattle with abhorrence, even though the refusal to kill vast number of useless cattle which exist in India today is detrimental to the nation." Even the Indian Ministry of Information formerly maintained that "the large animal population is more a liability than an asset in view of our land resources." Accounts from many different sources point to the same conclusion: India, one of the world's great civilizations, is being strangled by its love for the cow.

The easy explanation for India's devotion to the cow, the one most Westerners and Indians would offer, is that cow worship is an integral part of Hinduism. Religion is somehow good for the soul, even it if sometimes fails the body. Religion orders the cosmos and explains our place in the universe. Religious beliefs, many would claim, have existed for thousands of years and have a life of their own. They are not understandable in scientific terms.

But all this ignores history. There is more to be said for cow worship than is immediately apparent. The earliest Vedas, the Hindu sacred texts from the second millennium B.C., do not prohibit the slaughter of cattle. Instead, they ordain it as part of sacrificial rites. The early Hindus did not avoid the flesh of cows and bulls; they ate it at ceremonial feasts presided over by Brahman priests. Cow worship is a relatively recent development in India; it evolved as the Hindu religion developed and changed.

This evolution is recorded in royal edicts and religious texts written during the last 3,000 years of Indian history. The Vedas from the first millennium B.C. contain contradictory passages, some referring to ritual slaughter and others to a strict taboo on beef consumption. A.N. Bose, in *Social and Rural Economy of Northern India,* 600 B.C.–200 A.D., concludes that many of the sacred-cow passages were incorporated into the texts by priests of a later period.

By 200 A.D. the status of Indian cattle had undergone a spiritual transformation. The Brahman priesthood exhorted the population to venerate the
cow and forbade them to abuse it or to feed on it. Religious feasts involving
the ritual slaughter and consumption of livestock were eliminated and meat
eating was restricted to the nobility.

By 1000 A.D., all Hindus were forbidden to eat beef. Ahimsa, the Hindu
belief in the unity of all life, was the spiritual justification for this restriction. But it is difficult to ascertain exactly when this change occurred. An
important event that helped to shape the modern complex was the Islamic
invasion, which took place in the eighth century A.D. Hindus may have found
it politically expedient to set themselves off from the invaders, who were
beefeaters, by emphasizing the need to prevent the slaughter of their sacred
animals. Thereafter, the cow taboo assumed its modern form and began to
function much as it does today.

The place of the cow in modern India is every place—on posters, in the
movies, in brass figures, in stone and wood carvings, on the streets, in the
fields. The cow is a symbol of health and abundance. It provides the milk
that Indians consume in the form of yogurt and ghee (clarified butter),
which contribute subtle flavors to much spicy Indian food.

This, perhaps, is the practical role of the cow, but cows provide less than
half the milk produced in India. Most cows in India are not dairy breeds. In
most regions, when an Indian farmer wants a steady, high-quality source of
milk he usually invests in a female water buffalo. In India the water buffalo
is the specialized dairy breed because its milk has a higher butterfat content
than zebu milk. Although the farmer milks his zebu cows, the milk is merely
a by-product.

More vital than zebu milk to South Asian farmers are zebu calves. Male
calves are especially valued because from bulls come oxen, which are the
mainstay of the Indian agricultural system.

Small, fast oxen drag wooden plows through late-spring fields when
monsoons have dampened the dry, cracked earth. After harvest, the oxen
break the grain from the stalk by stomping through mounds of cut wheat and
rice. For rice cultivation in irrigated fields, the male water buffalo is preferred (it pulls better in deep mud), but for most other crops, including rain-
fall rice, wheat, sorghum, and millet, and for transporting goods and people
to and from town, a team of oxen is preferred. The ox is the Indian peasant's
tractor, thresher, and family car combined; the cow is the factory that produces the ox.

If draft animals instead of cows are counted, India appears to have too
few domesticated ruminants, not too many. Since each of the 70 million
farms in India require a draft team, it follows that Indian peasants should use

140 million animals in the fields. But there are only 83 million oxen and male water buffalo on the subcontinent, a shortage of 30 million draft teams.

In other regions of the world, joint ownership of draft animals might overcome a shortage, but Indian agriculture is closely tied to the monsoon rains of late spring and summer. Field preparation and planting must coincide with the rain, and a farmer must have his animals ready to plow when the weather is right. When the farmer without a draft team needs bullocks most, his neighbors are all using theirs. Any delay in turning the soil drastically lowers production.

Because of this dependence on draft animals, loss of the family oxen is devastating. If a beast dies, the farmer must borrow money to buy or rent an ox at interest rates so high that he ultimately loses his land. Every year foreclosures force thousands of poverty-stricken peasants to abandon the countryside for the overcrowded cities.

If a family is fortunate enough to own a fertile cow, it will be able to rear replacements for a lost team and thus survive until life returns to normal. If, as sometimes happens, famine leads a family to sell its cow and ox team, all ties to agriculture are cut. Even if the family survives, it has no way to farm the land, no oxen to work the land, and no cows to produce oxen.

The prohibition against eating meat applies to the flesh of cows, bulls, and oxen, but the cow is the most sacred because it can produce the other two. The peasant whose cow dies is not only crying over a spiritual loss but over the loss of his farm as well.

Religious laws that forbid the slaughter of cattle promote the recovery of the agricultural system from the dry Indian winter and from periods of drought. The monsoon, on which all agriculture depends, is erratic. Sometimes, it arrives early, sometimes late, sometimes not at all. Drought has struck large portions of India time and again in this century, and Indian farmers and the zebus are accustomed to these natural disasters. Zebus can pass weeks on end with little or no food and water. Like camels, they store both in their humps and recuperate quickly with only a little nourishment.

During drought the cows often stop lactating and become barren. In some cases the condition is permanent but often it is only temporary. If barren animals were summarily eliminated, as Western experts in animal husbandry have suggested, cows capable of recovery would be lost along with those entirely debilitated. By keeping alive the cows that can later produce oxen, religious laws against cow slaughter assure the recovery of the agricultural system from the greatest challenge it faces—the failure of the monsoon.

The local Indian governments aid the process of recovery by maintaining homes for barren cows. Farmers reclaim any animal that calves or begins to lactate. One police station in Madras collects strays and pastures them in a field adjacent to the station. After a small fine is paid, a cow is returned to its rightful owner when the owner thinks the cow shows signs of being able to reproduce.

During the hot, dry spring months most of India is like a desert. Indian farmers often complain they cannot feed their livestock during this period. They maintain the cattle by letting them scavenge on the sparse grass along the roads. In the cities the cattle are encouraged to scavenge near food stalls to supplement their scant diet. These are the wandering cattle tourists report seeing throughout India.

Westerners expect shopkeepers to respond to these intrusions with the deference due a sacred animal; instead, their response is a string of curses and the crack of a long bamboo pole across the beast's back or a poke at its genitals. Mahatma Gandhi was well aware of the treatment sacred cows (and bulls and oxen) received in India. "How we bleed her to take the last drop of milk from her. How we starve her to emaciation, how we ill-treat the calves, how we deprive them of their portion of milk, how cruelly we treat the oxen, how we castrate them, how we beat them, how we overload them" [Gandhi, 1954].

Oxen generally receive better treatment than cows. When food is in short supply, thrifty Indian peasants feed their working bullocks and ignore their cows, but rarely do they abandon the cows to die. When cows are sick, farmers worry over them as they would over members of the family and nurse them as if they were children. When the rains return and when the fields are harvested, the farmers again feed their cows regularly and reclaim their abandoned animals. The prohibition against beef consumption is a form of disaster insurance for all India.

Western agronomists and economists are quick to protest that all the functions of the zebu cattle can be improved with organized breeding programs, cultivated pastures, and silage. Because stronger oxen would pull the plow faster, they could work multiple plots of land, allowing farmers to share their animals. Fewer healthy, well-fed cows could provide Indians with more milk. But pastures and silage require arable land, land needed to produce wheat and rice.

A look at Western cattle farming makes plain the cost of adopting advanced technology in Indian agriculture. In a study of livestock production in the United States, David Pimentel of the College of Agriculture and Life Sciences at Cornell University, found that 91 percent of the cereal, legume, and vegetable protein suitable for human consumption is consumed by livestock. Approximately three quarters of the arable land in the United States is devoted to growing food for livestock. In the production of meat and milk, American ranchers use enough fossil fuel to equal more than 82 million barrels of oil annually.

Indian cattle do not drain the system in the same way. In a 1971 study of livestock in West Bengal, Stewart Odend'hal [1972] of the University of Missouri found that Bengalese cattle ate only the inedible remains of subsistence crops—rice straw, rice hulls, the tops of sugar cane, and mustard-oil cake. Cattle graze in the fields after harvest and eat the remains of crops left on the ground; they forage for grass and weeds on the roadsides. The food for zebu cattle costs the human population virtually nothing. "Basically," Odend'hal says, "the cattle convert the items of little direct human value into products of immediate utility."

In addition to plowing the fields and producing milk, the zebus produce dung, which fires the hearths and fertilizes the fields of India. Much of the estimated 800 million tons of manure produced annually is collected by the farmers' children as they follow the family cows and bullocks from place to place. And when the children see the droppings of another farmer's cattle along the road, they pick those up also. Odend'hal reports that the system operates with such high efficiency that the children of West Bengal recover nearly 100 percent of the dung produced by their livestock.

From 40 to 70 percent of all manure produced by Indian cattle is used as fuel for cooking; the rest is returned to the fields as fertilizer. Dried dung burns slowly, cleanly, and with low heat—characteristics that satisfy the household needs of Indian women. Staples like curry and rice can simmer for hours. While the meal slowly cooks over an unattended fire, the women of the household can do other chores. Cow chips, unlike firewood, do not scorch as they burn.

It is estimated that the dung used for cooking fuel provides the energy-equivalent of 43 million tons of coal. At current prices, it would cost India an extra 1.5 billion dollars in foreign exchange to replace the dung with coal. And if the 350 million tons of manure that are being used as fertilizer were replaced with commercial fertilizers, the expense would be even greater. Roger Revelle of the University of California at San Diego has calculated that 89 percent of the energy used in Indian agriculture (the equivalent of about 140 million tons of coal) is provided by local sources. Even if foreign loans were to provide the money, the capital outlay necessary to replace the Indian cow with tractors and fertilizers for the fields, coal for the fires, and transportation for the family would probably warp international financial institutions for years.

Instead of asking the Indians to learn from the American model of industrial agriculture, American farmers might learn energy conservation from the Indians. Every step in an energy cycle results in a loss of energy to the system. Like a pendulum that slows a bit with each swing, each transfer of energy from sun to plants, plants to animals, and animals to human beings involves energy losses. Some systems are more efficient than others; they provide a higher percentage of the energy inputs in a final, useful form. Seventeen percent of all energy zebus consume is returned in the form of milk, traction, and dung. American cattle raised on Western rangeland return only 4 percent of the energy they consume.

But the American system is improving. Based on techniques pioneered by Indian scientists, at least one commercial firm in the United States is reported to be building plants that will turn manure from cattle feedlots into combustible gas. When organic matter is broken down by anaerobic bacteria, methane gas and carbon dioxide are produced. After the methane is cleansed of the carbon dioxide, it is available for the same purposes as natural gas— cooking, heating, electric generation. The company constructing the biogasification plant plans to sell its product to a gas-supply company, to be piped through the existing distribution system. Schemes similar to this one could make cattle ranches almost independent of utility and gasoline companies; for methane can be used to run trucks, tractors, and cars as well as to supply heat and electricity. The relative energy self-sufficiency that the Indian peasant has achieved is a goal American farmers and industry are now striving for.

Studies of Odend'hal's understate the efficiency of the Indian cow, because dead cows are used for purposes that Hindus prefer not to acknowledge. When a cow dies, an Untouchable, a member of one of the lowest ranking castes in India, is summoned to haul away the carcass. Higher castes consider the body of the dead cow polluting; if they handle it, they must go through a rite of purification.

Untouchables first skin the dead animal and either tan the skin themselves or sell it to a leather factory. In the privacy of their homes, contrary to the teachings of Hinduism, untouchable castes cook the meat and eat it. Indians of all castes rarely acknowledge the existence of these practices to non-Hindus, but most are aware that beefeating takes place. The prohibition against beefeating restricts consumption by the higher castes and helps distribute animal protein to the poorest sectors of the population that otherwise would have no source of these vital nutrients.

Untouchables are not the only Indians who consume beef. Indian Muslims and Christians are under no restriction that forbids them beef, and its consumption is legal in many places. The Indian ban on cow slaughter is state, not national, law and not all states restrict it. In many cities, such as New Delhi, Calcutta, and Bombay, legal slaughterhouses sell beef to retail customers and to restaurants that serve steak.

If the caloric value of beef and the energy costs involved in the manufacture of synthetic leather were included in the estimate of energy, the calculated efficiency of Indian livestock would rise considerably. As well as the system works, experts often claim that its efficiency can be further improved. Alan Heston [et al., 1971], an economist at the University of Pennsylvania, believes that Indians suffer from an overabundance of cows simply because they refuse to slaughter the excess cattle. India could produce at least the same number of oxen and the same quantities of milk and manure with 30 million fewer cows. Heston calculates that only 40 cows are necessary to maintain a population of 100 bulls and oxen. Since India averages 70 cows for every 100 bullocks, the difference, 30 million cows, is expendable.

What Heston fails to note is that sex ratios among cattle in different regions of India vary tremendously, indicating that adjustments in the cow population do take place. Along the Ganges River, one of the holiest shrines of Hinduism, the ratio drops to 47 cows for every 100 male animals. This ratio reflects the preference for dairy buffalo in the irrigated sectors of the Gangetic Plains. In nearby Pakistan, in contrast, where cow slaughter is permitted, the sex ratio is 60 cows to 100 oxen.

Since the sex ratios among cattle differ greatly from region to region and do not even approximate the balance that would be expected if no females were killed, we can assume that some culling of herds does take place; Indians do adjust their religious restrictions to accommodate ecological realities.

They cannot kill a cow but they can tether an old or unhealthy animal until it has starved to death. They cannot slaughter a calf but they can yoke it with a large wooden triangle so that when it nurses it irritates the mother's udder and gets kicked to death. They cannot ship their animals to the slaughterhouse but they can sell them to Muslims, closing their eyes to the fact that the Muslims will take the cattle to the slaughterhouse.

These violations of the prohibition against cattle slaughter strengthen the premise that cow worship is a vital part of Indian culture. The practice arose to prevent the population from consuming the animal on which Indian agriculture depends. During the first millennium B.C., the Gange Valley became one of the most densely populated regions of the world.

Where previously there had been only scattered villages, many towns and cities arose and peasants farmed every available acre of land. Kingsley Davis, a population expert at the University of California at Berkeley, estimates that by 300 B.C. between 50 million and 100 million people were living in India. The forested Ganges Valley became a windswept semidesert and signs of ecological collapse appeared; droughts and floods became commonplace, erosion took away the rich topsoil, farms shrank as population increased, and domesticated animals became harder and harder to maintain.

It is probable that the elimination of meat eating came about in a slow, practical manner. The farmers who decided not to eat their cows, who saved them for procreation to produce oxen, were the ones who survived the natural disasters. Those who ate beef lost the tools with which to farm. Over a period of centuries, more and more farmers probably avoided beef until an unwritten taboo came into existence.

Only later was the practice codified by the priesthood. While Indian peasants were probably aware of the role of cattle in their society, strong sanctions were necessary to protect zebus from a population faced with starvation. To remove temptation, the flesh of cattle became taboo and the cow became sacred.

The sacredness of the cow is not just an ignorant belief that stands in the way of progress. Like all concepts of the sacred and the profane, this one affects the physical world; it defines the relationships that are important for the maintenance of Indian society.

Indians have the sacred cow, we have the "sacred" car and the "sacred" dog. It would not occur to us to propose the elimination of automobiles and dogs from our society without carefully considering the consequences, and we should not propose the elimination of zebu cattle without first understanding their place in the social order of India.

Human society is neither random nor capricious. The regularities of thought and behavior called culture are the principal mechanisms by which we human beings adapt to the world around us. Practices and beliefs can be rational or irrational, but a society that fails to adapt to its environment is doomed to extinction. Only those societies that draw the necessities of life from their surroundings without destroying those surroundings inherit the earth. The West has much to learn from the great antiquity of Indian civilization, and the sacred cow is an important part of that lesson.

41 Police Accounts of Normal Force

JENNIFER HUNT

My personal contacts with the police have been infrequent and brief. Nevertheless, I have seen a policeman handcuff a rape suspect to a tree and then slap him in the face in front of a group of citizen-witnesses. I have heard another threaten the life of a suspect he was escorting near a stream, saying he wished the suspect would attempt to flee so he "could shoot her and watch her body float down the river." And in Mexico, after recovering my billfold and apprehending the two men who had picked my pocket, the secret police offered to hold the culprits while I beat them. They felt that I *ought* to beat them because, as they said, the men had caused me (and presumably them) so much trouble. (I didn't, in case you are wondering.)

These events have convinced me that police violence is no random matter but is a regular part of the occupation. Sociological research bears this out. Why should this be? Is it because the police recruit people with sadistic tendencies? As a sociologist, Hunt does not look for explanations lodged *within* people, such as "personality types." Rather, she examines the occupational culture, *external* conditions that affect people's orientations, in this instance how occupational norms influence the behavior and attitudes of recruits.

If you were a social reformer and you wanted to decrease police violence, where would you start? Keep in mind what Hunt found—the virtual absence of differences by gender, the distinction between formal and informal expectations, and the strong support for "normal" violence that is built into this occupation—and the lessons from the Zimbardo experiment in Part VI.

THE POLICE ARE REQUIRED to handle a variety of peacekeeping and law enforcement tasks including settling disputes, removing drunks from the street, aiding the sick, controlling crowds, and pursuing criminals. What unifies these diverse activities is the possibility that their resolution might require the use of force. Indeed, the capacity to use force stands at the core of the police mandate (Bittner, 1980). . . . The following research . . . explores how police themselves classify and evaluate acts of force as either legal, normal, or excessive. Legal force is that coercion necessary to subdue, control, and restrain a suspect in order to take him into custody. Although force not accountable in legal terms is technically labeled excessive by the courts and the public, the police perceive many forms of illegal force as normal. Normal force involves coercive acts that specific "cops" on specific occasions formulate as necessary, appropriate, reasonable, or understandable. Although not always legitimated or admired, normal force is depicted as a necessary or natural response of normal police to particular situational exigencies. . . . Brutality is viewed as illegal, illegitimate, and often immoral violence, but the police draw the lines in extremely different ways and at different points [from] either the court system or the public. . . .

The article is based on approximately eighteen months of participant observation in a major urban police department referred to as the Metro City P.D. I attended the police academy with male and female recruits and later rode with individual officers in one-person cars on evening and night shifts in high crime districts.[1] The female officers described in this research were among the first 100 women assigned to the ranks of uniformed patrol as a result of a discrimination suit filed by the Justice Department and a policewoman plaintiff.

Learning to Use Normal Force

The police phrase "it's not done on the street the way that it's taught at the academy" underscores the perceived contradiction between the formal world of the police academy and the informal world of the street. This contradiction permeates the police officer's construction of his world, particularly his view of the rational and moral use of force.

In the formal world of the police academy, the recruit learns to account for force by reference to legality. He or she is issued the regulation instruments and trained to use them to subdue, control, and restrain a suspect. If threatened with great bodily harm, the officer learns that he can justifiably use deadly force and fire his revolver. Yet the recruit is taught that he cannot use his baton, jack, or gun unnecessarily to torture, maim, or kill a suspect.

When recruits leave the formal world of the academy and are assigned to patrol a district, they are introduced to an informal world in which police recognize normal as well as legal and brutal force. Through observation and instruction, rookies gradually learn to apply force and account for its use in terms familiar to the street cop. First, rookies learn to adjust their arsenals to conform to street standards. They are encouraged to buy the more powerful weapons worn by veteran colleagues as these colleagues point out the inadequacy of a wooden baton or compare their convoy jacks to vibrators. They quickly discover that their department-issued equipment marks them as new recruits. At any rate, within a few weeks, most rookies have dispensed with the wooden baton and convoy jack and substituted . . . the more powerful plastic nightstick and flat-headed slapjack.[2]

Through experience and informal instruction, the rookie also learns the street use of these weapons. In school, for example, recruits are taught to avoid hitting a person on the head or neck because it could cause lethal damage. On the street, in contrast, police conclude that they must hit wherever it causes the most damage in order to incapacitate the suspect before they themselves are harmed. New officers also learn that they will earn the respect of their veteran co-workers not by observing legal niceties in using force, but by being "aggressive" and using whatever force is necessary in a given situation.

Peer approval helps neutralize the guilt and confusion that rookies often experience when they begin to use force to assert their authority. One female officer, for example, learned she was the object of a brutality suit while listening to the news on television. At first, she felt so mortified that she hesitated to go to work and face her peers. In fact, male colleagues greeted her with a standing ovation and commented, "You can use our urinal now." In their view, any aggressive police officer regularly using normal force might eventually face a brutality suit or civilian complaint. Such accusations confirm the officer's status as a "street cop" rather than an "inside man" who doesn't engage in "real police work."

Whereas male rookies are assumed to be competent dispensers of force unless proven otherwise, women are believed to be physically weak, naturally passive, and emotionally vulnerable.[3] Women officers are assumed to be reluctant to use physical force and are viewed as incompetent "street cops" until they prove otherwise. As a result, women rookies encounter special problems in learning to use normal force in the process of becoming recognized as "real street cops." It becomes crucial for women officers to create or exploit opportunities to display their physical abilities in order to overcome sexual bias and obtain full acceptance from co-workers. As a result, women rookies are encouraged informally to act more aggressively and to display more machismo than male rookies. . . .

For a street cop, it is often a graver error to use too little force and develop a "shaky" reputation than it is to use too much force and be told to calm down. Thus officers, particularly rookies, who do not back up their partners in appropriate ways or who hesitate to use force in circumstances where it is deemed necessary are informally instructed regarding their aberrant ways. If the problematic incident is relatively insignificant and his general reputation is good, a rookie who "freezes" one time is given a second chance before becoming generally known as an untrustworthy partner. However, such incidents become the subject of degrading gossip, gossip that pressures the officer either to use force as expected or risk isolation. Such talk also informs rookies about the general boundaries of legal and normal force.

For example, a female rookie was accused of "freezing" in an incident that came to be referred to as a "Mexican standoff." A pedestrian had complained that "something funny is going on in the drugstore." The officer walked into the pharmacy where she found an armed man committing a robbery. Although he turned his weapon on her when she entered the premises, she still pulled out her gun and pointed it at him. When he ordered her to drop it, claiming that his partner was behind her with a revolver at her head, she refused and told him to drop his.[4] He refused, and the stalemate continued until a sergeant entered the drugstore and ordered the suspect to drop his gun.

Initially, the female officer thought she had acted appropriately and even heroically. She soon discovered, however, that her hesitation to shoot had brought into question her competence with some of her fellow officers. Although many veterans claimed that "she had a lot a balls" to take her gun out at all when the suspect already had a gun on her, most contended "she shoulda shot him." Other policemen confirmed that she committed a "rookie mistake"; she had failed to notice a "lookout" standing outside the store and hence had been unprepared for an armed confrontation. Her sergeant and lieutenant, moreover, even insisted that she had acted in a cowardly manner, despite her reputation as a "gung-ho cop," and cited the incident as evidence of the general inadequacy of policewomen.

In the weeks that followed, this officer became increasingly depressed and angry. She was particularly outraged when she learned that she would not receive a commendation, although such awards were commonly made for "gun pinches" of this nature. Several months later, the officer vehemently expressed the wish that she had killed the suspect and vowed that next time she would "shoot first and ask questions later." The negative sanctions of supervisors and colleagues clearly encouraged her to adopt an attitude favorable to using force with less restraint in future situations. . . .

At the same time that male and female rookies are commended for using force under appropriate circumstances, they are reprimanded if their participation in force is viewed as excessive or inappropriate. In this way, rookies are instructed that although many acts of coercion are accepted and even demanded, not everything goes. They thereby learn to distinguish between normal and brutal force. . . .

Accounting for Normal Force

Police routinely normalize the use of force by two types of accounts: excuses and justifications. . . .

EXCUSES AND NORMAL FORCE

Excuses are accounts in which police deny full responsibility for an act but recognize its inappropriateness. Excuses therefore constitute socially approved vocabularies for relieving responsibility when conduct is questionable. Police most often excuse morally problematic force by referring to emotional or physiological states that are precipitated by some circumstances of routine patrol work. These circumstances include shootouts, violent fights, pursuits, and instances in which a police officer mistakenly comes close to killing an unarmed person.

Police work in these circumstances can generate intense excitement in which the officer experiences the "combat high" and "adrenaline rush" familiar to the combat soldier.[5] Foot and car pursuits not only bring on feelings of danger and excitement from the chase, but also a challenge to official authority. As one patrolman commented about a suspect: "Yeh, he got tuned up [beaten] . . . you always tune them up after a car chase." Another officer normalized the use of force after a pursuit in these terms:

> It's my feeling that violence inevitably occurs after a pursuit. . . . The adrenaline . . . and the insult involved when someone flees increases with every foot of the pursuit. I know the two or three times that I felt I lost control of myself . . . was when someone would run on me. The further I had to chase the guy the madder I got. . . . The funny thing is the reason for the pursuit could have been something as minor as a traffic violation or a kid you're chasing who just turned on a fire hydrant. It always ends in violence. You feel obligated to hit or kick the guy just for running.

Police officers also excuse force when it follows an experience of helplessness and confusion that has culminated in a temporary loss of emotional control. This emotional combination occurs most frequently when an officer comes to the brink of using lethal force, drawing a gun and perhaps firing, only to learn there were no "real" grounds for this action. The officer may then "snap out" and hit the suspect.[6] In one such incident, for example, two policemen picked up a complainant who positively identified a suspect as a man who just tried to shoot him. Just as the officers approached the suspect, he suddenly reached for his back pocket for what the officers assumed to be a gun. One officer was close enough to jump the suspect before he pulled his hand from his pocket. As it turned out, the suspect had no weapon, having dropped it several feet away. Although he was unarmed and under control, the suspect was punched and kicked out of anger and frustration by the officer who had almost shot him.

Note that in both these circumstances—pursuit and near-miss mistaken shootings—officers would concede that the ensuing force is inappropriate and unjustifiable when considered abstractly. But although abstractly wrong, the use of force on such occasions is presented as a normal, human reaction to an extreme situation. Although not every officer might react violently in such circumstances, it is understandable and expected that some will.

SITUATIONAL JUSTIFICATIONS

Officers also justify force as normal by reference to interactional situations in which an officer's authority is physically or symbolically threatened. [In contrast to excuses, which deny responsibility for the act but recognize that the act is blameworthy, justifications accept responsibility for the act but deny that the act is blameworthy.—Ed.] In such accounts, the use of force is justified instrumentally—as a means of regaining immediate control in a situation where that control has become tenuous. Here, the officer depicts his primary intent for using force as a need to reestablish immediate control in a problematic encounter, and only incidentally as hurting or punishing the offender.

Few officers will hesitate to assault a suspect who physically threatens or attacks them. In one case, an officer was punched in the face by a prisoner he had just apprehended for allegedly attempting to shoot a friend. The incident occurred in the stationhouse, and several policemen observed the exchange. Immediately, one officer hit the prisoner in the jaw and the rest immediately joined the brawl.

Violations of an officer's property such as his car or hat may signify a more symbolic assault on the officer's authority and self, thus justifying a forceful response to maintain control. Indeed, in the police view, almost any person who verbally challenges a police officer is appropriately subject to force. . . .

On rare occasions, women officers encounter special problems in these regards. Although most suspects view women in the same way as policemen, some seem less inclined to accord female officers *de facto* and symbolic control in street encounters, and on a few occasions seem determined to provoke direct confrontations with such officers, explicitly denying their formal authority and attempting none too subtly to sexualize the encounter. Women officers, then, might use force as a resource for rectifying such insults and for establishing control over such partially sexualized interactions. Consider the following woman officer's extended account providing such situational justifications for the use of force:

. . . I'm sitting at Second Street, Second and Nassau, writing curfews up. And this silver Thunderbird . . . blows right by a stop sign where I'm sitting. And I look up and think to myself, "Now, do I want to get involved?" And I figure, it was really belligerent doing it right in front of me. So I take off after him, put my lights on and he immediately pulls over. So he jumps out of the car. I jump out of the car right away and I say, "I'm stopping you for that stop sign you just blew through. . . . Let me see your cards, please." Then he starts making these lip smacking noises at me everytime he begins to talk. He said, (smack) "The only way you're seeing my cards is if you lock me up and the only way you're gonna lock me up is if you chase me." And I said to him, "Well, look, I will satisfy you on one account. Now go to your car because I will lock you up. . . . And just sit in your car. I'll be right with you." He smacks his lips, turns around and goes to his car and he sits. And I call a wagon at Second and Nassau. They ask me what I have. I say, "I've got one to go." So as the wagon acknowledges, the car all of a sudden tears out of its spot. And I get on the air and say, "I'm in pursuit." And I give them a description of the car and the direction I'm going. . . . And all of a sudden he pulls over about a block and a half after I started the pursuit. So I got on the air and I said, "I got him at Second and Washington." I jumped out of my car and as I jumped out he tears away again. Now I'm ready to die of embarrassment. I have to get back on the air and say no I don't have him. So I got on the air and said, "Look, he's playing games with me now. He took off again." I said, "I'm still heading South on Second Street." He gets down to Lexington. He pulls over again. Well, this time I pulled the police car in front of him. . . . I go over to the car and I hear him lock the doors. I pull out my gun and I put it right in his window. I say, "Unlock that door." Well, he looked at the gun. He nearly liked to shit himself. He unlocked the door. I holster my gun. I go to grab his arms to pull him out and all of a sudden I realize Anne's got him. So we keep pulling him out of the car. Throw him on the trunk of his car and kept pounding him back down on the trunk. She's punching his head. I'm kicking him. Then I take out my blackjack. I jack him across the shoulder. Then I go to jack him in the head and I jack Anne's fingers. . . . The next thing they know is we're throwing him bodily into the wagon. And they said, "Did you search him?" We go to the wagon, drag him out again. Now we're tearing through his pockets throwing everything on the ground. Pick him up bodily again, threw him in. . . . So I straightened it out with the sergeant. . . . I said, "What did you want me to do? Let any citizen on the street get stopped and pull away and that's the end of it?"

In this instance, a male suspect manages to convey a series of affronts to the officer's authority. These affronts become explicitly and insultingly sexual, turning the challenge from the claim that "no cop will stop me" to the more gender specific one, "no woman cop will stop me." Resistance ups the ante until the suspect backs down in the face of the officer's drawn revolver. The force to which the culprit was then subjected is normalized through all the accounts considered to this point—it is situationally justified as a means to reestablish and maintain immediate and symbolic control in a highly problematic encounter and it is excused as a natural, collective outburst following resolution of a dangerous, tension-filled incident. And finally, it is more implicitly justified as appropriate punishment, an account building upon standard police practices for abstract justification, to which I now turn.

ABSTRACT JUSTIFICATIONS

Police also justify the use of extreme force against certain categories of morally reprehensible persons. In this case, force is not presented as an instrumental means to regain control that has been symbolically or physically threatened. Instead, it is justified as an appropriate response to particularly heinous offenders. Categories of such offenders include: cop haters who have gained notoriety as persistent police antagonizers; cop killers or any person who has attempted seriously to harm a police officer (Westley, 1970:131); sexual deviants who prey on children and "moral women"; child abusers; and junkies and other "scum" who inhabit the street. The more morally reprehensible the act is judged, the more likely the police are to depict any violence directed toward its perpetrator as justifiable. Thus a man who exposes himself to children in a playground is less likely to experience police assault than one who rapes or sexually molests a child.

"Clean" criminals, such as high-level mafiosi, white-collar criminals, and professional burglars, are rarely subject to abstract force. Nor are perpetrators of violent and nonviolent street crimes who prey on adult males, prostitutes, and other categories of persons who belong on the street.[7] Similarly, the "psycho" or demented person is perceived as so mentally deranged that he is not responsible for his acts and hence does not merit abstract, punitive force (Van Maanen, 1978:233–34).

Police justify abstract force by invoking a higher moral purpose that legitimates the violation of commonly recognized standards. In one case, for example, a nun was raped by a seventeen-year-old male adolescent. When the police apprehended the suspect, he was severely beaten and his penis put in an electrical outlet to teach him a lesson. The story of the event was told to me by a police officer who, despite the fact that he rarely supported the use of extralegal force, depicted this treatment as legitimate. Indeed, when I asked if he would have participated had he been present, he responded, "I'm Catholic. I would have participated."

Excessive Force and Peer Responses

Although police routinely excuse and justify many incidents where they or their co-workers have used extreme force against a citizen or suspect, this does not mean that on any and every occasion the officer using such force is exonerated. Indeed, the concept of normal force is useful because it suggests that there are specific circumstances under which police officers will not condone the use of force by themselves or colleagues as reasonable and acceptable. Thus, officer-recognized conceptions of normal force are subject to restrictions of the following kinds:

1. Police recognize and honor some rough equation between the behavior of the suspect and the harmfulness of the force to which it is subject. There are limits, therefore, to the degree of force that is acceptable in particular circumstances. In the following incident, for example, an officer reflects on a situation in which a "symbolic assailant" (Skolnick, 1975:45) was mistakenly subject to more force than he "deserved" and almost killed:

> One time Bill Johnson and I . . . had a particularly rude drunk one day. He was really rude and spit on you and he did all this stuff and we even had to cuff him lying down on the hard stretcher, like you would do an epileptic. . . . So we were really mad. We said let's just give him one or two shots . . . slamming on the brakes and having him roll. But we didn't use our heads . . . we heard the stretcher go nnnnnBam and then nothing. We heard nothing and we realized we had put this man in with his head to the front so when we slammed on the brakes his stretcher. . . . I guess it can roll four foot. Well, it was his head that had hit the front. . . . So, we went to Madison Street and parked. It's a really lonely area. And we unlocked the wagon and peeked in. We know he's in there. We were so scared and we look in and there's not a sound and we see blood coming in front of the wagon and think ". . . we killed this man. What am I gonna do? What am I gonna tell my family?" And to make a long story short, he was just knocked out. But boy was I scared. From then on we learned, feet first.

2. Similarly, even in cases where suspects are seen as deserving some violent punishment, this force should not be used randomly and without control. Thus, in the following incident, an officer who "snapped out" and began to beat a child abuser clearly regarded his partner's attempt to stop the beating as reasonable.

. . . I knock on the door and a lady answers just completely hysterical. And I say, "Listen, I don't know what's going on in here," but then I hear this, just this screeching. You know. And I figure well I'm just going to find out what's going on so I just go past the lady and what's happening is that the husband had. . . . The kid was being potty trained and the way they were potty training this kid, this two-year-old boy, was that the boyfriend of this girl would pick up this kid and he would sit him down on top of the stove. It was their method of potty training. Well, first of all you think of your own kids. I mean afterwards you do. I mean I've never been this mad in my whole life. You see this little two-year-old boy seated on the top of the stove with rings around it being absolutely scalding hot. And he's saying "I'll teach you to go. . . ." It just triggered something. An uncontrollable. . . . It's just probably the most violent I ever got. Well you just grab that guy. You hit him ten, fifteen times . . . you don't know how many. You just get so mad. And I remember my partner eventually came in and grabbed me and said, "Don't worry about it. We got him. We got him." And we cuffed him and we took him down. Yeah that was bad.

Learning these sorts of restrictions on the use of normal force and these informal practices of peer control are important processes in the socialization of newcomers. This socialization proceeds both through ongoing observation and experience and, on occasion, through explicit instruction. For example, one veteran officer advised a rookie, "The only reason to go in on a pursuit is not to get the perpetrator but to pull the cop who gets there first offa the guy before he kills him."

Conclusion

The organization of police work reflects a poignant moral dilemma: For a variety of reasons, society mandates to the police the right to use force but provides little direction as to its proper use in specific, "real life" situations. Thus, the police, as officers of the law, must be prepared to use force under circumstances in which its rationale is often morally, legally, and practically ambiguous. This fact explains some otherwise puzzling aspects of police training and socialization.

The police academy provides a semblance of socialization for its recruits by teaching formal rules for using force. . . . [T]he full socialization of a police officer takes place outside the academy as the officer moves from its idealizations to the practicalities of the street. . . .

. . . [J]ustifications and excuses . . . conventionalize but do not reform situations that are inherently charged and morally ambiguous. In this way they simultaneously preserve the self-image of police as agents of the conventional order, provide ways in which individual officers can resolve their personal doubts as to the moral status of their action and those of their colleagues, and reinforce the solidarity of the police community.

Notes

1. Nonetheless masculine pronouns are generally used to refer to the police in this article, because the Metro P.D. remained dominated by men numerically, in style, and in tone. . . .

2. Some officers also substitute a large heavy duty flashlight for the nightstick. If used correctly, the flashlight can inflict more damage than the baton and is less likely to break when applied to the head or other parts of the body.

3. As the Metro City Police Commissioner commented in an interview: "In general, they [women] are physically weaker than males. . . . I believe they would be inclined to let their emotions all too frequently overrule their good judgment . . . there are periods in their life when they are psychologically unbalanced because of physical problems that are occurring within them."

4. The woman officer later explained that she did not obey the suspect's command because she saw no reflection of the partner in the suspect's glasses and therefore assumed he was lying.

5. The combat high is a state of controlled exhilaration in which the officer experiences a heightened awareness of the world around him. Officers report that perception, smell, and hearing seem acute; one seems to stand outside oneself, and the world appears extraordinarily vivid and clear. At the same time, officers insist that they are able to think rationally and instantly translate thoughts into action; when experienced, fear is not incapacitating but instead enhances the ability to act.

6. This police experience of fear and helplessness, leading to a violent outburst, may be analogized to a parent's reaction on seeing his child almost die in an accident. Imagine a scene in which a father is walking with his six-year-old son. Suddenly, the boy runs into the street to get a red ball on the pavement. The father watches a car slam on the brakes and miss the boy by two inches. He grabs his son and smacks him on the face before he takes him in his arms and holds him. . . .

7. The categories of persons who merit violence are not unique to the police. Prisoners, criminals, and hospital personnel appear to draw similar distinctions between morally unworthy persons; on the latter, see Sudnow (1967:105).

42 Anybody's Son Will Do

GWYNNE DYER

Perhaps the strangest social institution is the military. A notable characteristic is how separated it is from the society that it is set up to protect. Its bases are isolated from the rest of society—like a prison, armed guards control who enters and leaves. Like a prison, too, the military has the power to force its members to remain for years against their will. It can even lock people behind bars if they refuse orders. Many of its members live apart from the rest of society; they shop at their own stores and go to doctors who serve only the military. They even play in their own recreational settings—the Department of Defense operates more bowling alleys than any other organization. The most visible sign of separateness is the dress—its members proudly set themselves apart by wearing uniforms that proclaim they are not one of us.

The strangest characteristic that sets the military apart from the rest of us, of course, is not these things, but that their business is killing. It becomes the military's task to turn civilians—who have learned contrasting values and ways of life—into soldiers. This means that civilians must learn to become killers. How does the military accomplish this? This is the question that Dyer answers in this selection.

You think about it and you know you're going to have to kill but you don't understand the implications of that, because in the society in which you've lived murder is the most heinous of crimes . . . and you are in a situation in which it's turned the other way round. . . . When you do actually kill someone, the experience, my experience, was one of revulsion and disgust. . . .

I was utterly terrified—petrified—but I knew there had to be a Japanese sniper in a small fishing shack near the shore. He was firing in the other direction at Marines in another battalion, but I knew as soon as he picked off the people there—there was a window on our side—that he would start picking us off. And there was nobody else to go . . . and so I ran towards the shack and broke in and found myself in an empty room. . . .

There was a door which meant there was another room and the sniper was in that—and I just broke that down. I was just absolutely gripped by the fear that this man would expect me and would shoot me. But as it turned out he was in a sniper harness and he couldn't turn around fast enough. He was entangled in the harness so I shot him with a .45, and I felt remorse and shame. I can remember whispering foolishly, "I'm sorry" and then just throwing up. . . . I threw up all over myself. It was a betrayal of what I'd been taught since a child.

—William Manchester

481

YET HE DID KILL THE Japanese soldier, just as he had been trained to—the revulsion only came afterward. And even after Manchester knew what it was like to kill another human being, a young man like himself, he went on trying to kill his "enemies" until the war was over. Like all the other tens of millions of soldiers who had been taught from infancy that killing was wrong, and had then been sent off to kill for their countries, he was almost helpless to disobey, for he had fallen into the hands of an institution so powerful and so subtle that it could quickly reverse the moral training of a lifetime.

The whole vast edifice of the military institution rests on its ability to obtain obedience from its members even unto death—and the killing of others. It has enormous powers of compulsion at its command, of course, but all authority must be based ultimately on consent. The task of extracting that consent from its members has probably grown harder in recent times, for the gulf between the military and the civilian worlds has undoubtedly widened: Civilians no longer perceive the threat of violent death as an everyday hazard of existence, and the categories of people whom it is not morally permissible to kill have broadened to include (in peacetime) the entire human race. Yet the armed forces of every country can still take almost any young male civilian and turn him into a soldier with all the right reflexes and attitudes in only a few weeks. Their recruits usually have no more than twenty years' experience of the world, most of it as children, while the armies have had all of history to practice and perfect their techniques.

> Just think of how the soldier is treated. While still a child he is shut up in the barracks. During his training he is always being knocked about. If he makes the least mistake he is beaten, a burning blow on his body, another on his eye, perhaps his head is laid open with a wound. He is battered and bruised with flogging. On the march . . . they hang heavy loads round his neck like that of an ass.
>
> —Egyptian, ca. 1500 B.C.

> The moment I talk to the new conscripts about the homeland I strike a land mine. So I kept quiet. Instead, I try to make soldiers of them. I give them hell from morning to sunset. They begin to curse me, curse the army, curse the state. Then they begin to curse together, and become a truly cohesive group, a unit, a fighting unit.
>
> —Israeli, ca. A.D. 1970

All soldiers belong to the same profession, no matter what country they serve, and it makes them different from everybody else. They have to be different, for their job is ultimately about killing and dying, and those things are not a natural vocation for any human being. Yet all soldiers are born civilians. The method for turning young men into soldiers—people who kill other people and expose themselves to death—is basic training. It's essentially the same all over the world, and it always has been, because young men every- where are pretty much alike.

Human beings are fairly malleable, especially when they are young, and in every young man there are attitudes for any army to work with: the inher- ited values and postures, more or less dimly recalled, of the tribal warriors who were once the model for every young boy to emulate. Civilization did not involve a sudden clean break in the way people behave, but merely the progressive distortion and redirection of all the ways in which people in the old tribal societies used to behave, and modern definitions of maleness still contain a great deal of the old warrior ethic. The anarchic machismo of the primitive warrior is not what modern armies really need in their soldiers, but it does provide them with promising raw material for the transformation they must work in their recruits.

Just how this transformation is wrought varies from time to time and from country to country. In totally militarized societies—ancient Sparta, the samurai class of medieval Japan, the areas controlled by organizations like the Eritrean People's Liberation Front today—it begins at puberty or before, when the young boy is immersed in a disciplined society in which only the military values are allowed to penetrate. In more sophisticated modern soci- eties, the process is briefer and more concentrated, and the way it works is much more visible. It is, essentially, a conversion process in an almost reli- gious sense—and as in all conversion phenomena, the emotions are far more important than the specific ideas. . . .

Armies know this. It is their business to get men to fight, and they have had a long time to work out the best way of doing it. All of them pay lip ser- vice to the symbols and slogans of their political masters, though the amount of time they must devote to this activity varies from country to country. . . . Nor should it be thought that the armies are hypocritical—most of their members really do believe in their particular national symbols and slogans. But their secret is that they know these are not the things that sus- tain men in combat.

What really enables men to fight is their own self-respect, and a special kind of love that has nothing to do with sex or idealism. Very few men have died in battle, when the moment actually arrived, for the United States of America or for the sacred cause of Communism, or even for their homes and families; if they had any choice in the matter at all, they chose to die for each other and for their own vision of themselves. . . .

The way armies produce this sense of brotherhood in a peacetime envi- ronment is basic training: a feat of psychological manipulation on the grand scale which has been so consistently successful and so universal that we fail to notice it as remarkable. In countries where the army must extract its recruits in their late teens, whether voluntarily or by conscription, from a civilian environment that does not share the military values, basic training involves a brief but intense period of indoctrination whose purpose is not really to teach the recruits basic military skills, but rather to change their values and their loyalties. "I guess you could say we brainwash them a little bit," admitted a U.S. Marine drill instructor, "but you know they're good people."

The duration and intensity of basic training, and even its major emphases, depend on what kind of society the recruits are coming from, and on what sort of military organization they are going to. It is obviously quicker to train men from a martial culture than from one in which the dominant values are civilian and commercial, and easier to deal with volunteers than with reluctant conscripts. Conscripts are not always unwilling, however; there are many instances in which the army is popular for economic reasons. . . .

It's easier if you catch them young. You can train older men to be soldiers; it's done in every major war. But you can never get them to believe that they like it, which is the major reason armies try to get their recruits before they are 20. There are other reasons too, of course, like the physical fitness, lack of dependents, and economic dispensability of teenagers, that make armies prefer them, but the most important qualities teenagers bring to basic training are enthusiasm and naiveté. Many of them actively want the discipline and the closely structured environment that the armed forces will provide, so there is no need for the recruiters to deceive the kids about what will happen to them after they join.

> There is discipline. There is drill. . . . When you are relying on your mates and they are relying on you, there's no room for slackness or sloppiness. If you're not prepared to accept the rules, you're better off where you are.
> —British army recruiting advertisement, 1976

> People are not born soldiers, they become soldiers. . . . And it should not begin at the moment a new recruit is enlisted into the ranks, but rather much earlier, at the time of the first signs of maturity, during the time of adolescent dreams.
> —Red Star (Soviet army newspaper), 1973

Young civilians who have volunteered and have been accepted by the Marine Corps arrive at Parris Island, the Corps's East Coast facility for basic training, in a state of considerable excitement and apprehension: Most are aware that they are about to undergo an extraordinary and very difficult experience. But they do not make their own way to the base; rather, they trickle in to Charleston airport on various flights throughout the day on which their training platoon is due to form, and are held there, in a state of suppressed but mounting nervous tension, until late in the evening. When the buses finally come to carry them the 76 miles to Parris Island, it is often after midnight—and this is not an administrative oversight. The shock treatment they are about to receive will work most efficiently if they are worn out and somewhat disoriented when they arrive.

The basic training organization is a machine, processing several thousand young men every month, and every facet and gear of it has been designed with the sole purpose of turning civilians into Marines as efficiently as possible. Provided it can have total control over their bodies and their environment for approximately three months, it can practically guarantee converts. Parris Island provides that controlled environment, and the recruits do not set foot outside it again until they graduate as Marine privates 11 weeks later.

> They're allowed to call home, so long as it doesn't get out of hand—every three weeks or so they can call home and make sure everything's all right, if they haven't gotten a letter or there's a particular set of circumstances. If it's a case of an emergency call coming in, then they're allowed to accept that call; if not, one of my staff will take the message. . . .
>
> In some cases I'll get calls from parents who haven't quite gotten adjusted to the idea that their son had cut the strings—and in a lot of cases that's what they're doing. The military provides them with an opportunity to leave home but they're still in a rather secure environment.
>
> —Captain Brassington, USMC

For the young recruits, basic training is the closest thing their society can offer to a formal rite of passage, and the institution probably stands in an unbroken line of descent from the lengthy ordeals by which young males in precivilized groups were initiated into the adult community of warriors. But in civilized societies it is a highly functional institution whose product is not anarchic warriors, but trained soldiers.

Basic training is not really about teaching people skills; it's about changing them so that they can do things they wouldn't have dreamt of otherwise. It works by applying enormous physical and mental pressure to men who have been isolated from their normal civilian environment and placed in one where the only right way to think and behave is the way the Marine Corps wants them to. The key word the men who run the machine use to describe this process is motivation.

> I can motivate a recruit and in third phase, if I tell him to jump off the third deck, he'll jump off the third deck. Like I said before, it's a captive audience and I can train that guy; I can get him to do anything I want him to do. . . . They're good kids and they're out to do the right thing. We get some

bad kids, but you know, we weed those out. But as far as motivation—here, we can motivate them to do anything you want, in recruit training.

—USM drill instructor, Parris Island

The first three days the raw recruits spend at Parris Island are actually relatively easy, though they are hustled and shouted at continuously. It is during this time that they are documented and inoculated, receive uniforms, and learn the basic orders of drill that will enable young Americans (who are not very accustomed to this aspect of life) to do everything simultaneously in large groups. But the most important thing that happens in "forming" is the surrender of the recruits' own clothes, their hair—all the physical evidence of their individual civilian identities.

During a period of only 72 hours, in which they are allowed little sleep, recruits lay aside their former lives in a series of hasty rituals (like being shaven to the scalp) whose symbolic significance is quite clear to them even though they are quite deliberately given absolutely no time for reflection, or any hint that they might have the option of turning back from their commitment. The men in charge of them know how delicate a tightrope they are walking, though, because at this stage the recruits are still newly caught civilians who have not yet made their ultimate inward submission to the discipline of the Corps.

> Forming Day One makes me nervous. You've got a whole new mob of recruits, you know, 60 or 70 depending, and they don't know anything. You don't know what kind of a reaction you're going to get from the stress you're going to lay on them, and it just worries me the first day. . . .
>
> Things could happen, I'm not going to lie to you. Something might happen. A recruit might decide he doesn't want any part of this stuff and maybe take a poke at you or something like that. In a situation like that it's going to be a spur-of-the-moment thing and that worries me.
>
> —USMC drill instructor

But it rarely happens. The frantic bustle of forming is designed to give the recruit no time to think about resisting what is happening to him. And so the recruits emerge from their initiation into the system, stripped of their civilian clothes, shorn of their hair, and deprived of whatever confidence in their own identity they may previously have had as 18-year-olds, like so many blanks ready to have the Marine identity impressed upon them.

The first stage in any conversion process is the destruction of an individual's former beliefs and confidence, and his reduction to a position of helplessness and need. It isn't really as drastic as all that, of course, for three days cannot cancel out 18 years; the inner thoughts and the basic character are not erased. But the recruits have already learned that the only acceptable behavior is to repress any unorthodox thoughts and to mimic the character the Marine Corps wants. Nor are they, on the whole, reluctant to do so, for they want to be Marines. From the moment they arrive at Parris Island, the vague notion that has been passed down for a thousand generations that masculinity means being a warrior becomes an explicit article of faith, relentlessly preached: To be a man means to be a Marine.

There are very few 18-year-old boys who do not have highly romanticized ideas of what it means to be a man, so the Marine Corps has plenty of buttons to push. And it starts pushing them on the first day of real training. The officer in charge of the formation appears before them for the first time, in full dress uniform with medals, and tells them how to become men.

> The United States Marine Corps has 205 years of illustrious history to speak for itself. You have made the most important decision in your life . . . by signing your name, your life, your pledge to the Government of the United States, and even more importantly, to the United States Marine Corps—a brotherhood, an elite unit. In 10.3 weeks you are going to become a member of that history, those traditions, this organization—if you have what it takes. . . .
>
> All of you want to do that by virtue of your signing your name as a man. The Marine Corps says that we build men. Well, I'll go a little bit further. We develop the tools that you have—and everybody has those tools to a certain extent right now. We're going to give you the blueprints, and we are going to show you how to build a Marine. You've got to build a Marine—you understand?
>
> —Captain Pingree, USMC

The recruits, gazing at him in awe and adoration, shout in unison, "Yes, sir!" just as they have been taught. They do it willingly, because they are volunteers—but even conscripts tend to have the romantic fervor of volunteers if they are only 18 years old. Basic training, whatever its hardships, is a quick way to become a man among men, with an undeniable status, and beyond the initial consent to undergo it, it doesn't even require any decisions.

> I had just dropped out of high school and I wasn't doing much on the street except hanging out, as most teenagers would be doing. So they gave me an opportunity—a recruit picked me up, gave me a good line, and said that I could make it in the Marines, that I have a future ahead of me. And since I was living with my parents, I figured that I could start my own life here and grow up a little.
>
> —USMC recruit

> I like the hand-to-hand combat and . . . things like that. It's a little rough going on me, and since I have a small frame I would like to become deadly, as I would put it. I like to have them words, especially the way they've been teaching me here.
>
> —USMC recruit (from Brooklyn), Parris Island

The training, when it starts, seems impossibly demanding physically for most of the recruits—and then it gets harder week by week. There is constant barrage of abuse and insults aimed at the recruits, with the deliberate purpose of breaking down their pride and so destroying their ability to resist the transformation of values and attitudes that the Corps intends them to undergo. At the same time, the demands for constant alertness and for instant obedience are continuously stepped up, and the standards by which the dress and behavior of the recruits are judged become steadily more unforgiving. But it is all carefully calculated by the men who run the machine, who think and talk in terms of the stress they are placing on the recruits: "We take so many c.c.'s of stress and we administer it to each man—they should be a little bit scared and they should be unsure, but they're adjusting." The aim is to keep the training arduous but just within most of the recruits' capability to withstand. One of the most striking achievements of the drill instructors is to create and maintain the illusion that basic training is an extraordinary challenge, one that will set those who graduate apart from others, when in fact almost everyone can succeed.

There has been some preliminary weeding out of potential recruits even before they begin basic training, to eliminate the obviously unsuitable minority, and some people do "fail" basic training and get sent home, at least in peacetime. The standards of acceptable performance in the U.S. armed forces, for example, tend to rise and fall in inverse proportion to the number and quality of recruits available to fill the forces to the authorized manpower levels. But there are very few young men who cannot be turned into passable soldiers if the forces are willing to invest enough effort in it.

Not even physical violence is necessary to effect the transformation, though it has been used by most armies at most times.

> It's not what it was 15 years ago down here. The Marine Corps still occupies the position of a tool which the society uses when it feels like that is a resort that they have to fall to. Our society changes as all societies do, and our society felt that through enlightened training methods we could still produce the same product—and when you examine it, they're right. . . . Our 100 c.c.'s of stress is really all we need, not two gallons of it, which is what used to be. . . . In some cases with some of the younger drill instructors it was more an initiation than it was an acute test, and so we introduced extra officers and we select our drill instructors to "fine-tune" it.
>
> —Captain Brassington, USMC

There is, indeed, a good deal of fine-tuning in the roles that the men in charge of training any specific group of recruits assume. At the simplest level, there is a sort of "good cop-bad cop" manipulation of recruits' attitudes toward those applying the stress. The three younger drill instructors with a particular serial are quite close to them in age and unremittingly harsh in their demands for ever higher performance, but the senior drill instructor, a man almost old enough to be their father, plays a more benevolent and understanding part and is available for individual counseling. And generally off-stage, but always looming in the background, is the company commander, an impossibly austere and almost godlike personage.

At least these are the images conveyed to the recruits, although of course all these men cooperate closely with an identical goal in view. It works: In the end they become not just role models and authority figures, but the focus of the recruits' developing loyalty to the organization.

> I imagine there's some fear, especially in the beginning, because they don't know what to expect. . . . I think they hate you at first, at least for a week or two, but it turns to respect. . . . They're seeking discipline, they're seeking someone to take charge, 'cause at home they never got it. . . . They're looking to be told what to do and then someone is standing there enforcing what they tell them to do, and it's kind of like the father-and-son game, all the way through. They form a fatherly image of the DI whether they want to or not.
>
> —Sergeant Carrington, USMC

Just the sheer physical exercise, administered in massive doses, soon has recruits feeling stronger and more competent than ever before. Inspections, often several times daily, quickly build up their ability to wear the uniform and carry themselves like real Marines, which is a considerable source of pride. The inspections also help to set up the pattern in the recruits of unquestioning submission to military authority: Standing stock-still, staring straight ahead, while somebody else examines you closely for faults is about as extreme a ritual act of submission as you can make with your clothes on.

But they are not submitting themselves merely to the abusive sergeant making unpleasant remarks about the hair in their nostrils. All around them are deliberate reminders—the flags and insignia displayed on parade, the military music, the marching formations and drill instructors' cadenced calls—of the idealized organization, the "brotherhood" to which they will be admitted as full members if they submit and conform. Nowhere in the armed forces are the military courtesies so elaborately observed, the staffs' uniforms so immaculate (some DIs change several times a day), and the ritual aspects of military life so highly visible as on a basic training establishment.

Even the seeming inanity of close-order drill has a practical role in the conversion process. It has been over a century since mass formations of men were of any use on the battlefield, but every army in the world still drills its troops, especially during basic training, because marching in formation, with every man moving his body in the same way at the same moment, is a direct physical way of learning two things a soldier must believe: that orders have to be obeyed automatically and instantly, and that you are no longer an individual, but part of a group.

The recruits' total identification with the other members of their unit is the most important lesson of all, and everything possible is done to foster it. They spend almost every waking moment together—a recruit alone is an anomaly to be looked into at once—and during most of that time they are enduring shared hardships. They also undergo collective punishments, often for the misdeed or omission of a single individual (talking in the ranks, a bed not swept under during barracks inspection), which is a highly effective way of suppressing any tendencies toward individualism. And, of course, the DIs place relentless emphasis on competition with other "serials" in training: There may be something infinitely pathetic to outsiders about a marching group of anonymous recruits chanting, "Lift your heads and hold them high, 3313 is a-passin' by," but it doesn't seem like that to the men in the ranks.

Nothing is quite so effective in building up a group's morale and solidarity, though, as a steady diet of small triumphs. Quite early in basic training, the recruits begin to do things that seem, at first sight, quite dangerous: descend by ropes from 50-foot towers, cross yawning gaps hand-over-hand on high wires (known as the Slide for Life, of course), and the like. The common denominator is that these activities are daunting but not really dangerous: The ropes will prevent anyone from falling to his death off the rappelling tower, and there is a pond of just the right depth—deep enough to cushion a falling man, but not deep enough that he is likely to drown—under the Slide for Life. The goal is not to kill recruits, but to build up their confidence as individuals and as a group by allowing them to overcome apparently frightening obstacles.

> You have an enemy here at Parris Island. The enemy that you're going to have at Parris Island is in every one of us. It's in the form of cowardice. The most rewarding experience you're going to have in recruit training is standing on line every evening, and you'll be able to look into each other's eyes, and you'll be able to say to each other with your eyes: "By God, we've made it one more day! We've defeated the coward."
>
> —Captain Pingree
>
> Number on deck, sir, 45 . . . highly motivated, truly dedicated, rompin', stompin', bloodthirsty, kill-crazy United States Marine Corps recruits, SIR!
> —Marine chant, Parris Island

If somebody does fail a particular test, he tends to be alone, for the hurdles are deliberately set low enough that most recruits can clear them if they try. In any large group of people there is usually a goat: someone whose intelligence or manner or lack of physical stamina marks him for failure and contempt. The competent drill instructor, without deliberately setting up this unfortunate individual for disgrace, will use his failure to strengthen the solidarity and confidence of the rest. When one hapless young man fell off the Slide for Life into the pond, for example, his drill instructor shouted the usual invective—"Well, get out of the water. Don't contaminate it all day"— and then delivered the payoff line: "Go back and change your clothes. You're useless to your unit now."

"Useless to your unit" is the key phrase, and all the recruits know that what it means is "useless in battle." The Marine drill instructors at Parris Island know exactly what they are doing to the recruits, and why. They are not rear-echelon people filling comfortable jobs, but the most dedicated and intelligent NCOs the Marine Corps can find; even now, many of them have combat experience. The Corps has a clear-eyed understanding of precisely what it is training its recruits for—combat—and it ensures that those who do the training keep that objective constantly in sight.

The DIs "stress" the recruits, feed them their daily ration of synthetic triumphs over apparent obstacles, and bear in mind all the time that the goal is to instill the foundations for the instinctive, selfless reactions and the fierce group loyalty that is what the recruits will need if they ever see combat. They are arch-manipulators, fully conscious of it, and utterly unashamed. These kids have signed up as Marines, and they could well see combat; this is the way they have to think if they want to live.

> I've seen guys come to Vietnam from all over. They were all sorts of people that had been scared—some of them had been scared all their life and still scared. Some of them had been a country boy, city boys—you know, all different kinds of people—but when they got in combat they all reacted the same— 99 percent of them reacted the same. . . . A lot of it is training here at Parris Island, but the other part of it is survival. They know if they don't conform— conform I call it, but if they don't react in the same way other people are reacting, they won't survive. That's just it. You know, if you don't react together, then nobody survives.
>
> —USMC drill instructor, Parris Island

> When I went to boot camp and did individual combat training they said if you walk into an ambush what you want to do is just do a right face—you just turn right or left, whichever way the fire is coming from, and assault. I said, "Man, that's crazy. I'd never do anything like that. It's stupid." . . .
>
> The first time we came under fire, on Hill 1044 in Operation Beauty Canyon in Laos, we did it automatically. Just like you look at your watch to see what time it is. We done a right face, assaulted the hill—a fortified position with concrete bunkers emplaced, machine guns, automatic weapons—and we took it. And we killed—I'd estimate probably 35 North Vietnamese soldiers in

492 / *Gwynne Dyer*

the assault, and we only lost three killed. I think it was about two or three, and about eight or ten wounded. . . .

But you know, what they teach you, it doesn't faze you until it comes down to the time to use it, but it's in the back of your head, like, What do you do when you come to a stop sign? It's in the back of your head, and you react automatically.

—USMC sergeant

Combat is the ultimate reality that Marines—or any other soldiers, under any flag—have to deal with. Physical fitness, weapons training, battle drills, are all indispensable elements of basic training, and it is absolutely essential that the recruits learn the attitudes of group loyalty and interdependency which will be their sole hope of survival and success in combat. The training inculcates or fosters all of those things, and even by the halfway point in the 11-week course, the recruits are generally responding with enthusiasm to their tasks. . . .

In basic training establishments, . . . the malleability is all one way: in the direction of submission to military authority and the internalization of military values. What a place like Parris Island produces when it is successful, as it usually is, is a soldier who will kill because that is his job.

PART IX Social Change

WHAT IMAGERY SHOULD WE USE? We are drifting in a small boat on a tumultuous sea of social change. Like a mighty wind, unpredictable events swirl around us, at times seeming to sweep us away. Like an out-of-control fire, change leaves us no refuge, threatening to overcome and devour us. Change is like a bullet unleashed from a rifle, which pierces whatever is in its path and cannot be stopped until its energy is spent.

Regardless of the imagery, vast social change is a basic fact of contemporary life—and this change can be ominous, threatening to cast us into the unknown. Nothing seems to remain the same. Familiar landmarks are torn down and replaced, seemingly overnight, by a supermarket or another of an endless chain of fast-food outlets. Farm fields and woods are paved over as they sprout malls and shopping centers. Computers change so rapidly that the one you bought a year or two ago seems hopelessly out of date. Afraid of divorce—and of making a commitment—the young postpone marriage, opting instead to take refuge in the temporariness of cohabitation.

Cell phones embedded in human teeth, with its electronic signals translated into vibrations that travel from the tooth to the inner ear. A glove that translates the hand signals of deaf people into words. C-cash for purchases on the Internet. A plane propelled by human muscle-power. "Smart cards" to control access and security. Interactive television and virtual reality. Long distance surgery, with patient and surgeon 3,000 miles apart. A wallet computer that is not only a credit card and a checkbook, but that also sends fax and e-mail. It also dispenses tickets for airlines and concerts, and, not incidentally, will pop a coke out of the soda machine.

Although change is an essential part of today's society, it is anything but new. Twenty-five hundred years ago, Heraclitus said, "Everything flows; nothing stands still." Six hundred years later, Marcus Aurelius Antoninus wrote, "The universe is change." A more recent observer of the social scene put it this way: "The only thing constant is the certainty of change."

Social change was indeed a part of past civilizations, too, but an essential difference distinguishes those changes and what we are experiencing today. Barring catastrophe in the form of human or natural disaster, change in ancient times was slow—sometimes so slow that even over generations its effects were barely perceptible. In all societies of the world, in fact, it was routinely the case that the father passed his occupation down to his son, who, in turn, passed it on to his son, and so on. Mothers, too, passed their occupation to their daughters. The society that children lived in was practically identical to that into which their parents had been born. Although the players had changed, the basic social institutions, with their routine ways of handling things, remained the same over generations.

The contrast with our situation is stark. Most children today take it for granted that they are different from their parents—some even being amazed if they notice similarities with them. Adolescents routinely assume that their parents will not understand them, for each represents a different world. With worlds so dissimilar, it is not uncommon for a grown child visiting his or her parents, following an absence of months or even years, to find that after "catching up"—about an hour or so—they have little or nothing left to talk about. Social change has sorted them into different worlds, their particular experiences imparting contrasting orientations to life and, in effect, making them different kinds of people—and strangers to one another.

"Adapt or die" may be the maxim under which living creatures exist. Only the organisms that adapt to changing circumstances survive, and humans are no exception. Confronted with challenge, humans adapt. They change their social institutions to match changing circumstances. The effects are highly visible as people modify their behaviors. But the consequences are hardly limited to the external, for they also penetrate people's inner life, changing their ideas, attitudes, and beliefs, their basic orientations to the world.

In the opening selection, Robin Leidner examines what is perhaps the broadest change affecting our lives today, the *McDonaldization of society*. This means that a rationalized efficiency is taking over many of the routine aspects of everyday life. Not everyone welcomes social change, of course. Jerry Savells focuses on the Amish, analyzing how this ethno-religious group resists social change in order to maintain its traditional way of life. Laura Miller then continues this theme by looking at men's resistance to the gender integration of the military. As we close the book with an analysis of changes that are sweeping the world, William Wishard points out that we currently find ourselves between two ages. You need not agree with his optimism to see the implications of the future diverging in two directions, with us as reluctant passengers.

In conclusion, I would like to add that you cannot escape being shaped by your experiences of the vast changes occurring in society. For you to make better sense of your transformative experiences, however, I highly recommend the sociological imagination—the idea with which we began this book.

43 Over the Counter at McDonald's

ROBIN LEIDNER

Rationalization means to make things efficient. It means to set up rules that reduce unexpected events, increase control and predictability, and lead to efficient outcomes. Rationalization has become a central part of life in U.S. society. We live in a world of fast-food restaurants, TV dinners, and instant oil changes. We know what to expect when we step inside a Burger King or a Taco Bell. We know what the decor will look like, what the employees will say to us, what items will be on the menu, even what our meal will taste like. Rationalization has led to almost identical experiences whether we visit one of these restaurants in Paris or in Muncie, Indiana.

The epitome of rationalization, however, is McDonald's. What Henry Ford was to the assembly line of auto production, McDonald's is to the assembly line of food production. As you read Leidner's analysis of McDonald's, think of how other aspects of your life are being "McDonaldized," such as package tours, franchised gyms and workout centers, and, at college, machine-graded multiple choice questions.

McDonald's

NO ONE EVER WALKS into a McDonald's and asks, "So, what's good today?" except satirically. The heart of McDonald's success is its uniformity and predictability. Not only is the food supposed to taste the same every day everywhere in the world, but McDonald's promises that every meal will be served quickly, courteously, and with a smile. Delivering on that promise over 20 million times a day in 54 countries is the company's colossal challenge. Its strategy for meeting that challenge draws on scientific management's most basic tenets: Find the One Best Way to do every task and see that the work is conducted accordingly.

To ensure that all McDonald's restaurants serve products of uniform quality, the company uses centralized planning, centrally designed training programs, centrally approved and supervised suppliers, automated machinery and other specially designed equipment, meticulous specifications, and systematic inspections. To provide its customers with a uniformly pleasant "McDonald's experience," the company also tries to mass produce friendliness, deference, diligence, and good cheer through a variety of socialization and social control techniques. Despite sneers from those who equate uniformity with mediocrity, the success of McDonald's has been spectacular.

McFacts

The relentless standardization and infinite replication that inspire both horror and admiration are the legacy of Ray Kroc, a salesman who got into the hamburger business in 1954, when he was 52 years old, and created a worldwide phenomenon. His inspiration was a phenomenally successful hamburger stand owned by the McDonald brothers of San Bernardino, California. He believed that their success could be reproduced consistently through carefully controlled franchises, and his hamburger business succeeded on an unprecedented scale. The basic idea was to serve a very few items of strictly uniform quality at low prices. Over the years, the menu has expanded somewhat and prices have risen, but the emphasis on strict, detailed standardization has never varied. . . .

Enforcement of McDonald's standards has been made easier over the years by the introduction of highly specialized equipment. Every company-owned store in the United States now has an "in-store processor," a computer system that calculates yields and food costs, keeps track of inventory and cash, schedules labor, and breaks down sales by time of day, product, and worker. In today's McDonald's, lights and buzzers tell workers exactly when to turn burgers or take fries out of the fat, and technologically advanced cash registers, linked to the computer system, do much of the thinking for window workers. Specially designed ketchup dispensers squirt exactly the right amount of ketchup on each burger in the approved flower pattern. The french-fry scoops let workers fill a bag and set it down in one continuous motion and help them gauge the proper serving size.

The extreme standardization of McDonald's products, and its workers, is closely tied to its marketing. The company advertises on a massive scale. In fact, McDonald's is the single most advertised brand in the world. The national advertising assures the public that it will find high standards of quality, service, and cleanliness at every McDonald's store. The intent of the strict quality-control standards applied to every aspect of running a McDonald's outlet, from proper cleaning of the bathrooms to making sure the hamburgers are served hot, is to help franchise owners keep the promises made in the company's advertising.

The image of McDonald's outlets promoted in the company's advertising is one of fun, wholesomeness, and family orientation. Kroc was particularly concerned that his stores not become teenage hangouts, since that would discourage families' patronage. To minimize their attractiveness to teenage loiterers, McDonald's stores do not have jukeboxes, video games, or even telephones.

You Deserve a Break Today: Conditions of Employment

Although McDonald's does not want teenagers to hang out on its premises, it certainly does want them to work in the stores. Almost half of its U.S. employees are under 20 years old. In recent years, as the McDonald's chain has grown faster than the supply of teenagers, the company has also tried to attract senior citizens and housewives as workers. What people in these groups have in common is a preference or need for part-time work, and therefore a dearth of alternative employment options. Because of this lack of good alternatives, and because they may have other means of support for themselves and their dependents, many people in these groups are willing to accept jobs that provide less than subsistence wages.

Traditionally, McDonald's has paid most of its employees the minimum wage, although labor shortages have now forced wages up in some parts of the country. Benefits such as health insurance and sick days are entirely lacking for crew people at most franchises. In fact, when the topic of employee benefits was introduced in a class lecture at McDonald's management training center, it turned out to refer to crew meetings, individual work-evaluation sessions, and similar programs to make McDonald's management seem accessible and fair.

The lack of more tangible benefits is linked to the organization of employment at McDonald's as part-time work. According to the manager of the franchise I studied, all McDonald's hourly employees are officially part-time workers, in that no one is guaranteed a full work week. The company's labor practices are designed to make workers bear the costs of uncertainty based on fluctuation in demand. McDonald's places great emphasis on having no more crew people at work at any time than are required by customer flow at that period, as measured in half-hour increments. Most workers therefore have fluctuating schedules, and they are expected to be flexible about working late or leaving early depending on the volume of business.

McDonald's wants both managers and workers to dedicate themselves to the values summed up in its three-letter corporate credo, "QSC." Quality, service, and cleanliness are the ends that the company's thousands of rules and specifications are intended to achieve. Kroc promised his customers QSC, and he believed firmly that if, at every level of the organization, McDonald's workers were committed to providing higher quality food, speedier service, and cleaner surroundings than the competition, the success of the enterprise was assured. McDonald's extraordinarily elaborate training programs are designed both to teach McDonald's procedures and standards and to instill and enforce corporate values.

Kroc approached his business with a zeal and dedication that even he regarded as religious: "I've often said that *I believe in God, family, and McDonald's—and in the office that order is reversed.*" Throughout the organization, Kroc is still frequently quoted and held up as a model, and nowhere is his ongoing influence more apparent than at Hamburger University.

Taking Hamburgers Seriously: Training Managers

McDonald's main management training facility is located on 80 beautifully landscaped acres in Oak Brook, Illinois, a suburb of Chicago. Its name, Hamburger University, captures the thoroughness and intensity with which McDonald's approaches management training, and it also suggests the comic possibilities of immersion in McDonald's corporate world. The company tries to produce managers "with ketchup in their veins," a common McDonald's phrase for people who love their work, take pride in it, and are extraordinarily hardworking, competitive, and loyal to McDonald's. A line I heard frequently at Hamburger U. was, "We take hamburgers very seriously here." Nothing I saw called this fixity of purpose into doubt.

Ensuring uniformity of service and products in its far-flung empire is a major challenge for McDonald's. In each McDonald's store, in regional training centers, and at Hamburger University, crew people, managers, and franchisees learn that there is a McDonald's way to handle virtually every detail of the business and that doing things differently means doing things wrong. Training begins in the stores, where crew people are instructed using materials provided by the corporation and where managers prepare for more advanced training. Management trainees and managers seeking promotion work with their store managers to learn materials in manuals and workbooks provided by the corporation. When they have completed the manual for the appropriate level, they are eligible for courses taught in regional training centers and at Hamburger University: the Basic Operations Course, the

Intermediate Operations Course, the Applied Equipment Course, and, finally, the Advanced Operations Course, taught only at Hamburger University. Altogether, the full training program requires approximately six hundred to one thousand hours of work. It is required of everyone who wishes to own a McDonald's store, and it is strongly recommended for all store managers. By the time trainees get to Hamburger University for the Advanced Operations Course, they have already put in considerable time working in a McDonald's store—two to three and a half years, on average—and have acquired much detailed knowledge about McDonald's workings.

The zeal and competence of franchisees and managers are of special concern to McDonald's, since they are the people responsible for daily enforcement of corporate standards. Their training therefore focuses as much on building commitment and motivation as on extending knowledge of company procedures. In teaching management skills, McDonald's also works on the personalities of its managers, encouraging both rigid adherence to routines and, somewhat paradoxically, personal flexibility. Flexibility is presented as a virtue both because the company wants to minimize resistance to adopting McDonald's ways of doing things and to frequent revision of procedures, and because managers must provide whatever responsiveness to special circumstances the system has, since crew people are allowed virtually no discretion. Hamburger University therefore provides a large dose of personal-growth cheerleading along with more prosaic skills training. . . .

The curriculum of the Advanced Operating Course includes inculcation with pride in McDonald's. Sessions are devoted to McDonald's history and McDonald's dedication to ever-improving QSC. Lectures are sprinkled with statistics attesting to McDonald's phenomenal success. Students hear the story of Ray Kroc's rise to wealth and prominence, based on his strength of character and willingness to work hard, and are assigned his autobiography, *Grinding It Out*. Kroc is quoted frequently in lectures, and students are encouraged to model themselves on him. They are told repeatedly that they have all proven themselves "winners" by getting as far as they have at McDonald's. The theme throughout is "We're the best in the world, we know exactly what we're doing, but our success depends on the best efforts of every one of you."

About 3,500 students from all over the world attend classes at Hamburger University each year. Those who complete the course receive diplomas proclaiming them Doctors of Hamburgerology. The course lasts two weeks and is extremely rigorous. Class time is about evenly divided between work in the labs and lectures on store operations and personnel management. In the labs, trainees learn the mechanics of ensuring that McDonald's food is of consistent quality and its stores in good working order. They learn to check the equipment and maintain its properly so that fries cook at precisely the right temperature, shakes are mixed to just the right consistency, and ice cubes are uniform. "Taste of Quality" labs reinforce McDonald's standards for food quality. For instance, in a Condiments Lab, trainees are taught exactly how to store vegetables and sauces, what the shelf lives of these products are, and how they should look and taste. Samples of "McDonald's quality" Big Mac Special Sauce are contrasted with samples that have been left too long unrefrigerated and should be discarded. The importance of serving only food that meets McDonald's standards is constantly emphasized and, a trainer pointed out, "McDonald's has standards for everything, down to the width of the pickle slices." . . .

LEARNING THE JOB

As a manager at Hamburger University explained to me, the crew training process is how McDonald's standardization is maintained, how the company ensures that Big Macs are the same everywhere in the world. The McDonald's central administration supplies franchisees with videotapes and other materials for use in training workers to meet the company's exacting specifications. The company produces a separate videotape for each job in the store, and it encourages franchisees to keep their tape libraries up-to-date as product specifications change. The Hamburger University professor who taught the Advanced Operating Course session on training said that, to keep current, franchisees should be buying 10 or 12 tapes a year. For each work station in the store, McDonald's also has a "Station Operation Checklist" (SOC), a short but highly detailed job description that lays out exactly how the job should be done: how much ketchup and mustard go on each kind of hamburger, in what sequence the products customers order are to be gathered, what arm motion is to be used in salting a batch of fries, and so on. . . .

THE ROUTINE

McDonald's had routinized the work of its crews so thoroughly that decision making had practically been eliminated from the jobs. As one window worker told me, "They've tried to break it down so that it's almost idiot-proof." Most of the workers agreed that there was little call for them to use their own judgment on the job, since there were rules about everything. If an unusual problem arose, the workers were supposed to turn it over to a manager.

Many of the noninteractive parts of the window workers' job had been made idiot-proof through automation. The soda machines, for example, automatically dispensed the proper amount of beverage for regular, medium, and large cups. Computerized cash registers performed a variety of functions handled elsewhere by human waitresses, waiters, and cashiers, making some kinds of skills and knowledge unnecessary. As a customer gave an order, the window worker simply pressed the cash register button labeled with the name of the selected product. There was no need to write the orders down, because the buttons lit up to indicate which products had been selected. Nor was there any need to remember prices, because the prices were programmed into the machines. Like most new cash registers, these added the tax automatically and told workers how much change customers were owed, so the window crew did not need to know how to do those calculations. The cash registers also helped regulate some of the crew's interactive work by reminding them to try to increase the size of each sale. For example, when a customer ordered a Big Mac, large fries, and a regular Coke, the cash register buttons for cookies, hot apple pies, ice cream cones, and ice cream sundaes would light up, prompting the worker to suggest dessert. It took some skill to operate the relatively complicated cash register, as my difficulties during my first work shift made clear, but this organizationally specific skill could soon be acquired on the job.

In addition to doing much of the workers' thinking for them, the computerized cash registers made it possible for managers to monitor the crew members' work and the store's inventory very closely. For example, if the number of Quarter Pounder with Cheese boxes gone did not match the number of Quarter Pounders with Cheese sold or accounted for as waste, managers might suspect that workers were giving away or taking food. Managers could easily tell which workers had brought in the most money during a given interval and who was doing the best job of persuading customers to buy a particular item. The computerized system could also complicate what would otherwise have been simple customer requests, however. For example, when a man who had not realized the benefit of ordering his son's food as a Happy Meal came back to the counter to ask whether his little boy could have one of the plastic beach pails the Happy Meals were served in, I had to ask a manager what to do, since fulfilling the request would produce a discrepancy between the inventory and the receipts. Sometimes the extreme systematization can induce rather than prevent idiocy, as when a window worker says she cannot serve a cup of coffee that is half decaffeinated and half regular because she would not know how to ring up the sale.

The interactive part of window work is routinized through the Six Steps of Window Service and also through rules aimed at standardizing attitudes and demeanors as well as words and actions. The window workers were taught that they represented McDonald's to the public and that their attitudes were therefore an important component of service quality. Crew people could be reprimanded for not smiling, and often were. The window workers were supposed to be cheerful and polite at all times, but they were also told to be themselves while on the job. McDonald's does not want its workers to seem like robots, so part of the emotion work asked of the window crew is that they act naturally. "Being yourself" in this situation meant behaving in a way that did not seem stilted. Although workers had some latitude to go beyond the script, the short, highly schematic routine obviously did not allow much room for genuine self-expression.

McDonald's window workers' routines were not intended to give them much leverage over customers' behavior, however. The window workers interacted only with people who had already decided to do business with McDonald's and who therefore did not need to be persuaded to take part in the service interaction. Furthermore, almost all customers were familiar enough with McDonald's routines to know how they were expected to behave. For instance, I never saw a customer who did not know that she or he was supposed to come up to the counter rather than sit down and wait to be served. This customer training was accomplished through advertising, spatial design, customer experience, and the example of other customers.

Additional cues about expected customer behavior are provided by the design of the restaurants. For example, the entrances usually lead to the service counter, not to the dining area, making it unlikely that customers will fail to realize that they should get in line, and the placement of waste cans makes clear that customers are expected to throw out their own trash. Most important, the majority of customers have had years of experience with McDonald's, as well as with other fast-food restaurants that have similar arrangements. The company estimates that the average customer visits a McDonald's 20 times a year and it is not uncommon for a customer to come in several times per week. For many customers, then, ordering at McDonald's is as routine an interaction as it is for the window worker.

Not surprisingly, then, most customers at the McDonald's I studied knew what was expected of them and tried to play their part well. They sorted themselves into lines and gazed up at the menu boards while waiting to be served. They usually gave their orders in the conventional sequence: burgers or other entrees, french fries or other side orders, drinks, and desserts. Hurried customers with savvy might order an item "only if it's in the bin," that is, ready to be served. Many customers prepared carefully so that they could give their orders promptly when they got to the counter. This preparation sometimes became apparent when a worker interrupted to ask, "What kind of dressing?" or "Cream and sugar?," flustering customers who could not deliver their orders as planned.

McDonald's routines work most efficiently when all customers accept their products exactly as they are usually prepared; indeed, the whole business is based on this premise. Since, however, some people give special instructions for customized products, such as "no onions," the routine allows for these exceptions. At the franchise I studied, workers could key the special requests into their cash registers, which automatically printed out "grill slips" with the instructions for the grill workers to follow. Under this system, the customer making the special order had to wait for it to be prepared, but the smooth flow of service for other customers was not interrupted. Another type of routine difficulty was customer dissatisfaction with food quality. Whenever a customer had a complaint about the food—cold fries, dried-out burger—window workers were authorized to supply a new product immediately without consulting a supervisor.

These two kinds of difficulties—special orders and complaints about food—were the only irregularities window workers were authorized to handle. The subroutines increased the flexibility of the service system, but they did not increase the workers' discretion, since procedures were in place for dealing with both situations. All other kinds of demands fell outside the window crew's purview. If they were faced with a dispute about money, an extraordinary request, or a furious customer, workers were instructed to call a manager; the crew had no authority to handle such problems.

Given the almost complete regimentation of tasks and preemption of decision making, does McDonald's need the flexibility and thoughtfulness of human workers? As the declining supply of teenagers and legislated increases in the minimum wage drive up labor costs, it is not surprising that McDonald's is experimenting with electronic replacements. So far, the only robot in use handles behind-the-scenes work rather than customer interactions. ARCH (Automated Restaurant Crew Helper) works in a Minnesota McDonald's where it does all the frying and lets workers know when to prepare sandwich buns, when supplies are running low, and when fries are no longer fresh enough to sell. Other McDonald's stores (along with Arby's and Burger King units) are experimenting with a touch-screen computer system that lets customers order their meals themselves, further curtailing the role of the window worker.

Overview

McDonald's pioneered the routinization of interactive service work and remains an exemplar of extreme standardization. Innovation is not discouraged at McDonald's; the company favors experimentation, at least among managers and franchisees. Ironically, though, "the object is to look for new, innovative ways to create an experience that is exactly the same no matter what McDonald's you walk into, no matter where it is in the world." Thus, when someone in the field comes up with a good idea—and such McDonald's success stores as the Egg McMuffin and the Big Mac were store-level inspirations—the corporation experiments, tests, and refines the idea and finally implements it in a uniform way systemwide.

McDonald's . . . does promise uniform products and consistent service, and to provide them the company has broken down virtually every task required to run a store into detailed routines with clear instructions and standards. For those routines to run smoothly, conditions must be relatively predictable, so McDonald's tries to control as many contingencies as possible, including the attitudes and behavior of workers, managers, and customers. The company uses a wide array of socialization and control techniques to ensure that these people are familiar with McDonald's procedures and willing to comply with them.

Most McDonald's work is organized as low-paying, low-status, part-time jobs that give workers little autonomy. Almost every decision about how to do crew people's tasks has been made in advance by the corporation, and many of the decisions have been built into the stores' technology. Why use human workers at all, if not to take advantage of the human capacity to respond to circumstances flexibly? McDonald's does want to provide at least a simulacrum of the human attributes of warmth, friendliness, and recognition. For that reason, not only worker's movements but also their words, demeanor, and attitudes are subject to managerial control.

Although predictability is McDonald's hallmark, not all factors can be controlled by management. One of the most serious irregularities that store management must deal with is fluctuation in the flow of customers, both expected and unexpected. Since personnel costs are the most manipulable variable affecting a store's profitability, managers want to match labor power to consumer demand as exactly as possible. They do so by paying all crew people by the hour, giving them highly irregular hours based on expected sales—sometimes including split shifts—and sending workers home early or keeping them late as conditions require. In other words, the costs of uneven demand are shifted to workers whenever possible. Since most McDonald's crew people cannot count on working a particular number of hours at precisely scheduled times, it is hard for them to make plans based on how much money they will earn or exactly what times they will be free. Workers are pressured to be flexible in order to maximize the organization's own flexibility in staffing levels. In contrast, of course, flexibility in the work process itself is minimized.

Routinization has not made the crew people's work easy. Their jobs, although highly structured and repetitive, are often demanding and stressful. Under these working conditions, the organization's limited commitment to workers, as reflected in job security, wages, and benefits, makes the task of maintaining worker motivation and discipline even more challenging. A variety of factors, many orchestrated by the corporation, keeps McDonald's crew people hard at work despite the limited rewards. Socialization into McDonald's norms, extremely close supervision (both human and electronic), individual and group incentives, peer pressure, and pressure from customers all play their part in getting workers to do things the McDonald's way.

Because franchisees and store-level managers are responsible for enforcing standardization throughout the McDonald's system, their socialization includes a more intensive focus on building commitment to and pride in the organization than does crew training. In fact, it is the corporate attempt at transforming these higher-level McDonald's people by making them more loyal, confident, flexible, and sensitive to others, as well as more knowledgeable about company procedures, that makes the extreme rigidity of the crew training workable. The crew people do not have to be trusted with decision-making authority, because all unusual problems are referred to managers. Their more extensive training gives them the knowledge and attitudes to make the kinds of decisions the corporation would approve. . . . In addition to thorough socialization, McDonald's managers and franchisees are subjected to close corporate oversight. Every aspect of their stores' operations is rated by corporate staff, and they are sanctioned accordingly.

Despite elaborate socialization and social controls, McDonald's stores do not, of course, carry out every corporate directive exactly as recommended. In the store I studied, managers did not always provide their workers with the mandated support and encouragement, crew trainers did not always follow the Six Steps of Window Service with the required eye contact and smile. There were many kinds of pressures to deviate from corporate standards. Nonetheless, the benefits of standardization should not be underestimated. As every Durkheimian knows, clear rules and shared standards provide support and coherence as well as constraint. Although some aspects of the routines did strike the participants as overly constraining, undignified, or silly, the approved routines largely worked.

Obtaining the cooperation of workers and managers is not enough to ensure the smooth functioning of McDonald's relatively inflexible routines. Customers must be routinized as well. Not only do customers have to understand the service routine and accept the limited range of choices the company offers, they also must be willing to do some kinds of work that are done for them in conventional restaurants, including carrying food to the table and throwing out their trash. Experience, advertising, the example set by other customers, and clear environmental cues familiarize customers with McDonald's routines, and most want to cooperate in order to speed service.

44 Social Change Among the Amish

JERRY SAVELLS

With change in contemporary society so common, and so extensive, how is it possible to hold it back? Most of us are engulfed in social change so vast that it sweeps over us like a tide. Like it or not, we have little choice but to adapt. Isn't this the situation for everyone who lives in an industrialized or post-industrialized society? Vast changes occur, and rapidly so. Our only choice seems to be how to adapt.

But not so for everybody. The Amish are an outstanding exception. This group of people, who broke from the Swiss-German Mennonite church in the late 1600s and settled in Pennsylvania around 1727, can now be found in about twenty states and Ontario, Canada. About 75 percent, however, live in just three states: Pennsylvania, Ohio, and Indiana. To protect their values, the Amish strategically control change. They maintain customs of dress, music, transportation, marriage, entertainment, and morality from the 1600s and continue to reject "worldly ways." How do they manage to resist such pressure? That is the focus of Savells' article.

THE AUTHOR VISITED EIGHT Amish communities in six states from 1982 to 1986: Berne and Milroy, Indiana; Ethridge, Tennessee; Intercourse and Bird-in-Hand, Pennsylvania; Kalona, Iowa; Plain City, Ohio; and Montezuma, Georgia. Face-to-face interviews were conducted with a select number of the local Amish population and some of the non-Amish population who have frequent contact with the Amish, i.e., local merchants who sell to the Amish, craftpersons, farmers, mail carriers, drivers of the local milk trucks who travel to Amish farms almost daily, and others. A structured twelve-page questionnaire has been used to collect research data using a stratified random sample selected from the New American Almanac (1983) and the Ohio Amish Directory (1981). At this time, 130 questionnaires and/or personal interviews have been completed with selected Amish families. An additional fifty interviews have also been completed among so-called "conservative Mennonite" families for future comparisons.

Although the sample is small, it is encouraging since the Old Order Amish have spurned many efforts from the scientific community to investigate their lifestyle. This particular effort gave new meaning to the term "field research," since it represents approximately 6,500 miles of driving, spread over thirty months.

The Amish interviewees were polite and cordial, but they typically do not welcome outsiders intruding into their lives. They were both retiring and private in their demeanor, since they have not been socialized to desire interaction with strangers. Their lifestyle and religion promote voluntary isolation and this has been a major obstacle to anyone intent on collecting research data via personal interviews. Since the religious concerns of the Amish hold top priority, they would not engage intentionally in any activity that would have the potential of embarrassing members in the same church district.

Sociological Considerations

A brief visit to the public library will reinforce the observation that the Amish cherish many social values once widely embraced in our agrarian society of the Colonial period—values which are largely the antithesis of those that emerged in a modern urban, industrialized society. The Amish typically emphasize the importance of humility, modesty, strong obedience to God, and social conformity; they abhor pride, social snobbery, individualism, and winning through competition. Family bonds and their faith are indeed the cornerstones of the Amish lifestyle.

Unfortunately, what limited information is available to the lay public about the Old Order Amish is often sensationalized and distorted. Yet, there is a distinct feeling of "separateness" and "difference" with numerous references to their horse-and-buggy transportation, somewhat drab clothing, and their aloofness (or overt resistance) to those things considered "trendy" or fashionable.

The Amish are very ethnocentric with a strong sense of social solidarity. There is a consciousness-of-kind evident in their thinking and quick sanctions directed toward the non-believer or those displaying evidence of weakness in their faith. Indeed, some sociologists might argue that the Amish practice of insularity—with a limited tolerance of any deviation—is a major reason why they have survived as a model of the extended family of the past.

In his professional writing, journalist Alvin Toffler has pointed out the disastrous consequences of modern materialism, self-serving lifestyles, hedonistic behavior, the transience and rootlessness of this culture, and extreme emphasis upon competition, money, and careerism to determine one's self-worth. The latter suggest experiences both alien and repulsive to Amish tradition; they abhor the concept of personal achievement rather than seeking to express God's will, the modern habit of "powerbrokering" to gain social advantages, and mutual manipulation. . . . Social change is evident—but carefully controlled and monitored. They work to preserve traditions of the past, emphasize the importance of humility and divine guidance in controlling their own destiny, and maintain a strong posture of serving God rather than the interests of humanity.

An Operational Definition of Change

The Amish do not live within a social vacuum. They are surrounded by accelerating currents of social, political, and economic changes which directly influence their quality of life. One reasonably expects the Amish to be vulnerable to pressures toward modernization. For example, many have been asked to sell their land for commercial development at inflated prices. The changing economic climate in these eight communities and the frustration of competing in a money market where "megabucks" and agri-business threaten the small farmer are having a definite impact upon the Amish way of life.

Amish farmers and the future of their children are often adversely affected by soaring land prices, and the foreign trade imbalance can mean a restricted market for some of their farm exports. Furthermore, when the Amish farmer needs to borrow money for spring planting, the interest rate at the local bank can be especially painful for the small farmer with a limited cash flow.

The Amish are forced to compete in a "money market" where agri-business and the profit motive often threaten some of their most cherished values. For example, our society promotes maximum efficiency, quality control through standardization, the accumulation of capital or wealth, competition among workers for career advancement, and the merits of mass production—basic trends essentially alien to the Amish pursuit of "devotedness, simplicity, and peace."

The Amish strongly advocate the "therapeutic value of real work." They believe that physical labor is good for mind, body, and soul in keeping with the biblical admonition of earning one's bread by the sweat of one's brow. Their work is labor-intensive, in contrast to the national marketplace dominated by the forces of technology and profit margins. Thus, the Amish do not view every new labor-saving device as desirable or progressive. . . .

Since life in any Amish community is ongoing, it is not possible or practical to totally isolate units of analysis, i.e., families, without the influence of outside variables. The Amish do not constitute an experimental group in a laboratory situation. Hence, one must be careful not to treat all indicators of social change as evidence of modernity. Some changes may be basically unique to one church district or community, and cannot be considered universal to all Amish. For example, the New Order Amish in both Kalona and Intercourse have accepted the practice of having closer contact with the outside world; some own cottage industries that cater to tourists and some have given their business cards to this researcher. In many Old Order communities this behavior would be unacceptable.

Pressures That Influence Modernization

The five major social institutions—family, religion, economics, education, and politics—were studied in this sample of Amish interviewees as an ethnographic method to identify and document patterns of modernity. Caution is both recommended and prudent to avoid the pitfalls of making global generalizations regarding the Amish lifestyle, since rules of behavior may vary among church districts or regions. The Amish define the behavioral expectations and boundaries of their communities through the *Ordnung*, the official rules of the Amish community. Any member found to have disobeyed the *Ordnung* would be subject to *Meidung*, or shunning. It is a measure of social and religious control still considered an acceptable practice by over eighty percent of the respondents in this study. This has the avowed purpose of encouraging the offender to seek forgiveness from God and other members of the church district as quickly as possible.

FAMILY

This institution is still greatly cherished by the Amish. It is not unusual to see three generations living together in either of the eight research sites. The average Amish family in this sample had seven children, but this researcher talked with some Amish families that had as many as thirteen children. Family size would appear to be more a reflection of age and economic security than sheer desire, since almost all Amish parents profess to want large families. Modern means of contraception are forbidden, unless medically prescribed to protect the health of the mother.

Several Amish parents were concerned that economic factors beyond their control represent a serious challenge to their children and may cause many of their youth to accept employment in occupations provided by outsiders. In Milroy, Indiana, several of the young married males commuted to Indianapolis with the assistance of a non-Amish driver to work as carpenters in the building industry—a situation that forces them to accommodate the expectations of a non-Amish employer. Being away from hearth and home was clearly not their first choice; it reduces the opportunities and time to share family activities. The subtle pressures of this experience can undermine cherished Amish values in the name of economic survival.

Amish parents prefer that their families remain self-supporting, since the daily sharing of work assignments tends to give prolonged contact between parent and child, with a "solidifying effect." The Amish still grow much of their food, provide for their own energy needs, and assume responsibility for their own well-being, rather than relying upon insurance companies, welfare programs, or Social Security to shield them from the hazards of life.

To help preserve this family-centered focus, Amish parents are careful to shield their children from the information explosion of our technological society—particularly as it is disseminated by the mass media and in the public schools. However, where outside employment is essential for survival, accommodation may become necessary through learning new skills or pursuing an advanced education.

The Amish family is still strongly patriarchal. The women's liberation movement has made very few incursions into any of these eight Amish communities. However, Amish women today are by no means totally subservient in a traditional sense. This researcher discovered that Amish women in some church districts can accept modest change without severe reprisals or shunning. For example, in Berne, it was a common practice for Amish women to use polyester cloth rather than 100 percent cotton for their family's clothing. Also, many of these clothes are now purchased, rather than handsewn. Some of the Amish wives in Berne used Mary Kay cosmetics, but only the creams, not the make-up. The latter is considered too "worldly."

RELIGION

The Amish in this sample show some gradual change in their religious practices. Over ten percent of the respondents had changed their religious preference from Old Order to New Order within the context of one generation. This change will definitely have a ripple effect for their children, grandchildren, and great-grandchildren. . . .

The Old Order Amish prohibit ownership of automobiles, telephones, and electricity in the home. However, farm tractors are now being used by the New Order Amish in some areas; in Kalona, tractors were acceptable if they had steel wheels, not rubber tires. The adoption of the latter would create too much mobility.

In both Plain City and Intercourse, diesel generators are now considered an acceptable innovation to supply the barn (not the house) with electricity.

The Amish dairy farmer—like all other dairy farmers—must meet state health standards regarding proper refrigeration of milk which is sold commercially. Hence, it is very difficult to pinpoint where the Old Order Amish religious practices actually end and their lifestyle begins since the two are often "one and the same."

A few of the Amish in Berne are now beginning to use cameras, especially to photograph their children, a practice that would have brought immediate censure a few years ago. Even when this practice is known to other family members, it is regarded as a taboo topic for everyday conversation. Most of the Old Order Amish interviewed in Berne still believe that the Bible forbids taking "graven images" of persons.

ECONOMIC CHANGES

The economic security in some of the families interviewed appeared to be more fragile than that of previous generations. Wherever possible parents are still subdividing their farms so that their children will have the chance to enjoy the fruit of their labor in farming. However, with a shortage of affordable and available land for farming, the younger generation has found itself increasingly dependent upon ties with the non-Amish sector of the local economy. In Berne and Intercourse, some of the local Amish men work in craft-related industries, such as factories that manufacture furniture (mostly handcrafted), coal or wood burning stoves, and carriages. In Kalona some of the Amish girls work in a local cheese factory that purchases the bulk milk produced on Amish farms. The waitresses in some of the local restaurants are also members of the local Amish community.

This trend toward outside employment leaves the Amish especially vulnerable to forces of economic recession and a stagnant national economy. Since the Old Order Amish prohibit their members from pursuing an advanced education which would make them more competitive in the national job market, they are often underskilled in jobs that require moderate levels of technological sophistication.

The Amish are also forbidden to accept employment where joining a labor union is a condition of the workplace; thus, they have minimal job security in a formal sense. However, the Amish in this sample remained cheerful and optimistic that God would provide for their daily needs.

EDUCATION

As one moves from the environment of the Old Order Amish to the New Order Amish, one expects that the number of years of formal education might increase with each successive generation. There is a definite trend in that direction, since some of the New Order Amish want to develop marketable skills at a trade school or by taking correspondence courses. In Montezuma this researcher interviewed a young female from a New Order Amish family who is a registered nurse.

The Old Order Amish still maintain their own schools in most of the communities studied. In Berne the Old Order Amish can send their children to the eighth grade in an Amish school where funds for operating the school are provided by the parents of the children who attend, and an Amish teacher is provided, or they are permitted to send their children to a public school in Berne—only through the ninth grade.

Very few of the children in Old Order Amish families remain in school after reaching age sixteen—the age at which they can quit according to most state laws. In order to comply with legal requirements some Amish children voluntarily repeat the ninth grade—a sacrifice to the expectations of their Amish parents.

One Old Order Amish mother of several children indicated that she wanted her sons and daughters to consider going to college, preferably a Mennonite college, where they could receive training to become a member of a "noble" profession. Then they could serve the Amish community directly in professions such as teaching, and medical or veterinary practice.

This researcher found that most of the Amish adults were reasonably well informed about news events on a global scale. Some Amish families subscribe to both *The Budget,* an Amish-related newspaper, and a local or regional newspaper. Some have subscriptions to such mass circulation magazines as *Time, Newsweek, U.S. News and World Report, Reader's Digest, and National Geographic.* Most of the Amish adults do travel out-of-state to visit relatives and for recreation. In Montezuma, one respondent had recently returned from a trip to Australia.

POLITICS

The Old Order Amish in each of these eight communities do not permit their members to pursue or hold public office. To say that the Old Order Amish are politically uninvolved is not accurate. For example, they have petitioned the Congress of the United States to be exempt from payment of Social Security taxes since they do not allow their members to collect Social Security benefits. They have also sought a favorable hearing in the courts to have their children exempt from both mandatory attendance at public secondary schools and conscription into the military service.

The Old Order Amish in this sample showed an aloofness to affiliation with either major political party. Less than fifteen percent of the male interviewees had voted in either the 1980 or 1984 United States presidential election, when one of the most conservative candidates in recent history was representing the Republican Party. The Amish fear that politics with either party would certainly invite reprisals from the opposite party. Thus, it is in their best interest to remain neutral—a strong statement for the separation of church and state.

MODERNIZATION

This researcher found that the majority of the social changes that are occurring in these eight Amish communities are the result of very careful, selective, conscious deliberation, i.e., planned change. . . . One respondent added a word of caution regarding their non-use of so-called modern technology: "We do not feel that electricity, the telephone, and the automobile are evil in themselves; rather, our non-use helps us to keep from being drawn into the mainstream of the world."

Thomas Foster, a respected scholar of the Old Order Amish, has suggested that one of the most significant factors reinforcing Amish self-sufficiency is their reliance upon appropriate technologies that complement their lifestyle and religious beliefs, i.e., their sustained, practical use of human labor and power from wind, water, horses, wood, and the sun. These small-scale, labor-intensive technologies greatly reduce the need for large capital investments while keeping a lid on operating costs compared to their non-Amish peers. Foster maintains that in Ohio, for example, the Old Order Amish can earn profits on 75 to 150 acres of land at a time when Ohio's non-Amish farmers, who use diesel tractors and other costly equipment, have difficulty making a decent profit on acreage twice as large.

Social Change Among the Amish

Change has been regarded as neither evil nor good among the Amish. It can work for betterment, or it can create havoc. The Amish perceive that much of what is regarded as "modern" or "progress" by contemporary standards remains a source of temptation for their young, and potential conflict and disharmony for their communities if not kept at a proper distance. For example, the Amish do not believe electricity, telephones, and driving an automobile are inherently evil, but they realize that these so-called modern conveniences would alter the Amish lifestyle and that of future generations.

The effects of this technology, e.g., high mobility with an automobile, would offer too much temptation and less concern for maintaining tradition.

Simply speaking, the Amish prefer not to become dependent upon these inventions, but prefer to maintain a quiet and simple life unfettered with the high-level complications of the modern world. Some outsiders feel the Amish have essentially avoided the acceptance of social change in order to maintain the pursuit of a Nirvana or heaven on earth. The Amish, on the other hand, rarely convey that they feel cheated by denying themselves in this life. . . .

Historians and sociologists have been aware that in other historical periods, religious ideology and practice have fueled powerful motivations for creating change—as seen in the kinship between the growth of Protestantism and industrialism in the Western World. Yet, the Amish have cited their religion as one of the most important reasons why they have essentially and successfully avoided much of the social change identified with the Industrial Revolution. Change is *not* welcome if it adversely affects their religious beliefs, their family stability, their nonresistant lifestyle, or if it creates too much conflict.

Where change has been accepted—and this can be measured figuratively more in inches than yards—it has ordinarily been seen as either an improvement of their ability to provide economically for their families or as reasonable for public safety and the public good. Two examples of the latter were the adoption in some states of batteries on horsedrawn transportation to provide flashing taillights at night as a safety precaution, and the adoption in some districts of diesel generators in their barns, primarily to cool and agitate milk in bulk tanks. To the Amish this is a preference, not a paradox. If it confuses outsiders, they do not feel a need to explain.

Although the vast majority of my sample had routine (daily or weekly) contact with outsiders, most felt that the average outsider did not understand their Amish lifestyle or values and the religious justification for the way they prefer to live. Thus, from an outsider's perspective, the Amish are resisting change simply to preserve tradition—but the Amish understand their actions to be "the will of God."

Summary and Conclusions

. . . Each generation experiences a certain amount of trial and error in finding norms and values that will best serve their unique needs. Tradition for the sake of tradition is hardly an answer to the complex problems facing the Amish. Although the Amish honor important traditions regarding their faith and their people, they also recognize that social and economic survival necessitates that some acceptance of change will be both normal and inevitable. As one Old Order Amish man remarked, "You cannot put a ship in the middle of the ocean and expect the deck to always stay dry."

Acculturation *is* occurring in the majority of Old Order Amish communities visited by this researcher, but it is neither rampant nor whimsical. Rather, social change has consistently been scrutinized carefully and accepted gradually—where the results could be monitored for any possible unwanted side effects. The Old Order Amish enclave is not so much a model of "paradise lost" as it is a model of "evasive innovation" to save and protect a small, but significant, religious minority who wish to be "in the world, but not of the world."

45 Women in the Military

LAURA L. MILLER

That we are immersed in rapid social change has become a taken-for-granted assumption of contemporary life. But the pinch of change is not felt to the same degree by everyone. A change may affect one person's life profoundly, while for others that same change merely provides an interesting topic of conversation. Some change is so moderate that we can adjust to the new aspect of life with little difficulty. Other change upsets us because it challenges our taken-for-granted assumptions about the way the world is and should be. Some people gain by change and like what is happening; others lose, and can't stand it. With perspectives so vastly different in our pluralistic society, some view the same change as long overdue; others insist that it should never have come about in the first place.

The women's movement represents profound social change. It has challenged taken-for-granted assumptions and brought deep consequences for our lives. But, as with other social change, not everyone has been touched in the same way. In this article, we look at the integration of women in the military, where women now occupy positions from which they were excluded just a generation ago. Miller focuses on how men react to the presence of women in formerly all-male jobs, noting that they are using techniques of resistance more commonly associated with the protests of minorities.

THE DATA PRESENTED HERE are taken from multiple stages of field research on active-duty Army soldiers from early 1992 to late 1994. I used a multimethod strategy to capture both large-scale attitudinal patterns and individual viewpoints. To collect the data, I traveled to eight stateside Army posts and two national training centers, where soldiers conduct war games on a simulated battlefield. I also lived with Army personnel for 10 days in Somalia during Operation Restore Hope, for seven days in Macedonia during Operation Able Sentry, and for six days in Haiti during Operation Uphold Democracy. . . .

Given the military context and the sensitive nature of some of the issues, [in my discussion groups and interviews] I relied on written notes rather than tape-recording. . . . I also collected large-scale survey data in order to analyze the relationships between soldiers' demographics and their attitudes on a wide array of issues. The ethnographic data were cross-validated by multiple stages of questionnaires totaling more than 4,100. . . .

In *Domination and the Arts of Resistance,* James C. Scott (1990) provides an extensive historical analysis explaining how powerless groups resist and subvert the efforts of those with power over them. His work demonstrates that people's fear of negative sanctions often drives them to resist in ways that cannot be traced to the initiator, or are lost in the anonymity of crowds. The greater the power exerted from above, the more fully masked the resistance from below. Scott provides numerous examples of the art of political disguise, including gossip, rumor, grumbling, folktales, possession by spirits, mass defiance, anonymous threats, symbolic inversion of the social order, and rituals of reversal such as carnival. Like much of the research on which he draws, Scott continues the Marxist tradition of dividing the world in two: those with economic power (the bourgeoisie, landlords, kings, the ruling class, employers) and those who depend on them or must serve them (the proletariat, peasants, serfs, slaves, workers). . . .

Scott's examples closely parallel behavior that I found in gender relations in the Army, except for one very significant anomaly: It is the structurally dominant group, Army men, who employ the strategies of resistance that are generally seen as the weapons of the weak. My research shows that some men devote a great deal of energy to resisting their women coworkers and commanders through methods such as sabotage, name-calling, foot-dragging, and spreading rumors. Women, paradoxically, do not appear to be using any of these strategies of the weak to gain power from men, according to either their accounts or men's.

What explains the use of weapons of the weak by the structurally dominant group but not by the subordinate minority? My investigation led me to social psychological studies of power. In this literature it is argued that people act according to perceptions of power based on their own experiences and knowledge, not according to some objective analysis of resources. . . . Frequently military men described themselves as unjustly constrained or controlled by military women. Furthermore, these men tend to believe that women's power is usually gained illegitimately and that women take advantage of their gender to promote their own careers. . . .

For example, enlisted men may not enjoy the privileges of their sex as much as men at the higher command levels, particularly in relation to women officers; also, in this era of organizational downsizing, male career officers sometimes blame their limited opportunities on increased participation by women. Thus not all military men experience male privilege, and even some of the more privileged members are constrained within the organization. . . .

In this article I first describe men's resistance in the form of gender harassment. Then I examine who is likely to oppose expanded or even current roles for women soldiers, and why gender harassment is a product of this opposition. I conclude with the implications of this case for gender and other minority relations as well as for the study of power and resistance.

Gender Harassment

DISTINGUISHING GENDER HARASSMENT FROM SEXUAL HARASSMENT

> Sexual harassment implies that you can only be harassed through sexual means. Women can also be harassed through the job in other ways. If your commander doesn't like you, you will encounter harassment, i.e., the shit details, made to work later than everyone else, constant field problems, low efficiency ratings, etc. It's more prejudice than harassment towards females in the Army. (black NCO [Non-Commissioned Officer] in administrative support)

Sexual harassment is not an analytically useful category because it may refer to situations as disparate as sexual assault, discrimination in promotion or assignment, sexual comments, and gender harassment. . . . In my analysis, I limit the term *sexual harassment* to unwanted sexual comments or advances.

Gender harassment refers to harassment that is not sexual, and is used to enforce traditional gender roles, or in response to the violation of those roles. This form of harassment also may aim to undermine women's attempts at gaining power or to describe that power as illegitimately obtained or exercised. Examples include men proclaiming "Women can't drive trucks" in the presence of female drivers or refusing to follow a superior's directives simply because that superior is a woman. Many Army women report that gender harassment on the job is more prevalent than sexual harassment.

Gender harassment also can be used against men who violate gender norms. For example, men who fail to live up to the "masculine ideal" by showing insecurity or hesitation during maneuvers may be called "fags" or "girls" by their comrades. . . . Because behavior that conflicts with one's gender role is stereotypically associated with homosexuality, both heterosexuality and traditional gender roles are enforced through gender harassment.

Because of the prevalence of gender harassment, workshops and policies that address only sexual harassment miss much of the picture. Women report that gender harassment can be just as disruptive in their lives as sexual harassment: it can interfere with their ability to do their work, with their private lives, and with their opportunities to receive some recognition and promotions. Gender harassment is often difficult to attribute to individuals, may not be recognized by command as a problem, and is often invisible in debates about harassment of women in the military. . . .

Gender harassment is hardly unique to military men and women; it is found in many studies of women in sex-atypical work. Examples of what I call gender harassment are scattered throughout studies of job climate, male coworkers' reactions to women, and subtle or covert sex discrimination:

> [We] also face another pervasive and sinister kind of harassment which is gender-based, but may have nothing to do with sex. It is a harassment aimed at us simply because we are women in a "man's" job, and its function is to discourage us from staying in our trades. (M. Martin 1988: 10)

SOME FORMS OF GENDER HARASSMENT

Below are some illustrative examples of gender harassment.

Resistance to Authority. Women who are officers or NCOs commonly complained of male subordinates, especially older enlisted men, who "just don't like answering to a woman." When given orders, they feign ignorance about what is expected of them, or engage in foot-dragging. This method is effective because the men do not risk the official reprimand warranted by an outright refusal to obey orders; yet they challenge women's authority by not complying completely. As one white NCO hypothesized, "Men are intimidated by women superiors and most try to undermine their work." Several women leaders reported having to "pull rank" more often than their male counterparts to get things done. . . .

Constant Scrutiny. Hostile men use constant scrutiny to catch individual women making mistakes, and then use the mistakes to criticize the abilities of women in general. Because of this scrutiny women often feel obligated to work harder than those under less supervision. Women report that they experience such scrutiny as relentless harassment, and that it can make them feel self-conscious and extremely stressed.

Both enlisted and officer women report that as women they are subject to closer scrutiny than men. When women are singled out for observation by suspicious peers and superiors, they often feel they have to work harder than their coworkers just to be accepted as equal members of the unit. . . .

The behavior of a few women is often projected onto the entire gender, but the same is not true for men. To illustrate, some women soldiers serving in the early phases of operations in Haiti pointed out that if the three soldiers who committed suicide there had been women, a discussion would have ensued: People would have asked whether women could handle the stress of deployments or separation from their families. Yet because they were "just men," they were reported as *soldiers,* and the suicides were not interpreted as saying anything about men in general. . . .

Women leaders are rendered less flexible than men because of the constant scrutiny. Sometimes they believe that the people watching them are waiting for them to make mistakes or deviate from regulations; this is a disconcerting environment in which to make decisions. As a result, some men as well as some women classify female superiors as unfair or "too hard." They prefer to serve under men, who have more freedom to bend the rules in favor of their troops: "Women seem to feel they have something to prove. They do, but should not abuse their soldiers [in the process]" (white enlisted man in electronics).

Scrutiny as a harassment strategy is particularly safe in the military because it fits into the functioning of the organization. One cannot be punished for seeking out and correcting errors, and it would be quite difficult to prove that women are being watched more closely than men.

Gossip and Rumors.   Army women are often the subject of untrue gossip about their sex lives. Repeatedly I heard that if a woman dates more than one man in the Army, she is labeled a "slut." If she doesn't date, she is labeled a "dyke." Unlike men, women who are promoted quickly or who receive coveted assignments are often rumored to have "slept their way to the top." At every post I visited, soldiers had heard the rumor (which has never been verified) that a few women soldiers in the Persian Gulf War made a fortune by setting up a tent and serving as prostitutes for their male counterparts.

Young Army women in particular feel that their personal lives are under intense scrutiny at all times, and that ridiculous lies can emerge from the rumor mill for no apparent reason. One enlisted woman was shocked when her commander took her aside one day and said, "Look, I know you're sleeping with all the guys in your unit." She could not imagine why he said that to her; who would have started such a rumor, or why; or why fellow soldiers—her friends—would have contributed to spreading the stories. . . .

Because rumors are usually untraceable, they cannot be addressed through a formal complaint system. Scott discusses the power of such strategies:

> Gossip is perhaps the most familiar and elementary form of disguised popular aggression. Though its use is hardly confined to attacks by subordinates on their superiors, it represents a relatively safe social sanction. Gossip, almost by definition, has no identifiable author, but scores of eager retellers who can claim they are just passing on the news. Should the gossip—and here I have in mind malicious gossip—be challenged, everyone can disavow responsibility for having originated it. . . .

The character of gossip that distinguishes it from rumor is that gossip consists typically of stories that are designed to ruin the reputation of some identifiable person or persons. If the perpetrators remain anonymous, the victim is clearly specified. There is, arguably, something of a disguised democratic voice about gossip in the sense that it is propagated only to the extent that others find it in their interest to retell the story. If they don't, it disappears. (1990:142)

Sabotage. I found evidence of sabotage, as a form of gender harassment, only in work fields that are nontraditional for women. Because these nontraditional occupations can be strenuous and dangerous, the sabotage of equipment can be quite threatening. . . .

In one instance of sabotage from my research, two women new to an all-male vehicle maintenance and repair unit arrived at work every morning to find that the heavy, difficult-to-change track had been removed from their assigned vehicle. After a few weeks, during which they patiently replaced the track each day, the harassment ended. They had earned the men's respect by proving their skills and their willingness to work hard. The men's doubts were dispelled when they decided that the women's abilities had earned them a position in the unit, and that they would not use their gender to exempt themselves from dirty and difficult work.

Sabotage of equipment and tools was reported by women in mechanical fields, but I never heard of sabotage in the form of disappearing files, erased computer data, jammed typewriters, hidden medical supplies, or misplaced cooking utensils.

Indirect Threats. Some soldiers reported that some of their fellow men would rape women who dared to enter infantry or armor units. The comments written on surveys include these remarks by a black enlisted man in the combat arms:

> The majority of men in the Army are sexist. I know, because I'm a man. Women in combat units would be harassed, if not raped. I say this because I've seen it and have nothing to hide. If you want the truth about issues, don't ask NCOs or officers. They'll tell you everything is all peaches and cream!! If you want the truth ask an E4 that's been in about 5 years. Women only have a fair shake as cooks or nurses. They'll be extremely harassed, if not molested, if they enter combat arms. I know, trust me.

Another infantryman echoed that assessment, although he proposed that male violence toward women is due to the conditions of deployments, not to sexism:

> In a situation where times are hard—less food, no showers, road marching, with 70–100 lbs ruck on your back, and [you] don't know when the next supply

shipment will be in, the male soldiers will start thinking of sex and the female soldiers may be raped or something.

Why Gender Harassment? Perceptions of Power and Limited Forms of Protest

Some men resort to gender harassment to protect changing gender norms, either because they personally prefer traditional norms or because they think that men and women are not capable of successfully working outside traditional roles. Many of these men believe that women's attempts to claim equality have resulted in favorable treatment for women who have been largely unwilling or unable to fully meet the demands of being a soldier. Gender harassment is an attempt to push women back into their more "natural" roles, restore the meritocratic order of the organization, and ensure that all soldiers on the battlefield can do their jobs and assist the wounded in times of war. Certainly these views are considered sexist by many, and potentially could cause problems for any soldier who expresses them openly in mixed company. Thus gender harassment is preferred as an often unattributable way to protest the expansion of women's roles and to attempt to balance scales that are perceived to be tilted in women's favor.

HOSTILE PROPONENTS AND ANOTHER VERSION OF EQUALITY

"Women should be given totally equal treatment and standards. But I don't see it happening." This assertion by a male Army captain expresses the views of many Army men. Rather than championing women's rights, however, this officer is among the men who feel that women, not men, are the privileged and powerful group in the military. These men oppose expanding women's opportunities because they believe that women already enjoy too many advantages in the organization and have not yet met the requirements of the roles they already fill.

Some men believe that women use the term *equality* to advance their personal interests, and that they would object if true equality were offered:

> My opinion is that if women want the right to be in combat roles, they should have to register with selective service. Also, if women want to be treated and have the same rights as men, they should be treated equally all of the time and not just when it is convenient for them. (white enlisted man)

Interview data reveal that most of the men who favor opening combat roles to women on the same terms as men do so only because they are confident that women will fail in those roles. I term this group "hostile proponents" of women in combat. Such hostile proponents reason that the issue of women in the combat arms will not be put to rest until women have been given the opportunity to prove their incompetence. For example, a male driver agreed that women should be allowed to volunteer for combat roles—until he dropped off the female officer who was traveling with us. As soon as she left our group, he added that he thought women should be allowed into combat because they would see how hard the combat arms really are, and no one would have to listen any longer to their complaints about wanting to be included. This "treat women the same to watch them fail" attitude was expressed in writing by a white NCO in the combat arms:

> My feelings are that women just want a door open that is closed. If they want to be totally equal with us, shave their head in basic training [and] give them the same [physical training] test as men. Women in the infantry would ruin male bonding and get soldiers killed or hurt trying to cover for them in combat. Try an all female infantry basic training and [advanced individual training] with the exact same standards as males.

These hostile proponents have found that they can voice their objections by appropriating the language of the feminist activists. Arguments that women should stay home and raise children can be denounced as sexist; agreeing with activists that women and men are "equal" and should be expected to be treated equally cannot. When women are kept out of certain occupations, feminists can continue to argue that women, given the chance, could perform as well as men. Hostile proponents believe that admitting women is a better strategy for reducing the credibility of such arguments because, they insist, the reality will prove the arguments false.

One resistant male soldier provided the formula "(Equal pay = equal job = equal responsibility = equal risk) = equal opportunity" to stress that equality should be sought across the board, not only in pay or opportunity. He was one of the many men who believed that the differential policies actually work in women's favor, disrupt the meritocratic order, and are likely to imperil soldiers in times of war.

A few combat soldiers in my survey were motivated by self-interest to support admitting women to their Military Occupational Specialties (MOSs). One such man, a black NCO, wrote:

> If women are allowed in combat they should be made to shave their heads like men, or let men grow their hair like women. And if women are allowed, field

duty would become better for men, because of [women's] needs. So therefore, I'm for them in combat. Yes, let them in.

Why do some Army men perceive themselves, and not women, to be the disadvantaged gender in the military? Although other respondents offer counterarguments to these men's opinions, I focus here on the viewpoint of men who regard themselves as underdogs. In this section I demonstrate how a structurally dominant group can perceive itself to be a disadvantaged group, and therefore resort to the types of resistance strategies that Scott attributes to the weak. The unifying theme of these examples is the belief that most military women do not take the same risks or work as hard as do military men, and yet are promoted more quickly than men because of their gender.

Easier Physical Training Standards. Both men and women reported that women's physical training requirements are not only different from men's, but easier for most women to meet than men's are for most men. Although this training is supposed to maintain physical fitness, most soldiers interpret it as a measure of strength. That the women's requirements are easier than the men's is seen by many as proof that women are less well qualified for physically strenuous work:

> I can't be adamant enough. There is no place for women in the infantry. Women do not belong in combat units. If you haven't been there, then you wouldn't understand. As far as equal rights, some women say they are as physically strong as a man. Then why are the [physical training] standards different? (white NCO in the combat arms)

Thus some soldiers argue that only one standard should exist for men and for women, and that such a standard should reflect the requirements of the job. A white lieutenant in intelligence and communications explained his view:

> The standards are never the same for men and women. The [Army Physical Fitness Test] is a perfect example. [W]hat most junior leaders feel (that I have discussed the topic with) . . . there should be no difference for either sex. [The Department of the Army] has established minimum standards and they should apply across the board, regardless of sex. Which means the female standards would have to go out the window. A man who can only do 18 pushups is unfit for service, so it should be [the same] for females. If a female can meet the same standards as me, I will gladly serve with, for, or over her. But if she can't I will also gladly chapter her out of the Army as unfit for service. I've seen action in Grenada and Iraq and know there are females who could've done my

job. Few, but some. However my wife, who went to Saudi, is 104 lbs., 5'4" and couldn't carry my 201 lbs. across the living room, much less the desert if I was wounded. Whose standards should apply?

In deployments and field exercises, the differences are most apparent. Some commanders find them difficult to know how to handle:

The topic about women in combat MOS's has finally cleared up with me, I have completed [platoon leadership training], and found that the women on my patrol team could not perform their squad duties. For example, being a 60-gunner, or radio operator I was patrol leader. I assigned the females on my team the 60 and the radio. After about 2 miles of patrolling, the females could not do their jobs. I was accused of being sexist, but when it came down to it, men had to take those assigned jobs in my squad from these women. I'm sure that there are some females that could "keep up" or "hang" with the men, but the fact is that women are not physically strong enough. (white enlisted man in the combat arms)

Pregnancy as an Advantage.   Some men find it unfair that women have an honorable option out of the service, deployments, or single barracks that men do not have: pregnancy. A white enlisted man in intelligence and communications wrote:

There seems to be a trend that females in the Army take advantage of free medical and have kids while serving. The 9 months of pregnancy limits them to no physical labor and is bad on morale. They are still a soldier, but they are only working at about 30% of their potential, forcing men or non-pregnant women to compensate.

A white lieutenant in the medical field noted, "I am currently in a unit with female soldiers, about 60–75% are pregnant or on some type of profile." "Profile" is a standing in which soldiers' physical abilities are limited; therefore they are exempt from physically strenuous tasks, including daily physical training. Pregnant women are among the most common sources of resentment and thus are targets of harassment. Pregnancy then, is another way in which some men feel that women are receiving equal pay and promotion, but are not doing equal work and not taking equal risks and responsibilities.

Better Educational Opportunities.   Many men feel that restrictions on women's roles are unfair not because they limit women, but because they appear to give women opportunities to receive more schooling than men, thus improving their chances for promotion. A white enlisted man wrote, "Most women are in rear units and have the chance to go to school and complete correspondence courses." A black NCO viewed these opportunities as tipping the balance in women's favor in competitions for promotion: "Of most of the units that I've served, the female soldier is more apt to attend schools, i.e., military and civilian. This constant trend allows them better opportunities for career progression."

Some men feel that with this extra training, women will be more qualified than men, with the result that "Most women are promoted above their peers" (white NCO). One white enlisted man expressed the view that it is wasteful to allow women to take coveted slots in combat-related training to help their careers when they are currently restricted from performing those tasks in the event of a real war:

> Each person male or female will perform according to his or her gifts. We cannot make that determination. Congress needs to get off its lazy butt and make a decision one way or the other. Until that time, it remains a waste of time and taxpayer's money to send women to combat related schools (jump schools and air assault, etc.) just for the sake of being "stylish" and to appease those women who whine about discrimination when they're not allowed to do something a male soldier does.

Exemption from Combat Arms as a Way to Faster Promotion, Better Assignments, and "Cushy" Jobs. In some units there is a hierarchy of assignments, which is sometimes disrupted by the way women are integrated. The lowest jobs are often the "grunt work"—hard, mindless labor. Some men protested to me that when women are assigned to such a unit, they are spared the grunt work and placed (often by male superiors) ahead of men for more desirable assignments. Not only are they excused from doing what men have to do; they also delay men's progress into better positions and sometimes have authority over the men they have bumped. A white lieutenant cited an example of the problems created because a man in a signal MOS can be assigned to a combat unit and required to do grunt work, but a woman is always assigned elsewhere:

> Currently, females in combat support roles (e.g., signal, chemical, [military police], medical services) can not hold a designated position in Combat Units. For example, females are allowed to serve in the signal corps, but they are not allowed to serve as a signal [platoon leader] in a combat arms unit. There is too much animosity towards females in a specific branch if they can't hold the same positions that their male counterparts [do]. The females are seen as getting the "cushy" jobs and interesting jobs as the males have to fulfill the combat roles. If a female can not hold a position in their designated specialty, they should not be allowed in that specific specialty.

These men view women not only as obtaining easier work, but as jumping up the hierarchy without earning it. As a white lieutenant explains, this can breed resentment:

> Chemical corps: females should not be allowed in this branch if they cannot serve in all positions. For example, they get sent to this division, but cannot serve in the infantry, armor, or forward artillery units. This leaves very few slots for them to fill. [The Army] does not manage this very [well] at all. As a new lieutenant, we must put in our time at the battalion staff level, first, then we are awarded a platoon at the chem company. (One company per division). [The Department of the Army] sends us more females than we have slots for, so they wind up being platoon leaders at the company ahead of the males who have put in their time at the battalions. A lot of hard feelings about this. They (females) should not be branched chemical or some of the other combat support branches.

Men complained that women are not required to do the heaviest or dirtiest part of any job, and that they can get away with it without reprimand because of their sex. Although men may find it humorous when Beetle Bailey shirks his assignments, they may become resentful when women have an unfair advantage based on their sex. One black enlisted man wrote: "Today all you hear in the Army is that we are equal, but men do all the hard and heavy work whether it's combat or not."

According to some men, women's current behavior is proof that most are unable or unwilling to do the work required of soldiers in the combat arms. Thus they resist putting their lives on the line with such soldiers: "I feel women are useless to the Army, most do not do their part when it comes to real work! Most won't change a tire, or pick up a box if it weighs more than 5 lbs. I would not go to war with women in or out of a combat role." Some of these conclusions are based on experience in the States:

> When given the same opportunity, most [women] look for excuses not to do the work. You in your position can not see it. However, I am exposed to it daily. The majority of females I know are not soldiers. They are employed. Anything strenuous is avoided with a passion. I would hate to serve with them during combat! I would end up doing my job and ⅔ of theirs just to stay alive. (black NCO in administrative work)
>
> I feel as if women in the military are ordered to do less work, get out of doing things such as field problems, and when it comes to doing heavy work, they just stand around and watch the work until it is completed. This is part of the reason I feel they could not handle a combat role because of a weaker physical and mental capability under such a stressful situation. I say this because it is proved in an everyday day of work. (black enlisted man in a technical field)

Women's gender identity traditionally has been tied to "delicacy," while men's identity has been tied to the ability to be tough and strong. So men may try to avoid work in general, but avoiding heavy labor in particular would make them look weak, cast doubt on their masculinity, and draw ridicule from other men about their "femininity." thus many men resent that women can avoid a great deal of dirty, heavy work and still succeed in the military, while men's lives are considerably tougher. Although men tend to lay most of the blame for "getting by" on women, this behavior could not persist unless the leaders allowed it.

Paternalism Allowing Women to Get Away with More. Both men and women may try to bend the rules, but when women succeed because of their gender, male coworkers may hold it against them. Several times women told me how they could avoid certain duties by complaining of cramps to particular male commanders. At the first mention of anything "menstrual" their commander would grimace and wave them away. (This did not work with women superiors, who sent them to sick call if they thought the cramps were serious.) Two women told me that they could hide off-limits items such as candy by placing tampons or underwear on top of the contents of their lockers or drawers. During inspections, their male commander took one look at their belongings, saw the personal items, and moved on, apparently too embarrassed to examine the rest of the contents.

As another example, one man wrote on his survey.

> I don't think women can withstand not being able to take showers for as long as men. When I was in the Gulf, we were ordered to use the water that we had only for drinking. But after one week the women were using our drinking water to take bird baths. This made me very upset.

This problem is framed as a matter of women's behavior, not the command's enforcement of rules.

Male commanders enforce rules differently for women, for several reasons. In the case of the water, the leader may have made this exception for women because he perceived them as more fragile than men, or felt that some sort of chivalry was appropriate. Padavic and Reskin (1990) call such behavior "paternalism," which they measured in their study of blue-collar workers according to whether women "had been relieved of some hard assignments, whether male coworkers had given them special treatment because of their sex, and whether their supervisors had favored them because of their sex" (p. 618).

Men in command positions sometimes fear disciplining women or pushing them to excel. These men worry that they will be accused of harassing women soldiers because of their gender, or of being insensitive to women's

needs or limitations. Also, some are too embarrassed about women's underwear or hygiene to perform the ritual invasion of privacy men must undergo.
As a result, even when sensitivity to women is intended, women receive privileges that men do not; this situation breeds disdain for women soldiers
among some of the men.

In the military, some believe that male leaders' unwillingness to push
women to excel creates a weakness among the troops that could have grave
consequences during a war:

> The more fundamental question is whether women should be in the military at
> all. They have served well, but are victims of a male dominated system which
> has always demanded less of them than they would (hopefully) of themselves.
> If every soldier in the U.S. Army today had been trained at the same low level
> of expectation that female soldiers routinely are, the U.S. Army today would
> either be dead or in Prisoner of War camps. (an "other race" major)

Quotas, Sex, and Other Paths to the Top.   As noted earlier, some men believe
that women can "sleep their way" to the top, and that quotas allow women to
receive undeserved promotions and assignments because of their minority
status. Some men also believe that women can and do challenge poor
performance reviews by claiming discrimination, and that they can use false
harassment claims to punish or remove men they do not like. The perception
is that women usually are believed over men in harassment cases; as a result,
men's careers are ruined by the whims of ambitious or vengeful women.

Most of these perceptions reinforce the view that women want the prestige and promotions that come with serving in the combat arms, but do not intend to make the same efforts as men: "They want equal rights, but don't want
to do what it takes to become equal" (white enlisted man in administration).

LIMITED FORMS OF PROTEST

When I asked men who opposed women in combat roles what they thought
would happen in the future, they all asserted that integration was inevitable. They concluded that women eventually would "have their way" despite any reasonable objections. Perhaps because women's gains have been
made gradually over the years, men perceive this progression not as a series
of slow, incremental change toward one goal but as a string of victories for
women over men.

One white major said, "As minorities, women have advantages." White
men were likely to have a similar attitude about race; for example, they
tended to think that nonwhite soldiers unfairly charge racial discrimination
to challenge negative performance reviews. One white NCO spoke for many
of his comrades in defining himself as a member of the oppressed minority:
"I feel that the white enlisted male has more prejudice against him than any

other sector in the military." He specified not only his gender but also his race and rank as contributing to his position.

Scott analyzes both the micro interactional forms of resistance by subjugated people and the outward rebellion of the powerless that occurs when "an entire category of people suddenly finds its public voice no longer stifled" (1990:210). I found the reverse among military men: a category of people who have assumed and enjoyed gender privilege, and who rebel because their public voice has been deemed sexist and has been silenced.

Because of the nature of the military organization, many forms of protest are not realistic options for men who contend that they are disadvantaged. Army men cannot strike, circulate petitions, organize rallies or demonstrations, walk out during the workday, or quit collectively in response to a policy change. (Before quitting they would have to meet their enlistment obligations or complete time-consuming formal exit procedures and paperwork.) Boycotts and "client preference" arguments are generally irrelevant here. Thus men who are silent in mixed-sex environments may be channeling their frustrations into underground grumbling.

I experienced firsthand evidence of men's perception that they must hide their opinions. Often the men who eventually voiced their objections to working with women were not initially forthright. When asked about gender issues, they first told me what they imagined I wanted to hear, or recited the "party line" that would keep them out of trouble should any statements be attributed to them. After calculating my opinion on the basis of my status as a young civilian woman conducting research on military women, they hesitated at my opening questions and then said reluctantly that they thought women should and could serve in any military roles. Then, when I raised an opposing argument (such as "So you don't see any problem with close contact between men and women serving in tanks together?"), their true feelings burst forth.[1]

In mixed-sex groups (particularly groups of officers), some of the men squirmed, rolled their eyes, or shook their heads, but did not speak up during discussions about gender. After I dismissed the group, I privately asked those men to stay behind, and asked them why they were silent but seemingly dissatisfied. They revealed that they refrained from participating because they believed that organizational constraints prohibited them from stating their true opinions, particularly in the presence of officer women. In this way I learned which arguments were considered legitimate in the organization (at least when women were present) and which would be censured. The opportunity to write anonymous comments on the formal questionnaires may have been particularly appreciated by soldiers who felt their views were controversial. Men were concerned that they would be held accountable for any statements that could be considered sexist; they feared an official reprimand and negative consequences for their career.

These soldiers' perceptions are evidence that the Army has made some headway in controlling men's willingness to make openly sexist statements. (Soldiers' self-censorship about gender contrasted sharply with their comments about allowing open gays and lesbians to serve in the military; men did not hesitate to make loud, violent threats against any gays they might discover.) Many of these men resent the inability to speak their minds. They believe that even if they could speak candidly, their concerns would not be addressed formally because they think women have the advantage in gender-based disputes. Therefore they express their resentment in ways that the institution cannot control.

Male soldiers interpret the "suppression" of some arguments against women as proof that those arguments are valid and that women have no legitimate counterargument. Thus some men are angry because they perceive women as having gained their power in the military illegitimately or as having taken advantage of that power. Others simply object to changing gender norms and increasing participation of women in non-traditional roles. This tension is exacerbated by the perceived prohibition against expressing their dissatisfaction. Therefore many men hold their tongues in public, but complain among themselves and retaliate with gender harassment. Although grumbling is certainly a part of military culture, the resistance strategies I found directed against women are rarely employed for similar complaints against male leaders or fellow soldiers in general.

Implications of Gender Harassment

The Army's formal sexual harassment [policies] in the 1990s have taught many men the definitions and the possible consequences of this behavior.

Yet improvements in controlling sexual harassment do not necessarily mean that women are now working in a supportive or even a tolerant environment. Although women can be hurt by public sexist comments that express doubts about their abilities, it is also debilitating when such comments are forced underground, where they cannot be challenged. In addition, because many men perceive themselves as unable to safely voice their concerns about women as coworkers, some men feel that gender harassment is a justified means of registering their complaints.

As previously disadvantaged groups gain some power in legislating discriminatory behavior, their opponents may come to rely on forms of resistance that are difficult to regulate. These implications go beyond gender and affect areas such as race, ethnicity, and sexual orientation. Even as minorities enjoy increased success in controlling overt harassment, they must recognize that people will seek other ways to express hostility. When minority groups call for equality, they should be prepared to be informed about inequities that favor them, and to learn how the language of equality might be used against them.

Underlying the cases in the resistance literature is the assumption that the reader is sympathetic to the oppressed groups; groups claiming oppression in fact are oppressed and are justified in their resistance. Resistance, then, has been treated as something constructive, which preserves human dignity and may lead to the overthrow of an unjust system. Thus nobody has asked how to eliminate the "hidden transcript" and dismantle underground forms of resistance. In the traditional dichotomous framework of resistance studies, that question would have been asked only by oppressors seeking compliance—seeking to use their power for manipulation or indoctrination.

But what do we say when the resisting group is not entirely powerless and does not wish to relinquish one of the realms in which it holds power? The powerful can appropriate for themselves the language and framework used to explain dominance and resistance. They can portray themselves as victims, as "silenced," when *they* suddenly are required to monitor their behavior in the presence of others. Is the attempt to regulate racist, sexist, and homophobic speech and behavior equivalent to the past suppression of minority groups' voices? Are we to be sympathetic when previously powerful groups develop underground resistance because their behavior is suppressed?

In this paper I have sought to demonstrate that in order to effectively examine power dynamics, studies of resistance must supplement cultural and structural analyses. Future work must recognize the importance of perceptions of power because such perceptions do not necessarily correspond to objective measures of power. These perceptions, however, strongly influence people's attitudes and behavior. In the military, soldiers' experience of gender varies according to rank, age, race, and occupational specialty.

Resistance studies also must move beyond seeing the world in terms of only two classes: the oppressors and the oppressed. This dichotomy cannot fully explain the dynamics of a world in which multiple hierarchies can make people simultaneously powerful and powerless relative to others. Future research must account for people's multiple statuses which result in a much more varied distribution of power than a dichotomous model would allow. The behavior of some military men toward women soldiers demonstrates that researchers must look for "weapons of the weak" in the hands of people at all levels of both perceived and structurally measured power.

46 Caught Between the Ages

WILLIAM VAN DUSEN WISHARD

One of the world's most significant changes is the *globalization of capitalism*. Capitalism won the Cold War, and except for a few holdouts (Cuba, North Korea, and China), socialism has been vanquished. Victorious with its heady success, capitalism is expanding rapidly into every nook and cranny of the planet. The so-called undeveloped nations ("undeveloped" only in a chauvinistic, ethnocentric sense of Western economic and political dominance, for they all have fully developed, intricate cultures) are part of this process. Eyeing the material wealth of the industrialized West and Japan, and the growing economic and military power of China, and mindful of the West's cultural dominance, like separated lovers many nations long to embrace capitalism. For their part, the most industrialized nations view the least industrialized nations as vast sources of cheap labor and natural resources.

The cultural dominance of the West, however, tears at identities that were laid down over centuries, posing a threat to traditional cultures. Some groups mildly resist these vast changes, pushing back slightly to protect elements of their culture. Others, like the French, more resentful of the changes, especially their being shunted into a closet relationship in world affairs, enact laws to limit English words in their mass media. Some, seeing their entire way of life crumbling, and fearful of the future they see arriving at a dizzying pace, strike back, hoping, as does Al-Queda, that by violence they can hold back the overpowering forces that have been unleashed against them. As Wishard points out in this selection, living in these times of vast change is certainly easier for us whose culture is dominant than it is for those whose cultures have been invaded.

NOTHING SO DRAMATIZES living between two ages as does the image of the fireball engulfing the World Trade Center, an image burned into the world's psyche September 11th. I'm not going to dwell on that event, except to say this. The image of the imploding World Trade Center must be seen as part of a panorama of images for its full significance to best be understood. The image, for instance, of death camps and crematoriums in Central Europe. The image of a mushroom cloud rising over the Pacific. Of Neil Armstrong stepping onto the Moon. Of Louise Brown, the first human to be conceived outside of the human body. Of a man standing near the summit of Mt. Everest talking on his cell phone to his wife in Australia. Of the first human embryo to be cloned. Of a computer performing billions of calculations in a second, calculations that could not have been performed by all the mathematicians who ever lived, even in their combined lifetimes. These are some of the images, representing both human greatness and depravity, that mark the end of one age and the approach of a new time in human experience.

It was in 1957 that Peter Drucker, who, more than any other person, defined management as a discipline, wrote: "No one born after the turn of the 20th century has ever known anything but a world uprooting its foundations, overturning its values and toppling its idols." So today I'm going to pursue Drucker's thought and suggest why I believe we're living at probably the most critical turning point of human history.

Between two ages. How are we to visualize the difference between those two ages? I offer some contrasts. From the dominance of print communication, to the emergence of electronic communication. From American immigration coming primarily from Europe, to immigration coming mainly from Asia and Latin America. From a time of relatively slow change, to change at an exponential rate. From economic development as a national endeavor, to economic development as part of a global system. From ultimate destructive power being confined to the state, to such power available to the individual. We could continue, but I think you see what I mean. We are in what the ancient Greeks called Kairos—the "right moment" for a fundamental change in principles and symbols.

Exactly what kind of era is opening up is far from clear. The only obvious fact is that it's going to be global, whatever else it is.

In the next few minutes I want to comment on three trends that are part of this shift between two ages. Let me start by stating my bias: I am bullish on the future. We've got unprecedented challenges ahead, clearly the most difficult humanity has ever faced. But I believe in the capacity of the human spirit to surmount any challenge if given the vision, the will, and the leadership.

With this in mind, let's look at some trends that are moving us from one age to the next.

First trend: For the first time in human history, the world is forging an awareness of our existence as a single entity. Nations are incorporating planetary dimensions of life into the fabric of our economics, politics, culture, and international relations. The shorthand for this is "globalization."

We all have some idea of what globalization means. In my view, globalization represents the world's best chance to enrich the lives of the greatest number of people. The specter of terrorism, however, raises the question as to globalization's future. Will the 1990's "go-go" version be one of the casualties of terrorism? Yes or no. The economic pace of globalization may slow down, and certainly reaction to America's "soft power"—what other nations see as the "Americanization" of world culture—will continue to grow. But other aspects may actually accelerate. For example, we're already seeing the increased globalization of intelligence, security, and humanitarian concerns.

Aside from that, globalization is far more than just economics and politics: more than non-western nations adopting free markets and democratic political systems. At its core, globalization means that western ideas are gradually seeping into the social and political fabric of the world. And even deeper, globalization is about culture, tradition, and historic relationships; it's about existing institutions and why and how they evolved. In short, globalization goes to the very psychological foundations of a people.

Look at what's happening. Nations are adopting such ideas as the sanctity of the individual, due process of law, universal education, the equality of women, human rights, private property, legal safeguards governing business and finance, science as the engine of social growth, concepts of civil society, and perhaps most importantly, the ability of people to take charge of their destiny and not simply accept the hand dealt them in life. For millions of people these concepts are new modes of thought, which open undreamt of possibilities.

Is this good? From our perspective it is. But what do other nations feel as America's idea of creative destruction and entrepreneurship press deeper into the social fabric of countries such as China and India; as American cultural products uproot historic traditions?

In the Middle East, American culture as exemplified by a TV program such as Baywatch generates a unique resentment. Such a program presents Islamic civilization with a different nuance of feminine beauty and the dignity of women. Baywatch, and American culture in general, lure Muslims into an awkward position. On the one hand, their basic human appetites respond at a primal level. So it becomes part of them. Yet on another level, they fear the invasion of this new culture is undermining something sacred and irreplaceable in their very social fabric. Yes, it's their own fault; they don't have to import such entertainment. Yet it all seems to be part of so-called "modernization."

All of which illustrates how hard it is for us Americans to appreciate the underlying differences between western ideas and the foundations of other nations. Take some of the basic contrasts between Asia and the west. The west prizes individuality, while the east emphasizes relationships and community. The west sees humans dominating nature, while the east sees humans as part of nature. In the west there is a division between mind and heart, while in the east mind and heart are unified.

I mention this to illustrate the deep psychological trauma nations are experiencing as they confront the effects of globalization. We Americans, raised on the instinct of change, say, "Great. Let tradition go. Embrace the new." But much of the world says, "Wait a minute. Traditions are our connection to the past; they're part of our psychic roots. If we jettison them, we'll endanger our social coherence and stability."

Remember, it took centuries for our political, social, and economic concepts to evolve in the West. They are the product of a unique western psychology and experience. Thus we cannot expect non-western nations to graft alien social attitudes onto an indigenous societal structure overnight.

Part of the upheaval created by globalization is the largest migration the world has ever seen, which is now under way. In China alone, 100 million people are on the move from the countryside to the city. In Europe, the OECD tells us that no country is reproducing its population; that the EU will need 180 million immigrants in the next three decades simply to keep its population at 1995 levels, as well as to keep the current ratio of retirees to workers.

As European population growth declines, and as immigration increases, the historic legends that are the basis of national identities tend to wane. As one British historian put it, "A white majority that invented the national mythologies underpinning modern European culture lives in an almost perpetual state of fear that it and its way of life are about to disappear." You realize what he means when you hear that the Church of England expects England to have more practicing Muslims than practicing Anglicans by next year. In Italy, the Archbishop of Bologna recently warned Italy is in danger of "losing its identity" due to the immigration from North Africa and Central Europe. This fear is the subtext for everything else we see happening in Europe today.

The question of identity is at the core of the world problem as globalization accelerates. It came sharply into focus in the 1960's when, for the first time in human history, we saw Earth from space, from the moon. An idea that had only existed in the minds of poets and philosophers suddenly became geopolitical reality—the human family is a single entity. We began to see national, cultural, and ethnic distinctions for what they are—projections in our minds. We lost the clarity of identity—Herder's "collective soul"—that had given birth and meaning to nations and civilizations for centuries.

In my view, it's this continuing loss of identity—or the threat of it—that helps fuel terrorism. Granted, there's an individual psychotic aspect to any terrorist. But the context in which they live is a loss of a personal sense of identity, as well as a subsequent psychological identification with the God-image.

One aspect of globalization we sometimes find irritating is America's global role and the resulting world perception of America. This perception is shaped by many factors, some of which we control, many of which we don't. For example, nations have historically felt a natural antipathy toward the world's strongest empire, whoever it happened to be at the time. And make no mistake, we are perceived, at a minimum, as an empire of influence. That said, in my view no great nation has used its power as generously and with as little intention of territorial gain as has America. Nonetheless, if we don't understand what other nations feel about America, globalization will not succeed, and neither will the war on terrorism.

Consider a comment by the Norwegian newspaper, Aftenposten: "in Norway, Nepal, and New Zealand, all of us live in a world that is increasingly shaped by the United States." Now let's play with that thought for a moment and consider a hypothetical situation.

Imagine how we would feel if the world were increasingly shaped by, say, China. Suppose China had produced the information technology that is the engine of globalization, technology that we had to buy and incorporate into our social structure. Picture Chinese currency as the medium of world trade. Further envision Chinese as the international language of commerce. What if Chinese films and TV programs were flooding global entertainment markets, undermining bedrock American beliefs, and values. Suppose China were the dominant military and economic world power. Imagine the Chinese having troops stationed for security and peacekeeping in over thirty countries around the world. What if the IMF and World Bank were primarily influenced by Chinese power and pressure. Suppose China had developed the economic and management theories that we had to adopt in order to compete in the global marketplace.

If this were the case, how would Americans feel? I'm not suggesting there's anything inherently wrong with U.S. world influence, I'm trying to illustrate the all pervasiveness of America's reach in the world in order to suggest why even our allies manifest uneasy concerns about America. Understanding this, and adjusting where warranted, is essential to the success of globalization, to say nothing of the future of America.

Consider another example. Think what it looks like to the rest of the world when we judge other nations on the basis of human rights and democracy, while at the same time systematically feeding our children a cultural diet considered by all religions and civilizations throughout history to be destructive of personal character and social cohesion. Two of America's foremost diplomats have commented on this anomaly. Zbigniew Brzezinski, former National Security Advisor to the president, writes, "I don't think Western secularism in its present shape is the best standard for human rights." He mentions consumption, self-gratification, and hedonism as three characteristics of America's definition of the "good life," and then says, "The defense of the political individual doesn't mean a whole lot in such a spiritual and moral vacuum."

George F. Kennan, one of the giant U.S. diplomatic figures of the past half century, says simply, "This whole tendency to see ourselves as the center of political enlightenment and as teachers to a great part of the rest of the world strikes me as unthought-thought, vainglorious, and undesirable." I might add these comments were made before September 11th.

Such comments perhaps seem almost unpatriotic. But America's ability to provide world leadership may depend on whether we have the capacity to consider such reactions, and see what truth there may be in them. It's what the Scottish poet Robert Burns wrote: "Oh would some power the gift to give us, to see ourselves as others see us!"

I emphasize these points because if we're going to build a global age, it's got to be built on more than free markets and the Internet. Even more, it's got to be built on some view of life far broader than "my nation," "my race," or "my religion" is the greatest. Such views gave dynamism and meaning to the empires of the past. But the task now is to bring into being a global consciousness. It must have as its foundation some shared psychological and, ultimately, spiritual experience, and expression. At the end of the day, globalization must have a legitimacy that validates itself in terms of a true democratic and moral order.

The second trend moving us between two ages is a new stage of technology development. This new phase is without precedent in the history of science and technology.

At least since Francis Bacon in the 1600's we have viewed the purpose of science and technology as being to improve the human condition. As Bacon put it, the "true and lawful end of the sciences is that human life be enriched by new discoveries and powers."

And indeed it has. Take America. During the last century, the real GDP, in constant dollars, increased by $48 trillion, much of this wealth built on the marvels of technology.

But along with technological wonders, uncertainties arise. Let me interject here that in 1997 I had a quadruple heart bypass operation using the most sophisticated medical technology in the world. So I'm a believer. Nonetheless, the question today is whether we're creating certain technologies not to improve the human condition, but for purposes that seem to be to replace human meaning and significance altogether.

The experts tell us that by the year 2035, artificial robotic intelligence will surpass human intelligence. (Let's leave aside for a moment the question of what constitutes "intelligence.") And a decade after that, we shall have a robot with all the emotional and spiritual sensitivities of a human being.

Not long after that, computers—will go at such a speed that the totality of human existence will change so dramatically that it's beyond our capability to envision what life will be like. But never fear, we're told. The eventual marriage of human and machine will mean that humans will continue as a species, albeit not in a form we would recognize today.

Thus arrives what some would-be scientific intellectuals call the "Posthuman Age." I emphasize, this is not science fiction. It is the projection of some of our foremost scientists.

Let's move from the general to the specific. Consider a remark by the co-founder of MIT's artificial intelligence lab and one of the world's leading authorities on artificial intelligence: "Suppose that the robot had all of the virtues of people and was smarter and understood things better. Then why would we want to prefer those grubby, old people? I don't see anything wrong with human life being devalued if we have something better." Now just absorb that thought for a moment. One of the world's leading scientists ready to "devalue human life" if we can create something he thinks is better. Setting aside the question of who decides what "better" is, to me, devaluing human life is a form of self-destruction.

The editor of *Wired* magazine says we're in the process of the "wiring of human and artificial minds into one planetary soul." Thus, he believes, we'll be the first species "to create our own successors." He sees artificial intelligence "creating its own civilization."

These are not "mad scientists." They're America's best and brightest, and they believe they're ushering in the next stage of evolution.

In sum, we're creating technology that forces us to ask what are humans for once we've created super intelligent robots that can do anything humans can do, only do it a thousand times faster? Why do we need robots with emotional and spiritual capability, and what does that have to do with the seventy percent of humanity that simply seeks the basic necessities of life? What will it mean to be able to change the genetic structure not just of an individual child, but also of all future generations? Do we really want to be able to make genetic changes so subtle that it may be generations before we know what we've done to ourselves?

What we're talking about is a potential alteration of the human being at the level of the soul. This is a work proceeding absent any political debate, certainly without the assent of elected leaders. Yet it will change the definition of what it means to be a human being. It's the silent loss of freedom masquerading as technological progress.

Many other questions come to mind, but two in particular. Will it happen, and what is driving this self-destructive technological imperative?

On the first question—will it happen—my guess is probably not. In my judgment, there is a major issue the technological visionaries disregard. That is the question of how much manipulation and accelerated change the human being can take before he/she disintegrates psychologically and physiologically.

What we're experiencing is not simply the acceleration of the pace of change, but the acceleration of acceleration itself. In other words, change growing at an exponential rate. The experts tell us that the rate of change doubles every decade; that at today's rate of change, we'll experience 100 calendar years of change in the next twenty-five years; and that due to the nature of exponential growth, the 21st century as a whole will experience almost one thousand times greater technological change than did the 20th century.

I hasten to add that these are not my projections. They are the views of some of America's most accomplished and respected experts in computer science and artificial intelligence.

Onrushing change is already producing mounting dysfunction. The suicide rate among women has increased 200% in the past two decades. Thirty years ago, major corporations didn't have to think much about mental health programs for employees. Now, mental health is the fastest growing component of corporate health insurance programs. Think of the corporations that now provide special rooms for relaxation, naps, music, or prayer and meditation. The issue now for corporations is not so much how to deal with stress; it's how to maintain the psychological integrity of the individual employee.

Other indicators of dysfunction tell us that teen suicide jumped 300% between 1960–90. Books are now written for eight and nine year old children advising them how to recognize the symptoms of stress, and to deal with it in their own lives. Anti-depressants and other character-controlling drugs are taken like aspirin. Rage has assumed a culture-like place in the national fabric, whether rage on the road, in stores, in schools, and even in a popular video game called "Primal Rage," and, most tragically, in families.

Now, project forward the predicted increased speed of computers and the resulting ratcheting up of the pace of life over the next decades, and you end up asking, "How much more of this can the human metabolism take?" It's not the case that sooner or later something will give way. The multiplying social pathologies indicate that individual and collective psychological integrity is already giving way.

The second question is, what's driving this self-destructive activity? Certainly we as consumers are a major part of it. We're addicted to the latest electronic gizmo; whether it's the ubiquitous cell phone to keep us in touch with everyone everywhere, or one of those Sharper Image CD players you hang on the shower head so you can listen to Beethoven while taking a shower.

But let me offer three views that suggest a deeper story. Consider the comment of a former Carnegie-Mellon University computer scientist hired by Microsoft as a researcher. In an interview with the *Washington Post,* the good professor said, "This corporation is my power tool. It is the tool I wield to allow my ideas to shape the world."

My power tool. What clearer expression of ego-inflation could there be?

A second comment comes from the editor of *Weird* magazine, who famously wrote, "We are as gods, and we might as well be good at it." The Greeks had a word for identifying ourselves with the gods—hubris, pride reaching beyond proper human limits.

Perspective on all this comes from within the scientific community itself.

Freeman Dyson is one of the world's preeminent theoretical physicists. He talks about the "technical arrogance" that overcomes people "when they see what they can do with their minds."

My power tool; we are as gods; technical arrogance. The Greeks had another word that was even stronger than hubris. Pleonexia. An overweening resolve to reach beyond the limits, an insatiable greed for the unattainable. It is what one writer terms the "Masculine Sublime," which he describes as the "gendered characteristics out of which the myths of science are molded-myths of masculine power, control, rationality, objectivity."

From the earliest times, everything in human myth and religion warns us about overreaching. From the myths of Prometheus in ancient Greece, to the Hebrew story of Adam and Eve; from the Faust legend to Milton's Paradise Lost; from Mary Shelly's Frankenstein to Stevenson's Dr. Jekyll and Mr. Hyde; from Emily Dickinson to Robert Oppenheimer's lament that "in some sort of crude sense, the physicists have known sin"; through all these stories and experiences that come from the deepest level of the human soul, there has been a warning that limits exist on both human knowledge and endeavor; that to go beyond those limits is self-destructive.

No one knows exactly where such limits might be. But if they don't include the effort to create some technical/human life form supposedly superior to human beings, if they don't include the capacity to genetically reconfigure human nature, if they don't include the attempt to introduce a "post-human" civilization, then it's hard to imagine where such limits would be drawn.

Keep in mind that myths are more than fanciful stories left over from the childhood of man. They emanate from the unconscious level of the psyche; that level which connects us to whatever transpersonal wisdom may exist. It's a level at which, as quantum physics suggests, there may exist some relationship between the human psyche and external matter. There may be some fundamental pattern of life common to both that is operating outside the understanding of contemporary science. In other words, we may be fooling around with phenomena that are, in fact, beyond human awareness; possibly even beyond the ability of humans to grasp. For at the heart of life is a great mystery which does not yield to rational interpretation. This eternal mystery induces a sense of wonder out of which all that humanity has of religion, art, and science is born. The mystery is the giver of these gifts, and we only lose the gifts when we grasp at the mystery itself. In my view, Nature will not permit arrogant man to defy that mystery, that transcendent wisdom. In the end, Nature's going to win out.

Some people are already searching for the wisest way to approach such potential challenges as the new technologies present. Bill Joy, co-founder and former chief scientist of Sun Microsystems, suggests we've reached the point where we must "limit development of technologies that are too dangerous, by limiting our pursuit of certain kinds of knowledge." His concerns are based on the unknown potential of genetics, nanotechnology, and robotics, driven by computers capable of infinite speeds, and the possible uncontrollable self-replication of these technologies this might pose. Joy acknowledges the pursuit of knowledge as one of the primary human goals since earliest times. But, he says, "If open access to, and unlimited development of, knowledge henceforth puts us all in clear danger of extinction, then common sense demands that we re-examine even these basic, long-held beliefs."

The third trend moving us between two ages is a long-term spiritual and psychological reorientation that's increasingly generating uncertainty and instability. This affects all of us, for we're all part of America's collective psychology, whether we realize it or not.

The best measure of America's psychological and spiritual life is not public opinion polls telling us what percentage of the population believes in God. Rather, it's the content and quality of our culture. For culture is to a nation what dreams are to an individual—an indication of what's going on in the inner life.

In my judgment, what's really going on is that the world is experiencing a long-term spiritual and psychological reorientation similar to what happened when the Greco-Roman era gave way to the start of the Feudal Age. That was a time of great disorientation and searching. The cry "Great Pan is dead," was heard throughout the ancient world as the traditional gods lost their hold on the collective psyche. The Greco-Roman world became awash in countless new religions and sects vying for supremacy.

Not too different from our times, beginning with Nietzsche's cry, "God is dead." When we look at what's happening today we see 1500 religions in America, including such anomalies as "Catholic-Buddhists." Beyond that, we see a smorgasbord of spiritual/psychological fare as seen in the popularity of books such as The Celestine Prophecy or the Chicken Soup series, in the rise of worldwide fundamentalism, in numerous cults such as "Heaven's Gate," in the New Age phenomenon, in interest in Nostradamus, in crop circles, in the supposed "Bible Code," in conspiracy theories, in fascination with the "other" as seen in movies such as "Planet of the Apes" or "Tomb Raiders," in the search for some extraterrestrial intelligence to save us from ourselves, and last but certainly not least, in terrorism, which, at its core, is a demonic hatred expressed in spiritual terms.

What happened in the Rome—early Feudal Age shift was played out over centuries. What's happening today has, yes, been evolving over the past few centuries. We see it first manifested in the emergence of the Faust legend; then in the Enlightenment's enthronement of the Goddess of Reason in Notre Dame and the ensuing acceptance of rationalism as life's highest authority; and in our own time in the ethos of "meaninglessness" that has virtually defined 20th century Western culture. But what's happening today—due to the 20th century electronic information technologies—is probably unfolding at a more rapid pace than the shift in the fourth-fifth-sixth centuries. For information technologies transmit not only information, but psychological dynamics as well.

While there are millions of devout Christians and Jews in America and Europe, the Judeo-Christian impulse is no longer the formative dynamic of Western culture, especially among the so-called "creative minority." Even so calm a journal as the Economist opines, "The West is secular." One need only look at the changing relationship between the roles of the priest and the psychologist to see what has been happening. Earlier in the 20th century, if someone had personal problems, he or she went to the priest for advice. Gradually that changed, and people started going to their psychologist. Recently, the leader of the Roman Catholic Church in England and Wales said that as a background for people's lives, Christianity "has almost been vanquished." His language mirrored a statement by the Archbishop of Canterbury who declared Britain to be a country where "tacit atheism prevails." Newsweek recently described Europe as a "post-Christian civilization." Throughout the continent, Newsweek reported, "churches stand empty."

Part of the psychological reorientation taking place is the breakup of our collective inner images of wholeness. For example, we used to talk about "heaven," which denoted the transcendent realm, eternity, the dwelling place of the gods. Now we just speak of "space," which has no spiritual connotation. We used to talk of "mother earth," which had a vital emotional association. From time immemorial, nature was filled with spirit. Now we just speak of "matter," a lifeless nature bereft of gods.

Thus transcendent meaning—which is the source of psychological wholeness is diminished. The function of symbolic language-words like "heaven" and "mother earth"—is to link our consciousness to the roots of our being, to link our consciousness to its base in the unconscious. When that link is devalued or discarded, there is little to sustain the inner life of the individual. So, few people are inwardly fed by any primal source of wholeness. In effect, our symbolic life and language have been displaced by a vocabulary of technology, a vocabulary that's increasingly devoid of transcendent meaning. The effect is a weakening of the structures that organize and, regulate our life-religion, self-government, education, culture, and the family.

As a result, the soul of America—indeed, of the world—is in a giant search for some deeper and greater expression of life. Despite the benefits of modernization, technological society offers no underlying meaning to life. Thus the search taking place is both healthy and normal—given the seminal shift to an entirely new epoch that is occurring as we speak.

What we're discussing is at the core of the crisis of meaning that afflicts not only America and Europe, but Asia as well. For example, the *Washington Post* reports from Beijing, "Across China people are struggling to redefine notions of success and failure, right and wrong. The quest for something to believe in is one of the unifying characteristics of China today." A report from the East/West Center in Hawaii notes the decline in family and authority in Asia, and concludes by saying, "Eastern religion no longer is the binding force in Asian society." So it's a global crisis of meaning we're talking about.

Let me briefly summarize what we've been discussing: (1) Globalization, possibly the most ambitious collective human experiment in history; (2) a new stage of technology the objective of which is to supplant human meaning and significance; and (3) a long-term psychological and spiritual reorientation. These are only three of the basic changes determining the future. And it's because of the magnitude and significant of such trends that I suggest the next three decades may be the most decisive thirty-year period in human history.

Glossary

Account One's version of an incident; often an excuse or justification for unexpected or inappropriate behavior. See *Excuse* and *Justification.*

Achieved status A person's position or ranking achieved at least partly through personal efforts (such as becoming a college student) or failings (such as becoming a skid row alcoholic).

Aggregate People grouped together for the purpose of social research because of characteristics they have in common. An example is U.S. females between the ages of 18 and 23 who wear contact lenses.

Alienation Used in a couple of different meanings. The first is Weberian, a sense of separation, of not belonging, of being estranged. This meaning includes the idea that one has little control over the social world; may also include the feeling that one's world is meaningless. The second is Marxian, a sense of being separated from and not identifying with the product of one's labor.

Anomie Normlessness; conflict between norms, weakened respect for norms, or absence of norms.

Anticipatory socialization Learning the perspectives of a role before entering it. See *Role* and *Socialization.*

Ascribed status A person's position or ranking assigned on the basis of standards over which the individual has little or no control, such as age, race, or sex.

Authority Power that is regarded as legitimate or proper by those over whom it is exercised.

Background expectancies (or assumptions) The taken-for-granted assumptions people have about the way the world is. See *Social construction of reality.*

Belief An idea about some part of the natural or social world; a view of reality.

Body language Communicating messages through the movement or positioning of the body; includes gestures and facial expressions.

Bureaucracy A form of organization that has several layers of authority, usually depicted by a pyramid. Decisions flow downward, accountability for fulfilling orders goes upward, rules are explicit, emphasis is placed on written records, resources are directed toward efficiently reaching the goals of the organization, the "bottom line" is of utmost concern, and the personal is kept separate from that which belongs to the organization. The reality of any particular organization does not necessarily match this *Ideal type.*

Case study An in-depth investigation of a single event, experience, organization, or situation in order to better understand that case or to abstract principles of human behavior.

548 / *Glossary*

Charisma Extraordinary personal qualities that attract followers. Charisma varies from simply a "magnetic" personality to qualities so extraordinary that they are assumed to be supernatural.

Charismatic authority Leadership exercised on the basis of charisma. See *Charisma* and *Traditional authority.*

Class See *Social class.*

Class conflict Karl Marx's term for the struggle between social classes; generally thought of as the struggle between the rich (and powerful) and the poor (and powerless), or those who own the means of economic production and those who do not.

Coding Fitting data into classifications so they can be analyzed.

Collective behavior Relatively spontaneous, unstructured, and transitory ways of thinking, feeling, and acting that develop among a large number of people.

Community Its primary meaning is that of people who inhabit the same geographical area and share common interests and feel a sense of "belonging." From this sense comes a derived meaning of people who share common interests and have a sense of "belonging" but who do not inhabit the same geographical area, such as in the phrase "a community of scholars."

Conflict theory The theoretical view that emphasizes conflict as the inevitable outcome in society due to its various groups competing for limited resources. See *Functionalism* and *Symbolic interactionism.*

Conformity Following social norms or expectations.

Conspicuous consumption Thorstein Veblen's term for a change from an orientation toward saving in the Protestant ethic to showing off wealth by the elaborate consumption of goods.

Content analysis Classifying the contents of presidential speeches, medical novels, situation comedies, and so on in order to identify and analyze its themes.

Control group The subjects in an experiment who are *not* exposed to the independent variable, as opposed to the experimental group who are subjected to this variable. See *Experiment, Experimental group, Independent variable,* and *Variable.*

Covert participant observation See *Participant observation.*

Crime An act prohibited by law.

Cultural diffusion The process by which items (or behavior, beliefs, and attitudes) from one culture are adopted by members of another culture.

Cultural relativity The view that one cannot judge the characteristics of any culture to be morally superior to those of another. See its opposite, *Ethnocentrism.*

Culture A way of life, or shared ways of doing things; includes nonmaterial culture (such as norms, beliefs, values, and language) and material culture (such as art, tools, weapons, and buildings). See *Ideal culture* and *Real culture.*

Culture lag (Cultural lag) A term developed by William F. Ogburn to refer to the material culture changing more rapidly than the nonmaterial culture.

Culture of poverty The distinctive culture said to exist among the poor of industrialized societies; its central features of defeatism, dependence, and a present time orientation are thought to trap people in poverty and to perpetuate it from one generation to the next.

Culture shock   The disorienting effect that immersion in an unfamiliar culture has on a visitor as he or she encounters markedly different norms, values, beliefs, customs, and other basic orientations of social life. No longer is the individual able to rely on the basics of his or her socialization.

Data   The information that scientists gather in their studies.

Definition of reality   A view of what the world or some part of the world is like. See *Social construction of reality.*

Dehumanization   The act or process of reducing people to objects that do not deserve the treatment given humans.

Demography   The study of the size, distribution, composition, and change in human populations.

Dependent variable   That which is being explained as the result of other factors; a variable or social phenomenon thought to be changed or influenced by another variable. See *Independent variable.*

Deviance   Violation of social norms or expectations.

Deviant   One who violates social norms or expectations. As used by sociologists, a neutrally descriptive rather than a negative term.

Deviant career   The main course of events during someone's involvement in deviance; generally refers to people who are habitually, or at least for a period of time heavily, involved in some deviant activity.

Differential association   If a person associates with one group of people, he or she will learn one set of attitudes, ideas, and norms; associating with a different group teaches a different approach to life. Such differential association influences people either to conform or to deviate.

Diffusion   The spread of an invention or discovery from one area or group to another.

Disclaimer   An excuse or justification for inappropriate behavior that is *about* to take place. Examples are: "Now don't get me wrong, but . . .;" and "Let me play the devil's advocate for a minute."

Discrimination   The denial of rights, privileges, or opportunities to others on the basis of their group membership. See *Minority group, Racism,* and *Sexism.*

Division of labor   A concept developed by Emile Durkheim to refer to the various ways in which work is divided, with some people specializing in financing or production, others in advertising or distribution, teaching or learning, and so on.

Documents   In its narrow sense, written sources that provide data; in its extended sense, archival material of any sort, including photographs, movies, recordings, and so on.

Double standard   More stringent expectations being applied to one group than to another. *The* double standard refers to attitudes and ideas more favorable to males than to females—often to males being allowed more sexual freedom.

Downsizing   A fancy way of saying that to reduce costs a company is firing workers.

Downward social mobility   Movement from a higher to a lower social position. See *Social class.*

Dramaturgical analysis Developed by Erving Goffman, this term refers to viewing human interaction as a theatrical performance. People are seen as actors, their clothing as costumes, what they do as parts they play, what they say as the delivery of lines, where they interact as a stage, and so on.

Dramaturgy Refers to theatrical performances. The same as *Dramaturgical analysis*.

Ecology The study of reciprocal relationships between organisms and their environment.

Education One of the primary institutions of society; it is designed to transmit values, skills, and knowledge from one generation to the next.

Ego Commonly used as a term to refer to the self; technically, Freud's term for the conscious, rational part of an individual.

Endogamy A cultural pattern of marrying *within* one's own social group. See *Exogamy*.

Ethnic cleansing Refers to killing people because of their ethnicity, with the goal of "cleaning out" an area for one's own ethnic group to inhabit.

Ethnic group A group of people with a sense of common ancestry, who generally share similar cultural traits and who regard themselves as distinct from others.

Ethnic stratification Groups of people who are stratified (or divided into layers) on the basis of their ethnic group membership. See *Social stratification*.

Ethnocentrism Using the standards of one's own group, culture, or subculture to evaluate the characteristics of other groups, cultures, or subcultures, generally from the point of view that one's own characteristics are superior. See *Cultural relativity*.

Ethnography A report or study that details the major characteristics of the way of life of a group of people; can be of an entire tribe, an entire village, or a small group within a large society, such as urban cabdrivers.

Ethnomethodology Developed by Harold Garfinkel, this term refers to the study of people's worlds of reality, their taken-for-granted background assumptions, and the ways by which they make sense out of their experiences.

Excuse An account of an event in which someone acknowledges that an act is blameworthy, but denies responsibility for the act. See *Account* and *Justification*.

Exogamy A cultural pattern of marrying *outside* one's social group. See *Endogamy*.

Experiment A study in which the researcher manipulates one or more variables (independent variables) in order to measure the results on other variables (dependent variables). See *Variable*.

Experimental group The subjects in an experiment who are exposed to the independent variable, as opposed to the control group who do not experience this variable. See *Experiment*.

Extended family A family consisting of two or more generations; they are *extended* beyond the nuclear family. See *Family* and *Nuclear family*.

False consciousness A term developed by Karl Marx to refer to members of the working class identifying with capitalists.

Family People who are related by ancestry, marriage, or adoption, who generally live together and form an economic unit, and whose adult members assume responsibility for the young. The form of the family varies remarkably from one culture to another.

Family of orientation The family into which one is born. See *Family* and *Family of procreation.*

Family of procreation The family that is created by marriage. See *Family* and *Family of orientation.*

Femininity Our behaviors and orientations as females. Assumed in sociology to be an expression not of biology but of cultural or social learning. See *Masculinity.*

Feral children Children who have been found in the wilderness, supposedly raised by animals. Not only do they possess no language, but also they exhibit few behaviors that we ordinarily associate with humans.

Field research Another term for *Participant observation.*

Field study Another term for *Participant observation.*

Fieldwork Another term for *Participant observation.*

Folk society A term developed by Robert Redfield to refer to small, traditional societies in which there is little social change.

Folkways Developed by William G. Sumner, this term refers to norms that people are expected or encouraged to follow, but whose violation is not considered immoral; the ordinary rules, usages, conventions, and expectations of everyday life, such as, in U.S. society, the use of deodorant. See *Mores.*

Formal organization A social group that is brought into existence to reach specific goals; often utilizes a bureaucratic mode of operation to achieve those objectives. See *Bureaucracy.*

Formal sanction A social reward or punishment that is formally applied; often a part of ritual recognition for achievement (such as receiving a passing grade in school, or being promoted at work) or failure (such as receiving a failing grade in school, or being fired from one's job). See *Informal sanction* and *Sanction.*

Functionalism The theoretical view that stresses how the parts of a society or social group are interrelated. Emphasis is placed on the contributions (functions) that one part makes for the adjustment or well-being of other parts. Each part, working properly, is seen as contributing to the stability of the whole. See *Symbolic interactionism* and *Conflict theory.*

Future shock A term developed by Alvin Toffler to refer to the dizzying disorientation brought on by the rapid arrival of the future.

Gender The social expectations attached to a person on account of that person's sex. Sex is biological, while gender is social. See *Femininity* and *Masculinity.*

Gender socialization Learning one's gender. See *Gender.*

Generalize To apply the research findings from a sample to a larger group.

Generalized other The ideas we have of the expectations of a major reference group, or even of society in general.

Genocide Killing an entire population, usually because of the group's biological and cultural traits.

Gentrification The process by which the relatively affluent move to decaying urban neighborhoods, renovate buildings, and displace the poor.

Gestures   The movement and positioning of the body to communicate meaning.

Heterosexuality   Sexual acts or feelings toward members of the opposite sex. See *Homosexuality.*

Hidden curriculum   The unwritten goals of schools, such as teaching obedience to authority and conformity to cultural norms.

Holocaust   The Nazi destruction, in death camps and by means of death squads, of Jews, gypsies, Slavs, homosexuals, the mentally retarded, and others considered threats to the purity of the so-called Aryan race.

Homosexuality   Sexual acts or feelings toward members of the same sex. See *Heterosexuality.*

Horizontal mobility   Movement from one social position to another that is approximately equivalent.

Human ecology   The reciprocal relationships between people and their environment.

Hypothesis   A prediction about how two or more variables are related. See *Variable.*

Ideal culture   The way of life represented by people's values and norms, rather than by their actual practices. See *Real culture.*

Ideal type   Developed by Max Weber, this term refers to a model or description of something that is derived from examining real cases and abstracting what appear to be the essential characteristics of those cases.

Identity formation   The process by which we develop a personal identity; our internalization of social expectations. The end result is that we come to think of ourselves in a certain way; that is, as we internalize people's reactions to us, we develop a "self."

Ideology   Statements or beliefs (especially of reasons and purposes) that justify a group's actions or interests; they buttress, uphold, or legitimate the existing social order.

Incest   Sexual intercourse with forbidden categories of kinfolk. See *Incest taboo.*

Incest taboo   A prohibition against sexual intercourse with specific categories of kinfolk. See *Incest.*

Independent variable   That which is thought to affect or to cause change in some other factor; the variable thought to influence another variable. See *Dependent variable.*

Informal sanction   A social reward or punishment that is informally applied, includes spontaneous gestures of approval or disapproval. Examples include staring, smiling, and gossip. See *Formal sanction* and *Sanction.*

Ingroup   The group to which an individual belongs, identifies, and feels loyalty. See *Outgroup.*

Institution   See *Social institution.*

Institutional(ized) racism   The use of social institutions to discriminate, exploit, or oppress a racial–ethnic group. See *Discrimination* and *Racism.*

Institutional(ized) sexism   The use of social institutions to discriminate, exploit, or oppress either males or females as a group. See *Discrimination* and *Sexism.*

Interaction   See *Social interaction.*

Interactional sociology   Studies of social life in which the emphasis is on social interaction. See *Participant observation, Qualitative sociology,* and *symbolic interactionism.*

Internalization Experiences becoming part of one's "internal" life—thinking, attitudes, and other orientations.

Interview Asking a respondent questions; can be face-to-face, by writing, or by some form of electronic communication such as by telephone, fax, or computer. See *Respondent.*

Interviewer bias Effects that interviewers have on respondents that tilt answers in some direction.

Involuntary associations Groups to which people belong, but about which they have little or no choice. Examples include grade school for youngsters and military service during periods of conscription. See *Voluntary associations.*

Justification An account of an event in which one accepts responsibility for an act, while denying that the act is blameworthy. See *Account* and *Excuse.*

Kin People who are related by birth, adoption, or marriage.

Kinfolk See *Kin.*

Kinship The network of people who are related to one another by birth, adoption, or marriage.

Labeling theory (or perspective) This perspective, which focuses on the effects of labels (or terms) on people, stresses that acts are not inherently deviant (or criminal) but are such only because those acts have been so labeled (or defined). Deviants are those on whom the label of deviant has been successfully applied.

Life chances The likelihood that an individual or group will benefit from their society's opportunities, goods and services, and other satisfactions in life.

Life course The stages of our life as we go from birth to death.

Life expectancy The average number of years that a person can expect to live.

Looking-glass self Charles Horton Cooley's term for the process by which people see themselves through the eyes of others. As people act, others react. In those reactions, people see themselves reflected. Perceiving this, they interpret its meaning, which yields a particular self-image.

Masculinity Our behaviors and orientations as males. Generally assumed in sociology to be an expression not of biology but of cultural or social learning. See *Femininity.*

Mass media Forms of communication that reach a large audience, with no personal contact between the senders and receivers of the message. Examples are movies, radio, television, newspaper, magazines, plays, books, video games, and the Internet.

Master status (or trait) A social status (achieved or ascribed) that cuts across most other social statuses and provides a major basis for personal and public identity.

Material culture See *Culture.*

Meanings The significance that something has to someone. Also called symbols, mental constructs, ideas, and stereotypes. See *Qualitative sociology.*

Methodology (Methods, Research designs) The procedures scientists use to conduct their studies.

Military-industrial complex The relationships between top leaders of the Pentagon and U.S. corporations by which they reciprocally support one another and thereby influence political decisions on their behalf.

Minority group A group of people who are treated unequally because of their physical or cultural characteristics. See *Discrimination.*

Mores (Pronounced more-rays) Developed by William G. Sumner, this term refers to norms whose violation is considered a moral transgression. Examples are the norms against murder and theft. See *Folkways.*

Negative sanction Punishment for disapproved behavior. See *Sanction.*

Neutralization (techniques of) Words and ways of thinking that help to deflect social norms and avoid social disapproval. An example is saying, "The circumstances required it" or, "I didn't know what I was doing."

Nonmaterial culture See *Culture.*

Nonverbal communication Communication by the use of symbols other than language. Examples are *Body language* and traffic lights.

Norms Rules concerning appropriate and inappropriate behavior by which people are judged and sanctions applied. See *Sanction.*

Nuclear family A family that consists of a husband, wife, and their children. See *Extended family.*

Operational definition The way in which a variable in a hypothesis is measured.

Organization A social unit established for the purpose of attaining some agreed-upon goals.

Outgroup A group toward which an individual feels hostility, tension, or dislike. See *Ingroup.*

Overt participant observation See *Participant observation.*

Participant observation A method of studying social groups in which the researcher participates in the group being studied. If the people being studied know the researcher is in their midst, this method is called *overt participant observation;* if they do not know they are being studied, it is called *covert participant observation.*

Peer group People who occupy a similar social status and who are usually close in age. Examples are one's playmates as a child and workmates as an adult.

Personal identity Our ideas of who we are. Roughly equivalent to self concept. See *Public identity* and *Self.*

Personality The personal characteristics or behavior patterns we come to expect of people.

Population The target group to be studied.

Positive sanction A reward for approved behavior. See *Sanction.*

Power The ability to get your way, even over the objections or opposition of others.

Power elite C. Wright Mills's term to refer to a small group of powerful people who have interlocking interests, and who make a nation's most important political decisions.

Prejudice Attitudes, ideas, and feelings, often negative; can be about people one does not know. See *Discrimination* and *Ethnocentrism.*

Prestige Favorable evaluation, respect, or social recognition.

Primary group People whose relationship is intimate, face-to-face, expressive, and extended over time. Examples are one's family and close friends.

Prostitution   The exchange of sexual favors for some gain, usually money.

Public identity   The ideas that others have of what we ought to be like. Roughly equivalent to the public social roles we play. See *Personal identity* and *Self.*

Qualitative sociology   Studies of social life in which the emphasis is on the *meanings* of people's experiences. The goal is to determine how people construct their worlds, develop their ideas and attitudes, communicate these with one another, and how their meanings affect their behavior, ideas about the self, and relationships to one another. See *Meanings* and *Quantitative sociology.*

Quantitative sociology   Studies of social life in which the emphasis is on precise measurement, or numbers. Sociologists who have this orientation stress that to understand human behavior we must use statistical techniques. See *Qualitative sociology.*

Questionnaire   An interview by means of a written form.

Race   A large number of people who share physical characteristics on the basis of which they regard themselves as a biological unit and are similarly regarded by others.

Racism   One racial–ethnic group dominating or exploiting another, generally based on seeing those they exploit as inferior. See *Discrimination* and *Ethnocentrism.*

Random sample   A sample in which everyone in the target population has the same chance of being included in the study.

Rapport   A feeling of trust and communication between people.

Rationalization (of society)   Weber's term for the process by which a society or other group adopts a bureaucratic orientation, with emphasis on efficiency, impersonal relations, and the bottom line.

Real culture   A people's actual way of life, as contrasted with the way of life that is expressed by their ideals. See *Ideal culture.*

Reference group   A group to which people refer when they evaluate themselves, their behavior, or actions they are considering.

Relative deprivation   Feeling deprived relative to what others have; a sense of injustice regarding the gap between the resources or rewards that one has and what others have.

Reliability   The extent to which studies produce consistent results.

Replication   The repetition of a study in order to test its findings.

Research methods   See *Methodology.*

Resocialization   Learning norms, values, and behaviors that contrast with one's previous experiences.

Respondent   A person who has been interviewed or who has filled out a questionnaire. (He or she has *responded* to the request for data.)

Rising expectations   A situation in which people who have accepted existing conditions in the past now feel that they have a right to better conditions.

Rites of passage   Rituals that mark someone's transition from one social status to another. Examples include bar mitzvahs, confirmations, first communions, weddings, graduation ceremonies, and funerals. Also known as *rites de passage.*

Role   The part played by a person who occupies a particular status. See *Status.*

Role conflict   If a person finds himself or herself torn between conflicting demands of two or more roles, that person is said to be experiencing role conflict. Examples include a student wanting to date on the same night that he or she is supposed to study for a final examination.

Role taking   Putting yourself in the shoes of someone else and seeing how things look from that perspective.

Sample   The individuals who are intended to represent the population to be studied.

Sanction   A social reward for approved behavior, or punishment for disapproved behavior. See *Negative sanction* and *Positive sanction*.

Secondary analysis   The analysis of data that have already been collected by other researchers.

Secondary group   The more formal, impersonal, and transitory groups to which people belong, such as an introductory course in sociology.

Self   The sense of identity that individuals have of themselves as a distinct person; this sense, idea, or conception is acquired through social interaction. See *Identity formation*.

Self-fulfilling prophecy   A false definition of a situation ("The bank is in trouble") that causes people to change their behavior ("People rush to the bank to withdraw their savings") and makes the originally false statement come true ("The bank is now in trouble as it does not have enough cash on hand to meet the unexpected demand for immediate withdrawals"). If the "prophecy" had not been made, it would not have come true.

Sex role   The behaviors and characteristics that a male or female is expected to demonstrate, based on cultural concepts of masculinity or femininity; assigned on the basis of one's sex organs.

Sex role socialization   Learning one's sex role. See *Sex role.*

Sexism   Males or females dominating or exploiting the other, with the exploitation generally based on seeing the other as inferior; usually used to refer to males dominating females. See *Discrimination* and *Ethnocentrism*.

Social change   Change in society; the change can be in social institutions (or some small part of them), culture, and people's behavior.

Social class   A large number of people who have about the same amount of social power. In our society, some sociologists (Weberian) see the primary bases as the amount of people's income and education and the prestige of their occupation. Other sociologists (Marxian) see the essential difference as people's relationship to the means of production—whether they are capitalists (own the means of production) or workers (work for capitalists).

Social class mobility   Changing one's social class, usually in relationship to that of one's parents. See *Social mobility.*

Social construction of reality   The process by which definitions of reality (views of what some part of the world is like) are socially created, internalized, and then taken for granted.

Social control   The techniques used to keep people in line or, if they step out, to bring them back into line. Examples include persuasion, rewards, gifts, coercion, ridicule, education, and punishment. See *Sanction*.

Social group   Any human group.

Social inequality   Any inequality between or among groups of people; sometimes refers to *social stratification*.

Social institution   The standardized ways that a society meets its basic needs. Examples include government and politics (for social order), education (for training in conformity and the transmission of skills and knowledge), and the military (for protection from external enemies and the implementation of foreign policy).

Social interaction   People acting and reacting to one another; as they do so, they influence each other's feelings, attitudes, and actions.

Social mobility   Movement from one social position to another. See *Downward, Horizontal,* and *Upward social mobility*.

Social stratification   Large groups of people who are ranked in a hierarchy that gives them different access to the rewards that their society has to offer.

Social structure   The ways in which the basic components of a group or society are related to one another.

Socialization   Refers to learning; the process by which people learn the way of life of their society, or learn to play specific roles.

Society   A group of individuals who share the same territory and participate in a common culture.

Sociobiology   The study of the biological bases of human behavior.

Sociology   The study of human society and social behavior; the study of how groups influence people and how people influence groups.

Status   One's position in a group or society, such as woman, mother, and plumber.

Stereotypes   A generalization (or idea) about people (or even animals and objects); a mental image that summarizes what is believed to be typical about these people.

Stigma   An indelible mark of social disgrace.

Stratification   See *Social stratification*.

Structural sociology   The study of social life in which the emphasis is on social structure, social institutions, and other group memberships. See *Quantitative sociology* and *Social structure*.

Structured interview   An interview that uses closed-ended questions.

Subculture   A group that shares in the overall culture of a society but also has its own distinctive values, norms, beliefs, and life style. Examples include cabdrivers, singles, prostitutes, muggers, physicians, and college students.

Subjective interpretation   See *Verstehen*.

Survey   The collection of data by having people answer a series of questions.

Symbol   Any act, object, or event that represents something, such as a traffic light, a gesture, or this definition. See *Symbolic interactionism*.

Symbolic interaction   People's interaction based on symbols. See *Symbolic interactionism*.

Symbolic interactionism   Developed by Herbert Blumer, this term refers to studying social life by focusing on people's symbols or meanings. Symbolic interactionists analyze how people communicate with one another especially how they change or refine their courses of action in anticipation of the reactions of others. See *Conflict theory* and *Functionalism.*

Techniques of neutralization   See *Neutralization.*

Technology   Tools or items used to accomplish tasks.

Theory   A statement that organizes a set of concepts in a meaningful way by explaining the relationship between them.

Total institution   Erving Goffman's term to refer to a place in which people are confined, cut off from the rest of society, and under the almost absolute control of the people in charge. Examples include prisons, the military, and convents.

Traditional authority   Authority that is legitimated by custom and practice. The explanation for something is, "We have always done it this way." See *Charismatic authority.*

Trust   The willingness to accept the definition that someone offers of oneself or of a situation and to play a corresponding role based on that definition.

Unobtrusive measures   Techniques of observing people who do not know they are being studied.

Unstructured interview   An interview that uses open-ended questions.

Upward social mobility   Movement from a lower to a higher social position.

Validity   The extent to which an *operational definition* measures what it is intended to measure.

Value conflict   Disagreement over goals, ideals, policies, or other expressions of values.

Value judgment   A subjective opinion based on one's own set of values.

Values   Ideas about what is worthwhile.

Variable   Any condition or characteristic that varies from one situation or person or group to another. Examples include age, occupation, beliefs, and attitudes. See *Dependent variable, Experiment,* and *Independent variable.*

Verstehen   A term used by Max Weber to refer to the subjective interpretation of human behavior; that is, because we are members of a group or culture, we gain insight and understanding into what others are experiencing, allowing us to interpret those experiences. See *Qualitative sociology.*

Vertical social mobility   Movement to a higher or a lower social position.

Voluntary associations   Groups that people join voluntarily, often because they want to promote some goal or to be with like-minded people. Examples include a church, a college class, and a bowling league. See *Involuntary associations.*

War   Armed confict between nations or politically distinct groups.

White-collar crime   Crimes committed by "respectable" people of high status, frequently during the course of their occupation.

References

Abel, G., J. Becker, and L. Skinner. (1980). "Aggressive Behavior and Sex." *Psychiatric Clinics of North America 3:* 133–151.

Abrahams, R. D. (1973). "Ritual for Fun and Profit (or The Ends and Outs of Celebration)." Paper delivered at the Burg Wartenstein Symposium No. 59, on "Ritual: Reconciliation in Change." New York: Wenner-Gren Foundation for Anthropological Research.

Aldrich, N. W., Jr. (1988). *Old Money: The Mythology of America's Upper Class.* New York: Knopf.

American Psychological Association. (1978). *Directory of the American Psychological Association.* Washington, DC: Author.

Amos, E. P. (1983). *Kansas Funeral Profession Through the Years.* Topeka: Kansas Funeral Directors' Association.

Aries, P. (1976). *Western Attitudes Toward Death: From the Middle Ages to the Present.* Trans. P. M. Ranum. Baltimore: Johns Hopkins University Press, p. 99.

Baltzell, E. D. (1958). *Philadelphia Gentlemen: The Making of a National Upper Class.* New York: Free Press.

Barclay, G., C. Tavares, and A. Siddique. (2001). "International Comparisons of Criminal Justice Statistics, 1999." London: U.K. Home Office for Statistical Research.

Barker, J. (1995)."White Working-Class Men and Women in Academia." *Race, Gender, and Class* 3(1): 65–77.

Bart, P. (1979). "Rape as a Paradigm of Sexism in Society—Victimization and Its Discontents." *Women's Studies International Quarterly* 2: 347–357.

Becker, H. (1953). "Becoming a Marijuana User." *American Journal of Sociology* 59: 235–243.

Benales, C. (1973, January). "70 Days Battling Starvation and Freezing in the Andes: A Chronicle of Man's Unwillingness to Die." *New York Times* 3.

Bendick, M. Jr., C. Jackson, and V. Reinoso. (1994). "Measuring Employment Discrimination through Controlled Experiments." *Review of Black Political Economy* 23: 25–48.

Berk, B. (1977). "Face-Saving at the Singles Dance." *Social Problems* 24(5): 530–544.

Birmingham, N. (1978, October). "Ask Me No Secrets." *Town and Country* 132: 181.

Bittner, E. (1980). *The Functions of the Police in Modern Society.* Cambridge, MA: Oelgeschlager, Gunn & Hain.

Black, D. (1983). "Crime as Social Control." *American Sociological Review* 48: 34–45.

Blumberg, R. L. (1979). "A Paradigm for Predicting the Position of Women: Policy Implications and Problems." In J. Lipman-Blumen and J. Bernard (Eds.), *Sex Roles and Social Policy.* London: Sage Studies in International Sociology, pp. 113–142.

Bourdieu, P. (1984). *Taste.* (trans. By Richard Nice). Cambridge: Harvard University Press.

Bourdieu, P. (1986)."Forms of Capital," in *Handbook of Theory and Research for the Sociology of Education*. Westport, CT: Greenwood Press, pp. 241–256.

Broude, G., and S. Green. (1976). "Cross-Cultural Codes on Twenty Sexual Attitudes and Practices." *Ethnology 15*: 409–428.

Brown, A. (2001). "After the Kader Fire: Labour Organising for Health and Safety Standards in Thailand." In J. Hutchison and A. Brown (Eds.), *Organising Labour in Globalising Asia*. London/New York: Routledge, pp. 127–146.

Brownmiller, S. (1975). *Against Our Will*. New York: Simon & Schuster.

Bureau of Justice Statistics. (1997, March). *Lifetime Likelihood of Going to State or Federal Prison*, by Thomas P. Bonczar and Allen J. Beck. Special report. Washington, DC.

Bureau of Justice Statistics. (2000). *Key Facts at a Glance: Number of Persons in Custody of State Correctional Authorities by Most Serious Offense 1980–99*. Bulletin. Washington, DC: Government Printing Office.

Bureau of Justice Statistics. (2001, August). *Prisoners in 2000*, by Allen J. Beck and Paige M. Harrison. Bulletin. Washington, DC: NCJ 188207.

Bureau of Justice Statistics. (2002). *Sourcebook of Criminal Justice Statistics*. Last accessed March 1, 2003. Available http://www.albany.edu/sourcebook.

Charmaz, K. (1980). *The Social Reality of Death: Death in Contemporary America*. Reading, MA: Addison-Wesley.

Chodorow, N. (1978). *The Reproduction of Mothering*. Berkeley: The University of California Press.

Coleman, J. S. (1988)."Social Capital in the Creation of Human Capital." *American Journal of Sociology 94*: 95–120.

Collins, R. (1971, December). "Functional and Conflict Theories of Educational Stratification." *American Sociological Review 36*(6), 1002–1019.

Collins, R. (1981). *Sociology Since Midcentury: Essays in Theory Cumulation*. New York: Academic.

Cookson, P. W., 3rd, and C. H. Persell. (1985). *Preparing for Power*. New York: Basic Books.

Davis-Floyd, R. E. (1992). *Birth as an American Rite of Passage*. Berkeley: University of California Press.

Dinnerstein, D. (1976). *The Mermaid and the Minotaur: Sexual Arrangements and Human Malaise*. New York: Harper Colophon.

Ditton, J. (1977). "Alibis and Aliases: Some Notes on Motives of Fiddling Bread Salesmen." *Sociology 11*(2): 233–255.

Domhoff, G. W. (1983). *Who Rules America Now?* New York: Touchstone.

Douglas, J., P. Rasmussen, and C. Flanagan. (1977). *The Nude Beach*. Beverly Hills: Sage.

D'Souza, D. (1995). *The End of Racism: Principles for a Multiracial Society*. New York: Free Press.

Durkheim, E. (1965). *The Elementary Forms of the Religious Life*. New York: The Free Press (1915 copyright by George Allen & Unwin Ltd.).

Eder, D. (1985). "The Cycle of Popularity: Interpersonal Relations among Female Adolescents." *Sociology of Education 58*: 154–165.

Eliot, G. (May Ann Evans Cross, 1872). (1981). *Middlemarch: A Study of Provincial Life*. New York: New American Library.

Enloe, C. (1989). *Bananas, Beaches and Bases: Making Feminist Sense of International Politics.* Berkeley: University of California Press.

Farrell, R., and J. Nelson. (1976). "A Causal Model of Secondary Deviance: The Case of Homosexuality." *Sociological Quarterly 17:* 109–120.

Fine, G. A. (1980). "The Natural History of Preadolescent Male Friendship Groups." In H. C. Foot, A. J. Chapman, and J. R. Smith (Eds.), *Friendship and Social Relations in Children.* New York: Wiley, pp. 293–320.

Fisher, G., and E. Rivlin. (1971). "Psychological Needs of Rapists." *British Journal of Criminology 11:* 182–185.

Freeman, C. (2000). *High Tech and High Heels in the Global Economy: Women, Work, and Pink-Collar Identities in the Caribbean.* Durham, NC: Duke University Press.

Freeman, R. B. (1987). "The Relation of Criminal Activity to Black Youth Employment." *Review of Black Political Economy* 16(1–2): 99–107.

Freeman, R. B., and H. J. Holzer, eds. (1986). *The Black Youth Employment Crisis.* Chicago: University of Chicago Press for National Bureau of Economic Research.

Friedman, N. L. (1974, Spring). "Cookies and Contests: Notes on Ordinary Occupational Deviance and Its Neutralization." *Sociological Symposium,* 1–9.

Friends of Women. (1988, February). *Friends of Women Newsletter [chotomaay khaaw phúan ying].* Bangkok: Friends of Women Group.

Gage, N. (1972). *Mafia, U.S.A.* New York: Dell.

Gagnon, J. H., and W. Simon. (1973). *Sexual Conduct.* Chicago: Aldine.

Gandhi, M. K. (1954). *How to Serve the Cow.* Bombay: Navajivan Publishing House.

Gilligan, C. (1982). *In a Different Voice.* Cambridge: Harvard University Press.

Goer, H. (1995). *Obstetric Myths versus Research Realities: A Guide to the Medical Literature.* Westport, CT: Bergin and Garvey.

Goffman, E. (1959). *The Presentation of Self in Everyday Life.* Garden City, NY: Doubleday Anchor Books.

Goffman, E. (1963). *Behavior in Public Places: Notes on the Social Organization of Gatherings.* New York: The Free Press.

Goffman, E. (1974). *Frame Analysis.* Cambridge, MA: Harvard University Press.

Goffman, E. (1983). "The Interaction Order." *American Sociological Review 48:* 1–17.

Goode, E. (1978). *Deviant Behavior: An Interactionist Approach.* Englewood Cliffs, NJ: Prentice-Hall.

Griffin, S. (1971, September). "Rape: The All American Crime." *Ramparts 10:* 26–35.

Gross, E., and G. Stone. (1964). "Embarrassment and the Analysis of Role Requirements," *American Journal of Sociology 70:* 1–15.

Gross, H. (1977). "Micro and Macro Level Implications for a Sociology of Virtue—Case of Draft Protesters to Vietnam War." *Sociological Quarterly* 18(3): 319–339.

Groth, N. (1979). *Men Who Rape.* New York: Plenum Press.

Halle, D. (1984). *America's Working Man* Chicago: University of Chicago Press.

Hammer, E., and I. Jacks. (1955). "A Study of Rorschach Flexnor and Extensor Human Movements." *Journal of Clinical Psychology 11:* 63–67.

Harvey, D. (1989). *The Condition of Postmodernity*. Cambridge, MA: Blackwell.

Hayano, D. (1977, June). "The Professional Poker Player: Career Identification and the Problem of Respectability." *Social Problems 24*: 556–564.

Hays, C. L. (2004, November 14). "What Wal-Mart Knows About Customers' Habits." *New York Times*.

Henslin, J. M. (1990). "It's Not a Lovely Place to Visit, and I Wouldn't Want to Live There." In R. G. Burgess (Ed.), *Studies in Qualitative Methodology II*. Greenwich, CT: JAI Press, pp. 51–76.

Herman, D. (1984). "The Rape Culture." In J. Freeman (Ed.), *Women: A Feminist Perspective*. Palo Alto, CA: Mayfield, pp. 20–39.

Heston, A., et al. (1971). "An Approach to the Sacred Cow of India." *Current Anthropology 12*: 191–209.

Hirschi, T. (1969). *Causes of Delinquency*. Berkeley: University of California Press.

Hochschild, A. R. (1983). *The Managed Heart: Commercialization of Human Feeling*. Berkeley, CA: University of California Press.

Hoebel, E. A. (1954). *The Law of Primitive Man*. Boston: Harvard University Press.

Holtz, J. (1975). "The Professional Duplicate Bridge Player: Conflict Management in a Free, Legal, Quasi-Deviant Occupation." *Urban Life 4*(2): 131–160.

Hughes, E. C. (1962). "Good People and Dirty Work." *Social Problems 10*: 3–11.

Hunt, J. "The Development of Rapport through the Negotiation of Gender in Field Work among Police." *Human Organization*.

Joey. (1974). *Killer: Autobiography of a Mafia Hit Man*. New York: Pocket Books.

Johnson, A. G. (1980). "On the Prevalence of Rape in the United States." *Signs 6*: 136–146.

Jordan, B. (1993). *Birth in Four Cultures: A Cross-Cultural Investigation of Birth in Yucatan, Holland, Sweden and the United States* (4th ed., rev.). Prospect Heights, IL: Waveland Press.

Kanin, E. (1957). "Male Aggression in Dating-Courtship Relations." *American Journal of Sociology 63*: 197–204.

Kanin, E. (1965). "Male Sex Aggression and Three Psychiatric Hypotheses." *Journal of Sex Research 1*: 227–229.

Kanin, E. (1967). "Reference Groups and Sex Conduct Norm Violation." *Sociological Quarterly 8*: 495–504.

Kanin, E. (1969). "Selected Dyadic Aspects of Male Sex Aggression." *Journal of Sex Research 5*: 12–28.

Kanter, R. (1977). *Men and Women of the Corporation*. New York: Basic Books.

Kasinsky, R. (1975, September). "Rape: A Normal Act?" *Canadian Forum*: 18–22.

Keyes, C. F. (1984). "Mother or Mistress But Never a Monk: Buddhist Notions of Female Gender in Rural Thailand." *American Ethnologist 11*(2): 223–241.

Kirkpatrick, C., and E. Kanin (1957). "Male Sex Aggression on a University Campus." *American Sociological Review 22*: 52–58.

Kirsch, A. T. (1982). "Buddhism, Sex-Roles and the Thai Economy." In P. Van Esterik (Ed.), *Women of Southeast Asia*. DeKalb, IL: Northern Illinois University, Center for Southeast Asian Studies, pp. 16–41.

Kirsch, A. T. (1985). "Text and Context: Buddhist Sex Roles/Culture of Gender Revisited." *American Ethnologist 12*(2): 302–320.

Klein, M., et al. (1992). "Does Episiotomy Prevent Perineal Trauma and Pelvic Floor Relaxation?" *Online Journal of Current Clinical Trials 1* (Document 10).

Kluegel, J., and L. Bobo. (2001). "Perceived Group Discrimination and Policy Attitudes: The Sources and Consequences of the Race and Gender Gaps." In Alice O'Connor, Chris Tilly, and Lawrence D. Bobo (Eds.), *Urban Inequality: Evidence from Four Cities*. New York: Russell Sage Foundation, pp. 163–216.

Kohn, M., and C. Schooler. (1983). *Work and Personality*. Norwood: Ablex.

Koss, M. P., and K. E. Leonard (1984). "Sexually Aggressive Men: Empirical Findings and Theoretical Implications." In N. M. Malamuth and E. Donnerstein (Eds.), *Pornography and Sexual Aggression*. New York: Academic Press, pp. 213–232.

LaFree, G. (1980). "The Effect of Sexual Stratification by Race on Official Reactions to Rape." *American Sociological Review* 45: 824–854.

LaFree, G. (1982). "Male Power and Female Victimization: Towards a Theory of Interracial Rape." *American Journal of Sociology* 88: 311–328.

Lamphere, L. (1987). *From Working Daughters to Working Mothers: Immigrant Women in a New England Industrial Community*. Ithaca, NY: Cornell University Press.

Langer, J. (1976). "Drug Entrepreneurs and the Dealing Culture." *Australian and New Zealand Journal of Sociology* 12(2): 82–90.

Lareau, A. (1989). *Work and Personality*. Norwood: Ablex.

Lee, R. (2000). *Unobtrusive Methods in Social Research*. Philadelphia: Open University Press.

Leidner, R. (1991). "Serving Hamburgers and Selling Insurance: Gender, Work, and Identity in Interactive Service Jobs." *Gender and Society* 5: 154–177.

Lester, D., and G. Lester. (1975). *Crime of Passion: Murder and the Murderer*. Chicago: Nelson-Hall.

Lesy, M. (1987). *The Forbidden Zone*. New York: Farrar, Straus & Giroux.

Leveno, K. J., F. G. Cunningham, S. Nelson, M. Roark, M. L. Williams, D. Guzick, et al. (1986). "A Prospective Comparison of Selective and Universal Electronic Fetal Monitoring in 34,995 Pregnancies." *New England Journal of Medicine* 315(10): 615–619.

Levi, K. (1975). *Icemen*. Ann Arbor, MI: University Microfilms.

Levine, S. B. (1980). "The Rise of American Boarding Schools and the Development of a National Upper Class." *Social Problems* 28 (1): 63–94.

Levi-Strauss, C. (1969). *The Elementary Structures of Kinship*. Boston: Beacon.

Llewellyn, K. N., and E. A. Hoebel. (1941). *The Cheyenne Way: Conflict and Case Law in Primitive Jurisprudence*. Norman: University of Oklahoma Press.

Locker, D. (1981). *Symptoms and Illness: The Cognitive Organization of Disorder*. London: Tavistock.

Lorber, J. (1984). *Women as Physicians: Careers, Status and Power*. New York: Tavistock.

Lunneborg, P. (1990). *Women Changing Work*. New York: Bergin & Garvey.

Luria, Z. (1983). "Sexual Fantasy and Pornography: Two Cases of Girls Brought Up with Pornography." *Archives of Sexual Behavior* 11: 395–404.

Lynch, C. (1999). "The 'Good Girls' of Sri Lankan Modernity: Moral Orders of Nationalism and Capitalism." *Identities* 6: 55–89.

Lyttleton, C. (1994). "The Good People of Isan: Commercial Sex in Northeast Thailand." *The Australian Journal of Anthropology* 5(3): 257–279.

Maas, P. (1968). *The Valachi Papers*. New York: G. P. Putnam.

Malamuth, N., S. Haber, and S. Feshback. (1980). "Testing Hypotheses Regarding Rape: Exposure to Sexual Violence, Sex Difference, and the 'Normality' of Rapists." *Journal of Research in Personality 14:* 121–137.

Malamuth, N., M. Heim, and S. Feshback. (1980). "Sexual Responsiveness of College Students to Rape Depictions: Inhibitory and Disinhibitory Effects." *Social Psychology 38:* 399–408.

Malinowski, B. (1954). "Magic, Science, and Religion." In *Magic, Science and Religion and Other Essays.* New York: Doubleday/Anchor, pp. 17–87. (orig. pub. 1925)

Martin, M. (Ed.). (1988). *Hard Hatted Women: Stories of Struggle and Success in the Trades.* Seattle: Seal Press.

Matza, D. (1969). *Becoming Deviant.* Englewood Cliffs, NJ: Prentice-Hall.

McCarthy, M. J. (1993, August 25). "James Bond Hits the Supermarket: Stores Snoop on Shoppers' Habits to Boost Sales." *Wall Street Journal,* B1, B8.

Mead, G. H. (1934). *Mind, Self and Society.* Chicago: University of Chicago Press.

Mead, G. H. (1934). (1962). *Mind, Self, and Society,* edited by Charles Morris. Chicago: University of Chicago Press. (orig. pub. 1934).

Meyer, T. J. (1984, December 5). "'Date Rape': A Serious Problem That Few Talk About." *Chronicle of Higher Education.*

Miller, P. Y., and W. Simon. (1981). "The Development of Sexuality in Adolescence." In Joseph Adelson (Ed.), *Handbook of Adolescent Psychology.* New York: Wiley, pp. 383–407.

Mills, C. W. (1956). *The Power Elite.* London: Oxford University Press.

Mills, M. B. (1997). "Contesting the Margins of Modernity: Women, Migration, and Consumption in Thailand." *American Ethnologist 24*(1): 37–61.

Mills, M. B. (1999a). "Enacting Solidarity: Unions and Migrant Youth in Thailand." *Critique of Anthropology 19*(2): 175–191.

Mills, M. B. (1999b). *Thai Women in the Global Labor Force: Consuming Desires, Contested Selves.* New Brunswick, NJ: Rutgers University Press.

Morgan, R. (1980). "Theory and Practice: Pornography and Rape." In L. Lederer (Ed.), *Take Back the Night: Women on Pornography.* New York: William Morrow, pp. 134–140.

Muecke, M. (1992). "Mother Sold Food, Daughter Sells Her Body: The Cultural Continuity of Prostitution." *Social Science and Medicine 35*(7): 891–901.

Muehlenhard, C. L., and M. A. Linton. (1987). "Date Rape: Familiar Strangers." *Journal of Counseling Psychology 34:* 186–196.

Oakes, G. (1990). *The Soul of the Salesman.* New Jersey: Humanities Press International.

Oda, M. (1983). "Predicting Sales Performance of Car Salesmen by Personality Traits." *Japanese Journal of Psychology 54:* 73–80.

Odend'hal, S. (1972). "Gross Energetic Efficiency of Indian Cattle in Their Environment." *Journal of Human Ecology 1:* 1–27.

Padavic, I., and B. F. Reskin. (1990). "Men's Behavior and Women's Interest in Blue-Collar Jobs." *Social Problems, 37:* 613–628.

Parcel, T., and E. Menaghan. (1994). *Parents' Jobs and Children's Lives.* Aldine de Gruyter.

Parsons, T. (1951). *The Social System.* Glencoe, IL: Free Press.

Pasuk, P., and C. Baker. (1995). *Thailand: Economy and Politics.* Kuala Lumpur, Oxford and New York: Oxford University Press.

Pavalko, R. M. (1988). *Sociology of Occupations and Professions* (2nd ed.). Itasca, IL: Peacock.

Pawdee, T. (1982). *Women, Migration and Employment: A Study of Migrant Workers in Bangkok.* Ph.D. dissertation. New York University.

Pettit, B., and B. Western. (2001, August). "Inequality in Lifetime Risks of Imprisonment." Paper presented at the annual meetings of the American Sociological Association. Anaheim, CA.

Pfuhl, E. (1978). "The Unwed Father: A Non-Deviant Rule Breaker." *Sociological Quarterly 19:* 113–128.

Pine, V. R. (1975). *Caretaker of the Dead: The American Funeral Director.* New York: Irvington.

Porpora, D., and L. M. Hui. (1987). "The Political Economic Factors of Migration to Bangkok." *Journal of Contemporary Asia 17*(1): 76–89.

Pred, A., and M. J. Watts. (1992). *Reworking Modernity: Capitalisms and Symbolic Discontent.* New Brunswick, NJ: Rutgers University Press.

Prentice, A., and T. Lind. (1987). "Fetal Heart Rate Monitoring During Labor—Too Frequent Intervention, Too Little Benefit." *Lancet 2:* 1375–1377.

Prus, R. (1989). *Pursuing Customers: An Ethnography of Market Activities.* California: Sage.

Rada, R. (1978). *Clinical Aspects of Rape.* New York: Grune & Stratton.

Read, P. P. (1974). *Alive: The Story of the Andes Survivors.* Philadelphia: J. B. Lippincott.

Reid, S. (1976). *Crime and Criminology.* Hinsdale, IL: Dryden Press.

Rogers, J., and M. Buffalo. (1974). "Neutralization Techniques: Toward a Simplified Measurement Scale." *Pacific Sociological Review 17*(3): 313.

Russell, D. (1975). *The Politics of Rape.* New York: Stein & Day.

Rustad, M. L. (1984). "Female Tokenism in the Volunteer Army." In F. Fisher and C. Sirianni (Eds.), *Critical Studies in Organization and Bureaucracy.* Philadelphia: Temple University Press.

Ryan, J., and C. Sackrey. (1984). *Strangers in Paradise: Academics from the Working Class.* Boston: South End Press.

Sampson, R. J., and J. H. Laub. (1993). *Crime in the Making: Pathways and Turning Points through Life.* Cambridge, MA: Harvard University Press.

Sanday, P. R. (1979). *The Socio-Cultural Context of Rape.* Washington, DC: U.S. Department of Commerce, National Technical Information Service.

Sanders. P. (2005, May 13). "Casinos Bet on Radio—ID Gambling Chips." *Wall Street Journal.*

Sandmire, H. F. (1990). "Whither Electronic Fetal Monitoring?" *Obstetrics and Gynecology 76*(6): 1130–1134.

Schaefer, R. T., and R. P. Lamm. (1998). *Sociology* (6th ed.). New York: McGraw-Hill.

Schofield, J. (1982). *Black and White in School.* New York: Praeger.

Scott, J. C. (1990). *Domination and the Arts of Resistance: Hidden Transcripts.* New Haven: Yale University Press.

Scully, D., and J. Marolla. (1984). "Convicted Rapists' Vocabulary of Motive: Excuses and Justifications." *Social Problems 31:* 530–544.

Scully, D., and J. Marolla. (1985). "Rape and Psychiatric Vocabulary of Motive: Alternative Perspectives." In A. W. Burgess (Ed.), *Rape and Sexual Assault: A Research Handbook.* New York: Garland Publishing, pp. 294–312.

Shiono, P., M. A. Klebanoff, and J. C. Carey. (1990). "Midline Episiotomies: More Harm Than Good?" *American Journal of Obstetrics and Gynecology* 75(5): 765–770.

Shover, N. (1996). *Great Pretenders: Pursuits and Careers of Persistent Thieves.* Boulder, CO: Westview.

Shy, K., D. A. Luthy, F. C. Bennett, M. Whitfield, E. B. Larson, G. van Belle, et al. (1990). "Effects of Electronic Fetal Heart Rate Monitoring, as Compared with Periodic Auscultation, on the Neurologic Development of Premature Infants." *New England Journal of Medicine* 322(9): 588–593.

Silvey, R. (2000). "Diasporic Subjects: Gender and Mobility in South Sulawesi." *Women's Studies International Forum* 23(4): 501–515.

Simmel, G. (1908). (1971). *On Individuality and Social Forms*, edited by Donald N. Levine. Chicago: University of Chicago Press. (orig. pub. 1908).

Skolnick, J. (1975). *Justice Without Trial.* New York: John Wiley.

Slevin, P. (2000, April 24). "Life after Prison: Lack of Services Has High Price." *Washington Post.*

Smith, D. (1976). "The Social Context of Pornography." *Journal of Communications 26:* 16–24.

Smithyman, S. (1978). *The Undetected Rapist.* Unpublished dissertation. Claremont Graduate School.

Social Register Association. (1986). *Social Register 1887*, Facsimile Edition. New York: Social Register Association.

Social Register Association. (1987). *Social Register 1988*, Vol. CII. New York: Social Register Association.

Statistical Abstract of the United States. (2006). Washington, DC: U.S. Government Printing Office.

Steele, S. (1991). *The Content of Our Character: A New Vision of Race in America.* New York: Harper Perennial.

Stephenson, J. S. (1985). *Death, Grief and Mourning: Individual and Social Realities.* New York: Free Press.

Sudnow, D. (1967). *Passing On: The Social Organization of Dying.* Englewood Cliffs, NJ: Prentice-Hall.

Sykes, G., and D. Matza. (1957). "Techniques of Neutralization: A Theory of Delinquency." *American Sociological Review* 22: 664–670.

Tanay, E. (1972). "Psychiatric Aspects of Homicide Prevention." *American Journal of Psychology 128:* 814–817.

Theobald, S. (2002). "Working for Global Factories: Thai Women in Electronics Export Companies in the Northern Regional Industrial Estate." In D. S. Gills and N. Piper (Eds.), *Women and Work in Globalising Asia.* London: Routledge, pp. 131–153.

Thorbek, S. (1987). *Voices from the City: Women of Bangkok.* London: Zed Press.

Thorp, J. M., and W. A. Bowes. (1989). "Episiotomy: Can Its Routine Use Be Defended?" *American Journal of Obstetrics and Gynecology 160* (5, Pt 1): 1027–1030.

Tokarczyk, M., and E. Fay. (Eds.). (1993). *Working Class Women in the Academy.* Amherst: University of Massachusetts Press.

Truong, T. (1990). *Sex, Money and Morality: Prostitution and Tourism in Southeast Asia.* London: Zed Books Ltd.

Turner, R. E., and D. Edgley. (1976, July). "Death as Theater: A Dramaturgical Analysis of the American Funeral." *Sociology and Social Research 60*: 377–392.

Turner, R. H. (1990). "Role Change." *Annual Review of Sociology 16*: 87–110.

Turner, V. (1979). "Betwixt and Between: The Liminal Period in Rites de Passage." In W. Lessa and E. Z. Vogt (Eds.), *Reader in Comparative Religion* (4th ed.). New York: Harper and Row, pp. 234–243. (orig. pub. 1964)

Uggen, C. (2000). "Work as a Turning Point in the Life Course of Criminals: A Duration Model of Age, Employment, and Recidivism." *American Sociological Review 65*(4): 529–546.

Uggen, C., M. Thompson, and J. Manza. (2000, November 18). "Crime, Class, and Reintegration: The Socioeconomic, Familial, and Civic Lives of Offenders." Paper presented at the American Society of Criminology meetings, San Francisco.

Van Esterik, P. (1982). "Laywomen in Theravada Buddhism." In P. Van Esterik (Ed.), *Women of Southeast Asia.* DeKalb, IL: Center for Southeast Asian Studies, Northern Illinois University, pp. 55–78.

Van Esterik, P. (1988). "Gender and Development in Thailand: Deconstructing Display." Toronto: York University, Department of Anthropology, Thai Studies Project Report.

Van Esterik, P. (2000). *Materializing Thailand.* Oxford, UK: Berg.

van Gennep, A. (1966). *The Rites of Passage.* Chicago: University of Chicago Press. (orig. pub. 1908).

Van Maanen, J. (1978). "The Asshole." In P. K. Manning and J. Van Maanen (Eds.), *Policing: A View from the Street.* Santa Monica, CA: Goodyear.

Veevers, J. (1975). "The Moral Careers of Voluntarily Childless Wives: Notes on the Defense of a Variant World View." *Family Coordinator 24*(4): 473–487.

Verlarde, A. (1975). "Becoming Prostituted: The Decline of the Massage Parlor Profession and the Masseuse." *British Journal of Criminology 15*(3): 251–263.

Warr, P. G. (1993). "The Thai Economy." In P. G. Warr (Ed.), *The Thai Economy in Transition.* Melbourne and Cambridge: Cambridge University Press, pp. 1–80.

Webb, E. J., D. T. Campbell, R. D. Schwartz, and L. Sechrest. (1966). *Unobtrusive Measures: Nonreactive Research in the Social Sciences.* Chicago: Rand McNally.

Wecter, D. (1937). *The Saga of American Society.* New York: Charles Scribner's Sons.

Weis, K., and S. Borges (1973). "Victimology and Rape: The Case of the Legitimate Victim." *Issues in Criminology 8*: 71–115.

West, D. J. (1983). "Sex Offenses and Offending." In M. Tonry and N. Morris (Eds.), *Crime and Justice: An Annual Review of Research.* Chicago: University of Chicago Press, pp. 1–30.

Western, B. (2002). "The Impact of Incarceration on Wage Mobility and Inequality." *American Sociological Review 67*(4): 526–546.

Western, B., and B. Pettit. (1999). "Black-White Earnings Inquality, Employment Rates, and Incarceration." Working Paper No. 150. New York: Sage.

Westley, W. A. (1966, March). "The Escalation of Violence through Legitimation." *Annals of the American Association of Political and Social Science 364*, 120–126.

Westley, W. A. (1970). *Violence and the Police: A Sociological Study of Law, Custom and Morality.* Cambridge, MA: MIT Press.

Wheeler, H. (1985). "Pornography and Rape: A Feminist Perspective." In A. W. Burgess (Ed.), *Rape and Sexual Assault: A Research Handbook*. New York: Garland Publishing, pp. 374–391.

Wilcox, L. S., et al. (1989). "Episiotomy and Its Role in the Incident of Perineal Lacerations in a Maternity Center and a Tertiary Hospital Obstetric Service." *American Journal of Obstetrics and Gynecology 160* (5, Pt 1): 1047–1052.

Willis, P. G. (1977). *Learning to Labor*. London: Saxon House.

Wilson, W. J. (1997). *When Work Disappears: The World of the New Urban Poor*. New York: Vintage Books.

Winfrey, C. (1980, February 2). "Society's 'In' Book: Does It Still Matter?," *New York Times*.

Wiseman, J. (1979). *Stations of the Lost: The Treatment of Skid Row Alcoholics* (2nd ed.). Chicago: University of Chicago Press.

Wolfgang, M., and F. Ferracuti. (1967). *The Subculture of Violence*. London: Tavistock.

Woods, A. S., and R. G. Delisle. (1978). "The Treatment of Death in Sympathy Cards." In C. Winick (Ed.), *Deviance and Mass Media*. Beverly Hills, CA: Sage, pp. 95–103.

Wuthnow, R. (1987). *Meaning and Moral Order*. Princeton: Princeton University Press.

Wright, E. *Class*. (1985) London: Verso.

Yablonsky, L. (1962). *The Violent Gang*. New York: Macmillan.

Appendix
Correlation Chart

TO HELP YOU INTEGRATE this fourteenth edition with whatever main text you may be using, I have matched the articles in *Down to Earth Sociology* with 25 chapter themes found in introductory texts. To make it easier for you to produce your syllabus, for each article I have listed its number, title, author, and the page number on which it begins. Because some selections in *Down to Earth Sociology* have more than one theme, they are listed for more than a single chapter.

Some instructors build their introductory course around the articles in *Down to Earth Sociology*. They supplement these selections with a few chapters of what is usually the main text. In this way, their students concentrate on primary sociological studies, rather than on secondary analyses. Regardless of your approach, because of the inherent interest of most of these readings, they help make sociology come alive. Instructors report that *Down to Earth* helps them give their students a more engaging introduction to sociology. I hope this is your experience, too.

I have also prepared an instructor's manual for this edition. I have written not only the usual multiple choice, essay, and true-false questions, but also suggestions for in-class activities. These activities are designed to make your class more lively, to arouse your students' interest in sociology, and to stimulate their sociological imagination. You may want to try some of these exercises, for from the feedback that I have received from instructors, they accomplish their purpose. I welcome any suggestions you might have for other in-class activities.

Again, my best wishes for your classroom success.

Jim Henslin

Culture

Deviance and Social Control

The Economy

Education

Formal Organizations

Gender

Law

Marriage and Family

Medicine

Military

Occupations

See Work and Occupations

Politics

Race and Ethnicity

Religion

Research Methods

Social Change

Social Class

Social Groups

Socialization

The Sociological Perspective

Urbanization and Urban Life

Work and Occupations

Name Index

Subject Index